An Introduction to Collective Bargaining and Industrial Relations

McGraw-Hill Series in Management

Fred Luthans and Keith Davis, Consulting Editors

Also Available from McGraw-Hill

Schaum's Outline Series
in Accounting, Business, & Economics

Most outlines include basic theory, definitions, and hundreds of solved problems and supplementary problems with answers.

Titles on the Current List Include:

Accounting I, 3d edition
Accounting II, 3d edition
Advanced Accounting
Advanced Business Law
Advertising
Bookkeeping and Accounting
Introduction to Business
Business Law
Business Mathematics
Introduction to Business Organization and Management
Business Statistics, 2d edition
College Business Law
Contemporary Mathematics of Finance
Cost Accounting I, 2d edition
Cost Accounting II, 2d edition
Development Economics
Financial Accounting
Intermediate Accounting I, 2d edition
International Economics, 3d edition
Macroeconomic Theory, 2d edition
Managerial Accounting
Managerial Economics
Managerial Finance
Marketing
Mathematics for Economists, 2d edition
Mathematics of Finance
Microeconomic Theory, 3d edition
Money and Banking
Operations Management
Personal Finance
Personal Finance and Consumer Economics
Principles of Economics
Statistics and Econometrics
Tax Accounting

Available at your College Bookstore. A complete listing of Schaum titles may be obtained by writing to:
Schaum Division
McGraw-Hill, Inc.
Princeton Road, S-1
Hightstown, NJ 08520

An Introduction to Collective Bargaining and Industrial Relations

Harry C. Katz
Cornell University

Thomas A. Kochan
Massachusetts Institute of Technology

McGraw-Hill, Inc.

New York   St. Louis   San Francisco   Auckland   Bogotá   Caracas   Lisbon
London   Madrid   Mexico   Milan   Montreal   New Delhi
Paris   San Juan   Singapore   Sydney   Tokyo   Toronto

*An Introduction to Collective Bargaining
and Industrial Relations*

Copyright © 1992 by McGraw-Hill, Inc. All rights reserved. Printed in
the United States of America. Except as permitted under the United
States Copyright Act of 1976, no part of this publication may be
reproduced or distributed in any form or by any means, or stored in
a data base or retrieval system, without the prior written permission
of the publisher.

2 3 4 5 6 7 8 9 0 DOC DOC 9 0 9 8 7 6 5 4 3 2

ISBN 0-07-033645-8

This book was set in Cheltenham Book by The Clarinda Company.
The editors were Alan Sachs, Dan Alpert, and Sheila H. Gillams;
the designer was Jack Ehn;
the production supervisor was Louise Karam.
The photo editor was Kathy Bendo.
R. R. Donnelley & Sons Company was printer and binder.

Library of Congress Cataloging-in-Publication Data

Katz, Harry Charles, (date).
    An introduction to collective bargaining and industrial relations
    Harry Charles Katz, Thomas A. Kochan
        p.   cm.—(McGraw-Hill series in management)
    Includes index.
    ISBN 0-07-033645-8
    1. Collective bargaining.   2. Industrial relations.   I. Kochan,
Thomas A.   II. Title.   III. Series.
HD6971.5.K38   1992
331.89—dc20   91-15906

To our many teachers

Contents

Preface

This book provides an introduction to collective bargaining and industrial relations. It is appropriate for students and industrial relations professionals including unionists, managers, and neutrals. The strength of this text lies in its logical coherence and its comprehensive coverage of contemporary developments.

Key Features

The key features of the text include the following:

- A three-tiered strategic choice framework guides the text in a unified manner (presented in Chapter 1).

- A thorough grounding in labor history (Chapter 2) and labor law (Chapter 3) assist students in learning the basics.

- Boldface key terms in text and an end-of-book glossary define the terms.

- The influence of business and union strategies is examined in Chapters 5 and 6 with numerous contemporary illustrations.

- The processes of contract negotiation (Chapters 8 and 9) and contract administration (Chapter 11) are considered, with frequent comparisons to nonunion practices and developments. Four grievance arbitration cases covering a range of current issues are offered in Appendix C.

- Thorough analysis of participatory processes and their relationship to collective bargaining are made in Chapter 12.

- The special aspects of collective bargaining in the public sector are spotlighted in Chapter 13.

- A separate chapter on comparative and international issues (Chapter 14) culminates the frequent comparisons made throughout the text. Chapter 14 includes discussion of Japanese, German, Polish, and Korean industrial relations developments; the emergence of a single EEC market; the pressures created by multinational corporations; and the lessons for the United States from foreign practices.

- Two mock collective bargaining exercises, one in the private sector (involving blue collar workers) and one in the public sector (involving police officers), in Appendixes A and B. A self-contained, easily useable PC disk is available that allows students to engage in contract costing and financial forecasting with the private sector bargaining exercise.

- An extensive Instructor's Manual.

Central Themes and Text Organization

The text follows a three-tiered strategic choice framework. We introduce the reader to collective bargaining by simultaneously moving across and downward through the three tiers of industrial relations activity. We move across the framework by examining how environmental forces shape collective bargaining, then turning to the process of collective bargaining, and continue moving across the framework by analyzing bargaining outcomes. As the discourse moves from the environment, to the bargaining process, and then to bargaining outcomes, it follows in the tradition of John Dunlop's seminal work, *Industrial Relations Systems.*

The text also moves downward through the three-tiered framework by examining how business and union strategies constrain the process and outcomes of collective bargaining. After considering strategic issues we analyze the middle tier of bargaining where contract negotiation and administration are so important. Further down we examine workplace issues such as the organization of work and communication procedures. We (along with Robert McKersie) originally developed this three-tiered framework in our book, *The Transformation of American Industrial Relations* (New York: Basic Books, 1986).

By examining the influence of business and union strategies on industrial relations this book provides a broader focus than most other introductory texts. Yet, we feel the student must understand the influence of Wall Street, production strategies, union choices, and other strategic forces in order to accurately comprehend how collective bargaining works in the modern economy.

A separate chapter examining participatory processes and their connections to collective bargaining (Chapter 12) is the result of our concern for workplace issues. Worker and union participation programs have become a central part of many labor-management relationships, particularly in the manufacturing sector and in public schools. Students and professionals must study this development to adequately prepare for the realities they will experience in the industrial relations world.

Our writing on participation is heavily influenced by the findings of our own field research. Nonetheless, in contrast to the *Transformation* book, this text is less prescriptive or predictive. Our goal in this text is to convey the challenges and issues posed by the new participatory processes. We hope that critics of these programs will learn as much from our discussion of these issues as will supporters of the programs.

The focus in this book also is broadened by our concern for international developments. We highlight international comparisons and pressures through examples throughout the text and focus on these issues in a separate chapter (Chapter 14). International events, including the democratization movements in eastern Europe and developing countries such as Korea and Taiwan, are some of the most exciting developments of the day. Readers should understand the central roles that industrial relations problems and labor unions play in these events.

Extensive coverage of developments in the nonunion sector also distinguishes this book from others. The nonunion sector is important in its own right given the decline in U.S. union membership. Furthermore, analysis of the nonunion sector contributes to an understanding of the pressures and changes occurring within the union sector.

The public sector has increased in importance as unionization has declined in the private sector. We examine the special features of the public sector in Chapter 13.

Our broad focus helps the reader gain a full understanding of collective bargaining. We present numerous illustrations throughout the text, some of which are highlighted as "cases." Knowledge of labor history and labor law help ground the reader in the workings of American collective bargaining. These topics are covered early in the book (Chapters 2 and 3).

Students also can expand their understanding of collective bargaining through the two mock bargaining exercises provided in the appendixes. The first of these exercises involves a fictitious private sector manufacturing firm, "D. G. Barnhouse." Full instructions for this exercise and recommendations gained from our own classroom experience are provided in the Instructor's Manual. A self-contained computer disk for use on an IBM PC is available at no charge from McGraw-Hill. This disk allows the student (even those with no previous computer experience) to cost Barnhouse contract settlement terms and forecast the financial and employment implications of alternative settlements. We have used this contract-costing disk in our classes and highly recommend it.

The second mock bargaining exercise, provided in Appendix B, involves the police of "Queen City." This exercise gives students a feel for the role that political and urban pressures exert in public sector bargaining.

The four grievance arbitration cases in Appendix C illustrate a range of contemporary developments and enable students to test their skills as third parties.

Instructor's Manual

In addition to suggestions about how to use the mock bargaining exercises and supplementary material for those exercises, the Instructor's Manual includes: a test bank, overhead transparency masters, answers to the end-of-chapter discussion questions, chapter outlines, lecture outlines, and a listing of recommended supplementary films (and videos) and the companies that sell those materials. In our teaching of introductory collective bargaining, we have found that the mock bargaining exercises and films help convey how bargaining really works. We would appreciate hearing your reaction to the text and these materials.

Acknowledgments

A number of people assisted in the development of this book and we are deeply grateful to all of them. Ben Whipple developed the remarkably simple contract costing program available for use with the D. G. Barnhouse mock bargaining exercise. Able research assistance was provided by Alex Bernstein, Dirk Obbink, and Amy Andrews. Secretarial and administrative support beyond the call of duty was provided by Diana Kennedy, Michelle Kamin, and Jackie Dodge. The staff of McGraw-Hill, Alan Sachs, Dan Alpert, and Sheila Gillams, improved this book in many ways.

We are also grateful for the expert guidance of the following manuscript reviewers: Trevor Bain, University of Alabama; Thomas P. Gilroy, University of Iowa; Richard B. Peterson, University of Washington; Lee Stepina, Florida State University; and Harold C. White, Arizona State University.

This book is dedicated to our many teachers. It was they who generated the spark that led us into the field of industrial relations, a field we continue to find stimulating and rewarding. We hope this book can generate similar sparks for the reader.

Harry C. Katz

Thomas A. Kochan

An Introduction to Collective Bargaining and Industrial Relations

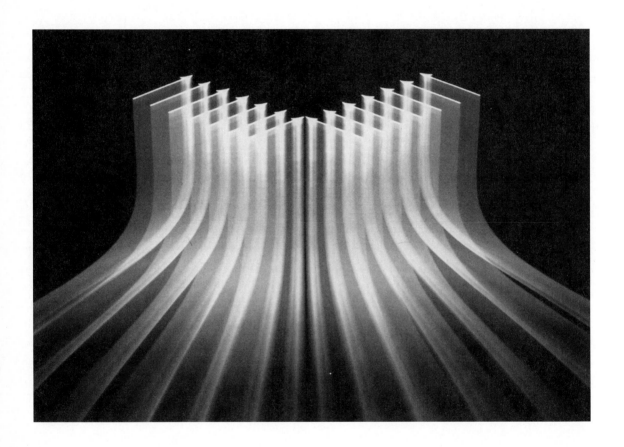

PART 1

INTRODUCTION

Chapter 1

A Framework for Analyzing Collective Bargaining and Industrial Relations

Whether we are at work or at leisure, we are affected by the conditions under which we work and the rewards we receive for working. Work plays such a central role in our lives and in society that the study of relations between employee and employer cannot be ignored.

This book traces how labor and management, acting either as individuals or as groups, have shaped and continue to shape the employment relationship. Employment is analyzed through the perspective of **industrial relations,** an interdisciplinary field of study that concentrates on individual workers, groups of workers and their unions and associations, employers and their organizations, and the environment in which these parties interact.

Industrial relations differs from other disciplines that study work because of its focus on labor and trade unions and on the process of collective bargaining. Thus this book describes how collective bargaining works and helps explain, for example, why it may lead to high wages in one situation and to low wages in another.

The study of industrial relations focuses on the key participants involved in the process, the role of industrial conflict, and the performance of collective bargaining. This chapter defines these various aspects of industrial relations and describes how this book analyzes them.

The Participants

The key participants (or parties) involved in the process of industrial relations are management, labor, and government.[1]

Management

The term **management** refers to those individuals or groups who are responsible for promoting the goals of employers and their organizations. In fact, management encompasses at least three groups: (1) owners and shareholders of an organization, (2) top executives and line managers, and (3) industrial relations and human resource staff professionals who specialize in managing relations with employees and unions. Management plays key roles in negotiating and implementing a firm's industrial relations policies and practices.

Labor

The term **labor** encompasses both employees and the unions that represent them. Employees are at the center of industrial relations. Employees influence whether the firms that employ them achieve their objectives, and employees shape the growth and demands of unions.

Government

The term **government** encompasses (1) the local, state, and federal political processes; (2) the government agencies responsible for passing and enforcing public policies that affect industrial relations; and (3) the government as a representative of the public interest. Government policy shapes how industrial relations proceed by regulating, for example, how workers form unions and what rights unions may have.

Assumptions about Labor and Conflict

More Than Just a Commodity

One of the most important assumptions guiding the study of industrial relations is the view that labor is more than a commodity, more than a marketable resource. For instance, because workers often acquire skills that are of special value to one firm and not to another, the possibilities for them to earn as much "in the labor market" as they can at their existing employer are limited. In addition, changing jobs often costs workers a lot: moving locations can be expensive and can also entail large personal and emotional costs. For these reasons and others, labor is not as freely exchanged in the open, competitive market as are other, nonhuman, market goods.

Furthermore, labor is more than a set of human resources to be allocated to serve the goals of the firm. Instead, employees are also members of families and communities. These broader responsibilities influence employees' behaviors and intersect with their work roles.

A Multiple Interest Perspective

Because employees bring their own aspirations to the workplace, industrial relations must be concerned with how the policies that govern employment relations, and the work itself, affect workers and their interests, as well as the interests of the firm and the larger society. Thus, industrial relations takes a **multiple interest** perspective on the study of collective bargaining and industrial relations.

The Inherent Nature of Conflict

A critical assumption underlying analysis of industrial relations is that there is an **inherent conflict of interest** between employees and employers. That conflict arises out of the clash of economic interests between workers seeking high pay and job security and employers pursuing profits. *Thus, conflict is not viewed as pathological.* Although conflict is a natural element of employment relations, society does have a legitimate interest in limiting the intensity of conflicts over work.

Common as Well as Conflicting Interests

There are also a number of common interests between employers and their employees. Both firms and their work forces can benefit, for example, from increases in productivity through higher wages and higher profits.

At the workplace there is no single best objective that satisfies all the parties. *The essence of an effective employment relationship is one in which the parties both successfully resolve issues that arise from their conflicting interests and successfully pursue joint gains.*

Collective bargaining is only one of a variety of mechanisms for resolving conflicts and pursuing common interests at the workplace. In fact, collective bargaining competes with these alternative employment systems. Not all employees, for example, perceive deep conflicts with their employers or want to join unions. In dealing with their employers, some workers prefer individual over collective actions. Others exercise the option of **exit** (quitting a job) when dissatisfied with employment conditions rather than choosing to **voice** their concerns, either individually or collectively.[2]

One of the roles for public policy is therefore not to require unionization and collective bargaining for all workers, but to provide a fair opportunity for workers to choose whether collective bargaining is the means *they* prefer to resolve conflicts and to pursue common interests with their employer.

Trade-offs among Conflicting Goals

Since many of the goals of the major actors—workers and their unions, employers, and the public or the government—conflict, it is not possible to specify a single overriding measure of the effectiveness of collective bargaining. Focusing on any single goal would destroy the effectiveness of collective bargaining as an instrument for accommodating the multiple interests of workers and employers in a democratic society.

Unions could not survive or effectively represent their members, for example, if employers were completely free to suppress or avoid unionization. Likewise, employers could not compete effectively in global or domestic markets if collective bargaining constantly produced wages or other conditions of employment that increased costs above what the market would bear.

The Three Levels of Industrial Relations Activity

This book uses a **three-tiered approach** to analyze the operation of industrial relations.[3] (Exhibit 1–1 provides the framework for this approach.) First we consider the environmental contexts of collective bargaining; then we look at the operation and outcomes of the bargaining system.

The top tier of industrial relations, the **strategic level,** includes the strategies and structures that exert long-run influences on collective bargaining. At this level we might compare the implications for collective

Exhibit 1–1   Conceptual Framework for the Study of Collective Bargaining

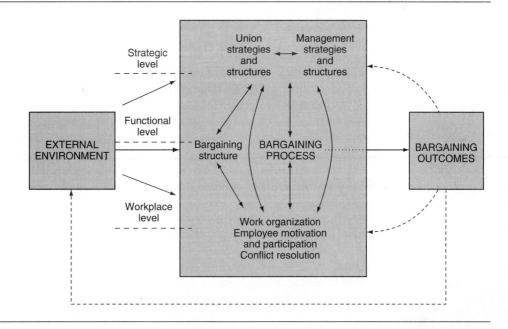

bargaining of a business strategy that emphasizes product quality and innovation against a business strategy that seeks to minimize labor costs.

The middle tier of industrial relations activity, the **functional level,** or collective bargaining level, involves the process and outcomes of contract negotiations. Discussions of strikes, bargaining power, and wage determination feature prominently here.

The bottom tier of industrial relations activity, the **workplace level,** involves those activities through which workers, their supervisors, and their union representatives administer the labor contract and relate to one another on a daily basis. At the workplace level adjustment to changing circumstances and new problems occur regularly. A typical question at this level, for example, is how the introduction of employee participation programs has changed the day-to-day life of workers and supervisors.

It is through the joint effects of the environment and the actions of the parties within this three-tiered structure that collective bargaining either meets the goals of the parties and the public or comes up short.

The Institutional Perspective

The perspective that guides our analysis of industrial relations was first developed by institutional economists at the University of Wisconsin. John R. Commons (1862–1945), the person who most deserves the title of "father of U.S. industrial relations," identified the essence of institutional economics as "a shift from commodities, individuals, and exchanges to transactions and working rules of collective action."[4] Commons and his fellow institutionalists placed great value on negotiations and on compromise among the divergent interests of labor, management, and the public.

The institutionalists in the United States were heavily influenced in their thinking by Sidney and Beatrice Webb, two British economists and social reformists, who were members of the Fabian socialist society. They viewed trade unions as a means of representing the interests of workers through the strategies of *mutual insurance, collective bargaining, and legal enactment.*[5]

In following the Webbs, the institutionalists rejected the arguments of Karl Marx. Marx argued that the pain of the exploitation and alienation inflicted on workers by the capitalistic system would eventually lead to the revolutionary overthrow of the system. He believed that workers would eventually develop a **class consciousness** that would pave the way for revolution and the ultimate solution to their problems—a Marxian economic and social system. Marx supported trade unions in their struggles for higher wages, but he believed they should simultaneously pursue the overthrow of the capitalistic system.

There were, however, some interesting similarities in the views of Commons, Marx, and the Webbs. Like Marx and the Webbs, Commons and other institutional economists rejected the view of labor as a commodity, for two fundamental reasons. First, the institutionalists saw work as being too central to the interests and welfare of individual workers, their families, and their communities to be treated simply as just another factor of production.[6]

Second, the institutionalists echoed the Webbs and the Marxist theorists by arguing that under conditions of "free competition" most individual workers deal with the employer from a position of unequal bargaining power. That is, in the vast majority of employment situations, the workings of the market tilt the balance of power in favor of the employer. The selection from Beatrice Webb's classic essay on the economics of factory legislation in Britain, shown in Box 1–1, amply illustrates this argument.

Box 1–1

Beatrice Webb on the Balance of Power between Employee and Employer

If the capitalist refuses to accept the workman's terms, he will, no doubt, suffer some inconvenience as an employer. To fulfill his orders, he will have to "speed up" some of his machinery, or insist on his people working longer hours. Failing these expedients he may have to delay the delivery of his goods, and may even find his profits, at the end of the year fractionally less than before. But, meanwhile, he goes on eating and drinking, his wife and family go on living, just as before. His physical comfort is not affected: he can afford to wait until the labourer comes back in a humble frame of mind. And that is just what the labourer must presently do. For he, meanwhile, has lost his day. His very subsistence depends on his promptly coming to an agreement. If he stands out, he has no money to meet his weekly rent, or to buy food for his family. If he is obstinate, consumption of his little hoard, or the pawning of his furniture, may put off the catastrophe; but sooner or later slow starvation forces him to come to terms. And since success in the higgling of the market is largely determined by the relative eagerness of the parties to come terms—especially if this eagerness cannot be hidden—it is now agreed, even on this ground alone, "that manual labourers as a class are at a disadvantage in bargaining."

Source: Mrs. Sidney Webb, ed., *The Case for Factory Acts* (London: Grant Richards, 1901), 8–9.

The institutionalists concluded that labor required protection from the workings of the competitive market and that unions could materially improve the conditions of the worker. This led them to advocate two basic labor policies: legislation to protect the rights of workers to join unions; and legislation on such workplace issues as safety and health, child labor, minimum wages, unemployment and workers' compensation, and social security.[7] Thus, in addition to making scholarly contributions, the institutionalists served as early advocates of the legislative reforms that became the centerpiece of the New Deal labor policy.

The Performance of Collective Bargaining

The performance of collective bargaining can be assessed by looking at how well it serves the goals of the parties involved and the public.

Labor's Goals

To see if collective bargaining is meeting labor's goals we can examine wages, benefits, safety conditions, and employee job satisfaction. In recent years a number of union-management experiments were designed to improve the quality of working life and employment security. Because many of these initiatives have expanded the traditional agenda of collective bargaining, their success or failure in serving workers' interests must also be assessed.

Management's Goals

Management is concerned with the effects of collective bargaining on labor costs, productivity, profits, product quality, and the degree of managerial control. Management also has goals for various personnel concerns, such as employee turnover, motivation, and performance. All of these indicate the extent to which collective bargaining aids or hinders employers' quests for competitiveness in the product market.

Management, particularly in the United States, historically has not been very sympathetic to collective bargaining. The vast majority of U.S. employers have resisted unionization of their employees and have often been only reluctant participants in collective bargaining. Managers tend to evaluate the performance of collective bargaining by comparing it with the nonunion alternatives.

The growing sophistication of human resource management strategies and the increasing competitive pressures from nonunion sectors have led more and more corporate managers to scrutinize the performance of their labor relations functions. Most top executives are trying to integrate their labor relations strategies with their business strategies. For example, firms in the steel, auto, aerospace, and retail industries have worked with unions to modify labor relations practices in order to make new investments in plant and equipment pay off.

The Public's Goals

Identifying the goals of collective bargaining for the public and the government is a more difficult task. Government labor policy requires the maintenance of industrial peace and union democracy. In addition, the government is concerned about the effects of collective bargaining on inflation and unemployment and on working conditions, such as safety and health, equal employment opportunity, and income security.

A free labor movement is important to any political democracy. So it is also necessary to assess whether public policies and private actions are producing a bargaining system that strengthens democracy at the workplace and in the society at large.

Since less than one-fifth of the U.S. labor force is now represented by trade unions, the regulation of employment conditions involves more than just collective bargaining. In some instances public policies preempt collective bargaining by creating alternative means through which labor-management issues are addressed, such as through government regulation of pensions.

The Plan of the Book

The chapters that follow analyze industrial relations by simultaneously moving across and downward through Exhibit 1–1. The framework in Exhibit 1–1 is broader and more dynamic than most models of collective bargaining. In particular, it emphasizes the range of choices management, labor, and government policymakers have in responding to environmental changes (such as increased competition or changes in technology), rather than in treating technology or competitive pressures solely as overriding constraints.

The following discussion provides a more elaborate description of the terms used in Exhibit 1–1. This material also sketches out in more detail the topics included in each chapter and their connections as the book moves across and downward through Exhibit 1–1. The reader may wish to return to this material from time to time as a review strategy to put the individual topics and chapters in perspective.

The Environment

The external environment sets the context for collective bargaining and strongly influences the bargaining process and bargaining outcomes. The **external environment** includes five key dimensions: the economic environment (micro and macro), law and public policy, the demographic context, social attitudes, and the technological context. The laws and public policies that regulate collective bargaining are a key aspect of the environment and are outlined in Chapter 3. Chapter 4 describes how each component of the environment influences the process and the outcomes of bargaining.

The environment often transmits its effects through the exercise of **bargaining power.** For example, a law that grants employees the right to strike is important because it facilitates the emergence of collective bargaining and thereby alters the balance of power between labor and management. The ensuing shift in the balance of power is particularly noteworthy to the extent that it leads to different employment conditions (such as higher wages) than would otherwise exist. In this way something in the external environment (a law) affects the frequency of bargaining (the bargaining process) and wage levels (a bargaining outcome).

Similarly, the economic features of product and labor markets affect the behavior of labor and management and the outcomes of collective bargaining. Workers and unions, for example, have more bargaining leverage and are able to win higher wages during contract negotiations when it is easier for striking workers to find temporary or alternative employment. Thus, an aspect of the macroeconomy (the unemployment rate) influences workers' bargaining power and bargaining outcomes (the wage settlement).

Do the provisions of typical collective bargaining contracts adequately address the needs of women in the work force, of youths, and of the elderly? Is the government enforcing the existing labor laws? These questions concern additional interactions between the external environment (in the first case, the demographic context; in the second case, the public policy context) and collective bargaining.

As the book traces how the various components of the environment affect the bargaining process and bargaining outcomes, the discussion moves across the middle tier of the framework outlined in Exhibit 1–1. At the same time it is important to be aware of how the *strategies and structures* of labor and management shape both the middle tier of industrial relations activity and exert impacts at the workplace. Thus, as the text moves across the framework the analysis also simultaneously moves downward through our three-tiered framework. The framework starts at the top by first considering the role played by labor and management strategies and structures.

The Strategic (Top) Tier

At the top tier of industrial relations activity are the strategies and structures that guide the long-run direction of U.S. industrial relations.

Management's Strategies and Structures   The strategies and structures of management are critically important in shaping the evolution of industrial relations. For instance, is a given company's top management content to work with its union(s) over the long run, or is it fundamentally committed to devoting its resources to nonunion pursuits and operations?

Chapter 5 analyzes the various strategic options available to managers, including the growing availability and sophistication of nonunion alternatives to collective bargaining. What leads management to aggressively seek to avoid unions in one case, whereas in another situation management is content to negotiate with the unions that represent its employees and to focus on improving the existing collective bargaining relationship? To help us understand what motivates management Chapter 5 contrasts the key features of some of the nonunion employment systems with those of both traditional union practices (the *New Deal system*) and the participatory practices that have recently emerged in a number of unionized settings.

While management strategies are important, so are the various structures that management uses to organize itself for industrial relations. The second part of Chapter 5 considers how management organizes its industrial relations staffs.

Labor's Strategies and Structures   Labor's strategies and structures also exert a critical influence on the course of industrial relations. The various aspects of labor's strategic issues are addressed in Chapter 6. For example, is a given union leadership committed to maintaining a distanced and adversarial posture in negotiations, or is it interested in exchanging new forms of flexible work organization for greater control over the design of the production process? In addition, should the labor movement focus on political action or seek to improve employment conditions through collective bargaining? These are but two of the strategic issues that face the labor movement.

The labor movement, like management, also structures itself in its efforts to shape industrial relations. Chapter 6 describes the organizational structure of the American labor movement and delineates the division in the responsibilities of the American Federation of Labor–Congress of Industrial Organizations (AFL-CIO), national unions, and local unions.

A key strategic issue, perhaps the single most important issue, for the labor movement today is the extent of the work force that belongs to a union. Chapter 6 traces current union membership figures and some of the trends. This chapter also explains why union membership as a fraction of the work force has declined so substantially in the United States.

The emphasis in this book on the strategic level of industrial relations activity contrasts with most traditional treatments of unions and employers. The traditional approach focuses on a narrow concept of the internal management structure for labor relations or on union wage objectives and internal politics. Today an understanding of the links between business and union strategies and collective bargaining is needed to interpret or to participate in the bargaining process.

The Functional (Middle) Tier

The middle tier of activity within a bargaining relationship encompasses the heart and soul of the bargaining process. This tier is the arena in which the process of contract negotiations takes place. It is here also that the terms and conditions of the labor agreement (the outcomes of bargaining) are established and periodically modified.

Union Organizing and Bargaining Structure   The formation of unions and workers' expression of interest in union representation precedes negotiations and the determination of bargaining outcomes. In the United States unions establish their right to represent workers in defined **bargaining units** through the vote of prospective members in a **representation election.** Thus, the first stage in our discussion of the process of bargaining (in Chapter 7) is consideration of how representation elections are held and the laws that regulate the conduct of those elections.

Unions have not fared very well in the representation elections held in the United States, particularly since the early 1970s. Thus an analysis of union organizing must consider some of the tactics management has been using to such great success and some of the recent steps taken by unions to increase their membership.

A critical factor that shapes the form and often the outcomes of organizing is the structure of the bargaining unit, the second major topic addressed in Chapter 7. **Bargaining structure** refers to the scope of employees and employers covered or in some way affected by the terms of a labor agreement. For example, are a number of different employers covered by a single collective bargaining agreement? Does a given company bargain with one union or with many? Does a given union represent workers with diverse or with homogeneous skills?

The structure of bargaining in the United States is highly decentralized: the U.S. Bureau of Labor Statistics estimates (no exact census has ever been attempted) that somewhere between 170,000 and 190,000 separate collective bargaining agreements currently exist in this country. This figure may overstate the actual degree of decentralization of bargaining, however. An informal process known as **pattern bargaining** often operates to tie separate agreements together, so that a change in one leads to similar changes in others within the same firm, region, or industry. For instance, the United Auto Workers union, which represents workers in both the auto parts and the auto assembly sectors, regularly has tried to extend the contract improvements it won in the assembly plants of the major manufacturers to the parts-producing plants owned by other companies. The strength of these patterns varies considerably over time; however, pattern bargaining remains an important feature of contemporary collective bargaining.

Chapter 7 explores how the structures of bargaining have undergone considerable change since the early 1980s. This analysis demonstrates the important links between bargaining structure and other concepts in the framework.

The Negotiations Process   At the heart of union/management relations is the negotiation of collective bargaining agreements, the topic that is the focus of Chapter 8. If a union wins the right to represent a group of workers, the next phase in the bargaining process involves the union's (and workers') efforts to negotiate a favorable collective bargaining agreement. The **negotiations process** is a complicated affair, involving tactics, strategies, and counterstrategies by both labor and management. What makes the subject of negotiations even more challenging is its dynamic nature.

Analysis of the process of negotiations considers the following sort of questions:

1. How can the dynamics of the negotiations process be described and explained?

2. What causes strikes to occur in some negotiations and not in others and to vary in frequency and intensity over time and across industries?

3. What role do union and business strategies play in shaping the negotiations process?

Chapter 8 examines the complete cycle of negotiations, starting with the presentation of opening offers and demands and proceeding through the signing of the final agreement.

Impasse Resolution   When labor and management reach an impasse in contract negotiations a variety of techniques can (and have) been used to settle the dispute. Chapter 9 assesses various **impasse resolution** techniques. This chapter examines the frequency of their use and some of the strengths and weaknesses of each.

Bargaining Outcomes   The bargaining process is important in its own right, but it is particularly relevant for its effects on workers' employment conditions, as analyzed in Chapter 10. Employment conditions are the most important **bargaining outcomes** that are shaped by collective bargaining.

Most, but not all, of the outcomes of the negotiations process are codified in the collective bargaining agreement. Exhibit 1–2 shows the range of the terms and conditions of employment that are covered in many labor contracts. This list illustrates that most of the agreements address, at the very least, the following sets of issues: (1) wage and fringe benefit levels, payment systems, and administration; (2) job and income security; (3) physical working conditions; (4) selected personnel management and plant operation practices; and (5) union and management rights and responsibilities.

Exhibit 1–2   **Standard Provisions in Collective Bargaining Agreements**

Establishment and Administration of the Agreement

Bargaining unit and plant supplements
Contract duration and reopening and renegotiation provisions
Union security and the checkoff
Special bargaining committees
Grievance procedures
Arbitration and mediation
Strikes and lockouts
Contract enforcement

Wage Determination and Administration

Rate structure and wage differentials
Incentive and bonus plans
Production standards and time studies
Job classification and job evaluation
Individual wage adjustments
General wage adjustments during the contract period

Job or Income Security

Hiring and transfer arrangements
Employment and income guarantees
Reporting and call-in pay
Supplemental unemployment benefit plans
Regulation of overtime, shift work, etc.
Reduction of hours to forestall layoffs
Layoff procedures, seniority, recall
Worksharing in lieu of layoff
Attrition arrangements
Promotion practices
Training and retraining
Relocation allowances
Severance pay and layoff benefit plans
Special funds and study committees

Functions, Rights, and Responsibilities

Management rights clauses
Plant removal
Subcontracting
Union activities on company time and premises
Union-management cooperation
Regulation of technological change
Advance notice and consultation

Plant Operations

Work and shop rules
Rest periods and other in-plant time allowances
Safety and health
Plant committees
Hours of work and premium pay practices
Shift operations
Hazardous work
Discipline and discharge

Paid and Unpaid Leave

Vacations and holidays
Sick leave
Funeral and personal leave
Military leave and jury duty

Employee Benefit Plans

Health and insurance plans
Pension plans
Profit-sharing, stock purchase, and thrift plans
Bonus plans

Special Groups

Apprentices and learners
Handicapped and older workers
Women
Veterans
Union representatives
Nondiscrimination clauses

Source: Adapted from Joseph W. Bloch, "Union Contracts—A New Series of Studies," *Monthly Labor Review* 87 (October 1964): 1184–85.

Nonetheless, the scope and content of bargaining agreements in the United States vary widely. Yet, because contract provisions define the rights and obligations of each of the parties, they furnish a starting point for assessing how well the interests of workers, employers, unions, and society are faring at the workplace.

Recently, a number of companies and unions have moved to simplify the rules contained in their agreements as part of their efforts to lower costs and to increase flexibility in managing human resources. The chapter addresses both the historical growth in the complexity of bargaining agreements and the more recent efforts to streamline some of the work rule provisions.

The Workplace (Bottom) Tier

The management of conflict and the delivery of due process are only two of several key activities that occur on a continuous basis at the workplace level of industrial relations activity. Other activities involve the motivation, participation, and supervision of individual workers and the structuring of work into jobs, groups, or teams. Should work be organized into highly fragmented jobs or, rather, placed in team systems of work organization? What does a shift to a team system imply for union leaders and the operation of the grievance system? These questions illustrate the issues being raised by the recent changes that have been occurring at the workplace level.

Administration of the Bargaining Agreement

Much of the workplace interaction between labor and management in unionized settings in the United States focuses on administration of the collective bargaining agreement. At the centerpiece of contact administration are the *grievance and arbitration* procedures analyzed in Chapter 11. Some analysts view grievance arbitration as *the* most significant innovation of the U.S. industrial relations system.

Grievance and arbitration procedures have been undergoing significant change with the growth of external laws governing health and safety, equal employment opportunity, and other matters that influence the rights of individuals and add to the responsibilities of both unions and employers. Chapter 11 considers how these external laws also influence the workplace.

Participatory Processes

The negotiation and administration of a collective bargaining agreement have traditionally provided a way for employees to participate in decisions that shape their work lives and employment conditions. In recent years there has been much effort to go beyond these procedures and to directly involve employees in making decisions. Chapter 12 analyzes the variety of *participatory processes* that have emerged, as it discusses the success of employee involvement and quality of work life programs. The text also assesses new forms of work organization, including team systems and quality circles, that have emerged as part of labor and management's efforts to improve productivity and product quality.

New participatory processes have sprung up at strategic levels as well as at the workplace level. The options range from new forms of employee ownership, to labor-management committees, to union representation on corporate boards, to the workplace processes discussed above.

Special Topics

Chapters 13 and 14 address selected topics that complete our understanding of collective bargaining in the modern economy.

Public Sector Collective Bargaining   The rules and procedures in public sector collective bargaining, examined in Chapter 13, differ from those used in the private sector in the United States. The public sector employs a wide diversity of employees, including public school teachers, municipal police and firefighters, and the office staffs of city, state, and federal governments. Public employees are not covered by the National Labor Relations Act (NLRA). This chapter considers the extent to which the theories presented in earlier parts of the book carry over to the public sector.

International and Comparative Industrial Relations   These days the industrial relations developments that are occurring around the world warrant the special attention they are given in Chapter 14. The labor movement has been at the forefront of the sweeping political changes occurring in the formerly Communist bloc and in developing nations such as Korea. In these countries the labor movement is as much concerned with political change as it is with the determination of work conditions on the factory floor.

International trade and competitiveness have moved to the forefront of economic policy in the United States. In particular, there is much discussion about whether the United States should try to imitate the industrial relations practices of its chief economic rivals. Chapter 14 reviews in detail the industrial practices in Japan and Germany. These two countries are informative because their practices are so different from those in the United States and because the performance of these economies has been so strong in recent years. Examination of industrial relations in other countries provides insight into American practice.

Labor Policy   Chapter 15 returns to a primary focus on issues in the United States. This concluding chapter assesses broad public and social policies and their effects on industrial relations. In the face of all the changes emerging in U.S. collective bargaining, this chapter also considers the various policy options and the merits and implications of the alternative policies.

Summary

The expansion of participatory processes is one of the many changes that have been occurring in industrial relations in recent years. Yet this is only one among many critical changes that have emerged. In the face of the wide-ranging changes that have come to industrial relations and collective bargaining, many of the earlier textbooks addressing those subjects have become out of date.

For some analysts the 1980s and early 1990s were remarkable because of the large number of labor concessions that occurred in these years. For others, it was the rapid decline of union membership that was so unusual. And for some other analysts it was the expanding worker and union participation programs that were most important. To us, each of these and other events were important, but it is even more important to understand how the various changes and events *fit together as a shift in the nature and form of industrial relations.*

We believe there has been a fundamental transformation in American industrial relations that includes shifts in the focus of activity from the middle level to both the strategic and the workplace levels. Concession bargaining, union decline, and participation programs and other events in the United States can all be understood as parts of this transformation.

We developed the model of industrial relations presented in Exhibit 1–1 in our efforts to comprehend the scope of the changes that are under way. We believe these changes in collective bargaining should be viewed as neither a fluke nor a special case but, rather, as an illustration of the dynamics of industrial relations.

One cannot gain an understanding of recent developments or the workings of industrial relations without a sense of history. Chapter 2 provides a historical perspective on the evolution of industrial relations in the United States. This chapter highlights some of the key events and turning points in that history as it provides a perspective on the wide-ranging changes that occurred in collective bargaining in the United States in recent years.

Discussion Questions

1. Name the actors, generally and specifically, who are involved in the collective bargaining process. MANAGEMENT, LABORERS, GOVERNMENT

2. Exhibit 1–1 is essential in understanding how this book is arranged and proceeds in its analysis of collective bargaining. Describe this figure and how it pertains to the study of collective bargaining.

3. One of the fundamental aims of collective bargaining is the reduction of conflict between employees and employers. What are some basic assumptions about labor and conflict in this book?

4. What are some of the ways in which we judge the effectiveness of collective bargaining, with respect to the different actors involved in the process?
   STRATEGIC LEVEL HAS MOST LEVERAGE

Suggested Readings

Dunlop, John T. *Industrial Relations Systems* (New York: Holt, 1958).

Kochan, Thomas A., Harry C. Katz, and Robert B. McKersie. *The Transformation of American Industrial Relations* (New York: Basic Books, 1986).

Webb, Sidney and Beatrice. *Industrial Democracy* (London: Longmans, Green and Co., 1920).

End Notes

1.   See John T. Dunlop, *Industrial Relations Systems* (New York: Holt, 1958).

2.   See Albert O. Hirschman, *Exit, Voice, and Loyalty: Responses to Declines in Firms, Organizations, and States* (Cambridge: Harvard University Press, 1970).

3.   For a summary of the theoretical and empirical research on which this model is based, see Thomas A. Kochan, Harry C. Katz, and Robert B. McKersie, *The Transformation of American Industrial Relations* (New York: Basic Books, 1986).

4.   John R. Commons, *Institutional Economics: Its Place in the Political Economy* (New York: Macmillan, 1934), p. 162.

5.   Sidney and Beatrice Webb, *Industrial Democracy* (London: Longmans, Green and Co., 1920).

6.   Commons, *Institutional Economics,* p. 559.

7.   For a discussion of the policies advocated by the early institutionalists and ultimately passed in the wave of New Deal legislation, see Joseph P. Goldberg, Eileen Ahern, William Haber, and Rudolph A. Oswald, *Federal Policies and Worker Status since the Thirties* (Madison, WI: Industrial Relations Research Association, 1977).

Chapter 2

The Historical Evolution
of the U.S. Industrial
Relations System

Collective bargaining is one means for organized groups of workers and their employers to resolve their conflicting interests. It is by no means, however, the only way to conduct industrial relations. Indeed, in the long history of industrial society, collective bargaining is only a recent arrival. Moreover, collective bargaining has had to adapt to changing times and changing values.

This chapter examines the evolution of industrial relations in the United States. Throughout American labor history there has been much violence and substantial hardships on the participants. At the same time, there was much ingenuity as economic expansion transformed a nation of immigrants into the world's leading industrial power. The history that follows highlights the individuals who played key roles in that transformation.

The Colonial and Preindustrial Era

From the beginning of colonial times to the Revolutionary War employment relationships were dominated by the master-servant principles inherited from British common law. Many early settlers gained their passage to the United States by becoming **indentured servants** to a shipowner. Under this arrangement, on arrival at a colonial port, the ships' captain sold the servant to an employer for a certain number of years (not to exceed seven). Many of these indentured servants were individuals seeking to escape their past problems or those forced to leave their home country. One observer described them as follows:

> Among those who repair to Bristol from all parts to be transported for servants to his Majesty's plantations beyond seas, some are

husbands that have forsaken wives, others wives who have forsaken their husbands; some are children and apprentices run way from their parents and masters, often-times unwary and credulous persons have been tempted on board by men-stealers, and many that have been pursued by hue-and-cry for robberies, burglaries, or breaking prison, do thereby escape the prosecution of law and justice.[1]

The Dominance of Agriculture

Colonial employers were eager for the arrival of these workers given the general shortage of labor for their farms and plantations. From 1609, when the first slaves were imported into Virginia, until 1808, when the slave trade was outlawed, indentured servants were supplemented by slaves brought from Africa and the East Indies. In this period agriculture was dominant and included large plantations in the south, farms in Quaker Pennsylvania, and family plots in Puritan New England.

Coinciding with these rural farming-based economies were a growing number of artisan services and manufactures—shopkeepers, toolmakers, and blacksmiths. One historian described the origins of the small business entrepreneurs as follows:

> A large proportion of the most successful manufacturers in the United States consists of persons who were journeymen, and in a few instances were foreman, in the work-shops and manufactories of Europe; who having been skillful, sober, frugal, and having thus saved a little money, have set up for themselves with great advantage in the United States.[2]

A Shortage of Skilled Labor

When a shortage of skilled labor appeared in the thirteen colonies, colonial leaders lobbied to have more skilled workers delivered to their shores to help take advantage of the opportunities for development. Captain John Smith of Jamestown put it this way:

> When you send again, I entreat you rather send but thirty carpenters, husbandmen, gardeners, fishermen, blacksmiths, masons, and digger up of trees' roots, well provided, than a thousand such as we have.[3]

Colonial employers complained that the shortage of skilled labor forced them to pay "excessive rates." One historian estimated that wages for skilled labor were 30 to 100 percent higher than those paid to comparable workers in England.[4] In response, employers and communities often lured skilled workers away from each other. This, in turn, led the Massachusetts Bay Colony and other colonial governmental authorities to try to regulate competition by putting an upper limit on wages. These early efforts at government regulation of the labor market generally failed in the face of the strong and growing demand for skilled labor.

Labor Force Diversity

From the beginning, our labor force was highly diverse—consisting of indentured servants, slaves, immigrants, well-paid skilled artisans, and small shopkeepers and farmers—both male and female and of all skin colors. This diversity became a hallmark of the American labor force and reduced the development of a class consciousness that helped unions develop in Europe. The American work-force diversity, coupled with expanding opportunities, led to little interest in collective organization in the preindustrial days of the eighteenth century.

Early Unionism

The development of unionism in the colonies was closely intertwined with the development of industry and the industrial revolution. Not all workers were able to easily adjust their work habits to fit the stringent time and disciplinary requirements of industrial work. Managers in the early mills and factories of New England had to impose strong discipline and extensive socialization on immigrants and other first-generation factory workers to make them adapt to the new work system.[5] Box 2–1 excerpts a disciplinary code imposed by a New England employer in the early 1800s. It illustrates the lengths some employers went to in their effort to maintain work discipline.

One reason employers had to go to such great lengths to maintain work discipline was because working conditions were harsh. Box 2–2 describes the working conditions in a southern cotton mill at the turn of the nineteenth century.

The First Trade Unions

The first groups of workers to challenge employers by joining together and demanding improved wages were skilled craftsmen. Most authorities cite the Federal Society of Journeymen Cordwainers, the union of Philadelphia shoemakers, organized in 1794 as the first modern trade union in the United States.[6] The shoemakers were joined by printers, carpenters, and other artisans in New York and a few other large cities.

Generally these unions started when workers jointly agreed on a new wage for their work and laid down their tools if employers resisted the new rate. In other cases, unions were spurred after employers posted wage cuts. Collective bargaining as we know it today did not really occur in the colonial period. Either the unilateral demands of one side were met and work continued, or employers replaced the strikers with workers

Box 2–1

GENERAL REGULATIONS
To Be Observed by Persons Employed by The
LAWRENCE MANUFACTURING COMPANY

1st.   All persons in the employ of the Company, are required to attend assiduously to their various duties, or labor, during working hours; are expected to be fully competent, or to aspire to the upmost efficiency in the work or business they may engage to perform, and to evince on all occasions, in their deportment and conversation, a laudable regard for temperance, virtue, and their moral and social obligations; and in which the Agent will endeavor to set a proper example. No person can be employed by the Company, whose known habits are or shall be dissolute, indolent, dishonest, or intemperate, or who habitually absent themselves from public worship, and violate the Sabbath, or who may be addicted to gambling of any kind.

2d.   All kinds of ardent spirit will be excluded from the Company's ground, except it be prescribed for medicine, or for washes, and external applications. Every kind of gambling and card playing, is totally prohibited within the limits of the Company's ground and Board house.

3d.   Smoking cannot be permitted in the Mills, or other buildings, or yards, and should not be carelessly indulged in the Board Houses and streets. . . .

Lowell, Massachusetts, 21 May 1833.

Source: William Cahn, *A Pictorial History of American Labor* (New York: Crown Publisher, 1972), p. 49.

willing to do the job for the wages they offered. In response, local unions began to coordinate their efforts.

Why Workers Formed Unions   What led workers during the process of industrialization to turn to unions to press their interests? John Commons (see Chapter 1) studied the formation of the earliest American unions in the shoe industry. He argued that unionism was a response to the competitive pressures (he labeled them **competitive menaces**) workers faced as a result of the expansion of the market. The competitive menaces led to lower cost competition (from "bad wares"), lower wages, and worsening employment conditions.

The increased competitive pressures were themselves products of the expansion of markets under way in the economy caused by innovations

Box 2–2

Southern Cotton Mill Towns of the 1800s

The cotton mill village was like one big white family closed off to the external world. Rows and rows of white clapboard houses lined dirt roads leading to the mill, while the mill owner lived some distance away in a mansion.

Workers, mostly women and children, labored sixteen hours a day for wages that were just enough to pay rent on their mill houses and their bills at the general store. Mill workers survived primarily on food grown in their own gardens. Mill owners not only encouraged child labor, they insisted upon it. Some mill villages provided schools, but most did not, and the majority of this first generation of mill workers grew up illiterate. The church was usually built on land owned by the mill which also provided its financial support. Thus sermons frequently followed the theme of hard work, deprivation, and suffering as the path to salvation.

Source: Victoria Byerly, *Hard Times Cotton Mill Girls: Personal Histories of Womanhood and Poverty in the South* (Ithaca, NY: ILR Press, 1986), p. 12.

---

in transportation. As markets expanded, the unity of production found in the position of the master shoemaker gave way to a division in work responsibilities as first journeymen and then assembly workers were used to make shoes. On the technological side there was a shift from hand tools to power machinery and the assembly line.

Although a social transformation was simultaneously occurring along with the increased competitive pressures, Commons argued that workers and early unions did not react against the work relations or the technology per se. Commons concluded that unions were a reaction to the ensuing deterioration in wages and working conditions. Thus, in Commons's view, workers turned to unions as a device to improve their lot and not as a mechanism to alter the social relations of production or to gain "control" of the production process.[7]

Early Court Reaction to Unionism   Employment relationships during the early years of industrialization in this country were governed solely by the **common-law traditions** carried over from Great Britain. Neither any constitutional provision nor any state or federal statutes explicitly addressed the rights of workers or the obligations of employers. It was left to the courts to develop their own prescriptions of the rights and responsibilities of the parties to employment contracts.[8]

Common-law rule generally translated into few enforceable contractual or implied rights for individual employees. Most courts, in fact, were outright hostile toward collective action by labor organizations.

The Conspiracy Doctrine

The actions of the shoemakers' union led to a famous trial in 1806 and a court decision that dominated rulings until the 1840s. A group of journeymen shoemakers (cordwainers) in Philadelphia joined together in 1804 and refused to work with people who were not members of their association. The shoemakers also won an increase in their wage rate. The employer of the shoemakers went to court to counteract the workers' and union's actions. A jury then convicted and fined the shoemakers on the grounds that they had formed an illegal **criminal conspiracy** through their union. The jury argued that the shoemakers' union was illegal on its own terms and had unjustly injured shoemakers who were not part of the union. Box 2–3 describes the Philadelphia shoemakers' case in more detail.

State and local courts in many jurisdictions followed the lead provided by this case. The courts found unions to be criminal conspiracies that impinged on industrial workers' "freedom" to contract with an employer. The courts issued decisions that limited the ability of workers to unionize or, once unionized, to use strikes, boycotts, or other forms of economic pressure.

The courts reflected the conservative, laissez faire economic and political culture of the country. Private property was to be protected; combinations of economic power, including combinations of labor power, were to be limited, and individual, (not collective) freedom to contract was to be preserved. All these principles worked against workers' efforts to build strong and durable unions.

Pre-Civil War Organizing Efforts

Political Initiatives   The combined effects of the criminal conspiracy doctrine and the economic depression that followed the end of the War of 1812 led to the disappearance of most of the early unions. Then around 1820, as the political and voting rights of male, white taxpayers gradually expanded, workers began to form **workingmen's political parties.** The two largest workingmen's parties were found in Philadelphia and New York. These parties were short-lived and generally disintegrated over internal disputes about which candidate to support in the election of 1832, which put Andrew Jackson in the White House.

The failure of the workingmen's parties to put together an effective political coalition to advance labor's interests was only the first in a long sequence of similar failed political efforts by labor parties over the course of U.S. history.

Labor's Economic Advances   Labor was making significant economic strides during these years, however. In the textile mills of New England workers successfully agitated for limitations on the use of child labor.

Box 2–3

The Shoemakers' Case and the Criminal Conspiracy Doctrine

In 1798, the Federal Society of Journeymen Cordwainers managed to boost the wages for making shoes to nearly $1 a pair. The journeymen shoemakers struck again in the fall of 1804, and gained an increase in wages to $2.75 for making a pair of cossack boots, regardless of how they were sold. But after Christmas, when retail orders dropped off, the employers paid a quarter less for "order work" boots (wholesale) and a quarter more for "bespoke" (retail) boots. This wage reduction led to a strike in 1805 when the journeymen demanded a flat price of $3 on both wholesale and retail work. The employers won the strike, and then turned to the courts.

A trial took place in the Philadelphia mayor's court. The jury was made up of merchants and craftsmen: two innkeepers, a merchant, three grocers, a hatter, a tobacconist, a watchmaker, a tailor, a tavernkeeper, and a bottler. A shoemaker called as one of the jurors was disqualified because of his occupation.

The prosecution (the employers) charged that the shoemakers (the defendants), "not being content to work and labour . . . at the usual prices and" had attempted "unjustly and oppressively to increase and argument the prices . . . and unjustly to exact and procure great sums of money for their work and labour." The shoemakers were said to have "unlawfully, perniously, and deceitfully" formed an organization that governed members and other journeymen through "unlawful and arbitrary bye laws, rules and orders."

Said the prosecutors, "Our position is that no man is at liberty to combine, conspire, confederate, and unlawfully agree to regulate the whole body of workmen in the city." These charges were brought under the rubric of English common law concerning criminal conspiracy.

The defense argued that any assembly could be judged unlawful under the prosecution's interpretation of conspiracy law. Said one defense lawyer, "A country dance would be criminal, a cotillion unlawful, even a minuet a conspiracy; and nothing but a horn pipe or a solo would be stepped with impunity!"

When the arguments were all in, the jury deliberated for one evening and returned a verdict of guilty. Each of the defendants was ordered to pay $8—about a week's pay—plus the costs of trial, and to "stand committed until the fines were paid."

Source: From Gloria Stevenson, "Cordwainers Put Their Soles into Bargaining," in *200 Years of American Worklife* (Washington, D.C.: U.S. Department of Labor, 1977), pp. 29–31.

The practice of working from "can't see to can't see" (sun-up to sundown) was first ended by skilled workers in New York, and gradually the 10-hour day became the accepted norm in surrounding industries. Later, Andrew Jackson's brand of people's democracy brought a recognition of the need for a public education system to provide the labor force needed for the expanding economy.[9]

The 1830s also brought the rise and fall of the first effort to create a National Trades Union. By this time, manufacturing was beginning to grow in New England and various small unions of skilled artisans had been formed. The goal of the National Trades Union, like the umbrella organizations that followed in later years, was to bring separate unions together to promote the interests of all workers. The National Trades Union met in annual conventions three times in New York between 1832 and 1837 and then collapsed in the depression of 1837.[10]

By the 1840s the great wave of immigrants from Europe was in full force. The skilled and highly disciplined northern European carpenters, mechanics, and farmers were joined by the poorer and less skilled Irish who, along with the slaves in the south, continued to expand the ethnic and religious diversity in the labor force. Some immigrants, such as the Jews from Russia and Poland who settled in tight communities in New York and several other large cities, carried a tradition of union organizing with them to the United States from Europe. In general, however, the ethnic diversity and competition among workers of different ethnic and skill levels made collective organization difficult.

The Utopian Movements   During the mid and late 1800s a number of new approaches to collective organization based on various utopian principles were put forward. The **utopians** proposed the creation of communities of citizens, workers, and managers who would work and advance together. Their aim was to avoid the divisive and dehumanizing effects of the factory system.

Box 2–4 summarizes the ideas of Horace Greeley, one of the most famous utopian thinkers. The utopian's vision must have sounded like an attractive alternative to workers in the nation's first factories, and these ideas gained a strong following. However, the diversity in the working class, the lure of rising real wages, and the opportunities to move west limited the appeal of the utopian cause.

The Means-Ends Doctrine: Commonwealth v. Hunt   Unions were helped by a shift in the courts' interpretations of the criminal conspiracy doctrine in the 1840s. The most famous decision came in 1842 in *Commonwealth v. Hunt.* In settling that case Judge Shaw concluded that unions per se were not illegal conspiracies. Judge Shaw argued that the court had to examine how unions pursued their goals.

Courts had to assess whether unions had abused their power or had violated the constitutional rights of workers or private property holders in taking any given action. Thus, a **means-ends doctrine** emerged in court decisions.[11] By the late 1800s judges had generally turned from restricting unions' right to exist to issuing injunctions that limited the ability of unions to strike, picket, or boycott employers. This shift in the courts helped unions, but it did not eliminate the many barriers that impeded their expansion.

The Yellow-Dog Contract   One way unions continued to be limited was through the employers' use of the common law in their dealings with employees. Employers in this period could require employees to sign a **yellow-dog contract,** a type of loyalty oath, that stated the employee would neither join nor participate in the activities of a union. Since courts would enforce these contracts as a condition of employment, employees could be fired if they later became involved with a union. Yellow-dog contracts also provided the basis for legal action against union organizers on the grounds that they were interfering with a contractual relationship.

The Labor Wars

From 1860 through the first decade of the twentieth century there was a series of bitter and sometimes violent struggles between workers and their employers. Some of these struggles remained local and concerned only groups of workers and a single employer, while others spread to include workers across the country.

The nation's coal fields were the site for some of the most violent disputes. Worker rebellions in coal were often triggered when mine owners unilaterally cut wages, in some cases by as much as a third.

The Molly Maguires   A secret association of militant Irish miners formed the **Molly Maguires** in 1862 to help striking mine workers resist wage cuts. The conspiracy lasted more than 10 years, when the Maguires were eventually infiltrated by a spy from the Pinkerton Detective Agency who had been hired by employers. The Pinkerton agent developed evidence (later judged by most historians to be of dubious validity) that was used to convict and execute 10 members of the Molly Maguires for murder.

The battles between the Molly Maguires and employers in the mining industry were only one example of the violent wave of strikes that occurred in the last third of the nineteenth century. Strikes in the railroad, steel, meat-packing, and other growing manufacturing industries often erupted into violent clashes between strikers, strikebreakers, local police, and, in some cases, private security forces.

Box 2–4

Horace Greeley

Among the most effective utopian reformers was Horace Greeley, the editor of the *New York Tribune.*

"The earth, the air, the waters, the sunshine, with their natural products, were divinely intended . . . for the enjoyment of the whole human family," stated Greeley. "But as society is now organized, this is not, and cannot be done. . . ."

The right of owning land is one thing," Greeley said. "The right to own thousands and even millions of acres of land is another. I condemn the system of land monopoly."

Greeley's voice, loud and shrill, was one of many being raised for the cause of "elevating the masses." As Emerson said: "Greeley does the thinking for the whole west." And, indeed, the words of Bayard Taylor, the writer, were accurate when he said: "The *Tribune* comes next to the Bible all through the west."

Perhaps of all Greeley's many directives to his readers, the one most remembered was "Young man, go west and grow up with the nation."

The fact that there were available lands in the west theoretically permitted a method of escape for the industrial workers. Some working men and women did go west to escape from industrial work.

Source: William Cahn, *A Pictorial History of American Labor,* 3rd printing (New York: Crown Publishers, 1976), pp. 71–72.

The hardships experienced by workers of this era produced a number of militant supporters who urged labor to fight back. One of the most colorful was a woman who became known as "Mother Jones." (See Box 2–5).

The Haymarket Affair

A major outburst of violence occurred in Chicago in 1886 in events that came to be known as the **Haymarket affair.**[12] Tensions had been building in Chicago after an employer initiated lockout of workers at the McCormick Harvester Works plant on the outskirts of the city. At one point a fight broke between strikebreakers who had crossed a picket line and the locked out workers. Police arrived to quell the fight and started shooting, killing four.

Horace Greeley *(Culver Pictures).*

A rally was called and 4,000 people gathered the following evening at Haymarket Square in Chicago to protest the shootings. After a peaceful meeting police arrived, and then a bomb went off. The police proceeded to open fire on the crowd, killing 10 and wounding another 50.

Eight anarchists were subsequently charged with the bombing and convicted, although no evidence was ever presented that linked these men to the actual bombing. Four of the men were hanged, one committed suicide, and the others served prison sentences that were later commuted by the governor of Illinois.

The Homestead Strike

Another illustration of the forces that confronted early American unionism comes from the **Homestead Strike** directed against the Carnegie

---

Box 2–5

"That's No Lady, That's Mother Jones"

During the late 1800s and early 1900s, when gunfire and bloodshed often accompanied workers' attempts to form unions, a sweet-faced old woman known only as Mother Jones tramped over most of the country's coalfields to encourage miners to organize and strike.

Mother Jones looked like a kindly grandmother. A mere 5 feet tall and weighing less than 100 pounds, she generally wore a genteel, lacetrimmed, black dress and a Victorian bonnet. But while Mother Jones appeared gentle, her words and actions were as hard as the life in the mines.

In 1917–18, 87-year-old Mother Jones told a group of striking West Virginia miners, "You goddamned cowards are losing this strike because you haven't got the guts to go out there and fight and win it. Why the hell don't you take your high-power rifles and blow the goddamned scabs out of the mines?"

The miners loved Mother Jones; mine owners, police, and many less radical union leaders looked forward to her death. She was arrested and jailed several times, once for allegedly conspiring to commit murder, stealing a machine gun, and attempting to blow up a train with dynamite. When she died at the age of 100, the priest who delivered her eulogy said, "Sometimes she used methods that made the righteous grieve. . . . but her faults were the excesses of her courage, her love of justice, the love in her mother's heart."

Source: From Gloria Stevenson, "That's No Lady, That's Mother Jones", in *200 Years of American Worklife* (Washington, D.C.: U.S. Department of Labor, 1977), pp. 104–108.

Steel Company in 1892. The Homestead mill had a longstanding wage agreement with the Amalgamated Association of Iron, Steel, and Tin Workers. Then Andrew Carnegie purchased the Homestead mills in 1889 and placed Henry Clay Frick in charge.[13]

In February 1892 Frick and the Amalgamated reached an impasse in their negotiations over a new contract after Frick demanded steep reductions in wages. The workers struck. Frick proceeded to erect barbed-wire fences around the plant, hired 300 Pinkerton (private security) guards, and began to hire strikebreakers. As the Pinkertons were being moved up the Ohio river to guard the plant, they were confronted by striking steelworkers. A battle followed in which a dozen men were killed on each side, and the Pinkertons were driven off.

The strike then spread to other mills, and so did the violence. The strike dragged on for months. With their personal and union coffers wiped out, the steelworkers eventually conceded and went back to work as nonunion workers. The Amalgamated was shattered as a union, and

Mother Jones *(Culver Pictures)*.

steel unionism was eliminated from many of the steel mills in the Pittsburgh area.

The Pullman Strike   Led by Eugene V. Debs in the early 1890s, the American Railway Union instigated a series of industrial actions against the railroad companies and the wage cuts they were demanding.[14] At one point the union had a membership of 150,000 workers. But then came **the Pullman strike.**

The employees of the Pullman Palace Car Company lived in a company-run town in Pullman, Illinois. They paid their food, utility, and tax bills to the company. In the depression year of 1893, the company cut workers' wages by 22 percent without any reduction in rents and other services; so employees asked for a wage increase. However, the company proceeded to fire some of the workers who tried to restore the wage cuts through negotiation. Pullman workers then appealed to the American

Box 2–6

Eugene V. Debs

Eugene Victor Debs, of Terre Haute, Indiana, was a locomotive fireman from 1871 until the depression of 1873 left him jobless. He was a local officer in the Brotherhood of Locomotive Firemen during the great railway strike of 1877. Although neither he nor his union took part in the strike, Debs was confused and stunned by its violence. He soon emerged as a national officer of the union and later as editor of its official publication. Over the next 15 years, interrupted only by a brief term in political office, Debs played a leading role in the firemen's union.

In the late 1880's, Debs changed from a man who shunned strikes and their associated violence to a socialist labor leader who envisioned the strike as a weapon to achieve economic justice. In 1892, disillusioned by the lack of unity among the railway unions, which remained divided along craft lines, he quit his Brotherhood job and undertook the organization of the American Railway Union (ARU), convinced that only the unification of all railway workers into one association could solve their problems.

An able organizer, shrewd and practical, Debs was immediately successful in his attempts to organize a union of all railroad workers. Within a year, 465 locals with a membership of more than 150,000 were enrolled.

Debs once said, "While there is a lower class, I am in it. While there is a criminal element, I am of it; where there is a soul in prison, I am not free."

Source: Patrick J. Ziska, "The Violent Years of Labor's Youth", in *200 Years of American Worklife* (Washington, D.C.: U.S. Department of Labor, 1977), pp. 99–103.

Eugene V. Debs *(UPI/Bettmann Newsphotos)*.

Railway Union for help, and a sympathetic work stoppage ensued on railroads across the country.

As the strike spread, a court injunction was issued on the grounds that striking railway workers were impeding the delivery of mail and interstate commerce. President Grover Cleveland sent in federal troops to enforce the order. Violence followed, including the burning of freight cars and other railway equipment.

Debs, who had been indicted for conspiracy in restraint of commerce, appealed to other trade unions to strike in support of the railway workers. Debs's appeal met with little support, and, facing a growing number of state and federal troops, the strikers returned to work defeated. Debs (see Box 2–6) went to jail but eventually emerged as the leading American socialist of his time.

The Need for National Unions

As transportation networks expanded across the country, workers were confronted by employers who could transfer goods and work across state borders. Up against these factors, local strikes and union action had limited power. The need for national labor organizations became ever more clear, and a number of national trade unions were formed.

The early national unions, such as the American Railway Workers, saw their membership fluctuate along with movements in the national economy.[15] When times were good, membership expanded and union powers increased. When the economy went into one of the severe recessions that marked early American industrialization, union membership waned as organized workers lost the power to press their demands.

The Knights of Labor

In 1869 the **Knights of Labor** emerged as one of the most important early national labor movements in the United States. The group was part fraternal society and part union. The Knights organized workers on a city-by-city basis across crafts. The philosophy espoused by the Knights proclaimed that all workers had common interests, regardless of skill or occupation.

The constitution of the Knights declared that the ultimate aim of the organization was the establishment of cooperative institutions. After this was accomplished, the Knights believed labor and capital could then live harmoniously together. To promote these objectives, the Knights favored organization, education, and cooperation.[16] With regard to trade union activities, the Knights advocated the substitution of arbitration for strikes. The Knights also favored such policies as the establishment of an eight-hour work day, legislative regulation of health and safety conditions, prohibition of child labor, and government ownership of railroads, telegraphs, and telephones. The Knights was a reformist organization seeking trade union and legislation action to limit the excesses of industrial society.

Terence Powderly (see Box 2–7) became head of the Knights in 1879 and had as his ultimate objective the establishment of producers' cooperatives. He felt that strikes and other union activities were destructive and

Box 2–7

Terence Powderly

"The working women and men of America, yes and of the world, have reason to hold in grateful appreciation the memory of . . . heroic women who struggle for freedom of opportunity for all," stated Terence V. Powderly, who was the Knights of Labor's most influential leader.

Source: William Cahn, *A Pictorial History of American Labor* (New York: Crown Publishers, 1977), pp. 115–120.

Terence Powderly *(The Bettmann Archive).*

incapable of bringing about the necessary political reforms. He favored negotiation and arbitration.

Splits eventually emerged within the leadership of the Knights concerning the extent to which the organization would devote its attention to trade unionism versus political activity. Many of the rank and file members of the Knights, in contrast to Powderly, favored the use of strikes and boycotts to achieve higher wages.

Membership in the Knights of Labor fluctuated greatly along with the national economy and the fortunes of local branches, peaking in 1886 at around 700,000.[17] Yet, by the late 1880s, the influence of the Knights was waning. The organization suffered from the bad publicity surrounding the violence that had emerged in the coal fields, at Homestead, and at Pullman. The Knights also suffered greatly from the publicity following events that occurred at Haymarket Square in Chicago in 1886.

The Industrial Workers of the World

The **Industrial Workers of the World (IWW)** provided workers with a radical alternative. The platform of the IWW was to organize labor into industrial unions that would take direct and vigorous action to improve working conditions (see Box 2–8). The IWW also favored the creation of an independent political party to work for the overthrow of capitalism and to establish instead a "co-operative commonwealth".[18] The membership of the IWW came largely from miners and lumber workers.

The IWW developed a reputation of a violence-prone band of misfits who were solely concerned with the overthrow of American institutions. Yet, while the strikes of the IWW were often raucous and sometimes turned violent, much of the violence was initiated by local authorities and vigilante groups, and IWW members were themselves often the victims of the violence.[19]

Although the platform of the IWW focused on the overthrow of capitalism, at its height the IWW led a series of strikes that focused on improvements in wages and working conditions. The IWW was never able to attain a large membership. The IWW suffered from a poor image and a tension between its bold political goals and the more practical objectives favored by much of its membership.

When World War I began, "Big Bill" (William D.) Haywood and other leaders of the IWW opposed U.S. involvement and favored neither side in the conflict on the grounds that only capitalists would benefit from the war. Haywood and other IWW activists were eventually tried for sedition, and the IWW faded from the scene.

Injunctions and Antitrust Rulings

Unions faced additional difficulties in the early 1900s when the courts began to find that union actions were a violation of **antitrust legislation.**

Box 2–8

Preamble of the Industrial Workers of the World

The working class and the employing class have nothing in common. There can be no peace so long as hunger and want are found among millions of working people and the few, who make up the employing class, have all the good things of life.

Between these two classes a struggle must go on until the workers of the world organize as a class, take possession of the earth and the machinery of production, and abolish the wage system.

We find that the centering of the management of industries into fewer and fewer hands makes the trade unions unable to cope with the ever growing power of the employing class. The trade unions foster a state of affairs which allows one set of workers to be pitted against another set of workers in the same industry, thereby helping defeat one another in wage wars. Moreover, the trade unions aid the employing class to mislead the workers into the belief that the working class have interests in common with their employers.

These conditions can be changed and the interest of the working class upheld only by an organization formed in such a way that all its members in any one industry, or in all industries if necessary, cease work whenever a strike or lockout is on in any department thereof, thus making an injury to one an injury to all.

Instead of the conservative motto, "A fair day's wage for a fair day's work," we must inscribe on our banner the revolutionary watchword, "Abolition of the wage system."

It is the historic mission of the working class to do away with capitalism. The army of production must be organized, not only for the every-day struggle with capitalists, but also to carry on production when capitalism shall have been overthrown. By organizing industrially we are forming the structure of the new society within the shell of the old.

Source: Paul F. Brissenden, *The I.W.W.: A Study of American Syndicalism,* 2d ed., (NY: Columbia University Press, 1920), pp. 351–52.

Federal antitrust legislation had passed Congress in an attempt to protect against the power acquired by expanding business combinations.

The Sherman Anti-trust Act   The Sherman Antitrust Act of 1890 declared illegal every contract, combination, or conspiracy that restrained trade across state boundaries. The act did not refer directly to unions because Congress had business trusts and monopolies in mind and not unions when passing the law. Nevertheless, courts began to apply the Sherman Antitrust Act to unions.

The most celebrated antitrust case against a union (the **Danbury Hatters case**) occurred in 1908. The United Hatters of America had called for a consumer boycott against the D. E. Loewe Company in an effort to gain union recognition. The union then went a step further and called for boycotts against other firms doing business with Loewe, a tactic known as a **secondary boycott.** The secondary boycott was directed at retailers, wholesalers, and customers and proved to be successful. Loewe and Company then went to court.

The U.S. Supreme Court eventually heard the case and ruled that unions were covered under the Sherman Antitrust Act. Specifically, the court directed the United Hatters to pay $250,000 in treble damages to the company.

The Clayton Act   Unions campaigned aggressively against the use of court injunctions and succeeded in gaining passage of the **Clayton Act** in 1914. The act declared that "the labor of a human being is not a commodity or article of commerce." Labor thought this language would lead to the end of labor injunctions. Yet courts interpreted the act narrowly, and unions continued to face judges who issued injunctions that limited the ability of unions to strike, picket, or boycott employers.

The Norris-LaGuardia Act   It was not until passage of the **Norris-LaGuardia Act** in 1932 that clear language outlawing the use of injunctions in most labor disputes was signed into law. The Norris-LaGuardia Act also outlawed yellow-dog contracts. Other provisions of the Norris-LaGuardia Act endorsed workers' rights to strike and to take other collective actions in their self-interest. These provisions foreshadowed the more comprehensive endorsement of collective bargaining that was to come with the passage of the National Labor Relations Act in 1935.

The Norris-LaGuardia Act lacked enforcement procedures. Thus, union recognition and collective bargaining remained a voluntary process between labor and management.

The Rise of The AFL

It was the **American Federation of Labor (AFL),** founded in 1886, that overcame the opposition of employers and the courts to build a membership able to survive the ups and downs of business cycles. The AFL was led by the former cigar maker Samuel Gompers (see Box 2–9) for all but one year between 1886 and his death in 1924.

Box 2–9

Samuel Gompers

Samuel Gompers was proud of being a "practical" man. He believed in applying sound business practices to the union movement. He was not a theorist, but was convinced of the importance to labor of fighting for immediate aims. Once asked the objectives of the A.F.L., he reportedly answered with one word: "More."

The A.F.L. under Gompers avoided politics in the usual sense. "No party politics, be they democratic, republican, populist, socialist or any other, shall have a place in the Federation," said Gompers. But the A.F.L. did play an important role, under pressure from its members, in helping win social and labor legislation, nationally and in the states. Gompers was skeptical of some legislative proposals supported by liberal leaders, even opposing as a socialist trend government health, unemployment insurance, and old-age pensions. Gompers believed labor's gains should be won largely by collective bargaining. But he did lend the A.F.L. influence, which was considerable, for or against numerous other legislative efforts.

Source: William Cahn, *A Pictorial History of American Labor* (New York: Crown Publishers, 1976), pp. 205–207

Samuel Gompers *(The Bettmann Archive).*

Business Unionism

The AFL espoused a **business unionism** philosophy. This philosophy was well expressed by Gompers when he said that "the trades unions pure and simple are the organizations of the wage workers to secure their present material and practical improvement and to achieve their final emancipation."[20] Business unionism cut a compromise between the reformist Knights of Labor and the radical IWW.

The AFL was in favor of political action through which labor would help its friends and punish its opponents, but it eschewed any permanent political alliances or long-term political objectives. The AFL strategy was to promote the organization of workers into unions that had **exclusive jurisdiction** (where only one union represented a designated group of workers). The AFL strove to use collective bargaining to achieve improved wages and working conditions.

The AFL was (and is) a federation of national unions. It does not negotiate collective bargaining agreements but, rather, acts as the representative of national unions in political activities and political lobbying. The AFL also provides assistance to national unions in their union-organizing activities.

Craft Focus

One of the guiding principles of the AFL was that workers should be organized into separate **craft unions.** For this, each trade—such as carpenters, printers, machinists, and the skilled trades within large manufacturing firms—was to organize workers engaged in these occupations, regardless of the industry or firm in which the workers were employed.

The Evolution of Management in Industrial Relations

A full understanding of industrial relations history requires an equally well grounded understanding of the evolution of managerial practices. There is a growing school of thought among historians that it is American *management,* more than American unions, that makes U.S. labor history and contemporary industrial relations practices unique.[21] At the heart of this uniqueness lie two interrelated features of American management—the desire for autonomy from government or any other institution that might limit management's prerogatives and a deep-seated opposition to unions.

The Origins of Factory Management

Over the course of the 1800s a continual expansion of potential markets for manufactured goods was made possible by the growth of the railroad, telephone, and telegraph industries. This increase in markets led employers to adopt the factory system and mass production technologies (the assembly line). Through the factory system employers gained from economies of scale and low production costs.

"If a man is dissatisfied, it is his privilege to quit." This oft-quoted statement of a steel industry executive during the McKees Rocks, Pennsylvania, strike in 1909 captures the prevailing philosophy of U.S. employers and their response to worker unrest in the years before World War I. Company executives asserted their rights as owners to treat labor as a commodity and to oppose challenges to their authority by unions.

The Drive System

To manage the expanding factories employers initially gave substantial power to line foremen, who were considered the **drive system** of management.[22] Hiring, firing, and general supervision of labor were all controlled by these foremen.[23] The arbitrary and often discriminatory treatment of workers by foremen created extremely high turnover rates among both unskilled and skilled workers. One estimate, for example, put turnover in auto plants before 1913 at 370 percent per year!

The costs of high turnover did not, however, go unnoticed by some managers. In 1913, for example, Henry Ford decided to introduce the $5 a day wage for his employees in an effort to lower employee turnover and to improve the performance of his auto assembly lines.

Around World War I the combination of tight labor markets, government pressure for wartime production, and a rising threat of unionization led a number of large firms to establish the professional personnel departments that are described in the next section. But the drive system continued to dominate the workplace in the majority of smaller establishments. And, regardless of whether foremen or personnel managers administered personnel policies, one managerial value held constant: unions capable of directly challenging management authority were to be avoided.

Scientific Management

The first important step toward establishing a professional personnel management function within the firm came with the introduction of **scientific management.** Although the ideas behind the scientific management movement can be traced as far back as the mid-1800s, Frederick Taylor's promotion of this movement in the first two decades of the twentieth century was critical. Scientific management blended economic incentives and industrial engineering techniques to produce the "one best way" for organizing work. By tying the individual worker's wages to output, it was assumed, the interests of the worker—economic rewards—and the interests of the firm—productivity—could be made compatible.

Box 2–10 describes how scientific management principles were applied on Henry Ford's assembly line. Management's function was to design the jobs and to supervise and compensate the work force so as to eliminate conflicts of interest between workers and the employer. Industrial engineering principles (such as time-and-motion studies) and incentive wages were employed to this end.

Scientific management stood in direct contradiction to the beliefs held by those who advocated collective bargaining. Instead of seeing conflicts of interest as an inherent part of the employment relationship, advocates of scientific management argued that appropriate task designs and wage systems could eliminate the sources of conflict between workers and employers. Because the optimal work system was to be determined through "scientific" engineering studies, there was no role for bargaining and therefore no need for union representation.

One lasting effect of scientific management was its advocacy of industrial engineering principles and a narrow division of labor in organizing work. This form of job design and work organization gradually became the standard in the mass-production industries, and unions inherited this form when they expanded their membership in the mass-production industries (such as auto, steel, and textiles) in the 1930s.

Welfare Capitalism, Human Relations, and the American Plan

By 1920 another competing method of management gained popularity. The **human relations movement,** (or **welfare capitalism**) stressed the social significance of work and work groups. Human relations theory predicted that satisfied workers would achieve higher productivity. The scientific management and human relations schools both believed that by following their principles employers could eliminate conflict with workers, thereby eliminating workers' need for union representation.

As the basic tenets of human relations gained influence over the 1920s, personnel departments gradually expanded in scope and influence. The departments centralized and standardized many of the functions that had previously been controlled by foremen. Hiring, firing, discipline, promotion, and compensation policies were developed and administered by the personnel staff. Foremen, in turn, were trained to follow these policies.

Management's Response to Unionism in the 1920s

Coinciding with the growth of progressive personnel policies during and after World War I was an aggressive **open shop movement.** This movement sought to discourage unionization through company-controlled independent unions and the expansion of pension, welfare, and profit-sharing programs. By the mid-1920s, these progressive personnel pro-

Box 2–10

Assembly Line

Scientific Management in the Auto Industry

Production efficiency in the final assembly of cars rose, but the soaring demand for Ford's Model T, introduced in 1908, rose even faster. Ford still had to rely on skilled mechanics to perform the complicated tasks in the Piquette plant—such as filing and fitting together the parts for transmissions and engines. These workers were not protected by union work rules, but their monopoly of mechanical skills and their crucial role in the production process enabled them to work at their own pace. Even the less-skilled assembly workers had some control over their work pace. As they pushed their bins from car to car, they could slow down to rest or to speak a word with their workmates. Beyond a certain point, supervisors simply could not force the men to adopt a faster gait or completely abandon their occasional socializing.

To gain greater control over the production process, Ford began to lay plans for a new plant in the rural village of Highland Park. It would be, he announced, the biggest

The Ford Highland Park assembly line *(Culver Pictures).*

grams were commonplace among the very largest firms in manufacturing and service industries.[24]

With the growth of progressive personnel policies came a corresponding growth in suppressive antiunion practices, such as industrial espionage, blacklisting of union members or supporters, strikebreaking, and

automobile plant in the world, employing new production methods that would revolutionize the auto industry.

Ford was not alone in seeking ways to spur production and lower labor costs. Factory owners had been mechanizing and deskilling certain kinds of production for many years, but after 1900, the nation's larger corporations attempted to do so on a broader, more systematic basis. The principles of this new "scientific management" were most vigorously espoused by Frederick Taylor, a former steel mill supervisor who became, after 1903, the nation's leading consultant on "productivity"—or worker output.

Like Ford, Taylor complained that in most workplaces—whether union or non-union—"The shop [is] really run by the workmen and not by the bosses. The workmen together carefully plan . . . just how fast each job should be done." Taylor's solution was simple: "All possible brainwork should be removed from the shop and centered in the planning or laying-out department." Management, in short, should redesign every job and divide it into dozens of simple, repetitive tasks performed by unskilled laborers or semi-skilled machine tenders. Skilled workers with their relatively high pay would no longer have to be tolerated in such large numbers. With deskilling, most craftsmen would be replaced, in Taylor's words, "by men of smaller attainments, who are therefore cheaper than those required under the old system."

When Taylor came to Detroit in 1909 and spoke to executives at Packard, Henry Ford was already planning to make his new Highland Park plant (dubbed the "Crystal Palace" because of its many windows) a model of "scientific management." Between 1910 and 1913, he put his ideas into practice by standardizing parts production and developing the auto industry's first moving assembly line. Where before entire engines had been built by a single mechanic with a few helpers, now the engine blocks were pulled past a line of over 100 workers. Each worker performed a specialized task as the engine (or its parts) moved past: one would ream bearings, one every seven seconds, all day long; the next would file bearings, one every 14 seconds, all day long; and the next would put bearings on camshafts, one every 10 seconds, all day long.

H. L. Arnold, writing of Ford in 1916, concluded that the company "desires and prefers machine operators who have nothing to unlearn, who have no theories of correct surface speeds for metal finishing, and who will do what they are told, over and over again, from bell-time to bell-time.

Source: Quoted from Steve Babson, *Working Detroit* (New York: Adama Books, 1984), pp. 29–31.

use of private police forces to disband picket lines. Company-controlled unions were set up in a number of chemical, oil, and other large firms.

The combination of progressive and suppressive policies to avoid unions was highly successful. Union membership fell from 5.8 million members in 1921 to fewer than 2 million members in 1931.

The Rise of Industrial Unionism

As the organization of production moved from small shops to large-scale mass production, the vast array of semiskilled and unskilled production workers were left without a basis for organizing. Furthermore, the AFL's emphasis on craft organizing made it difficult to counter the power of large-scale industrial corporations. For example, in 1919 a strike against the steel industry was called by 24 different unions with jurisdiction over different craft groups. The strike ultimately failed in part because of the inability of these unions to coordinate their efforts.

As a result, by the early 1920s a number of union leaders and socialists were urging the formation of new **industrial unions** that would organize all production and maintenance workers in a given industry, regardless of their skill level or craft. Since this approach to organizing would cut into the jurisdictions of many established craft unions, it was opposed vigorously by Gompers, by his successor as president of the AFL, William Green, and by other AFL union presidents.

The CIO Challenge to the AFL

The debate between the advocates of AFL craft unions and the advocates of industrial unionism came to a head at the AFL convention in 1935. At this convention John L. Lewis, president of the United Mine Workers and a leading spokesman for industrial unionism (see Box 2–11), lost a crucial vote on the issue of granting charters to industrial unions in the auto and rubber industries. A fight ensued, and Lewis landed a punch on the nose of "Big Bill" Hutcheson, president of the Carpenters' Union. Lewis and his supporters then stormed out of the convention and established the Committee for Industrial Organization as a rival federation to the AFL. Later this group changed its name to the **Congress of Industrial Organizations (CIO).**

The member unions in the CIO enlisted a large number of socialists as union organizers and, in general, projected a more militant image in collective bargaining than did many of the AFL unions. At the same time, the CIO and the AFL shared a commitment to the use of collective bargaining as the central means of achieving economic gains for their members.

The National Industrial Recovery Act

The great depression and its staggering unemployment raised doubts in the work force's mind about management's true commitment to progressive personnel policies. Labor unrest was rising, both in its frequency and its intensity. Encouraged by the passage of the **National Industrial Recovery Act (NIRA)** in 1933, Section 7(a) of which declared the rights of employees to self-organize, workers began organizing in greater numbers

Box 2–11

John L. Lewis: The Leader and His Strategy

No labor leader played a more important or colorful role in history from the 1930s to the 1950s than John L. Lewis. His skill in capturing the changed political climate of the Roosevelt administration is illustrated by the following handbill used in organizing coal miners in the 1930s.

> The United States Government Has Said LABOR MUST ORGANIZE. . . . Forget about injunctions, yellow dog contracts, blacklists, and the fear of dismissal. The employers cannot and will not dare to go to the Government for privileges if it can be shown that they have denied the right of organization to their employees. ALL WORKERS ARE FULLY PROTECTED IF THEY DESIRE TO JOIN A UNION.

Organize John L. Lewis did—5 million American workers into industrial unions in the major mass production industries of the nation in about 4 years.

· · ·

Lewis was the son of a Welsh immigrant coal miner. He went to work in the coal mines at 14 and his quick mind, strong personality, and gift for oratory soon won him election to Illinois union posts. In 1920 Lewis became president of the United Mine Workers of America. From that time until his death in 1960 he pursued the course of organizing the unorganized and representing workers in collective bargaining and political affairs with the vigor and style that is nicely captured in the following excerpt from one of his speeches:

> I have never faltered or failed to present the cause or plead the case of the mine workers of this country. I have pleaded your case from the pulpit and the public platform: in joint conferences with the operators of this country; before the bar of state legislatures; in the councils of the President's cabinet; and in the public press of this nation—not in the quavering tones of a feeble mendicant asking alms, but in the thundering voice of the captain of a mighty host, demanding the rights to which free men are entitled.

Source: Quoted from B. Kimball Baker, "The Great Depression," in *200 Years of American Worklife* (Washington, D.C.: U.S. Department of Labor, 1977), pp. 142, 150.

and strikes increased. By 1934 union membership and strike activity had returned to the levels reached in the years immediately after World War I.[25]

But in 1935 the Supreme Court ruled the NIRA unconstitutional. The stage was set for a crucial public policy debate, the ultimate outcome of which was the **New Deal** industrial relations system.

Box 2–12

The Great Depression

People perceived the Great Depression in different ways. Some looked at it dramatically, as did British economist John Maynard Keynes when he compared the situation in Europe and on the American continent to the Dark Ages. Others looked at it simply, like the 14-year-old Appalachian boy in Chicago who said, "See, I never heard that word 'depression' before. They would all just say 'hard times' to me."

The bare facts of the situation are eloquent enough. By early 1933 unemployment had increased to about 13 million—about 25 percent of the labor force. A third of these people were between the ages of 16 and 24. Hourly wages were down 60 percent. Industrial output was down by about half. On the farm, income was off by two-thirds, tenancy had doubled. 1 of every 4 farms was being foreclosed, and 500,000 farm families were living at the starvation level. A million transients were on the road, including 200,000 young people.

Unemployed autoworkers marched on the closed River Rouge Ford plant in Dearborn, Michigan, and four of them were shot by notorious "security guard" Harry Bennett and his thugs.

Former professionals and skilled tradespeople demonstrated potato papers and patent medicines in store windows and sold apples on street corners to the tune of a popular song, "Brother Can You Spare a Dime?" which reflected the desperate times.

A huge band of jobless veterans encamped in Washington and were routed in a needless show of military force which involved future war heroes named MacArthur, Eisenhower, and Patton.

Source: Quoted from B. Kimball Baker, "The Great Depression," in *200 Years of American Worklife* (Washington, D.C.: U.S. Department of Labor, 1977), pp. 140–141.

The New Deal Labor Policy

The election of Franklin D. Roosevelt as President in 1932, and the economic and social crises caused by the great depression (described in Box 2–12), gave rise to a new era in federal labor policy. Roosevelt introduced a series of new governmental programs designed to bolster citizens' purchasing power and to assist workers and the poor to cope with their economic hardships. The new programs included unemployment insurance, job creation, social security, and the minimum wage. Roosevelt's program became known as the New Deal.

The National Labor Relations Act

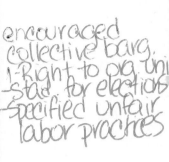

A critical part of the New Deal agenda was enactment of a new labor policy. The cornerstone of the new national labor policy was the **National Labor Relations Act (NLRA)** of 1935, also known as the Wagner Act after its chief legislative sponsor, Senator Robert F. Wagner of New York. The NLRA was important because it explicitly *encouraged* collective bargaining. The NLRA gave employees the right to organize themselves into unions, set standards for union elections, and specified unfair labor practices of employers.

John L. Lewis and his CIO colleagues quickly capitalized on this changing environment by, among other things, imploring workers to join unions with slogans such as "The President Wants You To Organize!" (See also Box 2–11.) It was in this new environment that the autoworkers in Detroit and the rubber workers in Akron refused to leave their plants and staged successful **sit-down strikes,** through which they gained collective bargaining contracts. Unrest and worker militance convinced many employers in the steel industry and others that unions and collective bargaining were to stay.

The Roots of the NLRA in American Practice and Experience

The NLRA did not constitute a completely new or untried way for resolving labor and management conflicts. Instead, the act embodied many of the principles and practices that had demonstrated their fit with American political values and with the practices of many unions and companies. The railroad, clothing, and other industries, for example, had developed ongoing relationships in the years before the depression.

The new law also codified many of the policies that had been recommended and pursued by the national War Labor Board (regulating wages and prices) in World War I and the National Labor Board that had been established under the now-defunct NIRA. The law also endorsed the pragmatic form of collective bargaining that had been promoted by the AFL.

Nonetheless, the law was not passed without vocal and vociferous opposition from employer groups. It was not until the NLRA was ruled constitutional by the Supreme Court in 1937, in the **NLRA v. Jones & Laughlin** case,[26] that most firms began to accept the inevitability of collective bargaining.

Indeed, it was not the law alone that produced the transition to what we will refer to as the **New Deal industrial relations system.** Instead, this turning point in industrial relations was brought about by the confluence of (1) a shift in political power that accompanied the depression and the election of the Roosevelt administration, which created the support needed to enact legislation in favor of worker and union rights to bargain; (2)

a shift in the strategy of the labor movement away from the craft union and voluntarist model of the AFL under Gompers to the industrial unionism model of organizing and representing workers promulgated by the CIO; and (3) the passage of a law that provided a stable foundation for collective bargaining.

This was indeed a unique confluence of events. The events surrounding passage of the NLRA were unique because, as labor historian Irving Bernstein has argued, the NLRA was passed at "the most favorable possible moment," when political support for improving the economic conditions of the nation's workers was at its historic high-water mark.[27]

The New Deal industrial relations system is examined below using the three-tiered model of the strategic, middle, and workplace levels of industrial relations practices.

The Middle Level: Collective Bargaining as the Cornerstone

The enactment of the NLRA signaled the choice of the middle tier of activity as the preferred forum for labor and management jointly to address and to resolve their differences. Once a majority of workers indicated that they wanted to be represented by a union, management was required by law to negotiate with that union over wages, hours, and working conditions.

It was hoped the NLRA would foster industrial peace. Peace would be encouraged, first, by replacing what had often been violent conflicts over union recognition with orderly election procedures and, second, by lending a degree of permanence to the union's right to represent the employees. Employers could no longer unilaterally terminate their recognition of a union during recessions.

The Strategic Level: Management Acts and the Union Reacts

Management rights to make strategic business decisions were left intact by the NLRA. As collective bargaining evolved, the principle "management acts and the workers react" became its key doctrine.[28]

Leaving strategic business decisions to management fit not only management's desire for control over the key decisions on resource allocation in the firm, but also the business unionism philosophy of the labor movement. Even the supporters of industrial unionism held to the view that unions should not seek to participate directly in managerial decision making or to gain control of private enterprise. Instead, unions sought to preserve their independence through the maintenance of a clear separation between union and management duties.

The American labor movement had a moderate agenda for political and social reform. Labor had no ultimate political goal of overthrowing the capitalist system but, rather, sought to improve workers' living standards gradually. Thus, at the strategic level, the New Deal system coincided with the values held by many in the ranks of the labor movement, as well as those held by management and the American public.

The Workplace Level: Job Control Unionism The arrival of established rules for collective bargaining did not produce a revolutionary new system for organizing work. The principles of scientific management had spread in industry as many employers became convinced of the need to rationalize the structure of jobs and the methods of pay. What collective bargaining did do was to codify many of the existing work systems within the labor contract.[29]

Labor Contracts

The writing of labor contracts met the needs of both management and labor. Labor reaped greater uniformity and fairness in workplace administration and thereby overcame much of the arbitrary power previously exercised by foremen. Management, in turn, achieved the work force stability necessary to take advantage of growing market opportunities. Government policymakers came to value the industrial peace this system provided during World War II, and they actively promoted this system.

The Post-World War II Evolution of the New Deal System

The New Deal system gradually diffused throughout the United States as union membership expanded from 3.5 million in 1934 to 17 million, or approximately 35 percent of the nonagricultural labor force, by the mid-1950s. Although the fifties proved to mark the peak of union penetration in the private sector economy, the New Deal principles continued to shape collective bargaining through the early 1990s. Within this long evolution, however, several distinct stages of development can be identified.

The 1940s: Institutionalization of Basic Principles

The exigencies of World War II demanded that labor and management maximize production of the goods needed to support the war, while avoiding both strikes and wage and price inflation. To help achieve these objectives, the Roosevelt administration established the national **War Labor Board (WLB)** in January 1942. The WLB was a tripartite agency, composed of neutrals who chaired boards of inquiry that included representatives of labor and management. Although the agency lacked any legal enforcement power, the tripartite structure, the national commitment to the war effort, and the implicit threat of more direct legislative intervention gave the "recommendations" of the agency considerable influence. From 1942 to 1945 the WLB succeeded in helping settle over 20,000 labor-management disputes.[30]

In carrying out this role, the board also used its offices to promote wider acceptance of collective bargaining. In fact, many of the actual contracts the board wrote remained in effect, with minor changes, throughout the postwar era.

In addition to its substantive role in helping gain acceptance of collective bargaining, the WLB served as a training group for many of the leading mediators, arbitrators, and government advisors who would later shape the evolution of collective bargaining in the decades that followed the war. Those professionals shared a deep commitment to a type of collective bargaining that involved little direct government intervention. George W. Taylor, chairman of the WLB and a leading teacher and neutral after the war, described his and his colleagues' views as follows:

> One conclusion invariably emerges whenever and wherever "the labor problem" is subjected to impartial analysis. It is: collective bargaining must be preserved and strengthened as the bulwark of industrial relations in a democracy. This is just another way of saying that organized labor and management should settle their own differences by understanding, compromises, and agreement without government interference. A rare unanimity of opinion exists about the soundness of collective bargaining as the most appropriate means for establishing conditions of employment.[31]

After the war ended and the WLB was disbanded, a surge of strikes overtook the nation, as illustrated in Box 2–13. The strikes were in part spurred by labor's efforts to gain wage increases that had been foregone during the war. In 1946 more production time was lost because of strikes than in any year before or since.

The strike wave, along with a general swing toward a more conservative political climate and a switch to Republican control of the Congress, contributed to the passage of the Labor Management Relations Act, known as the Taft-Hartley Act, in 1947. The act's amendments to the NLRA strengthened management's power at the bargaining table by limiting the union's rights to boycott the employer and by establishing a detailed set of rules that governed the union's obligation to bargain. It also designated the rights of the government to intervene in strikes that constituted national emergencies.

All of those changes reflected a shift in the public's view. The postwar strike wave had led many in the public to conclude that unions were too powerful.

Given this turn in the political environment, employers might have attempted, as in previous periods of labor history, to break from their union relationships. Collective bargaining had become sufficiently entrenched, however, and unions were viewed as sufficiently strong that a rebalancing of labor-management power occurred instead.

Throughout the 1940s management in the larger unionized firms had taken steps to professionalize their industrial relations staffs. The postwar strike wave further elevated the importance of trained professionals who could help stabilize labor-management relations by establishing formal procedures for negotiating and administering labor contracts. As the large firms adapted to collective bargaining, they served as examples for

Box 2–13

The Postwar Strike Wave

With the end of the war, the expected strike wave began. . . .
Forty-three thousand oil workers struck in twenty states on
September 16th (1945). Two hundred thousand coal miners struck
September 21st. . . . Forty-four thousand Northwest lumber
workers struck, seventy thousand Midwest truck drivers, forty
thousand machinists in San Francisco and Oakland. East Coast
longshoremen struck for nineteen days, flat glass workers for 102
days, and New England textile workers for 133 days. . . .

When G.M. failed to respond to a union offer to have all issues
settled by arbitration if the company would open its books for
public examination, 225,000 workers struck on November 21st. . . .
On January 15th, 1946, 174,000 electrical workers struck. Next day
93,000 meatpackers walked out. On January 21st, 750,000
steelworkers struck, the largest strike in United States history. At
the height of these and 250 lesser disputes, 1,600,000 workers were
on strike. On April 1st, 340,000 soft-coal miners struck. . . . The first
six months of 1946 marked what the U.S. Bureau of Labor Statistics
called the "most concentrated period of labor-management strife in
the country's history," with 2,970,000 workers involved in strikes
starting in this period.

Source: Jeremy Brecher, *Strike!* (San Francisco: Straight Arrow Books, 1972), pp.
227–228.

smaller organizations.[32] Thus, the rise of powerful unions had produced a
managerial response to professionalize labor-management relations.

Unions, too, faced and made a number of key strategic choices in the
1940s that had an important bearing on the shape of collective bargaining
in subsequent years. In the immediate postwar years conflicts emerged
inside unions over the role of Communists in the labor movement. The
net results of these battles were that the CIO expelled a number of
Communist-dominated unions (such as the United Electrical Workers)
and that some individual unions (such as the United Auto Workers)
purged Communist party members from leadership positions.

The 1946 round of bargaining in the auto industry illustrates the
choices union leaders made that were to affect the long-term development of collective bargaining. During the 1946 Auto Workers' strike
against General Motors, Walter Reuther, head of the General Motors
department of the union, called on GM to open its financial records to the
union. Reuther proposed limiting the UAW wage demands in return for a
pledge by GM not to raise prices. If those demands had been accepted,
it would have transformed collective bargaining by expanding union

influence over to strategic management issues. But as a result of his demands, Reuther came under heavy criticism from Philip Murray, president of the CIO. Murray urged Reuther to accept the more conventional steel industry wage pattern and to stay out of the managerial decision-making process in order to maintain labor's independence from management. Reuther eventually dropped his proposal and negotiated a conventional wage settlement.

The labor movement broadly chose not to press for inroads into managerial prerogatives and instead focused on improving wages and gradually expanding the scope of issues covered under the contract. Unions chose to follow the practices encouraged by the early administrators of the Wagner Act and nurtured by the members of the War Labor Board.

The 1950s: A Return to Hard Bargaining

By the 1950s few differences remained in the bargaining agendas or organizing strategies of the AFL and CIO unions. As a result, these two federations merged in 1955 to become the AFL-CIO. The merger allowed the member unions to focus their energies more directly on expanding the wage and benefit gains introduced in collective bargaining in the 1940s.

The early years of the 1950s saw collective bargaining spread throughout the major firms and unions in key sectors of the economy including steel, coal, rubber, meat packing, and transportation. The **scope of bargaining** also continued to expand and take up such topics as supplementary unemployment benefits, pensions, severance payments for workers dislocated by technological change or plant closings, and a variety of other fringe benefits and working conditions.[33]

But near the end of the decade a harder line in collective bargaining appeared as firms sought to limit any further expansion of the scope of bargaining or the influence of unions. The most visible example of this was General Electric's policy, which came to be known as **Boulwarism** after Lemuel Boulware, the architect of the policy and GE's vice president of industrial relations.[34] Boulwarism was a management strategy for regaining the initiative in bargaining. GE polled workers to determine their needs and then made one "firm and final" offer in negotiations. This offer reflected the financial condition of the firm and the results of the worker surveys. Boulwarism was eventually ruled by the courts to be a violation of the bargaining requirements in the NLRA. Boulwarism illustrates the aggressive position that had spread in management circles, however. By 1959, for example, at U.S. Steel a 116-day strike occurred over management's right to change work rules. Similar strikes broke out in the late 1950s in the railroad, airline, electrical products, and other industries.

Management's tougher stance paralleled a decline in labor's public image and political influence. In the late 1950s a series of congressional hearings highlighted corruption within the Teamsters and other unions. The culmination of the congressional debates over internal union affairs was the passage of the Labor-Management Reporting and Disclosure Act (Landrum-Griffin Act) as an amendment to the NLRA. As spelled out in more detail in the next chapter, Landrum-Griffin established reporting and disclosure requirements for union finances, specified the rights of individual union members, and regulated how union leaders could represent their members' interests.

Nonetheless, although many firms adopted a hard line in bargaining, collective bargaining continued in many sectors of the American economy in the 1950s. Only a few firms began to experiment with an alternative—a new form of nonunion human resource management. It was not until the turbulent 1960s that the latter spread.

The 1960s: Rank-and-File Unrest

The 1960s were marked by strong economic growth as well as social and political upheavals. These upheavals included the civil rights movement, urban riots, and wide-scale protests over continued expansion of the Vietnamese war. The economic growth and environment of protest fed employee militance at the workplace. This was exemplified by a growing number of contract demands, wildcat strikes during the term of the contract, and rank-and-file rejections of contracts negotiated by their union leaders.[35] At the same time, unions were beginning to reap success in organizing large numbers of public sector workers.

The 1960s were years of great challenge to management and union leaders alike. In the private sector the parties struggled to cope with pent-up pressures and conflicts at the workplace and in local unions. In the public sector labor and management searched for principles to guide the extension of collective bargaining to this new terrain.

Meanwhile, stimulated by governmental research and development expenditures to support the effort to catch up with the Soviet Union in the space race, the demand for white-collar, technical, and managerial employees expanded rapidly. What later came to be known as the high technology industries were born and flourished.

These forces had two effects on collective bargaining. First, the power of personnel and human resource management professionals grew as they were charged with satisfying the needs of the expanding highly skilled employees. The role of human resource professionals was further expanded by passage of new government regulations that covered the workplace, such as equal employment opportunity laws. Second, the high-technology organizations developed novel human resource strategies and policies. Unions found it very difficult to organize the expanding high tech firms.

As a result of these and other pressures, the late 1950s and early 1960s marked a turning point for union membership levels in the private sector. From the early 1950s to today growth in union membership has *not* kept pace with increases in the size of the labor force.

The 1970s: Stability and Atrophy

The 1970s may go down in American labor history as one of the least distinguished in the history of collective bargaining. As the economic pressures to change collective bargaining intensified, labor and management continued to follow the patterns of behavior that had developed in the earlier years. Management became preoccupied with holding the line against any further union gains in bargaining. And labor leaders seemed to push no further than preserving the gains they or their predecessors had achieved in collective bargaining in previous decades.

Interest in issues such as productivity improvement and the quality of working life began to surface in labor-management discussions. But little more than isolated and limited experimentation in collective bargaining resulted.

Government policymakers as well were stymied. A political stalemate emerged between labor and management, evidenced by the failure of Congress and a Democratic President to pass labor law reforms in 1978.[36] No party—labor, management, or governmental—successfully initiated any bold advance in bargaining practice, yet each seemed quite effective in constraining the actions of the others. Despite pressures from mounting foreign competition and domestic nonunion competition, union workers' wages grew more rapidly throughout the 1970s than did nonunion wages.

During the 1970s industrial relations professionals continued to emphasize the goals of labor peace and stability, while pressures for change continued to mount. As a result, they became more defensive and isolated from other managers within many corporations, and their influence with top executives began gradually to erode. It was not until a dramatic shift in the environment took place in the early 1980s, however, that these mounting pressures suddenly propelled the parties into an era of fundamental change in collective bargaining.

The 1980s: Experimentation and Change

The election of Ronald Reagan as President reflected a strong conservative shift in the political climate of the country. This shift was vividly illustrated early in Reagan's administration when he fired and permanently replaced air traffic controllers (members of the Professional Air Traffic Controller Union, PATCO) who had gone out on strike in August 1981.

PATCO had been engaging in an illegal strike over the terms of a new collective bargaining contract. Although the President's actions were directed at employees of the federal government, those actions sent a strong message to employers that the labor movement had lost not only much of its political power but also the public's support. The firing of striking controllers and the demise of PATCO solidified the resolve of employers to seize the initiative in collective bargaining.

The deep economic recession of 1981–83 further mobilized many employers to sidestep or even abolish collective bargaining. The rise in the value of the U.S. dollar against foreign currencies further reduced the competitiveness of U.S. producers that operated in foreign markets. Massive layoffs in key, highly unionized sectors resulted, reaching deep into union ranks and thereby cutting off the unions' primary source of bargaining power. Thus began the era of **concessionary bargaining** that entailed unions agreeing to wage cuts or freezes or in other ways giving back to employers previous gains. Box 2–14 lists some of the key events in concessionary bargaining.

The rate of decline in union membership not only continued during the 1980s, it accelerated. By 1985 the labor movement publicly acknowledged the depth of its membership crisis and called on its leaders to consider a variety of new strategies.[37]

At the same time, new forms of employee participation and new concepts of how to organize work appeared in some workplaces. Thus, on the one hand unions were negotiating concessionary agreements and losing members. On the other hand, some of the concessionary contracts included gains by providing employees with employment security or direct participation in business decisions. Employers were taking things away from unions while at the same time offering unions some of the very things they had always wanted.

Although these contradictory pressures did not hit all bargaining relationships with equal force, their cumulative effects posed fundamental challenges to the basic principles that underlaid the New Deal industrial relations system. There were changes occurring at all three levels of the traditional bargaining system.

At the workplace level unions were challenged by new forms of worker and union participation and by more direct communication between workers and management. At the middle level of industrial relations unions were making major concessions to their traditional wage settlements and **work rules** (such as fewer job classifications). Meanwhile, substantial strategic level changes were also occurring that often involved greater union involvement in strategic business issues.

The nature and extent of these changes varied considerably across the range of bargaining relationships in different industries and firms. By no means were they universal, and they may not prove to be lasting features of collective bargaining. But the new practices were in use in enough bargaining relationships to lead many American managers and unionists to discuss whether these new practices were superior to traditional collective bargaining.

Thus, the 1980s proved to be a critical period of experimentation and new strategic choices for management, labor, and government decision makers. All three of these actors must now decide which of the new ideas deserve to be encouraged and which of the traditional practices should be preserved.

Box 2–14

Key Events in Concessionary Bargaining

Case	Date	Significance
Chrysler-UAW	October 1979	Chrysler breaks from the historic patterns that had linked its contract with the UAW agreements at GM and Ford. COLA and other pay increases are postponed and later eliminated, and in exchange for these and other concessions Douglas Fraser, then president of the UAW, is put on the Chrysler board of directors.
Federal air traffic controllers (PATCO)	August 1981	President Reagan fires striking controllers, setting a significant example for other employers. (See Chapters 8 and 9.)
GM-UAW, Ford-UAW	March 1982	Early renegotiation of contracts brings pay and work rule concessions. The UAW wins profit sharing, employment security, and other quid pro quos in exchange.
Continental Airlines	September 1983	Claiming bankruptcy protection, Continental abrogates its collective bargaining agreements and lowers employee pay and benefits by approximately one-fourth. Employees then go on strike, but Continental continues to fly.
Boeing-IAM	October 1983	Boeing introduces lump sum bonuses (annual pay increases not later built into base pay) that replace the traditional annual base pay increases for machinists. The use of lump sums then spreads to a number of other industries and reappears in subsequent Boeing International Association & Machinists (IAM) contracts.
American Airlines	November 1983	American introduces a lower tier of pay (one-half of existing rates) for new pilot hires. Two-tiered pay then spreads to many other airlines and industries.
Hormel-UFCW	October 1984	A strike by Local P-9 (began in protest against wage cuts) at Austin, Minnesota, leads to a bitter dispute between the local and its national union, the United Food and Commercial Workers (UFCW). The local union is eventually put into receivership by the national union, and a settlement is reached keeping the Austin plant's wages in line with other Hormel plants and meat-packing companies.

Summary

The history of collective bargaining traced in this chapter reveals that developments in collective bargaining cannot always be accurately predicted by extrapolating from existing patterns of behavior. Incremental changes in the status quo did provide a good prediction for the relatively stable years of the 1950s and the 1970s. But events in the 1920s did not anticipate the arrival of industrial unionism and the enactment of the New Deal model in the 1930s. Furthermore, status quo bargaining in the 1970s was followed by the fundamental changes to the New Deal system in the 1980s.

The lesson is clear. Relations between labor and management are highly dynamic and adapt over time to changes in the environment and the wants of the participants.

It is also clear that collective bargaining gained acceptance in American society only recently and then only as part of a larger set of economic and social reforms. Furthermore, management and labor attitudes toward unions continued to shift over the last 40 years, in part, in response to shifts in environmental pressures. To understand the operation of collective bargaining, it is necessary to explore how forces in the environment interact with the strategies and structures of labor and management.

American labor history reveals the critical influence of labor law and public policy on the evolution of collective bargaining. Chapter 3 focuses on the evolution of American labor law, and Chapter 4 examines other environmental influences on industrial relations.

Discussion Questions

1. Briefly explain why workers joined unions, according to Commons.

2. Discuss the legal reaction toward unionization before the NLRA (1935).

3. Contrast the drive system and scientific management.

4. Outline the key eras that appeared in American collective bargaining after World War II.

Suggested Readings

Brody, Davis. *Workers in Industrial America: Essays on the Twentieth Century Struggle* (New York: Cambridge University Press, 1982).

Harris, Howell. *The Right to Manage* (Madison: University of Wisconsin Press, 1983).

Jacoby, Sanford M. *Employing Bureaucracy* (New York: Columbia University Press, 1985).

Lens, Sidney. *The Labor Wars: From the Molly Maguires to the Sit-Downs* (Garden City, NY: Doubleday, 1973).

Rayback, Joseph G. *A History of American Labor* (New York: Macmillan, 1966).

Salvatore, Nick, ed. *Seventy Years of Life and Labor: An Autobiography of Samuel Gompers* (Ithaca, NY: ILR Press, Cornell University, 1984).

End Notes

1.   Quoted from Henry Pelling, *American Labor* (Chicago: University of Chicago Press, 1960), p. 4.

2.   Ibid., p. 12.

3.   Thomas Brooks, *Toil and Trouble* (Chicago: University of Chicago Press, 1971), p. 2.

4.   Ibid., p. 4.

5.   Herbert Gutman, *Work, Culture, and Society in Industrializing America* (New York: Alfred A. Knopf, 1975).

6.   Neil W. Chamberlain and James W. Kuhn, *Collective Bargaining*, 3d ed. (New York: McGraw-Hill, 1986), pp. 6–8.

7.   John R. Commons, "American Shoemakers, 1648–1895," *Labor and Administration* (New York: Macmillan Co., 1913), pp. 210–264. On this issue Marxist theories and the institutionalist view of what early unions and workers wanted differed deeply. The Marxists claimed that unionism entailed an effort by workers to regain control over the production process. The institutionalists argued that workers and unions were primarily oriented (at least in the United States) toward improving workers' income and work conditions.

8.   Sanford M. Jacoby, "The Duration of Indefinite Employment Contracts in the United States and England: An Historical Analysis," *Comparative Labor Law* 5 (Winter 1982): 85–128.

9.   For a thorough historical analysis of labor developments during this period, see Joseph G. Rayback, *A History of American Labor* (New York: The Free Press, 1966), pp. 75–92.

10.   Brooks, *Toil and Trouble,* p. 28.

11.   For a good concise summary of the *Commonwealth v. Hunt* case and other legal doctrines in American labor history, see William B. Gould, *A Primer on American Labor Law* (Cambridge, MA: MIT Press, 1986).

12.   Rayback, *A History of American Labor,* pp. 166–168.

13.   Ibid., pp. 196–197.

14.   Rayback, *A History of American Labor,* pp. 200–207.

15.   Lloyd Ulman, *The Rise of the National Trade Union* (Cambridge, MA: Harvard University Press, 1958).

16.   Rayback, *A History of American Labor,* pp. 142–165.

17.   Ibid., p. 162.

18.   Ibid., pp. 238–249.

19. Ibid., p. 248.

20. Nick Salvatore, ed., *Samuel Gompers, Seventy Years of Life and Labor: An Autobiography* (Ithaca, NY: ILR Press, 1984).

21. Sanford Jacoby, ed., *Masters to Managers* (New York: Columbia University Press, 1990).

22. For a good discussion of the drive system and other aspects of American management, see Sanford Jacoby, ed., *Masters to Managers.*

23. In 1890 there were an estimated 90,000 foremen in American industry. By 1900 their numbers grew to 360,000. Robert Reich, *The Next American Frontier* (New York: Bantam, 1983).

24. Progressive personnel policies did not diffuse to many small firms or to industries such as railroads and mining. See Sanford M. Jacoby, *Employing Bureaucracy* (New York: Columbia University Press, 1985).

25. Ibid., p. 224.

26. *NLRA v. Jones & Laughlin Steel Corp.,* 301 U.S. 1 (1937).

27. Irving Bernstein, *The Lean Years* (New York: Houghton Mifflin, 1972).

28. For a discussion of the origins of this principle, see Robert F. Hoxie, *Trade Unionism in the United States* (New York: Appleton and Company, 1920).

29. Jacoby, *Employing Bureaucracy,* pp. 243–253.

30. See War Labor Board, *Termination Report of the War Labor Board* (Washington, D.C.: GPO, 1946).

31. George W. Taylor, *Government Regulation of Industrial Relations* (New York: Prentice-Hall, 1948), p. 1.

32. James N. Baron, Frank R. Dobbin, and P. Devereaux Jennings, "War and Peace: The Evolution of Modern Personnel Administration in U.S. Industry," *American Journal of Sociology* 92 (September 1986): 350–384.

33. For a description of these provisions, see the U.S. Department of Labor, Bureau of Labor Statistics series of publications called *Characteristics of Major Collective Bargaining Agreements* (Washington, D.C.: Bureau of Labor Statistics, 1979). See also *Basic Patterns in Union Contracts* (Washington, D.C.: Bureau of National Affairs, 1984).

34. Herbert N. Northrup, *Boulwarism* (Ann Arbor: Graduate School of Business, University of Michigan, 1964).

35. William E. Simkin, "Refusal to Ratify Contracts," in *Trade Union Government and Administration,* ed. Joel Seidman (New York: Praeger, 1970), pp. 107–148.

36. D. Quinn Mills, "Flawed Victory in Labor Law Reform," *Harvard Business Review* 52 (May–June 1979): 99–102.

37. AFL-CIO Committee on the Evolution of Work, *The Changing Situation of Workers and Unions,* (Washington, D.C.: AFL-CIO, February 1985).

Chapter 3

The Legal Regulation of Unions and Collective Bargaining

This chapter begins to move horizontally across the three-tiered framework by examining the legal regulation of industrial relations in the United States. Federal and state law is a key part of the environment that influences the collective bargaining process and bargaining outcomes (see Exhibit 1–1, the functional level). To understand how collective bargaining works, then, requires familiarity with labor law. This chapter describes the development of labor law in the United States and the major laws and administrative agencies that currently shape the conduct of collective bargaining.

The Conspiracy Doctrine

The major developments in U.S. labor policy are outlined in Exhibit 3–1. In the United States the earliest public policy statements about the legality of union formation and activity appeared in the decisions of state courts. From 1800 to 1890 the state courts relied on interpretations derived from British common law to regulate the conduct of unions and employers. The first landmark case among these decisions was the 1806 Philadelphia Cordwainers' case in which the court ruled that efforts by unions or other combinations of workers to raise wages were intrinsically illegal. In other words, unions were viewed as a form of criminal conspiracy.

The conspiracy doctrine changed after the 1842 Massachusetts decision in *Commonwealth v. Hunt* in which the court attempted to distinguish between legal and illegal means for achieving unions' ends. The court ruled that unions had a right to exist, but they were prohibited from using coercive pressures to achieve their goals.

Throughout the 1800s the courts viewed unions with hostility and suspicion. They had trouble fitting the idea of unions and collective activity

KNOW FOR TEST

Exhibit 3–1
Overview of Major Developments in U.S. Labor Policy

Date	Event	Description
1806	Cordwainers' case *conspiracy*	A combination of workers seeking a wage increase is a criminal conspiracy.
1842	*Commonwealth v. Hunt* *means/end doctrine*	Unions are lawful. Combinations of workers are allowed as long as lawful means are used to gain lawful ends. Courts still hostile to unions.
1890	Sherman Antitrust Act	"Every combination . . . or conspiracy in restraint of trade or commerce among the several states . . . is hereby declared to be illegal." Used by employers seeking injunctions for union activity.
1894	Debs case	A famous use of the injunction. Eugene Debs jailed for refusing to obey a court back-to-work order in the American Railway Union strike.
1906	Danbury Hatters case	Union boycott of goods in violation of the Sherman Act. Union is assessed triple damages.
1912	Lloyd-LaFollette Act	Public employees are allowed to request raises from Congress. Postal workers may organize, but not strike.
1914	Clayton Act	"Labor is not a commodity," but courts continue to find union acts illegal. *ended injunctions against unions*
✓ 1926	Railway Labor Act *first time unions okayed* *statutory right*	Railway workers are allowed to organize and bargain collectively. National Mediation Board added in 1934.
✓ 1932	Norris-LaGuardia Act	Federal courts are severely restricted in issuing injunctions against unions; yellow-dog contracts "shall not be enforceable."
1933	National Industrial Recovery Act (NIRA)	Workers are extended the "right to organize and bargain collectively through representatives of their own choosing . . . free from interference, restraint, or coercion of employers" [Sec. 7(a)].
✓ 1935	Shechter Poultry case	Supreme Court decision: NIRA is held unconstitutional.
✓ 1935	National Labor Relations Act (NLRA), or the (Wagner) Act *fundamental code governing employer, employee relationships*	Establishes organizing rights, unfair (employer) labor practices, and the National Labor Relations Board (NLRB).
1935	Social Security Act	Includes OASDHI (old age, survivors, disability, and health insurance) and OAA (old age assistance).
1938	Fair Labor Standards Act	Regulates wages and hours. Stipulates overtime pay and minimum wage requirements.
✓ 1947	Taft-Hartley Act	Amends the NLRA. Adds unfair union labor practices [Sec. 8(b)].
✓ 1959	Landrum-Griffin Act	Establishes a bill of rights for union members. Requires financial disclosing by unions. Lists guidelines for trusteeships and elections.
1962	Executive Order 10988	Encourages public sector bargaining. Requires maintenance of management rights. Orders added by Nixon in 1970 (Executive Order 11491). Followed by passage of state laws giving employees of local and state governments the right to bargain.
1962	Wage-price policies	Establish guideposts in 1962–66; set controls in 1971–73; set guidelines in 1978–79.
1964	Civil Rights Act, Title VII	Unlawful for employer or union to discriminate on the basis of race, color, religion, gender, or national origin.

Exhibit 3–1 *(continued)*
Overview of Major Developments in U.S. Labor Policy

Date	Event	Description
1970	Occupational Safety and Health Act (OSHA)	Establishes standards for on-the-job safety and health and the Occupational Safety and Health Administration.
1972	Supplementary Security Income Act	Effective January 1, 1974. Replaces OAA of the 1935 Social Security Act.
1974	Employee Retirement Income Security Act (ERISA)	Establishes minimum standards for private pension plans.
1978	Mandatory Retirement Act	"Age Discrimination in Employment Act"; outlaws mandatory retirement rules for workers up to age 70.
1978	Civil Service Reform Act	Establishes the Federal Labor Relations Authority (FLRA). Oversees and regulates labor relations in the federal government.
1989	Worker Adjustment and Retraining Notification Act	Requires employers to provide advance notice to employees affected by a plant closing or mass layoff.

into a constitutional system and a political ideology that emphasized individual action and freedom of contract, property rights, and laissez faire capitalism. As a result, the ability of workers to engage in collective action in pursuit of their goals was severely limited. In addition, the statutory void meant that legal challenges to union action largely were confined to local or state courts; there was little or no federal involvement in labor relations during this time.

The Sherman Antitrust Act

When federal laws were applied to unions, unions initially fared poorly. With application of the federal Sherman Antitrust Act, for example, unions found themselves being treated like any other commodity or factor of production. That is, the courts viewed unions as labor market monopolies to be limited, as were other combinations or conspiracies that aimed to restrict free trade in product markets.

In the 1800s and early 1900s, whether through implementation of the conspiracy doctrine or the Sherman Antitrust Act, courts also used injunctions to discourage strikes and other forms of union pressure against employers. With an injunction a court rules illegal a union action, such as a strike, and imposes penalties, such as jail, on individuals who defy court orders. In many ways injunctions were more punishing than were other court actions. For one thing, employers could gain injunctions against union actions more quickly.

The Clayton Act

Unions and union supporters lobbied hard for an end to labor injunctions. Finally, in 1914 the Clayton Act was passed. Unions hoped it would lead to an end to labor injunctions through the language the act contained, which distinguished labor from other commodities. Yet, union hopes were not satisfied as federal courts subsequently interpreted the Clayton Act narrowly and state courts continued to issue injunctions against union actions. Meaningful protection of union activities came only with the passage of federal legislation that granted unions the rights to exist and to strike.

Legislation Granting Rights to Collective Bargaining

Legal and public policy opposition to the formation of unions began to erode in the early twentieth century. First, the Lloyd-LaFollette Act of 1912 gave postal employees the right to organize. Then, during World War I, the War Labor Board adopted a policy statement that supported the right of private-sector workers to organize into unions and to bargain collectively. The **Railway Labor Act,** passed in 1926, gave railway employees the right to organize and to bargain collectively.

All of these laws and policies represented pragmatic adjustments in response to union power and labor turmoil. The already existing postal service and railroad unions used their power to obtain favorable legislation. Similarly, wartime production needs made it crucial to avoid disruptive strikes. In response, employers during the First World War agreed not to break those unions that already existed, setting the stage for a greater acceptance of unionization in later decades.

The Railway Labor Act

The Railway Labor Act continues today to regulate the conduct of collective bargaining in the railroad industry, as well as the air transportation industry, (which was added to the original act) in 1936. Given the continuing role of the act, we discuss its terms and administration in detail in this section.

Spurred by previous labor strife in the railroad industry, President Calvin Coolidge had urged the railroad companies and unions to develop procedures that would bring about industrial stability. In 1926 Congress passed the Railway Labor Act, closely following proposals that had been recommended by labor and management in the industry.

The act specifies that employees have the right to organize unions without employer interference and to bargain collectively through representatives of their own choosing. Railroad employers are obligated by the law to negotiate with the freely selected collective bargaining representatives of their workers. The chief purpose of the law was to establish a variety of procedures to reduce conflict in the railroads.[1]

A Test of Constitutionality   Given the previous resistance to collective bargaining and unionism expressed by the courts, the constitutionality of the Railway Labor Act was in question until a key ruling by the U.S. Supreme Court.

In the **Texas and New Orleans Railroad Company v. Brotherhood of Railway and Steamship Clerks case** of 1930 the company argued that the act impinged on its First and Fifth Amendment rights that gave the company control over the selection and discharge of employees. The Supreme Court rejected these arguments in that same year and went on to uphold the constitutionality of the Railway Labor Act. The Supreme Court stated that Congress had the right to become involved in labor relations in the railroad industry because of its interest in maintaining the flow of interstate commerce. The Court held that promotion of collective bargaining was of the "highest public interest," for such a procedure would prevent "the interruption of interstate commerce by labor disputes and strikes."[2] For the first time, the U.S. Supreme Court had recognized the authority of government to protect the right of workers to organize into unions and to collectively bargain.

Administration of the Act   In 1934 the Railway Labor Act was amended by Congress. A **National Mediation Board** was established and empowered to assist the collective bargaining process. The board, which still exists, is authorized to conduct elections to determine which union the employees desire for collective bargaining purposes. The union that receives the majority of votes is certified as the lawful representative of the employees. The board is also authorized to mediate disputes that arise between railway unions and companies during the negotiation of collective bargaining agreements.

The Norris-LaGuardia Act

The endorsement of collective bargaining provided in the Railway Labor Act was path breaking, but its effects on labor and management in the broad economy were limited by the fact that the act initially applied only to the railroad industry. Through the Norris-LaGuardia Act passed in 1932, Congress provided an even stronger endorsement of collective bargaining.

The Norris-LaGuardia Act allows private sector employees "full freedom of association, self-organization, and designation of representatives of (their) own choosing, to negotiate the terms and conditions of employment." The greatest practical impact of the act arose from the restraints it imposed on the issuance of labor injunctions. This earned the act its frequent alternative name of the "Federal Anti-injunction Act." Nevertheless, as mentioned in the discussion of antitrust acts above, state courts continued to issue frequent labor injunctions.

Congress justified the Norris-LaGuardia Act by pointing to the need for collective bargaining in modern society. Sections of the act state that, under prevailing economic conditions, the unorganized worker is at a disadvantage when confronted by the power held by large modern corporations. To redress this imbalance, the act endorsed collective bargaining and limited the power of the courts to intervene in labor disputes. To understand how Congress came to endorse collective bargaining, it is important to recognize that the Norris-LaGuardia Act was being debated (and passed) at a time when the U.S. economy was already in the midst of the great depression.

It is noteworthy that the Norris-LaGuardia Act did not grant to unions any new legal rights; it merely allowed them greater freedom to act by reducing interference from the courts.

The National Industrial Recovery Act

After the election of Franklin Roosevelt as President of the United States, the federal government took a number of steps to promote industrial recovery from the depression. A key part of the federal government's plan to promote recovery was contained in the National Industrial Recovery Act (NIRA), which passed in 1933. The law provided that business people across various industries could form groups and pass *codes,* a system of principles and rules, that would stipulate business plans and regulate prices. The hope was that collusion between businesses and the regulation of production and prices would stimulate output and the economy. Congress stipulated that each of these business codes would include a minimum wage for the workers covered by the code. Promoters of this feature of the act argued that higher minimum wages would increase the purchasing power of workers and thereby stimulate the economy.

Promotion of Collective Bargaining   The most significant clause in the NIRA for unions was Section 7(a), which provided legal protection for the right of workers to bargain collectively. As with minimum wages, the rationale for the promotion of collective bargaining was that it would elevate worker purchasing power and thereby stimulate the national economy and help bring the country out of the depression.

Section 7(a) contained two key principles: (1) that employees have the "right to organize and bargain collectively through representatives of their own choosing, and shall be free from interference, restraint, or coercion" from employers in the exercise of those rights; and (2) that no employee can be required as a condition of employment to join a company-dominated union.[3]

Supreme Court Ruling   The NIRA had important symbolic effects, but its direct effects were limited because it was ruled unconstitutional in 1935 by the Supreme Court. The Court held that the law illegally delegated power to the Congress and exceeded Congress's authority to regulate interstate commerce. Nevertheless, from 1933 (when the NIRA was passed) until 1935 (when it was struck down) union membership increased from 2.9 to 3.9 million.

The National Labor Relations Act

The most significant boost for unionism in the private sector of the U.S. economy came with passage of the National Labor Relations Act (NLRA) in 1935. The NLRA made unions and union activity (including strikes) legal in the private sector and did much more as well. As stated in its preamble, the purpose of the NLRA is to *promote* the orderly and peaceful recognition of unions and the use of collective bargaining as a means for establishing the terms and conditions of employment.

The NLRA was later amended. The Taft-Hartley amendments of 1947 added a list of unfair labor practices for unions and turned the NLRA into a detailed and comprehensive code of conduct for collective bargaining; the Landrum-Griffin amendments of 1959 added provisions that governed internal union affairs and sought to define the rights of union members vis-à-vis their union organizations and leaders. The provisions of these acts are summarized in Exhibit 3–2.

The importance of the NLRA can be conveyed through the following exercise. Before you began taking this course, how many of you knew that our current federal labor law not only says unions are legal but actually states a *preference* for collective bargaining? Given the active employer resistance to unions that prevails in our economy and the low esteem with which many in the public view unions, we would guess that this would be a surprise, if not a shock, to most Americans. We return to this inconsistency between the language of the NLRA and current attitudes later in this chapter and elsewhere in this book. For now, we only note it as a strange irony of U.S. public policy and practice.

Key Provisions of the NLRA

Since the NLRA is the most important law regulating industrial relations, we describe its key provisions in some detail here. Our description takes into account the Taft-Hartley and Landrum-Griffin amendments to the NLRA.

Section 1 The motivation for the NLRA is provided in Section 1. Congress states that actions by employers who deny employees the right to organize and who refuse to accept collective bargaining lead to labor strife and are harmful to the nation because these actions lead to the disruption of commerce. Congress goes on to conclude that, in the absence of collective bargaining rights, employees are at a power disadvantage relative to employers and this is harmful to the economy because it

Exhibit 3–2
The Major Features of the National Labor Relations Act, As Amended

Section	Provisions
National Labor Relations Act (NLRA; Wagner Act) 1935	
1	*Findings and policy:* An endorsement of collective bargaining, worker self-organization, and selection of representatives.
2	*Definitions:* Of *employer, employee, labor organization, unfair labor practice.*
3–6	*National Labor Relations Board:* Its establishment, authority, funding, and structure.
7	*Rights of employees:* Includes rights to self-organize and select representatives for bargaining.
8	*Unfair (employer) labor practices:* Prohibits interference with employee's Section 7 rights.
9	*Representatives and elections:* Majority's selection is exclusive bargaining representative. Board can define appropriate unit, certify employee representative.
10	*Prevention of unfair labor practices:* Board can issue cease and desist orders, take "affirmative action, including reinstatement of employees with or without back pay."
11–12	*Investigatory powers:* The NLRB can issue subpoenas, examine witnesses, etc. Refusal to obey may result in court contempt proceedings.
13–16	*Limitations:* Act does not limit the right to strike.
Labor-Management Relations Act (LMRA; Taft-Hartley Act) 1947 (amendments to NLRA)	
2	*Definitions:* Added supervisor, professional employee, agent.
3	*National Labor Relations Board:* Expanded from three to five members.
7	*Rights of employees:* Required to refrain from activities listed in section 7.
8	*Unfair labor practices:* Creates 8(b), Unfair Labor Organization Labor Practices.
9	*Representatives and elections:* Separate standards for professional employees, craft groups, guards. Expanded and defined election procedure.
Title II	*Conciliation of labor disputes:* In industries affecting commerce; national emergencies.
Sec. 301	*Suits by and against labor organizations.*
Labor-Management Reporting and Disclosure Act (LMRDA; Landrum-Griffin Act) 1959 (amendments to LMRA)	
Title I	*Bill of rights of members of labor organizations:* Includes freedom of speech and assembly, protection from dues increase without vote, and improper disciplinary action.
Title II	*Reporting by labor organizations:* Provides for reporting of officers' names, provisions for members' rights, annual financial statements.
Title III	*Trusteeships:* Defines reasons for trusteeships; provides for reports on all trusteeships.
Title IV	*Elections:* Guarantees regular local and national (and/or international) elections by secret ballot of all members in good standing.
Title V	*Safeguards for labor organizations:* Officials' Fiduciary Responsibility, requires bonding for all individuals who handle funds or property.

depresses worker purchasing power. Congress declares that it is the policy of the United States to encourage the practice of collective bargaining.

Section 2   Section 2 defines the terms used in the act. The most important definitions relate to the terms employer, employee, supervisor, and professional.

An **employer** includes "any person acting in the interest of an employer." Employers excluded from the act's coverage include federal, state, or local governments or any organizations owned by these agencies; companies subject to the Railway Labor Act; and union representatives when acting as bargaining agents.

Employees covered by the NLRA include individuals whose work has ceased due to a labor dispute or to an unfair labor practice. Employees continue to receive protection from the act after they leave an organization until they obtain "any other regular and substantially equivalent position." Individuals employed as agricultural laborers, as independent contractors, or by a spouse or parent; those in domestic service; and those covered by the Railway Labor Act are excluded from coverage by the act.

A **supervisor** is defined as any individual who has authority to "hire, transfer, suspend, layoff, recall, promote, discharge, assign, reward, or discipline other employees" if the exercise of the above authority "requires the use of independent judgment." Supervisors are excluded from coverage by the act.

A **professional employee** is any employee engaged in work "predominately intellectual and varied in character . . . involving the consistent exercise of discretion and judgement." Separate rules apply to how professional employees may be grouped with nonprofessional employees for bargaining purposes.[4]

Section 3   Section 3 establishes the National Labor Relations Board (NLRB). The board consists of five members appointed by the President and confirmed by the Senate. Members on the NLRB serve five-year terms. The NLRB can delegate authority to determine representation and election questions to its regional directors. The NLRB also has a general counsel who has the responsibility to investigate unfair labor practice charges and issue complaints.

Section 7   Section 7 grants to employees "the right to self-organization" and the right to "bargain collectively through representatives of their own choosing, or to engage in other concerted activities for the purpose of collective bargaining." Unions were thereby granted the right to picket and strike.

An employer may not discriminate against workers because they have participated in a strike. The employer, however, may hire either temporary or permanent replacements for striking workers. Striking workers who are permanently replaced can lose their jobs, even if the strikers offer to return to work, although such a striker has a right to recall if future openings appear at the workplace.[5]

Employers may **lock out** employees over mandatory subjects of bargaining. Thus, after bargaining in good faith with a union, an employer may lock out to force the union to agree to the employer's terms, even though the workers are content to accept present conditions and to continue bargaining.[6]

A strike that is part of a secondary boycott is illegal. Suppose a union has a labor dispute with an employer (called the *primary employer* because the dispute is primarily between this employer and the union). A way for the union to increase the pressure on this primary employer is to use union power against other employers *(secondary employers)*. For instance, a union in dispute with a manufacturing company may want to exercise leverage against the employer by extending a strike to a company that supplies parts to the manufacturing company. The NLRA does not allow any such *secondary boycott.*[7]

Section 8 Section 8 requires the employer and the union to bargain collectively with each other in good faith. **Bargaining in good faith** means that the employer and the representative of the employees "meet at reasonable times and confer in good faith with respect to wages, hours, and other terms and conditions of employment." The duty to bargain does not require either side to agree to a proposal or to make concessions.

Wages, hours, and conditions of employment are thus **mandatory subjects of bargaining.** If either side chooses to bargain over one of these issues, the other side is obligated to continue talks. In NLRB and court decisions, mandatory bargaining has been defined for those subjects that *directly affect* the employment relationship. There also are **permissible subjects of bargaining,** such as corporate advertising policy. Both sides can either refuse to bargain or voluntarily choose to bargain over a permissible subject. *Economic weapons,* such as striking or picketing, cannot be used to force agreement to proposals on a permissible subject. **Illegal subjects of bargaining** are topics that may not be lawfully included in a labor contract, such as a *closed shop* clause or a racially discriminatory clause. A closed shop provides that individuals must be a member of the union in order to be eligible for hire.

Section 8 also outlines *unfair labor practices* that can be committed by either employers or unions. These are actions that constitute violations of the rights specified in other parts of the act.

1. **Unfair Labor Practices by Employers:** An employer may not interfere with or coerce employees in the exercise of their Section 7 rights. The employer may not dominate or interfere with labor organizations or contribute financial or other support to these organizations.

   Employers also are forbidden from discriminating against individuals based on their views toward or activities in unions. Thus, an employer cannot intimidate a union by firing union activists or choose not to promote individuals because they are active supporters of a union. The act does allow employers and unions to negotiate collective bargaining agreements that require union membership as a condition of the continuation of employment (a *union shop* clause).[8]

2. **Unfair Labor Practices by Unions:** Unions cannot coerce employees in the exercise of their Section 7 rights. Unions cannot cause an employer to discriminate against employees who have been denied union membership except if such a denial was due to a failure to pay dues.

   Unions are not allowed to engage in or encourage individuals to strike or to refuse to handle goods in cases when the object is one of the following:
   a. Forcing an employer or self-employed person to join any labor or employer organization.
   b. Forcing an employer to bargain with a labor organization that is not a duly certified labor organization.
   c. Forcing an employer to assign work to employees unless the NLRB has ordered the employer to do so.
   d. Requiring employees to pay excessive union membership fees.
   e. Requiring an employer to pay for services that are not performed.
   f. Conducting unlawful picketing.

Section 8 also outlaws hot cargo clauses except in the construction and apparel industries. A **hot cargo clause** requires that employees not handle particular goods. Such clauses had been common in the trucking industry where they prevented drivers from handling goods manufactured by a nonunion firm.

Section 9   Section 9 provides that union representatives are selected by the majority of employees in a unit designated for such purposes (by the NLRB). A victorious union wins *exclusive representation* rights. This means that only one union gains the right to negotiate contracts for a designated bargaining unit. The act goes on to specify guidelines regarding how the appropriate bargaining unit is determined (we discuss this in Chapter 6).

Section 10   If the NLRB finds that an unfair labor practice has occurred, it is empowered to issue cease-and-desist orders and to order back pay to injured employees. The NLRB must petition a court of appeals for enforcement of its orders.

National Emergency Disputes

Title II of the NLRA includes procedures to be applied when a strike has caused a **national emergency dispute.** To avoid such cases the act creates the **Federal Mediation and Conciliation Service (FMCS)** and gives it the task of mediating labor disputes so as to assist the free flow of commerce.

When national emergencies arise out of labor disputes, a board of inquiry may be appointed by the President to conduct hearings and make recommendations for settling the dispute. The President can ask the attorney general to seek an injunction against the strike or lockout that is precipitating the national emergency. If an injunction is ordered, a 60-day cooling-off period follows. If no settlement is reached in the 60 days, the NLRB takes a vote among employees over management's final offer. If this does not produce a settlement, the President forwards recommendations to Congress to end the dispute.

Administration of the NLRA

The NLRB, a five-member board with a general counsel and fifty regional boards and staffs, administers the NLRA. The key functions of the NLRB are to supervise and conduct representation elections and to adjudicate charges of unfair labor practices.

Such charges start with a complaint filed by an employee, employer, or union with a regional NLRB office. The charge is investigated by the NLRB, and, if it is warranted, a hearing is conducted before an administrative law judge who makes a recommendation to the NLRB. The NLRB then can order cease-and-desist orders or dismiss the case.

Throughout the process the NLRB and its agents try to find a settlement to the charge. Suppose a union charges that organizers from its supporters were being harassed and threatened by their supervisors during a union election campaign. After investigating the charge, the NLRB might recommend as a settlement that the employer stop this action and post a notice promising not to continue the practice. Needless to say, the employer in this case might reject the proposed settlement, and the procedure would proceed.

After hearing the recommendation of the administrative judge, the NLRB has the power to award back pay to injured employees, but the NLRB cannot assess punitive damages. Furthermore, the board must turn to the courts to enforce its orders, and aggrieved parties can appeal NLRB decisions to the Federal Circuit Court of Appeals.

The Taft-Hartley Act

By the end of World War II labor unions had grown in strength and membership. The strike wave that occurred after the war stimulated hostility toward unions. Congress responded by passing the Labor-Management Relations Act (often referred to as the **Taft-Hartley amendments**) in 1947. The primary purpose of the act was to shift the balance of power more toward management and grant individuals more rights in their dealing with labor unions. The major provisions of the act include the following:

1. Section 7 was modified to protect employees' rights not to engage in union activities.

2. A list of unfair labor practices that could be committed by unions was added to Section 8 (see above).

3. Workers were allowed to decertify their unions. A majority of unionized workers thus can vote to get rid of union representation.

4. Employers were allowed to make anti-union statements during union organizing campaigns as long as they did not include threats of reprisals or promises of benefits.

5. Supervisors were excluded from the coverage of the NLRA.

6. Closed shops (in which union membership is required before an individual can be hired) were outlawed.

7. States were allowed to pass laws outlawing the union shop (*right to work* laws).[9]

8. Procedures for national emergency disputes were added.

The Taft-Hartley amendments excluded supervisors in the private sector from coverage under the NLRA. Section 2(11) of the amendments defines a supervisor as an employee

> having authority in the interest of the employer, to hire, transfer, suspend, layoff, recall, promote, discharge, assign, reward, or discipline other employees, or responsibly to direct them, or to adjust their grievances, or effectively to recommend such action, if . . . such authority is not a merely routine or clerical nature, but requires the use of independent judgment.

Thus, a supervisor is defined in terms of the duties the employee performs and the power the employee has to make key personnel management decisions or to exercise independent judgment.[10]

Although the law does not prevent supervisors from forming unions, it also does not provide any legal protection for such activity.

The Taft-Hartley exclusion of supervisors rested on the argument that if supervisors unionized, they would become less loyal to management and less committed to the goals of their employer. Plainly, some of the opposition to supervisory bargaining reflects a belief that management deserves a set of loyal representatives of its own interests. The actual legislative rationale for this policy, however, rested on assumptions about the responsibilities supervisors had at the time Taft-Hartley was enacted.

Two questions are immediately obvious. First, are the roles and powers of today's supervisors still the same as they were assumed to be in 1947? Second, would the negative organizational consequences hypothesized by the congressional majority in 1947 actually result if supervisors were given the same collective bargaining rights as other workers?

These questions have recently become the focal point of a debate over the rights of college faculty members to unionize and to bargain. In a test case decided in 1980 the Supreme Court ruled that the faculty at New York City's Yeshiva University had managerial responsibilities and therefore excluded them from coverage under the NLRA.[11] The Court reasoned that because the faculty members were involved in hiring, promotion, course assignment, and a variety of other managerial decisions that affected wages, hours, and working conditions, they fit the definition of supervisor embodied in the law. Thus, Yeshiva had no legal obligation to recognize a union of faculty members, and collective bargaining with faculty members in this university, as well as in several others, ended. Although many observers have criticized the logic of the Yeshiva ruling, and although the NLRB has subsequently found faculty members at several other universities to be eligible for coverage under the law, the debate over this question has intensified.

The Landrum-Griffin Act

The Labor-Management Reporting and Disclosure Act of 1959, commonly referred to as the **Landrum-Griffin amendments,** is primarily concerned with the internal practices of unions. The major purpose of these amendments to the NLRA is to protect union members from improper union conduct.[12] The law also is directed at eliminating arrangements between unions and employers that deprive union members of proper union representation.

Landrum-Griffin passed Congress in the aftermath of a series of well-publicized hearings on union corruption that were conducted by the McClellan Anti-Racketeering Committee in Congress. Much of the Committee's attention focused on the activities of the International Brotherhood of Teamsters and led to the expulsion of the Teamsters union from the AFL-CIO.[13]

Union Members' Bill of Rights

The Landrum-Griffin amendments include a "bill of rights" section for union members. Rights are stipulated for nomination of candidates for union office, voting in elections, attendance at membership meetings, and participation in the business transactions of unions. The act also regulates union dues and fees and affirms the right of any union member to sue the organization. The act provides that no union member may be fined, suspended, or otherwise disciplined by the union except for the nonpayment of dues, unless the member has been granted procedural safeguards.

The Regulation of Union Finances and Administration

Landrum-Griffin requires every labor organization to report its financial and administrative practices regularly to the **U.S. Department of Labor (DOL).** Information on the financial affairs of the union must be made available to union members.

The act makes union officers responsible for proper use of union funds. Union members are granted the right to sue union officers for relief on the grounds that officers have violated their financial obligations.

In addition, Landrum-Griffin regulates internal union elections. The act establishes requirements for the frequency of elections and regulates nomination, campaign rules, and election procedures.

The act also oversees how a union can regulate its local unions. The law specifically directs how and when local unions can be put into trusteeships. A trusteeship is a procedure by which the parent union (often the national offices of a union) suspends the autonomy of a local union. Typically, local unions are put into trusteeship if the parent organization feels there have been violations of the union's constitution or irregularities in the administration of the local union. Congress added these requirements after hearing reports of the misuse of trusteeships by certain national unions.

Landrum-Griffin imposes on unions requirements and obligations that go far beyond those imposed on corporations and other organizations. As a result, the internal operation and affairs of unions are under special scrutiny, and unions do not have the independence granted other private organizations.

The Value of Collective Bargaining

With passage of the NLRA, the U.S. federal government became committed to the promotion of collective bargaining. Since this commitment is so central to American labor law, it is useful to examine the rationale for this commitment in some detail.

The Contribution to Political Democracy

Collective bargaining involves the right to negotiate a labor agreement without direct interference from the government or other outside forces. The political rationale for collective bargaining can be stated simply: the right to form unions and carry out strikes is an essential component of political democracy. Walter Oberer and Kurt Hanslowe stated this premise succinctly:

One way of defining a free society may indeed be: a society the members of which are free to assert their individual interests collectively.[14]

The Need for the Right To Strike

Since the freedom to enter a contract also requires the freedom to reject a contract offer, the right to negotiate and the right to strike are closely related. Milton Konvitz stated this well in an article that explored the philosophical bases for the right to strike:

> Without the power to affect the course of events, a person or a group lacks the responsibility to reach decisions. Power is the source of responsibility. Without the right to strike, unions will lack the foundation for voluntary negotiation and agreement. If a free labor agreement—free collective bargaining in a free enterprise system—is in the public interest, so is the right to strike, which makes the free labor agreement possible.[15]

Additional Justifications for Collective Bargaining

Two additional justifications have been offered by industrial relations scholars for promoting and protecting collective bargaining. First, it is often argued that employees and employers have a better understanding of their needs, priorities, and problems than do outsiders. This suggests that more effective solutions to problems, or compromises that are more workable and acceptable to the parties, will be found in a bargaining process than where third parties constrain the participants from pursuing their own interests. Second, and perhaps more important, the parties may lose the capability to resolve their own problems once they begin to rely on outsiders for resolving their differences. The notion here is that effective problem resolution is a dynamic process that requires continual contact between the parties in dispute.

Yet we must be careful not to view the rights to form unions and to strike as unconditional. The exercise of these rights can, of course, conflict with other objectives of the larger society, including the public's interest in industrial peace and social stability. At times these objectives come into conflict.

Even though society has an interest in limiting conflicts that create social costs and social inconvenience, at the same time, the mere existence of public inconvenience is not in and of itself sufficient grounds to limit labor and management's right to negotiate and labor's right to engage in a strike if they cannot agree.

Given the important roles the negotiations process and the strike play in a collective bargaining system, on the one hand, and the potentially harmful impact a strike may exert on the public, on the other, it is not surprising that industrial relations scholars and the public often disagree on how well the process is performing. Archibald Cox, for example, once described the negotiations process as the "ideal of informed persuasion" because of the effective way the strike threat forces negotiators to face reality and make compromises.[16]

A Criticism of Unrestrained Collective Bargaining

Compare Cox's view with the following of Abe Raskin, longtime labor reporter and editor for *The New York Times:*

> The more ludicrous the whole performance of [collective bargaining] becomes, the more insistently learned scholars explain why it all makes sense and why any community action to protect itself by substituting reasons for the unrestrained exercise of force in settling labor disputes represents a stab in the back toward Nathan Hale, Paul Revere, and all the other apostles of American liberty.
>
> It is past time to arise and proclaim that the Emperor has no clothes. It is my conviction that, when all the people have to suffer because of the willfulness or ineptitude of economic power blocks, it is an affirmation—not a denial—of democracy to provide effective government machinery for breaking deadlocks.
>
> The question, in my estimation, is not whether to do it but simply how. I see no reason why in this institution alone, of all the facets of our society, we should exalt the right to make war as the hallmark of industrial civilization when we seek to exorcise it everywhere else, even in the global relations of sovereign powers.[17]

Thus, while the traditional supporters of the institution of collective bargaining seek to place walls around the process to promote and protect collective bargaining, others argue for greater governmental intervention to resolve disputes before strikes impose those costs on the public.

Public Sector Labor Law

The NLRA covers private sector employment relationships. Since passage of the NLRA, over 35 states have passed collective bargaining legislation that governs employees of state and local governments. In addition, collective bargaining rights were extended to federal employees through Executive Order 10988 in 1962. The Civil Service Reform Act of 1978 established a new Federal Labor Relations Authority (FLRA) to oversee and regulate the conduct of collective bargaining in the federal sector. A few states have extended bargaining rights to farm workers. Most of these state laws are modeled after the principles set forth in the NLRA, but they differ considerably in the procedures specified for implementing the principles.

Employment at Will

A central focus in collective bargaining is the negotiation and administration of procedures that provide employees with due process. **Due process in the union sector comes in part through contract negotiations and the grievance procedures**, topics examined later in Chapters 8 and 11. To understand the contribution of unionism to due process it is necessary to examine what takes place where unions are absent.

In the absence of a collective bargaining agreement, U.S. courts have applied a common law doctrine called employment at will.[18] The **employment-at-will doctrine** stipulates that the employee and employer are free to end the employment relationship at any time, for any reason, and without liability, provided that the termination does not violate any statutory or constitutional provisions. Application of this doctrine leads to the result that, in the absence of some sort of complaint procedure, nonunion employees have no recourse if they are discharged unless statutory or constitutional provisions are violated by the action.

The Scope of the Doctrine

Numerous state courts decided for the employment-at-will doctrine in the following situations:

1. When there is no written contract, no specified term of employment, and no employee handbook.[19] In these cases the employment-at-will doctrine prevails.

2. When the expiration of a collective bargaining agreement limits claims against an employer.[20] The court reasoned that an expired collective bargaining agreement does not constitute an implied contract. Such a contract would bind the parties in a manner inimical to the collective bargaining process and discourage good faith bargaining toward a new contract.

3. When an employee handbook is insufficient to establish exceptions to the employment-at-will doctrine.[21] The court held that handbooks merely contain guidelines, not express contractual undertakings, and the guidelines provide no support for a finding that the parties intended to bind themselves to anything but employment at will.[22]

Exceptions Imposed by State Courts

In recent years a number of state courts have modified application of the employment-at-will doctrine. It is state court decisions that regulate employment at will because there is no federal legislation to govern substantive employment rights.

Numerous state courts have awarded back pay and reinstatement to discharged employees on the following grounds:

1. When an employer's written policies constitute an implied contract, providing employment security. A contract can be implied by actions taken by the employer. This serves to limit the employer's discharges to **just cause,** namely, to cases where the employer has legitimate business reasons for a discharge.[23]

2. When a firm promises employment security in an oral or written agreement, or through actions that lead employees to expect employment security.[24]

3. When an employee is fired for refusing to violate a statutory policy.[25] Employees cannot be terminated for exposing or refusing to participate in employer conduct that violates statutory policy. In this case the court reasoned that there is no right to terminate a contract for an unlawful reason or a purpose that contravenes public policy. Such a privilege would encourage lawlessness, which the law is designed to prevent.

Thus, even with recent court modifications, nonunion employees have relatively few grounds to redress discharge. This is why allegations of insufficient due process arise frequently in union organizing drives.

Direct Regulation of Employment Conditions

Society also has seen fit to regulate certain employment conditions more directly than it does collective bargaining. In the United States federal regulations cover overtime hours (their limits and pay), minimum wages, unemployment insurance, pensions, and other issues. The Fair Labor Standards Act passed in 1938 includes many of the key regulations. As compared to other countries, however, the United States tends to have relatively little direct regulation of employment conditions (what is called **substantive regulation**). In western Europe, for instance, national laws directly set minimum wages and working conditions more extensively than do their counterpart regulations in the United States. (See Chapter 14 for examples.)

The extent of substantive employment regulation increased markedly in the United States during the 1960s and early 1970s (see Exhibit 3–1). Title VII of the 1964 **Civil Rights Act,** for example, gave the government a hand in workplace decisions on promotion, transfer, seniority, and other terms of employment. The Occupational Safety and Health Act (OSHA) of 1970 established standards for on-the-job health and safety and granted inspection and enforcement authority to the U.S. Department of Labor. The **Employee Retirement Income Security Act (ERISA)** of 1974 established minimum standards for private pension plans.[26]

In the late 1970s and 1980s U.S. public policy changed to a less interventionist style as policy returned to an emphasis on competitive markets at the micro- and macrolevels of the economy. Important developments at the microlevel include deregulation of the transportation and communications industries.

Seniority and Equal Employment Opportunity Policy Goals

Seniority provisions in collective bargaining often regulate which worker will be laid off and who is eligible for a promotion. The use of seniority in recent years has been restricted in order to attain equal employment objectives.

In the past, seniority had served in some cases to discriminate against minorities and women by establishing segregated seniority units or progression ladders. Some firms had set up departmentwide seniority units that systematically excluded blacks, women, and other minority groups such as Latinos and Asians from the most desirable jobs and progression ladders. Blacks and Latinos, for example, may have been hired only as laborers, while whites were hired into higher paying jobs in the maintenance department. Where this occurred, or where firms refused to hire minority or female workers at all, the effects of past discriminatory acts were perpetuated by the use of seniority criteria for either competitive- or benefit-status purposes.

Policy Goals

Satisfaction of **equal employment opportunity** goals has led courts (1) to ensure that present practices and seniority rules do not discriminate against any individuals or groups, (2) to avoid perpetuating the effects of past discrimination, and (3) to protect the interests of nonminority workers who are not responsible for the past discrimination but who may have indirectly benefited from it.

In an effort to remove artificial barriers to employment opportunities, Congress enacted Title VII of the 1964 Civil Rights Act. Its primary goal is to eliminate employment discrimination on the basis of "race, color, religion, sex, and national origin."

Key Court Decisions

The following statements represent the status, as of this writing, of some of the key court decisions concerning seniority and **affirmative action** plans.

1. Job-based or departmental seniority units are legal as long as there is no intent to discriminate. Before the Supreme Court announced this interpretation, virtually every lower federal court had held that a seniority system that perpetuated the effects of past discrimination was illegal.[27]

    Federal agencies have negotiated a number of "consent decrees" to settle civil rights class suits that had departmental seniority units excluding minority workers from the most desirable jobs. One such decree was in the steel industry: its effects were to change the seniority system from departmentwide to plantwide units and to provide a system of transfer rights to minority workers who had been discriminated against under the old system.

    A consent decree cannot be treated as binding on persons who are not parties to the proceedings in which it was negotiated.[28] Therefore, individuals adversely affected by a consent decree can challenge the decree in a later case.

2. Workers who have been discriminated against since the effective date of the Civil Rights Act (1965) may be entitled to both back pay and "constructive seniority" to make up for their losses. That is, a worker who was not hired in 1965 or later because of discrimination may receive both the back pay lost and the seniority credits he or she would have accrued since the date of the discriminatory act.[29]

    Section 1981 of the Civil Rights Act provides that "all persons . . . shall have the same right . . . to make and enforce contracts . . . as is enjoyed by white citizens." Section 1981 does not provide a separate remedy beyond those available under Title VII. The courts have held that the central premise of Title VII's make-whole policies of conciliation and voluntary compliance are preferred to Section 1981 court litigation fueled by prospects of big-money awards. Section 1981 strictly applies to discrimination that involves the "making and enforcement" of employment contracts and not to "post-formation conduct."[30]

3. Workers cannot be compensated (either through back pay or constructive seniority) for discrimination that occurred before the Civil Rights Act.[31] An individual has two years from the occurrence of a discriminatory action to file a charge of discrimination. A discriminatory act occurs when the decision is made and communicated to the employees.[32] The proper focus is on the time of the discriminatory act, not on the time at which the consequences of the act became most painful.

    Some violations are characterized as continuing and a charge may be filed at any time.[33] For instance, a seniority system that is discriminatory on its face may be challenged at any time as it is a continuing violation, whereas one that is neutral must be challenged within the specified time limit.[34]

4. The term affirmative action was introduced in 1961 in President Kennedy's Executive Order 10925. Employers and unions may voluntarily agree to modify their employment practices and introduce affirmative actions in order to remedy the effects of past discrimination. A central case is the one in which the company and the union agreed to admit to an affirmative action training program more minority workers than would have been eligible under the previous seniority rules.[35]

   An affirmative action is permissible under the following conditions:

   a. There is a "manifest imbalance" in the composition of the work force.

   b. The plan is "narrowly tailored" and designed to eliminate the imbalance in such a way that does not "unnecessarily trammel" the legitimate expectations of other workers.

   c. Race or sex are not the sole determinants in making any employment selection decision. The courts frown on employment selections based solely on race or sex. The employer must consider other pertinent factors such as experience and qualification.

   d. The preferences terminate once balance in the job category has been achieved.[36]

   The Supreme Court has adopted a strict "scrutiny standard" in determining whether an affirmative action plan is valid. An affirmative action plan is valid if there is a "compelling interest" for implementing the plan. In addition, the plan must be "narrowly tailored" to achieve its objectives.[37] The government must identify and document the existing discrimination suffered by the particular groups in the labor force and develop programs that are specifically designed to remedy that discrimination. In effect, governments can implement affirmative action programs only if they can prove specific acts of discrimination by a specific agency or institution.

5. Seniority systems may not be altered by a court for the benefit of workers who were not themselves victims of discrimination. Section 703(h) of the Civil Rights Act establishes seniority systems as exceptions to Title VII liability. In effect, "it is not unlawful for an employer to apply different standards of compensation, or different terms, conditions, or privileges of employment pursuant to a bona-fide seniority system . . . provided that such differences are not the result of the intention to discriminate because of race, color, religion, sex, or national origin." Therefore, an employer may follow an existing seniority system when making layoffs, even if the

effect is disproportionately adverse to recently hired blacks and women, as long as the seniority system is bona-fide.[38]

6. The burden of proving discrimination at all times remains with the plaintiff (the party alleging discrimination). Statistical disparities alone are insufficient to prove discrimination. The plaintiff(s) must demonstrate how the employment requirement producing the disparity was not relevant to the defendant's business needs and that the adverse impact resulted from a particular employment practice.

To rebut the charge of discrimination, the employer has the burden of producing evidence that there is a legitimate business necessity for the practice. The employer also may rebut the charge of discrimination by showing by the preponderance of the evidence that the same action would have been taken if there had not been any discrimination.[39] The employer need not show that the practice is essential or indispensable to the business but, rather, that the practice serves the "legitimate goals" of the employer.[40]

However, if an employer is found guilty of egregious discrimination, a court may order affirmative, "race-conscious" relief—such as minority hiring goals—even if those who will benefit from the affirmative action measures are not the actual victims of the employer's discriminatory practices.[41]

Important Administrative Agencies

This chapter has focused on the legal regulation of collective bargaining and unions. The administration of these regulations, critical to the functioning of collective bargaining, is in the hands of a variety of administrative agencies. Summarized below are the key activities of the most important administrative agencies operating in the labor area.

1. *National Labor Relations Board (NLRB):* Administers the National Labor Relations Act including the Taft-Hartley and Landrum-Griffin amendments. Key activities include designating bargaining units, conducting representation elections, and investigating and adjudicating unfair labor practice charges. The NLRB includes national and regional boards.

2. *U.S. Department of Labor (DOL):* Serves as the advisor to the President on labor issues. Conducts research and collects data on labor matters. Oversees the administration of a variety of regulations concerning equal employment opportunity, health and safety, and internal union affairs. Maintains a large staff in Washington, D.C., and regional offices.

3. *Federal Mediation and Conciliation Service (FMCS):* Offers mediation services to labor and management in their collective bargaining activities.

4. *National Mediation Board:* Administers the Railway Labor Act. Oversees union representation and provides mediation services to the parties during impasses.

5. *State and local agencies:* A variety of agencies regulate the conduct of public sector bargaining. Some of the agencies provide mediation services to parties engaged in collective bargaining in both the private and public sectors. Agencies also oversee the administration of state regulations dealing with employment conditions.

Summary

Labor laws are an important part of the environment that influences the conduct of collective bargaining. How workers join unions, the process of negotiations, the right to strike, and the scope of collective bargaining are all shaped by labor laws.

The National Labor Relations Act is the key labor law that governs collective bargaining in the private sector in the United States. The NLRA, passed in 1935, gives unions the right to strike, provides unions with exclusive jurisdiction, establishes representation election procedures, defines unfair labor practices, and in many other ways regulates collective bargaining. The National Labor Relations Board administers the NLRA, including the conduct of representation elections. A number of other administrative agencies also are involved in collective bargaining, including the Federal Mediation and Conciliation Service and the U.S. Department of Labor.

Significant issues addressed by the Taft-Hartley amendments to the NLRA, added in 1947, include union unfair labor practices, secondary boycotts, and representation limits on supervisors. The Landrum-Griffin amendments to the NLRA, passed in 1959, regulate union internal finances and governance.

Before passage of the NLRA, courts had restricted worker and union rights by applying conspiracy doctrines and injunctions. In the early 1900s a variety of laws, including the Clayton Act, the Norris-LaGuardia Act, and the Railway Labor Act, brought piecemeal changes to the regulation of collective bargaining. The NLRA established a comprehensive foundation for worker and union rights.

Separate state laws regulate public sector bargaining. As described in Chapter 13, the presence and scope of these laws vary greatly across states. Bargaining in the airline and railroad industry is regulated by the Railway Labor Act.

Frequently throughout the rest of this text reference is made to one of these labor laws as we discuss how collective bargaining works. Yet the influence of the law is often felt in combination with some other aspect of the environment. The next chapter examines how these other environmental factors shape collective bargaining.

Discussion Questions

1. How was the NLRA different from any previous labor law in the United States?

2. Describe what the NLRA requires regarding bargaining in good faith. How would you tell if labor and management in a particular negotiation actually were bargaining in good faith?

3. U.S. labor law is often said to put heavy emphasis on the procedural regulation of collective bargaining and to involve relatively little regulation of substantive bargaining outcomes. In what sense is this true?

4. Discuss whether collective bargaining in the railroads and airlines should be regulated with labor laws that differ from the laws that apply to other private sector employees.

Suggested Readings

Cox, Archibald. *The Law and National Labor Policy* (Los Angeles: Institute of Industrial Relations, University of California, 1960).

Gold, Michael Evan. *An Introduction to Labor Law* (Ithaca, NY: ILR Press, 1989).

Morris, Charles. editor, *American Labor Policy* (Washington, D.C.: Bureau of National Affairs, 1988).

Taylor, Benjamin J., and Fred Whitney. *Labor Relations Law,* 5th ed. (Englewood Cliffs, NJ: Prentice-Hall, 1987).

End Notes

1. Benjamin J. Taylor and Fred Whitney, *Labor Relations Law,* 5th ed., (Englewood Cliffs, NJ: Prentice-Hall, 1987), pp. 146–149.

2. Ibid., p. 147.

3. Ibid., p. 151.

4. Section 9(b) of the Taft-Hartley amendments to the NLRA prohibit the NLRB from including professional employees in a bargaining unit with nonprofessional employees unless the professional employees favor such a move with a majority vote. The formation of bargaining units is discussed in Chapter 7.

5. See Michael Evan Gold, *An Introduction to Labor Law* (Ithaca, NY: ILR Press, 1989): 44–45.

6. Ibid., p. 45.

7.   Ibid., p. 48.

8.   The Taft-Hartley amendments, as discussed in the following section, allow states to ban union shop clauses.

9.   Twenty states currently have right to work laws that ban the union shop.

10.   Charles J. Morris, ed., *The Developing Labor Law* (Washington, D.C.: Bureau of National Affairs, 1971), p. 204.

11.   *NLRB v. Yeshiva University,* 444 U.S. 672 (1980).

12.   Taylor and Whitney, *Labor Relations Law,* pp. 584–621.

13.   In 1989 the Teamsters reaffiliated with the AFL-CIO.

14.   Walter Oberer and Kurt Hanslowe, *Labor Law: Collective Bargaining in a Free Society* (St. Paul, MN: West Publishing, 1972), p. 42.

15.   Milton R. Konvitz, "An Empirical Theory of the Labor Movement: W. Stanley Jevons," *Philosophical Review* 62 (January 1948): 75.

16.   Archibald Cox, "The Duty to Bargain in Good Faith," *Harvard Law Review* 71 (1958): 1409.

17.   A. H. Raskin, "Collective Bargaining and the Public Interest," in *Challenges to Collective Bargaining,* ed. Lloyd Ulman (Englewood Cliffs, NJ: Prentice-Hall, 1967), p. 156.

18.   Sanford M. Jacoby, "The Duration of Indefinite Employment Contracts in the United States and England: An Historical Analysis," *Comparative Labor Law,* 5 (Winter, 1982): 85–128.

19.   *Merrit v. Edison Express* (South Dakota Supreme Court, 3/15/89).

20.   *Derrico v. Sheehan Emergency Hospital* U.S. Court of Appeals Second Circuit, New York, 844 F. 2d 22 (4/5/88).

21.   *Mursch v. Van Dorn Company* (Wisconsin Supreme Court, 7/25/88).

22.   *Pratt v. Brown Machine Co.* U.S. Court of Appeals, Sixth Circuit, Michigan, 855 F. 2d 1225, (9/7/88) and *Butterfield v. Citibank of South Dakota* (South Dakota Supreme Court, 3/15/89).

23.   *Berube v. Fashion Centre* (Utah Supreme Court, 3/20/89).

24.   *Bullock v. Automobile Club of Michigan* (Michigan Supreme Court, 6/6/89).

25.   *Volino v. General Dynamics* (U.S. District Court of Rhode Island, 4/07/88); *Cummins v. EG & G Sealol, Inc.* (U.S. District Court of Rhode Island, 6/30/88); and *Coman v. Thomas Manufacturing Co. Inc.* (North Carolina Supreme Court, 7/26/89).

26.   A by-product of this shift was a tripling of the number of regulatory programs administered by the U.S. Department of Labor. See John T. Dunlop, "The Limits of Legal Compulsion," *Labor Law Journal* 27 (February 1976): 67.

27.   *Teamsters v. United States,* 431 U.S. 324 (1977).

28.   *Martin v. Wilks,* 487 U.S. 1204 (1990).

29.   *Franks v. Bowman Transportation Company,* 424 U.S. 747 (1976).

30. *Patterson v. McLean Credit Union,* 485 U.S. 617 (1990).

31. *International Brotherhood of Teamsters v. United States,* 431 U.S. 324 (1977).

32. *Delaware v. Ricks,* 449 U.S. 250 (1980).

33. *Bazemore v. Friday,* 478 U.S. 385 (1976).

34. *Lorance v. AT&T Technologies,* 486 U.S. 1003 (1990).

35. *United Steelworkers of America v. Weber,* 443 U.S. 193 (1979).

36. Ibid.

37. *City of Richmond v. J. A. Croson Co.,* 484 U.S. 1058 (1990).

38. *Firefighters Local Union 1784 v. Stotts,* 467 U.S. 561 (1984).

39. *Price Waterhouse v. Hopkins,* 485 U.S. 933 (1990).

40. *Wards Cove Packing Company v. Antonio,* 487 U.S. 1232 (1990).

41. *Sheet Metal Workers Local 28 v. EEOC,* 478 U.S. 421 (1990).

Chapter 4

The Role
of the Environment

This chapter moves horizontally across the three-tiered framework by examining how the environment influences the bargaining process and bargaining outcomes at the functional level. The discussion focuses on five key aspects of the environment: the economic, public policy, demographic, social, and technological contexts of the bargaining relationship.

The environment is most important through its effects on the bargaining power held by labor and management, which determines bargaining outcomes. A union, for example, will be better able to gain a high wage and other favorable contract terms when the union has relatively high bargaining power. It is often something in the environment that determines whether a union has a lot of bargaining power in one situation and little power in another. Thus we start this chapter with a discussion of how the environment influences bargaining power and the bargaining process. For instance, the text traces how a low unemployment rate (an aspect of the economic environment) strengthens workers' ability to hold out on strike and thereby gives a union greater bargaining power.

The role of environmental factors is well illustrated by events in the 1980s as labor and management were forced to respond to threatening new forms of economic competition and a shift in national politics to conservative public policies. Both economic and political changes played a crucial role in the wave of concessionary bargaining that began in the early 1980s. To understand how the environment affected collective bargaining in the 1980s and in other periods a conceptual framework is needed.

A Conceptual Framework To Analyze the Environment

This book uses as a framework an extension of the model proposed by John Dunlop. Dunlop classified the industrial relations environment into three main influences: (1) the **economic context,** (2) the **technological**

context, and (3) the **locus of power** in the larger society.[1] This book also considers the influence of the **social context** and the **demographic context.** The underlying theme is that labor and management can influence the environment and the environment also influences them.

On the one hand, the external environment provides both incentives and constraints to labor and management in their efforts to meet their bargaining goals; thus it is important to consider how the environment shapes the power of the bargaining parties. On the other hand, the parties to collective bargaining also seek to mold their environment to better serve their needs; thus environmental influences are not entirely outside human control.

For example, since the 1920s, many textile, apparel, and other small, soft-goods employers have migrated from the northeast to the south, partly (if not primarily) to take advantage of a more favorable economic environment (such as lower labor costs).

More recently, many U.S. manufacturing firms have opened production facilities overseas or established joint ventures with foreign producers, thereby helping to create an economic environment of sluggish employment growth in their industries. In this way these firms have directly shaped the economic environment for collective bargaining.

The involved parties' ability to influence their environment is even more pronounced in the case of public policy because, quite simply, organized labor and management are the prime lobbyists influencing the public policies that regulate their own behavior. Consequently, in the long run the environment is to some extent influenced by the bargaining parties. Only in the short run should the environment be viewed as external and relatively fixed.

Bargaining Power

The environment is particularly influential through the effects it exerts on the bargaining power held by labor and management. **Bargaining power** can be defined simply as the ability of one party to achieve its goals in bargaining in the presence of opposition by another party to the process.

Sources of Power for Labor and Management

The bargaining power enjoyed by a union is heavily influenced by the union's and its members' abilities to withdraw their labor, usually (though not always) through a strike. Workers are more likely to win higher wages and other gains the more they are willing and able to sustain a strike. Moreover, strikes, once undertaken, are more likely to succeed the greater the costs of the strike to the employer. Thus, the employer's bargaining power is heavily influenced by their ability to withstand a strike. The simplest measure of bargaining power is the amount of strike leverage each party holds.

Workers can also withdraw their labor through more informal actions, such as "working to rule" (following rules strictly rather than pursuing effective work practices), the "blue flu" (large-scale worker absenteeism), and other means of slowing production. The discussion that follows focuses on the effects of strikes that entail workers who fully withdraw their labor. Nevertheless, many of the points raised carry over to less extreme forms of labor withdrawal.

How Strike Leverage Influences Bargaining Power

The relative degree to which workers and the employer are willing and able to sustain a strike is their **strike leverage.** More specifically, to measure each party's strike leverage, one needs to know what costs a strike would impose on each party and what alternative income sources there are available to each party to offset any income losses induced by a strike. The discussions of the environmental contexts that follow help us understand what determines strike leverage.

The Economic Context

Economic factors are particularly important in bargaining power and strike leverage. Economic factors can be separated into those that are macrolevel (economywide) and those that are microlevel (relevant only to a specific bargaining relationship). A common thread joins the macro- and microeconomic factors, however: both exert much of their influence through their effects on the bargaining power of the two parties.

The Microeconomic Influences on Bargaining Power

A number of microeconomic factors on bargaining power concern individual actors, either a worker or a firm. Strike leverage on both sides is where these factors coalesce.

Management's Strike Leverage   The more an employer is willing and able to sustain a strike, the more likely the work force will be to settle a strike before attaining all the union's goals. Employee strike leverage derives from the strike's influence on firm profits. The greater the profits lost by the firm, the more ready the firm will be to give in to labor's demands. During a strike a firm's profits are, in turn, shaped by a strike's effects on production and sales. Exhibit 4–1 diagrams the principal determinants of an employer's strike leverage: workers' ability to harm production, sales, and profits; and management's ability to find alternative means to maintain production, sales, and profits.

Exhibit 4–1   **Determinants of Management's Strike Leverage**

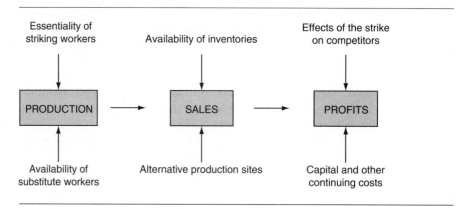

The effects of a strike on production: Once a strike has begun, the first indicator of workers' bargaining power is the degree to which the strike has impaired production and/or service. Workers who succeed in actually halting production because there are no readily available labor substitutes—supervisors, employees in or from another plant, strikebreakers, or automated equipment—have substantial strike leverage and bargaining power. In other words, these workers are *essential* to the production process. Craft workers, who are typically very difficult to replace because of their skills, often have significant strike leverage. For example, the high skill levels of electricians and repair machinists help explain why they earn so much more than production workers in the auto, steel, and textile industries.

The effects of a strike on sales: The power of a striking work group is tempered, however, if the halt in production does not lead to a reduction in sales. Employers can sever, or at least weaken, the link between production and sales if inventories are high or if alternative production sites can be used to produce what normally would be produced at the struck site. Whether alternative production is available is influenced by the bargaining structure (are the other sites covered by the same union or contract) and by the extent to which other workers at other sites join or support the strike.

The effects of a strike on profits: Finally, even if production and sales are stopped by a strike, the firm may not necessarily witness a serious decline in profits. For example, firms with relatively high ongoing capital or interest expenses have a harder time withstanding a loss of income caused by a strike. This helps explain why construction workers, who can temporarily halt costly construction projects, have so much bargaining power. In contrast, firms facing a strike that also shuts down all the competitors' operations have an easier time withstanding strikes because their lost sales and profits may be largely postponed rather than permanently foregone. Firms that have substantial savings or alternative income sources (such as from other lines of business) can more easily absorb the costs of a strike. Later sections of this chapter discuss how the recent growth in employers' nonunion operations has improved their strike leverage through this channel.

The Union's Strike Leverage   Consider the other side—the union's strike leverage. A union's strike leverage is determined by the ability and willingness of the work force to stay out on strike. The longer workers are willing and able to stay on strike, the greater the bargaining power held by the union representing those workers and the more likely they are to win favorable employment terms from an employer, other factors held constant.

Alternative sources of worker income: Workers' willingness to stay out on strike is heavily influenced by the degree to which alternative sources of income are available to the striking work force. Obviously, workers in unions that offer ample strike benefits can better afford to stay out on strike than can those in other unions. Likewise, when striking workers can more readily find temporary or part-time work that supplements any union strike benefits or when they have accumulated substantial savings or assets, workers are more able to sustain a strike action.

Worker solidarity: Another set of factors that influence worker strike leverage beyond the microeconomic environment is the attitude of union members. Workers' feelings of solidarity with one another influence whether picket lines will be honored, and any pent-up frustrations will influence workers' willingness to stay out on strike. In brief, strikes are highly emotional undertakings, and they depend on numerous factors, not simply the microeconomic environment.

The Wage-Employment Trade-off   Strike leverage determines whether workers are *able* to press for a higher wage settlement or other more advantageous contractual provisions. But higher wages often bring cuts in employment, and thus unions may, in same cases, choose not to raise wages as much as they could. This is called the **wage-employment trade-off.**

The key point is that there are employment effects from wage increases as well as direct wage gains. Unions sometimes moderate their wage demands given these employment effects. For example, autoworkers at Chrysler Corporation lowered their wage demands in 1980 because they feared that any higher wage payments by Chrysler would push the company into bankruptcy and Chrysler workers would then lose their jobs. This trade-off between wages and employment is therefore another important microeconomic influence on bargaining power and outcomes.

Marshall's Four Basic Conditions   Unions are more likely to consider the employment effects that result from a wage increase when these effects are greater. Why a wage increase leads to large reductions in employment in one situation and to only small reductions in employment in another is explained by **Marshall's Conditions.**

In his seminal analysis of labor and management bargaining power, Alfred Marshall argued that unions are most powerful when the **demand for labor** is highly **inelastic**—that is, when increases in wages will not result in significant reductions in employment in the unionized sector.[2] Marshall further proposed four basic conditions under which the demand for union labor would be inelastic: (1) when labor cannot be easily replaced in the production process by other workers or machines; (2) when the demand for the final product is price inelastic (that is, demand is not sensitive to changes in the price of the product); (3) when the supply of nonlabor factors of production is price inelastic; and (4) when the ratio of labor costs to total costs is small.[3] Let us address each of these conditions in turn.

The difficulty of replacing workers: The first condition, the degree to which *workers' are difficult to replace,* depends on the production technology. The more difficult it is to replace workers with machines or other workers, the less apt the workers will be to fear their displacement.

Unions can try to limit the ease with which management can introduce new technology by raising the costs of substituting other factors of production for union labor, but they face a dilemma in that strategy. Collectively bargained constraints on technological change may keep unions from losing employment, but slowing that rate of technological change may also constrain the rate of productivity growth, limiting the long-run potential for wage increases.

The demand for the product: Workers face less of an employment decline from raising wages if the demand for the product produced by these workers is not sensitive to the price of the product. This sensitivity (what economists call the *elasticity of product demand*) is a second key condition identified by Marshall. This condition is somewhat different from the other three in that it is influenced by consumer preferences and not by the actions of either the firm or the union. The elasticity of product demand depends on the willingness of consumers to substitute other products.

A modern-day illustration of this principle is the threat to union power raised by foreign imports that become more attractive to domestic consumers as wages and prices in the domestic unionized economy rise. The auto, apparel, steel, and electrical appliance industries are all recent cases in point.

Unions do try to influence consumer actions through "Buy Union" campaigns. Box 4–1 illustrates two different approaches to such cam-

Box 4–1

Examples of union efforts to influence consumer demand.

paigns. The ad on the right tells readers of the union newsletter where to find labels that identify whether various products are union made. The ad on the left is trying to discourage readers from purchasing a product the union claims is being produced by nonunion labor.

The supply of other inputs: Marshall's third condition is the responsiveness of the price of other inputs in the production process to the demand for those inputs (what economists call the *elasticity of supply of other factors of production*). When an employer turns to alternative inputs to economize on union labor, unions will be more able to push up wages (with less fear of employment cutbacks) if the price of other inputs rises little as their use increases. Thus, the more inelastic is the supply curve for alternative inputs, the greater is union power. Whereas Marshall's first condition concerns the degree to which it is *technologically feasible* to substitute machines or other factors of production for unionized labor, his third condition concerns the *costs* to the firm of increasing its use of alternative factors.

Labor's share of total costs: Marshall's fourth condition was that unions are more powerful when labor costs represent only a small proportion of total costs. This condition has often been restated as *the importance of being unimportant.* An employer is less likely to resist union pressure if a given wage increase affects only a very small proportion of the total cost of the product. Thus, a small craft unit, such as the skilled maintenance employees in a plant, is often less likely to meet management resistance to its wage demands than would a broad bargaining unit that represents all production and maintenance employees.[4]

Bargaining in the public sector demonstrates the difficulties unions experience when labor costs represent a large proportion of total production costs. Labor costs for local government often run between 60 and 70 percent of the budget, and in some jurisdictions occupations such as fire fighters run as high as 90 percent of the budget. When local government officials seek to control total budget costs, they take a very hard line in collective bargaining because the wages and salaries of public employees represent their largest controllable cost.

Do Unions and Workers Care about the Wage-Employment Trade-off?

All of the Marshallian conditions are based on the assumption that workers and unions are concerned about the employment effects of wage increases. If union members are willing to accept a slow rate of growth in employment or a decline in the number of union jobs as a trade-off for higher wages, the sources of power discussed above are less important.

Perhaps the classic example of a union that ignored the employment effects resulting from wage increases was the United Mine Workers of America (UMW) in the 1940s. UMW President John L. Lewis demanded high wage increases while giving employers a free hand to invest in labor-saving technology. The result was that, though mine workers' wages increased, employment in the industry declined sharply throughout the 1940s and into the 1950s.[5] Despite this decline, the union's leaders did not soften their demands for higher wages.

The industrial relations community has long engaged in a heated debate over the role the wage-employment trade-off actually plays in collective bargaining. Arthur Ross argued that political factors rather than employment consequences shape union wage policy. Ross also claimed that workers' wage demands are heavily influenced by their making comparisons with the wages of other workers or unions (by "orbits of coercive comparisons"), a practice that gives union leaders some leeway in defining their wage goals.[6]

John Dunlop had a very different view of union wage policy, claiming that unions do consider the employment consequences of their wage demands and that they may even try to maximize the employer's payroll.[7]

Concessionary bargaining in the 1980s offered evidence that unions and workers do consider the employment effects of higher wages, particularly when they might lead to a plant closing. Yet, as Ross asserted, political factors played an important role in shaping whether and to what extent employment was a concern in wage bargaining in the 1980s. Workers' willingness to accept concessions and what they won in exchange for those concessions was affected by a host of factors, including business and union strategies.

The Macroeconomic Influences on Bargaining Power

Economists refer to unemployment and the growth in national product or productivity as macroeconomic factors, those aspects of the whole economy that affect bargaining power through a variety of channels. A union's strike leverage, for example, depends in part on the availability of jobs—both for the striking workers and for their spouses or other family members who might help support the strikers. The higher the unemployment rate, the less likely striking workers or family members will be to find substitute employment and the more likely the family members normally employed will be on layoff.

Thus, during the upswing of a business cycle (as the unemployment rate declines) unions generally gain strike leverage. Conversely, the power of unions declines during periods of falling product demand and rising unemployment. The factors at work here include those discussed earlier regarding striking workers' needs for alternative income sources and employers' vulnerability to strikes when product demand is high. During periods of slack demand employers may, in fact, welcome a strike because they can then lower their inventories and use the strike as a substitute for layoffs.

Wage Flexibility over the Business Cycle   The connection between macroeconomic conditions and bargaining power is supported by evidence that the rate of wage increases in the economy responds to the business cycle. Wages rise more quickly in times of a growing economy, and they increase more slowly (or fall) in times of sluggish macroeconomic activity.

Nevertheless, declines in product demand and increases in unemployment have been shown to have a weaker downward effect on collectively bargained wage increases than on wage increases in the nonunion sector.[8] Unions tend to aggressively resist wage cutting, making it harder for union employers than for nonunion employers to cut wages or to moderate the pace of wage increases during recessionary periods. The fact that union wage rates are often set in multiyear agreements (labor contracts in trucking and the auto industry, for example, have traditionally been three years in duration) makes union wages less responsive than nonunion wages to changing economic conditions.

Incomes Policies   Incomes policies represent another macroeconomic factor that can affect bargaining power and collective bargaining. *Incomes policies* are direct efforts by the government (typically the federal government) to set wages and other employment conditions. Although incomes policies designed to limit precisely the size of wage and price increases have not been used in the United States in recent years, they had important effects on collective bargaining in earlier periods and in other countries.

For example, wartime administrations from World War I through the Korean war instituted tripartite boards that used various incomes policy techniques to stabilize wages. Between 1962 and 1966 the Kennedy and Johnson administrations formulated a set of **wage-price guideposts** as advisory or voluntary limits on wages and prices that union and management negotiators were asked to observe. In general, the guideposts recommended that wage increases be limited to the average long-term increase in the rate of productivity growth for the economy as a whole, initially specified as 3.2 percent. The guideposts were replaced by a more informal, case-by-case system of intervention known as *jawboning*, in which the President or his advisors privately negotiated with company and union officials to moderate their price and wage increases.

The first two years of the Nixon administration, 1969–70, brought a return to hands-off incomes policies. By 1971, however, administration advisors' concerns over wage escalation in construction brought about the establishment of the Construction Industry Stabilization Committee, a tripartite group that reviewed wage increases and later used its authority to reject increases it found were out of line. Later that year, in August, domestic and international economic conditions led the Nixon administration to impose the strongest and most direct form of incomes policies: **wage and price controls.** The first "phase" of the controls consisted of an economywide wage-price freeze, followed by a two-year period of gradually loosening controls. These wage and price controls were the first in peacetime during this century.

The next experiment with a formal incomes policy came in 1978. After several years of monitoring wage and price trends, the Carter administration announced a "voluntary" set of *guidelines* backed up by the threat that the government would refuse to purchase goods or services from employers that exceeded the wage or price standards.

It would be a mistake to assume, however, that the existence of controls either automatically reduced the aggregate rate of increases in wages and compensation costs to the target levels in the short run or reduced the longer run rate of wage and benefit increases. In fact, the record of incomes policies on both these scores is at best mixed.

The Reagan administration made no recourse to incomes policy, an absence of intervention that has been continued by the Bush administration to date. Not only were these administrations ideologically opposed to governmental regulation of wage bargaining (and many other economic affairs), but the pressure to institute controls weakened as the economy experienced low price inflation in the 1980s and early 1990s.

Exhibit 4–2 traces a number of the key macroeconomic variables in the United States. Many later sections of this book discuss U.S. economic trends, and the reader may find it useful to refer back to this chart. This book also frequently discusses how industrial relations behavior influences the economy's performance.

The Effects of Collective Bargaining on Macroeconomic Performance

The analysis of the macroeconomics of collective bargaining cannot close without identifying how bargaining outcomes in turn affect the economy itself. Bargaining outcomes not only illustrate the success of the macroeconomic policies designed to curb inflation and unemployment, but they also add a dynamic component of feedback to our framework. Bargaining outcomes influence the economic context for future collective bargaining negotiations and set the cycle of events in motion again.

The effects of collective bargaining settlements on the economy are complex and hotly debated by economists. There is much debate, for example, surrounding whether unions are the cause of inflation.

Do Unions Cause Inflation?   For union wage increases to lead *directly* to inflation, the union-nonunion wage differential would have to be ever widening. Although this differential did widen during the 1970s, it narrowed in the early 1980s, and, in any case, it has historically not been continuously increasing. Thus, even though union workers receive higher wages than do their nonunion counterparts, this earnings differential does not apparently produce inflation.

Furthermore, since unions represent less than 20 percent of the labor force, an increase in union wages will not be very inflationary unless union wage increases spill over to nonunion wages. Whether they do spill over to the nonunion sector has been widely debated, but there is little empirical evidence of this effect at an aggregate level.

A more significant way in which unions might cause the inflation rate to rise is through the slower response of union wages than nonunion

Exhibit 4–2
Macroeconomic Data for the United States, 1964–1989

Year	Inflation Rate[a]	Unemployment Rate[b]	Wage Increase in Major Collective Bargaining Settlements[c]	Productivity Increase (Output per Worker Hour)[d]	Unit Labor Cost Increase[e]	Contract Rejection Rate[f]	Incomes Policy[g]
1964	1.0%	5.2%	3.2%	3.9%	0.59%	8.7%	Guideposts
1965	1.9	4.5	3.8	2.5	0.79	10.0	Guideposts
1966	3.5	3.8	4.8	2.2	3.7	11.7	Guideposts
1967	3.0	3.8	5.6	2.2	3.2	14.2	Jawboning
1968	4.7	3.6	7.4	2.6	4.8	11.9	None
1969	6.2	3.5	9.2	-0.5	7.2	12.3	None
1970	5.6	4.9	11.9	0.3	6.5	11.2	None
1971	3.3	5.9	11.7	2.9	3.4	9.9	Controls
1972	3.4	5.6	7.3	3.0	3.4	10.1	Controls
1973	8.7	4.9	5.8	1.8	6.0	9.6	Controls
1974	12.3	5.6	9.8	-2.2	11.9	12.4	Decontrol
1975	6.9	8.5	10.2	1.8	7.9	11.2	None
1976	4.9	7.7	8.4	2.6	5.7	9.8	None
1977	6.7	7.1	7.8	1.5	6.0	11.5	None
1978	9.0	6.1	7.6	0.8	7.7	11.9	Guidelines
1979	13.3	5.8	7.4	-1.5	11.1	11.9	Guidelines
1980	12.5	7.1	9.5	-0.5	11.0	10.7	Guidelines
1981	8.9	7.6	9.8	0.9	8.4	8.9	None
1982	3.8	9.7	3.8	-0.6	8.3	n.a.	None
1983	3.8	9.6	2.6	3.3	1.0	n.a.	None
1984	3.9	7.5	2.4	2.1	1.8	n.a.	None
1985	3.8	7.2	2.3	1.4	2.8	n.a.	None
1986	1.1	7.0	1.2	1.9	2.2	n.a.	None
1987	4.4	6.2	2.2	0.7	3.1	n.a.	None
1988	4.4	5.5	2.5	1.4	3.2	n.a.	None
1989	4.6	5.2	4.0			n.a.	None

[a]Consumer price index taken from *The Economic Report of the President* (Washington, D.C.: Office of the President, transmitted to Congress February 1990), table C-61.
[b]The data are taken from U.S. Department of Labor, Bureau of Labor Statistics, *Handbook of Labor Statistics,* August 1989, table 26.
[c] The data are from *Current Wage Developments,* Bureau of Labor Statistics, G.P.O.; for 1976–82, from March 1983, table 15; for 1983–85, from March 1986, table 16; for 1986–90, April 1990, table 18. The figures represent wage adjustments in all industries for the first year of a contract.
[d]The data are from the *Handbook of Labor Statistics,* August 1989. The figures represent the output per hour of all workers in the non-farm business sector and are calculated from the annual percentage change based on the index in table 98.
[e]The data are from the *Handbook of Labor Statistics,* August 1989. The figures are calculated from the annual percentage change based on the index in table 98.
[f]The data are from the Federal Mediation and Conciliation Service, *Annual Report of the Federal Mediation and Conciliation Service* (Washington, D.C.: GPO, various years). The FMCS no longer kept these data after 1981.
[g]See text for descriptions of these terms.

wages to changing economic conditions. A number of studies have shown that wages in the unionized sector (or in highly unionized industries) respond less to increases in unemployment than do wages in the nonunion sector.[9] Thus, traditional strategies for reducing the rate of inflation by increasing the rate of unemployment and thereby holding down wage increases may be less effective for union wages than for nonunion wages.

The Political Influence of Unions on the Macroeconomy   Some observers have argued that all of these direct economic effects of unions on wages are less important in the overall wage-price inflationary spiral than are the political lobbying efforts of unions. For example, a wage-price spiral would continue only if the government pursues expansionary *monetary* or *fiscal policies,* or both. An *expansionary policy* encourages enough economic growth and allows the reemployment of any workers displaced by inflationary wage increases. Although the labor movement is certainly not the only lobbying group that supports expansionary monetary and fiscal policies, its support is a critical supplement to its more decentralized strategies to achieve individual wage and benefit agreements. Without an adequate rate of expansion and economic growth, collectively bargained wage increases would exert a greater toll on the employment opportunities of unionized members of the labor force.

The labor movement also supports a wide range of other economic and social policies that supplement its collective bargaining efforts. Again, it has been argued that many of these policies lead to a greater inflationary pressure than do the individually bargained wage increases. Some observers suggest, for example, that the union movement's support of full-employment policies, minimum-wage legislation, and various income-transfer policies such as unemployment compensation, workers' compensation, and social security all adds to the inflationary pressures in the economy.

Yet the effects of these policies on the economy as a whole are very unclear. Some economists claim that full-employment policies actually reduce inflationary pressures by promoting training and labor-market mobility and thereby expanding the available work force. And even if these policies were shown to contribute to inflationary pressures, it may be that these pressures are well worth the benefits provided by the policies.

Together macroeconomic and microeconomic forces act as one major set of determinants of the process and outcomes of collective bargaining. The factors described in the remainder of this chapter either supplement the economic forces or serve as the mechanisms through which the economic forces are translated into actual results in the collective bargaining system.

The Legal and Public Policy Context

Law and public policy influence the legal standing of unions, unions' bargaining power, and employment conditions. This section describes specifically how the law exerts these effects.

The Legality of Unionism and Union Activity

Public policy determines how easy it is for unions to form and sustain themselves. Imagine what would happen in a country where unionism was deemed to be illegal and workers were sent to jail if they tried to form unions or to carry out strikes. One would expect that under such a public policy there would be few unions and little activity carried out by organized representatives of workers. What would be the long-term consequences of such policies, and would this regime be sustainable?

With unions and union activity outlawed one would expect workers to exert little countervailing influence to other powerful social forces. Recent experience in the eastern European countries such as Poland, however, reveals the social conflict that can result under such a system. In Poland, the union, Solidarity, led a challenge to the Communist government, and unions were active in the overthrow of governments in other eastern European countries. Unionism has thus come to promote more than just the improvement of the working conditions of Polish workers. Events there and in other parts of the eastern bloc remind us of the role that unions can play as a democratic force in society.

Banning unions is one extreme. Legally requiring union membership is potentially the other extreme role that public policy may play. There is no democratic government that has chosen to follow this course. Rather, public policies toward unionism in the United States and other democratic countries have taken a middle course between the extremes of banning and requiring unionism. There exists sizeable variation across democratic countries in the regulations concerning which and how workers can join unions. In every country there also has been significant change in the regulations for unions over time.

The NLRA's Effects on Bargaining Power

The NLRA and state statutes governing public or agricultural employees in the United States do more than just give unions the right to exist. These acts exert sizeable effects on the process and outcomes of collective bargaining through their regulation of the actions by workers, unions, and employers in the course of collective bargaining. For example, the NLRA grants unions the right to strike and obligates employers to bargain in good faith. Without these rights the bargaining power of unions might be severely weakened.

The NLRA influences the bargaining power of workers and employers in a multitude of ways, and many of those effects are through subtle channels. For instance, as discussed in Chapter 3, the Taft-Hartley amendments to the original NLRA made it illegal for supervisors to join unions representing production workers.[10] By taking away the protection of the law, the passage of this amendment led to the demise of the numerous foreman unions that had formed. For those foreman unions the amendments had a clear effect.

The Effects of Direct Regulation of Employment Conditions

Society also has seen fit to regulate certain employment conditions more directly than it does collective bargaining. In the United States federal regulations cover overtime hours (their limits and pay), unemployment insurance, pensions, and a host of other issues. These regulations are clearly important to the extent they set employment terms. They also are important through their indirect effects on bargaining power. For instance, the fact that workers in some states can collect unemployment insurance while they are on strike makes those workers more able to sustain strike action and increases their bargaining power, if everything else is the same.[11]

An Illustration of Government Employment Regulation: Pensions

An example of how government has influenced employment conditions is found in the area of pensions. The *Employee Retirement Income Security Act (ERISA)* of 1974 has had profound effects on pensions. The act (1) specifies minimum standards for vesting of pension contributions, (2) requires more detailed reporting and disclosure of information about the plan to both employees and the government, (3) requires all future liabilities be fully funded on an annual basis and all past unfunded liabilities be amortized over a number of years, and (4) establishes an insurance protection program for workers affected by plan terminations. The costs of the termination insurance are met by a tax on existing plans.

The major policy problem created by ERISA lies in the potential liabilities to the government from the termination of major multiemployer plans. See Box 4–2 for an account of how the Pension Benefit Guarantee Corporation (empowered under ERISA to insure pension plans) acquired enormous liabilities as a result of the bankruptcy of the LTV Corporation. This and similar cases have added to the controversy surrounding ERISA.

Overall, ERISA is a good example of both the speed by which changes can be achieved through direct governmental regulation and the complex problems that result when the federal government attempts to establish uniform practices and standards in an area that previously was characterized by diversity.

Box 4–2

Multiemployer Pension Guarantees

The Pension Benefit Guarantee Corporation (PBGC) is a government agency that serves as statutory trustee for LTV Corporation's terminated pension plans. On June 18, 1990, the Supreme Court ruled that PBGC's decision to restore LTV's pension plans was consistent with the Employee Retirement Income Security Act (ERISA). The court reasoned that PBGC has broad authority to restore terminated pension plans to employers who negotiate "follow-on" pension plans that supplement the benefits paid by the PBGC.

After accumulating $2.3 million in unfunded liabilities under its three pension plans, LTV Corporation filed for bankruptcy under Chapter 11 (in July 1986.) As a result, LTV notified PBGC, which insured $2.1 billion of the company's unfunded pension liability, that it was unable to continue complete funding of its pension plans. Consequently, in January 1987, PBGC terminated LTV's pension plans and began paying benefits (though lower than those had the plan not been terminated) to LTV plan participants.

The decrease in benefits resulted in a United Steelworkers suit against LTV. In response, LTV negotiated a follow-on plan, that made up the benefit difference the participants lost as a result of the plan termination. Therefore, the follow-on plan put retirees in exactly the same position as had the pension plans not been terminated.

Section 4047 of ERISA empowers the PBGC to restore a pension plan when restoration furthers the interests of Title VII and ERISA. Based on its determination that a dramatic economic upturn in the steel industry had reduced the risk of large unfunded liabilities, the PBGC (in August 1987) decided to restore LTV's pension plans under ERISA. However, when the PBGC attempted to enforce the restoration order, a New York District Court ruled that PBGC's decision was arbitrary and capricious because of its reliance on the follow-on plan and insufficient evidence of LTV's financial improvement.

However, the Supreme Court reversed this decision in ruling that the PBGC is not required to consider federal labor and bankruptcy laws in returning a previously terminated pension plan to a private employer in bankruptcy proceedings. The court added that the PBGC properly interpreted Section 4047 in considering LTV's follow-on plan as a deciding factor for restoring the pension plan and that evidence of a substantial financial improvement is not necessary.

The PBGC's anti-follow-on policy is premised on the belief that employees will object more to a company's decision to terminate a pension plan if the company cannot use a follow-on plan to put employees in the same position. Thus, the decision is meant to discourage unnecessary unloading of pension obligations.

Source: Daily Labor Report (Washington, D.C.: Bureau of National Affairs): various issues from January 5, 1989, to June 19, 1990.

The Shift to Less Government Intervention

In the late 1970s and 1980s U.S. public policy changed to a less interventionist style as policy returned to an emphasis on competitive markets at the micro- and macrolevels of the economy. Important developments at the microlevel included **deregulation** of the transportation and communications industries.

Although deregulation was not motivated by labor policy concerns, it has had sizable effects on the process and outcomes of collective bargaining. Unions have trouble keeping wages out of competition and maintaining their penetration of any industry in the face of entry by new competitors. This has been well illustrated by the trucking industry since passage of the Motor Carrier Act of 1980, which reduced the regulation of industry pricing, and entry by the Interstate Commerce Commission. In the airline industry deregulation in 1978 spurred the growth of nonunion carriers and concessionary bargaining in the unionized airlines. In the communications industry deregulation in the 1980s has led to both a growth in the share of telecommunications markets that are served by nonunion companies such as MCI and the breakup of a national bargaining structure in the former Bell Telephone System.

In the 1980s and early 1990s the commitments of the Reagan and Bush administrations to free trade and floating exchange rates sparked heated debates over trade policy as the nation faced huge trade deficits and a loss of employment in those industries most threatened by foreign competition and imports. The increasing internationalization of the U.S. economy has also raised questions whether the labor law framework adopted in the 1930s is still appropriate.

The Labor Movement's Criticism of the NLRA—A Return to the Jungle?

Another serious challenge to the traditional NLRA system of labor regulation comes from within the labor movement itself. Several labor leaders have questioned whether labor unions would be better served if the NLRA were repealed and the parties returned to a variant of the public policy environment that prevailed before the 1930s. In 1984, Lane Kirkland, AFL-CIO president stated: "If by boycotting the [NLRB] one could divest oneself of the jurisdiction of the Board and go to the law of the jungle, I think that would be an option worth considering and I think we might very well be better off."[12] Although this option has not been pursued by the ranks of union leaders or members, it is noteworthy because it stands in dramatic opposition to the position traditionally held by U.S. labor leaders, who have been among the staunchest supporters of the NLRA.

This questioning of the ongoing value of the NLRA has arisen from union leaders' frustrations with both the current administration of the law and the union record of achievement in recent years, particularly in representation elections. Labor leaders (and others) argue that NLRA decisions and representation elections now come about only after enormous delays—caused in part by the lack of commitment to the original purposes of the NLRA exhibited by some NLRB members. The delays are also alleged to be the result of employer practices, such as the filing of numerous challenges and requests for postponement, which only serve to thwart the original intent of the NLRA for timely and fair elections. Overall, these critics argue that NLRB enforcement procedures operate to the advantage of management and against the original purposes of the law.

Labor leaders are also frustrated by the meager success unions are now having in representation elections and by the more general decline in union membership. They blame their lack of success on the current administration of the NLRA and stepped-up union-avoidance tactics on the part of management. And so they speculate whether unions and workers would be better served by a return to the law of the jungle than by a continuation of current practices.

The Demographic Context

Over the past decade the changing nature of the labor force has also caused many to question whether collective bargaining is obsolete. It is therefore important to examine the nature of those changes and to explore their implications for collective bargaining.

Changes in the demographic characteristics of workers or jobs will influence the needs and expectations of workers. These, in turn, may affect the individual's interest in union membership or willingness to stay out on strike.

Labor Force Trends

Since World War II the U.S. labor force has grown at an unprecedented rate, largely as a result of the postwar baby boom. The labor force is expected to grow at a slower rate in the 1990s than it did in the previous 20 years because baby boomers will no longer be entering the labor force but, rather, traveling through it. In fact, a slowdown in the growth of the labor force began in the late 1970s as the last of the boomers entered the labor force. In 1978 and 1979 the labor force grew by 2.7 million people, whereas in 1987 and 1988 it grew by only 1.8 million.[13]

As the trend continues, the median age of the labor force will change accordingly. The median age peaked in 1960 at 40.5 and remained relatively constant until the first of the baby boomers entered the labor force in 1970, at which time it declined significantly. The median age was 39.0

in 1970 and had fallen to 34.8 by 1982. But by 1995 it is projected to have risen again, up to 37.6, reflecting the aging of the baby boomers. In 1984 two-thirds of the labor force was at its prime working age (25–54); by 1995 three-quarters will be in that range.[14] By the turn of the century this generation will be nearing retirement and producing strains on private and public retirement systems.

These general patterns mean that over the course of this decade unions and employers will be faced with a young but aging work force as the baby boom cohort moves through its prime working years. As this happens workers will be in sharp competition for jobs at the higher levels of careers and occupations. Workers may become frustrated if their aspiration for upward mobility is not attainable. This could produce workplace conflicts and a heightened demand for employee participation and voice and, possibly, for union representation.

Over the longer run, 1995 and beyond, the problems of an aging population will become increasingly important, and the ratio of those not in the labor force to those in the labor force will increase—posing difficult problems indeed for all the actors in the industrial relations system.

Women in the Labor Force   The growing number of working women is the most significant labor force development of the last 20 years. In 1972 one-half of all women participated in the labor force; in 1988, 74 percent of women between the ages of 25 and 44 worked, and that fraction is expected to rise beyond 80 percent by 1995.[15] The general trend can largely be explained by women's changing marital status, educational attainment, and career expectations.

One component of the trend has been the increased participation in the labor force of women with young children. Women have been taking less time off from work for child rearing. In 1988, 57 percent of all mothers had entered the labor force before their youngest child was six years old. Moreover, about half of all mothers with infants one year old or younger were in the labor force, as compared to 39 percent in 1980 and 31 percent in 1975.[16]

Consequently, working mothers have begun to challenge employers and unions to meet their social needs. They pose a particular challenge because the propensity to work has been greater among the more highly educated women. Between 1975 and 1988 the labor force participation rate for female college graduates ages 25 to 64 rose from 61 to 80 percent.[17] In 1987 the college-educated labor force was 44 percent women, whereas in 1970 it was 32 percent.[18] Thus, in addition to being a growing component of the labor force, women may well become a vocal component. Their increasing numbers and their increasing education, militancy, and consciousness of women's issues may pressure employers and unions to change their postures toward female workers. Finally, women may present a new focal point for union-organizing campaigns.

Educational Attainment   The educational attainment of workers has increased over the last 20 years. In 1988 the median number of years of school completed for all workers was 12.7, or just slightly beyond a high school degree.[19] (It was 12.4 in 1970.) In 1970, 63.9 percent of all workers had graduated from high school and 12.9 percent had graduated from college. In 1988 those figures had risen to 85.1 percent and 25.3 percent, respectively.[20] Thus, the labor force is becoming more highly educated.

There is, however, an important caveat to consider in projecting the overall "quality" of the labor force. High rates of teenage unemployment (19.1 percent in 1989), high dropout rates from high schools (29.7 percent for whites and 34.7 percent for blacks in 1989), and the poor quality of education offered in urban and, particularly, in poor urban areas all suggest that a large number of new entrants in the labor force over the next decade will have little work experience, few skills, and a low potential for adapting to the rigors of organizational life.[21] Teenagers who grow up in areas with few or no jobs, high rates of crime, and poor schools will pose significant challenges to managers and union leaders of the future. Past experience has shown that it is difficult indeed for employers to reverse the effects of these liabilities.

These two separate educational patterns pose different but equally challenging problems to future managers and union leaders. The more highly educated workers may be less tolerant of authority, seek more involvement on their jobs, and demand more career development opportunities, while the educationally disadvantaged will require more remedial training to mold them into more literate, trainable, and motivated participants in the labor force.

Occupational and Industry Trends

As the supply characteristics of the U.S. labor force have been changing, so has the occupational and industry demand for labor. The most obvious trends in the occupational distribution since 1960 have been the growth of the white-collar sector and the decline of the blue-collar sector. Over half of the labor force is now classified as white-collar; in 1960 that proportion was 43 percent. As Exhibit 4–3 shows, as of 1988 the percentage of the labor force employed in service-producing jobs, the **service sector,** was 76.1 percent, whereas the percentage employed in goods-producing jobs was only 23.9 percent.

These major shifts in industry demand over the last 25 years have profound implications for collective bargaining. The portion of the labor force employed in manufacturing jobs, the traditional stronghold of unions, declined from 31 percent in 1960 to 18.4 percent in 1988. Furthermore, manufacturing industries have been migrating from the northeast and north central regions of the country to the south and southwest. There has been a sizeable movement of jobs away

Exhibit 4–3
The Relative Size of Industrial Sectors in the United States*

Year	All Service-Producing	All Goods-Producing	Manufacturing Only	Government Only
1919	52.6%	47.4%	39.4%	9.9%
1920	53.3	46.7	39.0	9.5
1930	59.3	40.7	32.5	10.7
1940	59.1	40.9	33.9	11.6
1950	59.1	40.9	33.7	13.3
1960	62.3	37.6	31.0	15.4
1970	66.7	33.3	27.3	17.7
1980	71.6	28.4	22.4	18.0
1988	76.1	23.9	18.4	16.5

*The percentages represent workers as a percentage of the total nonagricultural labor force.
Source: U.S. Department of Labor, Bureau of Labor Statistics, *Handbook of Labor Statistics* (Washington, D.C.: GPO, August 1989), calculated from table 68.

from the most unionized industries and regions to industries and areas where unions have traditionally been less successful in organizing workers.

There has also been a significant increase in the share of employment in **part-time jobs.** In 1963, 10.7 percent of all employees worked part-time; by 1988 that figure had grown to 18.4 percent. The percentage of employed youths 16 to 19 years old who worked on a part-time basis rose from 37.8 percent in 1963 to 64.3 percent in 1988.[22]

As part-time work has grown, so has the number of jobs being performed at home. **Home-based occupations** have grown in rank, partly in response to advances in information technologies that make it possible to perform production tasks at home while in communication with a business or businesses out of the home. This is especially true of several data-processing occupations. Both part-time workers and home-based workers are difficult to reach with union-organizing drives.

Is the U.S. Economy Deindustrializing?

The increase in the number of service and part-time jobs has spurred an intense debate. Barry Bluestone and Bennett Harrison claim that the growth in these jobs signals a decline in the manufacturing base of the U.S. economy (they call the process **deindustrialization**). They further argue that these shifts in job composition go hand-in-hand with increasing inequality in the income distribution. The better-paying jobs such as skilled trades, steel, and auto production jobs, they claim are disappearing and are being replaced by lower-paying service jobs.[23]

On the other side of the debate stand analysts such as Robert Lawrence who hold that the growth in the number of service and part-time jobs has been a response to the availability and desires of workers who want and are skilled for those jobs.[24] These observers see this as a sign of health in the U.S. economy and compare the job growth in the United States over the 1970s and 1980s to the sluggish employment growth in Europe over the same period.[25] There is a middle position in this debate, as well, with some disclaiming any deindustrialization but at the same time pointing to many persistent problems in the U.S. labor market.[26]

This debate subsumes a disagreement over both what the facts are and how the facts should be interpreted. Yet the debate is crucial to the future of the labor market because the issues at stake are of enormous importance. For if one decides that the labor market is relatively healthy, there is little reason to seek government policies to alter the outcomes in that labor market, and vice versa. Furthermore, any answer to the question whether deindustrialization or income inequality is taking place will affect government policy toward collective bargaining and many other labor market institutions.

The shift to greater service sector, part-time, and home-based employment has two indisputable implications for collective bargaining and union organizing. First, since part-time workers have looser attachments to a single employer than others (they are often only temporarily employed), union organizing among them is more difficult and probably requires nontraditional techniques. It is not surprising that the labor movement has vigorously opposed the growth of temporary and home-based work. It is unlikely, however, that labor's opposition will have any effect on the growth occurring in these types of employment relationships. Thus, to organize these workers, unions will need to develop policies and strategies that are tailored to their particular needs. One strategy that has been discussed within labor's ranks is to provide associate member status or individual forms of representation to these workers.[27] Other solutions may be developed outside the United States since the growth in temporary, part-time, and home-based work is a problem confronting labor movements all over the globe.

Second, the ease of replacing striking service workers makes it difficult for unions to acquire bargaining leverage through the strike. Several unions that represent service workers have been experimenting with strategies to broaden support for their demands within community groups such as churches. Service unions also have been experimenting with working to rule and other strategies that can exercise leverage against employers while not involving strike action.

Demographic Profile of Union Members

The average union member is more apt to be working in industries, occupations, and regions in which the demand for labor is either declining or growing at a slower pace than elsewhere in the economy. In addition, women, whose labor force participation is increasing rapidly, are underrepresented in the unionized sector.

There are many challenges posed for unions by these developments. The traditional constituency of unions—male, blue-collar, manufacturing, mining, construction, and transportation workers living in the northeast or north central regions—is declining in significance. Current union members are on average older and less well educated than the new entrants to the labor force. Unions may have difficulty adjusting to the demands of a younger, more vocal constituency.

Demographic Challenges for Unions

Demographic diversity can affect union policies. Once they join unions, people tend to try to shape union policies to reflect their own preferences. This process of political representation becomes troublesome to unions if members' views change rapidly. The very purpose of a union is to pursue the common goals of its members through the exercise of collective power. Thus, the more rapid the demography changes and the more heterogeneous the union constituency becomes, the greater the potential for internal conflict and the more difficulty the union will have in trying to establish bargaining priorities.

New union members sometimes have a difficult time creating an effective political base. This is a problem that sometimes confronts newly hired, younger workers as they try to influence the existing, often older, union leadership. Note the same problem faces women, racial and ethnic minorities, or any other new groups that move into union jobs. Until they can establish an effective political base and exert pressure on existing union leaders, their particular needs are not likely to be given as high a priority as they might desire.

In short, the demographic context of collective bargaining influences union membership, the attitudes union members have toward their jobs, and the skills workers bring to the job. If unions are unsuccessful at organizing the new work force, their membership will decline even further. If unions do succeed at organizing the new workers, they will face pressures for change—both within their own organizations and at the bargaining table. In any event, it is clear that any analysis of collective bargaining must account for the demography of the labor force.

The Social Context

What is the image of the union movement in the eyes of the American public? Is the society supportive of or hostile to unions? These are aspects of the social context that can affect industrial relations.

Polls that include questions about unions revealed a consistent decline in the public's image of unions from the 1960s to the mid-1980s. Gallup polls, for example, show a decline from 71 percent in 1965 to 58 percent in 1985 in the share of the population that "approves" of labor unions. More recently, however, the public's overall approval ratings of unions appears to have leveled off.

Although the public's image of unions has deteriorated since the 1960s, the public still generally approves of unions. Box 4–3 reports the findings of a public opinion poll of attitudes toward unions in 1989. Notice in this poll when the respondents were asked general questions about unions (questions 1 and 2), a large number were favorably inclined toward unions. Yet, as shown in the response to question 3, when the respondents were asked if they would join a union, the support for unions declined.

These responses are not unusual. Analysis of a wide range of poll data shows that the public and union members hold complex attitudes toward unions. For example, polls consistently have shown that the American public holds union leaders in low esteem. But, although skeptical of union leaders, the American public has continued to express strong approval of the *functions* unions perform in representing worker interests. Polls show, for example, that a majority of the population approve of unions in general and believe in the right of workers to join unions of their own choosing.[28] Thus, the majority of Americans apparently accept

---

Box 4–3

> ## An Opinion Poll on Unions
>
> Attitudes toward unions expressed in a public opinion poll conducted in 1989 were:
>
> 1. Overall, do you have a favorable or unfavorable opinion of unions?
>
>   44% Favorable
>   38% Unfavorable
>   18% Don't know
>
> 2. Are workers better off with a union?
>
>   49% Yes
>   31% No
>   15% Don't know
>
> 3. Would you join a union?
>
>   37% Yes
>   47% No
>   14% Don't know
>
> *Source:* American Public Opinion Index (Louisville, KY, July 16, 1989).

the legitimacy of unions as a means for protecting the economic- and job-related interests of workers.

American workers also seem to have a **dual image of trade unions.** On the one hand, the majority of workers see unions as big, powerful institutions in society that exert significant control over political decision making and elected officials, as well as over employers and union members. The majority also take a skeptical view of union leaders' personal motivations. On the other hand, an equally large majority of workers see unions as being helpful or instrumental in improving the working lives of their members. Evidently, then, most U.S. workers are skeptical of the political activities of trade unions but accepting of their collective bargaining activities.

The Technological Context

Technological change had a major role in workers' early efforts to look to unions as a way to alter their employment conditions. It also is clear that our economy is in the midst of ongoing technological changes that will have huge effects on future employment conditions. Yet, in the face of this agreement, many people still disagree over how and why technology influenced early unionization and what current technological changes imply for the future of industrial relations.

The Historical Debate over the Influence of Technology: Commons versus Marx

Both Karl Marx and John R. Commons believed that workers were spurred to join unions by technological change, the shift from craft systems of production to the hiring of wage labor, and the rise of the modern factory system. But they disagreed sharply over exactly why changes in technology and the organization of work had that effect.

To Marx the critical event in industrialization was the chasm that capitalist methods of production opened up between workers and the owners of the means of production. That chasm, according to Marx, would inevitably result in a worsening of working conditions, a profit crisis, and the emergence of a revolutionary class consciousness among workers. Followers of Marx went on to argue that it was the *loss of control* that workers experienced as a result of the shift in production methods and ownership that led them to form unions. To those observers collective bargaining was, and is, a continuing battle between workers and managers over control of the production process. Harry Braverman built on this argument and claimed that technological change typically leads to a lowering of the skills required in jobs **(deskilling)** as part of this battle for control.[29]

Commons, on the other hand, observed that the shift in production methods was itself a product of an expansion of the market brought about by urbanization and new transportation methods. To Commons, as the market expanded and the ownership of production changed, workers came up against a host of competitive menaces such as prison or child labor. Workers then turned to unions to protect themselves and to improve their standard of living. Commons and his students, such as Selig Perlman, argued that unions and workers sought *income and job security* rather than control of the production process.[30] Thus, although Marx and Commons differed sharply over the interpretation of unions' objectives, both saw the rise of capitalism as the spur to unionization.

To Clark Kerr, John Dunlop, Frederick Harbison, and Charles Myers it was the process of **industrialization** and not capitalism per se that brought forth the changes in the relationship between workers and employers that, in turn, led to unionization.[31] They argued that modern technology produced a need for rules to govern relations between workers and employers. Collective bargaining and contractually negotiated rules were a logical way to formalize and structure the rules required in modern industry. Given this framework, specific technological changes are important within collective bargaining because they result in changes in the relative bargaining power held by management or labor. In this regard, the industrialization thesis is closer to Commons than to Marx.

The Influence of Microelectronic Technology on Skill Levels

The recent expansion in the use of **microelectronic technology** has reignited the debate over the effects of technological change. To some this technology can open the way to less hierarchical, higher skilled work and further growth in real incomes. To others the new technology is being used to wrestle control away from the work force and to deskill workers now just as it allegedly was in the past.[32] These latter observers see little evidence of a shift away from the hierarchical forms of work organization. In fact, these modern proponents of the deskilling thesis argue that much of the concessionary bargaining of the 1980s illustrated management efforts to increase the pace of work and use new technology to weaken workers' bargaining leverage and skills. The deskilling thesis proponents also predict that new technology will lead to significant employment displacement and unemployment.

A number of behavioral scientists believe that new technologies serve to "unfreeze" existing practices and open up a variety of options for reconfiguring the organization of work, career ladders, compensation criteria, and other aspects of the employment relationship.[33] According to this view there is no single effect of technology on skills or worker power; rather, its effects depend on the choices made by decision makers and the way the new technology is implemented.

The High-Tech Paradox

The growing presence of Japanese manufacturing plants in the United States has produced some important new thinking about the concept of technology, its relationship to industrial relations practices, and its effects on economic performance. Part of the interest in Japanese manufacturing practices was fueled by what we call the **high-tech paradox:** evidence that America's highest technology plants are not our most productive. Instead, experience in the auto industry has demonstrated that the highest productivity and the best product quality in the industry is being achieved in those plants that effectively integrate new technologies and manufacturing practices with innovative human resource and industrial relations practices.

Evidence on this point includes case study comparisons of the relatively low-tech New United Motors Manufacturing Incorporated (NUMMI), a joint-venture GM-Toyota plant in California, with several other U.S. plants that had invested in the highest robotics, information processing, and materials handling technologies available. To the surprise of many industry and academic experts, NUMMI's productivity and quality record surpassed the performance achieved in these high-tech facilities.[34] The consensus explanation that emerged from these comparisons was that NUMMI did a better job of training, motivating, and involving the work force in the process of continuous improvement, and that they combined this human resource strategy with flexible work systems and advanced manufacturing practices such as just-in-time inventory control and statistical process quality controls.[35]

What emerged from this and other evidence was a hypothesis that it was the "integration" of new industrial relations and manufacturing practices that was the key to productivity and quality improvement and not just new technology alone. Evidence of this integration hypothesis also came from comparisons of the productivity and quality of an international sample of automobile assembly plants scattered around the world.[36] The integration of technology with solid human resources and industrial relations innovations is so important because it allows, as two analysts of the Japanese manufacturing practices put it, workers to "give wisdom to the new machines."[37]

Recent Environmental Pressures on Collective Bargaining

In the 1980s and early 1990s a number of changes in the environment placed unions at a distinct disadvantage. Macroeconomic recessions in 1980–83 and 1990–91 brought large numbers of layoffs and sharp increases in the unemployment rate. These events were exacerbated by increases in foreign competition and imports. The net effect of these macroeconomic and trade developments was sharp and prolonged employment declines. Between 1980 and 1984, for example, the Bureau of Labor Statistics estimated, approximately 2 million jobs were lost in manufacturing; of those, slightly more than half were the jobs of union members.[38] Employment in many industries dropped from previous peak levels, in most cases attained in 1979, to recession lows, in most cases reached in 1983. Declines over that period were 44 percent in the steel industry, 48 percent in the farm machinery industry, 50 percent in copper mining, and 39 percent in the auto industry.

The Unusual Depth of the Employment Declines in the 1980s

Unions had faced sharp employment declines before, during previous recessions. What made the declines of the 1980s so severe was their scale, their duration, and the failure of employment to rebound to previous levels when the economy recovered in the latter half of the decade. From 1980 to 1988 the number of manufacturing jobs in the United States declined by 882,000.[39]

Plant closings and the threat of further closings convinced many workers that these employment declines signaled a more permanent shift in the economic environment than was true in earlier recessions. Many unions feared that unless they agreed to concessionary modifications in their existing and new contracts, they would face even more substantial job cutbacks.

Pressure from Nonunion Competition

Unions also faced new competition in the form of growing numbers of domestic nonunion firms. In industries such as construction, trucking, textiles, and mining the share of nonunion production had risen substantially. Furthermore, even in traditional strongholds of unionism such as steel and autos, nonunion firms were entering the industry. Nonunion competition became an even greater threat as employers became more willing and able during strikes to shift production to nonunion sites. As a result, unions became less able to take wages out of competition, and, as predicted by our earlier theoretical discussion, their bargaining power declined significantly.

Heightened International Competition

The growing penetration of imports in several key manufacturing industries and the large trade deficit, carried the issue of the international economy straight to collective bargaining agendas. Foreign workers had become a major competitive threat to organized labor in the United States because it is very difficult for unions to take wages out of competition when goods and investments move easily across national and international borders. Perhaps the growth of the multinational companies is the modern-day equivalent of the competitive menaces faced by the Philadelphia shoemakers described so well by Commons.

A Conservative Swing in Political Ideology

Economic pressures were only part of the story, however. The labor movement in the 1980s and early 1990s encountered a conservative swing in political ideology. As the public grew warier of unions, strikers found their picket lines crossed by fellow workers and less support for strikes in the broader community. When unions sought recourse through the NLRB or the courts to block such management practices as the movement of operations to other sites or the abrogation of collective bargaining contracts during bankruptcy reorganization, they received little help.

Signs of Innovation in the Labor Movement

The economy, public policy, ideology, and demography had all taken a turn that would hamper the efforts of organized labor. And yet, in the face of all these environmental pressures, the union movement was exhibiting some signs of innovation and adaption. Concessionary bargaining in some firms and industries led to a broadening of the bargaining agenda and increased union involvement in managerial decision making. Moreover, the labor movement began to engage in serious soul-searching, as illustrated in the 1985 AFL-CIO report on potential new organizing and representational strategies.[40]

Summary

This chapter examines how the environment influences the bargaining process. The five key aspects of the environment are economic, public policy, demographic, social, and technological factors.

Important economic factors include those that operate at the firm level (called the microeconomic influences) and the state of the labor market and the overall economy (called the macroeconomic influences). The economic environment is most important through the effects it exerts on the bargaining power held by labor and management. Bargaining power is heavily influenced by strike leverage and the extent to which an increase in wages leads to a decline in employment (called the wage-employment trade-off).

Public policy shapes the rights of the parties and the procedures used in collective bargaining. There has long been a strong preference in the United States for labor laws that give employees, unions, and management the right to directly shape employment terms with limited interference from the government. The most important labor law in the United States is the National Labor Relations Act and its amendments. There also are substantive laws that directly influence particular employment conditions, such as pensions and equal employment opportunity rights, although we have relatively less substantive employment regulation by the government than do other countries.

Major demographic issues include the increased labor force participation of women that has occurred after World War II. The labor force is becoming more diverse and unions face a challenge in altering their policies to increase their appeal to the new workers, many of whom work in the service sector.

The public continues to express support for the general purposes served by unions. When asked about union leaders or the willingness to join unions, however, the public's attitudes toward unions turn less favorable.

Technology influences employment levels and bargaining leverage. In recent years there has been much debate over how technology is affecting worker skill levels. On the shop floor labor relations play an important role in shaping how well new technology is implemented. There is much recent evidence that the best-performing plants in the United States are those that successfully integrate human resource and technological improvements.

How well collective bargaining serves the interests of labor and management often depends on its ability to adapt to changes in the environment. Economic pressures on the U.S. collective bargaining system have steadily grown since foreign competition became threatening in the 1980s. There are also pressures from the other key environmental dimensions. To help build a better understanding of how collective bargaining could respond to these environmental challenges, the next chapter examines how collective bargaining works.

Discussion Questions

1. Define bargaining power and strike leverage.

2. Several microeconomic factors play a part in both a union's and an employer's strike leverage. Briefly describe some of these factors.

3. Since the early 1960s the federal government has engaged in income policies in an attempt to reduce wages and inflation. What are income policies? Give some examples.

4. Describe some of the ways the National Labor Relations Act influences the bargaining power of labor and management.

5. Briefly discuss some of the recent demographic trends in the work force.

Suggested Readings

Blauner, Robert. *Alienation and Freedom* (Chicago: University of Chicago Press, 1964).

Freeman, Richard B. *Labor Economics,* 2d ed. (Englewood Cliffs, NJ: Prentice-Hall, 1979).

Weber, Arnold R., and Daniel J.B. Mitchell. *The Pay Board's Progress* (Washington, DC: Brookings Institution, 1978).

End Notes

1. John T. Dunlop, *Industrial Relations Systems* (New York: Holt and Company, 1958).

2. Elasticity of demand refers to the *slope* of the demand curve for labor. The more inelastic is demand, the more vertical the demand curve and the less responsive is the demand for labor to any change in the price of labor. A perfectly elastic demand curve would be horizontal. Alfred Marshall, *Principles of Economics,* 8th ed. (New York: Macmillan, 1920), pp. 383–386.

3. Others have pointed out that for a low labor cost ratio to act as a source of power, as Marshall hypothesized, the elasticity of demand for the final product must be greater than the elasticity of substitution of nonlabor inputs in the production process. See Richard B. Freeman, *Labor Economics,* 2d ed. (Englewood Cliffs, NJ: Prentice-Hall, 1979), pp. 67–71.

4. Note, a small bargaining unit can be affected by employers that consider the "spillover" effects of a settlement negotiated with one small unit on the rest of the firm's work force.

5. Even if the union had tried to influence employment levels, it might not have been successful in the face of technological change in the industry.

6. Arthur M. Ross, *Trade Union Wage Policy* (Berkeley: University of California Press, 1948).

7. John T. Dunlop, *Wage Determination under Trade Unions* (New York: Macmillan, 1944).

8. Daniel J.B. Mitchell, *Unions, Wages, and Inflation* (Washington, D.C.: Brookings Institution, 1980), pp. 113–162.

9. See, for example, Farrell E. Bloch and Mark S. Kuskin, "Wage Determination in the Union and Nonunion Sector," *Industrial and Labor Relations Review* 31 (January 1978): 183–192.

10. The Taft-Hartley amendments do allow management to voluntarily bargain with a union representing supervisors. Such bargaining is extremely rare.

11. The effects of public policies on strike leverage are discussed in Robert Hutchens et al., *Strikes and Subsidies: The Influence of Government on Strike Activity* (Kalamazoo, MI: W. E. UpJohn Institute, 1989).

12. In "AFL-CIO Will Oppose Collyer Nomination as Board Counsel," *Daily Labor Report* 9 (May 1984): A–4.

13. *Labor Force Statistics* (Washington, D.C.: OECD, Department of Economics and Statistics, 1967–87).

14. All these figures come from various issues of *Special Labor Force Reports* (Washington, D.C.: U.S. Department of Labor, Bureau of Labor Statistics).

15. Calculated from U.S. Department of Labor, Bureau of Labor Statistics, *Handbook of Labor Statistics* (Washington, D.C.: GPO, 1989), tables 3 and 4.

16. *Labor-Force Statistics* (Washington, D.C.: U.S. Department of Labor, August 1988), Table C–12.

17. Ibid., table C–23.

18. Ibid., table C–22.

19. *Statistical Abstract of the United States* (Washington, D.C.: U.S. Department of Commerce, 1990), table 216.

20. *Labor Force Statistics,* 1988, table C–22.

21. Data regarding dropout rates are from U.S. Department of Commerce, Bureau of the Census, *Current Population Survey,* series P–20, no. 373 (Washington, D.C.: GPO, 1990). Unemployment rates are calculated from the *Statistical Abstract of the United States,* tables 248 and 249.

22. U.S. Department of Labor, *Handbook of Labor Statistics,* table 23.

23. Barry Bluestone and Bennett Harrison, *The Deindustrialization of America* (New York: Basic Books, 1982).

24. Robert Z. Lawrence, *Can America Compete?* (Washington, D.C.: Brookings Institution, 1985).

25. See, for example, Neal Rosenthal, "The Shrinking Middle Class: Myth or Reality," *Monthly Labor Review* (March 1985): 3–10.

26. See, for example, Paul Osterman, *Employment Futures* (New York: Oxford University Press, 1988).

27. AFL-CIO Committee on the Evolution of Work, *The Changing Situation of Workers and Their Unions* (Washington, D.C.: AFL-CIO, February 1985).

28. James L. Medoff, "The Public's Image of Labor and Labor's Response," photocopy (Cambridge, MA: Harvard University, 1984).

29. Harry Braverman, *Labor and Monopoly Capital* (New York: Monthly Review Press, 1984).

30. Selig Perlman, *A Theory of the Labor Movement* (Philadelphia: Porcupine Press, 1979 reprint of 1928 edition).

31. Clark Kerr, John T. Dunlop, Frederick Harbison, and Charles A. Myers, *Industrialism and Industrial Man* (Cambridge, MA: Harvard University Press, 1960).

32. David F. Noble, *Forces of Production* (New York: Oxford University Press, 1986); Harley Shaiken, *Work Transformed* (New York: Holt, Rinehart & Winston, 1984).

33. Richard Walton, "Work Innovations in the United States," *Harvard Business Review* 57 (July/August 1979): 88–98; Barry Wilkinson, *The Shopfloor Politics of New Technology* (London: Heinemann Educational Books, 1983); Stephen Barley, "Technology, Power, and the Social Organization of Work," *Research in the Sociology of Organizations,* ed. Samuel B. Bacharach and Nancy DiTomaso (Greenwich, CT: JAI Press, 1990).

34.   John F. Krafcik, "World Class Manufacturing: An International Comparison of Automobile Assembly Plant Performance," *Sloan Management Review,* 30 (1988): 41–52.

35.   Haruo Shimada and John Paul MacDuffie, "Industrial Relations and Humanware: Japanese Investments in Automobile Manufacturing in the United States," Sloan School of Management Working Paper (Cambridge, MA: MIT, 1986).

36.   John Paul MacDuffie and John F. Krafcik, "Flexible Production Systems and Manufacturing Performance," in *Transforming Organizations* ed. Thomas A. Kochan and Michael Useem (New York: Oxford University Press, forthcoming).

37.   Shimada and MacDuffie, "Industrial Relations and Humanware."

38.   Paul O. Flaim and Ellen Sehgal, "Displaced Workers of 1979–83: How Have They Fared?" *Monthly Labor Review* 108 (June 1985): 6.

39.   The number of manufacturing jobs in the United States was 20,285,000 in 1980 and 19,403,000 in 1988. These statistics are from *Statistical Abstract of the United States,* table 662, p. 402.

40.   AFL-CIO Committee on the Evolution of Work, *The Changing Situation.*

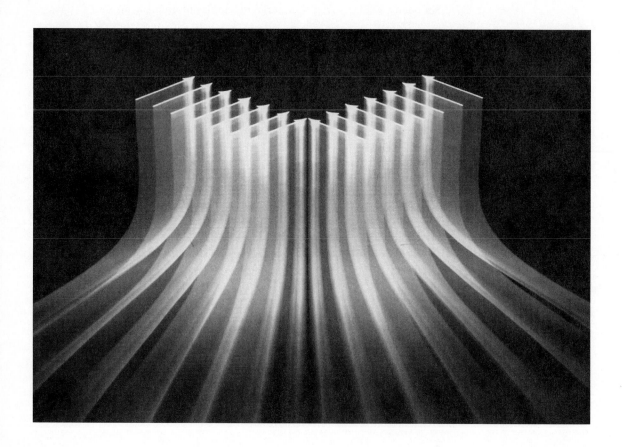

PART 2

THE
STRATEGIC LEVEL
OF INDUSTRIAL
RELATIONS

Chapter 5

Management Strategies
and Structures for
Collective Bargaining

Chapters 5 and 6 start the movement downward in our framework by considering how the strategies of both management and unions shape the course of industrial relations. Management is considered first because in recent years management has been the main initiator of change in industrial relations. It is management, for example, that has increased the growth of nonunion practices and pressured unionized plants for concessions. This chapter examines the strategic choices exercised by management and the structures management commonly uses to engage in collective bargaining. The text examines why and how management has pursued various industrial relations options.

Some of our attention will again focus on the role of the environment. For instance, heightened international competition is one environmental pressure that has played a critical role in shaping management's strategic actions. At the same time, management retains a high degree of choice in deciding industrial relations policies. Tracing managerial strategies in this chapter requires consideration of both the union and nonunion industrial relations systems that stand as alternatives before management.

Where unions exist, one of management's key tasks is to bargain and to administer contracts with those unions. So, although it is necessary to assess management's broad industrial relations strategies, this chapter also reviews how management practically prepares and structures itself to participate in the collective bargaining process.

Management's Strategic Choices—Theoretical Considerations

Management makes strategic choices in the design of personnel policies and through responses to employees' desires and expectations, including their demands for union representation. Management also makes strategic choices about its business plans, choices that are sometimes heavily based on consideration of the linkages between human resources and **business strategies.**

If the employees become unionized, management will attempt to use its bargaining power to shape collective bargaining processes and outcomes within the context of its bilateral relationship with the union. Although an employer's need to negotiate with union representatives will add various constraints to its strategic options in unionized settings, the employer's preferences for personnel policies are still heavily influenced by business strategies. Managers may have to make decisions regarding, for example, whether to continue investing in a given product line, whether to try to operate nonunion plants to produce a given product, or whether to supply a product by relying more heavily on the outsourcing of parts or production to another plant or firm. These decisions all influence management's bargaining leverage in any part of the firm covered by a labor contract.

Alternative Industrial Relations Systems

In the contemporary scene, management is constrained to choose among a handful of alternative industrial relations system types, or patterns. Each of these six patterns, described in Exhibit 5–1, has key personnel policies. Although it is clearly an oversimplification to try to fit every firm into one of these six patterns, this categorization scheme can help clarify the choices commonly made by management.

Nonunion Industrial Relations Patterns

Within the nonunion sector there is wide diversity in industrial relations practices. In broad terms nonunion industrial relations systems exhibit three basic patterns.[1] The common element across the three nonunion patterns is that management policy is influenced by management's desire to stay nonunion. At the same time, management policy also is guided by the firm's desire to pursue company objectives that may have very little to do with union status. Personnel practices are influenced, for example, by firm productivity and product quality goals. Note that these patterns are only ideal types, so some firms may contain elements of one or more patterns.

The Paternalistic Pattern   In the **paternalistic pattern** of industrial relations, personnel policies tend to be informally administered, and their administration involves substantial discretion by operating managers. A paternalistic firm would, for example, offer no formal leave and sickness policies, and its supervisors would grant paid leaves on a case-

Exhibit 5–1
Union and Nonunion Industrial Relations Patterns

Policy	Nonunion			Union		
	Paternalistic	**Bureaucratic**	**Human Resource Management**	**Conflict**	**New Deal**	**Participatory**
Rules	Informal	Formal	Flexible	Inflexible	Formal	Flexible
Management style	Managerial discretion	Rule bound	Strong corporate culture	Aggressive	Adversarial	Involvement
Complaint procedure	None	Written policies	Ombudsman	Excessive delays	Grievance system	Continuous problem solving
Work organization	Low skill	Detailed classifications	Teams	Detailed classifications	Detailed classifications	Teams
Pay procedure	Piece rates	Job evaluation	Pay-for-knowledge and contingent pay	Standard rates	Standard rates	Pay-for-knowledge and contingent pay
Job security	Temporary work	Cyclical insecurity	Employment stabilization	Unstable	Seniority-based layoffs	Employment security
Worker-manager relations	Hierarchical and personal	Hierarchical	Individual	Combative	Arms-length	Overlapping roles

by-case basis. Supervisors and other managers in these firms similarly exercise a high degree of discretion over other discipline and pay policies. The employment conditions of employees in these firms differ substantially across work groups, plants, and firms.

This pattern is common among small retail stores, such as grocery stores and gas stations, and in small manufacturing plants.[2] Managers in firms following this pattern like the discretion they gain through informal policies. Often these firms are family-owned or -operated with family members personally directing personnel policies. Family owners dislike losing control over decisions and particularly fear the reduction of control that would occur if unions represented employees. Union avoidance is often a prime policy objective in the firms that follow the paternalistic pattern.

The Bureaucratic Pattern   Larger firms find the diversity common to paternalistic firms too unsettling and costly. In their efforts to achieve economies of scale, larger firms find it advantageous to standardize and bureaucratize personnel policies, thereby creating a **bureaucratic pattern** of personnel administration. These firms have also come to realize that diversity can spur unionization if some employees believe other employees elsewhere in the firm are benefiting from more favorable policies.

The bureaucratic pattern is characterized by highly formalized procedures, such as clear (and typically written) policies on pay, leaves, promotion, and discipline. Firms that follow the bureaucratic pattern also make use of highly detailed and formalized job classifications and use job evaluation schemes to determine pay levels and job duties. Examples of firms that follow this pattern include most of the large, nonunion corporations that expanded in the post-World War II period.

The Human Resource Management Pattern   As an outgrowth of their efforts to increase flexibility and cost competitiveness while maintaining their nonunion status, a number of firms began to adopt a new pattern of personnel policies in the 1970s.[3] This sophisticated **human resource management** (HRM) **pattern,** like the bureaucratic pattern, relies on formal policies, but the nature of those policies is different from that traditionally found in nonunion firms. The HRM pattern includes policies such as **employment stabilization, team forms of work organization, skill- or knowledge-based pay,** and elaborate communication and complaint procedures.

Like the firms that follow the other nonunion patterns, the HRM firms vigilantly try to avoid unionization. Where they differ from the other nonunion firms is in the extent to which they consider union avoidance questions in decisions such as plant location. Union avoidance issues also influence how these firms design other personnel policies, such as employment stabilization and communication policies. In their efforts at union avoidance, as in so many of their personnel policies, the sophisticated HRM firms try to coordinate their various policies. The HRM firms also are noteworthy for the extensive measures they take in trying to induce employees to identify their interests with the long-term interests of the firm. Those measures include publishing company newsletters, offering salaries to all employees, and nurturing strong corporate cultures.

Among the best-known examples of mature companies that continue to apply some or all of these practices successfully are IBM, Proctor and Gamble, Delta Airlines, Eastman Kodak, Digital Equipment, Motorola, DuPont, and Michelin Tire.[4] Two companies that have been relatively successful using these strategies in more competitive environments and with less-skilled work forces are Marriott Hotels and Sears Roebuck.[5] A number of construction contractors, and even a few relatively new coal mines, have embarked on this approach in recent years.

The Role of Business Strategy in Shaping Nonunion Patterns

A number of factors influence which of these patterns are followed by nonunion firms. Management values and strategies play an important role. For instance, many of the sophisticated HRM firms had strong founding executives who helped initiate strong corporate cultures.[6]

Business strategy also makes a difference. The sophisticated HRM pattern seems to provide the advantage of more flexible and adaptable work organization through the use of team systems and skill-based pay.[7] These characteristics are particularly attractive to firms with rapidly changing technologies and markets. Thus, it is no surprise that many firms in high-technology industries follow the sophisticated HRM pattern.

Steel minimills illustrate how business strategy is linked to personnel practices. Among nonunion minimills those producing a wide variety of products ("market" mills) and those concentrating on high-quality products tend to follow the sophisticated HRM pattern, while those pursuing a low-cost and high-volume product strategy tend to follow a variant of the bureaucratic pattern.[8]

In sum, companies with sophisticated personnel systems are most likely to be those that enjoy an environment of growth, high profits, large-scale operations, and employees with sufficient skills to warrant large investments in human resource management. Furthermore, they must have highly trained personnel staffs to effectively monitor employee attitudes and the personnel practices of other firms.

Union Patterns of Industrial Relations

In firms where at least some of the employees are unionized industrial relations policies also follow distinct patterns. There are currently three dominant union patterns.

The New Deal Pattern   The form of collective bargaining in the United States that has dominated since World War II is the **New Deal Pattern,** which is characterized by highly detailed and formal contracts. This pattern includes grievance arbitration, seniority-based layoff procedures, numerous and detailed **job classifications,** and the standardization of pay.

The advantages to this pattern are that it is very good at providing stable labor relations. Some of that stability derives from the formal channels (such as the grievance procedure) through which problems can be addressed. These procedures are attractive to employees because they provide due process (see Chapters 3 and 11).

A subsequent section of this chapter examines the diversity that can exist even across plants that all follow this New Deal pattern. Nevertheless, firms that follow the New Deal pattern are clearly distinguished from the unionized firms that follow the other two patterns of collective bargaining: the conflict pattern and the participatory pattern.

The Conflict Pattern   Under the **conflict pattern** labor and management are engaged in a serious struggle over their basic rights. Often the issue in dispute is whether there will be union representation. The conflict pattern typically involves prolonged strikes. In some cases employees resort to sabotage or absenteeism to express their anger against employers in such a relationship.

Conflict imposes high costs on the firm through lost output or low productivity and costs on employees in the form of lost earnings. Because of the high costs to both parties of engaging in intense conflict, the conflict pattern tends not to be stable. The conflict pattern arises most often when a firm is trying to move from a union to a nonunion pattern or, sometimes, when a union tries to unionize a nonunion firm.

Eastern Airlines and the unions representing its employees were caught in a cycle of conflicts throughout the 1980s. Box 5–1 describes these events. Periodically, labor and management at Eastern shifted from conflict to experimentation with a participatory pattern of industrial relations. Yet, economic pressures and various actions taken by the parties led to the demise of those short-lived participatory experiments, the reemergence of heated conflict, and, finally, the demise of the airline.

The Participatory Pattern   A number of contemporary firms and unions have been experimenting with a **participatory pattern** of industrial relations, characterized by contingent compensation systems (linking firm or work group pay to economic performance), team forms of work organization, employment security programs, and more direct involvement by workers and unions in business decision making.

The participatory pattern tries to create mechanisms through which workers can directly solve production and personnel problems. Quality circle or team meetings are used to facilitate direct discussions between

---

Box 5–1

Conflictual Relations at Eastern Airlines

Eastern Airlines historically had been plagued by financial troubles, and these troubles were heightened by airline deregulation in the 1980s. After considerable conflict (but no strikes) between the company and its unions in the early 1980s, a truce was reached with the help of mediator William Usery, a former Secretary of Labor. From 1983 through 1985 a new labor-management partnership was formed in which labor was represented on the company's board of directors and employee participation programs were started to improve productivity. Then Eastern's economic troubles deepened in 1985 and the airline was sold to Frank Lorenzo, owner of Continental Airlines, who was known for his use of bankruptcy proceedings to introduce substantial reductions in pay and other employment terms at Continental in 1983.

Eastern's financial situation continued to deteriorate after the sale. Labor and management entered negotiations in 1988 with poor relations precipitated in part by Lorenzo's replacement of participation programs with hard bargaining tactics. The International Association of Machinists (IAM), representing 9,500 mechanics and ground service employees' struck Eastern Airlines on March 4, 1989, after over a year of negotiations and mediations had failed to produce a new agreement. There was much that separated the IAM and Eastern, including the IAM's demands for union security and Eastern's demands for further substantial major wage and work-rule concessions. In addition, there was much bad blood between the IAM membership and Lorenzo, who by then had become CEO of Eastern. Several efforts were made to mediate a settlement to the Eastern-IAM dispute.

The Railway Labor Act, which governs airline industry bargaining, requires the implementation of mediation when negotiations come to a standstill, yet all mediation efforts failed to find a settlement. After months of failed mediation and a rapidly increasing debt, Eastern sold a number of its assets (including the Eastern Shuttle to Donald Trump), laid off 4,000 employees, and closed operations in 14 cities.

The IAM attempted several strike strategies. First, the Machinists threatened to extend the strike to New York and Philadelphia commuter railroads. However, a District Court issued an injunction barring the Machinists and rail unions from engaging in sympathy strikes without exhausting all negotiation efforts under the Railway Labor Act. In addition, the IAM threatened using secondary boycotts.

The IAM did gain the support of Eastern's 3,000 pilots [represented by the Airline Pilots Association (ALPA)] and 5,500 flight attendants (represented by the Transport Workers Union (TWU)] who decided to honor the Machinists' picket lines and also walked out on March 4, 1989. The walkouts curtailed Eastern's operations and caused daily losses of $1 million. Eastern sought a federal court order to force the pilots and flight attendants back to work on the grounds that they were bound not to strike under their current contracts. A United States Court of Appeals, however, denied Eastern an injunction and the pilots continued their walkout.

Eastern filed for Chapter 11 bankruptcy five days after the ALPA and TWU walkouts. Under bankruptcy law, corporate financial and industrial relations are reviewed by the bankruptcy court, whose findings are final and binding. Eastern declared that its only practical alternative was a reorganization plan premised on a smaller airline or liquidation. The bankruptcy court approved the cancellation of the Machinists' contract and a $50 million cost-reducing package of wage, benefits, and work rule changes. For a while it appeared that Eastern would be sold to Peter Ueberroth (the former Commissioner of Baseball), but the deal fell through.

ALPA and Eastern then returned to the bargaining table assisted by a mediator. On April 2, 1989, Eastern pilots ended their walkout by ratifying a new collective bargaining agreement. The new pilots' agreement provided for a 25 percent reduction in pilot wages, employee contributions to medical and dental plans, and cuts in company retirement fund contributions. A similar back-to-work agreement was struck between Eastern and the TWU. Despite ALPA's and TWU's decision to end their respective walkouts, the Machinists continued their strike against Eastern.

To maintain its daily flight schedule, Eastern had been rebuilding its work force through the hiring of replacements. When the pilots and flight attendants voted to end their walkouts, Eastern adopted a policy of placing returning strikers behind the replacements that had been hired on recall lists when no positions were available. This policy was eliminated when a federal judge upheld ALPA's challenge and ruled that the Railway Labor Act guarantees returning strikers job rights ahead of newly hired trainees (replacements).

Meanwhile, the IAM, ALPA, and the TWU continued to argue before the bankruptcy court that Frank Lorenzo was using Eastern's assets for Continental's benefit (Lorenzo owned a sizeable block of Eastern and Continental stock and served as the chief executive officer of both carriers). The unions supported these allegations by pointing to Eastern's sale of its computer reservation system (System 1) to Texas Air (Eastern's parent company) for the low price of $1 million (analysts claimed that System 1 was worth a lot more). In addition, Eastern paid Texas Air (Eastern's parent company) an assortment of fees for things such as management, airplane rental, and fuel. Finally, there was evidence that Texas Air helped Eastern operate during the strike for a fee of $22.5 million.

The bankruptcy court eventually sided with the unions on this issue and ruled that Eastern's reorganization plan was a cover for illegal asset shifting from Eastern to Continental. The court held that Frank Lorenzo had squandered Eastern's money and was unable to reorganize the airline in a healthy and prosperous fashion. The bankruptcy court declared Frank Lorenzo unfit to retain fiduciary control over Eastern. On April 19, 1990, the court appointed Martin R. Shruge to serve as trustee and run Eastern, thereby stripping Lorenzo of any control of the airline.

The machinists also had filed a criminal complaint alleging Eastern managers of ignoring safety guidelines. After a 10-month investigation, a federal grand jury indicted Eastern for ignoring vital repairs and maintenance. In addition, Eastern managers were found guilty of falsifying work cards, log books, and other documents. As a result, Eastern was fined $30 million.

Box 5–1   (*continued*)

In August 1990 Frank Lorenzo sold his stock holdings in Continental Airlines to SAS airlines for a reported $35 million profit. Under the terms of the stock sale, Lorenzo cannot be associated with the airline industry in any way for seven years.

After further financial losses Eastern Airlines ceased all flights and operations on January 18, 1991. Subsequently, the assets of Eastern, including aircraft and landing slots, were auctioned to other airlines.

Source: Daily Labor Report (Washington, D.C.: Bureau of National Affairs; various issues from October 7, 1987, to June 18, 1990) and *The New York Times,* various stories in the issues November 6, 1988, July 26, 1990, August 3, 1990, and January 19, 1991.

---

supervisors and workers in many firms. In these firms workers also are called on to become involved in business decisions such as scrap control or issues concerning how best to implement new technology. Not all organizations that set out to create greater participation by employees, however, end up with more employee participation. There are a number of reasons for these failures, including supervisor or employee resistance to change. This pattern is discussed more fully in Chapter 12.

Management Attitudes toward Unionization

What influences whether management follows a union or a nonunion pattern? In part, the decision is a function of management's attitudes toward unionization. Much of U.S. labor history is a documentation of bloody organizing struggles and attempts by management to reduce the incentive for employees to join unions. Although the level of bloodshed has declined and the strategies used to oppose unionization have become more subtle over the years, management's vigorous opposition to unions continues to be very strong. Box 5–2 describes how a reporter felt anti-union animus on the shop floor of one of the country's major corporations.

Douglas Brown and Charles Myers aptly described the sentiments of perhaps the majority of U.S. management executives in an article written in the mid-1950s:

> It may well be true that if American management, upon retiring for the night, were assured that by the next morning the unions with which they dealt would have disappeared, more management people than not would experience the happiest sleep of their lives.[9]

Yet, even given the tenacious hold of this sentiment, some firms place a lower priority on remaining nonunion than others. Some employers have been pragmatic enough to recognize that in their situation either it is impossible to avoid unionization or the costs of attempting to avoid unions outweigh the potential benefits. These employers tend to be less aggressive in resisting unions. Thus, the intensity of employers' resistance to unionization, as well as the strategies they use to remain nonunion, has varied across firms and over time. Two union avoidance strategies stand out.

The Historical Evolution of Two Union Avoidance Strategies

As early as the 1920s two different strategies were used by employers to avoid unions: the direct union suppression approach (actively resisting any organizing drives); and the indirect union substitution approach (removing the incentives for unionization).[10] Why do some firms use the first strategy while others try the second?

The strategies used to avoid unionization are to some extent a function of the firm's financial resources. If a firm can afford the specialized personnel and employee relations staffs necessary to implement the strategy, it will use the union substitution approach. Those firms unable to absorb the expenses associated with the substitution approach tend to oppose unions by using the direct suppression strategies.

Environmental factors also influence whether and how management responds to the threat of being unionized. Factors that tend to lead management to a suppression strategy include the presence of a hostile political environment toward unions; employment of low-wage workers who have few labor market alternatives; an abundant supply of alternative workers; low recruitment costs; and a low-profit, highly competitive industry.

Increased Union Suppression

There is some evidence suggesting that the use of union suppression tactics has increased in the past 20 years. For instance, the number of employees illegally discharged by employers during organizing campaigns, as determined by the NLRB, increased tenfold from 1960 to 1975 and remained at a relatively high level throughout the 1980s and early 1990s.[11] Thus, management's use of suppressive tactics against union activists is not merely an artifact of pre-New Deal labor history but a significant feature of contemporary industrial relations.

At the same time, some firms continue to reduce employee incentives to unionize through the substitution strategy. Many workers reluctantly turn to unionization only after they have exhausted all other means to influence employer policies. Many firms try to use personnel policies to meet employee needs before workers become frustrated enough to turn to a union. Although many firms that institute sophisticated personnel

Box 5–2

Union Avoidance in Action—at Texas Instruments, If You're Pro-union, Firm May Be Anti-you

"It's like '1984'," says one worker as he waits for a machine in the lobby to read his badge and unlock the entrance door. "Big Brother is always watching for spies and for invaders from the union."

I am an invader of a different sort, a reporter who worked on the plant's electronics assembly line for three weeks to get a first-hand look at what labor unions say is one of the most calculated and effective antiunion operations in the country. The company didn't know I was a reporter when it hired me, and it has since strenuously objected to the way in which the story was obtained.

Texas Instruments—or TI—is the third largest nonunion company in the United States, after International Business Machines and Eastman Kodak. It earned $116.6 million last year—20% more than in 1976. In 1977, the company sold more than $2 billion of computers, calculators, semiconductors and other electronic products, ranging from digital watches to guided missiles. More than 45,000 employees work in the company's 15 U.S. plants.

. . . The company made its feelings about unions clear to me and the other new "TIers"—as we're called—during our first hour of orientation. A TI-produced videotape told us that unions were detrimental and were unnecessary for progress. An orientation booklet warned us that we might be approached by union organizers and asked to sign a union card. "We encourage you to do as a large majority of TIers all over the U.S. have done," the booklet ends, "and reject the union attempts to organize."

"Don't you mess with unions, girl," advises my assembly line's tough, kind group leader and a TI employee for 10 years in Dallas and Austin. "That's the one thing that'll put you out the door faster'n what you come in. If TI finds out you're even bending that way, well, you won't progress at TI. You'll be the first one laid off. They'll put you somewhere you can't make no trouble."

---

policies do so for business reasons and not solely to avoid unions, the effect of these policies is to lessen the incentive to unionize.

Many Firms Are Now Only Partially Unionized

Many firms now have some parts of their business unionized while other parts operate on a nonunion basis. Since the early 1970s there has been substantial growth in the fraction of the plants operating nonunion in those firms that have both union and nonunion plants.

In two Conference Board surveys, for example, industrial relations executives were asked to indicate which labor relations function was more important in their company: remaining as "nonunion as possible"

My casual conversations in which I express pro-union views trouble a few co-workers so much that they begin to avoid me. "Please don't talk to me on break anymore," one nervous fellow worker says. "If the company finds out I'm listening, I'll get fired."

Employee fear seems to be a major part of TI's antiunion defense system. TIers have heard how the company feels about unions, and they have also heard that TI swiftly terminates offenders.

To test TI's reputed union alarm mechanism, I tell [my group leader] a made-up story that I have been approached by another worker in the parking lot and asked to sign a union card. [She] immediately tells her supervisor, and a day later she mentions to me that she has already been questioned about her report by "higher-ups." "They called me on the carpet about it," she says. "They just always like to know where they stand, so's they can take action if they have to."

My plan was to work at the plant for a month, but by the end of my third week, my pro-union comments were so well known that I was referred to by some workers as "that union chick from Detroit."

Abruptly, right before Independence Day weekend, my supervisor pulled me from the assembly line and escorted me to the office of the chief of security at the Austin plant. [He] charged me with a "very serious, serious offense"—falsifying my application by omitting the fact that I am a college graduate. He has me sign a two-page document he has handwritten in my name, which explains that I falsified my application in order to obtain a job.

"You see how it works?" said one older colleague after hearing I had been fired. "They got you fair and square. Probably all of us here got something to hide."

Source: Reprinted with permission of *The Wall Street Journal,* Dow Jones and Company, Inc., 1978. All rights reserved.

or achieving the most favorable bargain possible with their existing unions.[12] In 1977, 31 percent of the firms responded that remaining as nonunion as possible was the more important function of the two. The majority of the firms with fewer than 40 percent of their employees organized assigned top priority to avoiding further union organizing; the majority of those that were more unionized gave priority to bargaining with their existing unions.

Among these same firms in 1983, however, 45 percent indicated that avoiding further unionization was their top priority. Thus, the number of firms assigning a higher priority to union avoidance than to bargaining increased by 14 percentage points over the six intervening years. One reason for this increase was that unions were losing members during those years, and it therefore became more feasible for firms to adopt an active union avoidance strategy.

The Influence of Union Structure on Management's Unionization Policies

Another factor that influences whether a union avoidance strategy will be used by a firm is the degree of centralization in how bargaining occurs in a firm. Those firms that deal with a single union across the whole company are less likely than others to resist unions vigorously in any newly opened facilities. In these bargaining relationships the dominant union has the leverage needed to engage top management decision makers at the strategic level of the firm—the level where the basic decision is made on whether to resist or to recognize a union. If a union cannot reach this level of managerial decision making, the firm can more easily adopt a union avoidance strategy.

General Motors Tries and Then Abandons a Southern Strategy

The history of the United Auto Workers (UAW) and General Motors (GM) illustrates this point. In the late 1970s, GM agreed to UAW demands and ended its **southern strategy** (opening nonunion plants in the south and resisting union-organizing attempts). In return for GM neutrality the UAW agreed to continue union commitment to quality-of-working-life and other workplace innovations in the existing union facilities. Since it represented production workers across GM plants the UAW had the foresight and the strength to induce GM to accept this bargain.

The Expansion of Double-Breasting

On the other hand, in some industries where unions lacked this strength, after becoming dissatisfied with their union contracts the companies were able to open either new, nonunion operations or operations organized by different unions. The construction industry is an example of the former strategy. A number of large, traditionally union contractors have developed what has been described as a **double-breasted strategy**—that is, the running of separate union and nonunion divisions. In a typical double-breasted construction firm, commercial business is performed by unionized employees while residential construction projects are carried out by unorganized employees of the firm.

Firms in the bituminous coal industry are examples of the latter strategy. A number of operators that have opened new mines in recent years have strongly resisted organizing drives by the United Mine Workers (UMW) even though they have contracts with the union in their other mines. In addition, some firms that have opened surface (strip) mines in the west have strongly opposed organizing efforts by the UMW and have managed either to remain nonunion or to be organized by the Union of

Operating Engineers (UOE) instead of the UMW. Because of this opposition, in 1989 the UMW bargained for and won a new provision in its collective bargaining agreements designed to organize new mines. The provision gives laid-off UMW members preferential hiring rights in new mines opened by UMW-organized companies.

Both the construction and the mining examples suggest that the performance of the existing union-management relationship will influence the intensity of opposition by highly unionized companies to the extension of organization to new operations. It also appears that the greater the difference between labor costs in union and nonunion firms in an industry, the more aggressively management will oppose any new union organizing.

The Influence of Attitudes Held by Top Executives

A firm's opposition to unionization is also influenced by another factor that is difficult to measure—namely, the philosophy of the top corporate executives. It is these individuals who make the ultimate decisions on how hard a line to pursue against unions. Although their decisions are based in part on the potential economic costs and benefits of avoiding unionization, they are also based on the executives' personal views of unions.

The contrast between U.S. employers and some of their European counterparts is evident, and it is often argued that European employers are less anti-union than their American counterparts. While there are no good conclusive tests of this, it is interesting to note that West German employers did not oppose extending their labor legislation, including the use of works councils and codetermination, to East Germany as part of the employment laws that would govern establishments after unification. German employers seem to take this extension for granted.

Overview of the Trends in Management Policies toward Unionization

Overall, management's recent choices of the industrial relations patterns described in Exhibit 5–1 are as follows:

1. In the majority of nonunion or weakly unionized firms, avoiding unions is a top priority.

2. Highly organized firms tend to be less strongly opposed to unionization of new plants, provided their economic and labor relations experiences with their present unions have been relatively favorable.

3. Firms of all types are strongly opposed to organization of white-collar employees, regardless of the firm's experiences with unions that represent their blue-collar workers.

Management Structures for Collective Bargaining

This section considers how management structures itself to engage in collective bargaining. This remains an important consideration for firms that have at least part of their work force represented by unions.

There are three basic characteristics of management's collective bargaining structure: the size of the labor relations staff in relation to the number of employees in the organization, the degree of centralization in decision making on labor relations issues, and the degree of specialization in decision making on labor relations. The latter concerns the extent to which decision-making power is placed in the hands of the labor relations staff instead of in the hands of the operating, or line, managers.

The term *labor relations staff* refers to staff with responsibility for handling union-organizing attempts, negotiations, **contract administration,** and litigation with regard to union activity. The term does not refer to personnel staff who handle, for example, recruitment, staffing, equal employment opportunity, safety and health, and wage and salary administration. It is interesting to note that a number of firms now integrate personnel and labor relations activities within a broad human resource management unit.

The management staff must first formulate industrial relations strategies.[13] Once basic strategic decisions are made, they must be implemented on a day-to-day basis. Management must allocate responsibility for decisions in a manner that allows the organization to adapt to new pressures from its environment. In short, management must develop a structure that enables the firm to bargain effectively and to manage its day-to-day relationship with the union.

When a firm's business strategy changes, there should be corresponding changes in management structure. This has been happening in recent years. As firms have shifted to business strategies that include tight cost controls, power has shifted from labor relations staff to line managers and human resource specialists.

Data from the Conference Board surveys mentioned earlier reveal common management industrial relations structures, as follows.[14]

The Size of the Labor Relations Staff

The majority of corporations included in the Conference Board surveys have labor relations staff at the plant, division, and corporate headquarters levels. Nevertheless, the number of staff members employed by these corporations in relation to the number of unionized employees varies greatly. In 1977 the 601 firms that responded to this question each employed an average of 13.4 labor relations professionals. The most common staffing level was one labor relations professional for each 200 to 400 union members, but there was much variation in staff levels across firms.

Larger industrial relations staffs exist in those firms where unions are more able to impose significant costs on the firm.

Centralization in Decision Making

In general, there is a high degree of centralization of the responsibility for labor relations policy inside firms. Most firms place primary responsibility for developing overall union policy at the corporate level, either in the hands of the top labor relations executive or in the hands of the chief executive officer.

In the majority of firms, the corporate labor relations executive also has primary responsibility for the following functions: developing union avoidance activities, responding to union-organizing campaigns, conducting contract negotiations or advising negotiators, drawing up the final contract language, costing union proposals, and doing the general background research for bargaining. Only the administration of the contract and general troubleshooting activities tend to be decentralized to the division or the plant level.

The top level of the corporation also plays a very active role in reviewing and approving major policy decisions on bargaining. In most firms the top executive of the corporation has to at least review and approve key decisions. In a number of firms the chief executive even has primary responsibility for the crucial decisions establishing the limits of discretion for the management negotiators, determining the issues over which the firm should take a strike, and approving the final package.

Specialization of the Labor Relations Function

There is evidence that power has shifted laterally within management structures in recent years. Labor relations specialists have been losing power to line managers and, to a somewhat lesser degree, to human resource specialists. The main reason for this is that firms now have less need for the traditional expertise of the labor relations specialist—that of achieving stability, labor peace, and predictability. Rather, firms want expertise in union avoidance, cost control, and flexibility in work rules.

This does not mean, however, that labor relations specialists are no longer necessary. Indeed, case studies reveal that lower level labor relations managers secretly delight in the "mistakes" some of the line managers and human resource management specialists make as they take greater control over critical labor relations decisions. In one large firm a career labor relations manager related to us the story of how the new vice president of labor relations who was transferred from another functional area had to call in the "old hands" to find out how the contract ratification procedures worked.

As a result of their continuing needs for technical expertise, most firms continue to depend on teams of labor relations specialists to conduct negotiations and implement policies and agreements. But a number of major firms have established strategic planning groups for labor relations, and others have used cross-functional teams to develop new bargaining proposals.

The careers of labor relations professionals are changing dramatically and thus pose new educational and training requirements. The industrial relations professionals of the future will need the following:

1. business, analytical, and planning skills

2. expertise in both traditional labor relations activities and personnel or human resource management activities

3. a thorough understanding of operating management issues

4. an ability to work as a member of a multidisciplinary team in implementing labor relations strategies and policies

5. skills in managing innovative labor-management **organizational change** efforts

Summary

Historically, management has accepted the general value that unions provide to American society, yet aggressively avoided the expansion of unionism. Although most managers accept in the abstract the principle that unions have a legitimate role to play in a democratic society, in practice managers continue to act on the belief that unions are either unnecessary or undesirable within their own organization.

Yet management also continues to be as pragmatic as ever. If the costs of union avoidance are too high—that is, if unions are too powerful to avoid—management will work with union leaders to develop the strategies needed to be competitive. Many firms have been able to pursue two strategies simultaneously: they avoid further unionization in one location in the firm, while they cooperate with the existing union at another. It remains to be seen if management will continue to enjoy such discretion and power in the years ahead.

Firms generally follow either a paternalistic, bureaucratic, human resource, conflict, New Deal, or participatory industrial relations pattern. For each of these patterns there is a set of basic personnel policies. Which of these patterns a firm prefers to follow is, in part, shaped by the firm's business strategy.

Where some of its employees are unionized, management turns to its industrial relations staff to represent its interests in collective bargaining. These staffs vary in their size, centralization, and specification.

Management makes a number of strategic choices in its relations with unions. These choices include decisions regarding how aggressively to resist the expansion of union representation and how to relate to any unions that represent employees in a firm. Management's strategic industrial relations choices appear to be influenced by the business strategy pursued by the firm. Management's strategic choices also are strongly influenced by the strategies chosen by unions. If the respective union that management must bargain with prefers a confrontational approach, for example, it is unlikely that management would then choose to promote a participatory pattern of industrial relations. The next chapter considers union strategy and structure.

Discussion Questions

1. Briefly describe the nonunion industrial relations patterns found in Exhibit 5–1.

2. Describe the union patterns of industrial relations found in Exhibit 5–1.

3. Contrast the primary two union avoidance strategies used by management.

4. Describe the three key aspects of management industrial relations staff structure.

Suggested Readings

Bendix, Reinhard. *Work and Authority in Industry* (New York: John Wiley, 1956).

Chandler, Alfred D., Jr. *Strategy and Structure* (New York: Anchor Books, 1966).

Foulkes, Fred. *Personnel Policies of Large Nonunion Companies* (Englewood Cliffs, NJ: Prentice-Hall, 1980).

Harris, Howell. *The Right to Manage* (Madison: University of Wisconsin Press, 1982).

Milkovich, George T., and Jerry Newman. *Compensation* (Plano, TX: Business Publications, 1984).

Slichter, Sumner, James J. Healy, and E. Robert Livernash, *The Impact of Collective Bargaining on Management* (Washington, D.C.: Brookings Institution, 1960).

End Notes

1. Topologies of industrial relations patterns with some similarities to this scheme are provided in Richard C. Edwards, *Contested Terrain* (New York: Basic Books, 1979) and in Alan Fox *Beyond Contract: Work, Power and Trust Relations* (London: Faber and Faber, 1974).

2. See Peter Doeringer, "Internal Labor Markets and Paternalism in Rural Areas," in *Internal Labor Markets,* ed. Paul Osterman (Cambridge, MA: MIT Press, 1984).

3. This sophisticated human resource management pattern developed in a few nonunion firms in the 1950s and had roots in earlier corporate policies of the 1920s (often labeled welfare capitalism; see Chapter 2).

4.   Delta Airlines is not a pure case of this nonunion pattern because its pilots are unionized.

5.   For a history of the personnel policies followed by Sears, see Sanford M. Jacoby, "Employee Attitude Testing at Sears, Roebuck and Company, 1938–1960," Working Paper Series 112 (Los Angeles: Institute of Industrial Relations, University of California, June 1986).

6.   For evidence on the role of the founding executives, see Fred Foulkes, *Personnel Policies in Large Nonunion Companies* (Englewood Cliffs, NJ: Prentice-Hall, 1980).

7.   See Thomas A. Kochan, Robert B. McKersie, and John Chalykoff, "The Effects of Corporate Strategy and Workplace Innovations on Union Representation," *Industrial and Labor Relations Review* 39 (July 1986): 487–501.

8.   See Jeffrey Arthur, *Industrial Relations and Business Strategies in American Steel Minimills* (Ithaca, NY: ILR Press, forthcoming).

9.   Douglas V. Brown and Charles A. Myers, "The Changing Industrial Relations Philosophy of American Management," in *Proceedings of the Ninth Annual Winter Meetings of the Industrial Relations Research Association* (Madison, WI: IRRA, 1957), p. 92.

10.   In earlier periods it was predominantly the larger companies that used the union substitution strategy (although many used both strategies simultaneously). In 1932, for example, 118 companies employing 1,000 workers or more accounted for 97 percent of all employees covered under employee representation (company union) plans. Harry Millis and Royal Montgomery, *Organized Labor* (New York: McGraw-Hill, 1945), p. 835.

11.   Richard B. Freeman and James L. Medoff, *What Do Unions Do?* (New York: Basic Books, 1984), p. 232.

12.   The 1977 Conference Board survey is described in Audrey Freedman, Managing Labor Relations: Organization, Objectives, and Results (New York: Conference Board, 1979). For the 1983 survey, see Audrey Freedman, *A New Look in Wage Bargaining* (New York: Conference Board, 1985).

13.   Alfred D. Chandler, Jr., *Strategy and Structure* (New York: Anchor Books, 1966), p. 15.

14.   The observations in the discussions that follow are derived from the Conference Board survey described in Freedman, 1983 and 1985.

Chapter 6

Union Strategies and Structures for Representing Workers

Unions design critical strategies just as management does. Yet, the scope of union decisions is somewhat wider because unions must decide to what extent they seek to promote worker interests through political channels versus collective bargaining. Unions must decide whether and how they will pursue political and legislative issues and determine the appropriate mix of federal, state, and local political or legislative activity. At the same time, all unions participate in collective bargaining to some degree; thus strategic choices must be made about how to represent workers' interests through bargaining and through daily activities at the workplace. For example, unions must decide how much of their resources and energy to devote to organizing new members and how they will structure their internal organization to represent their members.

Unions also make strategic decisions on the form of collective bargaining and other representational activities they will pursue. In recent years these questions have come to have renewed significance—even among well-established unions—as leaders have had to address whether and how to include involvement in strategic management or workplace issues as part of their representational strategy.

No question is more central to unions than membership. The lifeblood of unions and the source of their bargaining power are their members. This chapter traces union membership trends and also consider the various theories explaining the ups and downs that have occurred in union membership in the United States and other countries throughout history.

Unions and Politics

The U.S. labor movement historically has devoted the bulk of its efforts to collective bargaining as opposed to political action. In general,

American unions have followed a business unionism approach, as described in Chapter 2. Adhering to this philosophy, unions tend to avoid identifying with any overarching political ideology and instead focus on improving members' conditions of employment through collective bargaining. This is certainly evident when we compare U.S. labor to political unionists in other countries.

In the United States political system there is no labor party, as there is in a number of European countries. Furthermore, with few exceptions, U.S. unions have not identified themselves with a socialist political platform, another characteristic that is common among many European labor movements. But, these observations notwithstanding, researchers continue to debate how fully business unionism is an appropriate characterization of U.S. labor movement history, and contemporary unionists also continue to debate the proper role of unions in U.S. politics.

American Unions Do Have a Political Agenda

United States unions have historically played an important role as supporters of numerous welfare programs such as social security, medicare, and Aid to Families with Dependent Children. They also were strong supporters of the 1964 Civil Rights Act.

Unions also have been ardent and, again, successful supporters of federal legislation to protect and improve employment conditions. Here the list of federal programs includes the minimum wage, the Occupational Safety and Health Act, the **Davis-Bacon procedures,** and various pension regulations. AFL-CIO unions play an active role in the debates that surround federal legislation through the activities of the federation's **Committee on Political Education (COPE).**[1] Unions also remain an effective force in mobilizing voters in the United States.

U.S. unions are also active in state and local politics, both in the preparation of legislation and in the election of government officials. A number of state AFL-CIO and COPE organizations, community groups tied to unions, and local unions are very active in state and local affairs.

Is political action only a limited supplement to labor's search for job security? Or are U.S. workers not unlike their European counterparts—fully in possession of demands for social equality and political reform—but subject to much greater resistance to those demands from management and the courts? Labor historians have long debated these issues.

Current Debates in Unions over the Appropriate Role of Politics

The debate over the role of politics continues among the ranks of the U.S. labor movement. Some unionists have recently called for a reorientation of labor's strategy away from its traditional emphasis on collective bargaining and toward political action as the preferred means to labor's ends. Labor leaders such as Douglas Fraser (former president of the

UAW) have vented their frustration with union membership declines by expressing interest in an independent labor party.

Nonetheless, however frequent or well-publicized these calls for political activism may be, they have not been taken up in any widespread way. Despite all its recent problems, the labor movement in the United States has yet to make a fundamental change in its political orientation. Changes may come in the future, of course, but they would require a major break, not only from recent trends but from the long history of labor's involvement in U.S. politics.

Union Growth and Membership Characteristics

A central strategic question that faces any individual union and the labor movement as a whole is how much to focus their resources on the attraction of new members. Before exploring the factors that influence the growth of the labor movement, this chapter examines current patterns and recent trends in union membership. Recent data reveal a significant decline in union membership and illuminate some of the organizing and representational problems confronted by unions in the United States.

Union Membership Figures: The Loci of Membership

Exhibit 6–1 plots union membership as a percentage of the nonagricultural labor force over the years 1930 to 1990. As shown in the exhibit, union membership peaked in the mid-1940s at around 35 percent. By 1960 membership had declined to 31 percent of the nonagricultural labor force and by 1990 it had declined even further to 16.1 percent.

Union density (also called **union penetration**) levels vary substantially across industries, occupations, regions, and worker skill categories. The data reviewed below analyze how union membership varies across these dimensions.

Some regions of the United States exhibit high rates of unionization, whereas other regions have very low union membership. In 1984 New York and Michigan had the highest union densities in the nation, with, respectively, 39 and 37 percent of their labor forces organized.[2] At the other end of the spectrum were North and South Carolina—with less than 10 percent of their blue-collar workers organized—and Texas, Florida, and South Dakota, with union densities of less than 15 percent.

By Industrial Sector   These overall figures, however, mask major differences in union membership trends across industrial sectors. Exhibit 6–2 reports union membership data by industrial sector from 1930 to 1990. Although the percentage of manufacturing employees unionized declined from 42.4 percent in 1953 to 20.6 percent in 1990, the percentage of government employees in labor unions rose over the same period from 11.6 to 36.5 percent. Thus, the explosion of unions in government

Exhibit 6–1

Union Membership as a Percentage of the Nonagricultural Labor Force, 1930–90

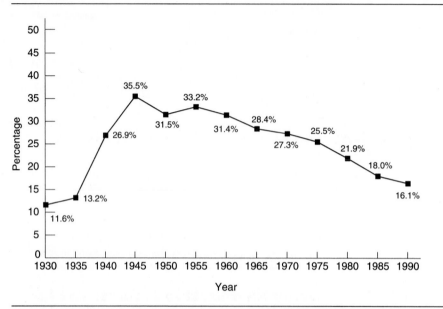

Note: The 1985 and 1990 figures are the percentage of employed wage and salary workers in all industries, private and public, who were union members. In 1980, this figure was 23.0 percent.
Sources: Reprinted by permission from Thomas A. Kochan, Harry C. Katz, and Robert B. McKersie, *The Transformation of American Industrial Relations,* p. 31. © 1986 by Basic Books. The 1985 figure is from Employment and Earnings, February 1987. The 1990 figure is from "News Bulletin," Bureau of Labor Statistics (Washington, D.C., February 6, 1991), USDL 91–34, p. 1.

employment during the 1960s and 1970s stands in stark contrast to the decline in manufacturing unionization.

Unionization in the **service sector** followed a different pattern. As Exhibit 6–2 shows, the percentage of service workers unionized rose from 9.5 percent in 1953 to 13.9 percent in 1975 but then fell to 5.7 percent in 1990.

By Occupation   Union membership also varies by occupation. Exhibit 6–3 presents estimates of the percentage of employees in major occupational groups that were members of trade unions in 1990. Within blue-collar ranks the highest levels of organization were in the semiskilled occupations (26.4 percent of operators, fabricators, and laborers were organized), followed by craft workers (25.9 percent were organized).

Among white-collar workers professional occupations were the most organized, at 21.4 percent, in 1990. Many of the unionized workers in those occupations were in the **public sector,** such as public school

Exhibit 6–2

Union Membership by Industrial Sector, 1930–1990*

Year	Manufacturing	Government	Services
1930	7.8%	8.5%	2.3%
1935	16.4	9.0	2.6
1940	30.5	10.7	5.7
1947	40.5	12.0	9.0
1953	42.4	11.6	9.5
1966	37.4	26.0	n.a.
1970	38.7	31.9	7.8
1975	36.0	39.5	13.9
1980	32.3	35.0	11.6
1983	27.8	36.7	7.7
1986	24.0	36.0	6.3
1990	20.6	36.5	5.7

*The figures represent the percentage of workers in each industrial sector who were members of a union.
Sources: Figures through 1980 are from Leo Troy and Neil Sheflin, *Union Sourcebook* (West Orange, NJ: Industrial Relations Data and Information Services, 1981). Data for 1983–1986 are from the U.S. Department of Labor, Bureau of Labor Statistics, *Employment and Earnings* (Washington, D.C.: GPO, January 1985 and January 1987). 1990 data are from "News Bulletin," U.S. Department of Labor, Bureau of Labor Statistics (Washington, D.C., February 6, 1991), USDL 91–34, table 2.

Exhibit 6–3

Union Membership by Occupation, 1990*

Occupational Classification	Percent Unionized
White-collar workers	
Executive, administrative, and managerial	6.0%
Professional	21.4
Technicians and related support	11.5
Sales occupations	5.0
Service occupations	13.8
Blue-collar workers	
Craft workers	25.9
Operators, fabricators, and laborers	26.4
Farming, forestry, and fishing	4.9

*The figures represent the percentage of workers in each occupation who were members of a union.
Sources: Data from "News Bulletin," U.S. Department of Labor, Bureau of Labor Statistics (Washington, D.C., February 6, 1991), USDL 91–34, table 2.

teachers. Service workers were less organized (13.8 percent).[3] Only 6 percent of executive, administrative, and managerial employees and 5 percent of sales workers were organized. Although unions still have not penetrated very deeply into the white-collar occupations, white-collar unionists are accounting for an increasing percentage of all union and association members.

By Demographic Group Union membership levels also vary by demographic characteristics. In 1990, 19.3 percent of all men and 12.6 percent of all women were members of unions.[4] Since 1970 the number of female union members has increased by almost 9 percent, whereas the figure for men has decreased by about 8 percent. The number of female unionists as a percentage of all union members has been rising: women made up 36.2 percent of all union members and 47.1 percent of employed workers in 1990.[5] Black workers are more likely to be members of unions than are whites. Bureau of Labor Statistics estimates for 1990 indicated that 21.1 percent of all black workers were union members, as compared to 15.5 percent of all white workers.[6]

Membership in the Large Unions A majority of members are concentrated in a few of the large unions. Exhibit 6–4 shows that in 1988 the five largest unions in the country were the National Education Association; the International Brotherhood of Teamsters; the United Food and Commercial Workers; the American Federation of State, County, and Municipal Employees (AFSCME); and the United Auto Workers. These five unions accounted for 46.5 percent of all union members in the country, and the ten largest unions accounted for almost three quarters (73.2 percent) of all union members.

The two fastest growing unions in the country since 1970 (where growth did not occur through merger) have been public sector unions. Between 1970 and 1988 AFSCME gained approximately 554,000 members (plus an estimated 206,000 members of the Civil Service Employees Association, which merged with AFSCME in 1978), and the American Federation of Teachers more than tripled in size. In addition, after 1970 the Service Employees International Union and the Communications Workers of America gained large numbers of new members.

Recent Union Membership Declines

By 1990 union membership among the total nonfarm labor force had fallen to 16.1 percent from its 1945 peak of 35.5 percent. Union membership as a percentage of the work force declined particularly rapidly after 1977 (when it stood at 23.8 percent). This resulted because the most highly unionized industries were hit hardest by the effects of the 1981–82 recession, by the declining competitiveness of U.S. manufactured goods on world markets, and by the economic and organizational restructuring under way within these industries.

Exhibit 6–4   **Membership in Individual Unions, Selected Years**

Union	Number of Members (in thousands)				
	1939	1960	1979	1983	1988
National Education Association (NEA)	0	0	1,594	1,444	1,700
Teamsters	442	1,481	1,975	1,616	1,600
Food and Commercial Workers (UFCW)	66	364	892	1,203	1,270
State, County, and Municipal (AFSCME)	27	195	942	955	1,100
Auto Workers (UAW)	165	1,136	1,520	1,026	1,003
Service Employees (SEIU)	62	269	597	644	850
Electrical Workers (IBEW)	136	690	922	869	790
Machinists (IAM)	178	687	735	540	750
Steelworkers (USW)	225	945	1,205	694	730
Communications (CWA)	71	269	523	578	700
Teachers (AFT)	32	56	452	457	660
Carpenters and Joiners	215	757	727	678	609
Laborers	158	443	537	461	371
Postal Workers	0	0	263	226	350
Plumbers	61	261	338	329	330
Operating Engineers	58	282	452	436	320
Hotel and Restaurant	221	435	398	344	293
Clothing and Textile (ACTWU)	240	273	316	251	281
Paperworkers	0	0	269	234	221
Musicians (AFM)	127	260	274	219	207
Garment Workers (ILGWU)	202	393	396	303	200

Sources: Data from Courtney D. Gifford, *Directory of U.S. Labor Organizations, 1990–91 Edition* (Washington, D.C.: Bureau of National Affairs, March 1990), appendix A, pp. 56–59; and Leo Troy and Neil Sheflin, *U.S. Union Sourcebook* (West Orange, NJ: Industrial Relations Data Information Services, 1985), appendix B, pp. B–1 to B–20.

As shown in Exhibit 6–4, from 1979 to 1983 alone the Steelworkers lost 511,000 members, the UAW lost 494,000 members, and the Machinists lost 195,000 members. Perhaps even more troubling for the labor movement is the fact that union election success did not improve in the mid- and late 1980s when the economy expanded.[7]

Although these numbers demonstrate the large magnitude of the decline in unionization, they conceal an even more important characteristic of recent unionization patterns. Over the 1960s and 1970s a significant nonunion sector emerged in virtually every industry we examined. This decline has been most surprising in industries that have historically been viewed as strongholds of unionism such as mining, construction, and trucking.

In the Coal Industry   In underground bituminous coal mining the nonunion sector has grown from virtually nothing to some 50 percent of the industry. Major companies are now operating completely nonunion mines, often in the heart of United Mine Workers territory, such as Kentucky and West Virginia.

In the Construction Industry   In construction nonunion shops have begun to arise even among large commercial operations. During the 1950s and 1960s open-shop construction companies had moved into residential and light commercial construction, but unionized companies continued to dominate the important, heavy construction sector. Starting in the 1970s, however, the situation changed; increasingly, major office buildings and large industrial sites are being built by nonunion labor. Overall, between 1975 and 1984 nonunion operations have grown from approximately 50 to 75 percent of all construction work.

In the Trucking Industry   Over-the-road (intercity) trucking presents a similar picture. Since its deregulation in 1980 the industry has experienced a sharp transformation. Approximately 30 percent of the large, unionized carriers went into bankruptcy and were replaced by smaller, independent, and generally nonunion companies. In time, many of the smaller firms also failed, so that by 1990 the largest three unionized carriers had increased their dominance and market share as a consequence of deregulation. Meanwhile, a variety of small and largely nonunion carriers had carved out specialized niches in the remaining parts of the market.

In Particular Companies   At the company level, data from a number of highly visible firms further illustrate this general trend. In the early 1960s General Electric had 30 to 40 nonunion plants, but by 1990 that number had roughly doubled as a result of the corporate restructuring and the opening of new, nonunion plants. Companies such as Monsanto and 3M have seen a drop in the representation rate for their production and maintenance workers—from approximately 80 to 40 percent or less. Similarly, some of the major companies in the auto parts industry, such as Dana, Bendix (now a part of Allied Signal), and Eaton, have developed sizable nonunion sectors.

American unions have faced serious declines in the share of the work force they represent since the early 1950s. What explains this decline? The next section considers in general terms the factors that influence union growth as general theories can help guide our analysis of recent U.S. experience.

Models of Union Growth

Two types of factors influence union growth. On the one hand, union growth is influenced by the state of the economy, which can be categorized as a cyclical factor. In addition, there are a host of historical, political, and social factors that have influenced unions' organizing success. These factors are often labeled as structural factors.

The Cyclical Factor

John R. Commons was one of the first to note that unions grew during economic prosperity and declined during economic downturns.[8] In the latter half of the nineteenth century union membership and the numbers of national unions rose and fell in sync with changes in the business cycle throughout that period.[9] Commons posited that as labor markets tightened during an upturn in the economy, workers became more aggressive in pursuing their goals while employers became less resistant to collective efforts by their employees. Tighter labor markets gave workers more bargaining power and thereby increased the payoffs to unionization. With the higher profit rates that accompany prosperity, employers had more to lose during strikes and unionization drives and therefore employers had fewer incentives to resist unionization.

This business cycle movement in union membership appears in other places and times. Analysis of union growth in the United States and in other countries reveals a persistent positive correlation between union membership and the strength of the economy.[10]

The Structural Factors

The Historical and Legal Influences   Although the business cycle clearly affects union growth, it is important to note that much of the growth in U.S. labor unions took place in only a few significant spurts. As Exhibit 6–1 shows, unionism flourished during the late 1930s and the early and mid-1940s. Public sector unionism also grew in a spurt, starting in the early 1960s. Evidence that cyclical factors are not the only influences on union growth comes from the fact that union growth did not rebound in 1985–1990 even though these were years of economic expansion.

Events during the great depression and the two world wars illustrate that the most dramatic increases in union growth have come during times of major social upheavals. Analysts argue that the political climate of the 1930s and later the social upheavals caused by the wartime economy provided workers with strong motivation to turn to unions.

The Influence of Laws and Public Policy   Union growth and decline also appear to be affected by the legal environment and public policy. It was not the effects of the great depression, but the encouragement to collective bargaining given by the NLRA that led to increases in unionization in the late 1930s and 1940s.

Union membership is low in states that have **right-to-work laws** and this is another illustration of how public policy can influence union growth. These laws make it illegal to require employees to join unions as a condition of employment (such laws exist in 20 states).

Another illustration of how public policy affects union growth is the growth of public sector unions in the 1960s and 1970s. This growth occurred after many states passed legislation that protects the rights of public employees to unionize and to bargain collectively. Unfortunately, it is not entirely clear which was the cause and which the effect in those public sector developments.

On the one hand, union membership has grown fastest in states that passed legislation granting public employee unions the right to collective bargaining. On the other hand, an already favorable political climate, the existence of a strong potential for organizing, and, in some cases, the beginnings of union organization in the public sector all contributed to the passage of the state laws in the first place and may be the real major causes of union growth. Thus, it is probably safest to conclude that in the public sector the passage of legislation is both partially a cause and partially an effect of union growth.[11] This simultaneous or reciprocal causality in the relationship between public sector unionization and legislation plagues other efforts to sort out the independent effects of public policy variables on union growth in general (and on many other aspects of collective bargaining as well).

In summary, union growth in the United States and in other countries is affected by cyclical economic factors and by a number of structural factors. The latter include public policies and major historical and social events.

Explanations of Recent Union Declines

American unions have experienced a sizeable decline in the share of the work force organized after the mid 1940s. Furthermore, in the early 1980s unions in the United States were losing members in numerical (absolute) terms, and the decline in the percentage of the work force in unions accelerated. What explains these events? Do the general theories discussed above apply, or are special explanations needed?

The next section uses a scheme offered first by Jack Fiorito and Cheryl Maranto to account for the decline that has occurred in American union membership.[12] There are six categories of factors that have contributed to this decline.

Factor 1: Structural Changes in the Economy and the Labor Force

Unions have had difficulty gaining new members in part due to changes that have occurred in the nature and location of jobs. Unions historically have had the greatest success in organizing urban jobs in the east, west coast, and north-central regions of the country. Yet jobs have been moving away from these regions. Unions also have had the greatest success with middle-aged males in blue-collar occupations. Again, the trends have worked against unions with the expansion of service and white-collar jobs, and young and female workers. Statistical tests suggest that roughly 40 percent of the decline in union membership (as a percentage of the work force) that occurred from the early 1950s to the 1980s can be explained by region, industry, and worker characteristics.[13]

It is important to note that union declines in particular regions or occupations were not independent of management or union actions. The shift in employment to the south in part reflected management's decision to take advantage of the region's labor costs—lower than those prevailing in the more highly unionized north—and managers' beliefs that the social and political climate of the south reduced employers' vulnerability to unionization. Similarly, while employment opportunities were shifting to the service sector, unions did not follow suit by reallocating their organizing resources to take advantage of that shift.

Factor 2: Union Avoidance through Employer Election Campaign Practices

There is also evidence that many employers increased their resistance to unions and that, specifically, management became very sophisticated in the tactics employed during election campaigns. Management's tactics include the use of consultants, direct discussion with employees, speeches by executives of the firm during election campaigns, and in some cases, threats. Management's resistance to unions during election campaigns appears to have contributed to low union win rates in campaign elections.[14]

Factor 3: Employer Substitution through Personnel Practices

Management does not always wait until an organizing election to try to convince its employees that unions are unnecessary. Management can adopt sophisticated personnel practices that serve to substitute, at least in part, for union representation. In particular, the human resource industrial relations pattern (described in Chapter 5) has as one of its chief objectives avoidance of union representation. One key way the personnel practices differ from the election campaign practices discussed above is their long-run nature. It is useful also to keep in mind that management may have a number of reasons for using these personnel practices, including the fact that these practices can contribute to the firm's performance and adaptability.

Factor 4: Government Substitution

The government, at both the federal and state levels, since the late 1960s in particular, has become more directly involved in shaping employment conditions. Governmental influence on the substantive conditions of employment comes in part through regulations for equal employment opportunity, health and safety, and pension rights and funding. It is possible that by passing this legislation the government has weakened the need for unions by, in effect, giving the work force many of the things that unions provide.

Does the increasing role played by governments in the regulation of employment conditions actually sizably restrain union growth? Union substitution does not seem consistent with the success unions have had in a number of countries in Europe and Scandinavia with even more active governments (often Social Democratic governments) and strong and growing unions. Perhaps union substitution has had more significant effects in the United States.

Factor 5: American Worker Ideology

Some historians argue that the American work force possesses an ideology that leads workers away from unionism. The claim is that the particular American culture of individualism and the absence of class or aristocratic traditions lead to a weak union appeal.

Seymour Martin Lipset, for example, contrasted American and Canadian ideologies and claimed that these explain the relatively higher union membership in Canada. Unions are stronger in Canada even though there are many similarities in the economic conditions in the two countries. Lipset argued that U.S. citizens are individualistic (and hence not attracted to unions) whereas Canadians are culturally attracted to unions and other "communal" organizations. In Lipset's view, it was the union growth that occurred during the great depression in the United States that was the exceptional event and not the decline that U.S. unions experienced after the mid 1940s.[15]

Yet, just as there is much debate as to whether business unionism is (or ever was) an appropriate characterization of the American labor movement, there is debate as to whether the ideology possessed by workers in the United States is so different from that held by workers in other countries.

Moreover, opinion poll data indicate that attitudes of the public toward unions are quite similar in Canada and the United States and have moved in the same direction over the postwar period.[16] This too casts doubt on the claim that worker or public ideology explains the differences in union growth rates in the two countries.

It also is debatable whether it is appropriate to speak as if worker ideology emerges independent of management actions or the strategies used by the labor movement. Maybe American workers *would* have reacted differently, for example, if management was less resistant to unions or if unions offered a different set of policies.

Factor 6: Internal Union Affairs and Actions

Unions may bear some of the blame for their organizing difficulties and decline. One argument along these lines is that American unions have suffered from corruption and sluggish adaptation to changing times. Analysts also point to all the poor publicity generated by the charges of corruption that plague the Teamsters union or the longshoring unions as part of the source of the low image the public holds of unions.

Others have argued that unions have done poorly in representation elections because they have not devoted enough resources to organizing. A number of critics have argued that labor no longer approaches the task of organizing new workers with the same enthusiasm or commitment as that which characterized the organizing drives of the 1930s.[17]

An analysis of overall trends in union election activity since 1950 shows that between 1960 and 1980 the number of elections held, the number of workers voting in those elections, and the unions' win rate in the elections held all declined.[18] As a result of these declines, the annual percentage of eligible workers in the labor force that became newly organized fell from about 1 percent in 1955 to less than 0.2 percent in 1980. That 1980 rate of new union organizing produced less than one-fifth the number of new union members that would have been needed just to offset the number of workers who left unions because they were leaving the labor force.

To summarize, there are a number of potential explanations of the decline that has occurred in the percentage of the American labor force that belongs to a union. It may also be the case that the best explanation is a combination of some of the factors described above.

Union Structures for Collective Bargaining

For a union to pursue its goals effectively in the collective bargaining process it must have an appropriate structure. The structure of a union not only is important to its success in collective bargaining, but it also directs the internal distribution of power and influence among union decision makers. The next section describes the governance and activities of the AFL-CIO, of national unions, and of local unions.

The AFL-CIO

The **AFL-CIO, a federation** of national unions, is the major labor federation in the United States. The primary roles of the AFL-CIO are to promote the political objectives of the labor movement and to assist the component unions in their collective bargaining activities. The AFL-CIO promotes the political objectives of unions through political lobbying and disseminating information to union members about political events and elections.

The federation has no formal authority over the collective bargaining activities of its member national unions and only rarely becomes directly involved in them. In recent years, however, the Building and Construction Trades Department and the Metal Trades Department of the AFL-CIO have played a more active and direct role in collective bargaining in selected construction projects and in the federal sector, respectively. Similarly, the Industrial Union Department has played a key supporting role in some coalition bargaining efforts in a number of industries. More generally, the staff departments of the federation offer extensive research and technical support to individual unions or to groups of unions experiencing common problems. In addition, competing unions turn to the federation to arbitrate their jurisdictional disputes.

The governance structure of the AFL-CIO is diagrammed in Exhibit 6–5. The supreme governing body of the AFL-CIO is the biennial national convention. The chief officer of the federation is its president, and the most influential policymaking body is the Executive Council. The president has traditionally been the major source of power in the federation—with significant influence over the Executive Council and the membership—because the president has the authority to interpret the constitution between meetings of the Executive Council and manages the federation staff.

The Structure of National Unions

The **national union** is the key body and the center of power within most trade unions in the United States. National unions often are actively involved in the negotiation of collective bargaining agreements. The national unions also sanction and provide assistance to their member local unions.

Craft versus Industrial Union Structure   It is important to understand how union jurisdiction influences how national unions perform their functions. Union jurisdiction determines the range of workers who can be legitimately organized by the union. Two of the most prevalent alternative union forms are craft or industrial unionism. A **craft union**'s jurisdiction is limited to workers in a specific trade (such as painters, electricians, or carpenters) or profession (for example, teachers, nurses, pilots, baseball players, and fire fighters). An **industrial union**'s jurisdic-

Exhibit 6–5
The Structure of the AFL-CIO

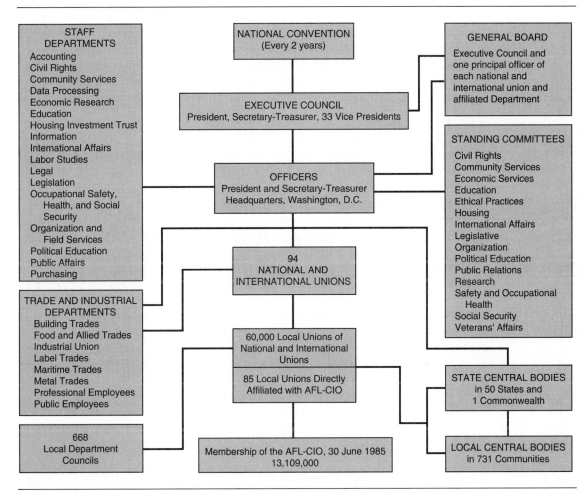

STAFF DEPARTMENTS
Accounting
Civil Rights
Community Services
Data Processing
Economic Research
Education
Housing Investment Trust
Information
International Affairs
Labor Studies
Legal
Legislation
Occupational Safety,
   Health, and Social
   Security
Organization and
   Field Services
Political Education
Public Affairs
Purchasing

NATIONAL CONVENTION
(Every 2 years)

GENERAL BOARD
Executive Council and
one principal officer of
each national and
international union and
affiliated Department

EXECUTIVE COUNCIL
President, Secretary-Treasurer, 33 Vice Presidents

STANDING COMMITTEES
Civil Rights
Community Services
Economic Services
Education
Ethical Practices
Housing
International Affairs
Legislative
Organization
Political Education
Public Relations
Research
Safety and Occupational
   Health
Social Security
Veterans' Affairs

OFFICERS
President and Secretary-Treasurer
Headquarters, Washington, D.C.

94 NATIONAL AND INTERNATIONAL UNIONS

TRADE AND INDUSTRIAL DEPARTMENTS
Building Trades
Food and Allied Trades
Industrial Union
Label Trades
Maritime Trades
Metal Trades
Professional Employees
Public Employees

60,000 Local Unions of National and International Unions

85 Local Unions Directly Affiliated with AFL-CIO

STATE CENTRAL BODIES
in 50 States and
1 Commonwealth

668 Local Department Councils

Membership of the AFL-CIO, 30 June 1985
13,109,000

LOCAL CENTRAL BODIES
in 731 Communities

Sources: U.S. Department of Labor, Bureau of Labor Statistics, *Directory of National Unions and Employee Associations, 1975* (Washington D.C.: GPO, 1977), p. 2; updated with information from Courtney D. Gifford, *Directory of U.S. Labor Organizations, 1986–87 Edition* (Washington D.C.: Bureau of National Affairs, 1986), pp. 1–4

tion typically encompasses all workers in a firm (such as, steel, autos, and coal mining).

The early U.S. unions were craft unions organized within local labor markets. From its formation in 1886 the AFL firmly adhered to the craft union principle as the cornerstone for organizing skilled workers. But as labor markets and product markets broadened with transportation improvements and the growth of mass production industries, the need to expand union jurisdictions became evident. Markets began to cross state lines, and unskilled workers became a significant part of the labor force, raising serious challenges to the appropriateness of the narrow, craft-based organizations.

In 1935 advocates of industrial unionism, led by John L. Lewis, president of the United Mine Workers, split with the craft union advocates in the AFL and formed what became in 1937 the Congress of Industrial Organizations (CIO). As the large industrial unions grew, corporations and markets continued to expand, and centralized bargaining became more popular—all of which helped to establish the national union as the central, or most powerful, structure in most industrial unions.

The Governance of National Unions   National unions typically are governed by a constitution and bylaws. Commonly there are annual or biennial conventions held by the national union in which officers are elected, rules and bylaws are modified, and policies are debated. The local unions that are branches of the national union send delegates to the national union convention, often with the number of delegates determined by the number of members in the local union.

National unions have elected officers that frequently include a president, secretary-treasurer, vice presidents (each of which might oversee certain of the covered membership in various companies or industries), and an executive board. The national union also commonly includes an administrative staff that is appointed by the president.

The staff of a national union implements policies in areas such as organizing, contract negotiation, grievance administration, health and safety, strike and welfare fund administration, and research. One important task performed by these staffs is communicating with organizations that are external to the union, such as other national unions, offices of the AFL-CIO, or governmental agencies. Another responsibility of the national union staff is to provide advice and assistance to the local unions within the national union.

The Local Union

For most unionized workers the most extensive interaction they have with the union that represents them is through their contact with and involvement in a **local union.** The individual employee can participate in local union meetings and vote in the elections that determine local union officers. It is the local union that is involved in the initial processing of a grievance and the direction of any strike or picketing activities.

If a local union is not linked to any national union (as is the case in some small manufacturing companies), the local union negotiates a collective bargaining agreement on its own. More typically, however, a local union is a branch of a national union and is thus governed by the constitution or bylaws of a national union. In addition to this formal connection, there is typically extensive contact between local and national union officers, especially during contract negotiations or contract administration.

The Division between Local and National Union Responsibilities In most industrial unionized settings, such as the steel, auto, textile, and mining industries, the unionized employee is covered by both a local contract and a contract that is negotiated at either the company or industry level. The local union negotiates the local contract, whereas the national union negotiates the company or industry contract.

When there are both local and higher level (company or industry) collective bargaining agreements, each agreement covers different subjects. The local contract (which might cover either a single plant or all the plants in a company) usually includes issues such as the work rules for job requirements and seniority rights and the wage rates paid for specific jobs. The company or national contract addresses matters such as the scheduled wage increase over the term of the contract and fringe benefits, and it sets out procedures for the grievance process.

The national union usually assists the local union during negotiation of the local collective bargaining agreement. The national union might provide an expert in negotiations who advises the local union during negotiations; in some instances the national union representative directs the union side in local negotiations. Or, the research staff of the national union may be involved by providing background information (about other wage settlements in the industry or economic trends) or technical assistance to the local union.

The local and national union staffs often have regular contact during the term of a labor agreement. National staff might provide, for example, technical assistance to a local union as it develops or implements health and safety or employee assistance programs. The national and local unions often coordinate their efforts during a union organizing drive. In addition, as discussed further in Chapter 11, in many unions it is the national union that decides whether an unresolved grievance is pressed to arbitration.

The Governance of Local Unions The local union typically includes a number of elected executive officers, including a president and a secretary-treasurer. Industrial unions frequently also have bargaining chairs and bargaining committees that lead the local union in contractual negotiations. In the construction industry and some other local unions a **business agent** directs the local contractual negotiations, handles grievances, and in other ways operates as the chief administrative officer of the local union.

Local unions are funded out of the dues paid by unionized employees. In large and well-funded unions the executive officers of the local union will be paid full- or part-time to carry out union duties. In many locals the union president is the only full-time paid position, and other officers carry out union-related duties part-time and perform their normal jobs at other times.

Union officers are involved in formulating the strategic direction of the local union, but for the average worker the most important person who represents the union is the **shop steward.** In a typical union, the steward provides union services at the shop floor level to 10 to 20 workers. It is the steward that becomes involved most quickly if a grievance or other dispute arises between a worker and a supervisor. Furthermore, workers often hear about union events or programs from their steward.

Political Life inside Local Unions   Local union officers and stewards are chosen for their positions through elections. Many local unions elect officers for two- or three-year terms. Local union elections are frequently highly contested, with a large number of candidates running for positions. There is rarely anything similar to a formal political party in local unions, although there are often slates (groups) of candidates who join together informally during their campaigns for union office.

Union Democracy

How extensive is the amount of democracy inside national and local unions? Although it is difficult to generalize, given the wide diversity that exists within unions, overall, there is much **union democracy.** Union officers are elected regularly through democratic election processes. Compared to the way the executives in corporations are chosen, the election of union officers is clearly more democratic.

There tends to be greater stability in national union officer elections than in local union officer elections. The presidents of many national unions, for example, are often reelected to serve for a number of terms. Some of the important and colorful figures in U.S. labor history were national union presidents, such as John L. Lewis (in the United Mine Workers) and Walter Reuther (in the United Auto Workers) who were elected for a number of terms.

In most unions there are regular debates over the strategic direction and positions the union should take in contractual negotiations with management, another sign of healthy democratic processes. There are rarely formal political parties inside unions like the national political parties that exist in the United States. Instead, debates and coalitions tend to be formed around specific issues and events.

Recently, for example, there has been active debate inside unions over whether unions should cooperate more extensively with management. Sometimes this debate is triggered by management's requests for changes in work rules that can lead to improvements in plant productivity. Critics of the cooperative approach argue that the union might unnecessarily give up gains that had taken years to win or might lose the capability to defend workers' interests.

Inside the UAW the debate described above has divided members who support the Administration caucus that has led the union for the last

Box 6–1

The Debate inside the UAW: The Administration Caucus versus the New Directions Movement

A heated debate and political infighting emerged inside the UAW in the 1980s, pitting the long-standing leadership of the union against the "New Directions movement." These debates upset the consensus that had prevailed among the national officers of the UAW regarding the union's negotiating strategy.

Walter Reuther had led a coalition that dominated the union from the mid-1940s until his death in 1971. Followers of Reuther continued to lead the union and maintained a tight-knit coalition, the administration caucus. In the mid-1980s the dominance of the administration caucus was challenged by the New Directions movement led by Jerry Tucker.

Debates focused on how the union should respond to the economic pressures and challenges posed by rising Japanese imports and increased Japanese auto production in the United States. These debates were triggered by the UAW's collective bargaining agreements with the auto companies in the 1980s in which the UAW accepted pay settlements that were below the pay increases the union had gained in previous contract settlements. The union also did not oppose the expansion of participation programs and team systems of work involving few job classifications on the shop floor.

The New Directions movement argued that the UAW had been too ready to give in to management's demands. In particular, supporters of New Directions claimed the team system and participation programs weakened the union's ability to defend workers' rights, increased the pace of work, and produced little real involvement by workers in company decisions. The New Directions movement opposed any collaboration with management.

The fight between the Administration caucus and the New Directions movement came to a head when Tucker entered the race for election as one of the UAW regional directors (against an Administration caucus candidate). Tucker narrowly lost his election bid in 1986, but the U.S. Department of Labor overturned the election on the grounds that there had been improprieties during the election. Tucker then won the new election and took office as the director of Region 5 (in the St. Louis area), a position which also made him a member of the UAW's national executive board.

In 1989 when Tucker ran for reelection he was defeated by a candidate supported by the Administration caucus. The Administration caucus went to great lengths to oppose Tucker and other individuals who ran on the New Directions' slate in other union elections. The staff members of the UAW were asked to contribute $500 each into a fund that was used to support campaigns against the New Directions candidates.

With Tucker's defeat the New Directions movement lost representation on the union's executive board, but the movement has been more successful in local union elections. A number of New Directions supporters have won election to union offices in various plants.

The debate continues over how the UAW should respond to economic pressures. Similar debates are under way in other American unions.

Source: "UAW Dissidents Hold National Conference; 500 Elect Tucker Organizing Coordinator," *Daily Labor Report* 204 (Washington, D.C.: Bureau of National Affairs), October 24, 1989, pp. A-3 and A-4.

40 years and supporters of the *New Directions movement.* Box 6–1 outlines some of the issues that separate the two sides in the debate currently under way.

Union Corruption

There are some instances of corruption inside unions. For many years, for example, there have been allegations that officers in the Teamsters union were linked to organized crime. Box 6–2 discusses the racketeering charges brought against the Teamsters by the Justice Department and how they were settled in 1989. It will be interesting to see whether the direct election of Teamsters officers included in the 1989 settlement leads to major changes in the leaders and policies of the union.

One can also point to particular local unions in which corrupt practices or corrupt leaders exist as evidence that unions do not maintain purely democratic institutions. Nevertheless, there is evidence of lively debates inside unions and the democratic selection of nearly all union officers.

Box 6–2

Racketeering Charges against the Teamsters Union

Since the 1930s there have been charges that a number of the officers of the Teamsters union were linked to organized crime. Four of the presidents who have led the Teamsters union since the 1930s have been indicted for criminal charges. Three of those presidents went to prison, and a number of union officers and challengers to the union leadership were killed under suspicious circumstances.

In the 1980s the Justice Department of the U.S. government brought a racketeering case against the union. The U.S. Attorney's complaint, filed in federal court against the union, claimed that there were at least 200 Teamsters' officials with proved or alleged connections to organized crime.

In 1989 the Justice Department and the Teamsters Union settled the racketeering case out of court. In the settlement the union (with 1.6 million members) agreed to have national union officers directly elected by member voting in 1991. This replaced the traditional election of national union officers by local union leaders. The settlement also appointed a number of individuals designated by the Justice Department to temporarily oversee the financial operation of the national union and to take over the direction of some of the local branches of the union.

Source: "1991 International Officers Election," in *Daily Labor Report* (Washington, D.C.: Bureau of National Affairs), June 12, 1990, p. A-16, and July 12, 1990, p. A-2.

Union Mergers

One of the key ways a national union can alter its governance structure and form is through a **union merger** with another union. One goal of the AFL-CIO merger in 1955 was to promote greater rationalization of union structures through mergers and consolidation of member unions.[19] Indeed, George Meany and Walter Reuther, then leaders of the AFL and CIO, respectively, expected the original 135 unions in the new federation to be reduced to approximately 50.[20] The number of unions in the AFL-CIO now stands at 94.[21]

The advantage of a merger for unions are the administrative benefits that accrue from greater economies of scale and the organizing and bargaining benefits from reduced interunion competition and rivalry. Small unions that lack the financial resources and professional expertise needed to adequately service union members can be absorbed into larger, more richly endowed organizations. Reducing competition among unions in the same industry or occupation can free up resources previously used in fighting with each other to improve collective bargaining or political efforts. And, finally, unions whose traditional occupational or craft jurisdictions have eroded can concentrate on helping their members adjust to the changing environment by protecting their job security and expending less of their effort on ensuring the institutional survival of the union.

Critics of merger activity, on the other hand, posit that mergers do not necessarily reflect the rational consolidation of outmoded union jurisdictions. Instead, they say, some mergers are simply opportunistic or expansionist in nature and arise out of union leaders' desires for greater memberships, larger treasuries, more stable jobs for themselves, and increased status and power within the labor movement. Critics also question whether mergers increase unions' administrative or collective bargaining effectiveness. They stress the negative consequences of large-scale unions for membership control and union democracy.[22]

In the face of the drops in membership, a number of unions entered financial crises and drastically cut back the size of their staffs in the 1980s. Thus, just as the workers in declining industries were facing layoffs, so were a number of union staff members.

In the 1980s a number of unions responded to financial pressures by merging. Mergers reduced the number of unions based in the United States over the 1980s by one-third.[23] Some small unions responded by merging in an effort to regain bargaining strength and staff economies through the creation of a larger union. In 1980, for example, the Aluminum, Brick and Clay Workers merged with the Glass and Ceramic Workers to form the Aluminum, Brick and Glass Workers International Union. Merger activity, particularly on the part of unions representing government workers enabled several of the nation's largest unions, such as AFSCME and the SEIU, to grow when the organized sector of the U.S. work force was declining.

Changes in technology, along with the rising administrative costs of running an effective union, are likely to continue the pressure for union mergers. At the same time, however, the political problems associated with merging two or more autonomous, and often rival, organizations into one body (with, obviously, only one president) will continue to limit the rate of mergers. Critical questions that must be addressed are: Do mergers produce the improved administrative and bargaining service they promise? Do they enhance unions' and their members' abilities to adapt to technological change? And do those benefits result without also yielding losses in union membership control and internal union democracy? These are questions worthy of attention.

Alternative Union Strategies: The 1985 AFL-CIO Report

In recent years union leaders have been forced to decide how far they are willing to extend bargaining beyond its traditional agenda. The ongoing strategic choices leaders make on this issue will have a profound effect on the nature of U.S. unionism and its future. Recognizing the crucial need for longer run strategic planning, a number of unions such as the Communications Workers, the Bricklayers, the Steelworkers, and the Auto Workers have created committees to examine alternative strategies for the future. This sort of planning is likely to become a more common part of union administration in the future.

One example of the union movement's consideration of new strategies is the 1985 report of the AFL-CIO Committee on the Evolution of Work.[24] The report stresses the need both (1) to develop more effective means for allowing organized workers to resolve—as individuals—the problems on their jobs and (2) to provide more individual membership options for those workers who are unable to establish (or who are disinterested in establishing) a formal collective bargaining relationship with their employer. The basis of these recommendations can be seen in the Harris poll conducted for the committee and in the committee's analyses of the growing number of workers who have only temporary or short-term attachments to a single employer.

For example, in 1990 approximately 20 percent of the employed labor force work in part-time jobs. In addition, a small but growing number hold temporary jobs, are consultants or independent contractors, or work for temporary-help agencies and thus are not attached to a single employer. This is clearly an increasingly important segment of the labor force. Unorganized part-time and temporary workers tend to be less interested in union appeals since they are less likely to be around to gain from any union benefits and they are less interested in paying union dues.

In response to the difficulties unions have had in organizing part-time and temporary workers, the AFL-CIO Committee on the Evolution of Work recommended that the union movement develop new strategies for representing these workers and nonunion workers in general.

The AFL-CIO committee recommended experimentation with an associate-membership option that would allow individual workers to join unions and receive benefits, such as inexpensive health care insurance, even if no collective bargaining unit existed at their place of employment. AFL-CIO then created a subsidiary organization called the **Union Privilege Program** that has begun to experiment with associate union and new union privilege programs. The AFL-CIO hopes these new programs will produce organizing leads and lead to broader political support for the labor movement (potentially from new associate members). It remains to be seen whether these expectations are fulfilled.

The Evolution of Work Committee has continued to meet, study, and debate alternative strategies for the future. Topics that in previous years might have been quickly rejected are now openly debated among union leaders. Examples of such topics include advocating European style works councils for the United States (see Chapter 14), union representation on company boards of directors, employee ownership, fundamental labor law reform, and enhanced political involvement. No consensus has been reached on these issues, but the very fact that U.S. labor leaders are debating these alternatives is quite interesting. Perhaps some bold new strategic choices will emerge from these discussions.

Summary

The union membership figures reported at the beginning of this chapter highlight one of the central challenges that face unions today. Unions' share of the U.S. labor force declined substantially since the early 1950s, a decline even more alarming given the inroads nonunion firms have achieved in many industries that were once bastions of union organization. Contributing to this decline have been innovative human resource and union avoidance policies adopted by some nonunion firms, structural shifts in the economy and labor force, the effects of recession and industrial decline, and unions' unproductive and, in some cases, only feeble efforts to counteract these developments.

Yet the outlook for the labor movement is not completely gloomy. The benefits of the human resource innovations that serve as a partial alternative to unionization have diffused to only a limited number of U.S. workers. And, many workers lack the long-term attachment to an employment relationship necessary to make the new human resource management models work. These include the growing numbers of temporary, part-time, or flexible-contract employees and the growing numbers of professionals who hold a greater attachment to their occupation than to their employer.

At the same time, although some workers remain suspicious of union leaders and labor institutions, many appear to be attracted to a representational system that addresses workplace and strategic issues when those issues have a direct influence on their employment security and working conditions. These unmet needs for workplace and strategic representation have led unions and the AFL-CIO to begin to rethink some of their basic strategies. But whether lasting and deep changes in unions' representational strategies follow and whether these changes are linked to a new union political strategy remain to be seen.

Collective bargaining is the most central activity carried out by unions in the United States, given the business unionist focus in the American labor movement. At the same time, American unions are active in political and community affairs. The national unions participate in activities that include bargaining, political lobbying, and organizing drives, and they oversee the operation of member local unions. The dominant federation of national unions is the AFL-CIO.

Unions rely heavily on the participation of their members to elect officers and form their policies and strategies. With few exceptions, there is much democracy in the internal operation of American unions. Democracy is evident in the wide-ranging debates now occurring in unions over how they should respond to membership declines and environmental pressures.

Discussion Questions

1. What is the basic union philosophy in the United States? Discuss some of the debates surrounding this philosophy.

2. Various demographic features or characteristics, such as type of occupation, physical location, and other demographic trends, play a large role in union membership. Describe some of these characteristics or features.

3. The text gives six possible explanations, offered by Fiorito and Maranto, for the recent decline in union membership. Briefly discuss these possible reasons.

4. The structure of a national union is extremely important in its ability to negotiate successful contracts with employers. Discuss the role union jurisdiction plays in this structure.

5. Since the merger of the AFL-CIO many unions have merged and consolidated their memberships and structures. What are some of the arguments the proponents use in defending this practice? What are some of the arguments against this practice?

Suggested Readings

Barbash, Jack. *American Unions: Structure, Government and Politics* (New York: Random House, 1967).

Dunlop, John T., and Derek C. Bok. *Labor and the American Community,* (New York: Simon and Shuster, 1970).

Sayles, Leonard R., and George Strauss. *The Local Union* (New York: Harcourt, Brace and World, 1967).

Ulman, Lloyd. *The Rise of the National Trade Union* (Cambridge, MA: Harvard University Press, 1958).

End Notes

1.   COPE is funded by voluntary contributions. Its activities include voter registration, efforts to encourage union members and supporters to vote, and the circulation of information on political matters and pending legislation.

2.   Courtney D. Gifford, *Directory of U.S. Labor Organizations, 1982–83 Edition* (Washington, D.C.: Bureau of National Affairs, 1982).

3.   The figures for unionism in the service sector reported in Exhibits 6–2 and 6–3 may appear inconsistent, but they are not. The tables utilize different definitions of "service" work. Exhibit 6–2 reports unionism by *industrial sector,* whereas Exhibit 6–3 reports unionism by *occupation.*

4.   "News Bulletin," U.S. Department of Labor, Bureau of Labor Statistics (Washington, D.C., February 6, 1991), USDL 91–34, table 1.

5.   Ibid., table 1.

6.   Ibid., table 1.

7.   See Gary N. Chaison and Dileep G. Dhavale, "A Note on the Severity of the Decline in Union Organizing," *Industrial and Labor Relations Review,* Vol. 23, No. 4, (April 1990): 366–373.

8.   John R. Commons, *A Documentary History of American Industrial Society,* Vol. 5 (Cleveland: Arthur H. Clark, 1911), p. 19.

9.   Lloyd Ulman, *The Rise of the National Trade Union* (Cambridge, MA: Harvard University Press, 1958), pp. 4–6.

10.   See Orley Ashenfelter and John H. Pencavel, "American Trade Union Growth, 1900–1960," *Quarterly Journal of Economics* 83 (August 1969): 434–448.

11.   Richard B. Freeman, "Unionism Comes to the Public Sector," *Journal of Economic Literature* 24 (March 1986): 42–86; Gregory Saltzman, "Bargaining Laws as a Cause and Consequence of Teacher Unionism," *Industrial and Labor Relations Review,* Vol. 38, No. 2, (April 1985): 335–351.

12.   Jack Fiorito and Cheryl L. Maranto, "The Contemporary Decline of Union Strength," *Contemporary Policy Issues,* n. 3 (July 1987): 12–27.

13.   Henry S. Farber, "The Extent of Unionization in the United States," *Challenges and Choices Facing American Labor,* ed. Thomas A. Kochan (Cambridge, MA: MIT Press, 1985), pp. 15–43.

14.   Common management campaign election tactics are discussed more fully in the next chapter.

15.   Seymour Martin Lipset, "North American Labor Movements: A Comparative Perspective," in *Unions in Transition,* ed. Seymour Martin Lipset (San Francisco: ICS Press, 1986), pp. 421–452.

16.   Peter G. Bruce, "Political Parties and Labor Legislation in Canada and the U.S.," *Industrial Relations* 28 (Spring 1989): 115–141.

17.   See Paula Voos, "Union Organizing: Costs and Benefits," *Industrial and Labor Relations Review* 36 (July 1983): 576–591.

18.   Richard B. Freeman, "Why Are Unions Faring So Poorly in NLRB Representation Elections?" in *Challenges and Choices Facing American Labor,* pp. 45–64; William T. Dickens and Jonathan S. Leonard, "Accounting for the Decline in Union Membership, 1950–1980," *Industrial and Labor Relations Review* 38 (April 1985): 323–334.

19.   For a comprehensive assessment of union mergers see Gary N. Chaison, *When Unions Merge* (Lexington, MA: D.C. Heath, 1986).

20.   Arthur Goldberg, *AFL-CIO: Labor United* (New York: McGraw-Hill, 1956), p. 229.

21.   "Overall Number of Unions Fell during 1980s Due to Mergers," *Daily Labor Report* (Washington, D.C.: Bureau of National Affairs, November 19, 1990), p. C–1.

22.   For a critical view of union mergers, see George W. Brooks and Sara Gamm, *The Causes and Effects of Union Mergers,* report to the U.S. Department of Labor (September 1976).

23.   See "Overall Number of Unions Fell during 1980s," p. C–1.

24.   AFL-CIO Committee on the Evolution of Work, *The Changing Situation of Workers and Their Unions* (Washington, D.C.: AFL-CIO, February 1985).

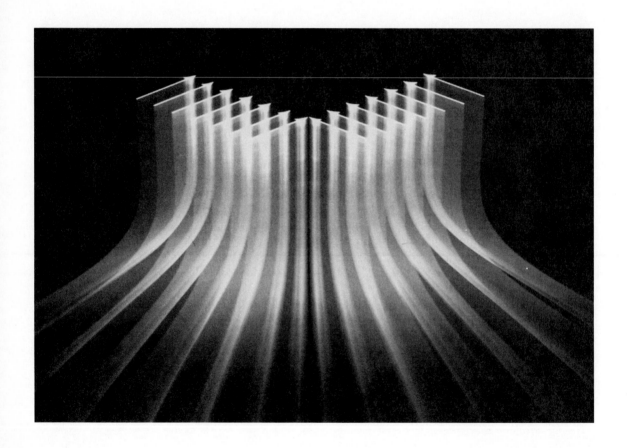

PART 3

THE FUNCTIONAL
LEVEL OF
INDUSTRIAL
RELATIONS

Chapter 7

Union Organizing
and Bargaining Structures

Chapters 7, 8, 9, and 10 examine the middle (functional) level of industrial relations activity. The focus in this chapter is on the election process that creates, or organizes labor into, new unions and the bargaining structures that determine which employees are covered by a collective bargaining contract.

In some ways the representation election is the most important step in collective bargaining. If unorganized workers vote not to be represented by a union, for instance, collective bargaining cannot proceed. On the other hand, positive expression of worker interest in such an election opens the way for subsequent bargaining.

Various environmental factors shape the parties' power and preferences in the organizing process. The law, for example, plays a prominent role in union organizing drives and representation elections. Environmental factors also exert an important influence on the determination of the formal bargaining structures through which a union and management engage in bargaining. Strike leverage and the economic environment, for example, are prominent not only in their effects on organizing success but also in shaping the parties' preferences for particular bargaining structures.

Union Organizing

Negotiations cannot take place until a bargaining representative has been duly certified as the exclusive representative of the employees. Normally, this requires that a union win a representation election (although an employer may voluntarily recognize a union if the union can demonstrate that it represents a majority of the employees involved).[1] The events and regulations that surround representation elections are described below.

The Organizing Process

The key steps in the organizing and representation election process are described in Box 7–1. Note that before the NLRB will schedule an election, at least 30 percent of the election unit must have signed an **authorization card** indicating they would like an election to be held. To understand how the organizing process works, it is useful to step back and first ask why an individual might seek union representation.

Why Workers Might Want Union Representation Evidence shows that for workers to express a preference for unionizing they must (1) be deeply dissatisfied with their current job and employment conditions, (2) believe that unionization can be helpful in improving those job conditions, and (3) be willing to overcome the generally negative stereotype of unions held by the population as a whole.

Workers might turn to unions because of their concerns with employment conditions or because they are unsatisfied with the process by which decisions are made at their workplace. Thus, workers might, for example, vote in favor of the union in the hope that subsequent contractual negotiations will improve wages. Or, a worker might be angered by a recent managerial decision, such as a layoff or a disappointing performance appraisal. In these cases the worker might turn to the union with the hope that the union will either improve future management decisions or, at a minimum, give employees greater voice in the process by which future decisions are made.

Union Campaign Practices Unions commonly rely on organizers to rally employee support during election campaigns. These organizers often include paid full-time staff from existing unions who travel from campaign to campaign. The union also often enlists some of the existing workforce to assist as organizers. Organizers and union supporters use a variety of mechanisms to try to promote a pro-union message. Group meetings are often held after work hours in a local church or community meeting room. Or, union supporters who have the opportunity to move around the plant (often these are craft workers) might spread the message during work hours.[2]

Management's Campaign Practices Management is rarely a passive observer in the election process. Management often tries to design personnel and other corporate policies far in advance of any representation election to dissuade employees from favoring union representation. It is useful to review these tactics because they can be as important to

Box 7–1

Steps in the Union-Organizing and Representation Election Process

1. Interested employees seek out a union to learn their rights and gain help in organizing, or a union seeks out a group of employees in order to explain their rights and explore their interest in organizing.

2. The union builds support for organizing among the employees and solicits their signatures on authorization cards.

3. When sufficient cards are signed to indicate substantial employee support, the union asks for recognition as the bargaining agent for the employees. If at least 30 percent of the employees have signed cards, the union can petition for an NLRB certification election. If over 50 percent of the employees have signed cards, the union can ask the employer for recognition, or, if this is refused and serious unfair labor practices are committed by the employer, the union can ask the NLRB for certification. If the employer does not voluntarily recognize the union, either party can petition for an NLRB certification election to determine whether the union has majority support.

4. The NLRB investigates to determine whether an election should be held. The board considers the issues of whether it has jurisdiction, whether there is sufficient interest among the workers, and whether there is already a bargaining agent or there had been an election within the past 12 months. Most importantly, the NLRB determines the appropriate bargaining unit.

5. If the NLRB finds that the conditions for an election have been met, it orders that one be held. Procedures of varying formality are used, depending on the level of disagreement between the parties. Expedited procedures can be used if the union has engaged in organizational or recognitional picketing.

6. With the election date set, campaigning on both sides intensifies. Restrictions apply to both union and management behavior during this period, in an attempt to maintain "laboratory conditions," that is, to allow the workers to make free, uncoerced choices.

7. Representatives of the NLRB conduct a secret-ballot election. An individual's right to vote can be challenged by the union, by management, or by the NLRB. If there are more than two choices on the ballot and no option receives a majority vote, a runoff election will be held between the two choices that received the most votes.

8. If the union wins the election, then, following any objections or appeals, the NLRB certifies the union as the exclusive bargaining agent for the employees. The employer has the obligation to begin negotiating a first contract. If the employer wins the election, there can be no further election for 12 months.

the election outcome as the tactics management might carry out during an election campaign.

Common strategies used by management before the onset of organizing campaigns to reduce the incentives to unionize include most, if not all, of the following:

1. Wages and fringe benefits equal to or greater than those paid comparable workers in the local labor market

2. A high rate of investment per worker in such employee programs as training and career development

3. Extensive efforts to stabilize employment and avoid layoffs as much as possible

4. Advanced systems of organizational communications and information sharing

5. Informal mechanisms for, or encouragement of, participation in decision making about the way work is to be performed

6. Development of a psychological climate that fosters and rewards organizational loyalty and commitment

7. Rational wage and salary administration, performance appraisal, and promotion systems that reward merit but also recognize seniority

8. A nonunion grievance procedure (usually without binding arbitration)

9. Location of new production facilities in rural areas or areas only sparsely unionized

Management does not always have the will or foresight to put all the above policies in place. And even where some of them are in place, election campaigns can arise.

If faced with a representation election, management typically will adopt a number of tactics in an effort to convince employees to vote against union representation. Management will call meetings with employees (these might be individual or group) to explain its case. Under the NLRA management is allowed to hold these meetings on company time and in company facilities (the law allows so-called **captive audience speeches** up to 24 hours before the vote).[3] During such a meeting a management spokesperson (such as the company president) might remind the employees of the direct costs of union membership (dues) or the potential losses in income employees could withstand during any strikes that ensue.

During the election campaign employers are not allowed by the NLRA to threaten to punish workers if they join or vote for a union. The NLRA also forbids employers from making promises to workers that might encourage them to reject the union. But an employer may make a prediction about the future if the prediction is based on fact. So an employer may say workers could be laid off if the union wins the election and successfully negotiates for a 50-cent raise—provided the employer has the evidence that a 50-cent raise would lead to layoffs.[4]

It is now common for firms to hire consultants or law firms to either shape or directly carry out management's campaign. The material in Box 7–2 depict some of the campaign literature issued by the union and management involved in the same organizing election. Imagine that you were an employee involved in this campaign and you received this literature. Would this material sway your decision to vote for or against union representation?

The Election Unit

The election unit serves as the basis for the bargaining unit. The **election unit** is the group of employees that the NLRB (or the appropriate state agency with jurisdiction over the employees involved) determines is covered under the appropriate statute and is eligible to vote in the representation election.

Two main decisions must be made to define the appropriate election unit. First, the range of employees to be included must be decided. This may involve choosing between a craft election unit structure (covering only workers in a single occupation) and an industrial election unit structure (for example, all the blue-collar production and maintenance workers within a plant) and between employees at one plant or location and employees at multiple plants or job sites. Second, the issue of who functions as a supervisor or manager must be decided because, since the passage in 1947 of the Taft-Hartley amendments to the National Labor Relations Act, supervisors have been excluded from coverage of the act.

The Scope of the Unit—The NLRB's Criteria   Since the composition of the electorate can influence the outcome of the election, the scope of the election unit is often a hotly contested issue. Quite simply, the union typically will seek an election unit that maximizes its ability to win the election, and the employer will seek a unit that minimizes the union's chances of winning. The NLRA states that the fundamental objective in choosing an election unit should be to ensure that employees have "the full freedom in exercising the rights guaranteed by this act."

The NLRB and the state and local boards normally consider the following general criteria in deciding on the appropriate election unit:

1. The community of interests among the employees

2. The potential effects of alternative units on stability in the labor-management relationship

3. The need to provide sufficient freedom of choice to professional and skilled employees

4. The history of bargaining or the employer's decision-making structure.

This fourth criterion is useful in resolving disputes between the parties over whether certain employees should be excluded because they perform supervisory or managerial functions.

Whether craft workers are put into the same election unit as production workers in the same plant (or company) is a difficult part of the election unit determination process. Although Section 9 (b) (2) of the Taft-Hartley Act was designed to limit the NLRB's ability to put craft workers into industrial election units, the board has consistently rejected petitions to exclude craft workers from the large industrial units. Indeed, the board has argued that the interdependence between craft workers and production workers warrants a single comprehensive unit.[5]

The NLRB has been somewhat more willing to grant professional employees a separate bargaining unit. Section 9(b) of Taft-Hartley prohibits the NLRB from including professional employees in a bargaining unit with nonprofessional employees unless the professionals decide by a majority vote to be included in a larger, more comprehensive unit.

Election Unit Determination in Hospitals The spread of bargaining to hospitals and the public sector has raised a number of questions about appropriate election units. Hospitals, for example, exhibit a wide range of fine distinctions among various professional and quasi-professional employees and vast differences in the nature of the tasks each group performs. The NLRB was asked to determine whether these various employees should be put into common election units when unions sought to organize various hospitals in the 1970s and 1980s. Should registered nurses, practical nurses, and nurses' aides all be included in a single unit, for example, or should they be separated into three distinct units for the purposes of a representation election? Should nurses be in the same election unit as hospital office or laboratory staffs?

The NLRB resolved these questions initially by establishing separate units for each of the following: registered nurses and laboratory specialists; business office and clerical employees; and service and maintenance employees. Later decisions of the NLRB, however, favored fewer and broader units. In 1990 the NLRB again reversed itself and decided to favor narrow units. Hospital employers then appealed this decision to the federal courts, where the debate continues.

Union Organizing Success Rates

Since 1974, labor unions have won slightly fewer than half of all the elections conducted. This figure declined steadily after 1964, when unions

Box 7-2

An Example of Management's Campaign Literature

April 1991

Dear Fellow Employee:

Think about the election which will be held here at the plant on April 21. It is extremely important that we consider some very important things. What has our company done for you over the years? We provide jobs and a job today, particularly a steady one, is not as easy to get and hold on to as it was at one time. You know and I know that your company pays good wages and provides good fringe benefits such as paid holidays, paid vacations, pension plan and a group hospital and life insurance plan. Also, NEVER FORGET THE CHRISTMAS BONUS EACH YEAR AND THE AMOUNT OF THE BONUS. Yes, your Company was interested in you long before the union organizers came along with their bill for union dues, assessments, per capita tax and all these other names the union boys have for getting money out of the paychecks of employees.

Who are these outside union organizers and why are they here? They live off money collected by the Union from members and they don't sell anything—except wild promises which they cannot guarantee. Now they have the nerve to ask you to help pay their expenses and their salaries. If this Union should win this election—though I know you will not allow this to happen as you have rejected this same bunch many times in the past years—one of the first things the Union would want is a "dues checkoff." This would mean that if you authorized it, union dues would be deducted from your paycheck and paid directly to the union. Yes, the Union wants to make sure they get their hook in you and keep it in you. Has the Union told you that this is what they will ask for? What about all the rules and regulations of this Union? There are two Union constitutions involved and they total over 95 pages. Were you given a copy of these rules and regulations by the Union organizers when they came to your home at night?

Talk this election over with your family. This is important to all of you. Remember—the Union did not give you your job and has never paid your wages and never will—the only thing a Union can truly guarantee is that Union members will have to pay the Union money—each and every month!

VOTE NO—MEANING NO UNION!

Sincerely,

John Smith
President

Strength.

That's what it takes to build a Union.
That's always what it takes to do what's right.

On Friday, just two days from now, we have a chance to show our strength.

—*It takes* **strength** *to talk seriously about the real issues: Insurance, 9-Day Rule, Seniority, Holidays, Funeral Pay, Favoritism, Respect on the Job.*

—*It takes* **strength** *to answer the tough questions.*

—*It takes* **strength** *to build an organization to make better lives for ourselves and our families.*

—*It even takes* **strength** *to sit there and listen to Mr. Smith's speeches knowing he refuses a fair, open, public debate.*

But we've done it. And we're proud of it!

We're strong. We're United. We're going to win!

For Our Families. For Our Future.

VOTE  YES !

won 61 percent of all the representation elections held. In 1988, unions won 46.3 percent (1,921 out of 4,153) of the representation elections held.[6] In large, multiplant companies unions have had trouble even securing enough signed authorization cards to certify to the board that an election should be held.[7]

Furthermore, even if a union wins a majority vote in a representation election this does not ensure that a first contract will be negotiated. The NLRA requires that employers (and the union) bargain in good faith, but the law does not require that the parties reach agreement. In fact, first contracts are won in only roughly two-thirds of newly designated units.

Research has shown that workers tend to become less inclined to vote for union representation if the election is delayed.[8] Studies also show that illegal employer behavior during the election campaign (a signal of aggressive employer opposition to bargaining) further reduces the probability that a first contract will be settled.[9] Evidence also shows that firms with previously poor worker-supervisor relations and low wages are more likely to commit unfair labor practice violations during election campaigns.[10]

Does the Election Campaign Influence How Workers Vote?

There is controversial evidence over the extent to which election campaigns actually affect how individuals vote in representation elections. In the 1970s, for example, Julius Getman, Stephen Goldberg, and Jeanne Herman studied more than 30 election campaigns and concluded that illegal campaign tactics by *either* employers or unions had little effect on individual voting or on election outcomes.[11] They therefore argued that the NLRB should expend less effort in regulating campaign conduct (specifically, by investigating the accuracy of campaign statements, promises of benefits, or threats by either party).[12]

Reanalysis of the Getman data and other studies of NLRB elections, however, shows that employer strategies both before and during election processes *do* significantly reduce the probability that a union will win an election.[13] Moreover, it also appears that employer opposition significantly reduces the chances that a union that wins a representation election will be successful in negotiating a first contract.[14]

Union Decertification

Unions gain members through winning union representation elections; they lose members through **decertification elections.** The 1947 Taft-Hartley amendments to the NLRA prescribed election procedures for decertifying a union.

The decertification elections held since Taft-Hartley have been far fewer than the representation elections, but in recent years their number has been increasing and unions have been losing an increasing percentage of these contests. The first year after passage of Taft-Hartley, for example, witnessed 97 decertification elections, or only 3 percent of the 3,822 representation elections held that year. That percentage held steady throughout the 1950s and 1960s but began creeping upward in the 1970s and held steady in the 1980s. In 1988 the ratio stood at 21 percent.[15]

Although decertification elections have increased, most union members appear to be satisfied by their unions and union leaders. In two national surveys, for example, union members gave largely positive ratings of their union representation overall. In a 1984 Harris survey 75 percent of the union members responding indicated they were satisfied or very satisfied with their unions. And in the 1982 National Longitudinal Survey of adult men, union members gave an even stronger endorsement of unionism in general. When asked how they would vote if a union representation election were held on their current job, 87 percent said they would vote to continue union representation.[16]

The Debate over Labor Law Reform

Unions' low win rate in representation elections has led to much debate over whether the endorsement of collective bargaining that is provided in the NLRA is being fulfilled. Remember, the original objective of the law was to assure that employees are able to exercise free choice regarding union representation, untrammeled by false promises or information, threats of reprisals or promises of benefits, or misuse of economic power by the employer or the union.[17] To carry out this objective, the NLRB (and most state labor boards) attempted to establish **laboratory conditions** for the election process. The notion was that workers should be free to judge whether they wanted union representation in an environment free of coercion and misinformation.

Advocates of **labor law reform** often argue that penalties imposed on employers who commit unlawful behavior during an election campaign are too weak. Furthermore, they claim that the procedures for remedying unfair labor practices and or holding representation elections are too protracted. Box 7–3 summarizes a number of the recommendations that have been made by advocates of labor law reform.

The last major congressional debate over labor law reform occurred in 1977 and 1978. Labor law reform bills introduced then would have imposed harsher penalties on labor law violators, required stricter time limits on the election process, and provided stronger remedies for victims of unfair labor practices. The bills were not passed (one bill passed the House of Representatives, but died in a filibuster in the Senate in 1978). In 1991, Congress debated labor law amendments that would limit employers' ability to hire permanent replacements during a strike. The debate continues over the performance of the nation's labor policies.

Box 7–3

Selected Proposals for Reforming Representation Election Procedures

1. Provide unions with rights of access to employees for campaign purposes equal to the access enjoyed by employers.

2. Stop attempting to regulate statements by employers or unions made as part of election campaigns.

3. Speed up the enforcement of current rules governing elections, and strengthen the penalties imposed on violators of the law by:
   a. using court injunctions to stop and/or remedy serious violations of the law, such as discriminatory discharges during campaigns;
   b. reinstating employees quickly, in time to allow union supporters to return to employment *before* the campaign is over and the vote is held;
   c. allowing employees or the union to sue for civil damages in cases of an employer's willful violation of an employee's rights; and
   d. lifting the constraint on the amount of the settlement available to an employee in cases where employer conduct exhibits a consistent pattern of illegal behavior. (Under current law a court can only award a settlement equal to the wages lost by an employee since the time of discharge.)

4. Conduct speedy elections, with a very short time allowed for campaigning.

5. Strengthen the ability of a union to strike to achieve a first contract by eliminating the ability of an employer to permanently replace strikers and by allowing other workers to boycott the goods of an employer on strike.

6. Require arbitration of first contracts if an impasse occurs.

Sources: Paul C. Weiler, "Milestone or Millstone: The Wagner Act at Fifty," in *Arbitration 1985: Law and Practice,* ed. Walter J. Gershenfeld (Washington, D.C.: Bureau of National Affairs, 1986), pp. 37–67, and Charles J. Morris, *American Labor Policy: A Critical Appraisal of the National Labor Relations Act* (Washington, D.C.: Bureau of National Affairs, 1987).

Nontraditional Union Organizing Tactics

Corporate Campaigns

Given the great difficulties they have been faced with by using traditional election campaign tactics, several unions have adopted more aggressive **corporate campaigns** and other tactics designed to increase the chances of organizing new workers. **Corporate campaigns** involve a variety of union efforts to bring public, financial, or political pressures to bear on top management.

In its extensive corporate campaign against the J. P. Stevens Company in the late 1970s, for example, the Amalgamated Clothing and Textile Workers Union (ACTWU) waged a successful national boycott of Stevens products, threatened to withdraw the union pension funds from banks that had officers on Stevens' board, and, eventually, after almost a decade of effort, negotiated its first contract with the company in 1981. Similar efforts have been mounted in recent years in attempts to organize the operations of such firms as Beverly Nursing Homes and Litton Industries.[18]

Most of the union corporate campaigns have been accompanied by strategies designed to influence the firm involved in the election indirectly by pressuring individuals or other firms that do business with or have interlocking directorates with the firm. These efforts attest to the unfairness labor leaders perceive and the frustrations they have experienced with the election process as it has been administered by the NLRB.

The AFL-CIO Organizing Institute

The AFL-CIO admitted the difficulties unions confronted in organizing in the well-publicized Evolution of Work report in 1985. In 1989 the AFL-CIO implemented one of the recommendations of the report by creating a new **AFL-CIO Organizing Institute.** The AFL-CIO has long had a department of organization and field services. The Organizing Institute is unique through its exclusive focus on organizing and through the clinical programs used to train new organizers. In addition to recruitment and training of new organizers, the institute also provides affiliated unions with strategic planning and analysis for organizing campaigns.

One of the purposes of the institute is to diffuse some of the successful organizing strategies used by affiliated unions. Unions such as the Amalgamated Clothing and Textile Workers Union and the United Food and Commercial Workers had above average success in their organizing. The campaigns of these unions use young, well-educated organizers and involve both extensive direct communication with prospective members and links to community groups such as churches.

The Organizing Institute uses experienced organizers in its clinical programs and also is experimenting with sending organizer recruits into the field to learn from active organizers. It is still too early to tell if the Organizing Institute will have a significant impact on union-organizing success.[19]

Voluntary Recognition

The NLRA allows employers to voluntarily recognize a union. The law, of course, also allows employers to remain neutral during a representation election campaign. In the 1940s and 1950s it was not uncommon for employers to either adopt **voluntary recognition** or maintain **employer election neutrality** during election campaigns. Employers' voluntary recognition of a union or neutrality in representation elections have declined relative to their use in the 1940s and 1950s. Nonetheless, there are some important exceptions to this trend.

The Xerox Case   Xerox is one exception. The Xerox Corporation has a bargaining relationship with ACTWU that dates back to the 1930s. Because Joseph Wilson, the company's founder, believed strongly in the value of a positive labor-management climate and relationship, the company has historically remained neutral or unopposed to ACTWU's representing Xerox production and maintenance workers when the company opened new plants. (Yet it is still the union's responsibility to seek and achieve recognition, either through an election or by presenting management with evidence that a majority of the workers have signed cards authorizing the union to represent them.)

Xerox shows that employer election neutrality can yield management some positive benefits. Relationships between the union and the company have been quite cooperative and innovative over the years. Xerox and ACTWU have been pioneers in introducing a variety of forms of employee participation and work organization redesign into their manufacturing bargaining units. In the 1980s the parties extended their participation efforts to joint discussions of where to build a new plant and how to design its work system.

The General Motors Case   The history of union recognition and its relationship to the existing bargaining units at General Motors Corporation is equally instructive. In the early 1970s GM opened a number of new, nonunion plants in the south and was successful in keeping them nonunion despite United Automobile Workers (UAW) efforts to organize them. But in its 1976 negotiations with the company, the UAW insisted that GM agree to remain neutral in future organizing efforts in the new plants, and the union prevailed. Then in 1979 the parties agreed to an accretion clause, which provided that any new plants opened that did work traditionally done by UAW members would automatically be included in the bargaining unit and represented by the union. The union achieved these provisions by making it clear to the company that the UAW could not continue to cooperate with GM in expanding quality of working life and other joint activities in existing sites if the company was determined to fight the union over union representation rights in the new facilities.

In 1985 GM and the UAW took this process one step further by jointly planning the design of the labor-management relationship and the work system to be included in a new division of the corporation created to build small cars. The agreement governing this new Saturn Division raised serious objections from conservative, anti-union groups. They argued that the agreement violated the NLRA because it established union recognition before employees had been hired and therefore did not give the new employees an opportunity to vote for or against union representation. The NLRB rejected this argument and let the agreement stand on grounds that there was a sufficient connection between the Saturn operations and other unionized GM facilities. Many of the workers who went to work at Saturn had previously worked at other GM facilities. Many of them applied for work at Saturn after becoming unemployed when their home GM plant closed.

The Xerox and GM cases illustrate how employer election neutrality can contribute positively toward fostering a more cooperative labor-management relationship. Union leaders often argue that management should provide unions the opportunity to benefit from new investments and represent employees in new establishments. In some cases management agrees and accepts unions in new establishments if the unions demonstrate flexibility and a commitment to labor-management cooperation.

One of the key strategic choices facing management is whether to contest unionism during a representation election or to voluntarily recognize the union in return for a more cooperative union-management relationship. The Saturn agreement is only the most visible of several that might become a model for those who make the latter decision.

Bargaining Structure

Once unionization occurs, whether through an election or some other procedure, then bargaining over a contract ensues. *Bargaining structure* refers to the *scope* of the employees and employers covered or affected by the bargaining agreement.

Labor and management do not necessarily bargain contracts that only cover election units. For example, the employees in the various plants of one employer represented by a union may wish to join together to negotiate a common contract covering the whole company. In the auto, rubber, and other industries where industrial unions are present there are companywide collective bargaining agreements. In addition, employees represented by the same union in a number of companies may prefer to ban together and try to negotiate a common contract covering all the companies. This occurs in the coal, construction, and trucking industries. Such company or industrywide bargaining may not develop if the employees (or unions) prefer to bargain in a more decentralized manner and thereby maintain plant level or company level bargaining.

Employee and union preferences are not the only determinants of the bargaining structure, however. Before we trace some of the determinants of bargaining structure, we need some definitions.

Definitions of Bargaining Structure

The **formal bargaining structure** is defined as the *bargaining unit,* or the *negotiation unit* —that is, the employees and employers who are legally bound by the terms of an agreement. The **informal bargaining structure** is defined as the employees or employers who are *affected* by the results of a negotiated settlement, through either *pattern bargaining* or some other nonbinding process.

The U.S. Bureau of Labor Statistics estimates that between 180,000 and 194,000 separate bargaining agreements currently exist in the United States. Many labor contracts in this country cover members of one local union at a single employment site.

The Decentralization of Bargaining Structure in the United States

In comparison to other countries, the United States has a highly **decentralized bargaining structure.** In many European countries, such as Germany and Sweden, many labor contracts cover entire industries or broad regions.[20] In recent years, however, many European employers have been arguing for greater decentralization of bargaining to allow individual firms the latitude to adjust to their particular economic circumstances.[21] Many U.S. employers are pressing for even further decentralization of the formal and informal structures of bargaining in this country, as well.

Types of Bargaining Units

The two primary characteristics of a bargaining structure are (1) the scope of *employee or union* interests represented in the unit, which can be either narrow craft or broad industrial or multiskill, and (2) the scope of *employer* interests represented in the unit, which can be multiemployer (centralized), single employer-multiplant, or single employer-single plant (decentralized).

Exhibit 7–1 illustrates this classification of bargaining structures. The vertical axis of the figure depicts the breadth of employee interests. For instance, in a single-employer-multiplant environment, a narrow bargaining unit might include only those craft or professional employees within one occupational class. Police, fire fighters, railroad workers, teachers, and airline pilots are examples of occupations typically represented in bargaining for narrow craft units. At the other end of the spectrum are the broad bargaining units that might include all the production and skilled employees in a firm. Such industrial unions bargain contracts that cover broad employee units in the auto, steel, farm equipment, state government, and textile industries.

Exhibit 7–1
Types and Examples of Bargaining Structures

EMPLOYEE INTERESTS COVERED	EMPLOYER INTERESTS COVERED		
	Multiemployer (Centralized)	Single-employer– Multiplant	Single-employer– Single Plant (Decentralized)
Craft (Narrow)	Construction trades Interstate trucking Longshoring Hospital association	Airline Teachers Police Firefighters Railroad	Craft union in small manufacturing plant Hospital
Industrial or Multiskill (Broad)	Coal mining (underground) Basic steel (pre-1986) Hotel association	Automobiles Steel (post 1986) Farm equipment State government Textile	Industrial union in small manufacturing plant

There are also intermediate cases in which more than one, but not all the various union-represented employees in a firm, bargain in the same unit. A manufacturing plant where a number of the craft workers bargain together would be such a case.

The horizontal axis of Exhibit 7–1 depicts the range, or the degree of centralization, of employer interests in the bargaining unit. A unit representing only one plant is an example of the most decentralized bargaining unit. An example of this is where a union negotiates a contract for the electrical (or production) workers in one plant.

A highly **centralized bargaining structure** covers all the plants of a number of companies with the same collective bargaining agreement. Although multiemployer bargaining units are relatively rare in the United States, some do exist. In the trucking industry, for example, a number of over-the-road (intercity and interstate) trucking companies have for a number of years bargained a single contract (the National Master Freight Agreement) with the Teamsters union to cover their unionized drivers. The coal industry has long had a master agreement negotiated with the United Mine Workers that covers the unionized mine workers in the mines of a number of coal companies. These multiemployer units are also found in the construction, longshoring, hotel, and (in some cities) hospital industries. In all these cases an employer association represents management at the bargaining table. These centralized agreements might cover a number of different employers either within a given locality (such as all of the voluntary hospitals in New York City) or within an industry (such as those coal producers that are members of the Bituminous Coal Operators' Association).

The intermediate case along the employer centralization dimension is found when a single contract covers multiple plants of one employer. The automobile, steel, farm equipment, textile industry, and many state governments use this intermediate bargaining structure. In these cases employers with more than one plant negotiate a single contract that covers employees in a number of plants as opposed to having a separate contract for each plant. Typically, these company agreements are supplemented with local agreements that cover those working conditions specific to a given plant.

Another intermediate employer case occurs in public school districts where commonly a single agreement covers all the unionized teachers across the various schools within the district. Police and fire fighters also commonly have one contract that covers the various (plant) sites in a city.

Determinants of Bargaining Structures

The major forces that affect the degree of centralization in bargaining structures are bargaining leverage, public policies, and organizational factors. How each of these factors influences bargaining structure is examined below.

Bargaining Leverage

Unions can increase their bargaining leverage if they organize a large share of the product market. One of the primary mechanisms for ensuring that wages are taken out of competition is to expand the bargaining structure to correspond with the scope of the market. But to achieve a high degree of employer centralization in the bargaining structure, unions usually must first organize a large proportion of the **product market** and then successfully maintain union coverage over time—a tall order.

This process is well illustrated by John R. Commons' famous account of early unionism among Philadelphia shoemakers. Commons described how in the absence of broad and aggressive unionism shoemakers were harmfully affected by the expansion of the shoe market (the product market) that had come about in the early 1800s because of improved transportation.[22] As it became possible for nonunion shoemakers outside the Philadelphia area to transport their products into the Philadelphia market and sell them at a low price, the bargaining power of the unionized shoemakers in Philadelphia was weakened. It therefore became important for the Philadelphia shoemakers to organize their fellow shoemakers from the surrounding areas and to see them covered under the same wage agreement to equalize and raise the price of labor.

Unions representing construction workers, for example, have a strong incentive to equalize the wage costs among competitive bidders on the same product. Thus, in the construction industry unions prefer bargaining with the multiple employers who are involved in a specific construction project. For example, where builders across a city bid for the contract to build an office building, the union representing carpenters in that city will try to bargain in a structure that spans the contractors across the city.

Employers Prefer Centralized Bargaining Structures in Some Cases   It should not be inferred that unions *always* gain (and employers always lose) a tactical advantage in larger or more centralized bargaining structures. Employers in the local service industries (such as hotels, restaurants, laundries, and local truck haulers) have often found it to their advantage to form associations and to bargain in multiemployer units.

For instance, consolidating the bargaining function allows employers to avoid being **whipsawed** by local union leaders. Union **whipsawing** occurs when a union negotiates a bargain at one plant or company and then puts pressure on the next plant or company to equal or surpass the contract terms just negotiated at the first site. The unions in the airline industry were able to follow this whipsawing strategy until the late 1970s. By consolidating the bargaining structure, however, employers can sometimes reduce the possibility of such union whipsawing. (Employers can also whipsaw a union when they gain a power advantage.)

Centralized Bargaining Can Stabilize Competition   In some cases a centralized bargaining structure can serve employer interests by stabilizing competition. Employers in small firms in a highly competitive industry may find it to their advantage to bargain centrally with a union. This can reduce the union's ability to whipsaw the small firms. If a strike occurs, the centralized bargaining structure also ensures that no single employer can gain an advantage because all the firms are shut down simultaneously.

The case in which an employer gains from centralized bargaining is well illustrated by the apparel industry. Employers have come to depend on the stability the apparel unions historically provided to their highly competitive industry. Labor costs are a significant component of total costs to the many small firms in the industry, and unionized employers are receptive to the wage standardization imposed by the union. Wage standardization ensures that competition across firms does not depend on their ability to gain low labor costs. The union representing apparel workers likes the centralized employer bargaining structure as this structure helps the union take wages out of competition.

Public Policies

Another crucial determinant of bargaining unit structures is the structure of the election unit imposed by the NLRB in a representation election. If the NLRB certifies the proper election unit to be an industrial unit, for example, this precludes a craft bargaining structure.

The influence of the NLRB is well illustrated by events at General Electric. For a number of years throughout the 1960s the unions representing General Electric (GE) workers attempted to engage in *coalition bargaining* but met with strong resistance from the company. **Coalition bargaining** would have meant that a number of the unions representing employees at GE would sit at the negotiating table even when the contract with only one union was under discussion. The NLRB decided to allow the unions to engage in this form of coalition bargaining with GE. Other influential board decisions have been made on whether the employer can withdraw from the multiemployer bargaining unit after having given proper notice before the start of negotiations or only after an impasse has been reached.

Some have argued that the NLRB has exhibited a strong preference for larger bargaining units and thus has aided in the trend toward greater centralization. George W. Brooks has been one of the most articulate critics of the board's preference for large production and maintenance bargaining units and against craft severance.[23] He argued that the preference for centralization reduced employees' free choice among alternative unions and made it impossible for individual members to effectively influence the direction of their unions. This, in turn, he believed, produced undemocratic and unresponsive unions.

Organizational Factors

The internal organizational characteristics of employers also have generated pressures to broaden the bargaining unit. In particular, the growth of large corporations and the centralization of managerial decision making have led unions to seek centralized bargaining structures. A fundamental principle underlying their efforts is that in many cases, unions will benefit if the structure of bargaining is coterminous with the level at which the critical management decisions are being made. That is, if management is making most industrial relations decisions at the company level, then the union would often prefer to have bargaining occur at this level as well.

Bargaining Structure in the Telephone Industry   The telephone industry illustrates how management's organizational structure has influenced bargaining structure. The gradual centralization of managerial decision-making power within AT&T that occurred from the 1940s through the 1970s led, first, to the merger of many of the independent unions of telephone workers into the Communications Workers of America (CWA), a national union, and, then, to the development of a centralized, nationwide contract and bargaining structure.[24] Box 7–4 provides a chronology of the structure of bargaining between the Bell System and the CWA as it evolved over the past 50 years.

After World War II, AT&T centralized its industrial relations policy-making in its corporate headquarters in New York. In the 1950s and 1960s, however, the CWA still bargained separately with each state affiliate of the Bell System. Consequently, throughout the 1960s the union sought to bring about a more centralized or national bargaining arrangement. Although CWA succeeded in negotiating a national contract in 1974, the breakup of the Bell System into regional telephone companies in 1984 forced a return to decentralized bargaining in the CWA's subsequent negotiations with the new regional telephone companies. But even after the breakup, since AT&T remained a company of national scope with a centralized management, bargaining involving AT&T employees remained centralized at the national level.

Bargaining Structure in the Trucking Industry On the other hand, the trucking industry illustrates how management may attempt to counter union centralization with a centralization of managerial decision-making power. In the 1950s James R. Hoffa, president of the Teamsters, sought to improve the bargaining power of the union and to consolidate his own power within the union by centralizing the structure of bargaining for the over-the-road (intercity and interstate) truckers. As Hoffa's drive succeeded, employers created a national truckers' association to conduct negotiations and to centralize some of the trucking firms' decision-making. Then, when the Teamsters lost market share to nonunion firms in the 1980s, a number of truck companies pulled out of the truckers' association and the bargaining structure in trucking started to decentralize.

Coordinated Bargaining In settings where no single union dominates in representing a firm's employees, the Industrial Union Department (IUD) of the AFL-CIO has attempted to coordinate bargaining. In recent years the IUD coordinated some 80 such contracts with its affiliated unions. The success of this coordinated bargaining, however, depends to a great degree on the ability and the willingness of the different unions to work together and to maintain the support of their **rank-and-file** members. Longstanding coordinated bargaining arrangements can be found in the electrical products, glass, and machinery industries and in a number of highly diversified conglomerates such as General Electric, Pittsburgh Plate Glass, and Textron.

The Influence of Diverse Labor and Management Interests

In order to participate in centralized bargaining local union officials or managers have to give up some of their independent authority and conform to centralized decisions and leaders. Needless to say, local union-

---

Box 7–4

The Evolution of a Bargaining Structure: AT&T and Its Unions

1855	AT&T incorporated to provide long-distance service linking the separate Bell Telephone companies.
1937	Bell System employee associations sever ties with the telephone companies to form a federation of local unions, the National Federation of Telephone Workers (NFTW).
1940	First collective bargaining agreement signed between New York Telephone and a local of the NFTW.
1940–45	Separate agreements signed with other Bell System companies: NFTW membership grows from 45,000 in 1939 to 170,000 in 1945. Telephone workers included in wage pattern set by "Little Steel" formula established by the War Labor Board.
1946	NFTW threatens to call a national strike against AT&T Long Lines in an effort to achieve a national pattern. Contract settled with intervention by the U.S. Secretary of Labor, with AT&T agreeing to use the agreement as a pattern for settlements with the Bell System companies. In 1946 difficulties in negotiating a national agreement serve as an impetus for NFTW to reorganize for more centralized control of the union.
1947	National strike against AT&T to get a national agreement is defeated. AT&T insists on local bargaining, claiming that they do not control the operating companies' labor relations policy. In the aftermath of the strike union membership falls below 50% in many places around the country. The Communications Workers of America (CWA) is then founded with the goal of achieving national bargaining with AT&T. Most Bell System workers join the CWA; some are represented by the International Brotherhood of Electrical Workers (IBEW); others remain in the Telephone Independent Union (TIU).
1951	U.S. Senate Labor Committee investigation finds that AT&T controls the labor relations of the operating companies. There are AT&T-controlled benefits plants, which limit the unions' ability to push for local bargaining over pensions.
1957	CWA establishes a Collective Bargaining Policy Committee centralizing bargaining strategy and coordination.
1959	Pattern bargaining begins with tacit agreement from AT&T. The first time benefits are negotiated between AT&T and CWA (10 years after the Inland case made them a mandatory subject and 8 years after the Senate investigation).

---

ists and managers are not always anxious to limit their own authority even where it may lead to a greater good for the whole organization. Having to conform to the wishes of a centralized authority is less painful where there are common goals. Thus, another factor that influences the emergence of centralized bargaining structures is the extent of diversity in the objectives across local actors and the degree to which there are traditions that generate organizational loyalty.

1968	The first national strike against the Bell System is led by the CWA and the IBEW. AT&T directly and openly involved in labor relations of operating companies. AT&T and CWA use federal mediator to reach agreement. IBEW tries to reach an agreement that differs from the CWA pattern and is defeated after a four-month strike.
1971	National strike against Bell System wins cost-of-living adjustments and **agency shop** provisions. AT&T openly coordinating negotiations. The New York local of the CWA tries to gain improvements on the pattern and leads a seven month strike which does not achieve the New York local's objectives.
1974	A two-tiered national bargaining framework is announced. The national agreement covers wages and benefits; local supplements cover specific working conditions and a portion of the wage increase granted in 1974 contracts.
1983	National bargaining breaks down under the pressure of the looming divestiture of AT&T. A three-week national strike follows involving 600,000 hourly employees of AT&T. This is the second largest strike in U.S. history.
1984	AT&T divestiture. Seven regional holding companies are established to provide local telephone service.
1986	A national agreement is signed with AT&T after a one-month strike by the CWA (the IBEW does not support the strike). Separate contracts are negotiated with the regional companies, with the CWA attempting to impose pattern bargaining across the regions and the regional companies stressing their individual needs and conditions. Within most of the regional operating companies a two-tiered bargaining structure is adopted, in which economic issues are settled at the regional level and other issues are negotiated at local companies. Strikes occur at some of the regional operating companies.
1989	The CWA and IBEW join together to conduct coalition bargaining with AT&T. A number of strikes occur at the regional operating companies over health insurance issues.

Sources: Information adapted from Marianne Koch, David Lewin, and Donna Sockell, "The Determinants of Bargaining Structure: A Case Study of AT&T," in *Advances in Industrial and Labor Relations,* vol. 4, ed. David Lewin, David B. Lipsky, and Donna Sockell (Greenwich, CT: JAI Press, 1989); Wallace E. Hendricks, "Telecommunications," in *Collective Bargaining in American Industry,* ed. David B. Lipsky and Clifford B. Dunn (Boston: Lexington Books, 1987), pp. 103–134; and input from Jeffrey Keefe.

For example, even though the wages and benefits of police and fire fighters are often similar, if not identical, there is very little joint police–fire fighter bargaining in U.S. municipalities. The rivalry between these two groups and their history of separate organizations has precluded formal coordinated or coalition bargaining in most cities. The major exceptions to this pattern occurred when cities experienced extreme financial crises.

Union leaders' opposition to consolidated bargaining units or to formal union mergers acts as an additional constraint on the centralization of negotiations. The reasons for this are very simple. Any consolidation of negotiating units or unions means that some leaders are going to lose influence, status, and perhaps even their jobs.

Resolving Different Issues at Different Bargaining Levels

It should be noted that even within centralized bargaining structures many issues are negotiated on a local basis. That is, in most cases the master agreement negotiated at the centralized level covers only broad issues, ones that are universal in scope, such as wage rates and fringe benefits. Issues that are either company- or plant-specific, such as safety and health conditions, seniority provisions, production standards, shift changes, and overtime distribution, are often left to more decentralized levels of the bargaining structure.

James W. Kuhn showed that the structure of bargaining extends even further down to the departmental or informal work group level, where individual supervisors and work groups often negotiate unwritten side agreements or in fact ignore certain provisions of the contract. He termed this activity **fractional bargaining.**[25] Indeed, one of the most important developments of the 1980s and 1990s has been the shift in bargaining down to lower levels.

Pattern Bargaining

Pattern bargaining is an informal means for spreading the terms and conditions of employment negotiated in one formal bargaining structure to another. It is an informal substitute for centralized bargaining aimed at taking wages out of competition.

Students of collective bargaining first began noticing the importance of pattern bargaining after World War II. The War Labor Board (WLB) had encouraged the development of pattern settlements, first, by attempting to fashion a national wage policy and, second, by making the comparison between proposed wage settlements and other industry, area, and national settlements a prime criterion for deciding wage disputes.

The WLB is not the only source of pattern bargaining, by any means. Even before centralized bargaining appeared, and in some cases before unions themselves, steel companies, among other concentrated industries, tended to adjust their wages in tandem by following the lead of a principal firm—in the case of steel, the U.S. Steel Corporation (now USX).[26] Once firms started following patterns in their pricing policies it was only natural that unions sought to create patterns in negotiated agreements covering these firms.

Although there are no precise empirical estimates of the number of employees who are affected by some form of pattern bargaining, a Conference Board survey of bargaining in 668 of the largest unionized firms in the private sector found the settlements of large units do spill over to many other workers, both within and outside the firm. On average, the employers responding to the survey estimated that the pattern established in their largest bargaining unit affected approximately two and one-half times as many employees outside the unit and within the firm, and another four times as many workers outside the firm but within the region or industry.[27]

Patterns within a Firm

The employees working within the same firm typically are very aware of what other employees in the firm are receiving in the way of pay or fringe benefits and very jealous of any differentials that emerge. The presence of internal promotion (and other features of an internal labor market) within a firm serve to heighten such comparisons. In the face of internal firm comparisons pattern bargaining follows where there is more than one negotiation that affects employees of the same firm. This is most common across the blue-collar employees of the same firm, but can also occur where unions represent both blue- and white-collar employees. At the Chrysler Corporation, for example, the United Auto Workers Union represents production workers and a number of technical and clerical staff in separate bargaining units. There is a history of strong pattern bargaining in the contracts that cover these employees.

Pattern Bargaining in Other Countries

From time to time economists who would like to see labor and management follow simple principles that link wage adjustments to macroeconomic trends look to Japan's **Spring Wage Offensive** as a model. During this annual bargaining process in Japan a tremendous amount of information sharing and discussion takes place among government, management, and labor leaders over economic trends and prospects for the coming year. Out of these discussions often emerges a general view of what the overall rate of wage increase should be for the next year. Then, individual companies and their unions "separately" negotiate increases that are consistent with this overall rate.[28]

The extreme diversity and decentralization of union and nonunion workplaces across the United States make a version of Japanese practice impractical here. Yet over the years there have been periods when something that approaches an interindustry if not a national pattern has been visible in the United States.

Some **interindustry pattern bargaining** was evident, for example, in the major bargaining rounds of the decade after World War II. In the early 1960s authors of two separate studies divided the manufacturing sector

into what were termed "key" and "nonkey" industries.[29] The key industries tended to be the highly unionized, more concentrated, heavy
durable goods industries. The studies showed that wages in those key
industries moved in identifiable cycles of bargaining in the postwar-to-
1960 period.

The most recent studies of the strength of national pattern bargaining
have concluded that, although wage interdependence continues to exist
among unionized industries, interindustry wage imitation was not as
strong after the 1970s as in the earlier bargaining rounds. Furthermore, it
is unlikely that national pattern bargaining will appear in the foreseeable
future given the diversity of union and nonunion wage-setting processes.

Intraindustry Pattern Bargaining

Perhaps the greatest extent of pattern bargaining in the United States is
the intraindustry variety (across firms in the same industry). The maintenance of patterns in the labor agreements negotiated across firms in the
same industry stabilizes competition over wages. The existence of dominant unions within an industry also facilitates the spread of such patterns
from one employer to another. Examples of this form of pattern bargaining are found in the auto, aerospace, and airline industries.

Negotiations at the NYNEX telephone company between the
Communication Workers of America (CWA) and the International
Brotherhood of Electrical Workers (IBEW) illustrate how pattern bargaining can emerge as an issue in negotiations. Box 7–5 describes the events
surrounding the negotiations and long strike that occurred at NYNEX in
1989. The CWA and IBEW wanted to bargain in a formal coordinated manner with NYNEX, but the company wanted to bargain separate contract
terms with each union. The company thought that separate contracts
would weaken the unions' power and allow contract terms to be tailored
to particular problems that arose in each bargaining unit.

After a long and bitter strike, the unions were able to coordinate their
settlement terms. This negotiation is also an interesting case as it illustrates how medical cost containment has become a controversial and
sometimes divisive issue in bargaining.

Intraindustry pattern bargaining can have drawbacks. A number of
problems result from overextending a pattern settlement to firms or to
different parts of an industry that are unable to absorb its costs.
Overextension is likely to reduce employment opportunities for the pat-
tern-following employees, encourage the entrance of new competitors
into the industry, and ultimately reduce the ability of the union to take
wages out of competition—which was the original purpose of pattern bargaining.

In moderation, however, pattern bargaining serves an important set of
functions in a collective bargaining system. It reduces the number of
strikes, since it not only serves as a standard for the acceptability of a

proposed wage settlement, but also helps to establish norms of equity among workers. And, like other forms of pattern bargaining, intraindustry patterns can help unions take wages out of competition where the pattern is supported by a union's ability to maintain union organizing.

The Trend toward Greater Decentralization

In the 1980s and 1990s a number of bargaining units underwent decentralization in their structure. The steel industry is an illustration. At the beginning of the 1970s the 10 largest steel companies negotiated as a group (although formally each company signed a separate contract). But by 1982 the number of companies that participated in the industry association had shrunk to eight; by 1986 the association had disbanded, and bargaining with the seven remaining firms began to take place on a company-by-company basis. Although the settlements that resulted after 1986 carried through many of the common features of the earlier ones, significant variations across the agreements were introduced: variations in wages, fringe benefits, profit sharing, work rules, and the extent of employee participation in management decision making.

In the 1980s and 1990s the number of firms in the coal and trucking industries declined substantially. Furthermore, there were major declines in the number of workers covered by multiemployer or industrywide contracts in these industries. In communications (as noted in Box 7–4) the national contract of the 1970s, which covered all Bell System employees, gave way to greater decentralization after AT&T's divestiture of the regional telephone companies in 1984.

Some of the decentralization in bargaining structures has been induced by public policies. By far the most significant effects of government policy on bargaining structures have come in recent years from the deregulation of product markets in trucking, airlines, and communications. In all of these cases, the effect of deregulation has been to open the industry to new entrants that start on a nonunion basis, pay wages and benefits below the unionized rates in the industry, and, in turn, put pressures on unionized firms to seek labor contract terms in ways that will meet the new competitors. As a result, firms in all three of these industries attempted to decentralize their bargaining structures.

As mentioned earlier, in trucking, before industry deregulation in 1980, the Teamsters had negotiated a national master freight agreement that covered over-the-road (intercity and interstate) truck drivers. Essentially all the major trucking companies that hauled freight between cities and states or across the country were covered by this single, national contract.

After deregulation, however, there was an influx of new, nonunion firms and small, independent contractors in the full-truckload portion of the industry. Furthermore, intense price competition emerged among the firms that remained highly unionized (essentially the "less than truck-

---

Box 7-5

1989 NYNEX Strike

The Communication Workers of America (CWA) and the International Brotherhood of Electrical Workers (IBEW) represent 60,000 employees at the NYNEX telephone company. On August 6, 1989, NYNEX employees went on strike after contract negotiations reached an impasse. This marked the first time that NYNEX faced a strike with both its unions united in their bargaining demands. The unions hoped to maintain a united front to create a precedent of coordinated bargaining with the company. Throughout the negotiations the CWA and the IBEW stressed that employees needed improved pay and job security. However, NYNEX emphasized that the company needed flexibility in pay and work rules so that NYNEX could effectively compete with unorganized companies in the new deregulated environment.

The unions' primary goal was to improve their members' standard of living through the preservation of health benefits, wage increases, wage protection against inflation through an uncapped cost-of-living adjustment (COLA), improved pensions, and preservation of union covered work. NYNEX, however, wanted to remove the COLA, claiming it was "uncontrollable and unpredictable," and insisted on shifting some of the costs of health insurance to the workers.

To support the strike, the union instituted various tactics such as asking the general public and striking union members to defer payment of their telephone bills until the settlement of the strike. Other strategies included urging the public to bypass the regional Bell companies by using other carriers for short-distance calls.

The health insurance issue was the major stumbling block in negotiations. Once the strike had started, NYNEX refused to return to the bargaining table with the unions' precondition that the cost-sharing medical expense plan be removed. NYNEX maintained that the previous (just-expired) contract called for employees to begin contributing to medical costs.

---

load" businesses that required large networks of terminals). The net result of these pressures was considerable decentralization in the bargaining structure. Several full-truckload companies broke out of the master freight structure and negotiated separate contracts with different wage payment and pension arrangements.

In the airline industry, deregulation has weakened the pattern bargaining that previously characterized negotiations across American, United, Northwest, and other major airlines. Under increased competitive pressure in the 1980s, pattern following gave way to a more varied pattern of company-specific adjustments, including two-tiered wage agreements (that is, wage settlements that lower the starting pay rates of future hires), changes in hours worked, wage cuts, profit-sharing plans, and employee memberships on company boards of directors.[30]

As a last resort, NYNEX and the unions agreed to submit their contract dispute to mediation (on October 12). NYNEX insisted on separate negotiations with the two unions. As a result, Malcolm R. Lovell, Jr., former undersecretary of labor in the Reagan administration, was selected to mediate the talks between NYNEX and the CWA. Donald White, dean of the Boston College School of Arts and Sciences, was chosen to mediate the talks between the company and the IBEW.

Nevertheless, the IBEW and the CWA successfully worked together in the mediated contract negotiations. Despite the company's refusal to bargain jointly, the unions maintained close communications and identical bargaining positions.

An agreement was reached between NYNEX and the IBEW on November 13, 1989, and ratified by a margin of better than 5 to 1. The new three-year contract preserved the health care provisions of the old contract with no requirement for employees to begin contribution to health insurance costs. The new contract, however, had lower wages than the union had sought although it did preserve cost-of-living adjustments to compensate for inflation between 2 and 5 percent in the second and third year.

Then, an agreement between NYNEX and the CWA was reached on November 22, 1989, and ratified by 85 percent of the membership. Following the pattern established in the IBEW agreement, the CWA contract also preserved the health care benefits of the old contract and instituted a COLA provision in exchange for lower wage increases than those originally offered by the company.

These agreements brought an end to a 17-week strike.

Source: Daily Labor Report (Bureau of National Affairs), various issues from April 4, 1989, to December 4, 1989.

Some observers have argued that pattern bargaining became insignificant in the 1980s.[31] This may be an overstatement, but there is strong evidence of greater variability in recent collective bargaining settlements across and within industries and even among different locations within the same firm. Moreover, the economic returns to unions from pattern bargaining seemed to decline after 1980.

Summary

This chapter discusses union organizing and bargaining structures. These two central issues emerge early on in the chronology of the bargaining process. Union organizing decides whether there will be bargaining in the first place, and then the parties' attention turns to the structure of bargaining.

An organizing campaign is initiated by union organizers, typically including some full-time paid organizers and shop floor employees. To receive authorization from the NLRB for a representation election the union needs to have 30 percent of the election unit sign authorization cards. Management typically launches a countercampaign in which it tries to convince employees not to vote for union representation. The NLRB regulates conduct during this organizing campaign including union access and management's use of captive audience speeches. There has been much debate in recent years over whether the NLRB has effectively maintained laboratory conditions in election campaigns.

The NLRB plays an important role in this process in decisions made about the appropriate election unit. The NLRB takes into account both the degree to which employees have common interests and the administrative concerns of management. There is much strategic interplay in this process as the union and management try to shape an election unit that increases the likelihood of victory in the eventual election.

The environment and bargaining power are important determinants of organizing outcomes. Power affects whether a union has enough muscle to win an election or to induce an employer to avoid an election and grant quick union recognition through automatic recognition procedures.

Unions have not fared particularly well in their organizing efforts over the last 25 years. Management has been aggressive in developing personnel policies that weaken the appeal of unions and in the conduct of countercampaigns against unionization. But unions have not been passive either, as they turned to corporate campaigns and other new organizing tactics.

Bargaining structure determines which unionized employees are covered by a collective bargaining agreement. The two key dimensions are the scope of employee interests covered—whether craft or industrial—and the degree of centralization in firm coverage—ranging from single-plant to multiple-company agreements.

Compared to other countries the United States continues as an example of relatively decentralized bargaining structures. During the 1980s and 1990s previously centralized bargaining structures in trucking, steel, coal, and many other industries either fragmented or collapsed.

To see the consequences of successful union organizing and the role played by the structure of bargaining requires a more elaborate account of the negotiation of the collective bargaining agreement. The next chapter turns to that issue.

Discussion Questions

1. Briefly describe the organizing process.

2. What are some common strategies used by management to keep unions out of the company?

3. Define what is meant by bargaining structures and discuss some of the determining factors of bargaining structures.

4. What is pattern bargaining and how does it affect informal bargaining structures?

Suggested Readings

Lipsky, David B., and Clifford B. Donn, eds. *Collective Bargaining in American Industry* (Lexington, MA: Lexington Books, 1987).

Seltzer, George. "Pattern Bargaining and the United Steelworkers," *Journal of Political Economy* 59 (August 1951): 319–331.

Somers, Gerald G., ed. *Collective Bargaining: Contemporary American Experiences* (Madison, WI: Industrial Relations Research Association, 1981).

Weber, Arnold R., ed. *The Structure of Collective Bargaining* (Chicago: Graduate School of Business, University of Chicago, 1964).

End Notes

1. It is also possible for the NLRB to order an employer to bargain with a union as a remedy for a representation election that involves extensive unfair labor practices on the part of the employer. This sort of "bargaining order" has been issued infrequently by the NLRB.

2. The NLRB can eliminate this practice if it interferes with the operation of the business.

3. The employer is not required by law to give the union the opportunity to respond to a captive audience speech.

4. Michael Evan Gold, *An Introduction to Labor Law* (Ithaca, NY: ILR Press, 1989), p. 27.

5. See *Mallenkrodt Chemical Works,* 162 NLRB 387 (1966).

6. National Labor Relations Board, *NLRB Annual Report* (Washington, D.C.: GPO, 1988), table 13.

7. Research also has shown that national union characteristics play a role in union success in certification elections. More specifically, unions with greater internal democracy, less centralized bargaining, lower strike activity, and larger size have greater success in organizing both blue- and white-collar workers than do other unions. See Cheryl L. Maranto and Jack Fiorito, "The Effect of Union Characteristics on the Outcome of NLRB Certification Elections," *Industrial and Labor Relations Review* 40 (January 1987): 225–240.

8. Myron Roomkin and Hervey Juris, "Unions in the Traditional Sectors: Mid-Life Passage of the Labor Movement," in *Proceedings of the Thirtieth Annual Meeting, December 28–39, 1977,* ed. Barbara D. Dennis, (Madison, WI: Industrial Relations Research Association, 1978), pp. 212–222.

9. William N. Cooke, *Union Organizing and Public Policy: Failure to Secure First Contracts* (Kalamazoo, MI: W. E. UpJohn Institute for Employment Research, 1985).

10.   Richard B. Freeman and Morris M. Kleiner, "Employer Behavior in the Face of Union Organizing Drives," *Industrial and Labor Relations Review,* vol. 43, no. 4 (April 1990): 351–365.

11.   Julius G. Getman, Stephen B. Goldberg, and Jeanne B. Herman, *Union Representation Elections: Law and Reality* (New York: Russell Sage Foundation, 1976).

12.   Instead, the authors proposed reforms that would deter employers' anti-union strategies carried out before the campaign. The Getman, Goldberg, and Herman study led to considerable debate and controversy, both in public policy circles and among researchers. A summary of the debate is in Stephen B. Goldberg, Julius G. Getman, and Jeanne M. Brett, "The Relationship between Free Choice and Labor Board Doctrine: Differing Empirical Approaches," *Northwestern University Law Review* 79 (1984), 721–735.

13.   See William T. Dickens, "The Effect of Company Campaigns: Law and Reality Once Again," *Industrial and Labor Relations Review* 36 (July 1983), 560–575.

14.   Cooke, *Union Organizing and Public Policy.*

15.   William T. Dickens and Jonathan S. Leonard, "Accounting for the Decline in Union Membership: 1950–1980," *Industrial and Labor Relations Review,* 38 (April 1985): 323–334.

16.   Stephen M. Hills, "The Attitudes of Union and Nonunion Male Workers toward Union Representation," *Industrial and Labor Relations Review* 38 (January 1985): 179–194.

17.   *Sewell Mfg. Co.,* 138 NLRB 66 (1962), pp. 69–70.

18.   A listing of corporate campaigns and analysis of their success is provided in Paul Jarley and Cheryl Maranto, "Union Corporate Campaigns: An Assessment," *Industrial and Labor Relations Review,* vol. 43, no. 5 (July 1990): 505–524.

19.   An interview with the first director of the new Organizing Institute is reported in *Daily Labor Report* (Washington, D.C.: Bureau of National Affairs), no. 116, June 6, 1989, p. C–2.

20.   See Industrial Democracy in Europe Working Group, *European Industrial Relations* (London: Oxford University Press, 1980).

21.   Ben C. Roberts, ed., *Industrial Relations in Europe* (London: Croom Helm, 1985).

22.   John R. Commons, "American Shoemakers, 1648–1895: A Sketch of Industrial Evolution," *Quarterly Journal of Economics* 25 (November 1919), reprinted and revised in *A Documentary History of American Society,* vol. 3, ed. John R. Commons (New York: Russell and Russell, 1958), pp. 18–58.

23.   George W. Brooks, "Stability versus Employee Free Choice," *Cornell Law Review* 61 (March 1976): 344–367.

24.   Marianne Koch, David Lewin, and Donna Sockell, "The Determinants of Bargaining Structure: A Case Study of AT&T," in *Advances in Industrial and Labor Relations,* vol. 4, ed. David Lewin, David B. Lipsky, and Donna Sockell (Greenwich, CT: JAI Press, 1989).

25.   James W. Kuhn, *Bargaining and Grievance Settlements* (New York: Columbia University Press, 1962).

26.   George Seltzer, "Pattern Bargaining and the United Steelworkers," *Journal of Political Economy* 59 (August 1951): 322.

27.   Audrey Freedman, *Managing Labor Relations* (New York: Conference Board, 1979).

28.   Kazutoshi Koshiro, "Development of Collective Bargaining in Post-War Japan," in *Contemporary Industrial Relations in Japan,* ed. Taishiro Shirai (Madison, WI: University of Wisconsin Press, 1982), pp. 205–258.

29.   Otto Eckstein and Thomas A. Wilson, "The Determination of Money Wages in American Industry," *Quarterly Journal of Economics* 75 (August 1962): 370–414, and John E. Maher, "The Wage Pattern in the United States," *Industrial and Labor Relations Review* 15 (October 1961): 1–20.

30.   Peter Cappelli, "Competitive Pressures and Labor Relations in the Airline Industry," *Industrial Relations* 24 (1985): 316–338.

31.   Audrey Freedman and William Fulmer, "Last Rites for Pattern Bargaining," *Harvard Business Review* 60 (March–April 1982): 30–48.

Chapter 8

The Negotiations Process
and Strikes

Chapters 8 and 9 examine the process by which unions and employers
negotiate collective bargaining agreements, continuing the analysis of the
middle (functional) level of industrial relations activity. This chapter
explains the dynamics of negotiations and the factors that lead to strikes;
the next chapter discusses impasse resolution.

Negotiations and strikes are the most visible parts of a collective bargaining system. Negotiations may set the terms of any contractual language, or they may produce the strikes that often provide headlines for
popular press coverage of collective bargaining.

The negotiations process involves a complex set of strategies and tactics. Good negotiators must possess the ability to stand firm in their positions while at the same time be alert to possible compromises that can
advance the interests of their side at the bargaining table.

To examine the various components of the negotiations process, this
chapter uses the framework developed by Richard Walton and Robert
McKersie.[1] This framework is particularly useful in identifying the wide
variety of pressures and competing interests that bear on the negotiators
and the negotiations process.

The Four Subprocesses of Negotiations

Although it may appear that the parties involved in the negotiations of a
labor contract are engaged in a simple give-and-take exercise, the negotiations process in fact involves a variety of pressures and interests.
Walton and McKersie argued that there are four **subprocesses of bargaining** within the negotiation of any collective bargaining agreement. The
four subprocesses are distributive bargaining, integrative bargaining,
intraorganizational bargaining, and attitudinal structuring. Each subpro-

cess and the interrelations between the various subprocesses are analyzed below.

Distributive Bargaining

- Win-Lose
- Zero-Sum
wage rates,
fringe benefits

Distributive bargaining involves those aspects of negotiations in which one side's gain is the other side's loss. Distributive bargaining is *win-lose* or *zero sum* bargaining. With distributive issues, what labor gains management must give up. Examples of distributive issues include wage rates and fringe benefits. With respect to the wage rate, labor gains more income from a higher wage, while management gives up some profit to pay the higher wage.[2] Similarly, workers lose when a fringe benefit (e.g., paid vacation time) is reduced, while management gains higher profits with the reduction of paid vacation time.

Since distributive issues involve gains for one side and losses for the other, these issues lead to conflicts across the bargaining table. Determination of how distributive issues are resolved involves the exercise of bargaining power. The union, for example, tries to convince management to agree to its request for a higher wage by threatening to strike if management does not give in to this demand. Meanwhile, management threatens the union with the loss of income associated with such a strike and might also point out to the union that such a wage increase entails additional costs to the work force in the form of reductions in employment. In this way, the components of bargaining power, strike leverage, and elasticity of demand for labor emerge as the critical determinants of how distributive conflicts are resolved.

Distributive issues are at the center of the negotiation of a collective bargaining agreement since disagreement over the distribution of labor's product lies at the core of labor-management relations. Nevertheless, it would be a mistake for either students of collective bargaining or participants in the bargaining process to lose sight of the fact that there are other dimensions to bargaining in addition to distributive issues.

Integrative Bargaining

- joint-gain
- win-win

Integrative bargaining issues are those in which a solution provides gains to both labor and management, leading to *joint gain* or *win-win* bargaining. Labor and management both gain when they resolve problems that are impeding productivity and organizational performance. If the productivity of the firm increases, for example, the employees can benefit in the form of higher compensation or shorter work hours while the firm can benefit in the form of greater profits.

There are numerous problems confronted at the workplace that provide the opportunity for integrative gains. Work is rarely performed in the most productive way possible: either cumbersome practices or outdated work rules often stand in the way of peak performance. Labor and management thus can improve firm performance by addressing such practices and either changing job classifications or seniority rules or in other ways creating procedures that promote high organizational performance.

The introduction of new technology often provides an avenue for integrative gains. Through the effective use of new technology productivity can increase, which can then provide rewards both to employees and the firm. Yet the mere introduction of new technology onto the shop floor does not lead readily to such productivity increases. Commonly technology works best if accompanied by changes in work practices—personnel levels might have to be reduced, training programs adopted, or reporting lines adjusted. Integrative bargaining would entail the negotiations surrounding how and to what extent these productivity-enhancing work rule changes are made as the new technology is introduced.

But why do the parties not automatically make integrative changes since such changes hold open the possibility of joint gain? In other words, why is integrative bargaining so difficult? The answer to this question is one of the key issues in industrial relations.

Why Integrative Bargaining Can Be So Difficult   Integrative bargaining is an ever-present and sometimes difficult component of the negotiations process for a number of reasons. For one thing, although integrative issues contain the possibility of providing joint gains to both sides, it is also true that the parties are simultaneously confronted with the question of how to divide up any joint gain. In effect, any integrative bargain also prompts the occurrence of distributive bargaining, and the difficulty in resolving this distributive issue can make integrative bargaining difficult.

Consider, for example, what happens when a new technology is introduced into a plant. If it is effectively introduced, the new technology provides the possibility of joint gains in the form of income to both employees and the firm. Yet, the involved parties cannot escape the fact that if productivity goes up when the new technology is implemented, it must then be decided how the increased income provided by that technology is divided. In this way, every integrative bargain prompts a distributive discussion. The problem for the bargaining parties is that it can be difficult for them to agree on how to resolve the distributive issue (namely, how to share the integrative gain). Thus, integrative solutions are sometimes blocked by labor and management's disagreement over how they would divide up the gains that result from problem resolution.

Integrative and Distributive Bargaining Involve Different Tactics   Integrative bargaining also can become difficult because the parties send confused signals and mixed messages to each other. This confusion springs from the fact that integrative and distributive bargaining entail very different tactics and negotiating styles. Exhibit 8–1 lists the different tactics used in distributive and integrative bargaining.

Remember, distributive bargaining concerns matters in which one side's gain is the other side's loss. To do well in such bargaining the negotiator typically finds it valuable to, among other things, overstate demands, withhold information, and project a stern and tough image. Effective integrative bargaining, on the other hand, involves first identifying and then solving problems. The tactics typically effective in such problem solving include open exchange of information, airing of multiple voices, and sharing of information. Distributive and integrative bargaining styles contrast sharply with each other.

The problem for both labor and management is that it is difficult to be effective at both distributive and integrative bargaining in the same negotiations. One side might set into a distributive bargaining mode just at the moment when the other side is ready for integrative problem solving. And when the latter party confronts hard distributive tactics it might become discouraged about the possibility of integrative bargaining, making it difficult for such bargaining ever to occur.

Integrative bargaining also can be difficult because the problems that impede productivity are not always obvious to the two parties, even when they agree on how to divide up the possible joint gains. If this does not make negotiations hard enough, consider as well that there are two other subprocesses in the bargaining process.

Exhibit 8–1   **Distributive versus Integrative Bargaining Tactics**

	Distributive Tactics	**Integrative Tactics**
Issues	Many issues	Specific concerns
Positions	Overstate real position at outset—"demands"	Focus on objectives; no final positions
Use of information	Information is power; hold it close, use selectively	Share information openly; treat as data
Communication process	*Controlled* Single spokesperson Use of private caucuses to air internal differences and discuss responses	*Open* Multiple voices Use of subcommittees
Interpersonal style	*Hard bargaining* Focused on own goals and interests Short run; not concerned about long-term relations Low trust	*Problem solving* Concern for mutual goals Concerned about long-term relations High trust

Intraorganizational Bargaining

Intraorganizational bargaining occurs when there are different goals or preferences *within* either side, either the union or management. For example, intraorganizational bargaining arises when the member of the union (or the union negotiating team) have different preferences regarding what the union should strive for during negotiations. Senior union members may prefer that the union focus its negotiating strategy around attainment of better pensions, whereas younger union members may prefer up-front wage increases. Or, the craft workers in the union might be in favor of restricting the use of outside contractors to maintain machinery in the plant, whereas production workers might be concerned with having safer conditions on the line.

Management may also have different preferences or opinions about what is feasible in negotiations. Corporate management, for example, may favor strict adherence to the seniority policies used in other plants of the company, whereas local plant management may prefer negotiation of a seniority procedure that has never been tried elsewhere in the company.

Intraorganizational conflict also can occur when one or both of the parties bring insufficient decision-making authority to the bargaining table. Nothing is more frustrating to negotiators than to realize they are engaging in what is called *shadow boxing* or *surface bargaining*—that is, bargaining opposite a representative who lacks the authority necessary to make commitments that will stick within his or her organization. Inadequate decision-making power or authority on the part of a negotiator greatly increases the probability of an impasse or a strike as the opponent turns to the strike to force the real decision makers to the bargaining table. This source of impasse is especially prevalent in the public sector or the quasi-public sector, such as not-for-profit hospitals.

Consider, for example, the severe intraorganizational conflict that appeared in the dispute between a teacher's union and a public school district, described in Box 8–1. This impasse was caused primarily by intramanagement conflicts. The union's only recourse was to call an impasse, bring in a mediator, and put pressure on the school board to resolve its internal differences and get on with the negotiations.

This example illustrates that intraorganizational conflicts are not solely a union phenomenon. It is true that the political structure of unions makes it more difficult for them than for most managements to resolve internal power struggles. Nonetheless, in firms where the locus of decision-making power is unclear or widely dispersed within management, open conflicts are also likely to occur and carry over into the negotiations process.

Intraorganizational conflict is common in the public sector because of its complex decision-making structures and numerous political con-

Box 8–1

Intraorganizational Conflict in a School District

Three years before the negotiations in question began, the teachers had engaged in a bitter strike. The board president and two other members of the current board were members of the board at the time of that strike and still bore extreme hostility toward the teachers. The other four members of the board held less antagonistic attitudes toward the teachers.

The board's professional negotiator was also a carryover from the strike. The relationship between him and the union was one of mutual and extreme distrust and antagonism. Thus, as the new negotiations got under way, the board and the teachers were still locked in a hostile relationship.

Shortly before negotiations began, the board had hired a new superintendent of schools. Repelled by the animosity between the teachers and the board, he sought to take a more conciliatory stance toward the union. Before long, bitter confrontations developed between the board's negotiator and the new superintendent.

During the summer months the superintendent held informal talks with the union president, and together they worked out a tentative agreement on a contract settlement, subject to board and union membership approval. The board refused to approve the agreement, partly because of objections by the board's negotiator. Throughout the course of the negotiations the superintendent tried to persuade the board to dismiss the negotiator.

Since these events took several months to transpire, the teachers pressured their union leaders into calling an impasse and began to engage in slowdowns and other forms of job actions short of a strike. During the months the superintendent and the negotiator were at loggerheads, each arranged separate meetings with the union representatives, one trying to work through a mediator and the other trying to keep the mediator out of the process. Meanwhile, both were lobbying members of the board to obtain the swing vote necessary to win the power struggle.

Obviously, no progress was made in negotiations until the internal dispute was resolved. The superintendent ultimately emerged as the victor in the power struggle, and the board dismissed its negotiator. The superintendent then brought in a new management negotiator with whom he could work, and a contract was successfully negotiated.

stituencies.[3] Multiemployer bargaining structures in industries where there is wide variation in the goals or financial status of the employers is another likely environment for intramanagement conflicts.

Attitudinal Structuring

Negotiations often involve a lot of uncertainty. Uncertainty arises from the difficulties the parties face in anticipating how much strike power they possess and the complications involved in interpreting each other's intentions.

Negotiations also can be extremely emotional. The stakes involved are usually high, and the tactics used—threats, bluffs, grandstanding for one's constituents, exaggerated anger—are hardly conducive to building rapport among the parties to the process.[4] Add to these the fact that any single round of negotiations typically is part of a larger and longer term power struggle between parties separated by an inherent conflict of interests. One can readily see why hostile attitudes can, and sometimes do, develop in a bargaining relationship and why they can constrain effective negotiations.

Consequently, **attitudinal structuring** (the degree of trust the respective sides feel toward each other) is another subprocess within bargaining. If labor and management, for example, have a high degree of trust in one another then it should be easier for the parties to engage in integrative bargaining since trust can facilitate the identification of problems (or solutions). In contrast, interpersonal mistrust can make it difficult to move from initial bargaining positions to compromise settlements. Mistrust hampers communications between the parties and can lead both parties to hold back on concessions they might otherwise be willing to make. Obviously, intense hostility can get in the way of serious discussion of the substantive merits of the issues.[5] Labor and management can try to build trust by meeting prior (or during negotiations) in forums that facilitate an open exchange of views and concerns. Trust can derive from a better understanding of why the other side holds its positions. Personality traits appear to play a role in trust building. Some personality traits, such as excessive authoritarianism, have been found to hinder the compromising necessary to bring about negotiated settlements.[6]

A recent study showed, for example, that the negotiators' "perspective-taking ability," that is, their ability to see the other party's point of view, enhances the likelihood of a negotiated agreement.[7] Those who are philosophically opposed to unions, on the other hand, and those who are opposed to the role managers play in a capitalistic society, on the other, may see bargaining issues as matters of great principle and thus find compromising difficult. Acceptance of the legitimacy of the other sides' point of view can facilitate conflict resolution. Its absence in negotiations increases the probability of an impasse.

Management's Wage Objectives in Negotiations

The formation of management's **wage objectives** (or **targets**) is a critical part of the negotiations process. Negotiators often have limits for bargaining, or the bottom-line terms they would accept short of taking a strike. The development of these wage targets is the heart of the internal management planning process that takes place before or during the early stages of negotiations.

Wages are important to management, but they are not the only critical issue addressed in a labor agreement. Yet the formation of management's targets for other bargaining issues occurs in a manner that is not very different from the formation of wage targets. Thus, the discussion that follows has general applicability.

Since top management is responsible for approving or authorizing any wage target in bargaining, the negotiating team must recommend targets that reflect top management's goals for the organization. To recommend too high a wage target risks rejection of the recommendations and the loss of influence that results from such a rejection. On the other hand, these targets play a pivotal role in the negotiations process once they are established because they indicate the negotiator's latitude for compromise.

Thus, the industrial relations staff has to develop bargaining targets that are realistic and achievable. The range of criteria that go into this decision-making process are discussed below.

Local Labor Market Comparisons

One factor an employer considers when setting their wage targets is the prevailing wage level in the **local labor market.** If the employer were to ignore the local labor market and allow wages inside the firm to fall low relative to wages at the other employment sites, high employee turnover might follow. Low wages also might produce a dissatisfied work force and difficulty in recruiting workers with the requisite ability to perform effectively. To set wages too high relative to the local labor market invites an excess of qualified job applicants and unnecessary costs.

Note this does not mean that the employer seeks to pay the lowest wage possible that will attract workers to a given job. Given a particular local labor market, the employer must choose the quality of employees it wishes to hire. The employer must decide if increasing the wage level will attract employees of sufficiently high quality and lower indirect personnel costs (such as training, turnover, and supervision).

Labor market comparisons are more likely to be used in bargaining relationships where the union is weak. Where unions are strong they use their bargaining power to do better than the local labor market and gain what they consider to be a fair wage.

The Firm's Ability To Pay

The effects of wage adjustments on the profits of the firm also influence management's wage target. Employers approaching the wage decision examine their **ability to pay** alternative wage increases. Ability-to-pay considerations are likely to be especially salient in small firms and in firms facing a weak union.

A union generally is reluctant to give a firm a lower settlement on ability-to-pay grounds unless the firm can demonstrate that a serious economic crisis would result otherwise. Union leaders and members often must be convinced that there would be sizable employment loss before they will agree to a low settlement. It took, for example, the threat of bankruptcy, along with government pressure, before the UAW agreed to give Chrysler wage concessions below the auto pattern in 1979. Ability-to-pay considerations have become more important in recent years. In response to heightened competitive pressures, management has preferred to shift away from externally driven wage criteria in favor of criteria that connect wages more closely to firm or worker performance. Thus, management has tried to shift away from factors such as wages in the industry or increases in the cost of living and toward the firm's ability to pay.

Internal Comparisons

Every negotiation is carefully watched by a firm's other employees. Management must consider how a wage settlement might influence the expectations and demands of other employees in the firm whether or not the other employees are represented by unions. Management, for example, often considers whether wage increases provided to unionized production workers will lead to pay increases for supervisors and other white-collar employees outside the bargaining unit. One reason management provides white-collar employees with pay increases is to weaken these employees' potential attraction to unionization.

The Union's Targets

Management must also take the union's preferences into account when setting targets for bargaining. Unless management is powerful enough to totally dominate bargaining, the management team will have to consider the potential acceptability of its wage offer to the union.

Unions will usually establish their own targets for wage bargaining. In setting those limits, union leaders employ two basic criteria for evaluating a proposed settlement: (1) the potential effects of the settlement on the real wages of the membership (the wage adjustment minus any increase in the cost of living), and (2) a comparison between the proposed settlement and settlements with other bargaining units or with other employees.

Comparisons with other units are important to unions for both economic and political reasons. Remember, the union's economic goal is to take wages out of competition. This leads unions to favor wage increases that maintain patterns. Union leaders also face pressure from their members to preserve "coercive comparisons" with the settlements achieved by other unions.[8] Rank-and-file union members often evaluate their leaders by comparing their own settlement to settlements achieved by leaders of other unions or granted by other employers.

Thus, the union tries to induce the firm to consider more than it might otherwise in wage setting. The union's bargaining power will determine the extent to which management actually takes into account the union's preferences.

The Dynamics of Management's Decision-Making Process

So far we have painted a rather static picture of management's decision-making. Yet the actual process of decision making over the course of a bargaining cycle (from the prenegotiation planning stage to the signing of the final agreement) is a dynamic one. The process is replete with ambiguities over who has the authority to set policies, conflicts among decision makers over the appropriate weight to be attached to different goals, and power struggles among competing decision makers.

The process by which management establishes bargaining strategies involves extensive intraorganizational bargaining, which is every bit as intense as the bargaining between the union and management. Because the successful resolution of internal differences is a prerequisite to a smoothly functioning bargaining process it is important to understand how firms prepare for negotiations.

To provide a more complete picture of how management prepares for collective bargaining, a typical case is described in Box 8–2 .[9] This firm is preparing to negotiate a contract with the major bargaining unit in its largest manufacturing facility. The contract traditionally sets the pattern for the economic settlements with several smaller units at other locations.

Before negotiations (or very early in negotiations) the labor relations staff tries to predict as closely as possible what it will take to get a settlement. But ultimately the staff is at all times ready to revise its estimates based on new or better information about the union's position as the negotiations proceed.

The case in Box 8–2 illustrates the diversity of interests that exists in the different levels within any modern organization. It shows that the development of a company strategy for negotiations is a highly political process, one in which the different goals of various groups must ultimately be accommodated. Although the labor relations staff serves as a key

Box 8–2

Management's Preparations for Negotiations: A Typical Firm

Input from the Plants
The first step in the process of preparing for negotiations takes place at the plant level. The plant labor relations staff holds meetings with plant supervisors to discuss problems experienced in administering the existing contract. From these discussions the staff puts together a list of suggested contract changes. At the same time, the staff also conducts a systematic review of the grievances that have arisen under the current contract and collects information on local labor market conditions and on the wages in other firms in the community.

The staff then holds a meeting with the plant manager who raises the industrial relations problems confronted in the plant. The plant's concerns are classified into two groups: those that are contractual problems, and those that should be addressed outside the negotiating process. In addition, the staff asks the plant manager to rank suggested contract changes on the basis of their potential for making a significant improvement in plant operations.

Input from Higher Levels of the Firm
Next a series of meetings are held at the division level involving the division labor relations staff, operations management at the division level, and the corporate labor relations director and staff. From time to time outside industrial relations consultants also sit in on these division-level meetings. Here the concerns of the various plants are evaluated against two criteria: (1) the operational benefits expected from proposed contract changes, and (2) the likelihood the changes desired can be achieved in the negotiations process.

The corporate labor relations staff plays a vital role in these division-level discussions, since the expected benefits of different contractual changes can be a matter of dispute across the various plants. In addition, the division labor relations staff is responsible for carefully examining the contract language that exists in the various local agreements for inconsistencies or problems that could be removed by clauses that reflect corporate labor relations preferences. Sometimes the plant labor relations representatives object to changes suggested at the division level because they do not correspond to the priorities of the plant officials and because the existing "discrepancies" may be serving a useful purpose in the plant.

The corporate labor relations staff works closely with the vice president for finance to develop the wage targets. Information on plant labor costs, corporate earnings, and the long-term financial prospects of the company and the industry are built into the wage target the corporate staff ultimately recommends.

Input from Research

A *research subgroup* within the labor relations staff of the company also carries out background research that is used in management's preparations for negotiations. At least a year and a half before the opening of formal negotiations the research staff begins to prepare the background information necessary for developing the company's proposals.

The researchers use a data base on employee demographic characteristics and analyze personnel statistics such as turnover, absentee, and grievance rates. They also monitor internal union developments, specifically, union convention resolutions, union publications, and union leader's statements about the upcoming negotiations. In addition, they survey plant managers for their views on their relations with the union and on the problems they would like to see addressed in the negotiations. The staff also consults plant labor relations staff members to obtain their suggestions. Note, this firm probably invests more resources and assigns more authority for bargaining preparation to its research staff than do most other corporations.

The research staff is ultimately responsible for putting together a summary report that goes to the vice president of industrial relations and the corporate director of compensation. These executives then work with the manager of the research and planning department to develop targets for bargaining.

The Final Steps in Management's Preparations

The final step in management's preparation for negotiations is a meeting involving the corporate labor relations staff, the chief executive officer, and the board of directors. At this meeting the corporate labor relations director presents for board approval the proposed wage targets and other proposed contract changes and the reasons for seeking the proposed changes. Sometimes this meeting does not take place until after the first negotiations session with the union. The industrial relations director might prefer waiting until then because it may be useful to hear from the union before making his recommendation to top management. This helps him identify both the relative importance the union is likely to place on pay issues and the intensity of the union's concern about other areas of the contract.

The industrial relations director described to us how he presents his recommendation to top management in this way:

> I always number my proposed target settlements as proposed settlement target number 1. Someone once asked me what that meant. I said that this is what I think it will take to get a settlement but I number it because I may have to come back to you at some point with my proposed settlement number 2 or even my proposed settlement number 3, et cetera.

participant in the development of the strategy, the concerns of operating management, financial staff, and other interest groups within the corporation are also integral to any final decision.

Union and Worker Involvement in Negotiations

This section reviews the common procedures followed by unions and workers during the negotiation of a collective bargaining contract. This material parallels the discussion of the procedures used by management in preparing for negotiations described above.

The Role of the Union Negotiating Committee

In negotiations with management the union is represented by a negotiating committee. The makeup of the **union negotiating committee** varies across unions, although it typically includes some union officers, support staff (such as members of the local or the national union's research staff, or both), and elected worker representatives. Often the leaders of the union's negotiating committee are the highest elected officers of the union covered by the collective bargaining agreement under negotiation. Some unions, such as local construction or trucking unions, tend to rely on hired business agents to lead their negotiations.

The negotiating committee will meet a number of times before the start of negotiations to formulate the union's list of demands and to begin to establish expectations regarding what the union can win in negotiations. Before these meetings the negotiating committee will solicit from union members their demands, either directly through membership meetings called to discuss the upcoming negotiations or in some cases through polls. In the UAW, for example, representatives elected from the local unions meet in a convention and vote on bargaining resolutions during preparations for companywide auto bargaining. Union members in the UAW are also consulted during the negotiation of plant contracts that supplement the companywide agreements.

A union negotiating committee typically also receives information and advice from the national union's research staff during its preparations for bargaining. The information provided frequently covers the financial performance of the company, forecasts the future performance of the company and the economy, and summarizes recent settlements in other unions or the pay improvements received by unorganized workers in the same city, firm, or industry.

Acquisition of Strike Authorization if at Impasse

If the union comes to an impasse with management during the negotiations and is considering going on strike over its unresolved disputes with management, two steps occur. In local contract negotiations the union's constitution typically requires the local to seek **strike authorization** from the national union. Strike approval is an important process because, among other things, it enables striking workers to receive strike benefits from the national union's strike fund.

A union considering a strike also typically will poll its members. The strike vote serves a dual purpose: it tells the union leadership whether the union's members support such an action, and it helps rally the workers around the purpose of the strike.

Contract Ratification

When an agreement is reached between the union's negotiating committee and management's representatives, the union proceeds through its **contract ratification** procedures. Here there is much variation in the exact procedures used by unions. Some unions first send a proposed agreement to a council made up of lower level union officers. This council would include local union officers when a companywide agreement is negotiated (as in the steel and auto industries). Union constitutions typically also require that the workers covered by a negotiated agreement vote on any proposed settlement.

There are some notable exceptions to the normal pattern of union member votes over proposed contracts. For instance, until the 1970s, coal miners represented by the United Mine Workers did not have the right to vote on new contracts negotiated by their national union leaders. The same was true of Teamster union members covered under the master freight agreement until this was changed in 1987. But in the usual case workers must approve contract settlements (often by majority vote). This sort of voting provides a mechanism for participatory democracy in this critical aspect of union decision making.

Union Leaders' Roles in Shaping Strategies

The actual bargaining demands of unions reflect more than just an averaging of their members' preferences. Several factors combine to produce the complex process by which union leaders arrive at their bargaining objectives.

First, in addition to considering the preferences of their members, union leaders must evaluate objectives in light of the probability that they can be attained. Unrealistic goals must be discarded during prenegotiation planning sessions or early on in negotiations.

Second, individual union members have varying political influence within the union. Older or more skilled workers, for example, may be more politically influential than other members. Thus, the objectives ultimately selected may reflect some workers' goals more than others.

Third, union leaders must also be concerned about the long-run survival of the union and must take steps to preserve those interests. There is always the risk that union leaders will emphasize union security at the expense of member preferences.

Finally, it should be recognized that a central job for union leaders, like all leaders, is to lead! Union leaders must weigh strategic options, make decisions, and secure the ongoing support of their members for those decisions.

One of the keys to union leadership is effective internal communication. Union leaders need regular upward communication from the rank and file and from local union officers. Effective union leadership also requires that decision makers communicate their activities and decisions back to the members. Unions use such techniques as opinion surveys, satellite hookups, and television advertising to communicate with their members.

The Cycle of Negotiations

Negotiations often proceed through a cycle in which the four subprocesses of bargaining emerge and interrelate.[10] A typical negotiations cycle is described below.

The Early Stages

In the initial stage of a negotiation the parties present their opening proposals. This stage often involves a larger number of people than will be involved in the negotiations of the final agreement. The union, for example, may bring in representatives from various interest groups and levels of the union hierarchy. These people participate in developing the initial proposals and later become involved in securing ratification of any agreement. The involvement of all these different representatives can smooth any intraorganizational bargaining within the union.

The union then presents proposals that cover its entire range of concerns. Some of the proposals will be of critical importance and will be at the heart of the discussions as the strike deadline approaches. Some are important but may be traded off at the last minute. Some may be translated into more specific demands at a later stage of bargaining or may be issues to which the union will assign a high priority in some future round of negotiations. Other issues are of low priority and will be dropped as negotiations proceed into the serious decision-making stages.

The Presentation of a Laundry List   The presentation by the union of a **laundry list** of issues serves several purposes. Such a list allows union leaders to recognize different interest groups by at least mentioning their proposals. Some unrealistic demands will be aired, the problems underlying these demands can be explored, and the employer can then reject these demands. This process takes the pressure off union officers who might otherwise appear to have arbitrarily nixed some group's pet proposal. In a laundry list either side also could introduce issues that it hopes could be pursued in future negotiations.

Initially presenting a long list of proposals and inflated demands might also be useful at camouflaging the real priorities of the union. Or, a long list of proposals could assist integrative bargaining by facilitating trades across issues.

Employer Behavior in the Early Phase   Employer behavior at the outset of bargaining varies considerably. Sometimes the employer will present a set of proposals to counterbalance the union demands. At other times the employer will receive the union demands and promise a response at a future negotiating session. Many management representatives prefer to delay making any specific proposal on wages or other economic issues until well into the negotiations process. Because the wage issue can be emotional and divisive, management often tries to resolve nonwage issues first.

Management may also initially try to camouflage its bottom-line position, and it, too, may have unresolved internal differences at the start of negotiations. In some firms a decision on the bottom line is not made until after the union offers its initial proposals and gives some preliminary indication of its priorities.

In the early stages the speakers for each side will argue strongly and often emotionally for the objectives of their constituents, both to carry out their representational obligations and to determine how strongly the opponent feels about the issues at stake. It should be no surprise that these initial stages are the forum for a good deal of grandstanding by both parties (grandstanding that may be a part of intraorganizational bargaining).

The Middle Stages

The middle stages of negotiations involve more serious consideration of various proposals. The most important tasks performed in the middle stages of bargaining are (1) to develop an estimate of the relative priorities the other side attaches to the outstanding issues, (2) to estimate the likelihood that an agreement can be reached without a strike, and (3) to signal to the other side those issues that might be the subject of compromise at a later stage of the process.

Often the parties choose to divide the issues into economic and noneconomic issues. The separation of issues may facilitate problem resolution and integrative bargaining. It is at these intermediate stages that any obstacles to a settlement may begin to surface.

The Final Stages

The final stages of bargaining begin as the **strike deadline** approaches. At this point the process both heats up and speeds up. Off-the-record discussions of the issues may take place between two individuals or small groups of representatives from both sides, perhaps in conjunction with a mediator. These discussions serve several purposes: to save face in front of one's constituents; to allow a fuller clarification of each party's position; and to explore possible compromises.

The bargaining taking place at the table, in many cases, is only the formal presentation of proposals and counterproposals. At this point the negotiators have a better idea of their opponent's bottom-line positions and they may have private discussions over what it will take to reach a settlement.

Whether the real bargaining occurs at the table or in the back room is less important than are the factors that determine whether a settlement will be reached without an impasse. In these final stages before a strike deadline each party is seeking to convince the other of the credibility of its threats to strike. Each side also is trying to get the other side to change its bottom line to prevent a strike. And each party is trying to accurately predict the other side's real positions on the issues to avoid backing into an unnecessary strike. At this stage, therefore, usually only a small number of decision makers are involved in the process.

Even if the key bargainers may agree on how a bargaining settlement could be reached, agreement is not yet assured. Because of their inability to sell a settlement to their constituents, the agreement might still not be reached without calling an impasse (see Chapter 9).

Strikes

The above provides an account of the various subprocesses involved in negotiations and a typical cycle of negotiations. To understand the outcomes of negotiations, the next section considers the role played by strikes and the threat of strikes.

How the Strike Threat Influences Negotiated Settlements

In negotiations the bargaining parties are unlikely to settle on terms that differ substantially from whatever terms they think would settle a strike if one were to occur. Consequently, strikes are an important determinant of both parties' bargaining power.

During negotiations both labor and management negotiators formulate expectations as to what might happen if the negotiations were to reach impasse and a strike were to follow. At the same time, both sides have a strong incentive to avoid a strike as each loses income during a strike.

During a strike workers give up foregone wages. They try to make up for those lost earnings by possibly taking a short-time job. Workers also turn to union strike benefits, the earnings of a spouse, or savings to support themselves and their families during a strike.

Firms lose foregone profits during a strike. They try to lessen the amount of profits lost through tactics such as bringing in replacement workers for the strikers, making sales out of any available inventories, or shifting production to an alternative site. The firm relies on assets or the earnings from other lines of business to meet any financial obligations (such as equipment expenses) during a strike.

The material below examines more closely the role played by the strike threat in the negotiations process and identifies the factors that lead to strikes.

The Hicks Model of Strikes *– know definition*

John R. Hicks developed a very insightful model to analyze the role played by strike leverage in shaping negotiated outcomes.[11] Exhibit 8–2 diagrams the **Hicks model of strikes.** To simplify the discussion, assume the parties are negotiating only over wages (or assume that all items in dispute can be reduced to monetary terms and represented by a simple wage).

In the Hicks model bargainers form an expectation of what they would eventually agree to if there was a strike. In case A in Exhibit 8–2, both par-

Exhibit 8–2   **The Hicks Model of Strikes**

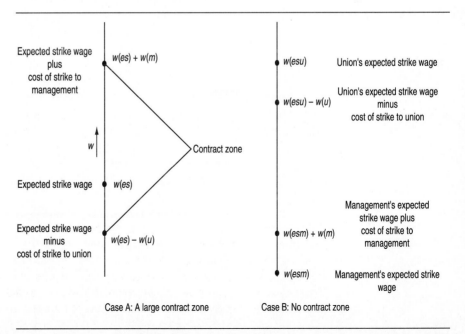

Case A: A large contract zone   Case B: No contract zone

ties expect that if there was a strike it would be ended with a wage settlement of $w(es)$. If a strike occurs, however, both labor and management will have to absorb income losses during the strike. Workers will forego earnings during the strike, and management will lose profits because of the stoppage in production.

Cognizant of these potential income losses, *during the negotiations* the parties should be able to find a negotiated wage settlement that they prefer over the wage settlement they would end up with at the end of a strike, $w(es)$.

The income management would lose during a strike would amount to an hourly wage cost to management of $w(m)$. Given that they expect a strike to end with a wage of $w(es)$, management should be willing *during negotiations* to agree to a wage as high as the expected strike outcome plus the cost to management of the potential strike, or $w(es) + w(m)$.

Labor in this case also expects a strike to end with a wage of $w(es)$. The income workers would lose during a strike would amount to an hourly wage cost to labor of $w(u)$. The workers, *during negotiations,* therefore, should be willing to accept a wage as low as the expected strike outcome minus the hourly cost of the strike to labor, or $w(es) - w(u)$.

The difference between what management is willing to accept during negotiations and what labor is willing to accept during negotiations creates a **contract zone** of potential settlements. Both sides should prefer to reach settlements in the contract zone during negotiations to the alternative of taking a strike and ending up with the strike wage outcome and income losses during the strike.

It is, of course, possible for there not to be a contract zone. Case B in Exhibit 8–2 diagrams such a situation. In this case management expects a very low strike outcome of $w(esm)$, while the union expects a very high strike outcome of $w(esu)$. Even in the face of the expected strike costs, $w(m)$ and $w(u)$, there is no contract zone because $w(esu) - w(u)$ is greater than $w(esm) + w(m)$.

The important point that Hicks noted is that, in this framework, there is *no* contract zone *only* if the parties have very different expectations of the strike outcome. The fact is that there is some true strike outcome. For labor and management to have divergent expectations from the strike outcome requires that one or both of the parties make **miscalculations** in their prediction of the strike outcome. One or both of the parties must be excessively optimistic regarding what it thinks will settle a strike for there not to be a contract zone.

Hicks was led to the conclusion that strikes occur only in the presence of miscalculation. The key point is that since a strike imposes costs on both sides, it should be less attractive than a negotiated settlement.

Strikes could also occur even if there is a contract zone, but in the Hicks framework this also requires miscalculation. Hicks argued that there may be situations where, even though a contract zone exists, the parties do not locate a settlement within the zone. This occurs because—

through either previous bluffing or intransigence—the parties are unable to find the negotiated settlements they both would prefer over the strike outcome.

In the Hicks model negotiators have great latitude to further their side's interests. Given a particular contract zone it is in management's interest to reach a settlement at the lowest wage in the contract zone, and it is in labor's interest to reach the highest wage settlement in the contract zone.

Furthermore, during negotiations it is in each side's interest to attempt to change the other side's expectation of the strike outcome. Management would like to convince labor that the potential strike outcome is in fact a very low wage, and labor has an interest in convincing management that the potential strike outcome is a very high wage. The risk the parties face is that in their efforts to change the other side's expectation of the potential strike outcome, they might engage in tactics (such as bluffing or threats) that result in miscalculations, a strike, and the income losses associated with a strike.

Some of the Sources of Miscalculation

Note that the negotiators may hold expectations of the potential strike outcome that are different from those held by their constituents. Orley Ashenfelter and George Johnson posited that strikes occur because union members have unrealistic expectations.[12] They argued that management has accurate expectations of the strike outcome and so do union leaders, but union members are overly optimistic about what can be achieved in a strike. Under these conditions, strikes are a device to lower union members' expectations. Although it is difficult to justify why, of the three parties, union members alone carry unrealistic expectations, the Ashenfelter and Johnson framework highlights that strikes may occur when union members and leaders have diverging expectations of the strike outcome.

Hicks's model is a very useful starting point for analyzing the negotiations process. To build on his approach requires an understanding of the factors that influence the willingness and ability of either side to engage in a strike. These factors determine the wage the parties expect they will end up with at the end of a strike. Furthermore, the Hicks framework suggests the need to uncover those factors that lead either side to be overly optimistic about the potential strike outcome or in other ways to miscalculate during negotiations.

Behavioral Sources of Strikes   Behavioral factors such as the degree to which labor is integrated into the surrounding social community may be one source of miscalculation that leads to strikes. In a classic study Clark Kerr and Abraham Siegel analyzed strike data across countries and industries, finding that strike rates were consistently higher in certain industries, such as mining and longshoring.[13] The authors proposed that behavioral factors peculiar to certain industries were at least partly responsible for the higher strike rates. Workers in longshoring and mining often have their own subculture, they are distant from major population centers, and their work involves harsh physical labor. Kerr and Siegel argued that workers in these industries are comparatively poorly integrated into society and take out their frustrations and isolation by instigating relatively frequent strikes.

In Hicks's terminology, Kerr and Siegel identified a set of factors—social and geographic isolation—that contribute to the likelihood of miscalculation in bargaining. Note that Kerr and Siegel also emphasized that strike occurrence may have very little to do with the issues on the bargaining table.

Militance as a Cause of Strikes   Strikes also may occur as a result of the militance of the work force or union. Marxist theorists have noted that there is a strong statistical association between strike frequency rates and the business cycle. Over time (and across countries) strikes tend to occur more frequently during business upturns. This association is difficult to explain with the Hicks model, which predicts that wage settlements should be higher during business upturns, but strike frequency should not increase during business downturns.[14]

Marxist theorists instead argue that the procyclical movement in strike frequency demonstrates that conflict is a product of the bargaining power held by labor. This **bargaining power model of strikes** focuses on the fact that strikes are typically initiated by the union and the work force. Thus, during periods when the union's bargaining power is relatively weak, the union is less likely to press its demands and less likely to resort to a strike in seeking more favorable contract terms.[15]

The bargaining power thesis also recognizes that strikes are frequently initiated by workers on the shop floor who are upset by management's actions or by official union policy (these sorts of strikes often would be counted as unauthorized, or wildcat, strikes). Workers are less likely to engage in this sort of shop-floor action when labor markets are slack and workers fear the possibility of layoff.[16]

It is important to recognize that negotiations involve a large number of issues, that what would actually occur in a strike is highly uncertain, and that labor negotiations typically occur repeatedly between the same parties. These factors make it extremely difficult to predict the settlement point or causes of an impasse in any given negotiations.

Strike Activity

Exhibit 8–3 presents the record of strikes in the United States involving more than 1,000 workers since 1950.[17] These figures illustrate the wide

Exhibit 8–3   **U.S. Work Stoppages Involving 1,000 Workers or More**

Year	Number of Work Stoppages[*]	Number of Workers Involved (000)	Days Idle during Month	
			Number (000)	Work Time Lost
1950	424	1,698	30,390	0.26%
1960	222	896	13,260	0.09
1965	268	999	15,140	0.10
1966	321	1,300	16,000	0.10
1967	381	2,192	31,320	0.18
1968	392	1,855	35,567	0.20
1969	412	1,576	29,397	0.16
1970	381	2,468	52,761	0.29
1971	298	2,516	35,538	0.19
1972	250	975	16,764	0.09
1973	317	1,400	16,260	0.08
1974	424	1,796	31,809	0.16
1975	235	965	17,563	0.09
1976	231	1,519	23,962	0.12
1977	298	1,212	21,258	0.10
1978	219	1,006	23,774	0.11
1979	235	1,021	20,409	0.09
1980	187	795	20,884	0.09
1981	145	729	16,908	0.07
1982	96	656	9,061	0.04
1983	81	909	17,461	0.08
1984	62	376	8,499	0.04
1985	54	324	7,079	0.03
1986	69	533	11,861	0.05
1987	46	174	4,481	0.02
1988	40	118	4,381	0.02
1989	51	452	16,996	0.07

*Includes strikes and lockouts lasting a full shift or longer.
Sources: Data from *Daily Labor Report* (February 1990): No. 34.

variation that exists over time in the frequency of strikes. The number of strikes annually between 1975 and 1989, for example, ranged from 40 to 298. Approximately two-thirds of all strikes are over negotiations of a new contract; the remaining one-third are (generally shorter) strikes called over other issues during the term of an agreement.[18]

Note that strikes occur infrequently. The total work time lost due to strikes has averaged well below one-half of 1 percent per year. The low aggregate strike frequency reported in Exhibit 8–3 is a product of the fact that for any particular negotiations, the probability that a strike will result is low. For instance, in her analysis of a large sample of negotiations that involved manufacturing workers, Cynthia Gramm found that 13.8 percent of the negotiations involved a strike.[19] The low frequency of strikes is consistent with Hick's prediction that both parties usually have strong incentives to avoid strikes.

International Comparisons of Strike Activity

When the number of work days lost due to strikes and the frequency of strike rates across countries are compared, the United States stands near the top of the list. Strikes in the United States tend to be longer and involve more workers than in most other countries.[20] Yet, Great Britain, Canada, France, and Australia frequently have even more days lost each year due to strikes than the United States does.

Strikes play different roles in various countries. In the United States strikes are tactical weapons wielded to induce employers to change their bargaining positions. Strikes in some European, South American, or Asian countries, however, often have political motives.

Strikes will also vary in occurrence across countries depending on the degree of freedom trade unions have in the legal system. In some countries unions or strikes are outlawed, and it is not surprising that strike rates tend to be low in such countries. In some other countries unions are dominated by the government or play a part in the government through a union-led political party.[21] These factors also affect strike frequency.

Strike Occurrence and Strategies in the United States

Strikes occurred very infrequently in the United States in the 1980s and 1990s. As Exhibit 8–3 shows, in 1988 there were only 40 strikes and only 0.02 percent of work time was lost to strikes.

The 1980s and 1990s witnessed very low strike activity for a number of reasons. Whereas strikes in other periods seemed to provide a positive return to union members, strikes in the 1980s and 1990s frequently appeared to be defensive weapons used only as a last resort by unions fighting for their continued existence. The strikes that did take place were often more hostile, violent, and emotional than the earlier strikes. Since strikes were so bitter they entailed greater costs to both sides, and, consequently, both labor and management had incentives to avoid their occurrence.

In some cases in the 1980s and 1990s pay and work rule improvements came only after bitter strikes that, in turn, occasionally ended with the elimination of union representation. Wilson Meatpacking and Continental Airlines, for example, underwent bitter strikes and used bankruptcy protection to impose substantially lower pay and less costly work rules after their unions refused to agree to those terms in negotiations. Other meat-packing and some trucking firms also used reorganizations in corporate ownership to gain lower labor costs. Some of those firms closed their unionized operations and then reopened them on a nonunion basis, hiring the same workers back on significantly less favorable terms.[22]

The 1980s, and 1990s generally, were characterized by employers' increasing willingness to hire worker replacements in an attempt to break strikes—if not the union itself. In firms such as Phelps Dodge, management succeeded in those efforts: the existing union was dislodged in a decertification vote held among the ranks of the new permanent strike replacements.[23] The hiring and status of permanent strike replacements also was a central issue in a strike at Greyhound described in Box 8–3.

A Workplace Slowdown as an Alternative to a Strike

Indeed, the declining utility of strikes has led a number of unions to search for alternative ways to bring pressure on employers without risking the costs of a full-scale work stoppage. Box 8–4 excerpts a *Wall Street Journal* story that summarized the return to one strategy from the past: the work slowdown.

The Role of Strategy in Negotiations and Strikes

To understand the course of negotiations and strikes it is necessary to consider the role played by management and union strategies. This provides another illustration of a point made throughout this book, that activities at one level of the industrial relations system interrelate with activities at other levels.

The Role of Management Strategies

Management strategies have a major effect on the negotiations process and on the strike record. For one thing, management's investment and product decisions affect bargaining power and negotiations strategies. For example, whether management chooses a low-cost, high volume product strategy rather than a high-quality, high-innovation strategy shapes the extent to which the employer is concerned with lowering wage costs.

In Airlines Negotiations Peter Cappelli analyzed the course of airline concessionary bargaining in the early 1980s and the role of manage-

Box 8-3

"Permanent" Replacements and the 1990 Greyhound Strike

The Amalgamated Transit Union (ATU) represents 9,435 drivers, office workers, and mechanics at Greyhound Lines, Inc. On March 2, 1990, Greyhound workers went on strike after failed negotiations. Once the strike started Greyhound hired "permanent" replacement drivers and continued to operate although at a reduced service level.

In an effort to avoid major disruptions in interstate commerce, the Federal Mediation and Conciliation Service (FMCS) then interceded and succeeded in reviving negotiations. However, contract talks once again came to a standstill when ATU refused Greyhound's proposal to tie all wage increases to profitability and driver's safety records.

During the strike there were a number of violent events (37 reported shootings of buses and three reported shootings directed at terminals). At one point Greyhound cancelled all negotiations until seven days without a violent incident had passed. Greyhound also filed a civil damage suit under the Racketeer Influenced and Corrupt Organizations Act (RICO), charging the ATU with attempted murder, arson, and interference with interstate commerce.

On May 22, 1990, the ATU made an unconditional offer to return to work. However, Greyhound declared that with the permanent replacements in place it would be unable to accommodate very many of the returning strikers. Instead, Greyhound offered to place the returning strikers on a recall list.

The ATU then filed charges with the NLRB claiming that Greyhound had not bargained in good faith and therefore had to rehire striking drivers and discharge the replacements. (Federal law prohibits management from hiring permanent replacements in strike situations caused by an unfair labor practice.)

Plagued by the strike, heavy debt, and a reported $56 million loss, Greyhound filed for Chapter 11 bankruptcy on June 4, 1990. While the ATU continues to try to get the strikers their jobs back, Greyhound has declared the strike over.

Source: Daily Labor Report (Bureau of National Affairs): various issues from February 26, 1990, to May 8, 1990.

ment strategy.[24] He pointed out that those airline carriers, such as USAir and Piedmont Airlines, that succeeded as regional carriers were under less pressure than other carriers to engage in concessionary bargaining. By servicing flights where they had monopoly power, the regional carriers managed to avoid intense price competition. Deregulation had led to

Box 8–4

> ## Finding Strikes Harder To Win, More Unions Turn to Slowdowns
>
> The union hall at the sprawling McDonnell Douglas Corp. plant resembles an Army field office. Union officials plot strategy on three huge maps hanging on a wall, and lookouts on the roof keep score on the union's efforts by counting airplanes rolling off the assembly line.
>
> The United Auto Workers local here is orchestrating a work slowdown—an increasingly popular weapon among labor unions. In a contract dispute, union employees are refusing to install parts without blueprints, and they are working to the minimums of their job requirements. The union also is weighing a plan to stage mass grievances by having hundreds of workers blow whistles whenever a member has a complaint against a foreman. . . .
>
> The fight at McDonnell Douglas suggests that the battleground between union and management may be shifting to the assembly line from the picket line. As managements have become more adept at fighting strikes, labor unions are dredging up old-time alternatives such as the slowdown. If the strategy proves out, it could reshape union-management confrontations.
>
> Such tactics are being taken up by unions as diverse as the flight attendants at AMR Corp's American Airlines and the Brotherhood of Boilermakers. The AFL-CIO's Industrial Union Department recently published a booklet teaching such techniques to its member groups. The manual, called, "The Inside Game: Winning with Workplace Strategies," has been so popular that the initial press run of 5,000 copies has been quadrupled.
>
> "If management is going to launch a broadside against us, then we're going to fight back. They won't know what to expect from one day to the next," says Joseph Uehlein, the department's director of special projects.
>
> *Source:* Alex Kotlowitz, *Wall Street Journal* (22 May 1987), p. 1.

intensified competition among the national carriers and pressure on these carriers to lower their labor costs.

Cappelli also noted that it was the financially stronger national airlines, such as American and United, that first secured pay and work rule concessions. These carriers could offer employment security in exchange for the concessions. Airlines such as Continental and later TWA, on the other hand, had to resort to more drastic measures to win concessions—namely, bitter strikes. The latter carriers faced the threat of bankruptcy, were under extreme pressure for immediate labor cost cuts, and found it difficult to trade any quid pro quos for the concessions.

Management's strategic initiatives altered the *process* of bargaining as well. To convince the work force that concessions were necessary, management introduced new communication tactics, some of which bypassed the traditional role unions played as an intermediary between management and workers. At American Airlines, for example, direct mailings outlining management's position to the employees played a critical role in labor negotiations held in 1983. Auto companies continue to use news broadcasts and analyses shown on video monitors on the shop floor to inform workers about industry developments.

In Steel Negotiations   The course of collective bargaining in the steel industry in the mid-1980s further illustrates the important role played by management's strategic choices on the process of negotiations. In 1986 bargaining for new national agreements at the major integrated steel mills took place on a company-by-company basis. This was in sharp contrast to the long tradition of coordinated national bargaining that had occurred between the United Steelworkers (USW) and the major steel corporations.

This decentralized bargaining produced a variety of outcomes across the major steel companies. Without taking a strike, the Wheeling-Pittsburgh, National, and LTV steel companies all reached contract settlements that included wage and work rule concessions, but provided USW members with profit sharing or stock payouts and enhanced forms of participation in business decision making. USX (formerly U.S. Steel) and the USW, in contrast, engaged in a 184-day strike in 1986 before reaching a settlement that did not differ substantially from the settlements reached at the steel companies that had peacefully negotiated agreements earlier in 1986.[25] Why the difference?

The most important factor appears to have been the history of poor relations between U.S. Steel and the USW. U.S. Steel had antagonized the USW and its members when, after winning pay concessions in the 1982 steel negotiations, it purchased the Marathon Oil Company. The Steelworkers had assumed, mistakenly, that the profits generated in large part through their concessions would be used for further investment in the company's steel operations. Furthermore, day-to-day relations between labor and management had become sorely strained at the plant level at U.S. Steel (and later USX).

To some extent strained labor relations was a common feature of companies throughout the steel industry, intensified in recent years by numerous plant closings and layoffs. But industrial relations were especially bitter at U.S. Steel. Management at a number of the other steel companies seemed to believe that gaining the confidence of the work force was critical to their recovery. They had devoted considerable resources to communication or participation programs geared toward that objective. U.S. Steel and later USX management, in contrast, focused on diversification as the focal point of their business strategy and discounted the value of worker and union participation.

The Role of Union Strategies

Airline bargaining also reveals how union strategies can influence the course of negotiations and strikes. As Cappelli demonstrated, the various unions representing pilots and flight attendants often were more willing to agree to concessions than was the International Association of Machinists (IAM), which represented airline maintenance workers. Part of the explanation for this divergence lies in ideology: the pilots and flight attendants were less opposed to concessions as a matter of principle than was the IAM, whose national leader repeatedly condemned concessions.

Labor market factors were also important. The pilots and flight attendants had a great deal of income to lose if their employer went bankrupt, unlike the airline maintenance workers, who could more easily find comparable employment elsewhere in the labor market.

Summary

This chapter begins by analyzing the four subprocesses that make up negotiations. Distributive bargaining concerns issues in which the gain of one party is a loss to the other side. There is no possibility of joint gain with distributive issues.

Integrative bargaining, in contrast, involves issues in which it is possible for both sides to gain from the resolution of problems. The successful introduction of new technology, for example, can increase the profits received by management and the income received by the work force. A number of factors can make the resolution of integrative issues difficult. The overuse of tactics oriented toward distributive bargaining can block an exchange of information and the identification of potential integrative solutions. In some cases the parties are not able to settle integrative issues because they do not agree on how to divide the gains that would follow from integrative problem solving.

Intraorganizational bargaining arises from the differences in preferences that exist within either the union or management side. For the union it may be that union leaders have different views than the rank and file, or older union members may prefer a contract settlement that differs from what younger union members prefer. Plant versus corporate management differences are a frequent source of intraorganizational bargaining within management's ranks.

Attitudinal structuring concerns the extent to which trust exists between the union and management. It is trust that often facilitates the settlement of integrative issues. There are frequent other interrelationships across the four subprocesses of bargaining.

Negotiations typically involve a complex cycle. Management engages in extensive preparation during the formation of its wage and other targets. Labor market data and other economic data are used by research staffs to prepare these targets. Similar preparations occur on the union side. Many unions engage in the polling of members to formulate their bargaining demands.

There are a number of explanations as to why the parties in some cases reach an impasse and a strike occurs. The Hicks model emphasizes the role that miscalculation can play as the precipitator of a strike. Behavioral factors and worker militancy can also produce strikes.

The empirical record demonstrates the general infrequency of strikes in the United States and the especially low rates of strike occurrence in the 1980s. Events in the 1980s and 1990s illustrate the role played by management and union strategies as a factor that shapes negotiations and strikes.

Strikes represent one potential outcome to negotiations. The next chapter examines various techniques and procedures used to resolve strikes.

The other potential (and more frequent) outcome to negotiations is a contract. After discussing impasse resolution in Chapter 9, we consider the range of various contractual outcomes that are produced by collective bargaining.

Discussion Questions

1. Describe the four subprocesses of negotiations developed by Walton and McKersie.

2. What are the key aspects of the three stages in a typical negotiations cycle?

3. Describe the Hicks model of strikes.

4. Give some examples of how management strategy influenced the course of negotiations or strikes in the 1980s or 1990s.

Suggested Readings

Brecher, Jeremy. *Strike!* (Boston, MA.: South End Press, 1972).

Fisher, Roger, and William Ury, *Getting to Yes: Negotiating Agreement without Giving In* (New York: Penguin Books, 1981).

Hicks, John R. *The Theory of Wages* (New York: Macmillan, 1932).

Morse, Bruce. *How to Negotiate the Labor Agreement,* 10th ed. (Southfield, MI: Trends Publishing, 1984).

Walton, Richard E., and Robert B. McKersie. *A Behavioral Theory of Labor Negotiations* (New York: McGraw-Hill, 1965).

Young, Oran R. *Bargaining: Formal Theories of Negotiations* (Urbana: University of Illinois Press, 1975).

End Notes

1.   Richard E. Walton and Robert B. McKersie, *A Behavioral Theory of Labor Negotiations* (New York: McGraw-Hill, 1965).

2.   It is, of course, possible that there is some joint gain associated with a higher wage rate if labor productivity increases when wages are raised. This might result from the greater motivation workers feel when their pay goes up or from the better qualified workers the firm can recruit when it offers a higher wage. We ignore such considerations in the text discussion.

3.   Thomas A. Kochan, George P. Huber, and L. L. Cummings, "Determinants of Intraorganizational Conflict in Collective Bargaining in the Public Sector," *Administrative Science Quarterly* 20 (March 1975): 10–23.

4.   See Roger Fisher and William Ury, *Getting to Yes: Negotiating Agreement without Giving In* (New York: Penguin Books, 1981).

5.   One empirical study found negotiator hostility to be a very strong predictor of public sector impasses, although it was not a strong predictor of strikes. See Thomas A. Kochan and Jean Baderschneider, "Dependence on Impasse Procedures: Police and Firefighters in New York State." *Industrial and Labor Relations Review* 31 (July 1978): 431–449.

6.   For evidence on the role of personality traits in bargaining, see Jeffrey Z. Rubin and Bert T. Brown, "The Social Psychology of Bargaining and Negotiations" (New York: Academic Press, 1975), pp. 1583–1596, and Max Bazerman, *Judgement in Managerial Decision Making* (New York: John Wiley, 1986).

7.   Margaret A. Neale and Max H. Bazerman, "The Role of Perspective-Taking Ability in Negotiating under Different Forms of Arbitration," *Industrial and Labor Relations Review* 36 (April 1983): 378–388.

8.   Arthur M. Ross, *Trade Union Wage Policy* (Berkeley: University of California Press, 1948), pp. 45–74.

9.   This case is a real firm we encountered in our field work. The firm preferred not to be identified by name.

10.   This cycle is discussed in Carl M. Stevens, *Strategy and Collective Bargaining Negotiations* (New York: McGraw-Hill, 1963), pp. 41–46.

11.   John R. Hicks, *The Theory of Wages* (New York: Macmillan, 1932), chap. 2.

12.   Orley Ashenfelter and George E. Johnson, "Bargaining Theory, Trade Unions, and Industrial Strike Activity," *American Economic Review* 59 (March 1969): 35–49.

13.   Clark Kerr and Abraham Siegel, "The Interindustry Propensity to Strike," in *Industrial Conflict,* ed. Arthur Kornhauser, Robert Dubin, and Arthur M. Ross (New York: McGraw-Hill, 1954), pp. 189–212.

14.   Recently economists have constructed models that involve "asymmetric information" to explain strike occurrence. These models rely on the notion that

management knows the profitability of the firm, whereas the union must guess profitability and use wage offers to get the firm to reveal its true profitability. See, for example, Joseph S. Tracy, "An Investigation into the Determinants of U.S. Strike Activity," *American Economic Review* 76 (1986): 423–436.

15.   Interindustry studies of strikes often yield results that support the bargaining power model of strikes. Specifically, these studies show that strikes are more frequent in industries with lower levels of unemployment, higher percentages of men in the work force, and a higher percentage of the work force organized. See David Britt and Omer Galle, "Structural Antecedents of the Shape of Strikes: A Comparative Analysis," *American Sociological Review* 39 (October 1974): 642–651.

16.   For an interesting analysis of both contract strikes and strikes between contract negotiations that is consistent with a bargaining power model of strikes, see Sean Flaherty, "Contract Status and the Economic Determinants of Strike Activity," *Industrial Relations* 22 (Winter 1983): 20–33.

17.   Strike activity can be measured in a variety of ways, depending on the purpose of the analysis including frequency, duration and breadth (size). For analysis of these issues see Robert N. Stern, "Methodological Issues in Quantitative Strike Analysis," *Industrial Relations* 17 (February 1978): 32–42.

18.   Data on the total number of strikes and the number of strikes during negotiations and between contracts (not shown in Exhibit 8–3) can be found in *Handbook of Labor Statistics* (Washington, D.C.: Bureau of Labor Statistics, U.S. Department of Labor, various years). For a discussion of the procedures and difficulties involved in collecting and compiling statistics on work stoppages, see *Handbook of Methods for Survey Studies,* Bulletin 1910 (Washington, D.C.: Bureau of Labor Statistics, U.S. Department of Labor, 1976), chap. 27.

19.   Cynthia L. Gramm, "The Determinants of Strike Incidence and Severity: A Micro-Level Study," *Industrial and Labor Relations Review* 39 (April 1986): 361–376.

20.   Comparative strike data are reported in Greg J. Bamber and Russel D. Landsbury, eds., *International and Comparative Industrial Relations* (London: Allen & Unwin, 1987), table A–19, p. 258.

21.   These issues are addressed more fully in Chapter 14.

22.   See "The Pork Workers' Beef: Pay Cuts Persist," *Business Week* (15 April 1985), pp. 75–76.

23.   The decertification vote and the United Steelworkers' efforts to challenge that vote are discussed in "Steelworkers To Challenge Vote Results," *AFL-CIO News* (16 February 1985), p. 2.

24.   Peter Cappelli, "Competitive Pressures and Labor Relations in the Airline Industry," *Industrial Relations* 24 (1985): 316–338.

25.   "USX Members in Nine States Approve Pact with Contracting Out Prohibitions, Profit Sharing," *Steelabor* 52 (January 1987): 12–13.

Chapter 9

Impasse Resolution Procedures

When labor and management fail to reach agreement on a labor contract through a negotiated settlement they may turn to a procedural technique to resolve the impasse. This chapter, still in the middle (functional) level of Exhibit 1–1, describes various impasse resolution techniques, shows how these techniques affect the negotiations process, and assesses how well the techniques perform in settling impasses.

The chapter first describes mediation, a process by which a third party tries to lead labor and management to a negotiated settlement through enhanced communication and recommendations. The discussion then turns to fact-finding, a more constraining procedure in which the third party makes their recommendations in a formal report. The next impasse procedure considered is interest arbitration where the parties are constrained to adhere to the decision of the third party, the arbitrator.[1]

As with our other aspects of collective bargaining, in the area of impasse resolution there are a number of new roles emerging. This chapter finishes by discussing how new third-party roles are emerging to better respond to the environmental pressures that confront the parties and to improve labor-management relations.

Mediation

Facilitator,
No power

Mediation is the most widely used, yet the most informal, type of third-party intervention into collective bargaining. In **mediation** a neutral party assists the union and management negotiators in reaching a labor agreement. A mediator has no power to impose a settlement but, rather, acts as a facilitator for the bargaining parties.

Mediators keep the parties talking, they carry messages between the parties, and they make suggestions. Mediators must rely on their persuasion and communication skills to induce the parties to reach a voluntary agreement. A mediator's power is limited by the fact that he or she is an invited guest who can be asked to leave by either labor or management.

The Federal Mediation and Conciliation Service

The National Labor Relations Act specifies that the party proposing changes in a contract (usually the union) must notify the Federal Mediation and Conciliation Service (FMCS) at least 30 days before the start of a strike. The law does not require the parties to use mediation if they reach an impasse; yet the FMCS includes a staff of experienced mediators who are always ready to assist the negotiating parties if they are invited. Most states have state mediation and conciliation agencies that also make mediators available to negotiating parties. Both federal and state mediators are typically available free of charge.

FMCS annual reports estimate that approximately 15 to 20 percent of all cases in which 30-day strike notices were filed involved at least some informal (by telephone) type of mediation, and between 8 and 10 percent involved a formal mediation effort. The FMCS, the U.S. Secretary of Labor, other members of the President's cabinet, or the President is sometimes brought into the mediation process in important disputes or those designated as national emergencies, as defined by Title II of the Taft-Hartley Act. Mediation also arises frequently in hospital collective bargaining as the 1974 amendments to the NLRA, which extended the act's coverage to private, nonprofit hospitals, specify that in those hospitals mediation has to take place before a legal strike can occur.

Mediation under the Railway Labor Act

The Railway Labor Act contains provisions for a mediation phase before a dispute can go to the next step of the impasse process. The staff mediators of the National Mediation Board, the administrative agency for the Railway Labor Act, serve as mediators in bargaining that occurs under the coverage of the Railway Labor Act.

Mediation in the Public Sector

Mediation is more commonly used in the public sector than in the private. Almost all of the bargaining statutes that cover state and local government employees call for mediation as the first phase of the impasse resolution process. In the state of New York, for example, between 30 and 50 percent of all public sector negotiations reached an impasse and required mediation. Other states have reported somewhat lower rates of reliance on mediation, but all states report rates that exceed the FMCS reported average for the private sector.

In the public sector mediation is the province of staff mediators employed by the various state agencies that administer the public employment bargaining statutes, and in some states it is the province of ad hoc, part-time mediators. These ad hoc mediators generally hold full-time posts as college professors, lawyers, or members of the clergy or in some occupation related to labor-management relations.

The Kinds of Impasses That Can Be Settled by Mediation

Mediation is most successful in addressing conflicts that arise from poor communications and misunderstandings caused, for instance, by one party or both becoming overcommitted to their bargaining positions or by a lack of experience on the part of the negotiators. Mediation is least successful, on the other hand, in resolving conflicts caused by the economic context of the dispute, such as the employer's inability to pay or major differences in the parties' expectations.

Where there is a wide divergence in the demands of labor and management, the mediation process is limited because here some form of outside pressure is necessary to induce the parties to make major changes in their bottom-line positions. Thus, the mediation process is best suited to helping the parties move marginally beyond their initial positions. Only in conjunction with some external pressure can mediation be expected to succeed in getting the parties to adjust their bottom lines and reach agreement when a large gap exists between them.

Mediation is also ill-suited to impasses that involve intraorganizational conflicts. Consider again the example of the teacher dispute described in Box 8–1, which involved major internal conflicts within the school board's management. In that case one mediation session was held before the internal split was resolved, but little progress was made. After the session ended the mediator was informed that the superintendent was going to try to get the board negotiator dismissed. For the next two months an internal power struggle ensued. The mediator kept in touch by telephone with all the parties (including, much to the dismay of the board's negotiator, the school superintendent), but no formal mediation session took place until the superintendent emerged as the victor of the internal battle and the board negotiator was replaced. Obviously, the mediator in this case had to walk a fine line in trying to convince management to resolve its internal conflicts so that negotiations could proceed.

The less the mediator becomes involved in trying to mediate disputes within one of the parties' organizations, the greater the likelihood that the mediator will be accepted by both parties and the more open the parties will be to the mediator. The difficulty for mediators is that the failure to resolve this sort of internal dispute can make it impossible to resolve the union-management dispute.

What Mediators Do

The ultimate objective of a mediator is to help the bargaining parties reach a settlement. Yet there is more to mediation than the final step that settles the contract. Mediation follows a continuously narrowing course as the mediator seeks to whittle away at the various issues in the dispute. Progress toward a settlement is possible without necessarily completely resolving any of the issues. In other words, progress has been made if the parties have succeeded in narrowing their differences over the open issues.

Mediation is also a device designed to help the parties "come clean without prejudice"—that is, to explore informally or off the record what would happen if they were to move away from their bottom-line positions. Mediators commonly undertake this exploratory effort to prevent the parties from miscalculating. Thus, one major function of mediation is to allow tacit bargaining to take place, either directly between the parties or indirectly by both parties' sharing confidential bargaining information with the mediator.[2]

The mediator also tries to prevent the parties from holding back on concessions they would be willing to make to avoid a strike. It is by no means an easy task for the mediator to identify what the resistance points of the parties are, since in most instances the negotiators are extremely wary of sharing this information openly with the mediator. Instead, the mediator must guess at the parties' positions from the statements they make and then try to get the parties to put forward their best offer.

The Traits of Successful Mediators

What are the traits of a good mediator? Perhaps the most critical requirement is that the mediator be acceptable to the parties. Because of the voluntary nature of this form of intervention, no mediator can function well without the trust of the parties.

Acceptability is also important because the mediator must obtain from the parties confidential bargaining information. This information, if used indiscriminately, could destroy a party's bargaining strategy. Although acceptability can be achieved by reputation, most experienced negotiators will be hesitant to divulge confidential bargaining information merely because the mediator has a good reputation. Thus, the early stages of most mediation efforts (when the mediator is not personally known to the parties) is often taken up with the mediator's attempts to establish his or her credibility.

Acceptability can also be lost as the process unfolds. When this occurs, a mediator may voluntarily withdraw from the case or the parties may seek other means of resolving the dispute.

The litany of desirable mediator traits often reads like a modified Boy or Girl Scout oath: A good mediator is trustworthy, helpful, friendly, intelligent, funny, knowledgeable about the substantive issues in question, and so on. Evidence suggests that nothing substitutes for experience as a quality that assists in a mediator's gaining of acceptance and in other ways promotes successful mediation. Mediation is an art that one must learn by trial and error through on-the-job training.[3]

The novice mediator has a very difficult time breaking into the occupation. Fortunately, not every collective bargaining dispute constitutes a national emergency, and so novice mediators do obtain on-the-job training in some of the less complex disputes before taking on the challenge of a major case.

Box 9–1 describes one of the most successful interventions by a mediator in recent years. Here, William Usery (a former Secretary of Labor) mediated a long and bitter strike involving the Pittston Coal Company and the United Mine Workers Union. In this case, as in many other mediations, it took the skills of an experienced third party to overcome the hostility that had developed between labor and management.

The Dynamics of Mediation

Like negotiations, mediation often proceeds through a cycle of different stages. The strategies used by a mediator will vary at different stages of the cycle.[4]

The Initial Stage: Gaining Acceptability During the initial stages of mediation the mediator is primarily concerned with achieving acceptability and identifying the issues in the dispute, the attitudinal climate between the parties, and the distribution of power within each negotiating team. The initial stages of mediation call for a relatively passive, questioning, and listening role on the part of the mediator. Normally the mediator will shuttle between the two negotiating teams to explore issues. Separate sessions with the mediator also give the parties an outlet for their pent-up emotions and frustrations.

In these stages the parties will often lash out at each other, exaggerate their differences, and try to convince the mediator of their own rationality and the unreasonableness of their opponent. It is in these early sessions that bonds of trust and credibility can be established between the mediator and the parties.

In short, in the early stage of mediation the parties are testing the mediator. Some of the same grandstanding that occurs in the early stages of the negotiating cycle is repeated at this point in mediation for the benefit of the newest entrant into the process.

The biggest challenges for the mediator at this stage are (1) to accurately diagnose the nature of the dispute and the obstacles to a settlement and (2) to get something started that will produce movement toward a final resolution. The mediator is often faced with the statement by one party that "we made the last move so the next move is up to them," only to proceed to the other side and hear the same thing. The mediator cannot let either party's hesitance to move first stop the process before it is given a chance. Neither party, in all likelihood, wants this to happen, or the mediator would not have been called in the first place.

Box 9–1

Pittston/UAW Strike: A Case of Successful Mediation

The United Mine Workers (UMW) represent 2,000 Pittston Coal Company miners in Kentucky, Virginia, and West Virginia. On April 5, 1989, 1,400 Pittston miners struck at 30 sites (affecting 80 percent of Pittston's coal operations) after more than a year of negotiations failed to produce a contract. Pension, health benefit, safety practices, work schedule, work rules (such as nonunion contracting), and job security issues brought the parties to impasse.

In 1987 Pittston had withdrawn from the Bituminous Coal Operators Association (BCOA), which negotiates on behalf of 14 major coal companies. As a result, in 1989 Pittston negotiated one on one with the UMW. Before the negotiations, Pittston had aroused the UMW's anger by transferring operations to nonunion subsidiaries (double-breasting) and by laying off 3,000 workers. In addition, Pittston refused numerous union offers for contract extensions and rejected proposals for mediation.

The major stumbling block in negotiations was Pittston's refusal to contribute to a multiemployer trust fund that paid the medical benefits of 6,000 Pittston retired miners. The UMW's health and pension benefits agreement with Pittston (which expired February 1, 1989) was provided through a multiemployer plan established under a UMW agreement through the BCOA. Pittston terminated its contribution to the funds when it withdrew from the BCOA in 1988. Instead, Pittston implemented a benefit plan when it declared a bargaining impasse. The plan called for worker copayment of medical bills.

The UMW used a number of strike strategies including a boycott of Pittston's lenders. The Bakery and Confectionery Union, for example, withdrew $23 million and the UMW withdrew $6.7 million from the Crestar Financial Corporation of Virginia. Furthermore, wildcat strikes spread into northern and eastern West Virginia idling 40,000 miners in 20

The Middle Stage: Probing for Potential Compromises   Once the mediator overcomes this stalemate, the next step is to begin an exchange of proposals and test for potential areas of compromise. At this point it is crucial that the mediator have made an accurate diagnosis of the underlying sources of conflict. The mediator is now beginning to intervene more actively by trying to establish a framework for moving toward a settlement. If the mediator has misjudged the underlying difficulties and tries to push the parties toward a settlement prematurely, or in a way that does not overcome some of the major obstacles, his or her credibility can be lost. For example, a retired mediator once told the following story about one of his early experiences while mediating a strike on the West Coast between the International Longshoremen's and Warehousemen's Union and the Pacific Maritime Association:

> I started the mediation in the normal way, and the parties responded by discussing their differences in a serious fashion. I

states. Although not sanctioned by the union, the wildcat strikes were sparked by reports that various coal companies were helping Pittston fill its orders during the strike. However, a U.S. District Court ordered the striking miners to end the wildcat strikes in sympathy with UMW members. As a result of these tactics, the UMW International incurred $63 million in fines levied by the courts for violating both injunctions that limited the union' picketing and court orders that limited protests and civil-disobedience tactics.

After failed attempts at mediation, negotiations were declared at an impasse and the company implemented its contract proposal. Pittston, however, was able to meet its sales commitments by continuing production through the use of contractors and supervisors, purchases from third parties, and the use of stockpiles. Nevertheless, Pittston acknowledged a $3.6 million loss due to the strike.

As a last resort, Labor Secretary Elizabeth Dole appointed former Labor Secretary William Usery as super-mediator to resolve the United Mine Workers' strike against Pittston Coal Group, Inc. A tentative agreement was then struck and approved on February 20, 1990, by 63 percent of the voting members. The agreement included significant work rule changes in exchange for job security guarantees and the maintenance of prestrike-level health benefits. Pittston achieved one of its work rule goals as the new contract permits round-the-clock shift rotations for continuous mine operations. The contract also permits Pittston to subcontract the transportation of coal and repair and maintenance work at Pittston mines.

Source: Daily Labor Report (Bureau of National Affairs): various issues between November 29, 1988, and February 21, 1990.

then broke the parties into separate caucuses. When I went to talk with the union team I found them playing cards. To my dismay, I could not convince them to stop playing cards and get down to the business of settling the strike. Instead, I was told to go back to my hotel room and that they would call me when they needed me. Later I learned that the major obstacle to a settlement in this case was a structural one—the longshoremen on the West Coast were waiting for the longshoremen on the East Coast to settle their contract so that they could then use it as a pattern for their own settlement.

During this second stage of the mediation process the mediator continues to probe to identify the priorities and bottom-line positions of the two parties. The mediator actively probes for possible acceptable solutions to the outstanding issues. Once the parties have begun to discuss specific proposals, the mediator attempts to determine whether their bottom-line positions are close enough. If they are, then the mediator presses for modifications that would yield an agreement.

The mediator's ability to estimate the parties' bottom-line positions is crucial at this stage, as is the timing. When the mediator judges the bottom-line positions to be close enough to push toward a settlement, he or she takes a more assertive role. The mediator can suggest compromises, push the parties to make compromises they earlier stated they would be unwilling to make, and, in general, try to close the gap between the parties. Engaging in such active tactics prematurely (that is, when the parties are still too far apart) damages the mediator's credibility and acceptability.

When conditions are not ripe for settlement, the mediator must hold back from overly aggressive tactics. When the situation is ripe, however, the mediator must take action or risk losing the opportunity to forge a settlement. The mediator's prior experience helps guide him or her in judging timing. At this point in the process the art in mediation comes to the fore.

The Final Stage: The Push To Compromise   As the pressure to reach a settlement builds and the mediator senses that the time for the final push toward resolution is at hand, the mediator becomes ever more aggressive. No longer passively listening to the parties' arguments and rationalizations, the mediator tries to get the parties to face reality and adjust their expectations. The mediator may push compromise solutions, while at the same time being careful to avoid becoming identified with a specific settlement point.

Overidentification with a solution that one or both parties rejects can limit the continued usefulness of the mediator. Thus, any compromises are proposed merely as recommendations.

The dynamics within each of the negotiating teams often change at this point as well. Frequently, team members will differ on the substantive issues. The mediator will often look to the professional negotiators on each team for help in dealing with the more militant team members. Sometimes the reverse is true as well: the negotiator will look to the mediator for help in calming a militant faction on the bargaining team.

These final-hour sessions often require that someone—the mediator, the professional negotiator, or both—convince the hard-liners that the best deal is at hand and that the final compromises necessary to reach a settlement should now be made. Again, the parties' confidence in the mediator is critical to the success of these final dynamics.

Sometimes the mediator is called on in these final stages to make what are called mediator proposals. Mediator proposals are riskier and more formal ventures than the many other suggestions a mediator will make during the course of an intervention. A mediator proposal is normally made only when both parties are close to a settlement and the mediator believes that by making the proposal the parties will come to agreement.

In some cases the mediator may make a proposal that the parties have already tacitly agreed to, but, for political or other reasons, they prefer not to offer themselves. Some mediators believe that a proposal should never be made unless the mediator is sure it will be acceptable to both parties.

The preceding description of the dynamics of mediation points out that mediators must be aggressive in pushing the parties toward a settlement—when the climate, timing, and pressures on the parties are right. The parties often prefer aggressive mediators, and the aggressiveness of the mediator has been shown to be related to the effectiveness of the mediation process.[5]

The Parties' Views of Mediation

The negotiators face risks during mediation and as a result they do not always welcome the mediator with open arms. Following is advice one negotiator offered to other negotiators regarding how best to act during mediation. Note the skepticism apparent in this negotiator's view of mediation.

1. Understand which contract items are essential and which are not. Mediators will be tempted to impose additional pressure on the side that cannot see the forest for the trees. Remember that all your demands will not be achieved and that compromise is inevitable in collective bargaining.

2. Be careful in revealing your final position on the remaining issues too quickly to the mediator. Negotiators should keep something in reserve for the mediator. The mediator expects both sides to bargain with him.

3. Control the flow of information from the negotiating team to the mediator. It is preferable to have a single spokesman in sessions with the mediator. Otherwise, members of your team might accidentally reveal your final positions in an informal, free-flowing discussion.

4. Be wary of pressure from the mediator. It may be mediator-generated pressure. Do not be rushed or panicked into unnecessary concessions.

5. Demand a meeting with the other side if unusual pressure or confusion results from separate meetings with the mediator. The other side is not a party to mediator-generated pressure or deception. A joint meeting will reveal the independent activities of the mediator.

6. Maintain informal, friendly contacts with your opponents. Private conversations between the chief negotiators or the lawyers will provide additional information and limit possible distortion or pressure by the mediator.[6]

The Potential Tension between What Is Right and What Will Bring a Settlement

In theory the mediator is not supposed to be concerned with the substance of the outcome. Instead, the traditional view is that mediation works because the job of the mediator is simply to bring the parties to agreement. Yet there are definitely times when mediators have trouble accepting this principle. Consider, for example, the mediator in the case told in Box 9–2. Here, the mediator could not let his personnel views of management's negotiating style get in the way of a settlement.

All mediators must struggle from time to time with the moral question of how far to compromise their personal values or perceptions of equity in attempting to fashion a contract settlement. The traditional answer to this question has been that the mediator's primary responsibility is to help the parties reach an agreement and to keep his or her values and preferences, or the values and preferences of the larger society, out of the process. According to this view, the mediator should *not* attempt to create a settlement that would be most consistent with "the public interest." The traditional view holds that the way the mediator best represents the public interest is by helping prevent or end an impasse.[7]

The moral dilemma is even more difficult to resolve if questions of individual rights are part of the settlement package preferred by one of the parties. Mediators will continue to struggle with this moral dilemma

---

Box 9–2

Report of a Frustrated Mediator

This dispute was resolved after one long night of mediation. The parties had been negotiating for over a year. A factfinding report had been issued, and considerable progress had been made on economic issues. The major remaining unresolved issue was whether these employees [janitors, bus drivers, and cafeteria workers in a school district] would have binding grievance arbitration in their contract. . . . It was clear that the [school] Board was adamantly opposed to binding arbitration. . . . The [mediation] process was made more frustrating by the condescending attitude that the district administrators took toward the members of the bargaining unit. Unfortunately, my role at this final step of the process was simply to get the union negotiators to face the reality that there was no way they could get an agreement containing binding arbitration. . . .

If I had let my own feelings toward the Board negotiating team surface during mediation, the process would have not only broken down but made it even harder for the parties to put this long and frustrating case behind them. Consequently, one walks away from this type of dispute with a lot of pent-up anger and frustration.

and decide how high a priority they are willing to put on the singular goal of achieving a settlement.[8]

Fact-Finding

Under **fact-finding** a third party (fact finder) is called in to study the issues that are in dispute between labor and management negotiators who have reached an impasse in their negotiations. After gathering facts the fact finder then makes a report or announcement that may be made public. The fact finder's report often includes recommendations of what the fact finder believes is an appropriate settlement of the impasse. Fact-finding is premised on the hope that the recommendations and a neutral report will bring sufficient pressure on the parties to induce them to accept the recommendations of the fact finder or to use them as the basis for a negotiated settlement.

Fact-finding is rarely used in the private sector (like mediation it is not required by the NLRA), but it is more commonly used in the public sector.[9] Fact-finding also has been used frequently in negotiations that are covered under the Railway Labor Act (the Railroad Mediation Board can call it into play). The national emergency dispute procedures of the NLRA also authorize the use of fact-finding as part of the process by which the President can call into action an emergency impasse resolution board.

The Performance of Fact-Finding

The record of fact-finding is mixed.[10] In most cases fact-finding recommendations do not generate the pressure needed to produce a settlement.[11]

Although the overall record of fact-finding has been less than spectacular, the procedure can make contributions to resolving certain types of disputes. It seems to be most useful as a supplement to mediation when one party is faced with internal differences and needs the recommendations of an expert neutral to overcome internal (intraorganizational) opposition to a settlement. Recall that the existence of internal differences was noted as a particularly difficult type of dispute for mediation to resolve.

Fact-finding also appears to work better with inexperienced than with experienced negotiators. This may explain why the effectiveness of fact-finding in the public sector seems to have declined over time. As the parties become more familiar with fact-finding and more adept at negotiating, they are apt to place less weight on the expert opinion of an outsider.

Fact-finding is less effective in overcoming serious disputes caused by a large gap between the expectations of one party and the bottom-line position of the other. The more experienced the parties, the less effective fact-finding will be in changing these expectations. On the other hand, as just noted, it can be a very useful device for one of the negotiators in convincing the rest of his or her constituents to face reality and reduce their expectations.

A Case of Fact-Finding

The following describes the use of fact-finding in a dispute between a teachers' union and a school district. A neutral [person] first attempted to mediate the dispute but was discouraged by both the professional negotiators for each side. They explained that they knew what their differences were and that if it was up to them alone they could settle the dispute without the help of a neutral party. The problem was that the school board was unwilling to accept what both negotiators agreed was a reasonable salary settlement, and one faction within the union was unwilling to compromise on a contract-language issue. The mediator therefore agreed to proceed directly to fact-finding. In the course of the hearing, the two negotiators presented their cases in ways that made it clear to the fact finder what they tacitly agreed to, and, therefore, what they wanted the fact finder to recommend. The fact finder's recommendations closely followed these tacit resolutions. Both negotiators used the "neutral's recommendations" in selling the tacit agreement to their constituents.

Interest Arbitration

Interest arbitration involves the use of a third party (an arbitrator) who is empowered to impose a settlement in a contract dispute. In interest arbitration the arbitrator is setting the terms of the contract. Thus, interest arbitration is different from grievance (or rights) arbitration, in which an arbitrator is used to settle a dispute during the term or over the implementation of an existing contract.

Interest arbitration is not used very often in the private sector in the United States. The few exceptions in the private sector have been national emergency disputes under the Taft-Hartley or Railway Labor acts or cases in which the parties voluntarily submitted their disputes to arbitration. Interest arbitration has been used more frequently to settle impasses in public sector bargaining.

The NLRA gives labor and management the right to strike over impasses and thereby avoids the use of interest arbitration. Many proponents of collective bargaining in the private sector have long argued that the right to strike (and, hence, the absence of interest arbitration) was essential for the preservation of free collective bargaining.

As one scholar put it, over 20 years ago:

> In the case against compulsory arbitration there are distinguished prosecutors galore, and the catalog of inevitable disasters runs the

gamut from simple bad decisions to dislocation of the economic foundations of free enterprise. The division is not liberal/conservative, nor labor/management—there is no division. All the principal authorities are in agreement.[12]

In this view interest arbitration should be limited to cases of dire national emergency or to disputes in which the parties themselves decide it is in their interest to submit their dispute to a procedural substitute for the strike.

The Use of Interest Arbitration in the Public Sector

As the demand for public sector bargaining became more vocal, however, policymakers had to make a difficult choice: unions were calling for collective bargaining rights, while elected officials were reluctant to grant public employees the right to strike. Because of the general disfavor accorded interest arbitration, most states initially turned to fact-finding as a compromise between the "dual evils" of the right to strike and compulsory interest arbitration. Later, about half the states that had endorsed collective bargaining for public employees turned to some form of arbitration for resolving disputes between city governments and their police and fire fighters.

Since interest arbitration primarily has been used in the public sector, the public sector record reveals how interest arbitration works. This record is discussed below along with occasional reference to experience with arbitration in the private sector.

Types of Interest Arbitration

Exhibit 9–1 outlines the differences among the various forms of interest arbitration. The exhibit starts by differentiating between voluntary and compulsory arbitration. **Voluntary arbitration** is a dispute resolution system in which the parties agree to submit their differences to arbitration. **Compulsory arbitration** is a system in which law requires the parties to submit their unresolved differences to arbitration if they cannot reach a negotiated settlement on their own.

Another important distinction is the difference between conventional arbitration and final-offer arbitration. **Conventional arbitration** (which can be either voluntary or compulsory) is a dispute resolution process in which the arbitrator is free to fashion any award he or she deems appropriate. Although the conventional arbitration award may be a compromise between the proposals of the employer and those of the union, the arbitrator is also free to accept either party's proposals or, for that matter, to go below the employer's offer or above the union's (although that rarely happens).

In **final-offer arbitration** the arbitrator must choose either the employer's proposal or the union's; the arbitrator may not fashion his or

Exhibit 9–1
The Terminology of Alternative Forms of Interest Arbitration

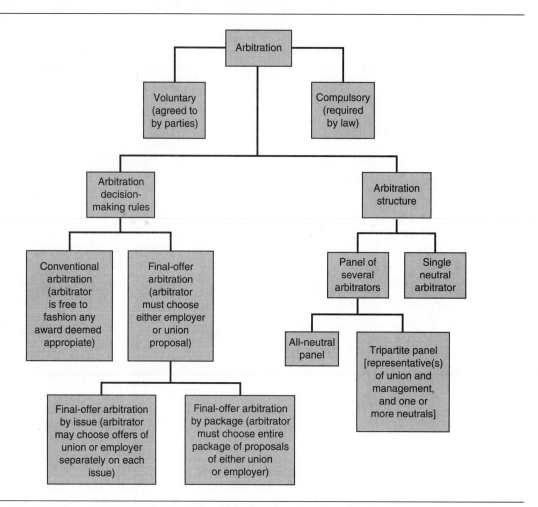

her own compromise. As a further distinction, final-offer arbitration may be handled on a total package basis—that is, the arbitrator must choose the complete offer of the employer or of the union on all issues. Or final offer arbitration can be handled on an issue-by-issue basis. The arbitrator, for example, might choose the employer's wage offer, the union's offer on health insurance, and the employer's offer on vacation days.[13]

There is yet another complication. The arbitrator can be an individual or a panel of individuals. Panels, in turn, can either be composed of all neutrals or can be tripartite. Tripartite panels are composed of one or more representatives of the employer, one or more representatives of the union, and one or more neutrals.

Debates over the Performance and Effects of Interest Arbitration

What does the use of interest arbitration do to the parties' ability to negotiate on their own? What kinds of settlements do arbitrators impose, and how do the arbitrators' settlements compare to the settlements labor and management reach on their own? Does interest arbitration actually prevent the occurrence of strikes? These questions are part of the controversy that surrounds the use of interest arbitration. The evidence on these issues is only summarized here because public sector experience with interest arbitration is examined in detail in Chapter 13.

Interest arbitration in the public sector has had a better record of preventing strikes than has fact-finding or bargaining without any impasse procedure. Although, obviously, no dispute resolution procedure, including interest arbitration, can prevent all strikes, interest arbitration appears to reduce the probability of strikes more than does fact-finding.

To date there is little evidence of excessive use of interest arbitration where it is available. The vast majority of disputes tend to be settled without resort to interest arbitration. Even in systems that have been followed for as long as 30 years, the rate of cases going to interest arbitration rarely exceeded 25 percent.[14]

The evidence of the effect of arbitration on contract terms is that arbitrators tend to impose settlements that are not very different from the settlements reached by parties bargaining where arbitration is not available as an impasse resolution procedure. The use of interest arbitration across a state (in settling public sector disputes) does appear to narrow the range of settlements by eliminating either extremely high or low settlements. The overall effect of interest arbitration on contract terms such as wage levels appears to be modest. Where an effect has been measured arbitration tends to lead to wage levels that are 5–10% higher than wages in jurisdictions where arbitration is not available.

Voluntary Interest Arbitration in the Private Sector

A number of voluntary interest arbitration schemes have been used in the private sector in electrical construction, large construction projects (such as the Cape Canaveral space center and the Alaska pipeline projects), and newspapers.

The **Experimental Negotiations Agreement (ENA)** was a voluntary interest arbitration plan first negotiated in 1972 between the United Steelworkers of America (USW) and the companies participating in a steel company bargaining association.[15] The parties gave up both the right to strike and the right to lock out for their contract negotiations. A three-person panel of arbitrators was to decide on the contract if the parties could not reach an agreement through negotiations. The ENA lasted for three rounds of contract negotiations. In each round the parties reached a contractual settlement without requiring an arbitrator's intervention.

The ENA was abandoned when industrywide bargaining was replaced in 1986 with separate company negotiations.

The only significant private sector use of interest arbitration now occurs in major league baseball in the setting of the salaries of players. The major league players and baseball club owners have, for a number of years, negotiated a master collective bargaining agreement. As stipulated in that master contract the salaries of individual players are determined through negotiations between each player and his respective club owner.

As Box 9–3 describes, the master agreement requires that a player's salary be set by an arbitrator if an impasse is reached between the player and the club owner in salary negotiations. Terms and conditions of employment for baseball palyers other than salary are not subject to interest arbitration.

Voluntary interest arbitration has also been used on an ad hoc basis as a conflict resolution device of last resort. From time to time difficult strikes, such as disputes between the U.S. Postal Service and postal worker unions, have been resolved with an agreement to arbitrate.

In voluntary interest arbitration schemes the parties normally limit the discretion of the arbitrator. The ENA, for example, prohibited the arbitrator from modifying the **union security, management rights, cost-of-living adjustment,** or local working conditions clauses of the contract. Moreover, local unions retained their right to strike over local issues. In baseball the arbitrator only rules on player salary (although other parts of the master baseball contract are subject to grievance arbitration).

The key to the negotiation of voluntary interest arbitration plans is that both parties must perceive benefits in agreeing to set aside the right to strike. Labor and management generally voluntarily accept interest arbitration only where strike costs are high.

Interest Arbitration Structure and Process

A wide array of choices is available for designing the structure of interest arbitration systems. These structural options determine the nature of the decision-making process in interest arbitration in important ways. In fact, the parties' choices of a particular structure reflects their fundamental views on the appropriate functions of an interest arbitration system. This section describes two divergent types of decision-making processes in interest arbitration and suggests how these are influenced by the structural design of the system.

A Combined Mediation-Arbitration Approach

The two decision-making processes available are (1) a mediation-arbitration process and (2) a judicial decision-making process. Advocates of the **mediation-arbitration** process view interest arbitration as an extension of the collective bargaining process in which the neutral arbitrator seeks to shape an award that is acceptable to the parties. Mediation-arbitration

Box 9–3

Major League Baseball Salary Arbitration Procedure

Eligibility
Any Player or Club may submit to salary arbitration with the consent of the other party. However, a player between three and six years of Major League service may submit to salary arbitration without the consent of the other party.

Selection of Arbitrator
The Players Association and the Player Relations Committee shall annually select the arbitrators.

Procedure
Within three days of salary arbitration submission, the Players Association and the Players Relations Committee exchange salary figures. The Player has the option of withdrawing within 7 days of the receipt of the Club's salary figure. And in the event the Club or Player reach a salary agreement before the arbitrator reaches his decision, the matter shall be withdrawn from arbitration.

Timetable and Decision
The Player and the Club submit the salary figures to the arbitrator at the hearing. The arbitration hearing is held as soon as possible after submission and scheduled between February 1 and February 20. The arbitrator may render his decision on the day of the hearing, and shall make every effort to decide no later than 24 hours following the close of the hearing. Finally, the arbitrator is limited to awarding only one or the other of the two figures submitted.

Conduct of Hearings
Each party is limited to one hour for initial presentation and a half-hour for rebuttal and submission. There are no continuances or adjournments.

Criteria
The criteria used in determining the Player's worth include the quality of the Player's contribution to his Club during the past season (including his overall performance, special qualities of leadership and public appeal), the length and consistency of his career contribution, the record of the Player's past compensation, comparative baseball salaries, the existence of any physical or mental defects on the part of the Player, and the recent performance record of the Club. In addition, any evidence relevant to these criteria may be submitted as evidence.

Source: Basic Agreement between the American and National League of Professional Baseball Clubs and the Major League Baseball Players Association, January 1, 1986.

places a premium on using the interest arbitration proceeding as a forum for continued negotiations or mediation, albeit with the arbitrator holding the ultimate authority to decide on the contract.

Those advocating the mediation-arbitration approach claim that no system of interest arbitration can hope to survive for long unless it produces outcomes that are acceptable to the parties. They also argue that the parties should maintain maximum control over the discretion of the arbitrator and should participate in the decision-making process as much as possible in order to maximize the amount and accuracy of the information used by the arbitrator in making the final decision.

A Judicial Approach

The countervailing view of interest arbitration holds that the arbitrator should focus on the "facts" of the case. In this judicial approach the arbitrator adheres strictly to predetermined criteria and is not influenced by the bargaining power or preferences of the parties.

The Influence of Arbitration Structure

The structure of an interest arbitration system can influence which of these two types of decision-making processes will prevail. The following structural features all favor a mediation-arbitration process:

1. Selection of the arbitrator by the parties

2. Use of a tripartite structure

3. Use of private ad hoc arbitrators appointed on a case-by-case basis or arbitrators who serve as long as they remain mutually acceptable to both parties

4. Use of decision-making criteria or standards that are flexible and can be assigned whatever weights are deemed appropriate to a given case

5. Forms of judicial review of the arbitration award that scrutinize only the procedural aspects of the process and not the substantive merits of the arbitrator's decision

The structural features favoring a judicial decision-making process, on the other hand, include selecting a single arbitrator (1) whose tenure for future cases is determined by someone other than the parties to the dispute, (2) who is required to apply predetermined weights to specified standards, and (3) whose decision can be reviewed by a court to determine whether the standards were appropriately applied in a given case.

Many state legislatures have been swayed by those favoring a mediation-arbitration process and most public sector interest arbitration systems have structural features favoring the mediation-arbitration approach. Whether the mediation-arbitration structure actually produces the outcomes predicted by its advocates—the greater acceptability of results and therefore its greater durability—remains a question for future research.

Nontraditional Dispute Resolution

The need for skilled third parties in conflict resolution and problem solving is not limited to the formal negotiations process. Indeed, in recent years a variety of new **dispute resolution** roles have emerged in settings where labor and management have been attempting to achieve fundamental changes in their bargaining relationships.

Neutrals, for example, are increasingly being called on to chair or facilitate labor-management committees, to serve as consultants to labor and management in quality-of-working-life programs, to facilitate the joint planning or design of a new plant or work system, or to work on other experimental projects designed to solve long-standing problems in a bargaining relationship. All of these roles require the skills of a labor mediator. In addition, however, these roles differ from traditional mediation or arbitration roles in several important ways.

First, most require that problems be addressed on an ongoing basis.[16] Often this requires that the parties first undergo a team-building effort to change their attitudes and to increase the level of trust they place in each other.

Second, these third parties must possess specialized knowledge of the substantive problems facing the parties. The third party is expected to be a consultant who brings technical expertise to bear on the problem and also is sensitive to the needs of both labor and management.

Third, the time horizon of the process tends to be very long. Whereas the traditional mediator is mainly concerned with achieving a settlement of the immediate impasse, third parties involved in these new roles must focus on the effects of any decision on the quality of the longer term relationship.

The behavior of the parties to these new processes is also significantly different from traditional labor-management behavior. For example, to be successful, long-term problem solving requires the parties to share information more readily than they do in traditional collective bargaining.

At the same time, however, the parties may still need to turn to the traditional mediation and arbitration processes. In short, effective conflict resolution and longer term problem solving are both critical to the success of contemporary collective bargaining relationships.

Key Organizations and Agencies Involved in Impasse Resolution

The key organizations and agencies that are involved in the resolution of impasses are summarized below.

American Arbitration Association (AAA): A private nonprofit organization that facilitates the process of arbitration. The AAA maintains lists of arbitrators and also makes available facilities that can be used for arbitration hearings. The AAA offers a number of seminars to train young arbitrators and to keep experienced arbitrators informed about emerging developments. Much of the arbitration work performed by AAA arbitrators is grievance arbitration, but AAA arbitrators do also become involved in interest arbitration.

Federal Mediation and Conciliation Service (FMCS): An agency of the federal government mandated by the National Labor Relations Act. The NLRA requires the FMCS be notified at least 30 days before a strike. The FMCS includes a staff of 250 mediators who offer their services to labor and management involved in impasses.

National Academy of Arbitrators (NAA): A professional society of experienced arbitrators. Most of the cases heard by NAA arbitrators are grievance arbitrations although NAA members are involved in interest arbitration.

National Mediation Board (NMB): An administrative agency created by the Railway Labor Act. One of the functions of the board is to mediate disputes between labor and management that arise in the transportation industries covered by the Railway Labor Act.

State mediation and conciliation Agencies: A variety of agencies exist at the state level to facilitate the mediation of labor impasses. In states that grant public employees bargaining rights there frequently exists a separate agency concerned with the public sector bargaining impasses. In New York, for example, the Public Employment Relations Board (PERB) provides mediation assistance among its many functions.

Summary

- Mediation
- Fact-Finding
- Interst Arbitration

This chapter describes the three major impasse resolution procedures—mediation, fact-finding, and interest arbitration. The use of these procedures has varied extensively. Mediation has been commonly used in both the private and public sectors. Fact-finding and interest arbitration, in contrast, have been used in the public sector, with only a few exceptions.

The procedures also vary in the degree to which they constrain the actions of labor and management. At one extreme is mediation, where the parties can, and sometimes do, either dismiss the mediator or ignore the advice given. At the other extreme is binding interest arbitration where the parties must follow the decision of the arbitrator.

The purpose of any impasse resolution procedure is to help the parties achieve a contract settlement that both labor and management find acceptable and a settlement that helps sustain a successful labor-man-

agement relationsip. Good mediators, fact finders, and arbitrators understand the issues that divide labor and management and have the ability
to offer creative solutions to these problems.

Discussion Questions

1. Describe the objectives of mediation.

2. What are the three stages that typically occur in a mediation?

3. Discuss some of the criticisms made of interest arbitration.

4. Contrast mediation-arbitration and judicial arbitration.

Suggested Readings

Cullen, Donald E. *National Emergency Disputes* (Ithaca: New York State School of
Industrial and Labor Relations, Cornell University, 1968).

Goldberg, Stephen B., Eric D. Green, and Frank E. A. Sander, *Dispute Resolution*
(Boston: Little, Brown, 1985).

Kolb, Deborah. *The Mediators* (Cambridge: MIT Press, 1982).

Pruitt, Dean G., and Jeffrey Z. Rubin. *Social Conflict: Escalation, Stalemate, and
Settlement* (New York: Random House, 1986).

Rubin, Jeffrey Z. *Dynamics of Third-Party Intervention* (New York: Praeger, 1981).

End Notes

1. The parties are constrained to adhere to the decision in a *binding* arbitration procedure. As discussed below there is occasional use of nonbinding arbitration.

2. Carl M. Steven, *Strategy and Collective Bargaining Negotiation* (New York:
McGraw-Hill, 1963), pp. 142–146.

3. One empirical study of mediation in the public sector did find a positive relationship between mediator experience (measured as the number of previous
mediation cases) and the effectiveness of mediation, especially effectiveness in
inducing movement toward settlement and in narrowing the number of issues
open in the dispute. See Thomas A. Kochan and Todd Jick, "The Public Sector
Mediation Process: A Theory and Empirical Examination," *Journal of Conflict
Resolution* 22 (June 1978): 209–240.

4. For analysis of mediation strategies, see Kenneth Kressel, *Mediation: An
Exploratory Survey* (Albany, NY: Association of Labor Mediation Agencies, 1972),
and Deborah Kolb, *The Mediators* (Cambridge: MIT Press, 1982).

5. One study shows a positive effect for mediator aggressiveness and further
noted that the more intense or difficult the dispute, the more aggressive the medi-

ator tended to be. See Paul F. Gerhart and John E. Drotning, "Dispute Settlement and the Intensity of the Mediator," *Industrial Relations* 19 (1980): 352–359.

6. Joseph F. Byrnes, "Mediator-Generated Pressure Tactics," *Journal of Collective Negotiations in the Public Sector* 7 (1978): 108.

7. Eva Robbins, *A Guide for Labor Mediators* (Honolulu: Industrial Relations Center, University of Hawaii, 1976).

8. For a good discussion of this dilemma, see William E. Simkin, *Mediation and the Dynamics of Collective Bargaining* (Washington, D.C.: Bureau of National Affairs, 1971), pp. 34–40.

9. Fact-finding is the most common form of dispute resolution for occupations other than police or fire fighters in the public sector (for the latter, interest arbitration is most common).

10. Fact-finding boards were highly successful in inducing settlements over the years 1926–40; that record deteriorated somewhat during the 1940s, 1950s, and 1960s and then improved again in the 1970s and 1980s.

11. A review of the experience with fact-finding suggested that its effectiveness declined over time on most of the criteria listed above. See Craig A. Olson, "The Dynamics of Dispute Resolution," in *Public Sector Bargaining,* 2d ed., ed. Benjamin Aaron, James L. Stern, and Joyce M. Najita (Washington, D.C.: Bureau of National Affairs, 1988), pp. 160–188.

12. Orme Phelps, "Compulsory Arbitration: Some Perspectives," *Industrial and Labor Relations Review* 18 (October 1964): 8.

13. Some final-offer procedures allow the arbitrator to choose the recommendation of a fact finder involved in an earlier step of the process.

14. Mark Thompson and James Cairnie, "Compulsory Arbitration: The Case of British Columbia Teachers," *Industrial and Labor Relations Review* 27 (October 1973): 3–17.

15. For a history of the ENA, see John Hoerr, *And the Wolf Finally Came* (New York: Praeger, 1987).

16. Stephen B. Goldberg, Jeanne M. Brett, and William Ury, "A Study in Metamediation," photocopy (Evanston, IL: School of Law, Northwestern University, 1987).

Chapter 10

Contract Terms
and Job Outcomes

For those engaged in collective bargaining and those who are trying to understand its consequences, the impact of collective bargaining agreements on job outcomes is of critical importance. This chapter continues the analysis of the middle (functional) tier of collective bargaining by examining the effects of collective bargaining on wages, fringe benefits, job security, and other bargaining outcomes. By comparing the wages, working conditions, and other job conditions of union and nonunion employees, it is possible to estimate the average effects of collective bargaining.

Rather than provide an exhaustive analysis of all the different ways bargaining affects employment conditions, this chapter focuses on union effects that are either the most common or the most controversial. This chapter also analyzes how collective bargaining outcomes have changed in recent years as labor and management have responded to the environmental pressures outlined in earlier chapters.

Tracing the Effects of Union Wage Increases

The relationship between job outcomes and unionization is complex. Changes in wages, for example, set off second-order changes in other job outcomes. Some of these second-order changes move in the same direction as the wage effects, whereas others move in the opposite direction. On the one hand, for example, an increase in wages may result in a corresponding, automatic *roll up* in such **fringe benefits** as sick leave pay, vacation pay, pensions, and unemployment benefits. On the other hand, a wage or benefit increase may create pressures for the firm to hold down costs by tightening work rules or other practices.

In this way the primary direct effects of unions set off a chain reaction. Primary union effects lead to adjustments by management and consequences for employment conditions. Once management makes adjustments and employment conditions are altered, unions typically react and try to modify management adjustments. This leads to secondary union effects on employment outcomes.

Exhibit 10–1 diagrams the chain reaction set off when a union raises wages. (Similar chains can be traced for other employment conditions.) There are three stages in this chain reaction.

Stage 1: Primary Union Effects

The **primary union effects** are on the compensation received by their members. If unions did not raise wages, they would have a hard time attracting and keeping members. Thus, the primary union wage effect is positive. The critical analytic question concerns the size of this and other primary effects.

Stage 2: Management Adjustments

Management takes a number of actions in response to the union's primary wage effects. The central motivation for the employer is to try to recoup the costs associated with union-negotiated improvements in wages through productivity increases or other measures.

Increases in labor costs result in some combination of the following responses by the firm: (1) a reduction in the scale of output and employment; (2) an increase in the price of the product; or (3) a substitution of capital for labor—all mechanisms for raising the marginal productivity of labor. These managerial reactions may lead to either higher prices or reduced employment opportunities, both of which are costly to society. At the same time, it should be recognized that society might value the union's primary effects, namely, the higher wages received by those employees covered by the union contract.

It is also possible that after identifying ways to recoup the costs initially imposed by a union contract, management ends up with productivity that is higher than it was before the primary union effects. Sumner

Exhibit 10–1
The Consequences of Union Effects on Wages

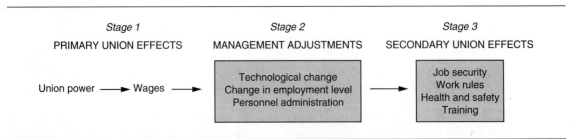

Slichter, in the 1940s, argued that such a **shock effect** was prevalent in management's response to early unionism.[1] Increases in wages, for example, may induce employees to quit less frequently and thereby reduce hiring and training costs to the firm. Higher wages also should attract better qualified workers for positions in the bargaining unit. In addition, improved wages might lead to employees who are more motivated and work harder.

Stage 3: Secondary Union Effects

If the employer reacts to a primary union effect by making at least some, if not all, of the adjustments discussed above, then employee welfare will be altered. The union might then take countervailing steps. This leads to **secondary union effects.**

If management responds to increased wage costs by reducing the number of jobs in the bargaining unit and increasing the pace of work, for example, the union may react to these changes in working conditions. The union might seek more elaborate job security language and stricter seniority rules in subsequent contract negotiations. The latter would represent secondary union effects on employment conditions.

Union Effects on Employment Conditions

The primary and secondary effects of unions on pay and working conditions depend on the union's bargaining power. The following sections review the empirical evidence regarding the magnitude of union effects on employment conditions.

Wages are of central importance to employees and employers. How do the earnings of union workers compare with what union workers would have earned if there had been no unions anywhere in the economy? This comparison is termed the **absolute union wage effect.** But because it is extremely difficult to estimate what employment conditions would have been in the absence of unions, most research has focused on assessing the relative union wage effect. The **relative union wage effect** compares the earnings of union and nonunion workers.[2]

The Empirical Evidence of Relative Union Wage Effects

Empirical studies indicate that the relative union wage effect averages 15 to 20 percent; that is, unionized workers earn roughly 15 to 20 percent more than nonunion workers. Relative union wage differentials increased in the 1970s and thus may have contributed to management's opposition to unions and the demand for concessions that followed in the 1980s. By the late 1980s the relative union wage differential had begun to decline.

Various studies also show that the wage effects of unions vary (1) over time, (2) over the course of the business cycle, (3) across occupations, (4) across industries, and (5) by workers' gender, race, education, and age.

Some of the key variations in union wage effects include the following:

1. Unions have a greater positive effect on the wages of blacks, and particularly black men, than on whites. There also is evidence that obtaining a union job and remaining on that job pays off more for black than for white youths.[3]

2. Unions reduce the effects of age and education on earnings. That is, unions increase the earnings of younger workers by raising the entry-level salaries on union jobs above what an inexperienced worker would be paid in a comparable nonunion job. At the upper end of the wage distribution, the effects of seniority provisions in union contracts protect older workers from wage erosion after they pass their peak productivity years.[4]

3. Unions have larger wage effects in some occupations. One study estimated the following union-nonunion pay differentials by occupation: laborers, 42 percent; transportation equipment operators, 38 percent; crafts workers, 19 percent; operatives, 18 percent; service workers, 15 percent; managers, 2 percent; clerical employees, 2 percent; and sales workers, 4 percent.[5]

4. Union wage effects also vary across industries. Union wages are relatively higher for white male, blue-collar workers: 43 percent in construction; 16 percent in transportation, communications, and utilities; 12 percent in nondurable goods manufacturing; and 9 percent in durable goods manufacturing.[6]

5. Unions reduce the white-collar/blue-collar wage differential in firms where blue-collar workers are organized. Unions also reduce intraindustry wage differentials by promoting wage standardization. The reduction in wage dispersion within an industry due to the presence of unions more than offsets the increase in earnings dispersion across industries, so that the net effect of unions is to reduce wage inequality among workers.[7]

6. Unions produce larger relative wage effects in less concentrated (less monopolistic) industries. This is because, even in the absence of unionization, highly concentrated industries would pay relatively high wages.[8]

Research Techniques

The following section discusses the techniques used by researchers to derive the findings discussed above. It may be of special interest to readers with statistical training. Statistical techniques and problems that are similar to those discussed below are involved in the analysis of union impacts on nonwage employment conditions as well.

The research technique most frequently used to measure relative union wage effects has been a regression analysis in which the wages of a pool of union and nonunion workers are used as the **dependent** (or outcome) **variable,** and the union status of each individual or group of workers is entered as an **independent** (or explanatory) **variable,** along with a series of controls for other determinants of wages.[9] The types of control variables normally included in these regression equations are (1) human capital or labor supply characteristics, such as worker age, education, experience, and training; (2) the region of the country; (3) worker race and gender (as measures of the effects of discrimination); (4) the industry and occupation; and (5) the size of the firm.

Several technical problems make it difficult to know if these estimates of the relative union effects provide a good approximation to the absolute effects of unions on employment conditions. The major problem in sorting out the net effects of unions is that union wages may spill over to the nonunion sector because to deter their employees from unionizing (the "threat" of unionization) nonunion employers may raise or, in the extreme case, match union-negotiated wage increases. The nonunion wage is therefore higher than it would be otherwise because of the **threat effect** of unionization. Thus, estimates of the relative union wage effect may understate the absolute effect of unions on wages because they do not fully account for the extent that union wages have spilled over to the nonunion sector.

On the other hand, by raising wages unions may induce unionized firms to cut back on employment. The workers displaced then seek employment in nonunion firms and industries. This **supply effect** results in lower wages for the nonunion workers. Thus, the supply effect leads to estimates of the relative union wage effect that may overstate the differential between union wages and the wages that would exist if there were no union. Researchers have not been able to identify whether the threat effects are larger than the supply effects of unions.

Another highly technical problem arises if union membership is influenced by wage levels.[10] Unions tend to organize high-wage industries or workers. As a result, the union coefficient in a single-stage regression equation captures both the effects of unions on wages (the true effect of interest here) and the effects of wages on unionization (that is, higher wage jobs attract more unionization). Estimates of the union's influence on wages may therefore be overstated or understated unless this reciprocal causality is accounted for.

Variation in Union Effects over Time

Union effects on wages and other employment conditions vary substantially over time. As with union growth there are both cyclical and structural factors.

The data show that unions have their largest relative wage effects during periods of recession because unions resist wage cuts whereas nonunion employees are not able to resist wage cutting during business downturns. As a result, unionized employees do relatively better than nonunion employees during business downturns. During business upturns, however, these relative wage effects decline.

Pay Concessions in the 1980s

Union bargaining power varies over time, in part as a product of changes in the economy. Collective bargaining in the 1980s, for example, produced wage outcomes that differed substantially from past patterns. It is useful to look closely at the pay concessions that occurred in the 1980s because the concessions illustrate how the economy can influence union effects.

Many collective bargaining agreements negotiated in the early 1980s either cut pay or did not provide a pay increase over the term of a contract (a pay freeze). These pay cuts or pay freezes were termed pay concessions. In 1982, 1.5 million workers, or 44 percent of those covered by newly signed major collective bargaining agreements, received first-year wage cuts or freezes.[11] In a summary of Bureau of Labor Statistics data on wage freezes and pay cuts in collective bargaining contracts covering 1,000 or more workers, Daniel Mitchell showed that between 1980 and 1984 about 50 percent of union members under those contracts experienced cuts or freezes lasting longer than one year.[12]

These wage concessions contributed to a nationwide drop in the rate of compensation increases, as illustrated in Exhibit 10–2. From 1982 to 1989 annual compensation rose between 1.6 and 3.4 percent, sharply lower than the rates of increase from 1979 to 1981 with annual raises of 6.6, 7.1, and 8.3 percent. Part of the decline in compensation increases reflected the diminishing contribution of cost-of-living adjustment (COLA) clauses in union contracts. Not only had the pace of inflation slowed, but, in a number of agreements, COLA payments were deferred or temporarily eliminated.[13]

Although the growth of nonunion wages and salaries was also slowing in the early 1980s, by 1983 nonunion employment costs had begun to rise faster than union costs (compare the figures in the second and third rows of Exhibit 10–2). The faster growth in nonunion earnings reversed the widening of the union-nonunion wage gap that had taken place in the 1970s.

By the late 1980s unions were doing relatively better in their wage negotiations than in the early 1980s. As the figures in the first row of Exhibit 10–2 show, compensation adjustments in 1989 were higher than any other year since 1981.

The use of two-tiered pay plans also declined. In 1990, two-tiered wage plans were mentioned in only 4 percent of all non-construction contracts.

Exhibit 10–2
Percentage Change in Compensation and Prices in the United States, 1979–90

	1979	1980	1981	1982	1983	1984	1985	1986	1987	1988	1989	1990
Compensation adjustments over the life of contracts covering 5,000 workers or more	6.6	7.1	8.3	2.8	3.0	2.8	2.7	1.6	2.6	2.5	3.4	3.2
Employment costs (wages, salaries, and benefits):												
Union	9.0	10.9	9.6	6.5	4.6	3.4	2.6	2.1	2.8	3.9	3.7	4.3
Nonunion	8.5	8.0	8.5	6.1	5.2	4.5	4.6	3.6	3.6	5.1	5.1	4.8
Annual percentage increase in the consumer price index (December to December)	13.3	12.5	8.9	3.8	3.8	3.9	3.8	1.1	4.4	4.4	4.6	6.1

Sources: For compensation adjustments, *Current Wage Developments* (March 1991), table 20; for employment costs from December to December, *Current Wage Developments,* calculated from various issues (1984–1991); for annual increase in the Consumer price index, *Economic Report of the President* (Washington, D.C.: GPO, February 1991), table B–62.

The proportion of contracts with two-tiered plans peaked at 11 percent in 1985.[14]

It is not clear whether the slowdown in union wage (and fringe benefit) advances that occurred in the 1980s represents a permanent change in the wage-setting process. On the one side in this debate are those who believe low union wages in the 1980s were caused by cyclical economic factors. Those on the other side of the debate believe union power was weakened by heightened international competition and other pressures. These analysts believe the intensified competitive pressures are unlikely to lessen for a long time.[15]

More research into this question will be needed to know whether a basic change in union wage setting has taken place, much less to determine the nature and causes of any such change. Whatever the future may tell us, there is no doubt that the wage settlements of the early and mid-1980s were small.

Union Effects on Wage Administration

Over the years, in addition to increasing wages, collective bargaining has introduced a number of innovations in the system of **wage administration.** Chief among these have been cost-of-living adjustments, deferred wage increases (sometimes referred to as **annual improvement factors**), **red circle wage rates** (stipulations that provide for rate retention to employees whose jobs are evaluated downward because of technological change), and **wage reopener** provisions (whereby the contract remains in force over several years, but wages are renegotiated at some specified point during the life of the agreement).[16]

In some industries, such as steel, the union and the employers have jointly developed complex systems for evaluating jobs and establishing a more rational structure of wage rates. In other industries, such as apparel, the unions and the employers negotiate and administer complicated **wage incentive** systems. The International Ladies' Garment Workers' Union, for example, provides technical advice to employers on incentive rates.[17]

Union Effects on Fringe Benefits

In general, unionized workers receive both a wider variety of benefits and a higher level of benefits than nonunion workers—for a variety of reasons.[18] A focus by unions on fringe benefits is long-standing.

During World War II, the War Labor Board first sanctioned and then actively encouraged bargaining over fringe benefits as a means of holding down the size of the basic wage increase. Since then unions have fought to broaden the scope of fringe benefits included among the mandatory subjects of bargaining. In the 1948 Inland Steel case the NLRB ruled that pension and retirement issues belonged on the mandatory list of subjects.[19] By the late 1950s the board had added to the list issues such as health insurance, sick leave, supplementary unemployment benefits, vacations, and holidays, and since then these have become standard provisions in almost all collective bargaining agreements.

The Sources of Unions' Demands for Fringe Benefits

Union demands for improvements in fringe benefits derive from a number of factors. For one thing, union membership typically includes a disproportionately high number of older workers and workers with longer tenure who are likely to place a particularly high priority on pensions and life insurance benefits. Furthermore, the preferences of these older union members are likely to carry much weight in union decision making because older union members tend to have greater political influence within unions.

Union concerns for certain fringe benefits also is a consequence of the fact that unionized employees exhibit low voluntary turnover (i.e., low quit rates). Since union members are likely to stay on their jobs for a longer time than do nonunion workers, they gain more from deferred benefits such as pension plans, vacation pay tied to seniority, early retirement, and disability retirement pay.

Employee demands for fringe benefits rise as employee income rises. Thus, as unions increase wages, their members will prefer to purchase additional fringe benefits over additional wage increases. This is compounded by the tax advantages associated with fringe benefits. Employees pay no income taxes on deferred benefits until they receive the benefits (if received as income, as in the case of a pension) and never pay tax on some benefits (such as medical care). Thus, workers will value an additional expenditure on fringe benefits more highly than the same expenditure on wages. This preference should increase as the wage level increases.

Trends in Fringe Benefit Provisions

For all the reasons discussed above, unionized employees exhibit a strong preference for fringe benefits. Research shows that unionized workers on average receive (1) a wider range of fringe benefits and (2) a greater percentage of their total compensation in the form of fringe benefits than do nonunion employees.[20] Among unionized private firms, for example, 22.7 percent of the total wage bill was allocated to fringe benefits, whereas among nonunion firms the fringe benefit allocation was 17.4 percent.[21]

The vast majority of unionized workers receive a comprehensive package of fringe benefits. The major breakthroughs in fringe benefit bargaining date back to the 1940s and early 1950s for such issues as pensions, vacations, sick leave, health and life insurance, and overtime. The 1960s and 1970s witnessed rapid escalations in benefit levels and the diffusion of these benefits across industries and workers. Survey research conducted by the U.S. Chamber of Commerce has documented the magnitude of the increase in fringe benefits. Employee benefits as a percentage of payroll for firms in the Chamber's surveys rose from 18.7 percent in 1951 to 37 percent in 1988.[22]

Union Effects on Work Rules

Employees are concerned with the difficulty and nature of their work at the same time that they are concerned with how much compensation they receive for performing that work. As a result, union effects extend beyond compensation. There are many **work rules** affecting matters such as the pace and difficulty of work that are of concern to unionized employees and, consequently, to unions. Below we review how unions generally influence some of the key work rules.

Protection from Arbitrary Treatment

Perhaps one of the most important effects of unions has been the protections they have secured for their members from arbitrary discipline, discharge, or denial of benefits. Unions pioneered the development of the principle of just cause for dismissal or discipline. Unions developed the grievance procedures ending in arbitration for adjudicating disputes over actions that violate the just-cause principle or some other term of the labor agreement. The installation of this system of industrial jurisprudence is often cited as one of the most distinct achievements of the U.S. collective bargaining system.

How does the union system of jurisprudence compare to practices in the nonunion sector? Although the number of nonunion grievance procedures has also swelled in recent years, most of them do not provide for binding arbitration by a neutral party.

Nonunion employees also receive some protection from statutory legal protections, although in most states (since state laws apply given the absence of federal law) these protections are limited.[23] The primary statutory protections available to workers dismissed, denied benefits, or denied promotions are those prohibiting such actions on the basis of discrimination by race, gender, age, religion, or support for union activity.

Seniority

Seniority plays a pivotal role in collective bargaining agreements, and the elaboration of **seniority rights** represents another important effect unions exert on employment conditions. Seniority rights are important to employees because they are used as a basis for allocating benefits and job opportunities to workers. Seniority rights are important to employers because they restrict the discretion they have in carrying out their personnel functions. And seniority is important to public officials as they administer equal employment opportunity labor policies.

Seniority is normally defined as the employee's length of service with the employer. In some cases, and for some purposes, it may be measured as the length of service in a particular department, job, or other subunit of the organization. Two types of seniority provisions commonly negotiated in collective bargaining agreements are benefit-status and competitive-status provisions. Benefit-status provisions tie increases in various economic benefits, such as vacations, pensions, supplementary unemployment pay, severance pay, and guaranteed annual wages, to the length of service with the employer. Competitive-status provisions make seniority a factor in personnel decisions, such as promotions, job assignments, layoffs, and transfers.

Seniority also plays a role in grievance arbitration. Most arbitrators will take the grievant's length of service into account in considering whether any disciplinary action taken against the worker was equitable, especially in light of a previously good personnel record.

As unionism developed in the United States, seniority emerged as an important bargaining goal of most unions as members viewed it as a means of curbing arbitrary treatment or favoritism in personnel decisions. Unions also came to support the notion that employees gain a property right to their jobs as their length of service increases.

Accordingly, unions argued that those employees with the longest service should (1) be entitled to the most secure jobs, (2) have the first opportunity to bid for better jobs as they open up, and (3) be accorded some deference in scheduling vacations and accruing other benefits.

Frequency and Common Forms of Seniority Language

Seniority provisions are mentioned as a factor to be used in promotion decisions in 83 percent of the manufacturing and 59 percent of the non-manufacturing agreements in a 1989 contract data base compiled by the Bureau of National Affairs (BNA).[24] The lower percentage in the nonmanufacturing contracts is largely attributable to the relative absence of these provisions in the construction industry. Of those contracts mentioning seniority in the BNA study only 5 percent specified that it be the sole criterion governing promotions within the bargaining unit. It served as a determining factor, provided the employee was qualified, in 43 percent of the contracts; as a secondary factor considered only when other qualifying factors were equal, in 25 percent of the contracts; and as a consideration equal to other factors in fewer than 1 percent of the contracts.[25]

Based on survey responses from about 400 firms Katharine Abraham and James Medoff concluded that in 1981 over three-quarters of hourly unionized employees worked in settings in which seniority had an important independent role in the promotion process.[26] Interestingly, the authors also found that seniority was used frequently in the nonunion sector as well, though not to as great a degree as within unionized firms. Over half of both hourly, nonunion employees and salaried, nonunion employees worked in settings in which seniority had an independent role in the promotion process.[27]

The Pros and Cons of Seniority Provisions

Seniority provisions protect the security of high seniority workers' incomes and jobs by reducing the threat of layoff by increasing the chances of bumping (displacing a newer employee when a layoff occurs). Seniority provisions also play an important role in shaping the career prospects of workers.

Both the scope of the seniority unit and the weight assigned to seniority in promotions affect the range of possible paths for upward mobility and the probability that an individual worker will obtain a promotion. Together the scope of the seniority unit and the weight given to seniority determine the expected length of time required to move up in the organization.

Strong seniority provisions improve the promotion chances of workers with average to below-average ability and motivation. These provisions may serve to slow the career advancement of younger employees who possess higher than average ability and motivation. Thus, seniority does not necessarily benefit all employees equally.

Seniority provisions offer employers both advantages and disadvantages. By increasing the economic and job security of workers as their tenure increases, seniority provisions should help stabilize the work force and reduce the number of valued workers who leave the firm. They also may reduce psychological stress and increase older workers' satisfaction with their jobs. Furthermore, if experience contributes to improved job performance, the use of seniority should help keep the most productive workers within the organization.

Seniority provisions reduce managers' and workers' uncertainty about the ongoing makeup of the work force. As a result, the employer can design jobs and training programs to ensure that job performance does improve with length of service, thereby simplifying the personnel function. Seniority provisions allow the employer to compute the probable movement of individual workers through different jobs in the organization over time.

All these benefits are greatest to those firms that have relatively routine and unchanging technologies in which individual worker differences have little affect on job performance. The more variable the technology and skill requirements, the greater the costs associated with strict adherence to seniority. In these cases employers will seek to limit both the scope of the seniority unit and the weight assigned to seniority in promotion decisions.

Strict adherence to seniority would entail large costs when jobs require great technical, professional, or artistic skill. It is hard to imagine, for example, seniority ever playing an important role in determining the starting lineup of a professional baseball team or the cast for a major motion picture.

The Importance of Seniority   This brief overview of the role of seniority provisions vividly illustrates why some see them as the heart of a collective bargaining agreement. Clearly, seniority provisions are among the most complex to negotiate and to modify as conditions change. The variations in the nature and strength of seniority provisions in union contracts attest to the ability of collective bargaining to fit a general principle to the specific circumstances of each bargaining pair.

Job and Income Security

In addition to its inherent importance to all workers, **job security** is of special concern to them because of how management adjusts to unions' primary effects. As unions increase wages and other labor costs they give employers reasons to make compensating adjustments in employment conditions that reduce employees' job security. An increase in labor costs, for example, leads firms to substitute technology for labor or to reduce the volume of production. Unions commonly respond to these adjustments by attempting to negotiate job and **income security** provisions that provide some protection from these adjustments or at least set rules about how the adjustment will be made (e.g., seniority rules regarding who gets laid off first if layoffs occur).

Some security provisions make it more difficult or costly for the employer to substitute either nonunion labor or capital inputs for union work covered under the contract. The union may also try to negotiate additional paid time off to reduce the employment losses or require the hiring of additional workers.

Employers frequently oppose demands for job and income security provisions because they (1) increase labor costs, (2) reduce employers' ability to adjust labor costs to fluctuations in business conditions, and (3) limit managerial discretion and freedom.

The comprehensiveness of the job and income security protections that unionized workers achieve is a function of the bargaining power of the union. Bargaining over these issues represents the classic conflict over the workers' desire for security and the employer's desire for autonomy and flexibility.

Job Preservation   Some job security provisions are geared toward preserving jobs. One way unions try to preserve jobs is by negotiating **work-sharing** provisions that cut the workweek during periods of slack demand rather than allow the layoff of employees. This practice is found in 18 percent of all union contracts and in almost all apparel industry contracts.[28]

One major disincentive to work sharing is that **unemployment benefits** in most states do not cover workers on a shortened workweek. In most states a complete layoff is necessary for unemployment eligibility, although a few states have begun to experiment with providing unemployment compensation to workers affected by a reduction in work hours. Most contractual work-sharing agreements limit the time period during which this alternative can be used to forestall layoffs. Most also limit the number of hours that will be reduced before commencing layoffs.

Other types of work rule provisions that are geared to preserving jobs are restrictions on the following: supervisors' rights to do bargaining-unit work; transferring employees and filling vacancies; the ratio of apprentices to journeymen; management's right to change the pace of work; and the extent of subcontracting. Many of these provisions are desired by the union for their contribution to increased safety and other reasons in addition to their effects on job preservation. Note that management sometimes complains that these procedures lead to their retaining more workers than are needed to perform the work, or what is referred to as featherbedding.

Income Security during Temporary Layoffs   When sales turn down firms commonly quickly try to reduce employment levels. This leads to layoffs that are temporary in duration if the laid-off workers are recalled when business improves. Temporary layoffs are a common occurrence in industries that produce durable goods such as automobiles or household appliances.

In the face of their experience with frequent layoffs over the post-World War period, unions in the United States developed a number of contractual provisions that address short-term layoffs. Many of these provisions provide income security rather than employment security.

The two major forms of income protection against short-term fluctuations in the demand for work are **supplementary unemployment benefit** (SUB) plans and **guaranteed annual wage** plans. The first major SUB plan to be negotiated was in the auto industry in 1955.[29] The United Auto Workers had originally sought a form of guaranteed annual income. Ford Motor Company, the target firm in that round of negotiations, countered with what has grown into the industry's SUB plan. The pattern set in the auto industry spread quickly.

The BNA data show that 14 percent of the contracts sampled in 1962 and 1989 had SUB plans.[30] Thus, like wage guarantees, most of the major SUB plans were negotiated in the 1950s. Since then the eligibility rules and benefits under those plans have been liberalized, but they have not spread to a significant number of other contracts or workers.

Work or pay guarantees were provided in 13 percent of major contracts in 1989.[31] This was up from 6 percent in 1966. The majority of these provide a limited weekly income guarantee for those who begin a given workweek; only a few provide long-term income maintenance in the absence of available work.

Programs in Response to Permanent Job Loss   Not all workers are recalled when laid off. As a result, another important set of collective bargaining clauses deals with permanent job loss caused by either technological change or a plant shutdown. Here the provisions address both job preservation and income protection. They include interplant **transfer rights** or transfer rights to other jobs within the plant or organization; early notice of technological change, a plant shutdown, or both; and relocation allowances.

Plant shutdown or relocation limitations are discussed in 25 percent of the BNA's 1989 contract file, up from 18 percent in 1983.[32] Early notice to the work force when a sizeable permanent layoff occurs is now required by federal law.

In the face of the substantial layoffs that occurred in many nonunion and unionized workplaces in the 1980s, Congress passed *The Worker Adjustment and Retraining Notification Act (S2527),* which took effect in February 1989. This law requires that employers provide advance notice to employees affected by plant closings: employers with 100 or more employees must give 60 days advance notice of plant shutdowns when they affect at least 50 workers at an employment site. In addition, the law contains a mass layoff provision, requiring advance notice in the case of layoffs that last more than six months and that affect 50 or more employees, 33 percent or more of the work force at a site, or more than 500 workers for any time frame.

Employment Security Initiatives in the 1980s and 1990s

Responding to the same pressures that induced Congress to require advance notice of plant closings, a number of recent collective bargaining agreements provided enhanced employment security through a variety of mechanisms. For example, American Airlines introduced lifetime job guarantees to workers on the payroll as of 1982. (The American Airlines contract also substantially lowered the pay of new hires.) The 1982 agreements at Ford and GM created a guaranteed income stream program to compensate high-seniority autoworkers permanently laid off because of plant closings or other reasons. In 1984 the two automakers instituted a *jobs bank,* guaranteeing income support or redeployment to workers displaced by technological change, outsourcing, corporate restructuring, or negotiated productivity improvements.

In their 1990–93 labor agreements with the UAW the auto companies adopted a host of measures that provided income security to workers. These contracts also increased the incentives for older workers to retire or quit. The auto companies hope that through attrition they can avoid the need to layoff workers and thereby avoid the high costs to the company for such layoffs imposed by clauses in their labor agreements.

Box 10–1 outlines the income security and early retirement features of the 1990–93 labor agreement reached between General Motors and the UAW. Agreements with similar terms were reached in 1990 at the Ford and Chrysler auto companies.

Why the Emphasis on Employment Security

The dominance of employment security as a quid pro quo for union concessions was hardly surprising in light of the extensive layoffs of the 1980s and 1990s. Over most of the post-World War II period employment insecurity had taken the form of layoffs that were temporary, and most workers were eventually recalled from layoff. The unions' response had been to bargain for income maintenance via unemployment benefits supplemental to the state unemployment insurance programs.

Faced with the extensive economic restructuring of industries that began in the late 1970s, workers with substantial seniority could no longer assume they would be called back. Plant shutdowns and the worldwide consolidation and technological updating of manufacturing facilities made recall less likely. As a result, workers and their unions shifted the bargaining agenda to demand greater guarantees of employment security.

The development of new work structures geared toward greater flexibility in the deployment of the work force has also spurred interest in employment security. Traditionally, plants were organized along the conventional lines of occupations commonly found in the external labor market, lessening the difficulties associated with layoffs by making alternative employment more easily available. But as firms pushed for fewer classifications and more firm-specific training, workers sought assurances of employment continuity. Without such assurances they feared

Box 10–1

The Income and Employment Security Features of the 1990–93 General Motors-UAW Contract

The 1990–93 General Motors-UAW labor agreement includes a number of income and employment security clauses. Perhaps the most innovative feature of the contract is the provision that workers laid off for any reason for more than 36 weeks during the term of the three-year agreement cannot be subject to further layoff. Rather, beyond 36 weeks of layoff workers qualify to receive full pay and benefits while they are placed in the jointly managed Jobs Bank. This provision goes beyond earlier Jobs Bank protections which applied only to workers laid off for specific reasons and excluded layoffs due to market-produced declines in the sales of autos.

The new contract also increases the incentives for workers to either retire or quit from GM and provides greater income support to workers on temporary layoff. The new contractual provisions include: older workers can go on "leave" at 85 percent of regular pay until eligible for retirement; pensions for workers who retire are raised 20 percent; early retirement benefits are raised 17 percent and the minimum retirement age is lowered; workers not eligible to retire who chose to voluntarily quit receive increased benefits (up to $72,000); high-seniority workers who are laid off can receive up to three years of supplementary unemployment benefits (at up to 95 percent of regular pay).

General Motors agreed to spend up to $4 billion over the term of the three-year agreement to fund the income and employment security provisions of the contract.

Source: Gregory A. Patterson and Joseph B. White, "GM-UAW Pact Allows Company To Cut Payroll in Return for Worker Buy-Outs," *Wall Street Journal* (September 19, 1990), p. A3.

---

their specialized training would make them ill-equipped for jobs elsewhere.

Employment security programs also became attractive because the teamwork systems being simultaneously introduced in many settings were particularly effective if employees were highly trained and committed to their work. Both of those attributes can be encouraged by enhancing workers' employment security.

Nevertheless, employment security programs as comprehensive as those negotiated in the auto industry to date are included in only a few other collective bargaining agreements in this country. The interesting question is whether these recent experiments with enhanced employment security will spread to other work sites in the future.

It also remains to be seen exactly how the new employment security programs are implemented and what their implications are. Some programs provide employment guarantees to only a subset of the work force, while others provide for the hiring of more temporary and part-time workers. As a result, these plans could engender intense political rivalries within unions—between those workers who have employment security and those who do not. It also remains to be seen whether employment security results in greater worker acceptance of flexible work rules and a greater bond of commitment between the firm and its work force.

Management's Response to Work Rules

The work rules provided in the labor contract, grievance procedures, seniority rights, or job security, all limit the amount of discretion management exercises at the workplace. Management usually takes a number of actions to expand its discretion over work rules.

Management Rights Clauses

One strategy management employs to limit the effects of restrictive work rules is to negotiate a **management rights** clause. In 1989 management rights statements appeared in 83 percent of manufacturing contracts and in 71 percent of nonmanufacturing contracts.[33] Some of the provisions were simple, general statements such as, "The supervision, management, and control of the company's business, operations, and plants are exclusively the function of this company." The majority of the provisions, however, enumerated a specific list of rights reserved to management, as in the following example:

> The rights to hire, promote, discharge or discipline for cause, and maintain the discipline and efficiency of employees are the sole responsibility of the corporation except that union members shall not be discriminated against as such. In addition, the products to be manufactured, the location of plants, the schedules of production, and the methods, processes, and means of manufacturing are solely and exclusively the responsibility of the corporation.

The obvious purpose of management rights clauses is to limit the territory of union influence and retain for management the freedom to run the organization. The traditional labor relations literature has articulated two views of the management rights concept; these are used by arbitrators and the courts in resolving disputes over contract interpretation. The **reserved, or residual, rights doctrine** takes the view that all rights not covered by a specific clause in the contract are retained by management. In contrast, the **implied obligations doctrine** assumes that the union recognition clause requires management to negotiate changes in terms and conditions of employment even in the absence of an express contract provision that covers the issue involved.[34]

The Residual Rights Doctrine   The residual rights doctrine has been most popular among management practitioners. Those supporting this view argue that it derives logically from the property rights that stockholders (or the public, in a governmental organization) delegate to management. The supporters claim that neither union members nor their representatives are directly accountable to stockholders. This view holds that unions should not have a right to infringe on the ability of management to act on the owners' behalf, except in the case of an issue over which management has agreed to share its authority by way of specific contract language.

The Implied Obligations Doctrine   The residual rights doctrine has been challenged by labor relations scholars and arbitrators who support the implied obligations doctrine. This position is worth examining because some courts have begun to use it as a rationale for limiting the firm's freedom to hire and fire at will.

Neil Chamberlain and James Kuhn, for example, proposed that while management may have a property right to allocate the resources needed to run the organization, the management of human resources requires the consent of the managed. They stated that workers are under no legal compulsion to cooperate with management.[35] Charles Killingsworth made a similar argument, noting that management's "right" to assert discretion over any subject is limited in a very practical way by its power to impose its will on employees. He noted that the residual rights doctrine is of little value as a legal principle because it ignores the power relationship between employer and employees.[36]

Productivity Bargaining

Where collective bargaining has produced work rules that inhibit labor efficiency, the parties can engage in **productivity bargaining** to eliminate those restrictions.[37] Productivity bargaining can take one of two forms: a one-time buyout of outmoded practices; or a long-term, joint union-management program for adjusting to technological change.

A highly publicized example of productivity bargaining occurred in 1960 when the Pacific Maritime Association, representing the west coast longshore industry, signed a Mechanization and Modernization Agreement with the International Longshoremen and Warehousemen's Union.[38] This agreement provided a $5 million productivity fund, wage and employment guarantees, and incentives for early retirement by high-seniority workers in return for an end to work rules that required multiple handling of goods and employment of more workers than needed as containerization swept through the docks.

In 1974 the International Typographical Union and the New York City newspapers negotiated an 11-year agreement that provided lifetime job security and early retirement incentives to typesetters in return for management's introduction of computerized technologies. The railroad industry also has periodically experienced productivity buyouts that involve quid pro quos exchanged for reductions in crew size.

Concessionary Work Rule Changes

In their efforts to slow the growth in unit labor costs and respond to environmental pressures, labor and management in the 1980s and 1990s often made changes in work rules part of their concessionary labor agreements. In itself, the negotiation of work rule change was not unusual. The tendency for employers to question work rule provisions more aggressively during periods of slack demand or intensified competition has been well documented in the collective bargaining literature. Slichter described just such an effect that resulted from the intensified competition between union and nonunion plants that took place historically during various recessions and the depression of the 1930s.[39] The 1958–59 recession also resulted in U.S. employers' taking a hard line on work rules and attempting to regain some of the prerogatives they had gradually lost during the business expansions of World War II and the early postwar years.[40]

The productivity bargaining literature of the 1950s and early 1970s represented another installment in the saga of how work rules are subject to periodic buyouts during hard times.[41] Finally, the 1972 recession prompted Peter Henle to document cases of "reverse collective bargaining" that came about under the downturn.[42] Nevertheless, although work rule concessions were a part of collective bargaining in the past, particularly during deep recessions, the recent depth and pervasiveness of these concessions is unprecedented in all the years since the great depression.

The general focus of management's demands since the early 1980s for concessions has been to increase its flexibility in human resource management. This push has been particularly salient in management proposals for broader job classifications, greater managerial discretion in allocating overtime, more liberal subcontracting rights, and restrictions on voluntary transfers or other movements across jobs.

In a number of trucking companies, for example, work rule changes involved drivers' taking on some loading tasks. In steel plants the concessions included increases in the pace of work, often accomplished through reductions in staffing levels. Airline pilots and flight attendants were induced to agree to increases in their flight hours. Autoworkers made concessions that limited the frequency of intraplant transfers (bumps) that were allowed during layoffs.

For many workers across industries, work rule concessions also brought reductions in the number of job classifications and a lessening of the role seniority plays in job transfers and job assignments. Exhibit 10–3

Exhibit 10–3

A Draft of Job Unification of Trades and Crafts in a Steel Works

NEW JOB CLASSIFICATION

EXISTING JOB CLASSIFICATION

Electrician
- Motor inspector
- Wireman
- Electrical repairman
- Wireman leader
- Power repairman
- Tack welding function

Electronic technician
- Instrument repairman
- Electronic repairman

Motor winder
- Winder

Mechanic
- Millwright
- Maintenance repairman
- Pipe fitter
- Rigger
- Welder
- Fitting fabricator
- Pipe repairman
- Roll shop machine repairman
- Maintenance repair layout man
- Sheeter
- Rigger leader
- System controller
- Rigger shop general layout man
- Weld shop equipment repairman
- General mechanic—rigger shop
- Layout man—dock

Crane repairman
- Crane millwright
- Crane inspector

Refrigeration repairman
- Refrigeration repairman

Machinist
- Machinist
- Bearing repairman

Mobile equipment repairman
- Mobile equipment mechanic
- Tractor repairman

Blacksmith
- Blacksmith
- Forger

Exhibit 10–3
(*continued*)

NEW JOB CLASSIFICATION   EXISTING JOB CLASSIFICATION

Industrial carpenter ————————————— Carpenter
                                          Painter
                                          Decorative painter
                                          Plasterer
                                          Sign painter

Bricklayer ———————————————————————— Bricklayer

Turbine and boiler ————————————————— Turbine repairman
    repairman   Boiler repairman

Roll turner ——————————————————————— Roll turner

Electrical helper ——————————————————— Motor inspector helper
                                          Wireman helper
                                          Instrument repairman helper
                                          Electronic repairman helper
                                          Repairman helper (winder)
                                          Repairman helper (yard)
                                          Tractor repairman helper
                                          Crane millwright helper
                                          Power repairman helper

Mechanical helper —————————————————— Millwright helper
                                          Welder helper
                                          Maintenance repairman
                                              helper
                                          Pipe fitter helper
                                          Rigger helper
                                          Machinist helper
                                          Blacksmith helper

Service helper ——————————————————————— Carpenter helper
                                          Painter helper
                                          Bricklayer helper
                                          Helper (roll shop)
                                          Turbine and machine
                                              repairman helper
                                          Turbine repair helper

Source: Takahara Yamagami, "The Survival Strategy for the U.S. Steel Industry," master's thesis (Cambridge: Sloan School of Management, Massachusetts Institute of Technology, 1987).

outlines how the National Steel Company reduced the number of job classifications for craft workers in one of its plants, as part of a concessionary contract signed in 1986. This reclassification illustrates what has become one of the major issues in contemporary collective bargaining, namely, the reduction in job classifications.

Other Critical Issues

Employee Turnover

Another way unions affect employment conditions is through a reduction in employee turnover. Attention to this union effect has been longstanding. In a classic article published in 1958 Arthur Ross asked whether a new industrial feudalism was developing through the spread of seniority, pension, layoff, and other job security provisions in union contracts.[43]

Studies using measures of job security provisions in contracts and studies using observations of individual workers have found that the presence of a union and the presence of these provisions do significantly reduce turnover. Richard Block found, for example, that the stronger the seniority provisions in bargaining agreements, the lower the quit rate in the industry.[44]

Freeman and Medoff showed that even after controlling for the wage level and job satisfaction (each of which alone would produce lower turnover rates), union membership was associated with a significantly lower probability of a worker's voluntarily leaving the job.[45] This finding was especially strong for older workers: The probability of older union workers' voluntarily quitting their jobs was very low.

Unions may lead to reduced turnover for a number of reasons. For one thing, unions reduce turnover because they make it less attractive for workers to leave the organization.[46] This union effect is likely to be strongest among those workers who have the least attractive alternatives in the external labor market, such as those subject to age, sex, race, or other forms of discrimination and those who have the least marketable skills. The effect is also likely to be stronger among older workers with more seniority. The older the worker, the greater the value of his or her pension, sick leave, and job security protections and the more difficult it is to find a new job with equivalent benefits and protections.

The effects of a union can also operate by giving employees greater voice at the workplace. If the union offers workers a viable alternative for voicing concerns on the job, union members may choose voice, rather than exit, as a means for addressing their dissatisfaction.[47] The grievance procedure may provide union members with a voice advantage.

Safety and Health

Another important job outcome influenced by collective bargaining is the health and safety of the work force. Unions historically have used three interrelated strategies to improve safety and health conditions at the workplace: (1) supporting governmental regulations that mandate or encourage safe practices; (2) negotiating safety provisions into bargaining agreements; and (3) encouraging the formation of joint union-management safety and health committees at the plant level. The labor movement, for example, was the driving force behind passage of the Occupational Safety and Health Act (OSHA) of 1970. The number of safety provisions in bargaining agreements has expanded considerably since then, as has the number of safety and health committees in unionized plants.

Unions can affect safety and health at the workplace in two ways. First, they can demand a higher compensating wage differential for workers exposed to higher risks. Although the evidence is far from conclusive, there is some indication that unions have been successful in obtaining a positive wage differential for risky jobs.[48] The differential, in turn, has both a direct effect and an indirect effect. The direct effect is obviously to compensate those workers who are exposed to risks. The indirect effect is to increase the employer's incentive to lower the risks on the job so as to avoid having to pay a compensating differential.

Second, unions can negotiate protections against job hazards, increased worker and supervisor training, and changes in the work environment that will eliminate the hazards. Whether these strategies are effective depends heavily on whether the parties have accurate information on the causes of injuries and occupational illnesses.

Exhibit 10–4 illustrates the range of safety and health provisions commonly found in collective bargaining agreements in 1989. A comparison

Exhibit 10–4   **Safety and Health Contractual Provisions in 1989**

	All Industries	Manufacturing
Provisions	86%	94%
General statement of responsibility	59	68
Company to comply with laws	33	33
Safety equipment	43	49
Company provides first aid	22	25
Physical examinations	33	34
Accident investigations	18	24
Hazardous work provisions	26	26
Safety committees	48	62

Note: Frequency expressed as percentage of industry contracts.
Source: Bureau of National Affairs, *Basic Patterns in Union Contracts, 1989,* 12th ed. (Washington, D.C.: GPO, 1989), p. 127.

of the percentages listed in this exhibit with comparable figures for earlier periods shows that all of these provisions became increasingly common over the last 20 years. For example, in 1970, 31 percent of the contracts in the BNA sample provided for safety and health committees; by 1989 that figure had risen to 48 percent.

Unions frequently also negotiate general contractual provisions stating that the employer is responsible for making the work environment safe or that the employer agrees to comply with applicable safety laws (something employers presumably have to do whether the union contract requires it or not). This sort of language allows the union to use the contractual grievance procedure to process safety complaints. The alternative is for the union to rely solely on either a joint union-management committee or complaints to the Occupational Safety and Health Administration, which is responsible for administering and enforcing OSHA.

In general, safety provisions were more common in manufacturing than in nonmanufacturing industries, and in all cases they were much more common in high-risk industries such as mining. Thus the probability that these provisions will be included in contracts depends partly on the magnitude of the risks found in the industry.

Recently, several major explosions in the petrochemical industry have heightened awareness of safety issues and raised a thorny set of labor-management relations issues. Box 10–2 reviews some of the events and the tripartite (labor, management, and government) initiatives that followed.

While the parties may be readily able to diagnose the causes of injuries, they have only recently begun to recognize the hidden, long-term development of illnesses. These illnesses can result from exposure to such health hazards as excessive dust, dangerous chemicals, and carcinogens.

Only in the last several years have most unions and many employers begun to address the problem of exposure to carcinogens and other health hazards in the workplace. Two main strategies are emerging. One is to compensate for the accumulated effects of past exposures by moving workers to safer jobs without loss in pay and by reforming workers' compensation systems to provide benefits not only to those disabled by injuries but also to those suffering from occupational diseases.

The other approach is to reduce workplace exposures. Here efforts take a variety of directions such as (1) supporting new or stricter governmental standards for exposure to polluted air, dust, toxic chemicals, radiation, and other potential carcinogens; (2) promoting the dissemination of information on toxic substances found at the workplace; and (3) negotiating provisions for more industrial hygienists, examinations by physicians other than company doctors, and so on.

Although unions and employers have been expanding their efforts to improve safety and health conditions over the past several years, there is

Box 10–2

> ### Safety and Contracting Out in the Petrochemical Industry
>
> In October 1989, 23 workers were killed in an explosion at a Phillips Chemical plant in Pasadena, Texas. In July 1990 another explosion 10 miles away killed 17 workers in an Arco chemical plant. Both instances involved contract maintenance employees who were working on the site.
>
> For years unions in the oil industry have argued that the increased use of temporary contract workers was both undermining the job security and the safety of regular employees in this industry. As a result of the Phillips' accident, OSHA initiated a major study of this issue. A tripartite (union, management, government and academic experts) steering committee oversees the study and advises OSHA on how to reduce risks in the industry. The research currently is under way, and the steering committee is engaged in hot debate over its preliminary findings.
>
> Whether a consensus can be forged around a set of recommendations remains to be seen. The problem involves a host of integrative issues (everyone is for improving safety and reducing risks). Distributive issues (the companies want to maintain the flexibility to subcontract out work and the union wants to limit this process) also arise. This example shows that the stakes in labor-management relations can be extremely high.

no conclusive evidence that their efforts have reduced the injury or illness rates of workers covered under bargaining agreements. There is evidence that unionized workers receive a higher compensating wage differential for hazardous work than nonunion workers. One study also has shown that the safety record of a coal mine was significantly improved as a result of a broader union-management experiment to improve productivity and the quality of work.[49]

Productivity

Perhaps the most critical issue in assessing the impact of unions and collective bargaining is how these institutions affect productivity and efficiency. This issue has become salient in recent years as the aggregate annual rate of productivity growth declined from 3.2 percent during the 20 years after World War II to 1.3 percent from 1980 to 1989 (see the figures in Exhibit 4–2).

Union-Nonunion Productivity Comparisons   A number of recent econometric studies have estimated the differences in **productivity** that are associated with collective bargaining at the industry or firm level of analysis. Some of the studies show higher productivity in unionized plants and industries. Because the productivity issue is so important, the results so controversial, and the statistical methods so complicated, this debate is reviewed in some detail below.

Using industry-by-state data, for example, Charles Brown and James Medoff estimated that collective bargaining was associated with a 20 to 25 percent higher rate of productivity in the manufacturing sector.[50] Other studies applying the same basic methodology found positive productivity differentials attributable to collective bargaining in the wooden furniture and cement industries.[51]

A number of measurement and statistical problems, however, plague these and other **cross-sectional** studies (these compare the productivity in union and nonunion observations at a given point in time). It is extremely difficult, for example, to measure the quality of labor inputs and control for their effects. If the higher wages firms pay for union workers result in work forces of higher quality, the union variable may mistakenly pick up some of this labor quality effect.

An even more serious issue of causality clouds productivity studies that are cross-sectional. Consider what unionization may imply for the long-run survival of firms and how this could affect cross-sectional analyses. Suppose firms vary substantially in their productivity because of various idiosyncratic factors, such as the special skills of the managers or work force in the firm or the locational advantages held by the firm. Unionization clearly results in higher compensation. In the long run, therefore, among firms that become unionized, those whose managers and workers have lower skills and productivity will be more apt to go out of business after unionization than those firms that have highly skilled and productive employees.

If the productivity of union and nonunion firms is compared after this process has proceeded, productivity is likely to be higher at the remaining union firms than at the nonunion firms. But this finding could result from the fact that the unionized firms that remained in business tended to have high productivity for a reason that had nothing to do with unionization. This example illustrates how cross-sectional analysis ignores dynamic processes and effects.[52]

Another difficulty in assessing average union effects arises because a high proportion of the new plants opened since 1960 are unorganized. As a result, the correlation between plant age and union status is strong: nonunion plants tend to be younger. Furthermore, as a plant ages, its work rules tend to become more rigid and cause a reduction in its economic performance. Given the association between unionized status and plant age and the fact that both exert independent effects on plants' economic performance, it is difficult to distinguish between the effects of each.

It also is important to bear in mind the difference between productivity in a single firm and the efficiency of the overall economy. Firms could raise their labor productivity by substituting capital for labor in response to higher union wages—that is, by increasing their capital-to-labor ratio. But this would lead to a lowering of the overall efficiency of the economy if the capital purchased by union firms in response to higher wage rates could have been put to better use elsewhere in the economy.

It is particularly difficult to reconcile the statistical evidence that Freeman and Medoff and others have provided, which shows positive union productivity effects, with descriptive evidence of the wide differences that exist in the work rules between union and nonunion plants. The work rule flexibility found in many nonunion workplaces is of particularly high value to firms faced with economic pressures that require flexible and high-quality production, as is the case with many firms today. Management certainly is acting as if the more flexible work rules present in many nonunion plants provide those plants with a significant productivity advantage.

There clearly is wide diversity in the evidence of the effects unions exert on productivity. At the same time, it is clear that this is an extremely important topic for future research and public policy.

The Diversity of Industrial Relations across Unionized Plants

When assessing the effects unions exert on productivity and other aspects of firm performance, it is important to account for the diverse outcomes that unionization produces across unionized workplaces (even within the same industry and even within the same firm). The data in Exhibit 10–5 illustrate this diversity among plants within one division of General Motors in 1979. Despite their common technology, union, and employer, the 18 plants observed exhibited a wide variety of grievance, discipline, and absenteeism rates.

Note, for example, that grievances per 100 workers varied from a low of 24 in one plant to a high of 450 in another plant. Absenteeism varied between 4.7 and 10.3 percent. There was also diverse performance on other industrial relations and economic performance measures across the auto plants. The economic performance indices in Exhibit 10–5 show considerable variation around their means.

What explains this diversity in performance across the plants? This is an interesting question particularly because all of the hourly employees in these plants are represented by the same union (UAW) and are covered by the same companywide contract (although each plant also has its own "local" collective bargaining agreement).

In part, the diversity in economic and industrial relations performance that exists in the plants may stem from differences in the work forces and the managerial styles in each plant. Or it may stem from the volatile nature of labor-management relations. In some plants the two sides seem

Exhibit 10–5
Measures of Industrial Relations and Economic Performance in 18 GM Plants, 1979

Performance Indicators*	Mean	Minimum	Maximum	Standard Deviation
Grievances	124.3	24.5	450.2	133.1
Absenteeism	7.4	4.7	10.3	1.7
Discipline	44.5	20.0	86.8	17.5
Contract demands	364.6	4.0	1163.0	196.4
Negotiation time	76.8	−110.0	532.0	143.4
Climate	2.9	2.2	3.8	.5
Product quality	127.6	122.0	137.0	3.7
Direct-labor efficiency	87.4	57.1	103.7	13.2

*Grievances=the number of grievances filed per 100 workers.
Absenteeism=the absentee rate as a percentage of straight-time hours, excluding contractual days off.
Discipline=the number of oral warnings, disciplinary leaves, and discharges assessed per 100 workers.
Contract demands=the number of contract demands submitted by the local union in triannual local contract negotiations.
Negotiation time=the number of days taken to reach settlement in local contract negotiations before (negative) or after (positive) settlement of the master agreement between GM and the UAW international.
Climate=an average score (based on a one to five response format) on five survey questions measuring the state of labor-management relations in the plant. The survey was administered to all managerial and supervisory employees in the plant. The higher the average score, the more cooperative the relations.
Product quality=an index derived from a count of the number of faults and demerits that appear in inspections of the product adjusted for differences in product attributes.
Direct-labor efficiency=an index comparing the actual hours of direct labor input to standardized hours adjusted for differences in product attributes.
Source: Harry C. Katz, Thomas A. Kochan, and Kenneth R. Gobeille, "Industrial Relations Performance, Economic Performance, and QWL Programs: An Interplant Analysis," *Industrial and Labor Relations Review* 37 (October 1983): 8.

to be caught in a low-trust dynamic, in which mistrust leads to ever-deteriorating industrial relations and economic performance and ever-deteriorating interpersonal relations. Nonetheless, the exact source of interplant diversity in industrial relations performance within the same organization remains something of a mystery, and an important subject for future research.

More germane to the union productivity issue is the fact that research conducted with this and other plant level data show that the plants with relatively good industrial relations performance also have relatively higher labor productivity and product quality. For example, the data show that lower rates of grievances and a higher degree of trust in the organizational climate (as measured by attitude surveys) are correlated with higher rates of labor efficiency and higher product quality.

Regression analysis further shows that the overall variations in industrial relations performance across the plants explain a significant portion of the variance in both labor efficiency and product quality, after controlling for the size of the plant and other plant characteristics.[53] Thus, in these plants industrial relations performance appears to have large effects on economic performance.

Summary

The presence of a union sets off a chain reaction in a wide range of economic and behavioral job outcomes that affect the goals of employees and employers. This chapter presents a framework for tracing these effects and summarizes the existing empirical evidence. Estimates of the "average" effects of collective bargaining must be interpreted with caution because there is much variation across union and nonunion workplaces.

The average effects of unions measured by research are as follows.

1.   Unions raise the wages of their members over those of comparable nonunion workers. The magnitude of this effect varies considerably over time and across occupations. The average wage effect is between 15 and 20 percent and is somewhat higher for nonwhites than for whites, for younger and older workers than for workers in their prime working years, and for blue-collar than white-collar workers.

2.   Concessionary bargaining has resulted in pay increases that are substantially below those of previous years. Debate is already under way over whether the low wage settlements of the 1980s signal a fundamental shift in the nature of wage setting.

3.   Unions increase the range of fringe benefits available to workers and the level of benefits provided. Some of this effect is due to the built-in relationship between wages and those fringe benefits that are tied to the wage rate, while some is due to the direct effect that unions have on benefits.

4.   Unions have negotiated a wide range of job security provisions. The most prominent union effect on job security lies in the protection against arbitrary discharge or discipline afforded union members through the grievance arbitration provisions found in most private sector labor agreements. Unions have also increased the security of long-service employees through the seniority provisions in labor contracts. A minority of unions have been successful in negotiating income security provisions that supplement the state unemployment compensation system during short, temporary layoffs.

A smaller minority of unions have negotiated provisions that protect the income and job security of employees who are affected by permanent job loss resulting from technological change. Again, the magnitude of these protections and benefits typically is set as a direct function of the worker's seniority. Recently some bargaining agreements have provided enhanced employment security in association with pay concessions or work reorganization.

5. Unions reduce turnover, primarily by increasing the value of the jobs held by union members over the value of the alternative jobs available in the external labor market. This effect increases directly with the seniority of the worker.

6. Unions have attempted to improve worker safety and health through a combination of negotiated provisions, labor-management committees, and federal legislation. Although contract provisions on safety and health have expanded over the past 20 years, we as yet have no conclusive evidence that the rate of injuries has declined in the union sector.

7. Assessing the unions' effects on productivity is a complicated exercise, in part due to the extensive variation that exists in union effects across unionized workplaces. The evidence is mixed. Some statistical evidence shows that unions raise productivity. Analysis of work rule flexibility across the union and nonunion plants of the same employer, however, suggests that unionization is associated with less flexible and more costly work practices. The impact of unionization on productivity may be mediated by age effects because unions tend to be in older plants. Plant-level industrial relations performance varies substantially across unionized workplaces, even within the same firm. Industrial relations performance appears to exert substantial effects on economic performance.

Thus, unions exert sizable effects on economic and job outcomes.

Discussion Questions

1. Wage increases set off a chain reaction. Describe the chain reaction.

2. Wages are of central importance to unions and their membership. Discuss some of the key variations in union relative wage effects.

3. Seniority is a vital issue in collective bargaining. Unions have argued that seniority protects against arbitrary treatment by the employer, but, with the advent of affirmative action, this has come under attack. It has been argued by some that seniority helps maintain, if not increase, the amount of racial discrimination in the workplace. Discuss the pros and cons of seniority systems.

Suggested Readings

Freeman, Richard B., and James L. Medoff. *What Do Unions Do?* (New York: Basic Books, 1984).

Hartman, Paul T. *Collective Bargaining and Productivity* (Berkeley: University of California Press, 1969).

Lewis, H. Gregg. *Union Relative Wage Effects: A Survey* (Chicago: University of Chicago Press, 1986).

Mitchell, Daniel J. B. "Shifting Norms in Wage Setting," *Brookings Papers on Economic Activity,* vol. 2 (1985): 575–609.

Shultz, George P., and Arnold R. Weber. *Strategies for Displaced Workers* (Westport, CT: Greenwood Press, 1966).

End Notes

1. Sumner Slichter, *Union Policies and Industrial Management* (Washington, D.C.: Brookings Institution, 1941).

2. H. Gregg Lewis, *Unionism and Relative Wages in the United States* (Chicago: University of Chicago Press, 1962).

3. Orley Ashenfelter, "Racial Discrimination and Trade Unionism," *Journal of Political Economy* 80 (May/June 1972): 435–464.

4. See, for example, George E. Johnson and Kenneth Youmans, "Union Relative Wage Effects by Age and Education," *Industrial and Labor Relations Review* 24 (January 1971): 171–179.

5. Farrell E. Bloch and Mark S. Kuskin, "Wage Determination in the Union and Nonunion Sectors," *Industrial and Labor Relations Review* 31 (January 1978): 183–192.

6. Orley Ashenfelter, "Union Relative Wage Effects: New Evidence and a Survey of Their Implications for Wage Inflation," in *Econometric Contributions to Public Policy,* ed. Richard Stone and William Peterson (New York: St. Martin's Press, 1978), pp. 31–60.

7. Richard B. Freeman, "Unionism and the Dispersion of Wages," *Industrial and Labor Relations Review* 34 (October 1980): 3–23 and Richard B. Freeman, "Union Wage Practices and Wage Dispersion within Establishments," *Industrial and Labor Relations Review* 36 (October 1982): 3–21.

8. James A. Dalton and E. J. Ford, Jr., "Concentration and Labor Earnings in Manufacturing and Utilities," *Industrial and Labor Relations Review* 31 (October 1977): 45–60.

9. See Lewis, *Unionism and Relative Wages* and Richard B. Freeman and James L. Medoff, *What Do Unions Do?* (New York: Basic Books, 1984).

10. See, for example, Greg Duncan and Frank Stafford, "Do Union Members Receive Compensating Wage Differentials?" *American Economic Review* 70 (June 1980): 355–371, and John Abowd and Henry S. Farber, "Job Queues and the Union Status of Workers," *Industrial and Labor Relations Review* 35 (April 1982): 354–367.

11. These figures are derived from *Current Wage Developments* (Washington, D.C.: Bureau of Labor Statistics, U.S. Department of Labor, various issues).

12. Daniel J. B. Mitchell, "Shifting Norms in Wage Determination," *Brookings Papers on Economic Activity,* vol. 2 (1985): 575–609.

13. Whereas COLA payments had accounted for 33.7 percent of the effective wage adjustments in major collective bargaining agreements in 1981, in 1983 they accounted for only 15 percent of those adjustments. See Robert J. Flanagan, "Wage Concessions and Long-Term Union Wage Flexibility," *Brookings Papers on Economic Activity,* vol. 1 (1984): 183–216.

14. "Two-Tier Wage Plans Slip to 4% of Contracts," *Daily Labor Report* 37 (February 25, 1991): B–3.

15. Some wage equations that accurately predicted wage settlements in the 1960s and 1970s overpredict the wages negotiated between 1980 and 1984, in some cases by as many as 3 percentage points annually. One example is the set of wage equations estimated by Mitchell, "Shifting Norms." Freeman, for example, used Current Population Survey data and found only a slight drop in the union-nonunion wage differential from 1977 to 1984 across a number of industries. He also found that the percentage of workers who took wage cuts or freezes in the early 1980s was well predicted by a simple equation using the inflation and unemployment rates from 1955 to the 1980s. See Richard B. Freeman, "In Search of Union Wage Concessions in Standard Data Sets," *Industrial Relations* 25 (Spring 1986): 131–145. For a more complete discussion of this evidence, see Thomas A. Kochan, Harry C. Katz, and Robert B. McKersie, *The Transformation of American Industrial Relations* (New York: Basic Books, 1986), pp. 110–111.

16. For a discussion of these and other wage administration provisions in union contracts, see U.S. Department of Labor, Bureau of Labor Statistics, *Major Collective Bargaining Agreements: Wage Administration Provisions,* Bulletin 1425–17 (Washington, D.C.: GPO, 1978).

17. Mitchell Lokiec, *Productivity and Incentives* (Columbia, SC: Bobbin Publishing, 1977).

18. The theoretical arguments and empirical evidence here draw heavily from Richard B. Freeman and James L. Medoff, *What Do Unions Do?* (New York: Basic Books, 1984), pp. 61–77.

19. Inland Steel Co. v. NLRB, 170 F. 2d 247 (1948).

20. See Freeman and Medoff, *What Do Unions Do?,* pp. 61–77.

21. See U.S. Chamber of Commerce, *Employee Benefits* (Washington, D.C.: U.S. Chamber of Commerce, 1989).

22. Ibid, Table 10.

23. See further discussion of employment at will in Chapter 10.

24. Bureau of National Affairs, *Basic Patterns in Union Contracts, 1989,* 12th ed. (Washington, D.C.: Bureau of National Affairs 1989), p. 87.

25. Ibid, p. 88.

26. Katharine G. Abraham and James L. Medoff, "Length of Service and Promotions in Union and Nonunion Work Groups," *Industrial and Labor Relations Review* 38 (April 1985): 408–420.

27. In a related study Medoff and Abraham found evidence that the earnings of nonunion employees exhibited substantial within-job differentials that were

associated with seniority and did not reflect employee productivity differences. See James L. Medoff and Katharine G. Abraham, "Experience, Performance, and Earnings," *Quarterly Journal of Economics* 95 (December 1980): 703–736.

28. Bureau of National Affairs, *Basic Patterns,* p. 69.

29. For a good description and analysis of SUB plans, see Audrey Freedman, *Security Bargains Reconsidered: SUB, Severance Pay, Guaranteed Work* (New York: Conference Board, 1978).

30. Bureau of National Affairs, *Basic Patterns,* p. 44.

31. Ibid., p. 41.

32. Ibid., p. 81. For an international perspective on plant closing limitations, see Bennett Harrison, "The International Movement for Prenotification of Plant Closings," *Industrial Relations* 23 (Fall 1984): 387–409.

33. Bureau of National Affairs, *Basic Patterns,* p. 79.

34. For a discussion of these two views, see Frank Elkouri and Edna Asper Elkouri, *How Arbitration Works,* 3d ed. (Washington, D.C.: Bureau of National Affairs, 1976), pp. 412–435.

35. Neil W. Chamberlain and James W. Kuhn, *Collective Bargaining,* 2d ed. (New York: McGraw-Hill, 1965), pp. 89–90.

36. Charles C. Killingsworth, "Management Rights Revisited," in *Arbitration and Social Change, Proceedings of the Twenty-Second Annual Meetings of the National Academy of Arbitrators,* ed. Gerald G. Somers (Washington, D.C.: Bureau of National Affairs, 1969), pp. 3–13.

37. See Robert B. McKersie and Lawrence C. Hunter, *Pay, Productivity and Collective Bargaining* (London: Macmillan, 1973).

38. Paul T. Hartman, *Collective Bargaining and Productivity: The Longshore Mechanization Agreement* (Berkeley: University of California Press, 1969).

39. Slichter, *Union Policies and Industrial Management.*

40. See the symposium "The Employer Challenge and the Union Response" in *Industrial Relations* 1 (October 1961): 9–56.

41. George P. Schultz and Robert B. McKersie, "Stimulating Productivity: Choices, Problems and Shares," *British Journal of Industrial Relations* 5 (March 1967): 3–18.

42. Peter Henle, "Reverse Collective Bargaining: A Look at Some Union Concession Situations," *Industrial and Labor Relations Review* 26 (April 1973): 956–968.

43. Arthur M. Ross, "Do We Have a New Industrial Feudalism?" *American Economic Review* 48 (December 1958): 903–920.

44. Richard N. Block, "The Impact of Seniority Provisions on the Manufacturing Quit Rate," *Industrial and Labor Relations Review* 31 (July 1978): 474–481.

45. Freeman and Medoff, *What Do Unions Do?*

46.   James G. March and Herbert A. Simon, *Organizations* (New York: Wiley, 1958).

47.   Albert O. Hirschman, *Exit, Voice, and Loyalty: Responses to Decline in Firms, Organizations, and States* (Cambridge: Harvard University Press, 1970) and Freeman and Medoff, *What Do Unions Do?*, pp. 94–110.

48.   Craig A. Olson, "An Analysis of Wage Differentials Received by Workers on Dangerous Jobs," *Journal of Human Resources* 16 (Spring 1981): 167–185.

49.   Paul S. Goodman, *Assessing Organizational Change* (New York: Wiley-Interscience, 1979).

50.   Charles Brown and James L. Medoff, "Trade Unions in the Production Process," *Journal of Political Economy* 86 (June 1978): 335–378.

51.   For the cement industry, see Kim B. Clark, "The Impact of Unionization on Productivity: A Case Study," *Industrial and Labor Relations Review* 33 (July 1980): 451–469. For the furniture industry, see J. Frantz, "The Impact of Trade Unions on Productivity in the Wood Household Furniture Industry," undergraduate thesis (Cambridge, MA: Harvard University, 1976).

52.   This is another example of the potential effects of selection bias in econometric analysis.

53.   Norsworthy and Zabala estimated that a 10 percent improvement in worker attitudes and behavior would have translated into a 3 to 5 percent reduction in the annual unit costs of production between 1959 and 1976. In turn, this reduction would have produced between $2.2 and $5.5 billion of annual savings in production costs over those years. See J. R. Norsworthy and Craig A. Zabala, "Worker Attitudes, Worker Behavior, and Productivity in the U.S. Automobile Industry, 1959–1976," *Industrial and Labor Relations Review* 38 (July 1985): 544–557. After controlling for the various factors that affect productivity in a sample of paper mills, Ichniowski found that productivity at the plants having the average number of grievances was 1.2 percent lower than productivity at plants with no grievances. Moving from zero grievances to the average level of grievances was estimated to reduce profits in a mill by approximately 15 percent. See Casey Ichniowski, "The Effects of Grievance Activity on Productivity," *Industrial and Labor Relations Review* 40, 1 (October 1986): 75–89.

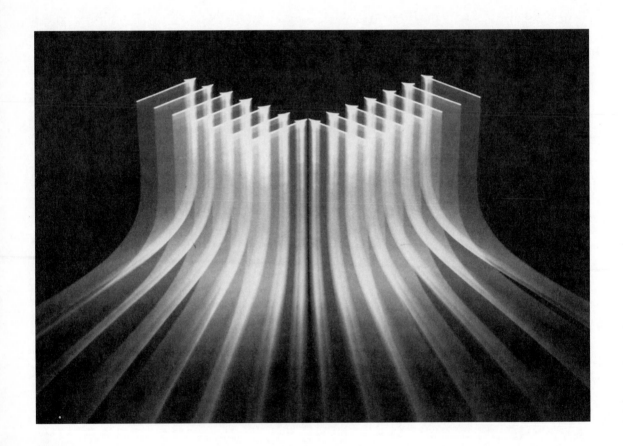

PART 4

THE WORKPLACE
LEVEL OF
INDUSTRIAL
RELATIONS

Chapter 11

Administering the Employment Relationship

Chapter 11 begins our examination of the workplace level of industrial relations, the third level of activities in Exhibit 1-1. The focus in this chapter is on the day-to-day employment relationship. In unionized settings this involves contract administration below the level of formal contract negotiations.

Collective bargaining agreements in the United States are elaborate and detailed documents. The existence of such extensive labor contracts contributed to the need for an orderly means for settling conflicts over interpretations of contract language.

Engrained in U.S. collective bargaining is the principle that "management acts and the union reacts," or, put another way, "it is management's job to manage and the union's job to grieve." This has led in unionized settings to reliance on grievance and arbitration procedures as mechanisms to resolve conflicts that arise at the workplace. The bulk of this chapter discusses how grievance and arbitration procedures operate.

In recent years in unionized settings, competitive environmental conditions and the increasingly complex needs of the labor force are giving rise to efforts to supplement formal contract administration procedures with more flexible mechanisms for resolving problems and conflict. Many large firms have established communication and informal complaint-handling processes for their nonunion employees, and increasingly they are instituting these for their unionized employees as well. Thus, this chapter also considers some of the new less formal mechanisms that are being used to settle problems at the workplace.

The Grievance Procedure

The grievance procedure specifies a series of steps to be taken to resolve a worker's complaint that management has not followed the terms of the collective bargaining agreement. The steps found in a typical procedure are outlined in Box 11–1. Each succeeding step in the decision-making process involves a higher level of the union and management organizations. The final step in this and most grievance procedures involves a hearing of the dispute and a final binding judgment by an arbitrator (acting as the third party).

Most often the grievance procedure comes into play when an employee has a complaint about the actions taken by the supervisor. Below we trace how an employee complaint makes its way through the typical grievance procedure.

Step 1: Step 1 of the procedure outlined in Box 11–1 gives the employee and his or her supervisor the opportunity to resolve the employee's complaint by talking about the problem. The supervisor might be unaware that there is a problem, and oral discussion might quickly resolve the issue. At this point, the employee's union steward might assist the employee in bringing the issue to the attention of the supervisor.

Step 2: If the grievance (complaint) is not resolved in these discussions, the employee can choose to drop the matter or to proceed to step 2 where the grievance is put in writing. In step 2 the union steward meets with a management representative and management eventually writes a response. The process of writing the grievance and management's response down on paper gives the parties the opportunity to formally make their cases, and this often serves to clarify exactly what is in dispute. At this and the previous step many grievances are resolved or dropped by the grieving party.

Step 3: Step 3 in the grievance procedure involves top line management, industrial relations staff, local union officers, and possibly national union staff. The involvement of higher level union and management staff consumes valuable time and resources, and for this reason the decision to press a grievance to the third step is not usually taken lightly.

Step 4: If the grievance has not been resolved at earlier steps, in step 4 it can be appealed to arbitration for a binding decision. It is important to note that it is the union and not the employee that decides whether or not to appeal a grievance to arbitration. Court decisions gave unions this power on the grounds that it was the union that created and "owned" the grievance procedure.

The Union's Decision to Go to Arbitration

It is not a simple matter for the union to decide whether or not to press a grievance to arbitration. The use of arbitration is costly (as discussed below, labor and management typically share the costs of an arbitration hearing). The union might decide to drop the grievance if it believes the

Box 11–1

Steps in a Typical Grievance Procedure

A. Employee-initiated grievance
   Step 1
      Employee discusses grievance or problem orally with supervisor.
      Union steward and employee may discuss problem orally with
      supervisor.
      Union steward and employee decide if (1) problem has been resolved
      or (2) if not resolved, whether a contract violation has occurred.

   Step 2
      Grievance is put in writing and submitted to production
      superintendent or other designated line manager.
      Steward and management representative meet and discuss grievance.
      Management's response is put in writing. A member of the industrial
      relations staff may be consulted at this stage.

   Step 3
      Grievance is appealed to top line management and industrial relations
      staff representatives. Additional local or national union officers may
      become involved in discussions. Decision is put in writing.

   Step 4
      Union decides on whether to appeal unresolved grievance to
      arbitration according to procedures specified in its constitution
      and/or bylaws.
      Grievance is appealed to arbitration for binding decision.

B. Discharge grievance
   Procedure may begin at step 2 or step 3.
   Time limits between steps may be shorter to expedite the process.

C. Union or group grievance
   Union representative initiates grievance at step 1 or step 2 on behalf
   of the affected class of workers or union representatives.

case is not winnable. Or, the union might drop the grievance even though
it thinks it can win the case if the union concludes that the issue in dispute is small and insignificant (and not worth the effort). The union might
also decide not to bring a grievance to arbitration if it believes the issue
is very important and should be brought up at the next contract negotiations. In this situation the union might fear that winning the case in arbitration would diffuse the employee's concern needed to later press the
union's case over the issue.

   Or, the union might decide to proceed to arbitration even if it believes
the case is not winnable, but the union officers feel an obligation to the
grievant (maybe because the grievant loyally supported the union over
the years) and cannot convince the employee to drop the issue.

The Reasons Why Grievances Are Filed

Employees commonly file a grievance when they think management is not fairly living up to the collective bargaining agreement. The grievance procedure provides a mechanism for workers to air their displeasure with management's actions, to change management's behavior, or to receive some form of compensation for management's actions.

Disagreements about employee discipline are a common source of grievances. Collective bargaining agreements commonly leave to management the right to discipline employees. Contracts often outline certain actions that can lead to discipline, such as repeated absenteeism or the failure to follow a direct order from a supervisor. An employee might file a grievance against a disciplinary action taken by management either because the employee contests management's claim that the employee did something wrong or because the employee believes too harsh a disciplinary action was imposed for whatever mistake was made by the employee.

When labor and management negotiate the collective bargaining contract they try to cover the major issues and write language that will guide future behavior. Yet the contract does not specify what is to happen under all circumstances. It would be impossible and too costly for negotiators to write contractual language that covers any but the most common events. Thus the parties also turn to the grievance procedure as a way to resolve issues that are not explicitly covered by the labor contract.

Many collective bargaining agreements, for example, specify that supervisors are not allowed to perform work that is commonly performed by someone in the bargaining unit. Unions favor this clause as a way to preserve work for union members and to prevent management from circumventing the terms of the contract by moving work out of the bargaining unit. When new technology is introduced into a plant it often changes the duties performed by existing workers and adds new types of work. Is the new work still in the bargaining unit, or can it be performed by a supervisor? It would be extremely cumbersome for labor and management to include language in the labor agreement specifying in detail what is to happen in every such case. Instead, the parties use the grievance procedure to resolve disputes that arise over this issue.

Furthermore, at all workplaces things frequently happen that were never anticipated by the parties when they were negotiating the labor agreement. What form of compensation, for example, should workers receive if they are sent home after a power outage forces the closing of a plant in the middle of the day? Should employees be paid for a full day's work in such a case? Should the amount of compensation vary, depending on how much of the work day the employees worked before being sent home? If language was not included in the labor contract that covered this type of occurrence and employees were upset by the compensation management decided to provide, then the employees might turn to the grievance procedure to settle the matter.

The filing of grievances can also serve other purposes. For instance, grievances may be filed by employees as a way to demonstrate employee concern for issues that are not addressed in the collective bargaining agreement. For example, employees may be concerned about the long-term health effects from working with video displays and vent their concern by filing grievances over the issue. In these sorts of cases the grievance procedure can serve the valuable function of warning management about problems that might otherwise be ignored.

Employees and their union also might use the grievance procedure as a tactical pressure device. The filing of grievances over an issue can serve, for example, to rally employee interest in bringing the issue to the bargaining table in the next contract renewal negotiation. In this sort of case the union may know that the filing of grievances will not lead to immediate changes in management's behavior but will put pressure on management and thereby increase its bargaining leverage.

The Historical Evolution of Grievance Arbitration

Arbitration is the common device stipulated in labor contracts to resolve grievances that are not settled in earlier steps (see step 4 in Box 11–1). Arbitration is a quasi-judicial procedure in which a third party settles a dispute by issuing a binding judgment. The use of arbitration to settle grievances that arise during the term of a collective bargaining is referred to as grievance (or rights) arbitration.

Arbitration developed early in the U.S. industrial relations system. Arbitration of minor disputes over the interpretation of agreements, for example, was mentioned in the Industrial Commission Report of 1902. Before World War II grievance procedures ending in binding arbitration were common in the clothing and anthracite coal mining industries.

The Spread of Arbitration

It took the strong advocacy of the national War Labor Board (WLB) during World War II for grievance arbitration to become a common practice across unionized industries. In many of the thousands of disputes it handled, the board encouraged the parties to include an arbitration clause in their bargaining agreement, and in some cases the board required it.

Within a few years the Taft-Hartley Act embedded grievance arbitration in national labor policy. Section 203(d) of the act states: "Final adjustment by a method agreed upon by the parties is hereby declared to be the desirable method for settlement of grievance disputes arising out of the application or interpretation of an existing collective bargaining agreement."

Court Encouragement of Arbitration

A series of Supreme Court decisions known as the **Steelworkers' trilogy** encouraged the use of arbitration and insulated many arbitration awards from judicial review.[1] These cases also gave grievance arbitration its protected status and exalted image.[2]

The three Steelworkers' trilogy decisions from 1960 are summarized in Box 11–2. These decisions provided that (1) the courts should rule only on questions about whether a dispute can be arbitrated, they should resolve any doubts about such questions by ruling in favor of arbitration, and they should not consider the merits of the grievance when deciding whether the case can be arbitrated; (2) the parties should view arbitration as the quid pro quo for giving up the right to strike; and except for issues that are specifically excluded from the arbitration clause, all disputes arising out of contract administration should be resolved by arbitration; and (3) the courts should not review the substantive merits of an arbitration decision but should confine their review to whether due process procedures were followed or whether the arbitrator exceeded his or her authority.

Judicial Deference to Arbitration

The Steelworkers' trilogy cases established the principle that the courts would not review disputes that were arbitrable. Subsequent court decisions, summarized in Box 11–2, continued that basic principle and added some modifications. In the Collyer decision of 1971, for example, the court deferred to an arbitrator to decide if an employer had violated the obligation to bargain in good faith when it unilaterally changed certain wage rates and job duties. This gave to an arbitrator the responsibility to rule on an unfair labor practice issue. In the Olin decision of 1984 the courts substantially further broadened the deferral of other unfair labor practice issues to arbitration (also see the United Technologies decision of 1984). Some of the other key court cases summarized in Box 11–2 affected aspects of arbitration that do not involve **judicial deference to arbitration.**

For many unions and managers the grievance arbitration procedures have evolved from a clinical approach to a more judicial approach. The clinical approach had been advocated by the WLB and applied frequently during the early postwar years.[5] The **clinical approach** emphasizes mediation of disputes, informality of procedure, and arbitrator discretion in helping the parties develop a working relationship and consistent policies for interpreting and administering the contract.

In the 1950s, as the environment for collective bargaining became more structured and a body of past precedents emerged, the arbitrator's scope of discretion narrowed. As the parties themselves became more professional, they came to demand a more judicial approach to arbitra-

Box 11–2

Key Court and Administrative Decisions that Affect the Conduct of Grievance Arbitration

Year	Case	Decision
1957	*Textile Workers v. Lincoln Mills*	Provided for court enforcement of arbitration awards.
1960	"Steelworkers' trilogy" 1. *Steelworkers v. American Manufacturing Co.*, 363 US 564 (1960)	Court should determine only arbitrability, i.e., whether issue is covered by the contract, and should not decide the merits of a case. Doubts about arbitrability should be decided in favor of sending the case to arbitration.
	2. *Steelworkers v. Warrior Gulf and Navigation Co.*, 363 US 574 (1960)	Disputes over contract terms are assumed to be arbitrable unless they are specifically excluded. Arbitration is viewed as the quid pro quo for giving up the right to strike during the term of the contract.
	3. *Steelworkers v. Enterprise Wheel and Car Corp.*, 363 US 593 (1960)	Courts should not review the substantive merits of the arbitrator's decision as long as the arbitrator's award is based on the content of the agreement.
1970	*Boys Markets, Inc. v. Retail Clerks, Local 770*, 389 US 235 (1970)	Courts may issue an injunction against a union forcing it to refrain from violating a no-strike clause or where an issue is covered by an arbitration clause in the contract.
1971	*Collyer Insulated Wire and Local Union 1098*, 192 NLRB 837 (1971)	NLRB will defer to arbitration disputes in which the issue could be decided either through arbitration (because it is covered by a clause in the bargaining agreement) or by NLRB ruling (because it alleges an unfair labor practice).
1974	*Alexander v. Gardner-Denver*, 415 US 36 (1974)	Arbitrator's decision on a claim involving discrimination covered under Title VII of the Civil Rights Act does not preclude judicial review of the award, nor does it prevent the employee from

Year	*Case*	*Decision*
		pursuing legal remedies through federal agencies or the federal court. Courts will hear the case de novo and decide it on its merits and will give the arbitrator's decision whatever weight the court deems appropriate.
1976	*Hines v. Anchor Motor Freight, Inc.* 424 US 554 (1976) preceded by several other key cases, especially *Steele v. Louisville & Nashville R.R.,* 323 US 192 (1944), and *Vaca v. Sipes,* 386 US 171 (1967)	An arbitration award should not be sustained by the court when the union has violated its duty to represent the grievant fairly. Federal courts will entertain suits of this nature on the basis of Section 301 of Taft-Hartley.
1983	*Bowen v. United States Postal Service,* 103 US (1983)	A union may be held liable for a portion of an award to an employee if the union has violated its duty of fair representation.
1984	Olin Corporation, 268 NLRB 86 (1984)	The NLRB expanded the Collyer doctrine of deferral to arbitration of disputes involving unfair labor practices. The NLRB will defer to an arbitrator's decision unless the arbitrator's award is "clearly repugnant" to the law. The NLRB retains the right to decide whether an arbitrator adequately considered the facts that would constitute an unfair labor practice.
1984	United Technologies, 268 NLRB 83 (1984)	The NLRB further expanded the Collyer doctrine of deferral to arbitration of disputes brought to the board before arbitration that both involve statutory rights and are covered by a collective bargaining contract.
1986	*AT&T Technologies v. Communications Workers,* Docket no. 84-1913, 7 April 1986	Courts, not arbitrators, should resolve disputes over arbitrability by examining the language found in the agreement giving rise to the issue.

tion. The **judicial approach** is more formal and legalistic. The clinical model of arbitration may have filled a void in an otherwise unstructured environment, but as the parties formalized their internal policies, they turned to arbitrators only in disputes in which their differences were clearly defined by the contract and the precedents that had arisen.

Thus, modern grievance arbitration, though still considerably more informal than court proceedings, has become dependent on the use of formal rules of evidence, examination and cross-examination of witnesses, submission of written briefs and posthearing briefs, and written transcripts. It is the heavy formality of the grievance arbitration procedure that has led some of the parties to recently search for alternative dispute-resolution procedures, a subject we discuss in more detail later in this chapter and in the next chapter.

The Functions of Grievance Procedures and Arbitration

Grievance and arbitration procedures serve the needs of three separate constituencies—labor, management, and society.

Employee Interest in Due Process and Fairness

The grievance and arbitration procedures serve the interests of workers by delivering industrial justice and by protecting workers who use the procedure from recrimination for having exercised their rights. If workers lose confidence in the efficacy of these procedures, they may turn to other potentially more costly and disruptive mechanisms to provide due process. Thus management often agrees to grievance and arbitration procedures to provide employees with due process because of the costs to management of the alternatives.

Recent events in major league baseball illustrate how grievance arbitration can protect employee rights. Box 11–3 describes the enormous financial settlement provided in arbitrators' awards to baseball players. The arbitrators in these cases protected players' rights by penalizing baseball club owners for colluding against players after they had attained "free-agent" status. Under the terms of the collective bargaining agreement covering players and owners, after a player plays for one club for a certain number of years, the player becomes eligible to become a free agent and is supposed to be able to freely market his services to the club that offers the highest salary.

Employer Interest in Labor Peace

Employers are also attracted to the grievance and arbitration procedures because they reduce the likelihood that disputes that occur during the term of a labor contract will lead to stoppages in production. In exchange

Box 11–3

Baseball Players Get $102.5 Million in Collusion Case

In what is believed to be the largest such award ever made in sports history, an arbitrator ruled that baseball club owners must pay players $102.5 million in lost salary for the 1987 and 1988 seasons. An estimated 300 players could receive money from the $102.5 million award. The number would exclude players who were in their first three years in the major leagues because they were not eligible for salary arbitration.

The arbitrator awarded the damages after the owners had been found in three separate cases to have colluded against free-agent players. Another arbitrator had previously awarded $10.5 million in damages for lost 1986 salary to players affected by the first episode of the owners' violation of their labor agreement with the players. The involvement and authority of both arbitrators derived from the grievance arbitration language in the collective bargaining agreements between the Major League Baseball Players Association and The Baseball Club Leagues.

With further hearings to be held into damages for lost salary for the 1989 and 1990 seasons and with possible interest added on to all of the money awarded, the final damages could approach $250 million.

The collusion dispute stemmed from the owners' efforts to end the escalation of salaries that had occurred since free agency was created in 1976. The owners contended that they had acted independently of one another in shunning free agents beginning with the winter of 1985–86, but the arbitrators found that the owners had violated the free-agent rule that says "clubs shall not act in concert with other clubs."

Source: Murray Chase, "Players Get $102.5 Million in Collusion Case," *New York Times* (September 18, 1990), p. D-25.

for accepting third-party arbitration of grievances, management commonly gains union acceptance of a clause eliminating the union's right to conduct a strike over an issue that is covered by the grievance and arbitration clause. The labor contract between General Motors and the UAW, for example, contains the following language:

> During the life of this agreement, the Union will not cause or permit its members to cause, nor will any member of the Union take part in any sitdown, stay-in or slow-down, in any plant of the Corporation, or any curtailment of work or restriction of production or interference with the production of the Corporation. The Union will

not cause or permit its members to cause nor will any member of the Union take part in any strike or stoppage of any of the Corporation's operations or picket any of the Corporation's plants or premises until all of the bargaining procedure as outlined in this Agreement has been exhausted, and in no case on which the Arbitrator shall have ruled . . . ."[3]

Some labor agreements exclude particular issues from coverage by the requirement to proceed to arbitration and allow the union to conduct a strike over unresolved grievances about these issues. **Production standards** (rules governing the pace of work) and health and safety issues are sometimes designated to be nonarbitrable. For health and safety disputes it may be impractical to require employees to follow management's orders and then wait for arbitration to settle disputes over the appropriateness and fairness of these orders. Thus some contracts allow workers to strike over health and safety issues.

Joint Interests in Continuity and Consistency

Another function served by the grievance and arbitration procedures is to address the common interests of labor and management. As Neil Chamberlain and James Kuhn noted, labor and management have a mutual interest in achieving continuity and consistency in the application of a collective bargaining agreement. They both also benefit from procedures that allow flexibility in addressing unforeseen developments and the unique needs of different groups and individuals.[4]

Finding the appropriate balance between uniformity and flexibility is a key challenge in administering the employment relationship. It is a particular challenge for grievance procedures and arbitration.

Society's Interest in Industrial Peace

Grievance and arbitration procedures serve the interests of society by preserving industrial peace during the term of the contract, by keeping industrial disputes from overloading the courts or regulatory agencies, and by ensuring that unions and employers comply with public policies governing employment. As we will show, this set of public functions is becoming increasingly complex and difficult to carry out.

How Arbitration Works

The core of the arbitration procedure is a hearing in which the labor and management representatives present their positions on the issue in dispute to an arbitrator. At some point after this hearing the arbitrator announces a judgment on the issue, a decision that is binding on the parties. Before the hearing the parties sometimes submit briefs to the arbitrator. Below are described each of the three components of arbitration—prehearing briefs, the hearing, and the arbitrator's decision.

The Components of Arbitration

Prehearing Briefs The management and union representatives can submit **prehearing briefs** to the arbitrator before the arbitration hearing. In these briefs the parties can present their views of the issues, express their positions, and describe the evidence that supports their position. Briefs vary in length, sometimes amounting to long documents similar in form to legal briefs presented in legal cases.

In some cases the parties jointly present prehearing **stipulations** to the arbitrator. These stipulations tend to be shorter than a brief and focus more around the parties' statement of the issue in dispute and some of the key facts in the case. Briefs and stipulations can make it easier for the parties in the arbitration hearing to quickly focus on the evidence and issues in dispute.

The Arbitration Hearing In the **arbitration hearing** the parties present their positions and evidence to support their cases. Hearings usually start with opening statements by union and management representatives. In disciplinary cases, management will commonly be asked to present their statement first.

The union and management representatives then present evidence to support their cases. Such evidence might include witnesses who observed particular events. If an employee is charged with committing an act that violates company policy, such as hitting a supervisor, for instance, management might call as a witness someone who saw the worker and supervisor interacting.

Critical to many arbitration hearings is evidence that documents past behavior, by either the employee or the company. As discussed below, the customs and past practices in the plant enter as important criteria in the arbitrator's decision process.

The hearing will typically end with closing statements by each side in which they summarize the key aspects of their case and their supporting evidence. The testimony given by witnesses or the other side during the hearing will sometimes lead the union or management representatives to alter their arguments during the course of the hearing. Thus it is not unusual for the parties' closing statements to focus on issues and evidence that differ substantially from the issues raised in the opening statements.

The hearing does not bring the presentation of evidence and arguments to a close. The parties can present their views in a posthearing brief, and they often do this in cases in which the issues in dispute are highly technical or complicated.

The Arbitrator's Decision   The arbitrator announces the **arbitrator's decision** sometime after the hearing. Some labor contracts stipulate time limits for these decisions. The arbitrator's decision can be written or oral and will vary, depending on the language in the labor agreement and the preferences of the arbitrator. Although arbitrators tend to follow similar procedures and look at similar kinds of evidence, the preferences of each arbitrator often play an important role in shaping their decisions.

In the decision the arbitrator commonly states the issues and facts in the case. The arbitrator also summarizes the contentions and claims made by the parties in the hearing or briefs. The arbitrator might discuss the merits of each side's evidence and claims. Of course, the most important part of the decision is the section that outlines the judgment reached by the arbitrator on the dispute. The arbitrator can uphold or deny the grievance and has substantial discretion in fashioning a remedy to the dispute.

In a grievance case in which a firm discharged an employee, for example, the arbitrator can deny the grievance and allow the discharge to stand, or the arbitrator can uphold the grievance and order the employer to reinstate the employee. If reinstatement is ordered, the arbitrator could order the company to pay the employee the full wages that have been lost due to the discharge. The arbitrator also could fashion a compromise settlement to such a case by ordering reinstatement but not ordering any back pay. Or, some other remedy might be ordered. The grievance-arbitration procedure grants to arbitrators substantial discretion to fashion any remedy the arbitrator believes is appropriate.

Arbitrators commonly see their task to be the resolution of the grievance. They do not commonly add substantial punitive penalties to their decisions. Thus, in the discharge case cited above, the best the employee could do is gain back the job, any back pay, and any lost rights (such as seniority lost while on discharge). The arbitrator would not assess a large punitive monetary penalty against the employer.

The Arbitrator's Decision Criteria

What does an arbitrator consider when deciding how to rule in a case? Below are outlined the criteria arbitrators commonly use in discipline and discharge cases. Discipline and discharge are used as the examples in part because these are frequent and important sources of grievances.

Discipline for Just Cause   Most labor agreements contain a clause stating that management has the right to **discipline** employees for **just cause.** Grievances over disciplinary actions arise so commonly in part because labor agreements rarely precisely define just cause.

In a discipline case the arbitrator must first decide if the employee actually carried out the act that management claims violates the labor agreement. If the arbitrator is convinced the act did not occur, then the grievance is upheld. In a case in which management alleges an employee hit a supervisor, for example, the arbitrator would rely on available evidence (possibly the testimony of eyewitnesses) to determine if the employee willfully did hit the supervisor. If the arbitrator concludes the act did occur (e.g., the supervisor was hit by the employee), the arbitrator must then decide if this act was a violation of the labor agreement.

Progressive Discipline   If the arbitrator concludes that the act did occur and it did violate the labor agreement, there remains the very important issue as to whether the discipline imposed by the company is appropriate. Arbitrators commonly require that management impose **progressive discipline**—namely, the penalties should increase in a stepwise fashion if there are repeated offenses. If an employee is absent once after a number of years of faithful service to the company, for example, an arbitrator is unlikely to uphold a penalty of discharge. Arbitrators will allow severe disciplinary penalties for repeated absences, however, and want those penalties to increase as the number of absences mount. The underlying principle is that discipline should be **corrective discipline** as well as punitive. Arbitrators commonly require that management take steps to assist employees in correcting their actions and performance. The common steps in progressive discipline are the issuance of an oral warning, suspension for some period of time, and then discharge. Needless to say, if the offense committed by the employee is so severe, such as destroying major company property, then the arbitrator might uphold immediate discharge.

The Importance of Past Practice   Arbitrators commonly rely heavily on the custom and **past practice** of management policy as a guide to decide grievance cases. If in the past employees in a firm have customarily been suspended for one week for their third unexcused absence, for example, an arbitrator would not allow a different disciplinary penalty on another employee for a similar offense unless there were extenuating circumstances. As a result, part of most arbitration hearings involves the union and management representative presenting their views regarding what past practice was for related cases. If a similar case has not arisen in the same firm, the parties (or the arbitrator) might turn to customary practice in another firm or industry to justify their actions.

Who Are The Arbitrators?

The people who serve as arbitrators usually have some expertise in industrial relations and the particularities of the industry in which the case arises. Some labor agreements provide for permanent arbitrators ("umpires") designated to handle all or some fraction of the grievances that arise during the term of a contract. The American Association of Arbitration (AAA) facilitates the process of arbitration. The AAA maintains an active list of arbitrators and can provide facilities for a hearing. A labor contract might stipulate that parties should turn to the AAA for a list of five arbitrators and then allow each side to cross off one name from the list to generate the arbitrator who will hear a particular case.

Some arbitrators work at arbitration as a full-time occupation. There are also many part-time arbitrators who are also industrial relations or law school professors.

The Connections between Grievance Procedures and Other Aspects of the Labor-Management Relationship

In many ways the operation of the grievance procedure is closely linked to other aspects of the labor-management relationship. The next section considers some of these linkages.

Contract Bargaining versus Contract Administration

The administration of a collective bargaining agreement does not operate in isolation from the events that take place in the negotiations process. The behavior and attitudes of the parties during negotiations typically carry over into the administration of the contract, and vice versa. This is not surprising, because the same factors that increase the level of conflict and reduce the ability of the parties to settle without an impasse in negotiations also increase the level of antagonistic behavior during the course of administering the contract.

The attitudinal climate (i.e., the level of trust between the parties) often carries over directly from contract administration to contract negotiations. When a large backlog of unresolved grievances piles up and adds to a hostile atmosphere between the parties during the term of the agreement, the negotiations process becomes a convenient forum for venting these hostilities. Similarly, when the grievance procedure or an arbitration decision has failed to resolve a problem, one party or the other can be expected to place a demand on the negotiation table to remedy the situation. On the other hand, vague or inconsistent language that was negotiated in a climate of distrust is likely to set the stage for conflict during the administration of the agreement.

The three basic functions served by any workplace industrial relations system are the following: conflict resolution and the assurance of due process; the supervision, motivation, and participation of individual workers; and the organization of work.[6] Exhibit 11–1 sketches the interrelationships among these three functions of workplace industrial relations and their effects on the performance of the firm and the fulfillment of workers' goals.

Researchers have found that cooperative attitudes between union and management officials increased the likelihood that grievances would be settled at the lower steps in the procedure.[7] Data from the auto industry show a positive correlation between the rate of grievances filed and two indicators of the intensity of conflict in local contract bargaining—name-

Exhibit 11–1   **The Functions of a Workplace Industrial Relations System: Interrelationships and Outcomes**

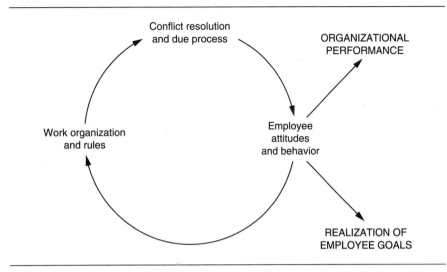

ly, the number of issues introduced into the negotiations and the length of time taken to reach a contract settlement.[8]

A comparative study of the dynamics of grievance settlements in two auto plants further illustrates this point. In the plant that exhibited a highly adversarial relationship, grievance rates and rates of appeal to higher steps in the procedure followed the cycle of bargaining. That is, the union in this plant would save up grievances and file them just before the start of contract negotiations to use this stockpile as a lever in negotiations and to rally the rank and file in support of the union's contract demands. In contrast, no such politicization of the grievance process occurred in a comparable auto plant that had a history of cooperative labor-management relations.[9]

James Kuhn found that a lot of bargaining commonly occurs at the work group level outside the formal grievance procedure. Kuhn found that work groups can engage in **fractional bargaining**—that is, informal bargaining with the supervisor to modify or even to ignore provisions of the agreement that do not suit the group's particular needs.[10]

The Impact of Technology

Changes in technology can render previous unit determination decisions obsolete by modifying how the work is performed, thereby raising the question whether the new jobs created should be excluded from the existing unit. Computer-aided design (CAD) serves as one example of just such a technological change. CAD can transfer drafting, model making, and other similar jobs from their traditional place within blue-collar production and maintenance units to the purview of design or manufacturing engineers, who traditionally have been either nonunion or in a separate engineers union and bargaining unit. In the aerospace industry, for instance, conflict has arisen over whether members of the machinists union or members of the professional engineers union should be given the work of maintaining the thousands of computers used in the firm.

Box 11–4 describes another technology-related dispute that was ultimately resolved by an arbitrator. In this case robots took over some of the tasks traditionally performed by blue-collar workers, and the issue was in part who should be given the job of bringing the robots on line and adapting their specifications to perform specific jobs.

This example illustrates an important feature of the structure of bargaining in the United States. Because so much rests on the definition of the boundary of the units, many fine legal distinctions have been drawn over the years. Labor and management often rely on these legalistic NLRB or arbitration rulings to modify the boundary to fit changing technologies or organizational practices.

As new technologies and new ways of organizing work are adopted, these issues will become more common. The parties will need to find better ways of resolving the issues than through arbitration or NLRB precedents. As the arbitrator quoted in Box 11–4 observed, it is generally preferable for the parties to develop their own principles for handling these issues as they arise, rather than to rely on an arbitrator to devise a viable solution after the fact.

The Japanese industrial relations system and some European systems may be better suited to respond to changing technologies than the U.S. system because they include both blue- and white-collar workers within the same union and the same election or bargaining unit. In Japan, for example, **enterprise unions** represent all blue- and white-collar workers within a single firm. In Germany most industrial unions include both the blue- and the white-collar workers employed within a company and an industry. In Great Britain, on the other hand, a tradition of not only separate blue- and white-collar unions but also a greater reliance on craft unions makes this problem potentially more troublesome than it is in our country. These issues are important because those industrial relations systems that make fine distinctions among election and bargaining units may be more likely than others to face difficulty in adapting to the new technologies now spreading across industries.

The Impact of Industrial Relations and Business Strategy

Differences in arbitration rates between Bethlehem Steel and the U.S. Steel Corporation (since renamed USX) illustrate the effects of different industrial relations and business strategies on grievance rates. Both of those firms experienced employment declines of approximately 70 per-

Box 11–4

Arbitrating over Technological Change

The Issue
Did the company violate the collective bargaining agreement when it assigned certain machining and fixturing work on robotics to non–bargaining unit personnel? If so, what shall be the remedy?

The Facts
The grievant and other bargaining unit personnel did fixturing work on production technology referred to as Robot No. 1. They did similar work for a while on Robots No. 2 and No. 3, but then this assignment stopped in 1984. In December 1983 the company formed a new department called Advanced Automation and Technology, and the fixturing work, what the company calls "development work," was given to non–bargaining unit engineering personnel assigned to the new department.

The Arbitrator's Discussion
In establishing the Advanced Automation and Technology department, the company made a major change that affects the allocation of work that previously had been done by tool room personnel. . . . In a world of changing technology and methods specific duties and responsibilities may shift within an organization. The issue in this case arises because of a shift from earlier technology (that is rather standard and can be adapted in a straightforward manner by bargaining unit personnel) to new technology that requires considerable experimentation by engineers and technicians.

And so we have a situation where an organizational change has shifted the function of preparing production technology, but it is not clear whether the new skills and duties that are involved belong in the bargaining unit or elsewhere in the organization. *Given the grey area that is involved in this dispute, it would be desirable for the parties to establish principles to guide the allocation of work.*

The Arbitrator's Decision
Given the fact that the union has not established conclusively that fixturing work for robotic technology belongs to the bargaining unit, it was not a violation of the collective bargaining agreement when the company assigned certain machining and fixturing work to non–bargaining unit personnel.

Nonetheless, given that the establishment of the Advanced Automation and Technology department represented a major decision with important consequences for the bargaining unit, . . . the parties are directed to negotiate in good faith over the effects of this change.

Source: Arbitration decision of Robert B. McKersie in the case of Northrup Corporation and United Auto Workers Local 1596, 1 July 1986. Adapted and used with permission of the arbitrator.

cent between 1966 and 1985. Over those years, while the number of grievance arbitration cases at Bethlehem declined in proportion to the decline in employment, the caseload at U.S. Steel remained stable even in the face of the employment decline.

The difference in the experiences of the two companies can be traced to their different labor relations philosophies and the different business strategies of the companies. Bethlehem Steel not only has had a relatively cooperative relationship with the Steelworkers union, it also has followed a business strategy of trying to remain active in the steel industry. U.S. Steel/USX on the other hand, has historically had highly adversarial relations with the Steelworkers. It also has taken steps to diversify its investments outside of steel and to seek greater bargaining leverage over the union by contracting out much work.[11] Thus, again, workplace-level activities are driven by, or at least are highly interdependent with, activities at higher levels of the industrial relations system.

Evaluating the Performance of the Grievance System

One important question about the effectiveness of the negotiations process is whether the parties can avoid strikes and impasses. Similarly, an important criterion for evaluating grievance and arbitration procedures is whether the parties can avoid a heavy caseload. The advantages of settling disputes informally or at the step closest to the site where the problems arise are large.

In fact, although the United States has a tradition of very formal grievance systems in unionized settings, informal practices have emerged at the workplace. Most employee complaints are resolved informally before they become formal grievances. The study by Lewin and Peterson, for example, found that between 16 and 40 percent of the employees in the unionized organizations they studied reported having discussed (and resolved) with their supervisors a problem about their contractual rights.[12]

Yet low grievance rates may be due to the fact that the union is not aggressively enforcing the terms of the contract. For this reason, evaluation of the use of the grievance procedure should be accompanied by consideration of the reasons for low use.

Time and Costs of Settling Grievances

Two criteria commonly employed to evaluate grievance procedures are the time taken to settle claims and the costs associated with processing them through to arbitration. The original purpose in developing the procedures was to find an expeditious and inexpensive substitute for court procedures. The parties themselves are increasingly concerned, howev-

er, with both the delays and the costs involved in following the procedures. Consider, for example, the following critique by John Zalusky, a
staff member of the AFL-CIO:

> The traditional labor arbitration procedure has grown in complexity
> until today it is taking on the appearance of a courtroom procedure.
> The presence of lawyers, use of transcripts, swearing in of
> witnesses, pre- and post-hearing briefs, and long delays
> throughout—in setting hearing dates, extending deadlines for the
> filing of briefs, and waiting for the decision—are all too common.
> The arbitration process is so large and cumbersome it is beginning
> to discourage industrial justice for two very basic reasons: cost
> and delay.[13]

The average time required to process a case through arbitration in
1987 was 310 days, or about 10 months. The estimated average cost to
the union in a case involving a lawyer, transcripts, and posthearing briefs
was estimated to be $2,700 (the cost to management on average may be
even higher given their heavy use of legal counsel).[14] These figures suggest that the modern grievance procedure may not be providing timely
due process.

The Effects of Arbitration Decisions

Another important aspect of the evaluation of grievance and arbitration
procedures is what happens after an arbitrator has reinstated a discharged employee. If the grievance procedure is effective in carrying out
industrial justice, a worker unjustly discharged should be able to return
to work and both perform well in the job and progress satisfactorily within the organization.

The procedure itself, however, may work against these results, in several ways. First, the delays involved in processing a case through arbitration may lead a grievant who has been discharged to seek alternative
employment; some reinstated employees therefore do not return to their
former jobs. Second, reinstated employees are put back on their jobs frequently against the will of their employers, often to the dismay of their
immediate supervisors, and sometimes to the dissatisfaction of their fellow workers. Some reinstated workers face hostility on their return to
work. Even if management, supervisors, and fellow workers make a good
faith effort to treat the reinstated employee fairly, the employee may distrust their intentions or lack the confidence to perform effectively. A
number of studies suggest that reinstated employees do not fit back into
the workplace.[15]

For example, one study showed that grievants in four firms, relative to
a comparison group of employees who had not used the grievance procedure, later received lower job performance ratings, had lower probabili-
ties of promotion, and were more likely to experience voluntary or invol-

untary turnover. Moreover, those grievants who had appealed their cases to the higher steps of the procedure later had more negative performance and promotion experiences than those who had settled at the lower steps. And those employees who had won their grievances—that is, whose grievances were found meritorious by either management or an arbitrator—had lower subsequent performance ratings than those whose grievances had been denied by management or an arbitrator. The same negative profile of aftereffects fit the supervisors of grievance filers. Relative to a comparison group, supervisors of grievance filers received lower performance ratings, were less likely to get promoted, and were more likely to experience involuntary turnover. This study suggests that grievance filers and their supervisors in the organizations studied faced considerable risk of retribution for using the procedure.[16]

An obvious implication of all this evidence is that both management and union representatives need to pay careful attention to what happens after a grievance is resolved.

Even in the face of the problem of retribution, the grievance procedures serve an important function as a common law of the shop. Management and union representatives often learn from grievance settlements and arbitration awards the appropriate interpretation of contract clauses and then adapt their behavior accordingly.[17]

In sum, the grievance and arbitration processes can have positive, learning effects or negative, retribution effects. Much depends on whether the management and labor representatives are committed to the goals the process was designed to foster.

The Duty of Fair Representation

In 1944 the Supreme Court held that, in return for the rights of exclusive representation, the union has the duty to represent all members of the bargaining unit "without hostile discrimination, fairly, impartially, and in good faith."[18] Since then, the union's **duty of fair representation** has become an important issue.

Four related developments brought the issue of fair representation to the fore:

1. The stringency of the standards the courts have used to judge whether an employee has been fairly represented by the union

2. The willingness of individual workers to bring claims against unions for failure to represent them fairly

3. The reluctance of unions to drop grievances of questionable merit short of arbitration for fear of being sued for failure to represent the grievant fairly

4. The resulting rise in the number of court cases that deal with this
    issue

The U.S. Supreme Court has defined the duty of fair representation to
prohibit "arbitrarily ignoring a meritorious grievance or processing it in a
perfunctory manner"; fraud, deceit, or bad-faith conduct in the handling
of a grievance; and refusal to handle a grievance out of personal hostility
toward the grievant.[19]

In *Hines v. Anchor Motor Freight, Inc.* (see Box 11–2) the court ruled
that both the employer and the union were liable for failure to handle
fairly an employee representation case.[20] The case involved an employee
whose discharge had been upheld in arbitration. After the arbitration
award was rendered, new evidence was discovered that proved the
employee was not guilty of the offense. Both parties were charged with
having failed to fully investigate the facts of the case in the original procedure. Essentially, a charge of negligence was applied to both the union
and the employer in this case.

In *Bowen v. United States Postal Service* the court went one step further by apportioning liability for back pay between a union and a company in a case in which an employee was reinstated after the union refused
to take the case to arbitration.[21]

Unfortunately, these various judicial efforts to clarify and specify the
standards to be applied in duty of fair representation cases have not
yielded unambiguous criteria for evaluating the union's performance. Box
11–5 extracts a comprehensive summary of the principles of the duty of
fair representation.

Responsiveness to Labor and Employment Laws

Events of the past two decades have raised concern about whether
grievance and arbitration procedures are responsive to public policies
that govern employee rights. Of chief concern is whether arbitration is
useful in resolving claims of discrimination raised under the protection of
Title VII of the Civil Rights Act. But the same concern also arises in claims
that involve alleged violations of regulations on safety and health, wages
and hours, pensions, disability benefits, workers' compensation, unemployment compensation, and many other regulations that may overlap or
even conflict with the provisions of the collective bargaining agreement.

The question is crucial because it has the potential to change the
functions of the arbitration procedure significantly or to reduce the status of arbitration as a conflict resolution procedure. Arbitration traditionally was favored because it was sensitive to the concerns of the parties.
The Supreme Court, in the Steelworkers' trilogy, argued that arbitrators
have special expertise in resolving private disputes.

Box 11–5

> ## Union Responsibilities under the Duty of Fair Representation
>
> First, the individual employee has a right to have the clear and unquestioned terms of the collective agreement which have been made for his benefit followed and enforced until the agreement is properly amended.
>
> Second, the individual employee has no right to insist on any particular interpretation of an ambiguous provision in a collective agreement, for the union must be free to settle a grievance in accordance with any reasonable interpretation thereof. The individual has a right, however, to be guaranteed that ambiguous provisions be applied consistently and that the provision mean the same when applied to him as when applied to other employees. Settlement of similar grievances on different terms is discriminatory and violates the union's duty to represent all employees equally.
>
> Third, the union has no duty to carry every grievance to arbitration: it can sift out grievances that are trivial or lacking in merit. But the individual's right to equal treatment includes the right of equal access to the grievance procedure and arbitration for similar grievances of equal merit.
>
> Fourth, settlement of grievances for improper motives such as personal hostility, political opposition, or racial prejudice constitutes bad faith regardless of the merits of the grievance.
>
> Fifth, the individual employee has a right to have his grievance decided on its own merits. The union violates its duty to represent fairly when it trades an individual's meritorious grievance for the benefit of another individual or of the group.
>
> Sixth, the union can make good-faith judgments in determining the merits of a grievance, but it owes the employees it represents the use of reasonable care and diligence both in investigating grievances in order to make that judgment and in processing and presenting grievances in their behalf.
>
> *Source:* Clyde W. Summers, "The Individual Employee's Rights under the Collective Bargaining Agreement: What Constitutes Fair Representation?" in *The Duty of Fair Representation,* ed. Jean T. McKelvey (Ithaca: New York State School of Industrial and Labor Relations, Cornell University, 1977), pp. 82–83.

Alexander v. Gardner-Denver

This positive view of arbitration has eroded with the growth of governmental regulation of the workplace. In *Alexander v. Gardner-Denver* (see Box 11–2) the Supreme Court departed from the trilogy doctrine in cases of claims concerning Title VII of the Civil Rights Act of 1964.[22] The Court ruled that an arbitrator's decision in a case involving a claim of discrimination does not preclude subsequent judicial review of the merits of the claim. The Court allowed the grievant to also pursue their claim with an appropriate administrative or judicial agency. Furthermore, the Court will hear such cases de novo—that is, the Court will make its own independent judgment of the merits of the claim and will apply whatever weight it deems appropriate to the arbitrator's decision.

This case thus rejected the trilogy doctrine that gave the arbitrator sole responsibility for judging the merits of the claim. As a result of the *Gardner-Denver* case, arbitrators in cases in which public law applies consider the rights accorded the grievant by public law.

Numerous cases have extended the Gardner-Denver decision to rights protected by statutes in addition to the 1964 Civil Rights Act. For instance, in *Barrentine v. Arkansas-Best Freight Sys.,* the U.S. Supreme Court extended the Gardner-Denver standard to individuals who sought remedy under the Fair Labor Standards Act following an adverse decision in arbitration proceedings.[23]

Should Arbitrators Ignore External Public Policies?

The arbitration community is divided over the issue whether arbitrators should consider the requirements of external laws when deciding grievances or instead confine their decisions to interpretations of the rights accorded by the bargaining agreement.[24] Those who advocate that the arbitrator stick to the bargaining agreement do so because they fear that considerations of external law will increase judicial scrutiny of arbitration decisions and that arbitrators may make erroneous interpretations of the law. They believe arbitration has not only been widely accepted as an institution by the parties but also assigned its protected status by the courts in the Steelworkers' trilogy precisely because arbitrators limit their decisions to issues in which they have special expertise. Thus, these advocates of minimal reference to external law are ready to trade off a reduced scope of jurisdiction in arbitration for protection of the status and autonomy that has been afforded labor arbitration since 1960.

Those who argue that arbitrators should play a more active role in resolving claims that involve public laws do so with full awareness that the arbitrator's role thereby shifts from one serving primarily the interests of the parties toward one serving public policies. The central arguments in favor of this new role are that arbitration is still cheaper, faster, and more efficient than the already overloaded judicial system. In this new role, it is argued, arbitration thus remains a useful procedure for resolving disputes that arise under collective bargaining.

Alternatives to the Grievance Procedure in the Union Sector

The costs and delays associated with the grievance procedure and arbitration have led labor and management to develop a number of innovative alternative procedures to cut down on excessive delays and costs.

Among these alternatives are several minor modifications of existing practices, such as keeping grievances oral as far into the procedure as possible to promote informal resolution, tightening time allowances at various steps of the procedure, and agreeing that oral settlements or settlements at intermediate steps of the procedure will not serve in any way as precedential. Box 11–6 describes a well-known and successful oral settlement procedure.

Expedited Arbitration

Expedited arbitration is a type of grievance arbitration in which the parties agree to speed the resolution of disputes. It has gained much attention in recent years. Expedited procedures bypass steps in the normal grievance procedure and impose tight time limits. Exhibit 11–2 illustrates the key features of five expedited arbitration schemes in practice.

A six-year review of one of these—the Steelworkers system—found that

1. Oral resolution cut the cost of the average grievance arbitration case to roughly $55 per party

2. More than half the grievances were resolved before arbitration

3. The awards almost always conformed to the time limits specified (see Exhibit 11–2)

4. The procedure has spread to other Steelworkers contracts in the aluminum, can, copper, and metals industries[25]

Expedited arbitration appears to be one viable strategy for reducing the costs and delays involved in many, merely routine cases.

Grievance Mediation

Another innovation that has gained in popularity is **grievance mediation,** which asks a third party to function as both mediator and arbitrator. In this procedure a neutral third party is asked to mediate a dispute and empowered to settle the dispute with an arbitration decision if mediation fails. The hope is that the mediator-arbitrator will be able to mediate settlements to many of the disputes and thereby reduce the frequency of arbitration.

A pioneering effort to use mediation to resolve grievances before they go to arbitration was developed and applied in the coal industry by William Ury, Jeanne Brett, and Stephen Goldberg.[26] These authors calculated that the average cost per arbitration case in the industry in 1985 was $1,300, whereas the average cost per mediation case was $309—a savings of roughly $1,000 per case. In addition, over the five-year period the average time lapse between the request for mediation and the resolu-

Box 11–6

International Harvester–UAW Procedure for the Oral Resolution of Grievances

Both parties agree that avoiding written grievances and the handling of oral grievances are dependent on the understanding and the continuing cooperation of management and union representatives and employees.

In this connection the parties encourage the expeditious consideration of complaints at the point of origin by bringing together people with the special talents and skills required for full exploration of the problem involved and by . . . joint investigation and resolution of differences within the framework of the labor contract.

The Company and the Union have established the following objectives:

1. Avoidance of grievances and misunderstandings.

2. Oral handling of grievances within the framework of our agreements.

3. Expeditious investigation and quick disposition of such grievances or problems.

4. In connection with the oral handling of grievances the parties further agree that since the retroactive provisions of the contract relating to grievance settlement are tied to dates on which written grievances are presented and processed through the procedure, that another form of control must be used. Although we believe that the new program should work to minimize problems of effective dates of the disposition of cases, it is agreed that reliance on recollection or memos should be adequate to avoid subsequent misunderstandings as to the date on which the problems were raised.

5. Procedure for disposition of unresolved Step 2 grievances.

Note: Although we cite the 1971 agreement, the practice was in existence for a number of years. For a description of the background and performance of this program, see Robert B. McKersie and William W. Skrapshire, Jr., "Avoiding Written Grievances: A Successful Program," *Journal of Business* 35 (April 1962): 135–52.

Source: Agreement between International Harvester and the International Union, United Automobile, Aerospace and Agricultural Implement Workers of America (1971), pp. 19–22.

tion of the case was 19 days, a period considerably shorter than the average of 52 days required to schedule an arbitration hearing and receive a written award. But even further testimony to the value of grievance mediation can be found in the high levels of satisfaction with the procedure itself reported by the management and union representatives and the miners who took part in it.[27]

Exhibit 11–2
Key Features of Five Expedited Arbitration Systems

Feature	United Steelworkers–Basic Steel Industry	American Arbitration Association Service	Allied Industrial Workers Local 562–Rusco, Inc.	American Postal Workers–U.S. Postal Service	Mini-Arbitration Columbus, Ohio
Source of arbitrators	Recent law school graduates and other sources	Special panel from AAA roster	FMCS roster	AAA, FMCS rosters	Its own Joint Selection and Orientation Committee from FMCS roster
Method of selecting	Preselected regional panels; administrator notifies in rotation	Appointed by AAA regional administrators	Preselected panel by rotating FMCS contacts	Appointed by AAA regional administrators	FMCS regional representative, by rotation
Lawyers	No limitation, but understanding that lawyers will not be used	No limitation	No lawyers	No limitation, but normally not used	No limitation
Transcript	No	No	No	No	May be used
Briefs	No	Permitted	No	No	May be used
Written description of issue	Last-step grievance report	Joint submission permitted	No	Position paper	Grievance record expected
Time from request to hearing date	Ten days	Approximately three days depending on arbitrator availability	Ten days	Approximately seven days depending on arbitrator availability	Not specified
Time from hearing to award	Bench decision or 48 hours	Five days	48 hours	Bench decision written award 48 hours	48 hours
Fees (plus expenses)	$100/half day; $150/day	$100 filing fee; arbitrator's normal fee	$100/half day; $150/day	$100 filing fee; $100 per case	$100/half day, 1 or 2 cases; $150/day, 1 or 2 cases; $200/day, 3 or 4 cases

Source: John Zalusky, "Arbitration: Updating a Vital Process," *American Federationist* 83 (November 1976): 4.

Conflict Resolution in Nonunion Settings

The absence of a union does not eliminate the need for conflict resolution systems at the workplace. Instead, means other than the traditional union grievance procedure must be used to perform this generic industrial relations function. If such means are not employed, according to Albert Hirschman's theory, employees who have no effective means to voice their discontent with any inequities they perceive may simply choose to exit the organization.[28] Indeed, evidence is ample that employee turnover rates are higher in nonunion than in union settings.[29] Some of this higher turnover may be traced to the lack of effective grievance or appeal mechanisms in nonunion settings.

Over the past two decades a number of employers have instituted complaint or appeal systems similar to grievance systems, as well as other communication and conflict resolution procedures for their nonunion employees.[30] The more formal of these procedures parallel union grievance procedures, except that only a few of them end in binding arbitration by an outside, or third-party, neutral. Profiles of three such nonunion procedures appear in Box 11–7.

Supplementing these formal procedures is a host of processes such as ombudsman offices, "speak up" programs, employee counseling services, and attitude surveys and related communications programs. Although the use of these various processes has expanded considerably in recent years, we are only beginning to accumulate empirical evidence on their performance as mechanisms for conflict resolution and due process.

The Ombudsman

One alternative to the traditional grievance procedure is to employ an **ombudsman** to help resolve problems, complaints, or conflicts between or among employees, supervisors, and managers. Within the typical organization chart the ombudsman reports either directly to the office of the chief executive or to the head of the human resource management department. Since the ombudsman's mandate is more open-ended than the mandate for a grievance procedure, ombudsmen play a more varied role in resolving conflicts and also often handle a broader range of issues than does the typical grievance procedure.

Box 11–8 lists a range of functions the typical ombudsman might perform. Indeed, the informality with which the ombudsman can approach this role is one of its distinct advantages.

The Performance of Nonunion Grievance Procedures

Critics of nonunion grievance systems argue that employees seldom use these systems either because they have little faith in the fairness of the

Box 11–7

Profiles of Nonunion Grievance Procedures in Three Firms

	Financial Services Firm	*Aerospace Firm*	*Computing Equipment Firm*
Step 1	Informal discussion with immediate supervisor	Written appeal filed with immediate supervisor	Written appeal filed with personnel officer, who meets separately with employee and immediate supervisor
Step 2	Written appeal filed with functional or departmental manager, who gives written response	Written appeal filed with personnel officer; hearing officer appointed to meet with employee's immediate supervisor and employee's representative	Written appeal filed with functional or facility manager, who meets separately with employee and immediate supervisor
Step 3	Written appeal filed with facility or business unit manager, who gives written response	Written appeal filed with corporate vice president of employee relations; VP, another management official, and employee's representative constitute board of inquiry	Written appeal filed with divisional or corporate vice president of personnel, who chairs a management appeals committee
Step 4	Written appeal filed with management appeals committee, which gives written response	Written appeal filed with adjustment board composed of outside arbitrator, management official, and employee's representative; board decisions are binding	Written appeal filed with chief executive officer, who makes final decision
Step 5	Written appeal filed with company vice president of human resources, who makes final decision		

Source: David Lewin, "Conflict Resolution in High Technology Firms," in *Human Resources in High Technology,* ed. Archie Kleingartner and Cara Anderson (Lexington, MA: Lexington Books, 1987)

Box 11–8

Functions of an Ombudsman *(confidentiality / credibility in organization)* neutral

- To give a personal and confidential hearing, to defuse rage, to provide a caring presence to those in grief about a dispute.

- To provide (and sometimes to receive) information on a one-to-one basis.

- To counsel people (confidentially) on how to help themselves, by helping to develop new options, by problem solving, by role playing.

- To conciliate (that is, to go between parties without bringing them face-to-face).

- To mediate by bringing parties together face-to-face.

- To investigate formally or informally, either with or without presenting recommendations.

- To arbitrate or adjudicate, although this is a rare function.

- To facilitate systems or procedural changes by recommending "generic" solutions, by upward feedback, internal memos, and "management consulting" with institutions, by public reports, by recommendations to legislatures, by supporting education and training.

The classic phrase describing most ombuds practitioners is "They may not make, or change, or set aside any law or policy or management decision; theirs is the power of reason and persuasion."

Source: Mary P. Rowe, "Notes on the Ombudsman in the United States, 1986," photocopy (Cambridge: Massachusetts Institute of Technology, 1986).

---

systems or because they fear reprisals. A study by David Lewin of the performance of grievance procedures in three high-technology, nonunion firms provides some support for these claims.[31] Grievance rates in these firms were well below the rates found in most union systems. Appeals to the higher steps of the procedures were also infrequent. Moreover, Lewin found that compared to employees who did not file grievances, grievance filers (and their supervisors) had lower performance ratings, lower promotion rates, and higher rates of turnover in the year after their use of the procedure. Finally, survey responses from two of the firms indicated that approximately one-third of those who did not file grievances chose not to do so because they either feared reprisals or believed there was little chance their appeal would be successful.

Thus, it appears the grievants in these nonunion firms exercised their right to use these procedures at considerable risk. If this pattern is at all representative of experiences in other firms, it supports some of the critics' arguments.[32]

The Nonunion Complaint Systems and Union Avoidance

The various conflict resolution systems in nonunion settings may serve important functions for employees and employers. These procedures can represent constructive additions to a modern industrial relations system, but they can also serve as a means of managerial control and union avoidance. Indeed, many firms that use these systems and many professionals who administer them will openly acknowledge that one of their purposes is to discourage unionization. A former General Electric executive stressed this point when commenting on the reason GE had established a nonunion grievance procedure (one that ends with a peer-review panel): "We took away a major union issue."[33]

To the extent that the express purpose of having these procedures is one of union avoidance, the history of grievance procedures has taken an ironic twist: what started as a unique and highly acclaimed innovation designed to deliver due process to employees has been transformed into an employer strategy for reducing employees' chances of achieving union representation and acquiring a truly independent grievance procedure. Thus, like many other human resource management innovations that are driven at least in part by union avoidance motives, nonunion conflict resolution systems are a double-edged sword.

Why Nonunion Employees Desire Complaint Procedures

Employees in nonunion firms seek complaint procedures in part because they desire a mechanism though which they might challenge discharge. Remember that in the absence of a collective bargaining agreement, U.S. courts have applied a doctrine called employment at will. The employment-at-will doctrine stipulates that both the employee and employer are free to end the employment relationship at any time, for any reason, and without liability, provided that the termination does not violate any statutory or constitutional provisions.

As discussed in Chapter 3, in recent years a number of state courts have loosened the application of the employment-at-will doctrine. Yet, even with the gradual expansion of nonunion complaint procedures and the courts' loosening of the employment-at-will doctrine, there is much controversy surrounding whether unorganized employees have an appropriate amount of due process. The importance of this as a public policy issue continues to grow as the percentage of the work force represented by unions declines.

Should Due Process Be Mandated by Federal Law?

As Jack Steiber has written, "The United States stands almost alone among industrialized nations in not providing statutory protection against unjust discharge or 'unfair dismissal' as it is commonly called in most countries."[34] Steiber and Clyde Summers have both vigorously championed instituting a comprehensive arbitration system to protect nonunion workers from unjust discharge. Summers argued that the fact that most nonunion employees lack due process protections while union employees have such a formal grievance procedure is a paradox in U.S. labor policy:

> The paradox becomes even more painful when we realize that employees in the United States protected by arbitration under collective agreements probably have more complete and sensitive protection against unjust dismissal, more efficient procedures, and more effective remedies than employees in any other country in the world. But employees in the United States who do not have arbitration available are almost alone in not having any general protection against dismissal without notice and without cause.[35]

Summers proposed for the nonunion sector building on the just-cause principle and the procedural guides that have developed in the union sector. He prefers to continue reliance on private arbitrators (who would need to be approved by state or federal agencies to have the force of law behind them) rather than to turn to a labor court or an administrative agency for adjudicating grievances by nonunion employees.

Support for requiring that nonunion employees be provided with complaint procedures that are similar to the kind of formal grievance procedures found in the union sector is high in academic circles but does not yet appear to be pervasive in the public at large. But support for Summers's position could grow if employee discontent with employer decisions were to build. Until then, arbitration will continue to be one of the key "premiums" provided to employees covered under collective bargaining contracts.

Summary

Grievance procedures historically have been the centerpiece of the day-to-day administration of the collective bargaining agreement. The grievance procedure provides a mechanism to settle disputes that arise during the term of a collective bargaining agreement. The grievance procedure typically includes successive steps involving higher union and management officials. The union has the right to decide if it wishes to push any unsettled grievance to a higher step.

The grievance procedure has been hailed as one of the most innovative features of the U.S. industrial relations system. Its centrality was due in part to the understanding that it was "management's job to manage and the union's job to grieve."

Collective bargaining agreements in the United States are elaborate documents that often include highly detailed job descriptions. The existence of such elaborate labor contracts contributed to the need for an orderly means for settling conflicts over interpretations of contract language.

Binding arbitration by a third party is the common device used as the final step of grievance procedures. Arbitrators commonly consider past practice at the workplace, the intent of the parties during contract negotiations, and fairness in fashioning their awards. In discipline cases arbitrators generally require that progressive and corrective discipline be applied.

The centrality of the formal grievance and arbitration procedures is now being challenged by a number of recent developments. The need for greater adaptability and competitive pressures have led some unions and managements to simplify how conflicts are settled.

Furthermore, public laws that govern a broad spectrum of employment issues, such as equal employment opportunity, are challenging the exclusivity of the private arbitration system. The courts have granted employees the right to pursue complaints concerning these matters in the courts as well as through the grievance procedure.

The expansion of worker involvement in business and strategic decisions also has led labor and management to rely less on the grievance procedure to solve problems. An effective industrial relations system in union settings now must be more than simply a grievance procedure. To keep in step with the times, the system must combine the strengths of a well-functioning grievance procedure with mechanisms to informally solve problems and enhance communication.

The next chapter describes how worker and union participation programs have supplemented formal complaint procedures and led to major changes in workplace industrial relations in some locations.

Discussion Questions

1. Describe the typical steps followed in a grievance case.

2. Grievance procedures meet the needs of several groups. Name these groups and discuss how the grievance arbitration procedures help meet their respective needs.

3. Grievance arbitration procedures are often very costly and time-consuming. What are some of the alternatives to this process in the union sector?

4. Although nonunion firms do not usually have a formalized grievance process with binding arbitration, these firms must also contend with conflict resolution at the workplace. What are some of the techniques nonunion firms use to resolve conflict?

Suggested Readings

Correge, Joy, Virginia A. Hughes, and Morris Stone, eds., *The Future of Labor Arbitration in America* (New York: American Arbitration Association, 1976).

Elkouri, Frank, and Edna Asper Elkouri. *How Arbitration Works,* 3d ed. (Washington, D.C.: Bureau of National Affairs, 1984).

Kuhn, James W. *Bargaining and Grievance Settlement* (New York: Columbia University Press, 1961).

Lewin, David, and Richard Peterson. *The Modern Grievance Procedure in the American Economy.* (New York: Quorum Books, 1988).

McKelvey, Jean T., ed. *The Changing Law of Fair Representation* (Ithaca, NY: ILR Press, 1985).

End Notes

1. For a good review of the historical development of court rulings on grievance procedures and arbitration, see Neil W. Chamberlain and James W. Kuhn, *Collective Bargaining,* 3d ed. (New York: McGraw Hill, 1986), pp. 151–153.

2. For a more thorough review of the development of grievance arbitration, see Robben W. Fleming, *The Labor Arbitration Process* (Urbana: University of Illinois Press, 1964).

3. *Agreement between General Motors Corporation and the UAW* (October 8, 1987), pp. 93–94.

4. Chamberlain and Kuhn, *Collective Bargaining,* pp. 151–153.

5. Charles C. Killingsworth and Saul Wallen, "Constraint and Variety in Arbitration Systems," in *Labor Arbitration—Perspectives and Problems: Proceedings of the National Academy of Arbitrators, 1964,* (Washington, D.C.: Bureau of National Affairs, 1965), pp. 56–81.

6. Harry C. Katz, Thomas A. Kochan, and Kenneth R. Gobeille, "Industrial Relations Performance, Economic Performance, and QWL Programs: An Interplant Analysis," *Industrial and Labor Relations Review* 37 (October 1983): 3–17.

7. James T. Turner and James W. Robinson, "A Pilot Study of the Validity of Grievance Settlement Rates as a Predictor of Union Management Relationships," *Journal of Industrial Relations* 14 (September 1972): 314–322.

8. Katz, Kochan, and Gobeille, "Industrial Relations Performance," pp. 8–9.

9. Nancy R. Mower, "The Labor-Management Relationship and Its Effects on Quality of Work Life," M.S. thesis (Cambridge: Massachusetts Institute of Technology, 1982).

10. James W. Kuhn, *Bargaining in Grievance Settlement* (New York: Columbia University Press, 1961).

11. "Bad Blood at Big Steel Could Lead to a Costly Strike," *Business Week* (19 May 1986), pp. 82–84.

12. David Lewin and Richard Peterson, *The Modern Grievance Procedure in the United States* (New York: Quorum Books, 1988).

13. John Zalusky, "Arbitration: Updating a Vital Process," *American Federationist* 83 (November 1976): 1.

14. *Federal Mediation and Conciliation Service—Fortieth Annual Report* (Washington, D.C.: FMCS Office of Information and Public Affairs, 1987).

15. Arthur M. Ross, "The Arbitration of Discharge Cases: What Happens After Reinstatement?" *Critical Issues in Arbitration: Proceedings of the Tenth Annual Meeting of the National Academy of Arbitrators, 1956* (Washington D.C.: Bureau of National Affairs, 1957), pp. 21–56, and Robert C. Rodgers, I. B. Helburn, and John E. Hunter, "The Relationship of Seniority to Job Performance Following Reinstatement," *Academy of Management Journal* 29 (March 1986): 101–114.

16. Lewin and Peterson, *The Modern Grievance Procedure.*

17. Thomas R. Knight, "Feedback and Grievance Resolution," *Industrial and Labor Relations Review* 39 (July 1986): 585–598.

18. *Steele v. Louisville & Nashville R.R. Co.,* 323 US 192 (1944).

19. *Vaca v. Sipes,* 386 US 171 (1967).

20. *Hines v. Anchor Motor Freight, Inc.,* 424 US 554 (1976).

21. *Bowen v. United States Postal Service,* 103 US (1983).

22. *Alexander v. Gardner-Denver,* 415 US 36 (1974).

23. *Barrentine v. Arkansas-Best Freight Sys.,* 101 S. Ct. 1437 (1981).

24. For a review of the different approaches, see David E. Feller, "The Impact of External Law upon Labor Arbitration," in *The Future of Labor Arbitration in America* (New York: American Arbitration Association, 1976), pp. 83–112, and David E. Feller, "The Coming End of Arbitration's Golden Age," in *Arbitration 1976: Proceedings of the 29th Annual Meeting of the National Academy of Arbitrators,* ed. Barbara D. Dennis and Gerald G. Somers (Washington, D.C.: Bureau of National Affairs, 1977), pp. 97–151.

25. Zalusky, "Arbitration: Updating a Vital Process".

26. William L. Ury, Jeanne M. Brett, and Stephen B. Goldberg, *Getting Disputes Resolved: Designing Systems To Cut the Costs of Conflict* (San Francisco: Jossey-Bass, 1988).

27. Stephen B. Goldberg, "The Mediation of Grievances under a Collective Bargaining Contract: An Alternative to Arbitration," *Northwestern University Law Review* 77 (October 1982): 270–315.

28. Albert O. Hirschman, *Exit, Voice, and Loyalty: Responses to Decline in Firms, Organizations, and States* (Cambridge, MA: Harvard University Press, 1971).

29. Richard B. Freeman and James L. Medoff, *What Do Unions Do?* (New York: Basic Books, 1984), pp. 94–107. The authors point out (pp. 104–107) that seniority systems, as well as grievance arbitration systems, reduce quit rates in union settings.

30. See Alan Balfour, "Five Types of Non-Union Grievance Procedures," *Personnel* 61 (March–April 1984): 67–76.

31. David Lewin, "Conflict Resolution in High Technology Firms," in *Human Resource Management in High Technology,* ed. Archie Kleingartner and Cara Anderson (Lexington, MA: Lexington Books, 1987).

32. Lewin and Peterson, *The Modern Grievance Procedure.*

33. "Letting Workers Help Handle Workers' Gripes," *Business Week,* (September 15, 1986), p. 82.

34. Jack Steiber, "The Case for Protection of Unorganized Employees against Unjust Discharge," in *Proceedings of the Thirty-Second Annual Meeting, IRRA, December 28–30, 1979,* ed. Barbara D. Dennis (Madison, WI: Industrial Relations Research Association, 1980), pp. 155–163.

35. Clyde W. Summers, "Arbitration of Unjust Dismissal: A Preliminary Proposal," in *The Future of Labor Arbitration in America,* Joy Correge, Virginia A. Hughes, and Morris Stone, eds., (New York: American Arbitration Association, 1976), p. 161.

Chapter 12

Participatory Processes

Unionized industrial relations systems now face intense environmental pressures, including those arising from the lower costs found in many nonunion workplace systems. In response to these pressures, labor and management in unionized settings have been introducing a wide range of innovations in their workplace systems. Central to these efforts are participatory processes that involve individual workers and union representatives in decision making. In many cases these participatory processes provide informal mechanisms of worker involvement that are supplements or alternatives to the grievance and arbitration procedures.

Participatory processes often are linked to alterations in the organization of work that simplify work rules and increase flexibility in management of the work force. Participatory processes are also frequently introduced along with new manufacturing methods such as **just-in-time inventory systems** or **cell manufacturing.** Furthermore, a number of the participatory processes have now evolved to increase the participation of workers and unions in strategic business decisions.

The efforts to expand worker and union participation have had varying degrees of success. Some experiments flourished, whereas others failed and were followed by a return to traditional practices and bitter labor-management relations. Both examples of success and failure are reviewed in this chapter.

Participatory programs also have stirred much debate within the ranks of the labor movement. Supporters of the programs argue that they can provide the sort of industrial democracy unions have long sought although rarely achieved in the United States. Meanwhile, critics of the programs claim that they lead to co-opted workers and to the weakening, if not the demise, of union representation.

Thus, an understanding of participatory programs is of interest for a number of reasons. It is useful first to provide some historical perspective.

The Evolution of Worker and Union Participation

Much of the effort to create new mechanisms of worker and union involvement in decision making involves what are called quality of working life (or employee involvement) programs. **Quality of working life (QWL) programs** are oriented toward improving organizational performance and the working life of employees. These programs operate at the lowest level of industrial relations activity, namely, down on the shop floor through the involvement of groups of workers.

Early QWL—Limited Success

Efforts to spark interest in QWL programs expanded in the early 1970s. Many of these early QWL programs sought to address a perception that modern factories alienated workers by providing repetitive job tasks and few avenues through which employees could provide direct input into matters that affected their work lives. The highly publicized 1972 *Work in America* report tried to spark interest in QWL issues by calling for workplace reforms that would reduce worker alienation (what was sometimes referred to as "the blue-collar blues").[1]

Most of the early promotion of QWL programs was unsuccessful. For example, the federal government's National Commission on Productivity and Quality of Working Life tried hard to stimulate interest and experimentation but managed only to generate pilot projects in a handful of manufacturing firms and one coal mine. The commission was eventually disbanded after it received a negative evaluation by the federal government's General Accounting Office and lost its political support.[2]

The early programs also ran into much opposition from labor and management, for several reasons. First, because these programs were largely initiated from outside the organizations, labor and management did not see a clear need to change. Second, many labor leaders and industrial relations managers resisted change because they believed that the proposed alternatives questioned the basic assumptions of the traditional form of unionism and the process of collective bargaining. Professionals on both sides of the table were skeptical of claims by QWL advocates that increased problem solving and participation could replace contractual rules that had been carefully bargained over the years.

Third, labor and management representatives also feared that informal problem solving would threaten their roles and status. Many labor leaders believed that QWL was simply another in the long line of managerial tactics to undermine collective bargaining and further weaken unionism. Since most of the QWL experience before the 1970s had been in nonunion firms and few of the advocates of QWL had much appreciation or understanding of unions, those fears were not unfounded.

Fourth, few line managers or top executives saw the bottom-line relevance of QWL. Instead, they tended to view QWL as a behavioral science fad that at most promised to improve job satisfaction and perhaps employee motivation. As we will see, this perspective was to change dramatically in the 1980s as line managers and an increasing number of top executives began to see participation and workplace innovations as keys to improving productivity and product quality.

The Rebirth of QWL in the 1980s

QWL was reborn in the 1980s as economic pressures intensified. Heightened economic pressure induced labor leaders and managers to find new ways to address their productivity, quality, and labor cost problems. By far most QWL efforts started out as narrow programs based on the premise that they be kept separate from collective bargaining issues and procedures. These narrow QWL programs were designed to increase individual and group problem solving around task-related issues.

Quality Circles   **Quality circles (QC's)** are an example of this narrow type of effort and the problems confronted by these narrow programs. In a typical QC program, the workers in one area of a plant met for one or two hours a week with their supervisor. Generally, higher management assigned QC's the task of identifying potential improvements in production and service delivery. The QC meetings were commonly held during normal work hours (the line might be stopped or meetings were added to the lunch hour), and workers were paid their normal hourly wage rate for their participation in these activities. (The latter was in contrast to how QC's operate in Japan where hourly workers typically attend QC meetings after work hours and are often not paid for their time.) Supervisors or other managers often played strong roles in the QC meetings. The supervisor, for example, might have led a discussion of statistical quality control techniques or taken the lead in listing priorities or communicating group recommendations to higher management.

Many companies initially reported large payouts from QC activities. For some companies scrap rates began to drop significantly after QC's were started up, and in others the groups were able to quickly identify methods for cost savings through changes in shop floor production processes.

The Limited Gains from Quality Circles   Over time the gains from QC's dissipated in company after company. At times workers became frustrated by, and in some cases stopped attending, QC meetings after management had rejected or ignored their suggestions and recommendations. In other cases workers continued to attend QC meetings but ran out of suggestions to offer because all their new suggestions required that changes be made in work rules or contractual clauses and these were deemed to be out of bounds to the QC. This latter problem arose because both management and the union typically defined QC activity as a supplement to normal collective bargaining. As a result, QC's were not normally authorized to address work rules, contractual issues, the nature of technology, or basic production methods. Other QWL efforts ran up against similar problems.

The Broadening of QC and QWL Programs

The most successful QC and QWL programs were those that eventually broadened to involve work rules, collective bargaining issues, and production methods (essentially all the things that initially had been kept separate from the participatory processes).[3] Unless this broadening occurred, the QWL change process was not able to address the important issues that affected economic performance and long-run employment security.

The Expansion of QWL at Xerox Not all narrow QWL processes made that transition successfully. In fact, by the mid-1980s articles had begun appearing in management journals criticizing many firms for treating QC's as just another short-lived fad.[4] One QWL program that did succeed in broadening its focus involved Xerox Corporation and the Amalgamated Clothing and Textile Workers Union (ACTWU) in Rochester, New York. As summarized in Box 12–1, there was an iterative broadening of QWL at Xerox. At each successive stage the parties had to reaffirm their commitment to expanding the problem-solving process while at the same time resolving conflicts that occurred in negotiations and in day-to-day contract administration. The parties' ability to manage the tensions between problem solving and labor-management conflict was critical in this case, as in so many others.

For example, less than two years into the QWL process the program came under fire from rank-and-file workers when management shifted to a business and manufacturing strategy based on greater concern for cost controls. But instead of abandoning QWL, the parties began to use it to search for ways to cut costs and save jobs. The study team in the wiring harness area represented the first such effort. This study team suggested changes in work organization that required contractual changes, and thereby they created the need for the QWL process to be integrated into the collective bargaining process. The parties did this in their 1983 negotiations by agreeing to use the wiring harness study team experience as a model for how to handle similar subcontracting decisions in the future. In return for this and several other work rule and pay changes, management in 1983 agreed to a no-layoff provision.

As Box 12–1 indicates, since 1983 Xerox and the ACTWU have broadened their joint efforts to allow autonomous work groups in some areas, to plan a new work system for a new plant, and to establish decentralized "business area work groups" (teams that manage their unit's own affairs and tailor their participation and problem-solving processes).[5] Xerox

---

Box 12–1

The Evolution of a QWL Program at Xerox

1980   QWL language put in collective bargaining agreement.
        Four joint Plant Advisory Committees and departmental steering committees established to create and support employee problem-solving groups.

1981   Over 90 problem-solving groups established.
        Outsourcing of 180 wiring harness jobs on hold pending analysis of joint Study-Action Team.

1982   Study-Action Team identifies over $3.2 million potential savings; jobs not subcontracted.
        Over 150 problem-solving groups exist in seven facilities.
        Massive layoffs of unionized and exempt personnel.
        First semi-autonomous work groups established on their own initiative.

1983   Contract includes no-layoff clause and mandated use of Study-Action Teams in all potential outsourcing situations, along with first-year wage freeze, co-payment medical changes, and a restrictive absenteeism control program.
        Strategic Planning Teams include the union to assess the future of the reprographic business.
        QWL training made mandatory, polarizing the work force.
        Study-Action Teams established in two additional areas, with work kept in-house in each case.

1984   Operating engineers' union withdraws from QWL in protest over issues of medical benefit changes.
        QWL groups decline in New Building Operations; informal pre-shift meetings emerge in their place.
        Study-Action Teams established in three areas, with work kept in-house in two cases.
        Employee attitude survey in Components Manufacturing (CMO) prompts top-level reexamination of QWL.

1985   Launch of Business Area Work Group concept at CMO.
        New plant built in Webster, New York, based on joint analysis and design team.

1986   Union supports flexible work assignments for hourly workers involved in new product development.
        Contract extends no-layoff guarantee; modifies restrictive absenteeism program; establishes classification for hourly group leaders; and contemplates pilot study of gains sharing—all with a mixture of hard bargaining and problem solving.
        Autonomous work groups increasingly established, prompted by early retirement of supervisors.

Source: Joel Cutcher-Gershenfeld, "New Path toward Organizational Effectiveness and Institutional Security: The Case of Xerox Corporation and the Amalgamated Clothing and Textile Workers Union," report to the Bureau of Labor Management Relations and Cooperative Programs, U.S. Department of Labor, 1987.

---

later won the prestigious Baldridge award for organizational excellence from the U.S. Commerce Department, and Xerox's participatory activities received much of the credit. Research also shows that the work areas in Xerox that had a greater intensity and wider range of cooperative activities had higher productivity and less scrap.[6]

Strategic Participation at Xerox   Several features of labor-management relations at the strategic level of Xerox helped increase the success of joint problem-solving efforts. Xerox has not resisted union organizing in its new facilities. In addition, top Xerox executives and ACTWU leaders meet periodically to share information and discuss long-range issues that affect the business. Thus, workplace QWL activities evolved in this case in an environment where strategic interactions reinforced worker and union shop floor participation.

New Channels of Communication

The expansion of participation processes is often associated with the elaboration of new channels of communication between workers and supervisors. Often such communication is supplemented by expanded communication between union officers and higher management. The mutual growth forums at Ford Motor Company described in Box 12–2 illustrate how this can occur.

Work Organization Restructuring—Links to QWL

As illustrated by the Xerox case, work reorganization became a central part of many participation processes. This occurred as a result of pressures for greater flexibility, higher quality, and lower costs. Yet altering

Box 12–2

UAW–Ford Motor Company Mutual Growth Forums

Both parties recognize that the need for change continues . . . and they must explore new methods of resolving their honest differences in orderly rational ways. . . . To provide such a new approach, to facilitate the process of continuing evolution and change, and to move the parties forward to new thresholds, Ford and the UAW have agreed to establish a Mutual Growth Forum that is intended to function—at both the local and national levels—as a highly visible new adjunct to the collective bargaining process.

"The forum does not replace collective bargaining, nor does it interfere in any way with the parties' grievance procedure. Rather, it provides a new framework designed to promote better Management-Union relations through better communications, systematic fact finding, and advance discussions of certain business developments that are of material interest and significance to the Union, the employees, and the Company."

Source: Letter of Understanding appended to the collective bargaining agreement between Ford Motor Company and the United Automobile, Aerospace and Agricultural Implement Workers of America (February 13, 1982).

work organization requires changing many of the practices that grew up under traditional collective bargaining. It is not surprising, therefore, that these changes do not come easily or without a great deal of internal debate within unions and companies.

Although there are many cases in which change is being introduced incrementally within existing work sites, the most significant examples of work organization restructuring are in new plants or in plants that are being completely retrofitted with new technology or new products. In particular, examples can be found in most auto, steel, and other basic manufacturing firms, as they upgrade their facilities in an effort to be competitive with the newest nonunion and foreign producers in their industry. Following the 1987 contract negotiations with the major steel companies, for example, the United Steelworkers and seven of the top eight steel firms began a series of industrywide joint training programs designed to diffuse knowledge and support for teamwork systems throughout their operations.[7]

It may be easier to see work restructuring when it occurs in a manufacturing site. Yet, now team and other new work systems are being used in many technical and service arenas. Team-based management also is being introduced into elementary and secondary education. In some hospitals radiology technicians are now taking on some diagnostic and machine maintenance responsibilities. Although the development of new work systems is diffusing unevenly in these settings, technological and other pressures are leading to the spread of team systems of work among white-collar jobs.[8]

The Links between Teamwork, Participation, and Work Restructuring

Teamwork systems require a fundamental reorganization of workplace relations because they replace multiple and narrow job classifications with jobs that are broader in scope, that involve workers in making discretionary judgements, and that require investments in training. Typically, work teams do their own inspections since they must take responsibility for quality performance. In some cases the teams also do their own scheduling, task assignment, certification of workers' skill levels, material handling, housekeeping, and routine repair work. Team and other participatory meetings also provide a forum for the sharing of information on financial performance and business matters.

New Roles for Supervisors

Traditional supervisors often are replaced with team leaders who are often, but not always, members of the bargaining unit rather than members of the first line of management. Finally, some teamwork systems use a pay-for-knowledge system of compensation, in which individuals are paid according to their skills (often measured by how many jobs in the work area they can perform).

In one auto plant under a pay-for-knowledge plan workers were paid $13.20 per hour and were required to be proficient at two different jobs in the work area. If the workers could perform five different jobs in their work area, they received 30 cents more per hour; they received another 30 cents more per hour if they could perform eight different jobs in their work area and another 30 cents per hour if they were proficient at all the jobs in their work area. Under pay-for-knowledge schemes workers are paid their skill rate each day regardless of whether they are actually assigned to a job that requires the use of their level of skill.

The Expansion of Teams

In some team plants there exists a top "administrative" team, which includes the plant manager and the chairman of the local union's bargaining committee, giving the union access to a broad array of financial and other strategic information as a matter of course and a significant role in the governance of the organization. One key to the success of this type of arrangement is local union participation in the initial design of the plant's new organizational structure.

Managing the Overlap between Participation, Work Restructuring, and Collective Bargaining

As participatory processes expand and become meshed in work restructuring, a union that represents workers at such a site faces a challenge regarding how to manage and coordinate the overlap. On the one hand, unions are tempted to try to maintain a clear and sharp separation between participatory activities and collective bargaining procedures and issues. Drawing such a separation can help the union leadership, particularly when a participatory program has just begun and some workers (or union officers) remain skeptical of the program's objectives and implications. One way the parties try to accomplish this separation, for example, is through the adoption of a rule declaring that during team meetings workers cannot raise issues that are normally dealt with through the grievance procedure or the collective bargaining agreement.

Although separating participatory processes and collective bargaining issues might make sense in this early phase, over time if the participatory process matures, the line between collective bargaining and participatory process blurs. In the Xerox case described above, for example, in their effort to lower production costs the wire harness study team began to make recommendations that altered job descriptions and transfer rights.

Changes in Contractual Procedures That Emerge from Participation

As unions and workers participate more directly in decisions, labor and management often find that the formal procedures outlined in the labor agreement become less important. In some firms as team meetings begin to tackle serious issues they become a forum for workers to air complaints. The parties then make alterations that might otherwise be processed through the grievance procedure.

As an illustration of modification of the grievance procedure, Box 12–3 describes how the Dayton Power and Light Company and the Utility Workers Union radically altered the language governing the resolution of grievances. The language described in this box grew out of a broad transformation that occurred in the relationship between Dayton Power management and their union and work force. In 1986 labor and management at Dayton Power replaced their 114-page labor agreement with a "Compact" that was only 13 pages long. In that compact the issue resolution procedures outlined in Box 12–3 replaced the traditional four-step grievance procedure previously used at the firm.

The three-year compact adopted in 1986 (and renewed in 1989) at Dayton Power also introduced a no-layoff clause and a new incentive pay system that paid workers bonuses if the performance of their work area exceeded a target. All these contractual changes were accompanied by a shift in the management of the company that decentralized authority into service areas. Events at Dayton Power illustrate how increased worker and union participation can be linked to changes in the labor agreement and managerial practices.

An Issue for Unions: How Far To Go in Lessening Formal Rules and Procedures

The unions at the sites described above want to allow the participatory process to evolve and to produce the very kind of innovations that can lead to improved cost competitiveness and employment security. Yet the unions also do not want to abandon the important roles that remain for the grievance procedure and formal negotiations.

How then can a union maintain a proper balance between direct worker involvement in decisions and the union's representation responsibilities? The answer seems to lie in a shift in union and union officer roles. The union must allow participation to proceed, but must continuously coordinate and oversee this process and the connections to collective bargaining. This requires that union committee persons, for example, stay in tune with what transpires in any team meetings in their jurisdiction. The union also should discuss the participatory programs at union meetings and report about any role the union plays in participatory activities in the union newsletter and other official communication channels.

A number of cases show that if the union ignores or maintains an arms-length distance to a participatory process, at some point a con-

Box 12–3

A New Approach to Conflict Resolution: Issue Resolution in the Dayton Power–UWUA Compact

The following language appears in the 1989–1993 collective bargaining agreement of the Dayton Power and Light Company and the Utility Workers Union of America, Local 175. This language appears in the section of the contract entitled "issue resolution." This language replaces the traditional four-step grievance procedure outlined in previous labor agreements between these parties.

The success of our mutual relations under this agreement depends on our commitment to address issues in a fair and responsible way. It is a matter of trust. It is the method we have chosen to avoid an agreement of rigid and unnecessary detail which hinders both management freedom and employee opportunity. Through mutual pledges to approach concerns in a problem-solving manner, we have established the following procedures for issues which arise among us.

A. *Unlimited Referral*—There is no limit on the nature of issues which may be referred to this process by employees, the Union, or the Company. The process will be used to advance positive ideas as well as to examine perceived wrongs. The only qualifications are that the affected person(s) certify the issue as a responsible one of genuine concern and thereafter participate first hand in its resolution. Employees will be paid scheduled rates for work time required for issue resolution. Union representatives may participate as they choose in any phase of issue resolution.

B. *Procedure*—An issue should be addressed promptly between the affected person and those with the resources and authority to resolve the issue. The initiator and responder have the responsibility for introducing the issue constructively, for identifying the necessary participants and resources for the resolution of the issue, and any further necessary interaction to resolve the issue.

   If not resolved within twenty (20) days, the issue will be jointly defined in writing and referred to the appropriate management and Union personnel to review the process/issue before the issue may be referred to mediation.

C. *Mediation*—The Mediation Panel will be composed of a Union representative, a Company representative and a neutral Umpire. No issue shall be referred to arbitration until the neutral Umpire and one other panel member certify they have failed to handle the matter satisfactorily.

D. *Arbitration*—Upon failure of mediation, the neutral Umpire shall reconvene the panel as arbitrators and conduct such hearing as is required, with the Umpire serving as the neutral Arbitrator. The Arbitrators shall have no power to add to or subtract from or modify the terms of this agreement. The Arbitration Panel shall announce their decision or resolution as speedily as possible in writing, and it shall be binding upon the parties. The parties shall bear their own costs of mediation and arbitration. The neutral Umpire's fee will be split equally between the Union and the Company.

E. *Discharge Cases*—Employee discharge cases shall be referred directly to the appropriate Company officer, and may be subject to mediation upon mutual agreement. The mediation Umpire shall not serve as a discharge Arbitrator. Arbitrators for discharge cases will normally be selected through the Federal Mediation and Conciliation Service.

Source: The Compact, Local 175, UWUA, AFL-CIO and the Dayton Power and Light Company, November 1, 1989, pp. 5–6.

frontation develops or the participatory process withers. This may be just the outcome a union opposed to participation wants, but for unions that support participation, it can be an unfortunate development.

New Union Roles   Union oversight and coordination of participatory processes can be assisted through **joint steering committees** or planning boards. In addition, individuals who serve in the role of **facilitators** in joint activities play a critical role in mediating any tensions that arise. Some of the best facilitators are former union officers as these people tend to be well respected by the work force and adept at fashioning compromises. The net result is the creation of a complex set of committees and new jobs (e.g., facilitators) that serve to bridge and coordinate participation, work restructuring, and collective bargaining.

Exhibit 12–1 outlines the organizational chart of Xerox and illustrates how expanded participation by workers and unions can be integrated into a business structure. The union's coordinating role (and balancing act) becomes ever more important where the participatory process evolves to the point that it includes strategic business issues.

The Expansion of Joint Activities   As participatory programs expanded to include discussion of work organization, they became one among a growing number of joint activities operating in contemporary unionized settings. Other joint activities commonly in existence in unionized settings include employee assistance programs (alcohol and drug abuse counseling and assistance), health and safety committees, absentee programs, training and education activities, and community service programs. These programs are all joint as each is administered (and often funded) by both union and management representatives.

Many of these joint programs started long before the expansion of participatory processes. Nevertheless, the economic and social pressures that led to an expansion in participatory processes in the 1980s and 1990s also were prompting the expansion of other joint programs. Absentee programs, for example, were also expanding because of cost-control pressures.

The simultaneous expansion of so many joint activities has combined to bring a restructuring of the job responsibilities of union representatives. In many unionized settings, union officers now spend as much (or even more) of their time in joint activities than they do in traditional arms-length activities characterized by opposing labor-management interests.

This trend has led to changes in job titles and job funding. With the expansion of joint activities, there are many more union jobs in which the jobholder's responsibility is to function as a facilitator. Many of these positions are funded out of jointly managed funds.[9]

Joint activities have increased not only in number of job positions. For many unionized plants it is the degree of success of the joint activities

Exhibit 12–1   **ACTWU/Xerox Joint Process 1990—Organizational Chart**

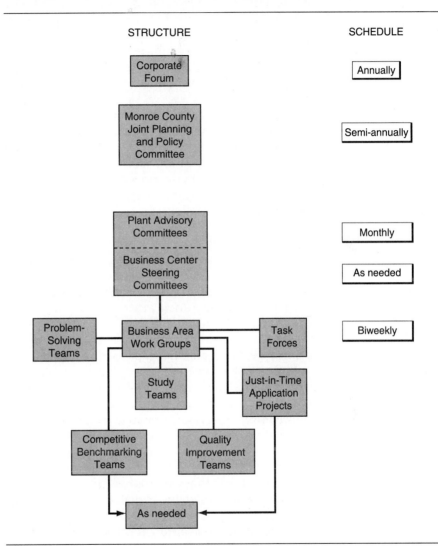

that will determine whether a plant survives in the future. The increased number and importance of joint activities poses new challenges to union representatives as they define and seek member support for their mission.

Worker and Union Participation in Strategic Decisions

In some plants worker or union involvement in strategic issues came about through formal committees such as the administrative team described earlier. In other cases workers and union officers are drawn into strategic issues on a gradual and informal basis. An example of this evolutionary course occurred in a number of auto plants after workers and union representatives were placed on planning committees that operate at the plant level. These committees were given the task of developing modifications in work rules and other manufacturing practices to keep work in the plant (and avoid outsourcing) or to help the plant win bids on new work.

In order to keep or win new business, these committees typically went on to develop methods to reduce costs and improve product quality. Like the wire harness study teams that operated at Xerox, these committees were drawn into strategic issues as the participants gained access to financial and operating information that previously had only been available to plant management as part of efforts to develop cost-reduction strategies.

The Sources of Failure   Not all of these committees proved to be successful as it was difficult to generate sustained improvements in plant productivity or quality that matched competitive alternatives. In some cases it was management's inability or reluctance to make necessary changes in manufacturing practices that was needed to attain competitive plant performance. Nevertheless, through this evolution the line between participation and collective bargaining blurred as what started as workplace participation expanded to include strategic business issues.

Strategic involvement by workers or unions historically has been rare in the United States because it goes against the grain of the core principle that "management manages and unions grieve." This principle has been central to the traditional American collective bargaining system. It is only in recent years that this principle has been challenged. Some labor leaders have come to believe that effective representation of their members' long-run interests requires influencing managerial decisions before they are made rather than only addressing the effects of these decisions after the fact through collective bargaining.

The Types of Strategic Involvement   The mildest form of strategic interaction is that of information sharing and prior consultation between management and labor, as illustrated by the periodic meetings described above between Ford executives and union officials. More significant forms are represented by the plants described earlier where the union leader is formally included in the plant manager's administrative staff and attends management staff meetings.

Another form of involvement comes in joint strategic planning of new facilities or in implementing other major organizational changes. The governance structure of the Saturn Corporation, a subsidiary of General Motors, exhibits many of these features (see Box 12–4). What is noteworthy at Saturn is the extent to which the union (UAW) plays a role in busi-

Box 12–4

GM–UAW Saturn Agreement

Organizational Structure of Saturn:

Strategic Advisory Committee
Does long-range planning. Consists of Saturn president and his staff and top UAW advisor
Manufacturing Advisory Committee
Oversees Saturn complex. Includes company and elected union representatives and specialists in engineering, marketing, etc.
Business Unit
Coordinates plant-level operations. Made up of company representatives, elected union adviser, and specialists
Work Unit Module
Groups of three to six work units led by a company "work unit advisor"
Work Units
Teams of 6 to 15 workers led by an elected UAW "counselor"

Key Industrial Relations Principles:

- Team forms of work organization with few job classifications

- Performance-based bonuses with all employees paid normal earnings on a salaried basis

- 80 percent of the work force protected against layoffs except in case of "catastrophic" events

- Worker and union participation in decision making

Source: Memorandum of Agreement between Saturn Corporation and UAW (Detroit: General Motors Corporation, July 1985).

ness and strategic decisions in the plant. The local officers of the UAW at Saturn participate in a wide range of issues, including choosing parts suppliers (and considering how much union representation at these suppliers versus cost and product quality attributes should count in the choice process). Employees and union officers at Saturn also have had a role in planning which technologies are used in the plant complex and decisions on how to configure the car assembly process.

The Debate Surrounding Participatory Programs

There is much debate within the ranks of workers, unionists, and academicians over the nature and consequences of participatory programs. Critics of these programs argue that they do not lead to real increases in the extent of worker or union involvement in decisions. Instead, the critics claim that the participatory programs are used by management to increase the pace and difficulty of work. These critics claim, for example, that team systems are used to put peer pressure on workers and remove the independent voice provided through union representation. To them teams and other participatory programs are part of **management by stress.**[10] The critics also argue that participatory programs are designed as a halfway house in the transition from union representation to nonunion operation.

The proponents of participatory processes see things differently. They admit that the pressure of heightened international and nonunion competition has led to increases in work pace and many pay concessions. But the proponents claim that increased worker and union participation in decision making can lead to both cost reductions and improvements in employment security, as well as more interesting work. To the proponents of participation, if a union becomes forcefully involved in a participatory process (possibly through the joint committees discussed above), the union can gain greater involvement in the very issues that are of critical importance to workers. What better way for the union to carry out its historic mission of representing workers' interests than to be involved in work restructuring and the strategic business decisions that shape workers' lives, say the proponents.

It may be impossible to resolve this debate through abstract argumentation. The test will come as participatory processes and work restructuring evolve. In the end, workers and unions will learn whether the critics or proponents are correct as a result of what they experience.

Assessing the Effects of Participatory Processes

Management seems convinced that participatory processes and work organization reforms can contribute significantly to improved productivity and product quality, and a number of unionists are coming to a similar judgment.

Research shows that the narrowly defined QC types of QWL programs have only small positive effects on product quality and negligible effects on productivity.[11] It is also clear that complex political dynamics and conflicts commonly emerge throughout the evolution of participatory programs and these sometimes lead unions to withdraw their support for the programs.[12]

Studies also show that the auto plants with the highest productivity and product quality are not those with the most advanced technology, but, rather, they are those that *integrate* their human resource strategy with their production processes.[13] Data show that as of early 1987 the

New United Motors Manufacturing, Incorporated (NUMMI), plant had the best productivity and product quality of all auto plants not only within GM but in all of North America. Although this plant has older technology than GM's most modern plants, it links the "humanware" and the "hardware" components of technology tightly together.[14]

Research also shows that the participatory programs are often accompanied by work rule changes. Consistent with the integration argument discussed above, evidence suggests that the biggest payouts to work rule changes occur where workers are simultaneously increasing their involvement in decision making.[15]

Yet we must be extremely careful not to overgeneralize from the small number of research studies in this area. Furthermore, research must be careful to isolate the effects of participation from the many other changes that often are occurring simultaneously, such as the introduction of new technology. Clearly, further research is needed to reach definitive conclusions on the effects of worker and union participation.

Union Representation on a Company's Board of Directors

Formal representation on the **board of directors** of a company is another way unions have achieved involvement in strategic business decisions. Starting with the addition of a UAW representative to Chrysler's board as part of the federal government's loan guarantees in 1980, a number of firms—for example, Weirton Steel, several airlines (Eastern, Western, Pan American, Republic), a small number of trucking firms, and various manufacturing firms—added union representatives to their boards in return for union concessions in other areas of the contract. In all of these cases the union in question represented a significant number of the firm's employees at the time board representation was granted.

The experiences surrounding employee participation at Rath Packing Company are described in Box 12–5. The Rath story is not a successful one as Rath eventually went out of business, which ended the experiment with employee board representation. Nevertheless, Rath is an interesting case because it illustrates some of the complex dynamics associated with union representation on a company board and the difficulties board representation poses for union leadership. In the Rath case a former union officer at one point became the chief executive of the company and in that role had difficulty convincing workers at Rath of the need for subsequent pay and other concessions. Eastern Airlines at one stage also experienced a period of union representation on its board, eventually went out of business, and has some parallels to the Rath case.

It would be wrong to conclude from Rath or Eastern Airlines that board representation is doomed to fail. But we do know that union influence on the employer's board of directors ultimately will require new

Box 12–5

Board Representation at Rath Packing Company

The threat of bankruptcy at Rath Packing Company in Waterloo, Iowa, in 1978 led the local union to negotiate an employee buyout of the corporation, effected in 1980. Through an employee stock ownership plan the workers and managers gained 60 percent of the company's stock and 10 of 16 seats on its board of directors. Although leaders of the international union, the United Food and Commercial Workers, advised against this plan, the local union and rank-and-file workers viewed it as the only alternative to company bankruptcy and the loss of their jobs.

Subsequent relations between management and the union officials at Rath vacillated between highly cooperative and highly adversarial, leading researchers Tove Hammer and Robert Stern to compare them to a yo-yo. Specifically, the initially cooperative pattern first gave way, after two years under the new arrangements, to a more adversarial pattern. Political pressures had been building up within the union as economic losses continued, no significant changes in plant operations or management were observed, and workers began questioning what had happened to the $5 million in wage and benefit deferrals they had conceded in the original negotiations. As these pressures escalated, the union began demanding that its representatives on the board vote as a unified block and promote the union's list of proposals at board meetings. The parties later returned to a more cooperative relationship when the chief executive officer was replaced and several union officials moved into key managerial positions. Adversarial relations came to the fore again, however, when financial losses continued to accumulate, management demanded further wage concessions, and the workers called a wildcat strike over a work rule dispute. The company ultimately filed for protection under Chapter 11 of the bankruptcy code. Although the labor contract was set aside by the court, the company eventually went out of business.

Source: This description draws heavily from Tove H. Hammer and Robert N. Stern, "A Yo-Yo Model of Cooperation: Union Participation in Management at the Rath Packing Company," *Industrial and Labor Relations Review* 39 (April 1986): 337–349.

---

communication and managerial skills and technical knowledge on the part of the worker representatives.

The evidence suggests that board membership by unions or employees on its own does not yield substantial payouts for workers or employers. To have lasting, positive results, this initiative has to be linked to the changes in collective bargaining and at the workplace that are discussed in other parts of this chapter.

Employee Ownership

A more radical form of workplace participation is that which follows after employees purchase a business from their employer. Recent history holds several examples of employee buyouts in the face of impending plant shutdowns. Box 12–6 describes the chronology of events that surrounded the evolution of **employee ownership** and QWL programs at former A&P supermarkets in the northeast region. As discussed in this box, research reveals high economic performance in supermarkets that transferred either to employee ownership or introduced extensive employee involvement.

The Views of the Labor Movement toward Employee Ownership As in the case of codetermination, the labor movement has for the most part been unenthusiastic about employee ownership as a means of averting threatened plant shutdowns. The objections raised typically mention both economic and organizational concerns. The union leaders' chief organizational concern is that their members' perceived need for the union will wither away under an employee-owned firm, since the employees would essentially be bargaining against themselves.

The empirical evidence accumulated to date should at least partially allay these fears, since member support for the union has remained strong in nearly all the cases reported. Several studies have examined the effects of employee ownership on workers' attitudes toward their union and on the union as a bargaining organization.[16]

The major conclusions to emerge from these case studies are that (1) the majority of employees still believe there is a strong need for union representation; (2) the role of the union changes in that it becomes a quasi-partner in making some of the strategic decisions the union would not have made under its former status; (3) the collective bargaining process remains an important decision-making forum within the organization; (4) the majority of blue-collar workers still prefer to see the bargaining process handle the traditional issues of wages and fringe benefits; and (5) new forums for decision making outside of collective bargaining often arise.

The major economic reasons for union leaders' opposition to employee takeovers are that the ventures create pressures to cut wages and fringe benefits in order to save jobs. Union leaders are also concerned with the effects any concessions at the plants would have on wage levels in other unionized firms in the industry.

Union leaders worry that employee takeovers encourage worker investments in the oldest, least profitable, and least-likely-to-succeed plants in private industry. The leaders argue that if the plant could be made profitable, either the existing employer would not want to pull out or other forms of private capital could be attracted to take over the plant and save the jobs.

Box 12–6

Worker Ownership and Employee Involvement at A&P Supermarkets

Chronology

February 1982	A&P announces the closing of its 29 remaining Philadelphia supermarkets in 20 days. (Such notification is required under its local union contract.) 2,000 workers would be displaced by these closings.
March 1982	Local 1357 of the United Food and Commercial Workers (UFCW) proposes employee purchase ("buyout") of the closed stores and holds meetings to get pledges from workers.
May 1982	A&P/UFCW sign agreement to sell two stores to workers ("O&O" stores) and reopen most others as Super Fresh stores.

The May 1982 agreement between A&P and the UFCW created two worker owned and operated stores ("O&O" stores). The agreement also created Super Fresh, a new subsidiary of A&P, which reopened many of the other closed A&P stores. Super Fresh incorporated new methods of management, a quality of worklife program to provide employee participation in decision making, and a revenue-based bonus plan to provide pay incentives to workers. The Super Fresh agreement included A&P's promise to eventually open 20 Super Fresh stores and to give preference to former A&P workers in hiring. In exchange, the UFCW agreed to wage cuts of 20 percent and some fringe benefit concessions.

Eventually, 38 former A&P employees became worker/owners in the two O&O supermarkets and over 1,500 displaced A&P employees became Super Fresh employees.

The Super Fresh subsidiary later expanded as all remaining A&P stores in southeastern Pennsylvania, southern New Jersey, and northern Delaware were transferred to Super Fresh. By mid-1983 there were 50 Super Fresh stores.

The extent of QWL and employee involvement has since varied substantially across the Super Fresh stores. Employer involvement is greater in the 20 original Philadelphia stores. In some Super Fresh stores QWL has hardly been implemented.

Research shows that the O&O stores, compared to the Super Fresh stores, have better sales growth, greater improvement in labor productivity and labor costs, a higher proportion of full-time (versus part-time) workers, and relatively more workers at the top of the pay scale. Worker-owned stores and those Super Fresh stores with extensive QWL activities had comparable profits and productivity.

Surveys of store employees found that O&O worker/owners perceived more participation in decision making than did Super Fresh workers. Workers at Super Fresh stores with extensive QWL programs reported greater involvement in decisions than their counterparts in non-QWL Super Fresh stores.

Source: Arthur Hockner, Cherlyn S. Granrose, Judith Goode, Elaine Simon, and Eileen Appelbaum, *Job-Saving Strategies: Worker Buyouts and QWL* (Kalamazoo, MI: W. E. UpJohn Institute for Employment Research, 1988).

Workers, managers, and the labor movement in the United States at this point in time generally view employee ownership as a strategy of last resort for saving jobs. Although some advocates of employee ownership also see it as a strategy for introducing industrial democracy and worker participation and for redistributing power within organizations, there is little evidence that these objectives either rate high in the minds of workers faced with this option or actually are achieved once the transfer of ownership takes place. Instead, the case studies to date have found that the predominant reason employees supported the ownership option was to save their jobs.[17]

Furthermore, although more democratic decision-making methods and structures did develop in some of the cases studied, a traditional division of labor between managers and line workers still remained in most of the employee-owned firms. And the workers continued to perceive this division as legitimate and necessary to the success of the enterprise. At the same time, however, the evidence shows the majority of blue-collar and white-collar workers wished they had had more influence over decisions that affected their jobs than they were given under the employee-owned firms.[18]

The Impact of Worker Ownership on Economic Performance

Finally, an extremely interesting and important question is whether worker-owned firms outperform other firms.[19] As at Super Fresh, the available evidence from other sites suggests that firm performance improves in those employee-owned firms in which employee involvement in decisions is broadened.[20]

Employee ownership appears to work best in small firms where the work force is relatively stable and committed to the community and to the organization, and where the workers are skilled enough to be able to improve plant productivity and economic performance through higher motivation and higher levels of individual and group performance.

Employee Stock Ownership Plans

Another response to threatened bankruptcy has been to take advantage of favorable tax treatment and create an **employee stock ownership plan (ESOP).** Proponents view ESOPs as a form of workers' capitalism, while opponents believe the plans put workers' pensions and assets at risk without providing any real increase in worker involvement in business or workplace decisions. The trucking industry illustrates how one union has wrestled with these issues.

ESOP's in the Trucking Industry

Between 1983 and 1985, 16 trucking firms organized by the Teamsters negotiated ESOP's. They did so in response to a continuing shrinkage in firms' and union employment in the industry after deregulation and after Teamster rank-and-file members had rejected a concessionary bargaining agreement negotiated between industry and international union representatives. After this contract rejection the Teamsters adopted a company-by-company approach to financial crises. When a company and union turned to an ESOP, the union demanded and achieved minority representation on the board of directors of the company and a management plan for how the 15 percent pay cut that served as the quid pro quo for the ESOP would be used to bolster the business.

In all cases the Teamsters sought employee ownership up to a maximum of 49 percent of the company's stock. This approach followed the union's conventional philosophy of leaving management in control of the enterprise and responsible for making the basic decisions. Worker and union influence on the board was achieved indirectly through Teamster-nominated board members, but not through putting a union official on the board. Thus, the union followed a *limited engagement strategy* toward its role in an ESOP plan or an employee-owned firm.[21] That is, once the board representative was chosen, the union made no further efforts to use its access to strategic decision-making to promote additional organizational changes.

In none of these trucking firms have there been significant changes in worker involvement at the workplace. Nearly all of these firms have undergone mergers and further ownership changes, and in several of these cases the representative of the workers and the union on the board played a key role in safeguarding the workers' jobs and financial interests in the acquisition negotiations. Nevertheless, in none of the firms did the ESOP lead to significant improvements in the economic performance of the firms or major subsequent changes in labor-management relations.

The Impact of an ESOP on Firm Performance   What is the general evidence on the organizational performance of the firms with ESOP's as compared to that of conventionally owned firms? There is some evidence that ESOP firms do not perform relatively well.[22] Yet this poor performance may be due to inadequate controls for the influence of other differences across the firms studied (i.e., the ESOP firms may well have done relatively poorly even if conventionally owned and financed).[23] As with other recent changes in industrial relations, more research is needed to assess the effects of new practices.

Participation through Labor-Management Committees

In some highly competitive industries that involve numerous employers and a single union or a small number of unions, industrywide **labor-management committees** historically were used to discuss problems of mutual interest. Those committees represented early efforts by unions to participate in issues of broad (strategic) concern outside of formal collective bargaining processes.

The Retail Food Case   One example was a committee started in 1974 as part of the federal government's wage and price control program. The initial stimulus to form the Joint Labor-Management Committee (JLMC) of the retail food industry came from the federal government in the early 1970s.[24] The federal government also sponsored the formation of a retail industry subcommittee of the National Pay Board as part of its efforts to control wage and price inflation.[25] The JLMC has succeeded in supporting or conducting several major long-term research projects investigating industry problems, including a study of the effects of new technology in stores and warehouses and a study of the occupational safety and health standards governing warehouses.

The Textile Industry Case   In the men's clothing industry the Tailored Clothing Technology Corporation (TC 2) program has been under way since 1980.[26] This project represents a dramatic example of a union's (the Amalgamated Clothing and Textile Workers Union, ACTWU) becoming involved at a very early and basic stage in a research and development effort to mechanize production to help stem the flow of imported goods. In contrast, most unions in the United States limit their involvement with new technology to its consequences—that is, they seek to address technology only after management has made the strategic decision to introduce it.

The ACTWU and the International Ladies' Garment Workers' Union (ILGWU) have been involved in strategic matters throughout the history of the garment and textile industries. These industries are characterized by having many small employers and substantial ease of market entry (and also substantial involuntary exit). The union has historically served as a stabilizing force in the organized portions of these industries. During the early 1900s, for example, the unions provided technical assistance in running many of the small shops on a modern basis.[27] By doing this they were able to transform what otherwise would have been a proliferation of sweatshops into enterprises capable of providing a living wage and acceptable working conditions.

Currently, a labor-management committee also is at work in the men and boys tailored clothing (suits and sport coats) industry. The committee was formed after the 1987 contract negotiations had reached an impasse over the question of whether to allow unionized firms to import garments from abroad in addition to manufacturing in the United States. A joint committee worked on this issue for two years with the help of an outside facilitator and a grant from the Federal Mediation and Conciliation Service.

An agreement eventually was reached that provided for an experimental program in which firms were allowed to import a fraction of their production in return for employment guarantees and a commitment to reinvest in their U.S. manufacturing facilities. The committee is now working on new approaches to recruitment, training, compensation, and the organization of work. Thus, the long tradition of union-management cooperation continues in this industry despite (or perhaps because of) the intense international competition that faces the parties.

Industrywide committees are often far removed from the attitudes and behaviors of individual employers, local union officials, and rank-and-file workers. Consequently, their efforts to introduce employee and union participation change must be supplemented with efforts at the workplace level. The committees can be very useful, however, in drawing links between participation and formal bargaining processes.

Summary

Although the new participatory processes represent a departure from the traditional collective bargaining system, experience suggests that they cannot operate in isolation from collective bargaining. Collective bargaining reforms seem to work best when they are associated with consistent changes across all three levels of industrial relations activity; that is, workplace changes must be reinforced by changes at the collective bargaining and strategic levels, and the same is true for changes at the other two levels.

The ultimate success of QWL programs and other workplace reform efforts depends on the ability of the organization to reinforce and sustain high levels of trust. That trust, in turn, depends heavily on the extent to which the strategies and events unfolding at the higher levels of the industrial relations system are consistent with and linked to the development of greater trust at the workplace.

To achieve tangible rewards, the expansion of worker participatory programs and the introduction of new forms of work organization have often been accompanied by changes in the contract terms negotiated in collective bargaining. The expansion of shop-floor worker participation has also been spurred by increased worker and union involvement in strategic issues. This involvement is critical because it both assures the unions that worker participation is not a step toward the demise of union representation and helps convince workers and the union that enhanced employment security will follow.

But expansion of the process to the strategic level of decision making does not occur easily or automatically. Management tends to closely guard its control over issues that have traditionally been viewed as its prerogatives. Thus a strong union presence and active union support for the process are essential. Nonunion firms and firms with weak unions are unlikely to develop or sustain a full form of worker participation.

Strategic involvement by employees or unions still occurs in isolated cases and probably will diffuse only gradually. Significant internal debate and conflict within management and labor ranks still exists over the wisdom of taking on these new roles. Opponents within the labor movement cite fears that unions will be co-opted into supporting managerially controlled and potentially unpopular decisions. These critics believe that union independence will be compromised and rank-and-file dissent will grow. And managers who are not committed to allowing workers or unions greater participation in strategic decisions may be an even more formidable barrier.

Only in crisis settings or settings in which unions have both the strength and the desire to demand greater involvement in managerial issues has participation extended beyond a single issue or a short period of time. Furthermore, union involvement at the strategic level has generally emerged only in settings in which unions already represent a large percentage of the firm's work force.

It is difficult to make predictions about the future course of increased union and worker involvement in business decisions. Participatory programs are so new that in some cases labor and management have yet to confront the tough economic and political problems that often led to the demise of the earlier joint initiatives at the national and industry levels. Furthermore, since most participatory plans have not lasted long, it is impossible to know how U.S. workers would react to sustained involvement and whether the recent efforts are likely to evolve toward even greater union and worker engagement in strategic business decisions.

Nevertheless, although cases like the Saturn auto plant are still in their infancy, their growing numbers indicate that labor and management in this country are moving through an important period of experimentation with new strategies in organizational governance. If these new strategies and experiments are diffused and institutionalized, they will lead to a fundamental departure from traditional collective bargaining.

Discussion Questions

1. Give a brief overview of how participatory programs evolved in the union sector from the 1970s on.

2. Participatory programs provide challenges to unions and their leaders. Discuss how unions might be able to manage the overlapping roles of participation, work restructuring, and collective bargaining.

3. Participatory programs have been the subject of much debate. Briefly describe this debate.

4. How do labor leaders and unions generally view employee ownership?

Suggested Readings

Cooke, William N. *Labor-Management Cooperation: New Partnerships or Going In Circles?* (Kalamazoo, MI: W. E. Upjohn Institute for Employment Research, 1990).

Klingel, Sally, and Ann Martin, eds. *A Fighting Chance: New Strategies To Save Jobs and Reduce Costs* (Ithaca, NY: ILR Press, 1989).

Kochan, Thomas A., Harry C. Katz, and Robert B. McKersie. *The Transformation of American Industrial Relations* (New York: Basic Books, 1986).

Kochan, Thomas A., Harry C. Katz, and Nancy R. Mower. *Worker Participation and American Unions: Threat or Opportunity?* (Kalamazoo, MI: W. E. Upjohn Institute for Employment Research, 1984).

Whyte, William Foote, Tove Helland Hammer, Christopher B. Meek, Reed Nelson, and Robert N. Stern. *Worker Participation and Ownership: Cooperative Strategies for Strengthening Local Economies* (Ithaca, NY: ILR Press, 1983).

End Notes

1. *Work in America,* A Report of a Special Task Force to the Secretary of Health, Education and Welfare (Cambridge, MA: MIT Press, 1973).

2. "GAO Report Finds Productivity Center's Accomplishments Limited," *Daily Labor Report,* no. 103 (May 26, 1978), pp. A5–A6.

3. Thomas A. Kochan, Harry C. Katz, and Robert B. McKersie, *The Transformation of American Industrial Relations* (New York: Basic Books, 1986), pp. 62–65.

4. See, for example, Edward E. Lawler III and Susan Mohrman, "Quality Circles after the Fad," *Harvard Business Review* 63 (January–February 1985): 64–71.

5. For a full case study of events at Xerox, see Joel Cutcher-Gershenfeld, "New Path toward Organizational Effectiveness and Institutional Security: The Case of Xerox Corporation and the Amalgamated Clothing and Textile Workers Union," report to the Bureau of Labor Management Relations and Cooperative Programs, U.S. Department of Labor, 1987.

6. See Joel Cutcher-Gershenfeld, "The Impact on Economic Performance of a Transformation in Workplace Relations," *Industrial and Labor Relations Review,* 44 (January 1991): 241–260.

7. "Steelmakers Want To Make Teamwork an Institution," *Business Week* (May 11, 1987), p. 84.

8. See Stephen R. Barley, "Technology as an Occasion for Structuring: Evidence from Observations of CT Scanners and the Social Order of Radiology Departments," *Administrative Science Quarterly* 31 (March 1986): 78–108.

9. The joint Human Resource Center of General Motors and the UAW has an annual operating budget of more than $300 million.

10. The term management by stress is used by Mike Parker and Jane Slaughter in *Choosing Sides: Unions and the Team Concept* (Boston: South End Press, 1988). Also see Guillermo J. Grenier, *Inhuman Relations: Quality Circles and Anti-Unionism in American Industry* (Philadelphia: Temple University Press, 1988).

11. See, for example, Harry C. Katz, Thomas A. Kochan, and Kenneth R. Gobeille, "Industrial Relations Performance, Economic Performance, and QWL Programs:

An Interplant Analysis," *Industrial and Labor Relations Review* 37 (October 1983): 3–17; Harry C. Katz, Thomas A. Kochan, and Mark Weber, "Assessing the Effects of Industrial Relations and Quality of Working Life Efforts on Organizational Effectiveness," *Academy of Management Journal* 28 (September 1985): 509–527; and Paul S. Goodman, *Assessing Organizational Change: The Rushton Quality of Work Experiment* (New York: Wiley-Interscience, 1979).

12.   Goodman, *Assessing Organizational Change.*

13.   John Paul MacDuffie and John F. Krafcik, "Flexible Production Systems and Manufacturing Performance," in *Transforming Organizations* ed. Thomas A. Kochan and Michael Useem (New York: Oxford University Press, 1991).

14.   Haruo Shimada and John Paul MacDuffie, "Industrial Relations and Humanware," *Sloan School of Management Working Paper* (Cambridge: Massachusetts Institute of Technology, 1987).

15.   Harry C. Katz, Thomas A. Kochan, and Jeffrey H. Keefe "Industrial Relations and Productivity in the U.S. Automobile Industry," *Brookings Papers on Economic Activity,* vol. 3, 1987, pp. 685–715, and Cutcher-Gershenfeld, "The Impact on Economic Performance."

16.   See, for example, Tove H. Hammer and Robert N. Stern, "Democracy in Work Organizations," unpublished manuscript, (Ithaca: New York State School of Industrial and Labor Relations, Cornell University, 1988), and Joseph Blasi, *Employee Ownership: Revolution or Ripoff?* (Cambridge, MA: Ballinger, 1988).

17.   Hammer and Stern, "Democracy in Work Organizations."

18.   Tove H. Hammer and Robert N. Stern, "Employee Ownership: Implications for the Organizational Distribution of Power," *Academy of Management Journal* 23 (March 1980): 78–100.

19.   One of the difficulties in answering this question is that worker-owned firms may tend to be those that were already in poor health when the employees bought them. Thus, to succeed in identifying the independent influence of worker ownership, researchers need to control fully for the influence of other factors that influence organizational performance, but this is very hard to do.

20.   Conte and Tannenbaum examined 98 U.S. and Canadian firms whose employees held substantial amounts of their employer's stock shares and found a strong relationship between the amount of equity held by nonmanagerial employees and company profit levels. See Michael Conte and Arnold Tannenbaum, "Employee-owned Companies: Is the Difference Measurable?" *Monthly Labor Review* (July 1978): 23–28.

21.   Kochan, Katz, and McKersie, *The Transformation,* p. 193.

22.   One study compared 51 large firms that had had ESOPs for at least 10 years with 51 matched, conventional firms. See P. T. Livingston and James B. Henry, "The Effects of Employee Stock Ownership Plans on Corporate Profits," *Journal of Risk and Insurance* 47 (September 1980): 491–505.

23.   For a comprehensive review of the evidence on ESOPs, see Hammer and Stern, "Democracy in Work Organizations."

24.   See Albert Rees, "Tripartite Wage Stabilization in the Food Industry," *Industrial Relations* 14 (May 1975): 250–258.

25.   The federal government tried to persuade other industries to form joint committees at that time but was rebuffed by either labor or management in each case. The parties in the retail food industry agreed to continue the committee as a privately funded and constituted entity after federal regulators discussed the possibility of greatly reducing federal regulations in the industry if the parties did so.

26.   See Kochan, Katz and McKersie, *The Transformation,* pp. 187–189.

27.   See Jesse Thomas Carpenter, *Competition and Collective Bargaining in the Needle Trades, 1960–1967* (Ithaca: New York State School of Industrial and Labor Relations, Cornell University, 1972), and Steven Fraser, "Dress Rehearsal for the New Deal: Shop Floor Insurgents, Political Elites, and Industrial Democracy," in *Working Class America,* ed. Michael A. Frisch and Daniel J. Walkowitz (Urbana: University of Illinois Press, 1983), pp. 212–255.

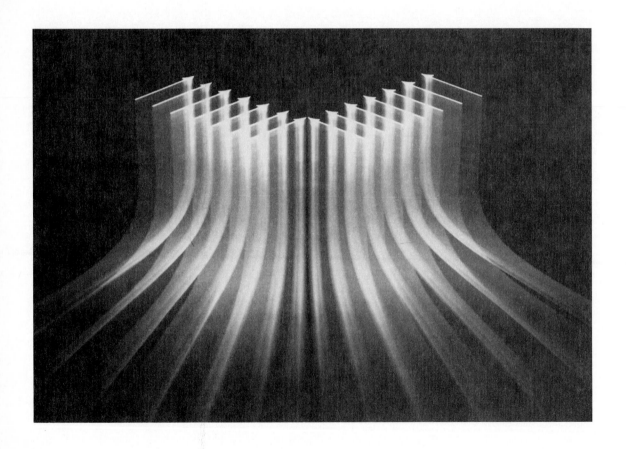

PART 5

SPECIAL TOPICS

Chapter 13

Collective Bargaining
in the Public Sector

Collective bargaining has spread rapidly in the public sector since the early 1960s, to the point that, today, 37 percent of federal, state, and local government employees are represented by either a union or an employee association that is not formally chartered as a union. This alone makes the public sector experience worthy of a separate chapter in this book—especially at a time when, each year, fewer and fewer private sector employees have union representation.

This chapter applies the general framework developed in the previous chapters to examine industrial relations in the public sector. It is important to recognize at the outset, however, that the public sector is a special case of bargaining and employment practice. Government is not just an employer and a provider of services, but a provider of *public* services, and as such the public sector bargaining system must be particularly responsive to the demands of the public.

There has been much debate about the appropriate legal regulation of public sector collective bargaining. Some analysts have argued that the unique nature of government as an employer makes collective bargaining, as traditionally practiced in the private sector, inappropriate for the public sector. Other observers would allow the traditional type of collective bargaining, but in a shape and form adapted to meet the special circumstances of the public sector.

The first section of this chapter examines the historical phases through which public sector bargaining has passed. The following sections review the practice and outcomes of public sector bargaining and consider how bargaining in the public sector actually compares to bargaining in the private sector. The text then considers on normative grounds whether the legal regulation of public sector unions should be different from that of private sector bargaining.

The Evolution of Public Sector Collective Bargaining

The percentage of all federal, state, and local government employees who were members of unions underwent dramatic growth in the 1960s and early 1970s, rising from 12.8 in 1960 to 20.6 in 1974. Other public employees had joined associations, such as the National Education Association, many of which also engaged in collective bargaining by the 1970s. By 1974, 37.7 percent of all public employees were members of a bargaining organization (whether it was a union or an association that engaged in collective bargaining).[1] Exhibit 13–1 shows the estimated public sector membership of the major unions that represented public employees in 1983.

The 1960s and Early 1970s: The Era of Growth

Factors that contributed to the expansion of public sector unionism in the 1960s and 1970s included the growth in government budgets throughout the 1960s and early 1970s, the example of civil disobedience set by civil rights and other groups in the 1960s, and the passage of laws favorable to public sector collective bargaining.

The Mid- and Late 1970s: The Taxpayers' Revolt

The economic environment for public sector bargaining, however, tightened sharply in the mid-1970s as a consequence of slowdowns in the economy and in response to a conservative political tide that questioned the value of many government expenditures. A number of state and local governments had begun to face major fiscal problems. Moreover, taxpayer resistance to public expenditures created a backlash against public employees and reduced the political influence of public sector employee organizations.

New York City, the prime example of the fiscal crises of the cities in the 1970s, hovered on the brink of bankruptcy for several years. Eventually, the city accepted an emergency financial control board composed of representatives of the state government, private sector, unions, and the federal government. Between 1974 and 1979 the number of employees on the city payroll declined through a combination of layoffs and attrition.[2]

Other cities faced similar fiscal crises.[3] In the fall of 1975 voters in San Francisco altered municipal procedures in a number of ways to the detriment of city employees.[4] Wage and pension-setting procedures were modified, and city craft workers received pay cuts that averaged $2,000 and went as high as $4,500 annually for some workers. Those craft workers then went on strike but were resoundingly defeated, returning to work a month later under management's salary terms.

Exhibit 13–1
Public Sector Union Membership, 1983

Teachers[a]

Education Association; National (Ind.)	1,444,000
Teachers; American Federation of (AFL-CIO)	457,000
University Professors; American Association of (Ind.)	58,000
State and Local Government	
State, County and Municipal Employees; American Federation of (AFL-CIO)	955,000
Service Employees' International Union (AFL-CIO) (1985)	560,000[c]
Governmental Employees; Assembly of (Ind.)	340,000
Fire Fighters; International Association of (AFL-CIO)	157,000
Police; Fraternal Order of (Ind.)	150,000
Teamsters, Chauffeurs, Warehousemen and Helpers of America; International Brotherhood of (Ind.) (1985)	150,000[c]
Laborers' International Union of North America (AFL-CIO) (1985)	85,000[c]
Communications Workers of America (AFL-CIO) (1987)	85,000[d]
Nurses' Association; American (Ind.) (1987)	25,000[e]
Automobile, Aerospace and Agricultural Implement Workers of America; International Union, United (AFL-CIO) (1987)	25,000[d]
Postal Service	
Postal Workers Union; American (AFL-CIO)	226,000
Letter Carriers; National Association of (AFL-CIO)	203,000
Letter Carriers' Association; National Rural (Ind.)	40,000
Post Office Mail Handlers (Laborers' International Union of North America, AFL-CIO)	40,000
Federal Government[b]	
Government Employees; American Federation of (AFL-CIO)	218,000
Treasury Employees Union; National (Ind.)	47,000
Federal Employees; National Federation of (Ind.)	34,000
Metal Trades Council (AFL-CIO) (1985)	24,000[f]
Government Employees; National Association of (Service Employees' International Union, AFL-CIO) (1985)	23,000[f]
Machinists and Aerospace Workers; International Association of (AFL-CIO) (1985)	12,000[f]

Note: The table was prepared by Mark Nakamura.
[a]Includes support personnel in schools and faculty and support personnel in higher education.
[b]Includes employees covered by the Civil Service Reform Act. Independent agencies such as the Tennessee Valley Authority are not included.
[c]From Richard B. Freeman, *Unionism Comes to the Public Sector,* 24 J. Econ. Lit. 41, 46 (March 1986); based on discussions with union officials.
[d]Based on discussions with union officials.
[e]Calculated from data in U.S. Bureau of the Census, *1980 Census of Population: Vol. 1, Characteristics of the Population; Ch. D, Detailed Population Characteristics; Part 1, United States Summary,* PC80-1-D1-A (Washington, D.C.: GPO, 1984); U.S. Bureau of the Census, *1982 Census of Governments: Vol. 3, Government Employment; No. 3, Labor-Management Relations in State and Local Government,* GC82(3)-3 (Washington, D.C.: GPO, 1985); and discussions with ANA officials. A small but indeterminate number of ANA members are represented by other organizations for collective bargaining purposes.
[f]Based on discussions with the U.S. Office of Personnel Management.
Source: James L. Stern "Unionism in the Public Sector," in *Public-Sector Bargaining,* 2d ed., Benjamin Aaron, Joyce Najitu, and James L. Stern, (Washington, D.C.: *Bureau of National Affairs,* 1988) p. 54.

New York's and San Francisco's financial problems received tremendous national attention and helped fuel taxpayer resistance to further growth in public budgets. As a result, nine states adopted new tax or spending limitations. The most widely publicized example, California's Proposition 13, was approved by the voters in 1979. This constitutional amendment limited property taxes to 1 percent of the real market value and tax increases to 2 percent per year.[5]

Although public sector employers may have grown more resistant to union demands in the mid- and late 1970s, they did not aggressively try to remove their unions. In this way, the institutions of collective bargaining in the public sector have exhibited much more stability than have their counterparts in the private sector.

The Early 1980s: The PATCO Strike

The one important exception to union stability in the public sector was the Professional Air Traffic Controllers Organization (PATCO). In August 1981 PATCO led its members on a strike. The controllers wanted their employer, the federal government, to increase their wages and benefits. President Reagan then fired the strikers on the grounds they had violated a no-strike clause in their employment contract. The government called in military controllers who, along with supervisors and some controllers who crossed picket lines, kept the air traffic system functioning (though limits were imposed on certain flights).

The striking controllers were never rehired, and the Federal Labor Relations Authority eventually decertified the union. (In 1987 the new controllers voted in a new union.) Some analysts argue that the firing of the controllers had enormous ramifications by legitimizing a hard line in bargaining by other public and private sector employers.

The Mid- and Late 1980s: Institutional Stability and Some Gains

The firing of PATCO strikers may have contributed to the wave of concessionary bargaining that occurred in the private sector in the 1980s. Nevertheless, it is important to note that public sector collective bargaining underwent a relatively calm period in the 1980s. In part, this stability resulted from the absence of extreme economic pressures. Public sector unions did not face international competition, and the growth of alternative nonunion suppliers was modest in the public sector in comparison to what confronted many private sector unions.

Furthermore, public sector management did not use strategic business actions or in other ways exert pressure for radical changes in the process of collective bargaining to the extent that occurred in the private sector. Team systems of work and new forms of direct communication between supervisors and workers, for example, were diffused in the public sector much less widely than in the private sector.

By the mid-1980s, the political tide had begun to turn back in favor of the public sector. Some politicians and observers were claiming that cutbacks in government spending had gone too far.

At the same time, public attention was turning to the problems in American primary and secondary education. Many newspaper editorials argued that weaknesses in the nation's schools, particularly in comparison to Japanese schools, were contributing to American trade and competitive problems. The Carnegie Commission, among others, issued reports charging that public education was inadequate and that part of the solution lay in upgrading the salary and status of public school teachers.[6] Evidence in support of that charge came from the fact that school districts were having difficulty recruiting science and math teachers because of competition from the computer industry.

All these factors added strength to the claims of public employee unions, especially the teachers unions. These pressures also spurred experimentation in industrial relations practices. As discussed in more detail at the end of this chapter, extensive employee and union participation in business decisions began to surface in the public schools by the late 1980s.

To summarize, the 1960s witnessed rapid expansion in public sector union membership and militancy. But in the mid-1970s a taxpayers' revolt emerged and slowed the gains of public employee unions. Then in the mid-1980s teachers and other public employee groups benefited from public concerns over the adequacy of public services and saw their bargaining power rebound.

Public employees and unions, like their private sector counterparts, have felt the effects of changing environmental pressures. But the environmental pressures and the changes that emerged within public sector collective bargaining were different in some ways from events in the private sector. In contrast to the private sector, there was much continuity and stability in the process of public sector collective bargaining throughout the 1970s, 1980s, and 1990s.

The Legal Regulation of Public Sector Unionism

Federal, state, and local government employees are all excluded from coverage under the NLRA. Separate legal regulations govern collective bargaining in each of these sectors.

Federal Employees

Federal employees received the rights to unionize and to negotiate over employment conditions other than wages or fringe benefits through Executive Order 10988, signed by President Kennedy in 1962. This order was subsequently extended by President Nixon in Executive Order 11491.

In 1970, as part of its effort to reform the postal service, however, Congress provided postal employees the right to engage in collective bargaining over wages, hours, and working conditions.

In 1978 Congress replaced the executive orders of Presidents Kennedy and Nixon with the first comprehensive federal law providing collective bargaining rights to federal employees. This law was part of a broad reform of civil service procedures and policies. Title VII of this law (Public Law 95-454) protects the rights to organize and to bargain collectively on conditions of employment. The law continues to exclude pay and fringe benefits from the scope of bargaining.

Collective bargaining in the federal sector is regulated by the Federal Labor Relations Authority. Responsibility for impasse resolution is vested in the Federal Services Impasse Panel. The panel may use mediation, fact-finding, or arbitration to resolve disputes. The right to strike is prohibited.

State and Local Government Employees

As of 1990, all but 10 states had legislation that provides at least some of their state or local government employees with the rights to organize and to bargain collectively. Exhibit 13–2 lists these states by the type of coverage provided. Of the 40 states, 25 have passed comprehensive laws that cover a number of occupational groups; the others that have not yet enacted public sector bargaining laws are primarily in the south.

Comprehensive collective bargaining laws for state and local employees were first passed in a number of states during the late 1960s and the early 1970s. In the 1980s, on the other hand, only two states, Illinois and Ohio, passed such comprehensive laws. Instead, the recent years have been witness to a number of revisions to the laws that were passed in earlier years. Those amendments expanded the scope of collective bargaining to new issues, covered new employee groups, strengthened the agencies charged with administration of the laws, or modified the dispute resolution procedures.

The Diffusion of State Bargaining Laws   Public sector bargaining laws were passed earliest and are most comprehensive in those states with liberal political histories, high levels of expenditures per capita on government services, and above-average growth in personal income between 1960 and 1970.[7] States with public sector laws also tend to be those with a relatively high percentage of their private sector employees unionized.

The pattern of legal enactment experienced in the public sector conforms to the hypothesis that public policy reflects the existing political balance of power and social norms. Legal enactment does not appear to make up for power imbalances. That is, laws that provide bargaining rights were passed where government expenditures were already

Exhibit 13–2   **State Public Employees Collective Bargaining Laws**

Coverage	States
All-inclusive laws	Florida, Hawaii, Iowa, Massachusetts, Minnesota,* Montana, New Hampshire, New Jersey, New York, Oregon[†]
All employees, separate laws	Alaska, California, Connecticut, Delaware, Illinois, Kansas, Maine, Nebraska, North Dakota, Pennsylvania, Rhode Island, South Dakota, Vermont, Wisconsin
Some employees covered	
Teachers	Indiana, Maryland, Tennessee
Police and fire fighters	Kentucky,[‡] Texas[¶]
Fire fighters	Wyoming
Police, fire fighters, and public school employees	Oklahoma
All but state civil service	Michigan, Washington
Local employees and teachers	Nevada
Fire fighters and teachers	Alabama, Georgia, Idaho
All but teachers and police	Missouri[§]
State-classified service	New Mexico
All but judicial	Ohio
No laws	Arizona, Arkansas, Colorado, Louisiana, Mississippi, North Carolina, South Carolina, Utah, Virginia, West Virginia

*Excludes employees in charitable hospitals.
[†]This category also includes the District of Columbia.
[‡]Qualified for certain cities.
[¶]Conditional on municipal vote.
[§]By Executive Order.
Sources: *Government Employee Relations Report* (Washington, D.C.: Bureau of National Affairs, July 1986), and *Public Sector Bargaining* (Washington D.C.: Bureau of National Affairs, 1988), Chap. 6.

relatively high and where labor had the greatest influence. Similar laws have not yet been passed in the states where wages are lower and the unions are weaker.

Variations in the political effectiveness of occupational groups also influence the nature of the laws that govern different groups within each state. Police and fire fighters, for example, tend to have the most comprehensive statutes and to have impasse resolution procedures that end in arbitration rather than in mediation or fact-finding. Teachers also fare better than other local employees in the majority of states. State government employees tend to have the least comprehensive forms of collective bargaining rights and impasse procedures.[8]

Studies of public sector union growth suggest that the state bargaining laws accelerated unionization. States that enacted laws had relative increases in unionization in the ensuing years. Furthermore, the more favorable the laws were to unions, the greater the growth of unionization. At the same time, however, the passage of laws favorable to public sector unions and collective bargaining appears to have been partially *caused* by the presence of unions that grew before the laws.[9] Thus union growth and legal regulation of public sector bargaining appear to have a complicated interrelationship.[10]

Legal Regulation of the Right To Strike   No state provides public employees with the right to strike equivalent to that specified by the NLRA for private sector workers. Nevertheless, some states do provide a limited right to strike.[11] Pennsylvania, for example, permits strikes by nonuniformed employees if they do not endanger the public health, safety, or welfare of its citizens.

At the same time, some states do not allow any public sector strikes, and some impose harsh penalties on public sector strikers. In New York, for example, the **Taylor Law** provides a "two for one" penalty under which a striking employee is penalized one day's pay for each strike day, which is in addition to the day's pay the employee loses while striking. Under the Taylor Law, the struck employer is responsible for collecting the monetary penalty and also keeps the money raised by the strike penalty.

The Frequency of Strikes   Strikes do occur in the public sector, however, even in states that have laws making such strikes illegal. In fact, public sector strikes appear to be most likely to occur in states without a law regulating public sector collective bargaining.[12] Strikes are least likely to occur in states with a public sector bargaining law that provides compulsory interest arbitration.[13] At the same time, strike penalties, when they are enforced, do appear to affect the frequency of strikes.

The types of employees involved also appear to affect the propensity to strike. Teachers in large districts, for example, are more likely to strike than are teachers in small districts. Strike propensities also vary substantially across other public sector occupations.[14]

The Bargaining Rights of Supervisors   The bargaining rights of supervisors differ substantially in the public and private sectors. Most state laws *do not exclude* public sector supervisors from collective bargaining, which diametrically opposes the Taft-Hartley restrictions on supervisor union involvement in the private sector. Some state laws do require supervisors to form separate bargaining units from rank-and-file employees, however.

Why are public sector supervisors treated differently? Unlike in the private sector, where supervisors are assumed to have the authority to make independent judgments on critical personnel functions, in the public sector many of those functions are often handled by a civil service commission. Moreover, there are many more levels of supervisors in the public sector hierarchies, and many individuals with the title of supervisor do not serve as bona fide supervisors.[15] Some have also argued that there exists a community of interests between supervisors and their subordinates in the public sector. Although not everyone agrees that public sector supervisors should be treated differently, to date the law has evolved differently in the public sector.

Calls for Federal Legislation Affecting State and Local Employees   The failure of the remaining states to provide collective bargaining rights for public employees has spurred calls for federal legislation to extend bargaining rights to all public employees. Movement on this issue has been blocked by two obstacles. The most formidable is the constitutional question whether the federal government has the authority to mandate collective bargaining legislation that covers state and local employees.[16] A second major obstacle has been the inability of various labor unions to agree on the form the legislation should take. Three different approaches for federal regulation of public sector collective bargaining have been advocated:

1. A simple extension of the National Labor Relations Act and the jurisdiction of the National Labor Relations Board to cover state and local employees

2. Special comprehensive legislation that takes into account the unique characteristics of public employees

3. A minimum-standards law of collective bargaining rights for state and local employees, with the specific form of the legislation left to the states

Like its private sector counterpart, public sector collective bargaining is influenced not only by collective bargaining legislation, but also by other regulations in state and federal statutes. Chief among these are the laws, outlined previously, that govern taxation. Also important are civil service laws and procedures. One of the more difficult issues that has arisen in the public sector, as collective bargaining has spread, is how to resolve conflict between the rights provided public employees in collective bargaining statutes and the provisions of other laws.

Differences in the Bargaining Process between the Public and Private Sectors

The more public sector employees are able and willing to sustain a strike and the less employers are willing and able to withstand a strike, the greater will be the bargaining power held by these employees.

Furthermore, public sector employees will have greater bargaining power the less employment drops over the long run in response to an increase in labor costs. These are the same conditions that influence bargaining power in the private sector. Thus in the public sector bargaining power is determined by the same basic set of factors as it is in the private sector.

But what about the level of bargaining power held on average by public and private sector unions. Does unionism or the right to strike give public employees excessive power? Are there differences in the way collective bargaining occurs in the public and private sectors that produce vastly different outcomes in the two sectors?

To resolve whether public sector unions have more power than private sector unions, it is necessary to consider how environmental factors influence union bargaining power. As in the private sector, this requires analysis of Marshall's conditions and the trade-off between wages and employment (the elasticity of demand for labor).

How Marshall's Conditions Operate in the Public Sector

Alfred Marshall's first condition states that employees have more bargaining power (face a smaller reduction in employment from an increase in wages) when it is difficult for management to substitute other factors of production for employees. On this score public employees, on average, should have more bargaining power than private employees do. It is difficult, for example, to substitute machines for public employees that provide many public services. Machines would be hard-pressed to substitute for public school teachers or police and fire fighters.

Some substitution of capital for labor is feasible even for public services: computers can at least partially substitute for teachers, police can acquire more cars and other equipment, and fire fighters can use more and better equipment. Nevertheless, public employees probably gain some advantage due to the relative difficulty to substitute other factors for employees.

Marshall's second condition concerns the price elasticity of demand for the final good. Here again public employees, on average, should have an advantage over most private employees. Government is typically the sole provider of a public good or service. A public employer cannot typically go out of business or move to some other area to escape higher labor costs. As a result, the demand for many public goods is relatively price inelastic. This makes public employment relatively insensitive to increases in wages.

Marshall's third condition concerns what happens to the price of substitute factors of production if the demand for them increases. Here there is no clear difference between the public and private sectors.

With regard to the fourth Marshallian condition, the importance of being unimportant, public employees are likely to be at a disadvantage. In most cases, labor costs make up a substantial share of total production costs. The ratio of labor to total costs varies in the public sector from a high of around 90 percent in police and fire departments to a low of between 60 and 70 percent in education and other public services. This means that wage increases have a significant effect on total increases in government budgets. Labor costs are a prime target for cost-cutting efforts when the public demands lower taxes and expenditure levels. In the long run, then, the high percentage of labor costs to total costs may act as a major impediment to public employee union power.

On net, Marshall's conditions predict that the demand for public services is relatively price-inelastic so that increases in labor costs should lead to relatively small declines in employment.

Shifts in the Demand for Public Services

Marshall's conditions concern the responsiveness of employment to price (wage) changes in the short run when other environmental influences on bargaining power are constant. The bargaining power held by public employees after the mid-1970s, however, was limited by the fact that environmental pressures were building. Tax revenues were declining in some jurisdictions, and the public expressed a reduced demand for many public services. These pressures led to cutbacks in government expenditures. The decline in the public's demand for government services was, in part, a product of the public's reaction to the advance in relative earnings public employees had received over the late 1960s and early 1970s.

The taxpayers' revolt was to some extent a delayed "price effect." The public had reduced its demand for public services in response to the rising cost of those services. Thus, the long-run demand for labor in the public sector is much more elastic than the short-run demand for labor.[18] It just takes a while for politicians to reduce employment levels significantly in response to wage increases.

Strike Leverage—Public versus Private

The strike leverage of public employees is influenced by their ability and willingness to sustain income losses as a result of a strike. Just as in the private sector, striking employees in the public sector rely on alternative sources of income, such as temporary jobs or the earnings of other members of the household. The critical factor that confronts public employees is the high penalty they face if they choose to strike.

In the private sector the employer's willingness to continue a strike is heavily influenced by the firm's ability and willingness to sustain the income losses that result from the shutdown in production and sales during the strike. In the public sector income is not necessarily tied to sales and production. Public agencies typically collect revenue through taxes and do not charge explicitly for services.[19] Thus, during a strike the public employer generally continues to receive revenue and consequently is not under pressure to agree to the strikers' demands as a result of fears of potential bankruptcy. Nor do public agencies typically face competitors who may continue to produce during a strike and thereby strip the struck employer of customers. This absence of a link between strikes and employer revenues clearly works in favor of public employers during strike situations.

The public employer may not lose income during a strike, but a strike can certainly anger the employer's constituents, namely, the public. The public is sometimes hard-pressed to do without certain public services, such as police and fire protection, education, and hospital services. These can be called essential services. Few substitutes for these services can be made available quickly, and the absence of these services can create hardships and, in some cases, health risks to the public.

Public services vary substantially in the degree to which they are essential. Police and fire protection may well be essential services, but do city clerks and engineers provide essential services? Parents may vocally complain when schools are closed by striking teachers, but when social workers strike do cities or states hear any public outcry?

Moreover, how the public reacts to strikes varies significantly over time. In the late 1960s and early 1970s public agencies frequently did not resist the demands of striking public employees. Yet in the mid- and late 1970s taxpayers often seemed eager to confront striking public employees as part of efforts to lower taxes and the cost of government. The public's willingness to sustain public sector strikes seems to sway with political and economic winds.

Financial Sources of Governments

To fully appreciate the special pressures that arise in public sector bargaining, it is important to understand the sources of revenue on which public employers rely. Local governments obtain the greatest proportion of their revenue from state governments. In 1988, 29.1 percent of local government revenues came from that source. Property taxes and aid from the federal government provided, respectively, 24.8 percent and 4.2 percent of local government funds in 1988.[20] The amount of federal aid to states and local governments grew considerably in the 1970s, but its growth slowed markedly in the 1980s.

Beyond these direct tax-based sources of revenues, local and state officials can generate funds from user charges and borrowing. In addition to the limits imposed by the credit and debt capital markets, the revenue-generating capacity of local government is constrained by (1) the size of the tax base in the community, (2) the willingness of the public to tax itself, and (3) constitutional or other legal limitations on the amount of taxes local governments raise.

Public Sector Bargaining Structures

Key aspects of bargaining structure are the degree of centralization in employer interests in the formal bargaining structure and the breadth or scope of employee interests included in bargaining units.

The Degree of Centralization

Collective bargaining in the public sector is highly decentralized. Almost all bargaining is done on a single-employer basis, that is, with a particular government or agency. There are a few isolated examples of formal multi-employer bargaining.

A number of factors have contributed to the continuation of decentralized bargaining in local governments. The diverse financial conditions that exist in local governments make both employers and unions hesitant to consolidate bargaining units.[21] Another pressure that limits centralized bargaining is that local governments like decision-making autonomy.

Nonetheless, information sharing and informal coordination do occur across state and local governments. As public sector bargaining has grown, so has the number of organizations of labor relations professionals in the public sector. These groups share information and conduct surveys to assist one another in the conduct of their separate negotiations.[22]

In some states, such as New York, school districts are organized into area associations that correspond to county or comparable regional subdivisions. Many of these associations pool the funds of member school districts and hire a single labor relations professional to represent them. This practice has produced pattern following as the professional negotiators developed consistent policies and contract provisions across the various school districts. And, because the teachers unions in these districts also normally rely on only a small number of business agents, the professional negotiators on both sides of the table in any given geographic region tend to be the same people.

There is some recent movement toward greater centralization in the financing of public education. If this continues, it may lead to greater centralization in teacher bargaining. The pressure for centralization in school financing comes from courts ruling that the existing heavy reliance on local property taxes to fund public education violates state constitutions. Box 13–1 describes one such court decision on New Jersey school financing. In recent years a number of state governments have shifted toward state sales or income taxes to replace the local property tax. As a result, public school financing is becoming more centralized and may become substantially more centralized if the court decisions described in Box 13–1 spread. As school financing becomes more centralized it is likely that school collective bargaining structures will also eventually become more centralized. Imagine how awkward it would be if bar-

Box 13–1

> ## Public School Aid from a New Jersey Supreme Court Decision
>
> On June 5, 1990, the New Jersey Supreme Court unanimously ruled in *Abbott v. Burke* that New Jersey must ensure that the poorest school districts spend as much on their children's education as the wealthy suburbs do. Unlike past decisions, the verdict does not establish a ceiling on spending by the wealthy as long as the state increases spending for poor districts.
>
> The New Jersey Supreme Court decision declared the financing of the public school system through property taxes unconstitutional. As a result:
>
> 1. Poor districts must receive enough state aid to enable them to spend as much per pupil as wealthy districts.
>
> 2. Wealthy districts can continue to increase their spending if they choose. However, the state must then increase aid to the poorer districts.
>
> 3. A system of minimum aid must be contingent on need.
>
> 4. The manner by which to close the gap between the poor and rich districts can be achieved by any manner except forcing persons of poorer districts to pay higher property taxes.
>
> In the last two years, Supreme Courts of Montana, Kentucky, and Texas have struck down their state's school financing systems. Similar cases are pending in Connecticut and Alaska.
>
> *Source:* "New Jersey Ruling to Lift School Aid for Poor Districts," *New York Times* (June 6, 1990), p. A–1.

gaining over public school teacher contracts continued on a local school district basis in states in which most of the revenues funding the schools come from the state government. This is an issue worth watching in the future.

The Scope of Bargaining Units

Bargaining in the public sector tends to follow occupational lines more than is the case in the private sector. A city government is likely to have separate bargaining units for police officers, fire fighters, blue-collar workers (either in one citywide unit or separate departmentwide units), and various professional groups. Public schools tend to have separate units for teachers, clerical and secretarial employees, bus drivers and maintenance employees, and school principals.

The rivalries that separate police and fire fighters in many cities effectively limit the potential for coalition bargaining with these two groups. Nevertheless, in the vast majority of municipal governments, the wages and fringe benefits of police and fire fighters are tied to each other through pay parity or pattern following.

State governments also tend to have a relatively large number of occupational or departmental groups. There has been a recent trend to consolidate some of these units into large, statewide units.[23]

Management Structure in the Public Sector

In the public sector managerial authority and responsibility is widely shared. As a result, collective bargaining in the public sector is multilateral and not bilateral as it is in the private sector.

Consider the typical elementary (or secondary) public school district. Each of the following groups have some managerial role to play in any collective bargaining that exists between the school district and its employees: the district superintendent, the professional industrial relations administrators who report to the superintendent, the elected school board, the mayor of the city in which the district resides, the citizens who approve school tax measures and elect the school board, the parent groups active in the community (including the PTA), the state legislature and the state governor who regulate state educational aid, the state education department officials who regulate school programs, the federal education department officials who regulate school expenditures and school programs, and possibly other parties.

Not only is managerial authority divided among a number of actors, but also there tend to be substantial differences in the goals of the various public sector managers. This arises because public sector organizations usually lack a clear hierarchy of decision makers to facilitate internal conflict resolution. Conflicts between the mayor and the city council, for example, are as likely to occur in collective bargaining as they are over other political issues. The consequence is that the internal conflicts within management's ranks frequently spill over into the formal negotiations process.[24]

Given this complex array of managerial interests and the diffusion of power, the role of the management negotiator in the public sector is a difficult one. Like the representative of any employer, the management negotiator must serve in the dual capacity of (1) coordinating internal organizational interests and (2) representing the organization in its dealings with the union. The more internal diversity there is and the more power is shared among different individuals, the more difficult the internal coordination role becomes.

When unions have considerable access to elected officials, the management negotiator may find it particularly difficult to hold elected officials together as a united management team.

The Negotiations Process in the Face of Multilateral Bargaining

Multilateral bargaining is a negotiations process that includes more than two distinct parties. In multilateral bargaining no clear dichotomy exists between the union and the management organization. Multilateral bargaining leads to novel bargaining techniques. One frequently observed union tactic in public sector negotiations, for example, is the "end run," in which union officials try to sidestep the formal management negotiating team and take their proposals before an alternative group—city council representatives, school board officials, or even the city or state legislature. As illustrated in Box 13–2, another tactic is intervention by elected government officials who act on their own to try to influence the course of negotiations, primarily because they want to impose their own settlement terms on the parties.

Still another form of multilateral negotiations occurs when a decision-making group rejects a negotiated agreement and refuses to implement it. Civil service commissions, school boards, or city councils, for example, often must ratify the final agreement. At the ratification stage constituent political pressures may come to bear on officials to change the terms and conditions of the bargain.

Yet another example of multilateralism arises when community interest groups become involved in the negotiations process. As the scope of bargaining in teacher negotiations expands to deal, for example, with issues of student discipline, the curriculum, or the welfare of minority interests, community groups step up their involvement in negotiations.

Multilateral bargaining also has emerged in jurisdictions that face fiscal crises. In these cases state and federal authorities, public employee pension managers, and private sector business leaders all have usually demanded some say in negotiated outcomes in return for their financial support.

A Case Study of Multilateral Bargaining: AFSCME and the State Government of Wisconsin

The presence of multilateral bargaining is nicely illustrated by the events that surrounded a strike of state employees in Wisconsin. The previous contract had been settled through an end run around the management negotiators, in an agreement worked out in consultations between Wisconsin's governor and Jerry Wurf, then president of the American Federation of State, County and Municipal Employees (AFSCME). The memory of this end run carried over to the next contract negotiations.

Box 13–2

A Case of Multilateral Bargaining

The following excerpts from *Boston Globe* articles report a quintessential case of multilateral bargaining that occurred in 1986 in a strike involving Boston school bus drivers, the Boston superintendent of schools, and the mayor of Boston.

Laval S. Wilson, Boston's school superintendent, sharply criticized Mayor Flynn last night after receiving a letter from the mayor outlining proposals to end the 11-day-old strike by 600 school bus drivers. The letter also went to the drivers' union president.

"I believe we are now in a critical time in the negotiations, and feel that in the best interests of the schoolchildren of our city, both sides should seriously consider [the attached] proposals as options for breaking the current logjam and getting all of our kids back into the classrooms," Flynn wrote to Wilson and the union president James Barrett.

. . . Sounding angry and frustrated after receiving the letter . . . Wilson said in a telephone interview, "I think it's completely out of bounds for the mayor to put something in writing with proposals to both sides, and to make it public through the press as if these are the ways we can solve the strike. . . . It's unfortunate that the mayor is intruding directly on the negotiating process," said Wilson, adding that negotiations should only include the drivers, bus companies, and the School Department.

In a follow-up article the next day the political dialogue continued:

[Superintendent Wilson:] "I don't like someone undermining the negotiations process. We can't have two superintendents running Boston's public schools."

[Mayor Flynn:] "I could care less about the School Committee members whining about political turf. The Boston school system is not the private political domain of the superintendent and the School Committee."

The strike ended the following day with a negotiated agreement. The *Globe* article on the settlement stated:

Flynn took credit for bringing about negotiations that led to a proposed settlement. "A more harmonious relationship is in everybody's interest." . . . Asked if he was worried about Boston being labeled as a strikebreaker Flynn responded, "You bet I am. I'm not about to become another Calvin Coolidge." [In 1919 Calvin Coolidge broke a Boston police strike that is thought to have been the first strike by public employees in the United States.]

Source: Boston Globe (January 17, 18, 19, 1986).

These negotiations were further complicated by an agreement between the parties to open negotiations to the public. Moreover, in the early negotiations sessions, which were characterized by much verbal sparring but little substantive negotiating, the union negotiators repeatedly protested that the management negotiators lacked adequate authority to bargain. In the background of the formal negotiations was a highly complex political situation. An interim governor took office at about the time the contract expired. Supervising the management negotiating team were the Secretary of the Department of Administration, the governor, and a bipartisan committee of the state legislature. The negotiators therefore were reporting to a set of administrative and elected officials who were separated by a long history of interparty rivalry over who should control the course of labor negotiations.

Thus most of the sources of impasse that we discussed earlier were factors in this dispute. The parties had a history of difficult bargaining. In previous negotiations the governor and other political officials who were not present in formal negotiations usually had become involved as the negotiations process heated up. The decision-making structure on the management side was highly complex, with power shared among a number of competing political and administrative officials. Furthermore, intense political rivalries and differences existed among these management officials. The union and management negotiators distrusted each other, and the membership and union officers displayed a willingness to engage in militant action from the start of the negotiations. The fact that the bargaining unit covered employees in all parts of the state ensured that this dispute would become a major political issue statewide. Thus the presence of all these potential sources of impasse indicated that bargaining would be difficult.

The dispute was settled only after the following sequence of events.

1. The state employees went on strike for 15 days, during which time the governor declared a state of emergency, called out the National Guard, and transferred physically and mentally handicapped patients from state to private institutions.

2. A court injunction was issued against the strikers.

3. An ad hoc, out-of-state mediator was brought in.

4. The governor and national officials from AFSCME entered the negotiations process.

5. The Joint Legislative Committee on Labor rejected a settlement that had brought the employees back to work.

6. Further negotiations and mediation efforts among the governor, representatives of the legislative committee, and the union took place.

7. The negotiated strike settlement was modified and approved by the legislature.

8. The state attorney general pursued contempt-of-court proceedings against the striking workers over the objections of the governor.

This case provides a good illustration of how diverse political pressures can affect the course of public sector collective bargaining.

The Effects of Public Sector Bargaining on Outcomes

Studies of collective bargaining in the public sector have found the following effects. (You may want to contrast these with the private sector bargaining outcomes described in Chapter 10.)

Wage and Other Compensation Outcomes

Although the magnitudes of the estimates on wages and costs vary across the studies, the vast majority of the studies have found a wage differential between unionized and nonunionized public employees.[25] These estimates also indicate, however, that the wage effects of collective bargaining in the public sector are not greater than the effects of collective bargaining in the private sector. The public sector union–nonunion wage differential is typically in the range of 5 to 15 percent. That is, unions do not appear to exert a stronger effect on the wages of public employees than they do on the wages of private employees.

There also is evidence that collective bargaining has had a positive effect on selected fringe benefits of public employees. Unionism leads to higher pension benefits, fewer hours and days worked, and increased time off with pay.[26] The large pension increases won by unions suggest that the simple wage differential seriously underestimates the compensation effects of bargaining.

The Dynamics of Union Effects on Pay

Historical or **longitudinal data** also reveal that unions have raised relative earnings and point out some interesting dynamics in union wage effects. Exhibit 13–3 reports ratios of the average annual earnings of public school teachers to the average annual earnings of private sector workers, and the same ratios for police earnings to private sector worker earnings. The data show that from 1960 to 1975 teachers' relative earnings increased (from 1.05 to 1.18), as did the relative earnings of police (from 1.01 to 1.06). These increases in relative earnings may at first glance not appear large, but it should be kept in mind that the U.S. earnings distribution typically shows a high degree of stability across occupations. In the face of that record these are indeed sizable changes.

The important point to note here is that the period 1955 to 1975 was the one during which teacher, police, and other public sector unions increased both their memberships and their militancy. The growth and militancy of unions at the time may well have contributed to the relative earnings advances achieved by these public employees. At the same time, however, government expenditures were also growing over this period, and it is difficult to know how much of the increase in public employees' relative earnings should be attributed to their unions.

The data in Exhibit 13–3 also indicate a sharp decline in both teachers' and police relative earnings from 1975 to 1980. This was the era of

Exhibit 13–3   **Longitudinal Evidence on the Relative Earnings of Teachers and Police, 1960–88**

Year	Teachers versus Private Sector Workers*	Police versus Private Sector Workers†
1960	1.05	1.01
1965	1.12	1.01
1970	1.26	1.08
1975	1.18	1.06
1980	1.09	1.00
1985	1.20	1.09
1988	1.33	1.19

*Data in this column are ratios of the mean annual earnings of all elementary and secondary public school teachers to the mean annual earnings of production and nonsupervisory workers in the private nonfarm sector. Teacher data are from the *Estimates of School Statistics* (Washington D.C.: National Education Association, various years). Production worker earning data are from U.S. Department of Labor, Bureau of Labor Statistics, *Handbook of Labor Statistics* (Washington, D.C.: GPO, 1989), table 81.
†Data are ratios of the mean annual earnings of all local police to the mean annual earning of production and nonsupervisory workers (the latter are the same figures as those used to calculate the teacher earning ratio). Police earnings are from *The Municipal Year Book* (Washington, D.C.: International City Management Association, various years).

the taxpayers' revolt, and it appears that the revolt had substantial effects on public sector earnings after 1975. However, in the mid- and late 1980s relative pay in the public sector rose again to levels far beyond those in 1975. These relative pay increases followed the shift in public concerns to issues of the adequacy of public education and public safety. The recent relative rise in public sector pay may also be a product of the slow growth in private sector pay, just as the fall in relative public sector earnings in the late 1970s likely was in part due to the rapid inflation in private sector pay rates in that period.

The Effects on Public Sector Budgets

Did the increases in expenditures on employees' salaries and benefits result in major budgetary reallocations from other areas? Evidence comparing employment in union and nonunion cities suggests that public sector unionism raises or at least does not lower employment in the public sector. Apparently public sector unions are able to lobby for greater government expenditures to eliminate any employment displacement caused by higher earnings.[27]

Union Effects on Public Administration

There is little doubt that collective bargaining has had a profound effect on both the process and the substance of personnel administration in public employment. As in the private sector, collective bargaining has increased the formalization of personnel practices and reduced the discretion of management in matters of discipline and discharge, promotions, transfers, and work assignments.[28]

Case studies of both successful productivity improvement programs and of resistance by public sector unions to changes in work rules have been reported. There have been a few cases of successful labor-management committees in the public sector.

Studies find that the effect of collective bargaining on the quality of public services is influenced by how well management adapts to the presence of the union.[29] As in the private sector, the effects of public sector unions and collective bargaining on the economic performance of the employer depend on the effectiveness of the relationship between the union and the employer.

The Use of Interest Arbitration

Some form of **interest arbitration,** arbitration that determines contract terms, is available in 20 states for the resolution of impasses in negotiations between local governments and at least some of their employees. Police and fire fighters are the groups most frequently covered by the procedure. There is a wide variety of forms of interest arbitration, including conventional, final offer, and various combinations of mediation, fact-finding, and interest arbitration.

Does Interest Arbitration Perversely Affect Collective Bargaining?

There is much controversy in the industrial relations community over the long-term consequences of binding interest arbitration.[30] Some claim that interest arbitration violates the spirit of free collective bargaining. Interest arbitration also has been criticized on the grounds that the availability of these procedures reduces the parties' incentive to bargain, thus imposing a **chilling effect** on the negotiations process. The parties avoid making compromises they might otherwise be willing to make because they fear the fact finder or arbitrator will split the difference between their stated positions.

A management negotiator, for example, may believe that it is better to go into fact-finding or interest arbitration offering only 4 percent when management would actually be willing to offer 6 percent to avoid a strike or impasse. By going in at 4 percent, the negotiator may increase the probability that the arbitrator (fact finder) will award (recommend) 6 percent. Put differently, if the negotiator were to enter the procedure offering 6 percent, this may increase the probability that the recommendation or award will be for something greater than this amount. The same rationale, it is argued, drives the union negotiator. Thus, the bargaining process is chilled: each party tends to hold back concessions rather than lay its best offer on the table.

These procedures also may suffer from overuse even in the absence of a chilling effect if they are not as economically costly as the strike. Remember, it is the income losses suffered during a strike that spurs the parties to negotiate a settlement. Third-party procedures may lead to lower income losses.[31]

Furthermore, use of interest arbitration may serve political objectives for the union or management negotiators by allowing them to pass the blame on to the arbitrator. Parties faced with difficult internal conflicts may prefer to pass the buck to the fact finder or arbitrator and let themselves off the hook.[32] There is also the worry that these procedures would favor one side or the other. This would occur if the arbitrators make awards that are different from what the parties would end up with if interest arbitration were not available as an alternative.

There is also concern that these procedures are inherently conservative and that they favor the party that seeks the fewest deviations from the status quo. Thus some fear that the presence of these procedures stifles innovation in bargaining or new breakthroughs in contract terms.

Evidence on the Effects of Interest Arbitration

Most negotiations that occur where interest arbitration is available are settled without the use of arbitration. In states where it is available, interest arbitration is used in between 3.8 and 29 percent of negotiations.[33] The variance in usage across states is partially a function of the different forms of arbitration used. **Final offer arbitration,** where the arbitrator must choose between the parties' final offers, for example, appears to produce lower usage rates than does conventional arbitration. Is the usage of arbitration unusually high? The evidence shows that it is not. The rate of interest arbitration usage cited above is in the same range of the frequency of strikes in the private sector.[34]

Even though the overall usage of interest arbitration is not high, it is still possible that particular bargaining units become addicted to the procedure once they use it. Is this "narcotic effect" evident? To answer this question, researchers have analyzed the experience of the individual bargaining units over successive rounds of negotiations. The data suggest that the existence of interest arbitration does not erode bargaining to the point that even a substantial majority of bargaining units become dependent on the procedure. But larger units with the most complex bargaining relationships are more likely to rely heavily on the procedures.[35] The evidence consistently shows that in those states where interest arbitration is available, strikes occur less frequently than in states where arbitration is not available.[36] At the same time, the data show that even in states that require interest arbitration, strikes sometimes do occur.

The Impacts of Interest Arbitration on Contractual Outcomes

Numerous analysts have studied the effects of interest arbitration on bargaining outcomes. A number of researchers have found that the availability of interest arbitration has led to slightly higher wage settlements and more favorable nonwage contract terms.[37] There is also evidence of less variation in collective bargaining outcomes across municipalities in states that make interest arbitration available.

Judgments about the appropriateness of interest arbitration should take into consideration these contract effects and the lower incidence of strikes that results from the availability of interest arbitration noted earlier. To date, the public generally appears to be satisfied with the use of interest arbitration, particularly for police and firefighters, as an alternative to the right to strike.

Participatory Programs and Work Restructuring in Public Schools

Under pressure to lower costs and improve service quality a number of public sector sites began in the late 1980s to turn to work restructuring and participatory programs. Many bold experiments were initiated in elementary or secondary public schools.[38] Developments in the public schools are examined below. Particular emphasis is placed on comparing public sector experience to what has been transpiring in the private sector (described in Chapter 12).

The History of School Reforms

Many school districts began to alter the roles and responsibilities of teachers, principals, and district administrators starting in the late 1980s. There were a proliferation of programs under names such as school improvement teams, lead (or master) teachers programs, school-based management, site-based management, and many others.

Reforms came in response to pressures to improve the education of students. In 1983 a well-publicized report by the Carnegie Commission, *A Nation at Risk,* argued that weaknesses in elementary and secondary schools were contributing to America's economic problems by producing a poorly trained work force.[39] One Educational Testing Service study of 13-year-olds in six countries found that U.S. students ranked last in math skills and next to last in science. There was also pressure building in the schools as an outgrowth of the wide ethnic diversity among the school-age population.

Public schools also were facing heightened social problems, including alarming rates of drug dependance among youth, reports of frequent illiteracy among high school graduates, and high student truancy rates. All of this was occurring in a fiscal environment in which state governments and the public were expressing reservations about making substantially larger contributions to the public schools.

The employees who worked in schools, including administrators, teachers, and support staff (clerical and custodial school employees) were being asked to improve learning without substantial increases in expenditures. Thus public schools came under pressure to improve productivity and lower costs, just like many private sector firms and employees.

The "Low-Cost–Hierarchical" School Reform Strategy

As in the private sector, there was a wide divergence of opinion over what was the appropriate way to restructure schools. At one extreme were those who claimed that what was needed were tighter controls over classroom activities and more strict adherence to hierarchical lines of authority among school employees. The notion here was that tighter controls and greater standardization would lead to greater work effort by teachers and other employees and stronger discipline in the classroom.

A number of techniques were advocated in this strategy. There was support for stricter and more frequent testing of teachers. Others recommended greater use of merit pay that would reward higher performing teachers with monetary incentives. Some argued that school management needed to take a harder line in collective bargaining with teacher unions. A hard line was recommended to gain concessions in contractual work rules that would increase the hours of work and give school administrators more flexibility in teacher allocations (promotions, transfers, and classroom assignments).

In many ways this strategy was the public schools counterpart to the low-cost business strategy pursued by some private sector firms. This strategy relied on greater control by administrators and *less* participation in decisions by teachers and support employees.

A "Decentralization-Participation" School Reform Strategy

At the other extreme was a strategy that relied on decentralizing decision-making authority within school systems. Decentralization would provide teachers and support staff with *greater* participation in decisions. Box 13–3 describes the types of and mechanisms for reforms along these lines initiated in six school systems.

Advocates of this strategy argued that involving teachers more extensively in decisions would improve the quality of education. The hope was (and is) that with decentralization and participation teachers would be

Box 13–3

How Six Schools/School Districts Achieved Reform		
School Districts	*Types of Reforms Initiated*	*Mechanisms for Change*
ABC United School District, Cerritos, California	A streamlined management organization and partially decentralized budget process, which has increased funds for schools and school-level control of funds	Management associations of school administrators, which meet regularly with the district superintendent
	Districtwide curriculum development and evaluation by teachers	A Curriculum Master Plan Council and subject-area committees made up of teachers from each school and management facilitators
	Mentor teachers	Selected by teacher committees
	Instructional resource teachers	Appointed by administration
	Teacher involvement in staff development and in-service training; selection of principals; determination of disciplinary procedures, and development of new instructional techniques	School site councils, departmental forums, off-site retreats, and staff development workshops
Cincinnati (Ohio) Public Schools	A peer appraisal plan, new teacher allocation methods to relieve overcrowded classrooms, new grading and promotion standards, improved professional teaching and learning conditions, and career ladders for new teachers	Joint union-administration committees
	Improvement of certain low-performing neighborhood schools through implementation of all-day kindergarten programs and several other reforms	A joint planning committee for identifying eligible pilot schools and conducting a selection process: teacher involvement in specific improvement plans
Dade County (Florida) Public Schools	School-Based Management, Shared-Decision Making program which has included a wide variety of school reforms, such as a new bilingual and basic skills curriculum,	A joint union-administration task force to oversee the school-based improvement program and various school-site structures to carry out reforms, such as quality circles,

School Districts	Types of Reforms Initiated	Mechanisms for Change
	nontraditional staffing techniques, and new scheduling procedures	faculty councils, and departmental committees
	Satellite learning centers established at business sites	A joint union-administration program implemented in conjunction with the business community
	Saturday morning tutorial programs, established at inner-city schools	Regular teachers, who are paid for their extra tutorial work
	Dade Academy of the Teaching Arts, a nine-week professional development program for teachers based at a functioning high school	Mentor teachers who work with other teachers; overall project is collaboratively run by the administration and union with participation of consultants from local universities
	Partners in Education, a school improvement program focused on inner-city schools	A joint program of the administration, union, as well as other local organizations; teacher-administration school committees
	Teacher Recruitment Internship Program	A collaborative project between the University of Miami, the school district, and the American Federation of Teachers
Duluth (Minnesota) School System	Participative Management/Quality of Work Life process, which has focused on improvements in instruction, teacher evaluation, staff development, and budgeting to increase school-level control over financial resources	A districtwide Quality of Work Life Steering Committee, composed of school board and central administration representatives, school principals, and union members; joint school-level quality circles and problem-solving groups
Hammond (Indiana) School District	A School Improvement Process, which has included improvements in such areas as curriculum development, instructional strategies, professional development, peer evaluation, disciplinary procedures, staffing needs and hiring, and scheduling	Joint school improvement teams, which may set aside elements of the master contract in order to carry out improvement plans

---

Box 13–3   *(continued)*

How Six Schools/School Districts Achieved Reform

School Districts	*Types of Reforms Initiated*	*Mechanisms for Change*
Jefferson County Public Schools, Louisville, Kentucky	A districtwide restructuring effort including the following components: Professional Development Schools, participation in the Coalition of Essential Schools, a school district/ University of Louisville project to redefine the induction process for the teaching profession, Learning Choice Schools, and a Middle Grades Assessment Program	At district level, led by the Gheens Professional Development Academy, a human resource development center for teachers and principals; at school level, a variety of teams and other participative structures

Source: Jerome M. Rosow and Robert Zager, *Allies in Educational Reform: How Teachers Unions, and Administrators Can Work Together For Better Schools* (New York: Work in America, 1989, pp. 27–28.

---

freed to innovate in classroom instruction and respond to student needs quickly. Even within the decentralization-participation strategy there was much diversity in the techniques being tried.

School Improvement Teams   Some school districts introduced *school improvement teams* with a committee of 10 to 15 members that typically included a principal and some teachers, parents, and support staff who would meet for a few hours each week to work on specific tasks. In some cases the principal would run the team meetings.[40] A team might study how guidance services might be better provided to students or might focus on the problems that surround the introduction of a new reading program in a specific school.

School improvement teams are analogous to the quality circle programs initiated in many private firms in the early and mid-1980s. As one would expect, school improvement teams faced problems and limitations that were similar to those experienced by private sector quality circle programs. Teachers on the improvement teams, for example, sometimes deferred to the authority of the principal or became frustrated when suggestions offered by teachers were later turned down by higher levels of school district administration.

School improvement teams sometimes were constrained by the myriad of regulations that surround public education. If an improvement team wanted to extensively restructure work rules in order to address a problem, for example, it could be constrained by district, state, or collective bargaining policies and rules.

Lead Teacher Programs   **Lead** (or master) **teacher programs** were often part of the decentralization-participation strategy. The goal here was to allow experienced and committed senior teachers to serve as mentors and role models for younger teachers. In addition, lead teacher programs provided a mechanism through which financial incentives could be provided to superior teachers. The latter was a way to cope with the fact that typically teacher salary schedules are stringently based on seniority with no mechanism allowed for rewarding meritorious performance.[41] Lead teachers performed the following activities: clinical supervision support, teaching demonstration classes, reviewing curriculum options, analyzing student test data and attendance records, and facilitating communication between teachers and administrators.

School-Based Management   An extreme reform adopted in some school districts was **school-based management.** School-based management typically included teams (either school- or building-based) composed of teachers, administrators, parents, students, and local community leaders. The range of issues such teams become involved in has included curriculum, teaching strategies, the hiring of administrators, professional development, discipline, and school schedules. The objective here is to give the teams at the school or building level latitude over the use of resources, budgeting, and time. At the core of school-based management is getting teachers directly involved in making decisions on scheduling, redeploying teachers, or teaching methods.

School-based management (and related reforms) attempt to create more flexibility in school systems that are otherwise constrained by regulations and rules. In some cases it is the state regulations that are most constraining. In North Carolina, for example, state school aid had been provided in 76 line items. Before 1987 schools were not allowed to transfer funds from one line item to another regardless of local priorities or needs.[42] School-based management experiments in North Carolina proceeded only after the state legislature agreed to waive fund transfer limitations for districts engaged in the reform process.

In some other cases it is the collectively bargained rules that must be altered to facilitate school-based management reforms. Some school-based teams, for example, developed new schedules that put some of the curriculum in large classrooms and thereby freed up teacher time for one-on-one student–teacher interaction. To implement this change the teachers unions would have to waive the contractual limitations on class size that is included in many teacher collective bargaining agreements.

Even in the face of the tensions between school reforms and participatory processes, the national teachers unions (particularly the American Federation of Teachers) have generally supported participatory restructuring. Yet there is much diversity in the stance taken by local teachers unions toward participatory processes.[43]

The Problems Inhibiting New Efforts   Since participatory programs in the public schools are so similar to participatory programs adopted in the private sector it is not surprising that many of the same problems arise. Many school-based management programs, for example, have been inhibited by principals or district administrators who are reluctant to give up control and allow teachers or parents greater input into decisions. In this way principals and administrators are expressing the same fears as those exhibited by supervisors and top executives in the private sector.

The school-based management and related reforms also create a critical issue concerning the relationship between collective bargaining and participatory processes. What is the role left for a contractual grievance procedure when a teacher can turn to a building-level team to solve a workplace problem? Can a sharp dividing line be drawn between the collective bargaining process and participatory processes? What will the role of the teachers union be if school-based teams take on extensive decision-making authority? These issues will be central to the evolution of participatory programs in the public schools and, interestingly, have clear parallels to the issues that are emerging in private sector participatory programs.

Accountability Programs

A number of school reforms, whatever their strategic focus, include efforts to establish greater **accountability** for educational attainment. Accountability programs focus on the generation and monitoring of data on student progress (test scores), student attendance, or teacher performance. The pressure for closer accountability derives in part from the public's concern over the quality of education and the apparently relatively poor educational attainment of U.S. school-age children.

The implementation of accountability programs arises in some districts as an outgrowth of the expansion of participatory processes. With the weakening of formal hierarchies between teachers and administrators, school districts are turning toward accountability measures to assess teacher performance.

The Effects of School Reforms on School Outcomes

Which of the school reform strategies lead to concrete improvements in student performance, and what are the costs (or savings) produced by various reforms?[44] Unfortunately, there is very little hard evidence about whether or how school reforms affect educational quality. In part, the lack of knowledge stems from the fact that the reforms have not been around long enough to demonstrate effects. In addition, complexities in the educational process make it extremely difficult to measure the effects of even long-lasting programs.

Assessing the payouts from school reforms remains one of the critical challenges for the future. It is also important to note that unionization and collective bargaining are likely to remain a central part of public education whatever the course of school reforms.

Normative Premises

How should industrial relations in the public sector be legally regulated? American labor law is governed by the premise that in the private sector (1) an inherent conflict of interests exists between employees and employers and (2) workers should have the right to pursue their interests through a union if they so choose. Furthermore, there is a strong preference for the process of free collective bargaining in which labor and management are given the opportunity to resolve their problems without extensive third-party interference.

Yet government differs from a private sector employer because, although government officials have traditional managerial responsibilities, the government is elected by the public. The public thereby has a dual role to play in public sector industrial relations. The public acts at the same time as citizens who regulate the provision of public services and as consumers of public services (paying for the public services as taxpayers). The problem for public policy is how to maintain the rights of employees to influence their employment conditions, through collective bargaining if they so desire, while maintaining citizens' rights to influence governmental action.

Criticisms of Public Sector Bargaining

Harry Wellington and Ralph Winter, among others, have taken the extreme position that government's primary responsibility—to represent the public interest—makes collective bargaining inappropriate for the public sector.[45] Critics of public sector bargaining also claim that if labor unions are granted the rights to exclusive representation and negotiations, they will achieve undue political power.

The Virtues of Public Sector Bargaining

We believe these positions ignore employee interests and inaccurately assess the actual effects of public sector collective bargaining. It is our view that public employees, like private sector employees, have an inherent right to participate in the determination of their working conditions. Why should the mere fact that an employee works for the government strip that employee of the right to influence employment conditions through collective bargaining?

Furthermore, the charge that collective bargaining leads to a perverse distortion of governmental decision making is not supported by the facts. The evidence discussed in this chapter shows that public sector unions have had a modest impact on employee pay and other working conditions. In fact, where they exist, public sector unions influence governmental decision making as but one among the many interest groups participating in this process. Public employee representation seems to enhance rather than detract from the process of representative democracy. Our argument does not necessarily imply that public sector collective bargaining rights should be identical to those in the private sector. Because a variety of interest groups are affected by governmental decisions their diverse interests must be taken into account in the collective bargaining process. Public policy must balance these objectives.

Summary

The questions in this chapter are as follows. (1) Has collective bargaining increased the political access and influence of public sector employees? (2) Has the strike proved to be a strong source of power in the public sector? (3) Have dispute resolution procedures, particularly binding interest arbitration, led to outcomes injurious to the public welfare? Early fears that public sector bargaining would tip the balance of power in favor of the unions have proved to be overly simplistic.

There has been a diverse range of experience in public sector bargaining. Cities, for example, developed various responses to public employee unions. There also were major shifts over time in the public's reaction to public employee demands and unionism. Wide differences also have appeared in the economic power of police, fire fighters, teachers, and other public employees. Therefore, it is inappropriate to generalize across public sector collective bargaining experiences.

Unionism in the public sector does not appear to warp the democratic process. The evidence also suggests that the strike has not consistently proven to be a one-sided source of union power. Furthermore, analysis of wage effects finds that the union–nonunion wage differential does not appear to be larger in the public sector than in the private sector.

Public sector unions do appear to have raised some fringe benefits substantially and to have increased the total amount of governmental expenditures and employment. Yet these effects are hardly significant enough to warrant any call for a dismantling of public sector bargaining. Finally, there is no evidence that the presence of interest arbitration has seriously perverted the collective bargaining process in the public sector.

Work restructuring and participatory programs have emerged as a central issue in the public sector, particularly in public schools. Here, as in the private sector, there are a variety of experiments under way. Many similarities prevail in the problems that arise in public and private sector restructuring including issues surrounding the relationship between participatory processes and collective bargaining. Furthermore, at this point we have little hard evidence on the effects reforms exert on educational outcomes.

What are the long-term consequences of a system that relies heavily on both third-party neutrals and outside advocates? What are the long-term effects of a system whose outcomes depend more on public choices and political decisions than on the direct constraints of the economic market? These are issues that will continue to be debated as experience unfolds. At the very least, the emergence of public sector bargaining has stimulated thought and analysis around these questions. In doing so it has opened the door to new ways of thinking about how collective bargaining can be adapted to new environments. The public sector has proven to be a valuable laboratory for experimentation and should continue to be so in future years.

Discussion Questions

1. What factors contributed to the growth of public sector unions and public sector collective bargaining in the 1960s?

2. There is debate over whether public sector unions have more power than those in the private sector. Evaluate the power of public employee unions in terms of Marshall's Conditions.

3. Describe the structure of most public sector collective bargaining.

4. Discuss the pros and cons of giving public sector employees the right to strike.

Suggested Readings

Aaron, Benjamin, Joyce Najita, and James L. Stern, eds. *Public-Sector Bargaining,* 2d ed. (Washington, D.C.: Bureau of National Affairs, 1988).

Freeman, Richard B. "Unionism Comes to the Public Sector," *Journal of Economic Literature* 24 (March 1986): 41–86.

Lewin, David, Peter Feuille, Thomas A. Kochan, and John T. Delaney, *Public Sector Labor Relations: Analysis and Readings,* 3d ed. (Lexington, MA: Lexington Books, 1987).

End Notes

1. Public employee union membership figures are traced in John F. Burton, Jr., and Terry Thomason, "The Extent of Collective Bargaining in the Public Sector," in *Public-Sector Bargaining,* 2d ed., ed. Benjamin Aaron, Joyce M. Najita, and James

L. Stern (Washington, D.C.: Bureau of National Affairs, 1988), pp. 1–51; and Richard B. Freeman, "Unionism Comes to the Public Sector," *Journal of Economic Literature* 24 (March 1986): 41–86.

2.　See Joan P. Weitzman, "The Effect of Economic Restraints on Public Sector Collective Bargaining: The Lessons from New York City," in *Government Labor Relations: Trends and Information for the Future,* ed. Hugh D. Jascourt (Oak Park, IL: Moore, 1979), pp. 334–346.

3.　We trace the broad wage trends in the public sector in more detail later in this chapter.

4.　The events in San Francisco are analyzed in Harry C. Katz, "Municipal Pay Determination: The Case of San Francisco," *Industrial Relations* 18 (Winter 1979): 44–59.

5.　For a description of Proposition 13 and the measures adopted in the other eight states, see "COPE Charts Impact of States' Spending and Tax Limitations," *Government Employee Relations Report* 812 (May 28, 1979): 14–17.

6.　See Carnegie Forum on Education and the Economy, *A Nation Prepared: Teachers for the Twenty-First Century* (Washington, D.C.: Carnegie Foundation, 1986).

7.　Thomas A. Kochan, "Correlates of State Public Employee Bargaining Laws," *Industrial Relations* 12 (October 1973): 322–337.

8.　Ibid., p. 327.

9.　There are examples of sizable public sector union growth in some states, such as Ohio, that did not have laws favorable to public sector unions.

10.　It is difficult to identify statistically the independent influence the law exerted on union growth. It is possible that passage of a law favorable to public sector unions was a reflection of factors that would have spurred the growth of unions even if the law had not been passed. See Gregory Saltzman, "Bargaining Laws as a Cause and Consequence of the Growth of Teacher Unionism," *Industrial and Labor Relations Review* 38 (April 1985): 335–351. Other studies are reviewed in Freeman, "Unionism Comes."

11.　A comprehensive summary of public sector strike experience is found in Craig A. Olson, "Dispute Resolution in the Public Sector," in *Public-Sector Bargaining,* 2d ed., ed. Benjamin Aaron, Joyce M. Najita, and James L. Stern (Washington D.C.: Bureau of National Affairs, 1988), pp. 160–188.

12.　See Casey Ichniowski, "Arbitration and Police Bargaining: Prescriptions for the Blue Flu," *Industrial Relations* 21 (Spring 1982): 149. Evidence on this issue is not unambiguous. See John F. Burton, Jr., and Charles E. Krider, "The Incidence of Strikes in Public Employment," in *Labor in the Public and Non-Profit Sectors,* ed. Daniel S. Hamermesh (Princeton: Princeton University Press, 1975), pp. 161–170, and James L. Stern and Craig A. Olson, "The Propensity To Strike of Local Government Employees," *Journal of Collective Negotiations in the Public Sector* vol. 11, no. 3 (1982): 201–214.

13.　See Olson, "Dispute Resolution."

14.　Stern and Olson, "The Propensity To Strike."

15. Stephen L. Hayford and Anthony V. Sinicropi, "Bargaining Rights Status of Public Sector Supervisors," *Industrial Relations* 15 (February 1976): 44–61.

16. The issue of federal jurisdiction arose in *Joe G. Garcia v. San Antonio Metropolitan Transit Authority et al.,* 105 US 1005 (1985), and *National League of Cities v. Usery,* 426 US (1976).

17. One early study (and many later studies) concluded that, on average, the demand for labor in the public sector was more inelastic than the demand for labor in the private sector. See Orley Ashenfelter and Ronald G. Ehrenberg, "The Demand for Labor in the Public Sector," in *Labor in the Public and Non-Profit Sectors,* ed. Daniel S. Hamermesh, (Princeton: Princeton University Press, 1975), pp. 55–78.

18. Robert J. Thornton, "The Elasticity of Demand for Public School Teachers," *Industrial Relations* 18 (Winter 1979): 86–91.

19. There are some exceptions to this, such as the tolls collected on roads and fees collected at parks.

20. Calculated from *Facts and Figures on Government Finance* (Washington, D.C.: Tax Foundation, 1990), table F–12.

21. The ups and downs of coordinated bargaining across various unions in New York City are traced in David Lewin and Mary McCormick, "Coalition Bargaining in Municipal Government: New York City in the 1970s," *Industrial and Labor Relations Review* 34 (July 1981): 175–190.

22. Peter Feuille, Hervey Juris, Ralph Jones, and Michael Jay Jedel, "Multi-Employer Negotiations among Local Governments," in *Public Sector Labor Relations: Analysis and Readings* David Lewin, Peter Feuille, Thomas A. Kochan and John T. Delaney, eds., 3d ed. (Lexington, MA: Lexington Books, 1987), pp. 110–113.

23. Some cities have consolidated their bargaining units. As mentioned in Chapter 4, between 1967 and 1977 New York City reduced the number of its bargaining units from 400 to just under 100.

24. Thomas A. Kochan, "City Government Bargaining: A Path Analysis," *Industrial Relations* 14 (February 1975): 90–101.

25. For a review of these studies see Freeman, "Unionism Comes." Also see David Lewin, Peter Feuille, Thomas A. Kochan, and John T. Delaney, "The Impact of Unions on Public Sector Wages," in *Public Sector Labor Relations,* (Lexington, MA: Lexington Books, 1987) pp. 397–405.

26. Ibid.

27. See ibid. These studies of union effects on expenditures had difficulty detecting whether higher government expenditures are caused by the same factors that cause public sector unions to grow or by the unions themselves.

28. See David T. Stanley, *Managing Local Government under Union Pressure* (Washington, D.C.: Brookings Institution, 1972); Hervey Juris and Peter Feuille, *Police Unionism* (Lexington, MA: D.C. Heath, 1973), pp. 125–150; Lorraine McDonnell and Anthony Pascal, *Organized Teachers in American Schools* (Santa Monica, CA: Rand Corporation, 1978), pp. 75–82; George Sulzer, *The Impact of*

Labor-Management Relations upon Selected Federal Personnel Policies and Practices (Washington, D.C.: Superintendent of Documents, 1979).

29. See McDonnell and Pascal, *Organized Teachers,* and Sulzer, *The Impact of Labor-Management Relations.* For an analysis of the consequences of technological change, see David Lewin, "Technological Service," in *Workers, Managers and Technological Change: Emerging Patterns of Labor Relations,* ed. Daniel B. Cornfield (New York: Plenum, 1986), pp. 281–309.

30. Carl M. Stevens, "Is Compulsory Arbitration Compatible with Collective Bargaining?" *Industrial Relations* 5 (February 1966): 38–52.

31. The costs associated with arbitration include the costs of the uncertainty associated with guessing what the arbitrator will do and any direct costs (such as fees) associated with use of the procedure. See Henry S. Farber and Harry C. Katz, "Interest Arbitration, Outcomes and the Incentive to Bargain," *Industrial and Labor Relations Review* 55 (October 1979): 55–63.

32. One study that compared the causes of impasses under arbitration and the causes of strikes found, for example, that internal political and attitudinal sources of conflict were more important in causing impasses than in causing strikes. Thomas A. Kochan, Mordehai Mironi, Ronald G. Ehrenberg, Jean Baderschneider and Todd Jick, *Dispute Resolution under Factfinding and Arbitration* (New York: American Arbitration Association, 1979), pp. 99–111.

33. See Olson, "Dispute Resolution."

34. Cynthia Gramm, "The Determinants of Strike Incidence and Severity: A Micro-Level Study," *Industrial and Labor Relations Review* 39 (April 1988): 361–76.

35. For conflicting conclusions on whether arbitration induces a narcotic effect, see Thomas A. Kochan and Jean Baderschneider, "Dependence on Impasse Procedures: Police and Firefighters in New York State," *Industrial and Labor Relations Review* 31 (July 1978): pp. 431–439; and Richard J. Butler and Ronald G. Ehrenberg, "Estimating the Narcotic Effect of Public Sector Impasse Procedures," *Industrial and Labor Relations Review* 35 (October 1981): 3–20.

36. See Olson, "Dispute Resolution."

37. For example, Craig A. Olson, in "The Impact of Arbitration on the Wages of Firefighters," *Industrial Relations* 19 (Fall 1980): 325–339, found that arbitration leads to higher firefighter compensation. Peter Feuille, John Thomas Delaney, and Wallace Hendricks, in "The Impact of Interest Arbitration on Police Contracts," *Industrial Relations* 24 (Spring 1985): 161–181, found that the availability of arbitration improves the earnings and other contract provisions of police. A few studies showed that interest arbitration had no effect on salaries. David E. Bloom, in "Collective Bargaining, Compulsory Arbitration, and Salary Settlements in the Public Sector: The Case of New Jersey's Municipal Police Officers," *Journal of Labor Research* 2 (Fall 1981): 369–384, found no salary effects of arbitration in New Jersey.

38. Samuel B. Bacharach, ed., *Education Reform: Making Sense of It All* (Boston: Allyn & Bacon, 1990).

39. *A Nation at Risk,* National Commission on Excellence in Education, A Report to the Secretary of Education, U.S. Department of Education, April 1983.

40.   The principal's role is in some ways comparable to that of the supervisor in a private sector firm. One important difference between the private and public sectors is that in many school districts principals and other administrators are represented by a union. Remember, the public sector is not covered by the NLRA (and the Taft-Hartley amendments).

41.   The controversy that surrounds merit pay is discussed in Samuel B. Bacharach, David B. Lipsky, and Joseph B. Shedd, *Paying for Better Teaching: Merit Pay and Its Alternatives* (Ithaca, NY: Organizational Analysis and Practice, 1984).

42.   See "North Carolina's Lead Teacher/Restructured School Pilot Project: An Interim Report," Public School Forum of North Carolina, *The Forum* (Spring 1988): 1–15.

43.   See Bureau of Labor-Management Relations and Cooperative Programs, U.S. Department of Labor, *Participatory Leadership: School and the Workplace,* Report 138 (Washington, D.C.: GPO, 1990).

44.   Skepticism about the payout from school-based management is expressed in Betty Malen, Rodney T. Ogawa, and Jennifer Kranz, "Unfilled Promises," *The School Administrator* (February 1990), pp. 3–32 and 53–60.

45.   This argument can be found in Harry H. Wellington and Ralph K. Winter, Jr., *The Unions and the Cities* (Washington, D.C.: Brookings Institution, 1971).

Chapter 14

International and Comparative Industrial Relations

An excellent way to gain perspective on one's own industrial relations system is to compare it to systems found in other countries.

The U.S. industrial relations system is unique in many ways. The United States, for example, has one of the lowest rates of unionization of any advanced democratic economy, and its rate of unionization has fallen faster in the past twenty years than that of any other industrialized country in the world. Furthermore, American management opposes unions more strongly than managers in most other countries. Unions in the United States are less closely tied to political parties than are their counterparts in Europe, Australia, and many developing countries. Strikes in the United States also tend to last longer and occur more frequently than those in many other countries.

Other differences between industrial relations in the United States and practices elsewhere are noted throughout this chapter. Through a comparative perspective it is possible to assess whether there are any features of the industrial relations systems in other countries that should be imported and applied in the United States. This question is now on the minds of many industrial relations practitioners in the United States.

There are other reasons why an international focus on industrial relations practice is important. The U.S. economy is becoming more international as exports and imports make up a larger share of total gross national product. The **trade deficit** has emerged as a critical policy issue. Exhibit 14–1 presents statistics on the U.S. trade deficit and trade flows. As a result of increased trade U.S. managers and unionists are more frequently exposed to and involved in the industrial relations practices of other nations. The globalization of the economy requires a globalization of our understanding of industrial relations.

The three-tiered framework is used in this chapter to study industrial relations in countries other than the United States. A comparative

Exhibit 14–1   **United States Imports and Exports, 1930–88**

Year	Exports as share of GNP (%)	Imports as share of GNP (%)	Balance of trade (exports-imports) ($ billion)
1930	5.2%	4.3%	1.0
1935	4.5	4.3	.1
1940	5.3	3.6	1.7
1945	7.6	4.8	6.0
1950	5.0	4.2	2.3
1955	5.5	4.4	4.4
1960	5.6	4.5	5.7
1965	3.8	3.0	5.3
1970	4.2	3.9	2.7
1975	6.7	6.2	9.1
1980	8.1	9.0	−24.2
1985	5.3	8.6	−132.1
1988	6.6	9.0	−119.8

Sources: Data on exports and imports from *Statistical Abstracts of the United States* (Washington, D.C.: U.S. Department of Commerce): 1961 ed., table 1195; 1990 ed., table 216. GNP data from *Statistical Abstract of the United States* (Washington, D.C.: U.S. Department of Commerce, 1990), table 690.

assessment of industrial relations should take account of the substantial institutional differences that exist across countries. However, the wide diversity in industrial relations practices around the globe makes it infeasible to present even a cursory examination of all of them. As a framework for an international perspective, then, this chapter examines in detail the key features of the industrial relations systems in Germany[1] and Japan.

This chapter includes a focus on Germany and Japan for a number of reasons. First, these countries have had strong economic growth over the last 30 years, and they now play very important roles in world trade.[2] Second, this economic success has drawn attention to their industrial relations practices as some analysts argue that these industrial relations systems *caused* their high economic growth. The industrial relations systems in Japan and Germany are widely discussed as models that might be appropriate for other countries. Third, Japan and Germany warrant special attention because their industrial relations practices are so different—both from each other and from the practices that exist in the United States. Thus they nicely illustrate the diversity that exists in industrial relations.

This chapter also considers the key international industrial relations issues that have emerged in recent years—the effects of firms that operate in more than one country (multinationals), the integration of the

European Economic Community, and the role of labor in the political democratization that is occurring in countries such as Poland and Korea. The final section of this chapter examines whether it is feasible to import the industrial relations practices of other countries into the United States.

Industrial Relations in Germany

The distinguishing feature of industrial relations in Germany is the presence of **codetermination.**[3] Codetermination procedures are mandated by German federal law and apply to all enterprises in the country whether or not employees in those enterprises belong to unions.

Codetermination

There are two key parts to German codetermination: employee representation on company boards and works councils.[4] Codetermination provides a parallel form of representation to employees that is in addition to the union representation available to German workers. At the same time, although codetermination and collective bargaining procedures are formally distinct forms of worker representation, there are many close connections between the operation of these two channels of representation and the individuals involved in each.

Board Representation   German federal law mandates that employees elect representatives to the **supervisory boards** of all German companies.[5] The number of representatives elected to the supervisory board by employees varies by the size of the firm and the industry (special provisions cover the coal and steel industries). Exhibit 14–2 describes the various codetermination requirements and the number of employees affected by these procedures. To understand the implications of these procedures it is helpful to examine the nature of German company board structure.

German firms have a two-tiered board structure. The supervisory board (*Aufsichtsrat*) is the higher ranked board and has the responsibility to control managerial performance and appoint top managers. The lower managing board (*Vorstund*) runs the firm on a day-to-day basis and implements most managerial decisions.

Employee representatives to the supervisory board are elected proportionately from the ranks of blue- and white-collar employees. The law also reserves two or three (depending on the size of the board) of the supervisory board seats for union delegates. In impasse situations, the chair of the supervisory board (the chair is nominated by shareholders) can vote to break the tie. Employee representatives on the supervisory board often run on slates associated with particular unions and are often active in unions (and frequently are union officials).

Exhibit 14–2   **Codetermination Rights in Germany**

Form of Codetermination	Sector	No. of Employees Covered (millions)
Full parity codetermination in supervisory boards and a labor director in management board; works councils	Coal and steel industries	0.6
Counterbalancing parity in supervisory boards; works councils	Large companies with more than 2000 employees	4.1
One-third of seats for employee representatives in supervisory boards; works councils	Smaller and medium-sized companies	0.9
Works councils	Other private enterprises with more than five employees	9.4
Personnel councils	Public service	3.6
No institutionalized workers' participation	Private enterprises with less than five employees	3.0

Source: Sueddeutsche Zeitung, (February 27, 1979).

The consequences of employee representation on supervisory boards varies across companies and is sometimes hard to detect. Some analysts claim that employee board representation has provided a major contribution to the low strike frequency that has been characteristic of the German industrial relations system over the post-World War II period (discussed below).

Wolfgang Streeck, for example, documented how employee representation on the Volkswagen board influenced that company's expansion into the United States. In that case employee and union involvement did not stop the company from making a major investment outside Germany, but it did alter the timing and scale of the investment.[6] In general, representation on the supervisory board appears to provide employees and unions a meaningful amount of access to and involvement in the formation of strategic business decisions.

Works Councils   The second major component of the German codetermination structure are the **works councils** mandated by federal law for all private enterprises with more than five employees. Works councils have many rights to information, consultation, and codetermination. The 1972 Works Constitution Act, for example, authorized works councils to be involved in the resolution of all of the following:

Discipline	Monitoring of employee performance
Daily working hours and breaks	
Temporary short-time or overtime work	Safety regulations
	Welfare services in the establishment
The setting of job piece rates	
Pay systems	Administration of housing for employees
Suggestion schemes	
Holiday schedules	

Works councils also codetermine any changes in the pace of work or the working environment. In the event of any major operational changes in the enterprise, the law requires that the works council and the employer negotiate over the change. If management wants to lay off employees it must negotiate with the works council and reach agreement (specified in a "social plan") on the factors that determine who gets laid off and the compensation arrangements for those who are laid off.

The works councilors are elected by all employees in a firm regardless of union affiliation. Nevertheless, works councilors usually cooperate closely with union officers or hold union office themselves. Works councils cannot call a strike, but they can sue management in a case of a breach of contractual rights.

Union Representation and Structure

Unions also play an important role in the German industrial relations system. Unions represented 41 percent of the German work force in 1989 (see Exhibit 14–3), and union membership (as a fraction of the work force) has been steady since 1960.[7] Unions provide representation through the negotiation of collective bargaining agreements and typically are actively involved in the codetermination processes, in some cases through the union activists or officers that serve either as employee representatives on a supervisory board or as works councilors.

German unions also are generally active in political and social life and issues. The largest federation of German unions, the Deutscher Gewerkschaftsbund (DGB), is closely aligned to the Social Democratic Party (SPD).[8]

Collective Bargaining in Germany Collective bargaining in Germany is generally highly centralized. Most collective agreements are reached at the industry or regional level. The most important unions in the private sector represent workers in one or more industries. IG Metall, for example, represents workers in the metal working industries.[9] German labor law does not give unions exclusive representation rights. More than one union can (and often does) represent employees at a work site, even among employees who perform similar jobs.

Exhibit 14–3

Economic and Labor Data from the European Economic Community Countries

Country	Labor Force (million)	Per Capita GDP ($)	Unionization Rate (%)	Hourly Compensation Cost in Manufacturing ($)
Belgium	4.2	11,802	70	15.68
Denmark	2.8	13,241	80	15.88
France	24.0	12,803	19	12.99
Greece	3.9	6,363	30	4.61
Ireland	1.4	7,541	45	9.86
Italy	24.0	12,254	39.6	12.87
Luxembourg	0.2	14,705	NA	10.63
Netherlands	6.0	12,252	32.5	16.30
Portugal	4.5	6,297	25	2.73
Spain	13.2	8,681	NA	8.75
United Kingdom	28.1	12,340	42.3	10.56
West Germany	28.3	13,323	41	18.07

Sources: Most of the data are for 1989. Data sources include the *Handbook of Labor Statistics* (August 1989), *Background Notes* on each EC nation published by the United States Department of State, Bureau of Public Affairs, and *Foreign Labor Trends,* U.S. Department of Labor, Bureau of International Labor Affairs. These data are reported in James B. Dworkin and Barbara A. Lee, "The Implications of Europe 1992 for Labor-Management Relations" Harry C. Katz, ed., in *The Future of Industrial Relations,* (Ithaca, NY: Institute of Collective Bargaining, 1991).

Employers are commonly represented by an employer association in industry or in regional collective bargaining.[10] Once an agreement is reached between a union and an industry association over wages and other basic employment terms, these terms are extended by law to other employees and firms in that industry. Distinctions between unionized and nonunionized workers are not allowed in collective bargaining agreements.

There are often "ordinary" collective bargaining agreements that last only one year and include pay in their terms. These ordinary agreements are signed under "framework" agreements that last for a number of years. Plant-level negotiations between the works council and management typically supplement the industry agreements.

Strike Rates in Germany Over the post-World War II period, Germany has had a lower strike frequency than the other major industrialized countries.[11] A number of hypotheses explain why this may be so. Some analysts argue that the low strike rate is a product of the conflict mediation accomplished through the codetermination system. Others say that it is possible that German workers and employers strove particularly hard to avoid strikes during this period because of their fear that strikes could bring a return to the social instability and turmoil that had occurred before the rise to power of Adolf Hitler and the Nazis. It could also be that the low strike rate is a *product* of the economic success of the German economy over the last 30 years as much as it is a *cause* of that success.

Working Time Reduction   There was a marked exception to the pattern of infrequent strikes in Germany in 1984.[12] Then there were long strikes that involved large numbers of workers in the printing and metal working industries. In those strikes unions and employers were at an impasse over the unions' demands for a reduction of weekly work hours from 40 to 35 hours without any loss in pay.

In part, unions were attracted to a reduction in the number of working hours as a device to address the high unemployment rates (particularly high by German standards) that emerged in Germany in the early 1980s. Employers claimed that such a reduction would make German goods less competitive in international trade and thereby lead to a net reduction in employment.

The 1984 strikes were eventually settled by a compromise that reduced the number of work hours to 38.5 but allowed these hours to vary during the day for different groups of workers in a plant. One of the by-products of this compromise is that it served to decentralize collective bargaining in Germany by increasing the role played by local negotiations and the works council. This is one of the ways that recent changes in German collective bargaining bear some similarity to changes under way in the U.S. industrial relations system. In both systems the workplace level of industrial relations has increased in importance.

Vocational and Apprenticeship Training

Supporting German labor management relations is a very strong vocational and **apprenticeship training** system. High school–aged youth must choose among three educational tracks around age 16: a college-bound program, an apprenticeship vocational school program, or a general education program.

Over 70 percent of high school graduates who do not go on to college enter the labor force as graduates of a vocational educational program. The apprenticeship programs in the vocational schools are overseen by a joint business-labor group that sets the qualifications for each occupational program. This system of training and certification provides German employers with a highly skilled labor force and is often cited as one of the key sources of Germany's economic success.

In summary, the German model of industrial relations stresses formal, legally mandated structures for worker representation and training; code-termination, board representation, works councils, apprenticeship training, and the extension of collective bargaining terms across all the firms in an industry. Through these formal structures, German unions and employers have achieved high levels of wages and social benefits, strong productivity performance, flexibility in the use of human resources, and low rates of strike activity.

Given the relative success of the German model, it is not surprising that its major features were extended by law to what was formerly East Germany as part of German reunification. Moreover, the transition occurred without significant opposition from either management or labor. This too attests to the high level of acceptance by German society of unions and the codetermination system.

Industrial Relations in Japan

Enterprise Unionism

The distinguishing feature of Japanese industrial relations is the central role of enterprise unions.[13] Enterprise unions in Japan represent both the white- and blue-collar employees of a firm, regardless of occupation and includes management staff. Of the firm's full-time employees, only the higher level managers do not belong to the enterprise unions. Thus foremen and line workers belong to the same enterprise union, and foremen often play a very active role in union affairs. Newly acquired employees to the firm (other than managers) automatically become union members and pay dues to the enterprise union through a dues check-off system.

Union and Employer Federations

The enterprise unions commonly are associated with industry **union federations,** which are, in turn, affiliated with union confederations.[14] Employers commonly belong to counterpart federations, the **employer federations.** Both union and employer federations provide advice and engage in political lobbying but do not become directly involved in enterprise-level collective bargaining.

Although industrial, craft, or general unions are rare in Japan, some important exceptions do exist. Furthermore, while most collective bargaining occurs at the enterprise level (between an enterprise union and the management of a firm), industry-level collective bargaining does occur in private railways, bus services, textiles, and some other cases.

The Lifetime Employment Principle

Japanese firms, particularly the large ones, tend to hire new employees upon their graduation from school (high school graduation for blue-collar workers and university graduation for managers), and the employees stay employed with that firm until they reach retirement age. This is **lifetime employment.** To avoid laying off "permanent" employees during business downturns, Japanese firms transfer workers across work areas and sometimes into training. If a large firm faces extreme financial difficulties it might also shift some of its work force to other firms in its **trading group.** The trading groups are firms linked together through either common owners or close business connections.[15] These employees are in effect loaned across companies and return to their original firm if it recovers.

The internal movement of permanent employees within and across firms is facilitated by the fact that workers receive extensive training and often rotate across jobs in a work area (or across work areas) during their work careers. This, like many of the other industrial relations practices in Japan, leads employees to strongly identify their personal interests with those of the firm.

Japanese firms can fulfill their promise to avoid laying off "permanent" employees because they also employ large numbers of workers on a part-time or temporary basis. These workers then fall outside the lifetime employment system.

In addition, workers retire relatively early in Japanese firms. Traditionally the average retirement age was 55; today it has risen to 60 in the face of declines in the number of new workers entering the Japanese work force.

Many employees promoted to supervisory and/or management were previously union members and some were union leaders. Furthermore, the movement between union and management careers can go both ways. When conducting an interview with a vice-president of the Honda Motor Workers Union a few years ago, one of the authors was struck to discover that this person had at one point been a manager at Honda and after serving in a management personnel staff job had decided to run for union office. This practice is not uncommon.[16]

Lifetime employment is not guaranteed through a contractual clause or any other binding agreement between Japanese firms and their workers or unions. Rather, firms *promise* to try to avoid layoffs. Firms do lay off workers if they are faced by extreme financial pressures, however. This informal arrangement is typical of Japanese industrial relations. Few of the distinguishing features of the Japanese system are the products of legal requirements, nor do they appear in formal contractual language. Instead, Japanese practices are shaped heavily by norms and customs that have built up over the years.

The enterprise union system just described is typical of large firms in Japan; by some estimates it covers one-third of the Japanese work force. But this system is found to a lesser extent in small and medium-sized firms, even though smaller firms often serve as supplier or subcontractor to a large firm.[17] Wages, for example, are typically 15 to 30 percent lower in the small firms, and there is less employment security.

Pay Determination in Japan

Most pay agreements are set in annual negotiations that occur between a firm and the enterprise union. Many pay negotiations occur in the spring as part of the annual national spring offensive (*Shunto*). In this offensive enterprise unions and managements consider guidelines issued by their respective union and employer associations and give special attention to wage settlements reached in negotiations at a handful of key firms.

Workers typically are paid on a salary basis. Workers also commonly receive annual bonuses that are on the order of five months' salary, although the exact size of the annual bonus varies somewhat in response to the firm's financial performance and management's assessment of individual worker performance.

Workers' pay grades are heavily influenced by an individual's seniority with the firm. **Seniority-based pay** in combination with the lifetime employment system produces a pay system with a heavy role for age. Thus workers who perform identical jobs can receive pay rates that vary significantly as a function of their age and performance appraisal.

Performance Appraisal   The fact that blue-collar workers receive regular **performance appraisals** (many workers are assessed twice a year) is another important feature of Japanese industrial relations. In a given year a worker who receives a top performance evaluation can receive up to a 10 percent larger pay increase than a worker who receives a poor performance appraisal. Over a worker's career these appraisal-based pay differences can add up and produce sizable differences in pay levels across employees. A worker's promotion and career path will also be heavily influenced by the cumulative effects of performance appraisals.

In the United States, in contrast, while many nonunion firms regularly appraise the performance of their employees, it is very rare (virtually unheard of) for blue-collar workers to undergo performance appraisals in traditional unionized settings.

Broad Job Definitions   Jobs in Japan tend to be defined relatively broadly on the shop floor even for blue-collar workers. Such broad **job definitions** go along with the practice of rotating workers across tasks and the provision of substantial training to the work force. In addition, the strong links between pay rates and worker age and individual performance lessen the role exercised by job task in pay determination. Some analysts argue that the breadth of job definitions contributes significantly to the flexibility in the Japanese production system.[18]

The Role of Consultation in Japanese Industrial Relations

The labor relations system in Japan relies heavily on informal **consultation** between labor and management to settle disputes. Grievance and arbitration procedures are often included in enterprise-level collective bargaining agreements, but these procedures are rarely used. Instead, grievances are typically settled through consultation at the work shop level. In addition, consultation over broader issues commonly occurs in labor-management committees that operate at the plant and company level. Workers also have input into shop floor production issues through the quality circles that often meet regularly.[19]

Union strength in these labor-management discussions is directly related to their membership and independence from management influence. One of the troubling issues confronting Japanese unions is declining membership. Union density in Japan stood at around 35 percent of the labor force from the early 1950s on through 1973. Since then, union membership (as a percentage of the work force) has fallen to 25.9 percent as of 1989. Some analysts wonder if this decline is an inevitable product of enterprise unionism.

Debates continue about the extent to which enterprise unions are truly independent from management influence. This arises as an issue not only because of the enterprise nature of union structure but also because of the heavy role played by labor-management consultation in the Japanese system. Critics see in this consultation the cooptation of independent unionism, whereas others see an industrial relations system that successfully mediates conflict as it provides gains in the form of high levels of employee commitment, economic growth, pay, and employment security.

Industrial Relations in Multinational Firms

A **multinational firm** engages in economic activity in more than one country. Over the last 40 years multinational firms have expanded greatly, to the point that they now assert a major influence on world commerce and the conduct of industrial relations in nearly every country.[20] This section considers why and the extent to which industrial relations in a multinational firm is different from that in a firm that operates solely in one country.

The framework developed in earlier parts of this book can be used to understand how industrial relations works in a multinational firm. The basic nature of the conflict between labor and management and the logic of how the environment affects the bargaining process and bargaining outcomes is not fundamentally altered because a firm operates in more than one country. Furthermore, it also makes sense to distinguish between strategic, middle, and workplace levels of industrial relations in multinational firms just as we can in firms that are solely "domestic." Thus, the three-tiered framework applies to multinational firms.

Problems Created by Multinationals for Management and Labor

A firm's operation in more than one country does add pressures to the conduct of industrial relations. The most important factors are the extensive cultural, legal, and institutional differences that multinational firms face and the bargaining power advantages that multinational operation provides to management.

For management, the key decision that emerges from the diverse political and social institutions that they face in different countries is how much to centralize the direction of industrial relations. At one extreme, industrial relations management can be centralized in the corporate offices of the multinational. Alternatively, local management in each country in which the multinational operates can be allowed to independently direct industrial relations.

For labor, the key problem created by multinationals is responding to the bargaining power advantage that management gains from its ability to shift production and capital across country boundaries in the multinational firm.

The Pressure of Diversity   The management of a multinational enterprise confronts cultural, legal, and institutional diversity. Cultural diversity arises from the fact that workers in different countries often view work differently, attach different meanings to work, and place different demands on their unions.[21]

Of course, management in *any* firm faces some diversity across workers in their culture and attitudes toward work. Some workers are concerned most about their pensions, whereas others may be most concerned about their current income and pay little attention to deferred compensation. Some workers have strong work ethics and would like to work on their own, whereas others may need constant supervision. The extent of this cultural diversity widens, however, as the firm crosses national boundaries. As a result, for example, compensation policies that work in one country may be inappropriate in another. Or, communication and motivation techniques that succeed in one culture will fail in another.[22]

There is also wide diversity in the legal regulation of industrial relations and employment conditions and the institutions shaping industrial relations across countries. In some countries, for example, national laws recognize workers' rights to form unions and carry out strikes; in other countries unions are outlawed or dominated by the government. In some countries the national government extensively regulates the substance of employment conditions. Commonly in Europe, for example, national governments stipulate employee rights to challenge dismissal (and government labor courts hear such cases), whereas, as we have discussed, in the United States in the nonunion sector employment at will is the rule.

The labor movement also differs markedly in its ideology and form across countries. In European countries, for example, labor unions are often affiliated with a particular political party. In France, the two most important unions and their political affiliations are, respectively, the CGT (affiliated with the Communist Party) and the CFDT (affiliated with the Socialist Party). By contrast, in the United States (and some other countries) unions are not formally linked to any political party.

Furthermore, the structure of unions differs markedly across countries. In Germany, for example, IG Metall represents workers across firms in metal working industries such as auto, steel, machine tools, and electronics. In contrast, in Canada (as in the United States) there are a variety of craft and industrial unions and only a few unions (such as the Teamsters and SEIU) that include workers from a number of industries.[23]

The Degree of Industrial Relations Centralization   The presence of so much diversity in culture, law, and institutions poses control and coordination problems for the multinational firm. Management's problem is how to pursue companywide objectives through industrial relations policies in the face of all the diversity that arises across the multinational firm. Traditionally, multinational firms responded to this problem by maintaining a high degree of local control (decentralization) in the direction of industrial relations.[24] Analysts of multinational firms, in fact, generally conclude that the administration of industrial relations is more decentralized than other management functions such as finance or marketing.

Multinationals found that there were substantial benefits to be gained from the decentralization of industrial relations. These benefits include the ability to respond flexibly to the diversity discussed above. By allowing local managers in each country to fashion industrial relations policies, these managers could create policies and procedures that fit with local conditions and events.

In recent years, however, multinational firms have begun to increase the central control and administration of industrial relations. Centralization of a corporate function has always had the advantage of providing consistency and scale economies. Yet diversity in local environments overwhelmed these advantages in the past.

Why then the switch to more centralized control? The explanation appears to lie in the fact that multinational firms are becoming more global in their strategies and organizational form.[25] The emergence of global firms leads management to strive to integrate their internal operations and policies. If production across national boundaries is integrated, for example, it makes less sense for the multinational firm to maintain wide variation in industrial relations policies.

This trend provides another illustration of one of the central themes of this book—namely, that managements are increasingly striving to link industrial relations more closely to business strategy. Increased globalization induces multinational firms to first develop particular business strategies and then align their production and industrial relations systems with those business strategies. This is not very different from the pressures at work in domestic firms. The special dilemma for industrial relations managers in the multinationals, however, is that culture, law, and institutions retain much of their international diversity at the same time that globalization has increased the premium on coordination and centralization.

The Power Advantage Provided to Management by Multinational Operation

The expansion of economic activity across national boundaries poses a bargaining power disadvantage for workers and unions. Multinational operation allows management to shift production and capital across national borders and raises the competitive pressures facing the work force. The concepts discussed earlier in this book illustrate how this can happen.

If faced by a strike in their operations in one country, management can gain a bargaining power advantage from multinational operation if it can turn to alternative production facilities in other countries or substitute workers in other countries for those out on strike. In many ways, the expansion of the firm across multinational boundaries is an extension of the same forces that were at work in early industrialization. As John Commons noted, the expansion of markets in early industrialization created "competitive menaces" for workers and weakened the bargaining leverage of unions.

Multinational operation confronts workers with new competitive menaces. Imagine, for example, the pressures faced by high-paid western European (or North American) workers because multinational firms operating in their countries can shift production to countries in which workers receive hourly wages that are a fraction of those received in western Europe (or North America).

The primary way a union could counter the advantages management gains from the expansion of markets is to expand the union's jurisdiction so it is coextensive with the boundaries of the multinational. If this were accomplished, the resulting **multinational unionism** would be better able to remove competition across workers in the different locations in which the multinational operates.

Multinational Unionism

In the United States at the start of the twentieth century unions expanded their jurisdiction by shifting from local or regional unions to become national unions.[26] How successful have unions been at following a similar strategy and becoming multinational? This section examines that issue.

The expansion of firms across national boundaries creates strong incentives for unions to expand their jurisdiction across national boundaries and create multinational unions. Even though there are some examples of multinational unions or at least the coordination of policies of national unions, overall, their occurrence has been infrequent.[27] Let us consider why this has been so and then look at some counter-examples.

The Difficulties Unions Face   Unions have found it difficult to become multinational because of the wide diversity that exists across countries in culture, law, and institutions as discussed above.[28] It is difficult enough for a union operating in one country to maintain cohesion and solidarity across its members. When the economic and cultural differences, communication difficulties, and fears that exist across workers in different countries are added on top of the normal problems, the maintenance of solidarity becomes a nearly insurmountable problem.

Consider the problems that multinational operation in less developed as well as highly industrialized countries creates for union solidarity. Workers in a less developed country, who earn low wages and face few employment alternatives, are generally very reluctant to support the bargaining demands of their high-wage counterparts in developed countries. There are strong short-run incentives for the workers in these two countries to view each other as competitors.

Furthermore, imagine how hard it is for a union to communicate to its members if those members speak a variety of languages. Indeed, the managers in a multinational firm typically have a lot of awareness of company objectives and worldwide activities, whereas workers and unions, in contrast, are often hard-pressed to gain information about such activities.[29]

The merger of independent unions across national borders has not been a solution to multinational pressures. The merger of independent unions is difficult enough even within a single country where there are strong bargaining power advantages to be gained. Even greater impediments exist for such a merger if it were to involve two unions based in different countries that represent workers at the same multinational firm.

It is most likely that the structure of two unions that might consider merging would not be similar even if the workers were employed by the same firm. Auto workers in the United States, for example, are represented by an industrial union (UAW), whereas auto workers in Germany belong to a union that spans industries (IG Metall). Similar problems exist even if the two unions were to merely coordinate their bargaining demands.

Examples of Multinational Unionism   Even in the face of the many impediments to international solidarity and coordination that confront unions, some multinational unionism has followed the expansion of multinational firms. There are, for example, a number of **international trade secretariats** that provide information to member unions and coordinate activities across national borders. These secretariats are autonomous agencies that cover particular industries or groups of industries. The International Metalworkers Federation, one of the most active of these secretariats, includes members from many less developed as well as highly industrialized nations. Among its many activities, it issues research reports to its members.

Many of the secretariats have a close working relationship with the International Federation of Free Trade Unions (ICFTU). The ICFTU includes affiliated unions that represent 48 million workers around the world. The ICFTU includes non-Communist unions. The World Federation of Trade Unions (WRTU) at one time represented 134 million workers in the Communist unions that were affiliated with it.[30] Nevertheless, the political differences that traditionally separated these federations and many of their member unions have impeded coordination across these and other union federations.

There also are some cases in which unions in different countries have coordinated their response to the actions taken by a particular multinational firm. Box 14–1 describes two recent situations in which unions in different countries cooperated in putting pressure on a multinational firm.

The potential integration of the European market has been a spur to joint union activities. The next section discusses these developments as they are both important in their own right and informative of the issues involved in multinational unionism.

European Integration, 1992

December 31, 1992, is the deadline set by the 12 nations that make up the **European Economic Community** (EEC) to become a single economic market.[31] The integration of Europe (or steps made toward integration even if the deadline is not met) will have major consequences on industrial relations, and industrial relations issues likely will influence the form of integration. This section reviews the history of **European integration** and the industrial relations issues that have surfaced.

The Goals of Integration

A central goal of European 1992 integration is to eliminate trade barriers across the 12 member states of the European Economic Community and to allow the free movement of workers across national borders. Economic integration will remove explicit trade restrictions and tariffs and create greater standardization in government regulations over such matters as products and taxes. Labor relations and other employment laws and policies, now vastly different across the 12 countries, are to be

Box 14–1

Displays of Union Solidarity across National Borders

Case 1: Janitors and the World Bank

The Service Employees International Union (SEIU) enlisted the aid of the International Federation of White Collar Workers (FIET) to mount worldwide pressure on the World Bank in Washington, D.C. to organize 250 janitors. FIET's membership totals 9 million members in 94 countries. FIET joined forces with 276 affiliated unions in the United Kingdom, Japan, West Germany, and France to pressure the World Bank to bargain with the janitors. Through a number of measures the unions in various countries publicized the janitors' claims and sought to embarrass the World Bank, an organization concerned with its public image.

Case 2: The UFCW v. Delhaize Corporation

Local 400 of the United Food and Commercial Workers (UFCW) was involved in a dispute with an American subsidiary of the Delhaize Corporation in North Carolina over labor relations policies of its Food Lion subsidiary. The dispute centered around the union's contention that Delhaize paid substandard wages and provided few benefits to its employees. The union struck in an effort to gain competitive wages and benefits. In an unusual display of solidarity between a French and a U.S. union, the Syndicat des Employes Techniciens et Cadres (SETCA) initiated a series of unannounced work stoppages in France as a show of solidarity to the United Food and Commercial Workers.

Source: The two cases are discussed in the *Daily Labor Report* (Washington, D.C.: Bureau of National Affairs): October 25, 1988, pp. A11–12; November 11, 18, 1988, pp. A4–A5.

"harmonized" in accordance with directives and regulations issued by the bodies governing the European Economic Community.[32]

For both labor and management, **harmonization** could bring a host of costs and benefits.[33] Because so much is at stake, there already has been much disagreement over the exact content and form of labor harmonization. To date, there has been only modest progress by the EEC in specifying how and around what standard industrial relations will be integrated, and it is likely that this will continue to be the focus of much debate and controversy in the years ahead.

Pre-1992 Structure of Industrial Relations in the EEC

The regulation of industrial relations and employment conditions varies widely across the 12 EEC member nations. The labor movements in the countries also vary substantially in their ideological orientation, organizational structure, and strength.

Unionization rates of the 12 countries were presented in Exhibit 14–3. Compared to the United States, many of the EEC nations are highly unionized, yet, as these figures show, there is wide variation. For example, France has a unionization rate of 19 percent, whereas 80 percent of the Denmark work force and 70 percent of the Belgium work forces are unionized.

Living standards and hourly labor rates also differ markedly across the countries, as reported in Exhibit 14–3. West Germany's hourly labor costs ($18.07), for example, are substantially greater than those in Greece ($4.61) and Portugal ($2.73). It is these wage differences that are at the root of the labor movement's fears that 1992 integration could lead to a lowering of labor standards in Germany and other high-wage countries.

There also are substantial differences in the industrial relations laws and practices in the 12 nations. In Germany, for example (as discussed earlier in this chapter), federal law mandates an elaborate system of works councils and employee representation on corporate boards (also required in Luxemborg and Denmark). In Ireland, in contrast, there are no formal legal requirements for works councils or employee representation on corporate boards.[34]

The structure of union representation also varies substantially across countries. In Spain, for example, unions within a single industry tend to be divided along political lines (this is also characteristic of France). In Germany, Belgium, and Denmark unions often span industries.

EEC Regulation of the "Social Dimension"

There has been heated debate among representatives from the 12 nations and between labor and management over what is often referred to as the **social dimension** of European integration. The social dimension includes the regulations, directives, and possible eventual laws that will govern employment and industrial relations policies in the 12 EEC countries. The EEC already has adopted a variety of health and safety standards, provisions to encourage labor mobility across national borders, and special commissions to address these issues.

Three directives that address worker rights in the event of layoffs, employer bankruptcies, or the sale or merger of a company have been adopted by the EEC. These directives require member nations to change their laws, if necessary, to conform to the intent of the directive.[35] Other directives have been proposed and hotly debated, but, as of this writing, no other directives have been adopted, a fact that reflects the differences of opinion that persist across countries and between labor and management.

Perhaps the most controversial was the "Vredling Directive," proposed but then tabled in 1983. This directive would have required employers to inform and consult workers before making any important decisions.[36] A second stalled proposal would have required that workers be given seats on boards of directors of companies operating in the EEC.

A major event in EEC regulation of the social dimension was the issuance of a **Social Charter** in May 1989.[37] Box 14–2 lists the basic topics addressed by the Social Charter. The charter includes giving workers the right to form and join unions and the ability to resort to collective action (i.e., strikes) in the event of conflicts of interests (this right is presently mandated by law by many, but not all, of the EEC countries). The Social Charter is a declaration of principles without legal force and leaves it up to member countries to develop specific policies. The charter extends an apparent retreat by the EEC from strict harmonization of labor standards and the avoidance of central regulation of industrial relations issues.

The exact terms of regulation of the social dimension that emerges from integration of the EEC market remain to be seen. There is much debate that will transpire as the December 1992 deadline is approached. Furthermore, the implementation of directives, charters, or other regulations will be heavily influenced by subsequent actions taken by governments within the respective countries, as well as by the actions taken by unions and managements.

Box 14–2

EEC Social Charter Summary: Fundamental Social Rights—Title I

1. The right to freedom of movement

2. The right to free choice of occupation and fair remuneration

3. The right to improved living and working conditions

4. The right to social protection

5. The right of freedom of association and collective bargaining

6. The right to vocational training

7. The right of men and women to equal treatment

8. The right of workers to information, consultation, and participation

9. The right to health protection and safety at the workplace

10. The protection of children and adolescents

11. The protection of the rights of elderly and disabled persons

Source: James B. Duorkin and Barbara A. Lee, "The Implications of Europe 1992," in Harry C. Katz, ed., *The Future of Industrial Relations* (Ithaca, NY: Institute of Collective Bargaining, 1991).

Labor's Concerns about Integration

Unions are particularly worried that the harmonization of labor standards will bring a lowering of labor standards. In this way European unions are reflecting fears similar to those held by American trade unionists as they confronted the expansion of markets, transportation, and communication systems across the United States at the start of the twentieth century. As Commons and others pointed out, unions' fears of the competition created by expanding markets are well founded.

At the same time, the heightened trade and associated economic development that may follow from market integration could provide benefits to labor. Large gains may be received by workers and unions in the countries that currently have lower labor standards if integration leads to greater investments in those countries.

The steps being taken to centrally regulate industrial relations in the integrated market also provide the possibility of union gains. Through European integration and the creation of a strong oversight regulation provided by the EEC, unions might be able to raise labor standards to levels they were unable to otherwise accomplish. This is the primary reason why, for example, the British unions favor European integration. Many of the directives (adopted or proposed) and the Social Charter extend aspects of the employee and union representation now provided in Germany to countries that have not on their own seen fit to extend such rights.

So, it is not clear that unions (or workers) will necessarily lose from market integration. Much depends on how market integration is regulated.

Management Concerns over Europe 1992

Managements operating in either one country or multinationally stand to benefit from the reduction in trade restrictions that will come with market integration.[38] In the pre-1992 economic system, multinational corporations confront a myriad of regulations and a variety of industrial relations practices in the countries in which they operate. Market integration, therefore, could greatly simplify the management of industrial relations across the EEC countries. Integration also could greatly increase the flexibility within corporate operations by easing the movement of people and operations across national boundaries. European managers see 1992 as offering their firms more strategic options as to where to locate and what business and labor relations strategies to pursue. They hope this will bring increased managerial discretion.

At the same time, management in Europe (and in multinationals headquartered outside of Europe) are worried about the possible restrictions and heightened labor costs that might follow from increased EEC regulation of industrial relations. Management's fears here are the reciprocal of the labor worries discussed above.

Management would like to have greater freedom to move workers and capital, in part to achieve greater flexibility and to take advantage of the lower costs found in some of the EEC countries. Yet the integration of markets simultaneously has created a centralized regulatory process that might give unions and workers bargaining leverage to counter management's moves. Management's worry and the union's hope is that EEC centralized regulation accomplishes what in other situations is attained by labor through collective negotiations between an individual employer and a union.

This explains some of the motivation for management to oppose the Vredling Directive and many others of the proposals being debated. Management generally prefers that the regulation of industrial relations and employment conditions be left to the member nations or to the parties at the firm level and that centralized regulations be avoided.

Industrial Relations in Developing Countries

Even with the diversity in the industrial relations practices and institutions found in the United States, Japan, and the EEC countries, there are still many similarities among them. In all these countries, for instance, national laws give workers the right to join unions and these unions have the right to strike.[39] Furthermore, although the exact terms of union-government and union-management relations vary across the countries, in all the countries labor unions are independent from government or management dominance. Unions are independent in the sense that they generally exercise free will and conduct democratic elections to determine union leadership and union policies.

Workers and labor unions do not possess such rights in countries that lack democratic governments and political pluralism. In these countries, in contrast, workers are denied the right to join unions. If unions exist at all, they are typically dominated by the government and/or employers. Yet history suggests that the outlawing or dominance of independent trade unions does not eliminate labor conflict, and in some ways only postpones and intensifies it. In the end, all countries are forced to wrestle with how to structure industrial relations in a manner that provides workers with enough representation at least to satisfy those workers while also maintaining social stability and economic growth.

In the 1980s and early 1990s these issues have come to the fore as **democratization** movements arose in many developing countries. The next sections review developments in Poland and Korea, countries with very different cultures and histories. At the same time, these two countries nicely illustrate how the labor movement and industrial relations issues are at the center of the democratization processes.

Industrial Relations and Political Change in Poland

In July 1980 the Polish government announced steep price increases in basic foodstuffs for the third time in a 10-year period. In 1980, as in 1970 and 1976, workers responded with protests, but unlike the previous two occasions, the strikers did not return to work after the government agreed to repeal the price increases. Rather, the workers at the Lenin Shipyard, under the leadership of Lech Walesa, demanded the right to establish a free and independent trade union. After a two-week sit-in strike and intensive public negotiations, the trade union **Solidarity** was born.

Throughout the remainder of 1980 and 1981, the government came under increasing pressure from the Soviet Union and elements of the Communist Party to erode the power of Solidarity. The union, in turn, persisted in its attempts to enforce the spirit of the Gdańsk accords, and at its national congress in August 1981 went one step further by supporting the cause of free trade unionism throughout the socialist bloc. The months after the congress were marked by a further deterioration of the Polish economy and growing tension between the trade union and the government. The crisis of authority culminated in the imposition of martial law, the imprisonment of Solidarity leaders, and the repeal of the union's legal mandate.

In the years that followed martial law, the government's attempts to implement economic reform were undermined by the absence of a social accord. Refusing to allow the emergence of consultative institutions, yet recognizing the need for societal consensus, the government decided to hold a popular referendum in the fall of 1987 to legitimate its economic reform program. Despite the government campaign, the proposed referendum was voted down.

Without a comprehensive program for restructuring the Polish economy, it was only a matter of time before a restive work force would once again attempt to organize. Indeed, in the spring and summer after the failed referendum, workers in a number of key industrial establishments went on strike. Despite the determination of the striking workers, the government did not yield to their demands. Finally, after the intervention of Lech Walesa, the strikers returned to work with the understanding that the relegalization of Solidarity would be Walesa's central demand at the upcoming "roundtable" discussions.

After a number of false starts, Solidarity and government representatives finally began the roundtable talks in February 1989, and two months later an accord was reached. Under the terms of the roundtable agreement, Solidarity was allowed to register as a trade union, and a new constitution was to be introduced which included the establishment of a democratically elected Senate and a restructured parliament. In June 1989 Solidarity candidates were swept into office, paving the way for Poland's transition to a market economy. Then in December 1990 Lech

Walesa won a landslide victory in Poland's first direct presidential elections.

Severe challenges confront the Polish economy and Poland's political leadership. By the year 1991 there were signs that Poland's transition to a market economy would involve severe economic dislocation. The unemployment rate was rising and industrial output was falling. Solidarity also faces challenges as it attempts to work with a government whose rise to power was the result of support received from the trade union movement. Solidarity is torn between its desire to provide political leadership while remaining independent of the government in a new pluralistic Poland.

Industrial Relations and Political Change in Korea

Trade unions in Korea have not attained the status and strong political role acquired by Solidarity. Rather, Korea is struggling with the issue of how far to democraticize its political system and the role that trade unions and collective bargaining will play in Korean society.

The post-World War II history of Korea is marked by authoritarian rule by governments in league with the military. Nevertheless, periodically, violent political protests have erupted to challenge that rule.[40] Labor unions have played leading roles in those political protests. At the same time, collective bargaining has not been allowed to take hold as the government regularly has either dominated unions, outlawed strikes, or imposed wage settlements.[41]

In the middle of 1987 there was another upsurge in protests and strikes. This upsurge began when the ruling Democratic Justice's Party presidential candidate (and eventual victor in a subsequent election), Roh Tae-Woo, pledged his support for popular elections to determine a new president of the Republic of Korea. The subsequent democratization process unleashed popular protests and demands among Koreans, particularly within the trade union movement.

A massive strike wave followed, along with a rapid rise in union membership and a wage explosion. On May 2, 1990, for example, there were violent protests in the port city of Ulsan when 30,000 workers from affiliated Hyundai companies held rallies at work sites to protest a massive police raid that had occurred earlier on strikers at the Hyundai Heavy Industries Company.

Worker protests were in part directed at existing trade unions and union leaders. There was an array of unions affiliated with the Korean Federation of Trade Unions. Yet protesting workers opposed the complicity that had existed between these unions and the government and employers. Protesting workers not only demanded higher wages and better working conditions but also sought procedures that would allow the emergence of unions that were independent from government and managerial dominance. Some new unions sprang up in response to these demands, such as Chunnohyop, a new federation of independent unions, even though the government did not recognize their legitimacy.

The protest wave cooled down by mid-1990, although violent strikes continued to periodically erupt. There were also continuing debates across Korean society as to how to provide greater stability in industrial relations while at the same time meeting workers' demands for greater democratization and higher wages.

Similarities in the Issues in Poland and Korea

What is similar about events in Poland and Korea? Poland was attempting to radically transform its economy through the introduction of markets and incentives. At the same time, Poland was creating new democratic institutions to replace those that had been Communist dominated.

Meanwhile, Korea approached the issue of how to structure and stabilize industrial relations from a very different political and economic history. In Korea it was autocratic and military rule that had previously dominated and controlled the labor movement. Furthermore, Korea had undergone enormous economic growth since 1960. It was not confronted with the issue of creating a market economy.

Yet in both Poland and Korea, as in many other developing countries, how to create and sustain more democratic and stable industrial relations were major political and economic issues. In both countries, in the long run the suppression of industrial relations and independent unionism proved to be neither socially stable nor economically productive.

Should the U.S. Import Industrial Relations Practices from Abroad?

In the United States persistent trade deficits, sluggish productivity, and adversarial labor-management relations have led to an intense debate among industrial relations professionals and policy makers. The debate concerns whether the United States should import what appear to be more successful industrial relations practices found in other countries.

Can Japanese practices be transferred to the United States? Here, one confronts the question of the origins of the Japanese system. On the one side stand those who claim that the development (or success) of the Japanese industrial relations system is a product of the particular culture that exists in Japan. The claim is that it is either worker homogeneity or the willingness to sacrifice personal goals for group objectives that makes the Japanese industrial relations system possible. On the other side in this debate are those who assert that Japanese practices can be used in other countries and do not require the presence of any particular pre-existing work or social culture.

Recent developments in the United States suggest that at least some of the Japanese practices appear to be transferable. The auto plants operating in the United States that are owned by Japanese parent companies (the Japanese transplants), for example, use some Japanese work practices and maintain very high product quality and labor productivity.[42]

In this debate we are also heavily swayed by those who point to the role played by historical factors in the evolution of Japanese industrial relations. The Japanese industrial relations system, for example, did not take on many of its now widespread features until after World War II. Furthermore, the introduction of new practices in Japan after the war occurred after militant unions were defeated in a series of strikes in the early and mid-1950s.[43] Many of these strikes culminated in the purging of union militants and their replacement with more moderate leadership. This suggests to us that while culture may influence the form and operation of the Japanese industrial relations system, that system does not depend on a particular worker culture.

There also is much debate about the virtues of the practices found in other countries. Some argue, for example, that industrial relations practices provide little positive contribution to the economic success of Japan or other countries. Others claim that even though economically successful, industrial relations practices in Japan or elsewhere are not attractive because of their alleged adverse social or political consequences.[44]

But suppose one believes that foreign practices can and should be imported. The question then turns on whether *individual* industrial relations practices can be imported or whether a *whole system* needs to be imported from the start.

One position in the debate over the importation of foreign practices is that all managers and labor leaders should constantly be looking globally for the *best* practice. After looking globally, managers can then implement innovative practices that work elsewhere as quickly as possible to avoid falling behind in international competition.

Yet, to get imported industrial relations practices to work well, it may be necessary to import other social and economic practices. This debate is illustrated below with two issues: (1) the quality circles (QC's) and team forms of work organization commonly found in Japan, and (2) the works council and codetermination system found in Germany.

The Debate over Quality Circles and Work Teams

The introduction of quality circles and team systems became the biggest management fad of the 1980s. Much of the impetus for the widespread experimentation in American firms with quality circles and team forms of work organization was the success Japanese firms experienced with these practices. Yet many of the resulting quality circle and team programs failed or achieved limited success in the United States.

Much of this failure was due to the fact that the relationship between the QC's or team structures and other industrial relations and management practices were not fully understood or appreciated. Management, for example, raced to introduce quality circles and team meetings, but failed to grant real authority to participants in these new groups. When at some sites workers saw the suggestions that arose out of QC or team meetings ignored, they became cynical about the new participatory processes.

Even when shop floor industrial relations procedures were modified by quality circles or teams, often gains were limited by continued adherence to traditional management methods at higher levels of firms. At some sites workers became disillusioned with QC's or teams when they saw management outsource an operation and allow little worker or union input into such a decision.

These experiences lent support to the critics of importing foreign practices. Some concluded from these failures that to succeed, quality circles and teams required implementation of the full Japanese system including practices such as lifetime employment, seniority-based pay, and enterprise unionism.

Some QC and work team experiments did succeed in the United States, and they continue to evolve. Success came to QC's and team systems where other industrial relations practices gradually changed so as to accommodate and support new practices. In this way American labor and management did not simply imitate or apply the "foreign" practice. Rather, foreign practices were modified to fit with American practices. The gradual expansion in the worker participation process at Xerox described in Chapter 12 illustrates how this has been done.

A key lesson from this experience is that one need not try to adopt an entire system of labor-management relations to benefit from the experience of others. But neither can one simply pick a single practice and introduce it without recognizing that changes in other practices are required for successful adaptation.

The Debate over Works Councils and Codetermination

A similar debate is now emerging over whether German-style works councils or employee representation on company boards of directors should be adopted in the United States. There already is some movement toward German-style codetermination in the new participatory practices that are emerging in some unionized settings in the United States (see Chapter 12).

Will the United States experiments blossom and spread to the point that a full-fledged variant of codetermination emerges? It is difficult to see how codetermination could emerge *incrementally* since codetermination (at least of the German form) entails legally mandated procedures. It appears to us that at some point major changes in American labor and corporate legislation would be required.

Perhaps codetermination will someday come to the United States. If it does, we would bet that what will emerge will not be a carbon copy of the German system, but, rather, Americanized arrangements that fit within our industrial relations system. Over time our system would likely be altered in this process in ways that are hard to foresee.

Summary

There are substantial differences in the way industrial relations are practiced in Germany, Japan, and the United States. In the United States collective bargaining is relatively decentralized and the written collective bargaining agreement plays a central role. The American collective bargaining system is also noteworthy for its heavy reliance on grievance and arbitration procedures.

In Germany, by contrast, codetermination procedures are central. These procedures provide employees with parallel representation from unions and works councils. Collective bargaining in Germany usually occurs on a regional or industrial basis and produces annual labor agreements.

In Japan, enterprise unions are dominant, and these unions represent both blue- and white-collar employees in a firm. Disputes tend to be settled and information exchanged through a variety of consultative procedures. Worker seniority and the economic performance of the firm influence worker earnings, and annual bonuses are an important share of worker compensation.

Interest in international comparisons of management and labor practices is currently at an all-time high. Interest has been spurred in part by the expansion of multinational firms. The process of collective bargaining and the determinants of bargaining power do not change fundamentally as a firm moves multinational. Yet unions generally see their bargaining leverage weakened as firms expand production across country borders.

Interest in comparative industrial relations also has been stimulated by the changes occurring throughout Europe and in the democratization movements under way in many developing nations. All countries must wrestle with the issue of how to structure industrial relations. Some governments choose to suppress collective bargaining. Experience suggests this inevitably leads to social conflict.

The problems that are now confronting the U.S. labor movement have led a number of union leaders to look abroad in general, and to Europe in particular, for new ideas. Business leaders, too, are increasingly convinced that they must look globally for innovative ideas.

In the future all industrial relations professionals will be expected to be well versed in both domestic and international industrial relations practices. Yet, importing ideas from other countries without careful thought is exceedingly dangerous. For successful innovation, imported practices must be meshed with domestic practices.

Discussion Questions

1. Briefly describe how codetermination works in Germany.

2. Describe three significant ways industrial relations in Japan differ from industrial relations in the United States.

3. What are some of the factors that make it difficult for unions to coordinate their efforts across national borders?

4. Why are some unionists worried about European integration? What are some of management's concerns about European integration?

Suggested Readings

Bamber, Greg J., and Russel D. Landsbury, eds. *International and Comparative Industrial Relations* (London: Allen & Unwin, 1987).

Berghahn, Volker R., and Detlev Karsten. *Industrial Relations in West Germany* (Oxford: Berg Publisher, 1987).

Cole, Robert E. *Japanese Blue Collar* (Berkeley and Los Angeles: University of California Press, 1971).

Cusumano, Michael. *The Japanese Automobile Industry* (Cambridge, MA: Harvard University Press, 1986).

Flanagan, Robert J., and Arnold R. Weber, eds. *Bargaining without Boundaries* (Chicago: University of Chicago Press, 1974).

Gladwin, Thomas N., and Ingo Walter. *Multinationals under Fire* (New York: Wiley, 1980).

End Notes

1. Throughout this chapter we refer to Germany even though some of the history recounted refers to the history of West Germany. With the unification of Germany the national laws of West Germany were extended to what was previously East Germany, including laws about industrial relations. Needless to say, unification has brought substantial changes to industrial relations practices and institutions in what was formerly East Germany.

2. From 1960 to 1980 the annual rate of growth in productivity in manufacturing in the United States, Germany, and Japan was, respectively, 2.7, 5.4, and 9.4 percent. See Patricia Capdevielle and Donato Alvarez, "International Comparisons

of Trends in Productivity and Labor Costs," *Monthly Labor Review* 104 (December 1981), p. 16.

3.   This section draws heavily from Friedrich Fuerstenberg, "Industrial Relations in the Federal Republic of Germany," in *International and Comparative Industrial Relations,* Greg J. Bamber and Russell D. Landsbury, eds. (London: Allen & Unwin, 1987), pp. 165–186.

4.   The major federal laws establishing the codetermination structure were the Codetermination Acts of 1951 and 1976. At the same time, there were long historical traditions to this system. Works councils were first established by law in 1916, in industries that were important for the economy in the First World War, and they became obligatory under the Works Council Act of 1920. See Fuerstenberg, "Industrial Relations in the Federal Republic of Germany," for more on this history.

5.   Supervisory boards generally meet four times a year.

6.   Volkswagen initially planned to open an American car assembly plant and stamping facility right at the time when layoffs were spreading within German auto plants. The union at Volkswagen became involved in this decision through board representation and opposed the initial plans. Volkswagen then reduced the scale of its investment and delayed the project. See Wolfgang Streeck, *Industrial Relations in West Germany* (New York: St. Martin's Press, 1984).

7.   These figures refer to union membership in West Germany alone. Union membership as a fraction of the work force since 1950 in a number of countries is reported in "Appendix," table A-17, p. 257 in Greg J. Bamber and Russell D. Landsbury, *International and Comparative Industrial Relations.*

8.   The DGB had 17 affiliated unions with 7,745,000 members as of 1983.

9.   In 1983, IG Metall had 2,536,000 members.

10.   The Confederation of German Employers' Associations (BDA) is the employer counterpart to the DGB. It includes 46 branch employer federations that engage in collective bargaining. One important exception is the negotiation of a company-wide collective bargaining agreement at Volkswagen. This is because of the special financial and legal status held by Volkswagen. See Streeck, *Industrial Relations in West Germany.*

11.   Comparative strike data are reported in "Appendix: Comparative International Data" in Greg J. Bamber and Russell D. Landsbury, *International and Comparative Industrial Relations,* table A-19, p. 258. Trade unions are required by law to poll their members, and before they call a strike, at least 75 percent of the members must vote for a strike.

12.   We are referring to events that occurred in what was then West Germany.

13.   Enterprise unions are 94.9 percent of all trade unions in Japan and represent 85.6 percent of organized employees.

14.   In 1982 labor federations in the private sector joined together to form Zenminrokyo (Japanese Private Sector Trade Union Council). Then in 1989 most private and public sector unions became affiliated with the new Rengo (Japanese

Trade Union Confederation). See *Labor-Management Relations in Japan* (Tokyo: Japan Institute of Labor, 1990), p. 19, figure 2.

15.   In earlier years these trading groups formed the *zaibatsu* that were outlawed after World War II.

16.   It remains to be seen if this sort of career movement continues in the future. It may not, due to the professionalization of managerial training and career development.

17.   The modern day extension of the traditional *zaibatsu* system often links large and small firms together into close business relations. For example, upon their retirement from the large "parent" firm, senior executives often then move on to serve as executives of one of the smaller firms in the same group.

18.   See Michael J. Piore and Charles F. Sabel, *The Second Industrial Divide* (New York: Basic Books, 1984).

19.   An informative account of life on the shop floor in Japan is provided in Robert E. Cole, *Japanese Blue Collar* (Berkeley and Los Angeles: University of California Press, 1971).

20.   On the growth of multinationals and the particular issues they pose, see Thomas N. Gladwin and Ingo Walters, *Multinationals under Fire* (New York: Wiley, 1980).

21.   See Jan H. Katz, "Cultural Issues in International Business," *Handbook of International Business,* ed. Ingo Walter (New York: Wiley, 1988) pp. 11-1–11-17.

22.   Ibid.

23.   The member local unions within the Teamsters and SEIU are craft or industrial rather than multiindustrial like IG Metall.

24.   See Duane Kujawa, "Labor Relations of U.S. Multinationals Abroad," in *Labor Relations in Advanced Industrial Societies: Issues and Problems,* ed. Benjamin Martin and Everett M. Kassalow (New York: Carnegie Endowment for Peace, 1980), pp. 15–17.

25.   See Alfred D. Chandler, Jr., "The Evolution of Modern Global Competition," in *Competition in Global Industries,* ed. Michael E. Porter (Cambridge, MA: Harvard Business School Press, 1986), pp. 405–448.

26.   See Lloyd Ulman, *The Rise of the National Trade Union* (Cambridge, MA: Harvard University Press, 1958).

27.   A study of 134 U.S.-based multinational firms found that only 10 percent of them had ever experienced labor actions taken against them across national frontiers. See David C. Hershfield, *The Multinational Union Challenges the Multinational Company* (New York: The Conference Board, 1975), p. 12.

28.   See Lloyd Ulman, "The Rise of the International Union," in *Bargaining without Boundaries,* ed. Robert J. Flanagan and Arnold R. Weber (Chicago: University of Chicago Press, 1974), pp. 37–69.

29.   For a discussion of unions' and workers' lack of information about the multinationals they bargain with, see Richard Prosten and Raymond MacDonald, "A

Union View of the Multinational Problem," in *Labor Relations in Advanced Industrial Societies: Issues and Problems,* ed. Benjamin Martin and Everett M. Kasselow (New York: Carnegie Endowment for Peace, 1980), p. 8.

30.   Enormous changes are under way in the WRTU in the face of the democratization occurring in eastern Europe. Another important international union federation is the World Confederation of Labor (WCL), which includes Christian unions, representing 15 million workers worldwide.

31.   The EEC countries are listed in Exhibit 14–3.

32.   The governance structure of the European Economic Community includes a legislative, executive, and judicial branch. The European Commission is the executive branch and proposes legislation to the Council of Europe, which sends all successful legislation to the Council of Ministers for preliminary approval. The Council then sends the legislation to the European Parliament and the Economic and Social Committee for their reactions. Each nation's representatives to the European Parliament are elected directly, and representation is proportional to a nation's population. If the Council enacts legislation, it is then sent to the 12 EEC member nations for implementation. The Court of Justice enforces any treaties. For further details, see James B. Dworkin and Barbara A. Lee, "The Implications of Europe 1992" in Harry C. Katz, ed., *The Future of Industrial Relations* (Ithaca, NY: Institute of Collective Bargaining, 1991).

33.   It should be noted that EEC legislative enactments would not replace national industrial relations laws or practices. EEC legislative enactments refer to *firm-level* industrial relations only, and, thus, within the subsidiary levels of a firm, national enactments would apply. At the same time, policies *within* firms would surely be significantly affected by any EEC regulations of firm policies.

34.   A number of other EEC countries require works councils. See James B. Dworkin and Barbara A. Lee, "The Implications of Europe 1992."

35.   For example, directive 75/129, adopted in 1975, requires the employer to consult workers through their representatives, with the goal of reaching agreement on ways to avoid layoffs or methods to either reduce the number of workers affected or the consequences of layoff. See James B. Dworkin and Barbara A. Lee, "The Implications of Europe 1992," pp. 9–10.

36.   The proposed requirements in the Vredling Directive were not very different from what already is required by law in Germany and the Netherlands.

37.   The United Kingdom opposed the social charter, but the other 11 states supported it.

38.   Note that all firms do not necessarily benefit from expanded trade. Some companies will lose the protections provided by government regulations or suffer when confronted by greater direct competition from firms in other EEC countries.

39.   This is true with regard to private sector unions.

40.   In 1960 trade unions played a leading part in the violent protests that culminated in the fall of the government, under Syngman Rhee. In 1980 violent protests again swept the country as workers demanded worker and union rights as well as improved wages and working conditions. See Russell Landsbury and Join Zappala, "Korean Industrial Relations in Transition: The Relevance of Australian

Experience," unpublished paper, Department of Industrial Relations, University of Sydney, Australia, 1990.

41.   See Mario F. Bognonno and Sookon Kim, "Collective Bargaining in Korea," *Papers and Proceedings of the 34th Annual Meeting,* (Madison, WI: Industrial Relations Research Association, 1982), pp. 193–201.

42.   See John Paul MacDuffie, "The Japanese Automobile Transplants: Challenges to Conventional Wisdom," *ILR Report,* vol. 26, no. 1 (Fall 1988): 12–18.

43.   Michael Cusumano, *The Japanese Automobile Industry* (Cambridge, MA: Harvard University Press, 1986).

44.   As discussed above, some people argue that the Japanese system of enterprise unionism lacks democratic and independent worker representation and thereby should neither be emulated nor imported.

Chapter 15

The Future of U.S. Labor Policy and Industrial Relations

This book has traced how changes in the environment are challenging many traditional collective bargaining practices in the United States. In recent years there has been much experimentation in industrial relations among a significant number of companies and unions. At the same time, conflicts emerged between a number of unions and employers and the nation experienced a significant decline in union representation.

Which of these two developments will dominate labor-management relations in the future? Will experiments with new forms of worker participation diffuse and become the foundation for a new model of U.S. industrial relations? Or will unionism continue to decline and experimentation with new industrial relations practices halt as labor and management lock horns?

The U.S. economy recently has experienced large and persistent trade deficits and sluggish productivity growth.[1] Concern for the competitiveness of the U.S. economy abounds, as illustrated by the number of highly publicized commissions seeking solutions to this problem.[2] The U.S. economy also has been plagued by stagnation in real wages for the average worker and growing inequality in the distribution of income.[3] These economic pressures create additional challenges for labor policy.

The task for national labor policy is to improve the competitiveness of the economy while simultaneously improving the standard of living of U.S. workers. This chapter examines the alternative strategies that labor policy might follow in the future and explores the implications of these choices.

When considering future possibilities it is necessary to examine the various channels through which the government can influence the conduct of collective bargaining. The most important federal statute affecting collective bargaining is the National Labor Relations Act. Government labor policy includes administration of this statute and other statutes dealing with collective bargaining such as the Railway Labor Act.

The nation's labor policy is also shaped by an array of regulations that govern employment conditions, training, and other aspects of the labor market. Industrial relations and employment conditions also are affected by economic and social policies. The social security system, for example, affects worker earnings and retirement decisions.

Thus, national labor policy includes general economic and social policies, labor relations policies, and employment and human resource policies. Exhibit 15–1 outlines the key components of our current national labor policy.

The History of Government-Promoted Labor-Management Dialogue

One way public officials tried to exercise leadership in the labor area in the past was through the promotion of labor-management dialogue. Previous "dialogue" efforts are reviewed below. This history is worth reviewing as there is much recent discussion about the possibility of increasing labor-management dialogue as a way of addressing the economic pressures that are confronting the country and collective bargaining.

National-Level Committees

A number of national labor-management committees have tried to change industrial relations practices.[4] At the turn of the century, for example, various national investigative commissions examined labor conditions and problems. Industrial relations commissions issued reports in 1880, 1902, and 1915. The 1915 commission, for example, cited the absence of industrial democracy and inadequate working conditions as two of the most serious social problems of the time. The reports of these commissions were used as background material by those who wrote the New Deal labor legislation in the 1930s.

Other labor-management committees were created during wartime. Both Presidents Woodrow Wilson and Franklin Roosevelt created national war labor boards to promote labor peace and wage stability during World Wars I and II, respectively. These boards were generally successful in fulfilling their mandate during the course of the wars. Both, however, failed to keep labor and management working together at the national level after the wars.

While every President from the 1930s through the 1960s established one or more top-level labor-management advisory committees to deal with various issues, this tradition was abandoned in the 1970s, 1980s, and 1990s. Instead, several *private* national level committees have been formed in recent years.

Exhibit 15–1   **Selected Components of National Labor Policies**

General Economic and Social Policies	Labor Relations Policies	Employment and Human Resource Policies
Aggregate monetary and fiscal policies	Railway Labor Act	Wage and hour legislation (e.g., Fair Labor Standards Act, Davis-Bacon Act)
Incomes policies	Norris-LaGuardia Act	Equal employment opportunity laws, regulations, and enforcement efforts
Trade policies	Wagner Act	Occupational Safety and Health Act
Immigration policies	Taft-Hartley Act	Employee Retirement Income Security Act
Antitrust policies	Landrum-Griffin Act	Unemployment insurance system
Regulation of multinational corporations	Civil Service Reform Act of 1978, Title VII	Social security system
Environmental protection policies	Postal Reorganization Act of 1970, Public Law 91-375	Workers' compensation system
National health insurance proposals	"Little Wagner acts" at state level	Job Training Partnership Act and related employment adjustment programs
Energy policies	State employee bargaining laws and policies	Programs to improve labor-management cooperation
Productivity improvement and capital formation policies		
Industry regulatory policies (hospitals, transportation, etc.)		
Welfare policies		

Former Secretary of Labor John T. Dunlop, for example, continues to meet with his *labor management group* composed of a small number of union and corporate presidents, founded in the mid-1970s. This group discusses various labor policy issues *other than* collective bargaining problems. Their view is that collective bargaining issues are best discussed at more decentralized levels between the parties that are directly involved. Bargaining issues, they believe, are too controversial to be settled through national labor-management dialogue.

Malcolm Lovell, a former Undersecretary of Labor, leads the *Collective Bargaining Forum* composed of top union and corporate leaders.[5] In contrast to Dunlop's group, the forum discusses long-term strategies for improving collective bargaining. Excerpts from one of the Forum's reports is contained in Box 15–1.

The record shows little direct effect of national forums on the practice of collective bargaining. A number of factors have made it difficult to change labor-management relations through national level dialogue in the United States. Such inhibiting factors include the highly decentralized structure of U.S. collective bargaining; the absence of a unified labor movement; a diversity of interests within the management community; and a lack of consensus across labor, management, and government officials concerning appropriate public policies.

Nevertheless, the fact that these groups continue to be formed and gain the participation of busy top labor and business leaders suggests that they serve some useful purpose. It may be that their central function is to help labor and management better understand their areas of mutual interest.

Local and Regional Government Dialogue Efforts

There have also been a number of efforts to promote labor-management dialogue at local and regional levels of the country. These labor-management committees usually include labor and management representatives and key community politicians. Almost all have been started under the active leadership of one individual.[6] The Jamestown, New York, committee, for example, developed largely out of the efforts of the former mayor of the city.

Area (local or regional) committees have tended to grow out of an economic crisis, such as plant closings. This was the motivation in Jamestown. In a few communities, such as Toledo, Ohio, the initial stimulus was a high number of strikes.[7]

Area committees have mobilized community resources to attract new business and encouraged local educational institutions to respond better to industrial needs. Area committees also have attracted federal and state economic development funds. Area committees, however, rarely have been able to convince employers or local unions to change collective bargaining practices. Recommendations of area committees for collective bargaining are often resisted by plant-level managers and union officers on the grounds that they interfere unwarrantedly with the prerogatives of these individuals.

The Common Failure of National and Area Labor-Management Committees

Our participation in a variety of national and area labor-management committees has left us with an uneasy feeling. None of these efforts

Box 15–1

Toward a New Labor Management Compact

In 1988, the Collective Bargaining Forum (an informal working group of major union and corporate leaders) adopted a statement of principles. The statement includes the following:

> We recognize that the institution of collective bargaining is an integral part of American economic life. We recognize that unions cannot be expected to expand their work with management to improve the economic performance of domestic enterprises and to help those firms adopt to technological, market, and other changes, if they are not accepted by employers and public policy makers as having a legitimate and valued role in the strategic decisions of the enterprise and in public policy making. It was also clear to us that employers need to expand their cooperative efforts with unions to revitalize U.S. industry and retain and expand opportunities for secure well-paid jobs for American workers. . . . The Forum, therefore urges adherence to the following principles:
>
> Acceptance in practice by American management both of the legitimacy of unions and a broader role for worker and union participation.
>
> Acceptance in practice by American unions of their responsibility to work with management to improve the economic performance of their enterprises, in ways that serve the interests of workers, consumers, stockholders, and society.
>
> Encouragement of a public policy which assures choice, free from any coercion, in determining whether to be represented by a union and which is conducive to labor-management relations based on mutual respect and trust at all levels.
>
> Acceptance by American corporations of employment security, the continuity of employment for its work force, as a major policy objective that will figure as importantly in the planning process as product development, marketing, and capital requirements.

The Forum also developed a "Compact" covering procedures needed to put its principles into practice. This compact suggests a new set of obligations and responsibilities which transcend and expand traditional collective bargaining relationships. The compact states, "Our purpose is to formulate standards or 'rules of the game' with respect to certain fundamental aspects of the relationship." The *Compact* suggests standards for governing joint efforts to improve the economic performance of U.S. enterprises: acceptance of unions within companies and in American society; the promotion of employment security, worker participation, and empowerment; improved conflict resolution; diffusion of innovations in labor management relations; and development of common positions on public policy issues.

Source: Labor-Management Commitment: A Compact for Change, Views from The Collective Bargaining Forum. Distributed by the U.S. Department of Labor, Bureau of Labor Management Relations and Cooperative Programs, Report No. 141, 1991.

seems to be producing reforms sufficient to stem job losses or slow declines in union membership; none have changed the attitudes of employers who are ideologically opposed to unionization; none have produced a new coherent strategy to foster employee participation; and none have produced a consensus over changes in national labor policy.

Perhaps these are expectations that go well beyond what these committees can deliver. But, if major reforms in collective bargaining do not come from the normal policymaking processes of government, nor from labor-management committees, one might reasonably ask from where, if at all, will these changes come?

Alternative Directions for Future National Labor Policy

There are three possible strategic directions for future national labor policy. One approach would continue the labor policies of the 1980s and early 1990s. The emphasis would be on further deregulation of product markets and reliance on the market to determine employment conditions. This strategy would emphasize the policies shown in column A of Exhibit 15–1 and deemphasize the policies in columns B and C.

Alternatively, the strategy could focus on the policies in column B in Exhibit 15–1 and marginally reform the National Labor Relations Act. The goal in this second policy approach would be to increase the power of labor and restrict the expansion of nonunion practices.

A third policy approach would seek to substantially alter collective bargaining and promote supportive economic policies. The focus in the third policy approach would be to diffuse the recent experiments transforming industrial relations practice (discussed in Chapter 12).

The three policy approaches are discussed in more detail below.

Strategy 1: Reliance on Deregulation and the Market

One strategy for national labor policy would involve extension of the deregulation wave that began in the late 1970s. The primary objective of deregulation is to increase product market competition.

The federal government has been reducing regulation of the labor market since the mid-1970s, and the first policy approach would further limit federal regulations. From 1960 to 1975, for example, the number of employment regulations administered by the U.S. Department of Labor tripled. In the deregulation era after 1975, in contrast, no major new labor regulations were enacted.[8]

Furthermore, in the 1980s and early 1990s the benefit levels in many social welfare and employment programs were either frozen or reduced, and programs were conservatively enforced.[9] The federal budget for employment and training activities, for example, was cut substantially. The number of Occupational Safety and Health Administration employees was reduced by 25 percent in the early 1980s alone. Benefit cuts or freezes would be extended in the first policy approach.

A shift in labor policy administration also appeared after 1980 in the decisions of the National Labor Relations Board. During the terms of Presidents Gerald Ford and Jimmy Carter in the 1970s roughly 28 percent of the board's unfair labor practice decisions were in favor of employers. In the 1980s, after President Reagan appointed two new members and a new chairman, the board decided 60 percent of its cases in favor of employers.[10] Continuing to favor employers in the administration of the NLRA would also be a part of the first policy approach.

The Case for Further Deregulation   Why not extend the deregulation policies pursued in the 1980s and allow market forces even freer rein to determine employment conditions? The basic argument in favor of product market deregulation and limited labor market regulation is twofold. First, market forces are extremely efficient in allocating labor. Efficiency derives, in part, from the pressure the market puts on labor and management to maximize profits.

Second, if market pressures are blocked, inefficient practices can persist. Society not only bears the cost of the output foregone while resources are misallocated, but often must help the parties absorb the costs of later adjustments to market pressures. Some would argue that the decline in the competitiveness of the U.S. steel industry illustrates the inertia that can set in when management and labor believe that their actions will be protected from market forces.[11]

Even if one does not like the outcomes generated by market forces, it is not clear that appropriate alternative policies can be successfully designed or implemented.[12] This also recommends limited regulation of product and labor markets.

Criticisms of a Market and Deregulation Policy Approach
There are, however, many costs and problems created by a deregulation policy approach. Normative arguments against reliance on the market alone to determine employment conditions were effectively articulated in the early years of this century by institutional economists of the Wisconsin School. The institutionalists stressed that labor is more than an economic commodity and that conflicts of interest between employees and employers are inherent and enduring. Put simply, competitive labor markets may leave too many workers in a weak bargaining position with their employers and give workers too little job security.

For these reasons the early institutional economists supported policies designed to allow workers to accumulate "property rights" in their jobs. The institutionalist believed that such a policy would be equitable. Moreover, if the workplace is to reflect the democratic values of the broader society, the institutionalists argued that employees should have a chance to influence managerial decisions that affect employment conditions.

The Potential Consequences of Further Declines in Union Membership   One might also worry what would happen if union representation continues to shrink. If union decline continues, management's abuse of its power might eventually produce an even more adversarial form of collective bargaining and costly conflict.

Moreover, as unions decline, they may lose the capacity to innovate as their members and leaders see their security erode. A lack of union innovativeness could, in turn, reinforce employers' resolve to avoid unions. Thus, further union decline might create a reinforcing cycle of intensified conflict, reduced innovation, and declining competitiveness. The conflict that emerged between Eastern Airlines and its unions in the 1980s illustrates this scenario (see Box 5–1).

The Costs to Workers of Adjusting to Economic Changes   Any future labor policy will have to address the fact that union membership is heavily concentrated in the oldest and most mature sectors of the economy. Those sectors will undoubtedly continue to reduce employment levels and shift large numbers of workers across jobs and occupations. Employment adjustments will occur in these mature sectors as a consequence of new labor-saving technology, the development of new products, and the adoption of new business strategies.

Many of the jobs being eliminated in mature industries are high-wage jobs held by union members. Older workers displaced from these jobs are not well trained to fill any of the new high-skilled jobs being created. A painful transition confronts those displaced older workers who have to accept low-wage jobs. Market forces alone may not fully smooth these adjustment processes.[13]

What Will Be the U.S. Comparative Advantage in World Trade: Low Wages or High Skills?   The events that followed deregulation of the airline and trucking industries suggest that deregulation may greatly reduce workers' power to resist management's efforts to minimize labor costs. Deregulated industries have experienced widespread pay and work rule concessions, reduced employment security, and a lack of innovation in labor-management relationships.[14] Once product market competition increased after deregulation, management often found it easier to cut labor costs than to compete through managerial reforms, technological innovation, or product innovation.

If the government were to promote further deregulation, then the minimization of labor costs might spread as a business strategy. Yet labor cost minimization may in the long run be self-defeating as American firms that compete on the basis of labor costs may not fare well in world trade. The problem is that workers in newly industrializing countries receive very low wages. U.S. firms may be unable (or unwilling) to keep wages low enough to compete through low costs with firms in developing countries.

American firms, however, might be more successful if they pursued the comparative advantages derived from high technology and product innovativeness. Few dispute that the comparative advantage of the U.S. economy lies in its high-technology, high-quality products and in its ability to adapt rapidly. These traits require skilled employees who are strongly committed to their employers. Thus, reducing labor costs may help save some jobs in the short run, but in the long run the U.S. economy and workers' interest may be better served if employers invest in the quality of their human resources. Yet, it does not appear that market forces alone will adequately push employers toward a high-skills human resource strategy.

All the reasons discussed in this section suggest the need to supplement the market with labor policies. But what should the policies be? Here, there is much debate. Below are sketched two alternative strategies.

Strategy 2: The Promotion of Traditional Collective Bargaining

A second alternative for future labor policy is to actively support traditional collective bargaining and the principles promoted by the NLRA. This would require, among other things, marginally reforming the NLRA and its administration. The reforms would make it more difficult for employers to oppose union-organizing efforts and make it easier for unions to achieve first contracts after they win a representation election.[15]

Following in the New Deal tradition, the focus of this strategy would be on procedural rules that specify the rights of the parties and place limits on each party's rights to use power. This policy approach is based on the belief that the parties can use collective bargaining to promote their long-term interests without imposing undue costs on society. Changes along these lines might come about if unions were able to help elect a President and a congress more sympathetic to their objectives.

But this policy approach may no longer suit the needs of many firms and employees. A new industrial relations system might better meet today's economic pressures.

Strategy 3: A New Industrial Relations System

We believe the new industrial relations system summarized in Exhibit 15–2 would help labor and management address the economic pressures that are now confronting our nation.[16] Industrial relations innovation

Exhibit 15–2   **Elements in a New Industrial Relations System**

Strategic Level

Information sharing between management and workers

Worker and union participation and representation

Cross-functional consultations

Integration of industrial relations with business and technology strategies

Functional Level

Contingent compensation

Employment continuity and security

Strong commitment to training and development

Workplace Level

Employee participation

Flexible work organization

Grievance procedures with communication and due process supplements

along these lines could provide valuable improvements in productivity and living standards while providing equitable due process.

Workplace industrial relations in the new system would feature employee participation in workplace decisions, flexibility in the organization of work, and extensive informal communication between labor and management. The goal is to develop trust and avoid the conflict often found in traditional collective bargaining relationships. Another major goal of the workplace system is to increase flexibility by moving away from detailed contractual provisions and narrow job descriptions. At the same time, workplace procedures should facilitate employee input into decisions and due process.

At the middle level of the new industrial relations system gains-sharing or profit-sharing arrangements would be encouraged. The parties must be careful, however, not to let the shift to these "contingent" compensation procedures erode workers' standards of living. The goal here is to make wages responsive to current economic conditions. Employee training and career development also would be encouraged at the middle level. Employment and income security programs can contribute toward this end.

At the strategic level, the new system would break with the principle that it is management's job to manage the enterprise and the union's job solely to negotiate over the effects of management actions. Instead, the new system would encourage information sharing and consultation between management and worker representatives. No single form of worker involvement at the strategic level is anticipated, in keeping with the variety of mechanisms already being developed by labor and management.

In the new system, the exclusive representation provided by unions to workers in a bargaining unit would be modified. Employee-management councils that provide representation to a cross-section of blue- and white-collar workers would be allowed. The parties would be encouraged to create consultation procedures involving employees from a variety of occupations. These consultative procedures could supplement formal negotiations.

The complete features of this new system cannot yet be found in any employment relationship in the United States. Yet, each of the features of the new system is currently used somewhere in both union and nonunion firms. The new system builds on these experiences and brings together some of the reform proposals that have been advocated in recent years.

The Need to Integrate Labor, Economic, and Social Policies in Strategy 3

The third policy approach to labor policy would promote the new industrial relations system and support this system with other economic and social policies. Diffusing a new industrial relations system will require the active support of federal and state policy makers and significant shifts in the strategies of management and labor. Below are outlined steps the government, labor, and management could take to encourage spread of the new industrial relations system.

Government Strategies   Major reform of the NLRA is necessary to achieve the new industrial relations system envisioned in Exhibit 15–2. Industrial relations over the past decade has included frequent employer unfair labor practices, weak remedies for unfair labor practice violations, and low rates of union success (and long delays) in achieving first contracts. Respect for the NLRB should be reestablished. Furthermore, employees should be assured of their right to decide if they choose union representation without employer interference.

Current policy encourages the parties to begin worker representation in an adversarial proceeding with the hope that eventually their relationship will mature and become more cooperative. A more affirmative policy that promotes participative industrial relations is necessary.

Legal Impediments to Participation   Other legal constraints on the participation by employees, supervisors, and middle managers in decision making should be removed. The restriction of bargaining rights for supervisors contained in the law is outmoded. These restrictions conflict with the contemporary decentralization of managerial decision making.[17]

Box 15–2 excerpts a discussion paper on supervisor representation issued by the U.S. Department of Labor. Stephen Schlossberg and Stephen Fetter strongly argue that the supervisory/nonsupervisory

Box 15–2

Labor-Management Cooperation in the Future

More and more large and progressive companies are embracing labor-management cooperative programs tailored to the particular needs of their operations. . . . The Department of Labor supports and encourages the adoption of such cooperative efforts between labor and management. Yet such arrangements do not fit easily within the framework of labor and related statutes that evolved out of the confrontation and industrial conflict of the 1930's. For example, the Supreme Court, construing the legislative intent of the National Labor Relations Act (NLRA), wrote in a 1981 decision that "Congress had no expectation that the elected union representative would become an equal partner in the running of the business enterprise. . . ." More recently, two pace-setting labor-management agreements involved in GM's Saturn project were challenged as unfair labor practices. These charges were dismissed, but the mere possibility of their full prosecution has the potential to deter parties from attempting dramatic and innovative cooperative initiatives in the future.

The Department of Labor, therefore, has embarked on a study of labor laws and practices that may inhibit improved labor-relations. . . . The ultimate goal of the study is to reach consensus on policy recommendations for interpretation of modification of the laws so that they support both the ingredients and the goals of labor-management cooperation rather than conflict with them.

. . . The laws as applied embody certain concepts that may not reflect practical arrangements that make sense in the real world of dealings between labor and management. For example, in its 1980 decision under the NLRA involving Yeshiva University, the Supreme Court . . . concluded that the faculty members were "in effect, substantially and pervasively operating the enterprise." Therefore, as managerial employees, they were not covered under the Act. This conclusion, unfortunately, could jeopardize a desired method of operation . . . and, if extended beyond the educational setting, could cast doubt on the most innovative features of other cooperative agreements such as those in the steel and auto industries, among others.

Source: Stephen I. Schlossberg and Stephen M. Fetter, *U.S. Labor Law and the Future of Labor-Management Cooperation* (Washington, D.C.: U.S. Department of Labor, 1986), Executive Summary, pp. 1–2.

distinctions found in the law do not encourage employee participation and labor-management cooperation.

Without reform of the law, first-line supervisors and middle managers are in an untenable predicament. On the one hand, changes in technology and personnel policies have reduced the power and status of supervisors and given rank-and-file employees more influence.[18] On the other hand, supervisors remain unprotected by the law if they engage in collective efforts to improve their employment conditions.

Given their precarious position, it is not surprising that supervisors so often find ways to block workplace innovations. This resistance to change is likely to continue unless supervisors are involved more meaningfully in the change process.

Likewise, constraints on the "mandatory" and "permissible" scope of bargaining no longer make sense. Strategic business decisions have serious consequences for employment and income security. Effective employee representation, therefore, requires employee participation in strategic business decision making at an early stage of the process.

The Need for Changes in Other Government Policies   The diffusion of the new industrial relations system should be accompanied by changes in other federal economic and social policies. An extensive employment and training policy, for example, is needed to assist workers transitioning across employers or occupations. The unemployment compensation system should be altered to cover a higher percentage of the unemployed and encourage the acquisition of new skills. Many other employment regulations should be modified to spur productivity and improve living standards.

Macroeconomic policies should promote economic expansion and productivity growth. Support for basic education and research should be increased in the United States in light of the support given to such activities by our economic competitors.

Government policy alone, however, cannot spark changes in industrial relations. The diffusion of a new industrial relations system requires the active support of management and labor.

Management Values and Strategies   U.S. managers will influence the diffusion of reforms in industrial relations through their values and their business strategies. In a new industrial relations system, management will have to accept a broad role for unions and workers in strategic decision making. Yet, opposition to unions is a deep-seated value of many U.S. managers. This is a significant barrier to the diffusion of a new system of industrial relations.

If management adheres to this oppositional view of unionism, efforts to unionize new groups of employees will be highly adversarial. Unions probably will lose a majority of these contests and fail to achieve contracts in a significant number of the representation elections they do win. This will further discredit NLRA procedures in the eyes of workers and union representatives. In cases in which unions do achieve recognition through an adversarial contest, the adversarial relationship likely will carry over to the subsequent bargaining relationship.

At the workplace level this hostile climate will strengthen the position of those union leaders who favor traditional adversarial relationships with management. Distrust will inhibit the flexibility and participation necessary for the new system of industrial relations.

The Role of Business Strategies   Not all business strategies are equally compatible with the industrial relations reforms proposed in Exhibit 15–2. Business competition based on low labor costs undermines worker trust, flexibility, and adaptability. Yet, because unions have difficulty in taking wages out of competition, many firms now are tempted to pursue a low-wage business strategy. The distrust that develops in firms that pursue low-wage strategies makes participative practices impossible.

Business strategies that move work to different locations in response to variations in labor costs also are incompatible with a new system of industrial relations. A low-cost production strategy can divert management's attention away from the need to develop other comparative advantages. Firms that focus on low-cost strategies tend to give too little attention to the development of advantages based on technology, labor skills, and product innovation.

Other business strategies that limit worker trust also need to be avoided if industrial relations innovations are to take hold. The buying and selling of productive assets as mere short-run financial instruments without attending to the employment consequences borne by those actions has negative effects. Thus, corporate takeovers that meet only short-term corporate objectives have dysfunctional consequences on industrial relations. Corporate financial maneuvers should either be limited by public policy or required to provide compensation to the affected work force.

Technological Strategies   Technological strategies that maintain managerial control and maximize labor-savings lead to deskilled and unmotivated workers. These technological strategies limit the opportunity for organizational learning and improvement.

More consistent with new industrial relations practices is a "social technical" approach to new technology. Sociotechnical policies use technology to decentralize decision making in organizations and upgrade worker skills. The upgrading of skills occurs by broadening job tasks and blurring traditional distinctions between white- and blue-collar work.[19] Thus, as with business strategy, U.S. management should follow technological strategies that reinforce the diffusion of industrial relations reforms.

Is it likely that a majority of U.S. managers quickly will adopt values and strategies that support the diffusion of a new industrial relations system? If history is any guide, the answer is clearly no. Most managers are likely to prefer either traditional practices or incremental change. Yet, with international and domestic competition increasing, technology changing rapidly, and worker aspirations intensifying, the need grows for extensive changes in industrial relations. Economic pressures, and pressures from government and unions, may eventually induce management to make major changes.

Union Strategies   Labor leaders face a similar strategic choice regarding whether to support the diffusion of a new system of industrial relations. At present the leaders of the U.S. labor movement are deeply divided in their view of recent innovations. The reluctance of union leaders to strongly support participation in managerial decision making stems, in part, from leaders' fears that they will be co-opted. Union leaders worry that increased participation will lead them to support management's goals at the expense of their members' interests.

Union leaders will have to reassess their views if industrial reforms are to diffuse. Without the strong support of the labor movement, it is difficult for management to take the risks associated with the introduction of new practices. Visible support from union leaders is also necessary to convince public policy officials, rank-and-file workers, and the public that a new industrial relations system is possible. Even union leaders' passive acceptance of new practices is unlikely to suffice.

If they do become more heavily involved in strategic business issues, union leaders will have to become more expert in communicating with their members about their participation. Otherwise, members will remain suspicious of union leaders' new roles. Furthermore, union leaders will have to match increased participation in business decisions with increased member participation in internal union affairs.

Why should labor leaders embrace a new industrial relations system and adopt the new roles it requires of them? The answer to this question is quite simple: union leaders have to do so if they are to represent the interests of their current members effectively and organize new members.

The scope of industrial relations activity has broadened in recent years to involve more activities above and below the level of traditional collective bargaining. Strategic decisions made at the top of corporations and interactions at the workplace are now as important as the negotiations process. Union leaders, therefore, have to acquire the ability to influence decisions made at the strategic and workplace levels as well as in collective bargaining negotiations. If they do not, their influence over the future of industrial relations will continue to decline.

Summary

This book began by presenting a normative perspective on industrial relations and a broad framework for analyzing industrial relations. The text then explored how the strategic choices of the parties interact with environmental conditions to shape industrial relations. It seems appropriate, therefore, that this final chapter poses the strategic choices now faced by labor, management, and governmental decision makers regarding the future of industrial relations.

The field of industrial relations has a heritage of close connections between research, teaching, public policy, and private practice. The fostering of this tradition would help the parties address the challenges that now face industrial relations.

Discussion Questions

1. What are some of the key components of the current U.S. national labor policy?

2. Briefly outline the deregulation-market approach to national labor policy. Discuss some of the strengths and weaknesses of this approach.

3. Describe the key features of the new labor policy advocated by the authors.

4. How could the government encourage the diffusion of the new industrial relations system recommended by the authors if it chooses to do so?

Suggested Readings

Heckscher, Charles C. *The New Unionism* (New York: Basic Books, 1988).

Kochan, Thomas A., Harry C. Katz, and Robert B. McKersie. *The Transformation of American Industrial Relations* (New York: Basic Books, 1986).

Osterman, Paul. *Employment Futures* (New York and Oxford: Oxford University Press, 1988).

Piore, Michael J., and Charles F. Sabel. *The Second Industrial Divide* (New York: Basic Books, 1984).

End Notes

1. For two different views of the consequences of U.S. trade deficits, see Robert Z. Lawrence, *Can America Compete?* (Washington, D.C.: Brookings Institution, 1984), and Otto Eckstein, Christopher Caton, Roger Brinner, and Peter Duprey, *The DRI Report on U.S. Manufacturing Industries* (New York: McGraw-Hill, 1984).

2.   President Reagan established two such groups: the White House Conference on Productivity and the President's Commission on Industrial Competitiveness. Numerous other study groups have issued recommendations for restoring the nation's international competitiveness, and several additional university groups and others involving labor, management, government, and university representatives are working on this issue.

3.   See Bennett Harrison and Barry Bluestone, *The Great U-Turn* (New York: Basic Books, 1988).

4.   Various names, including commission or board, were attached to these labor-management committees.

5.   The forum was established in the early 1980s and continues to meet.

6.   Joel Cutcher-Gershenfeld, "The Emergence of Community Labor-Management Cooperatives," in *Industrial Democracy: Strategies for Community Revitalization,* ed. Warner Woodworth, Christopher Meek, and William Foote Whyte (Beverly Hills, CA: Sage, 1985), pp. 99–120.

7.   Ibid., pp. 81–92.

8.   John T. Dunlop, "The Limits of Legal Compulsion," *Labor Law Journal* 27 (February 1976): 67.

9.   Data on changes in the funding and administration of labor policies during the Reagan administration years are found in Sar A. Levitan, Peter E. Carlson, and Isaac Shapiro, *Protecting American Workers: An Assessment of Government Programs* (Washington, D.C.: Bureau of National Affairs, 1986).

10.   F. Ray Marshall, "The Act's Impact on Employment, Society, and the National Economy," in *American Labor Policy: A Critical Appraisal of the National Labor Relations Act,* ed. Charles J. Morris (Washington, D.C.: Bureau of National Affairs, 1987), p. 33.

11.   For a discussion of the decline of the steel industry, see Robert W. Crandall, *The U.S. Steel Industry in Recurrent Crisis* (Washington, D.C.: Brookings Institution, 1981). For a historical analysis of labor relations in the steel industry through the mid-1980s, see John Hoerr, *And the Wolf Finally Came* (New York: Praeger, 1987).

12.   Paul Krugman, "Targeted Industrial Policies: Theory and Evidence," in *Industrial Change and Public Policy,* a symposium sponsored by the Federal Reserve Bank of Kansas City (Kansas City: Federal Reserve Bank, 1983), pp. 125–126.

13.   Paul Osterman, *Employment Futures* (New York and Oxford: Oxford University Press, 1988).

14.   Kirsten R. Wever, "Changing Union Structure and the Changing Structure of Unionization in the Post-Deregulation Era," in *Proceedings of the Thirty-Ninth Annual Meeting, IRRA,* December 28–30, 1986, New Orleans, ed. Barbara D. Dennis (Madison, WI: Industrial Relations Research Association, 1987), pp. 129–136.

15.   See Charles J. Morris, ed. "Preface," *American Labor Policy: A Critical Appraisal of the National Labor Relations Act* (Washington, D.C.: Bureau of National Affairs, 1987). For a discussion of a variety of different proposals for reform of the NLRA and the NLRB, also see Paul Weiler, *The Law at Work: The Past*

and Future of U.S. Labor and Employment Policy (Cambridge, MA: Harvard University Press, 1990).

16.   We developed Exhibit 15–2 with our colleagues after a longitudinal study of the innovations in industrial relations practice introduced in a number of collective bargaining relationships. See Thomas A. Kochan and Joel Cutcher-Gershenfeld, *Diffusing and Institutionalizing Innovations in Industrial Relations* (Washington, D.C.: Bureau of Labor Management Relations and Cooperative Programs, U.S. Department of Labor, 1987).

17.   James P. Begin and Barbara A. Lee, "NLRA Exclusion Criteria and Professional Work," *Industrial Relations* 26 (Winter 1987): 83–95. See also Barbara A. Lee and Joan Parker, "Supervisory Participation in Professional Associations: Implications of North Shore University Hospital," *Industrial and Labor Relations Review* 40 (April 1987): 364–381.

18.   Leonard A. Schlesinger and Janice A. Klein, "The First Line Supervisor: Past, Present, and Future," in *Handbook of Organizational Behavior,* ed. J. Lorsch (Englewood Cliffs, N.J: Prentice-Hall, 1987), pp. 370–384.

19.   See Larry Hirschhorn, *Beyond Mechanization* (Cambridge, MA: MIT Press, 1984), and Shoshana Zuboff, *In the Age of the Smart Machine* (New York: Basic Books, 1988).

Appendix A

Private Sector Mock Bargaining Exercise

The following materials provide the basic data for a mock exercise in collective bargaining in the private sector. The exercise involves the D. G. Barnhouse Company and the union representing Barnhouse's blue-collar employees, the United Metal Products Workers. Both the company and union names, as well as the material and data, are fictitious.

The students should divide into company and union negotiating teams. Three members per side are recommended. The roles on the union bargaining committee include a representative from the national union, the president of the local union, and a senior employee who is a shop steward in the local union. The roles on the management bargaining committee include the company director of industrial relations, the company director of production, and a general supervisor.

All negotiators should receive the materials that follow. There are also additional company and union supplemental materials available in the Instructor's Manual for the text. Negotiators should receive *either* company *or* union supplemental materials.

The task confronting the negotiators is to bargain a new contract covering Barnhouse's unionized employees. A copy of the expiring agreement and other pertinent data are included in the materials that follow.

After reading the materials, students should meet with their team before bargaining to formulate their team's demands and any strategy they may choose to follow in negotiations. Students may want to consult other collective bargaining agreements available in a library or sources of economic data. The U.S. Department of Labor, Bureau of Labor Statistics, publishes a number of economic reports on a regular basis. The Bureau of National Affairs publishes a number of reports tracing recent collective bargaining agreements.

 ### BARGAINING BETWEEN D. G. BARNHOUSE CO., INC. AND THE UNITED METAL PRODUCTS WORKERS

At the turn of the twentieth century, Mr. Donald Grayson Barnhouse, a highly skilled lathe craftsman, opened a small shop in which he made specialty machine tools. Based on very little financial capital—he had only about $1,000 available from savings and small personal loans—but a great deal of entrepreneurial stamina, he scraped together enough used tools to open his shop on the outskirts of Grandville, Illinois. After 10 years in operation, D. G. Barnhouse had gained a steady enough business to support himself and his small family, but had been able to take on only one apprenticed employee.

By 1915, however, Barnhouse's luck began to turn as small auto companies began to be built in the general vicinity of Grandville. His company, D. G. Barnhouse Co., Inc., had developed a reputation for quality, which soon led nascent area auto companies to buy tools from him. Thus, D. G. Barnhouse Co. (DGB) began to be looked on as one of the foremost suppliers to the auto industry.

By the mid-1920s DGB began diversifying into several new kinds of lathes, which came to be in higher and higher demand as the decade progressed. These were now produced in the machine tool plant DGB had built up over the previous decade. DGB had also maintained the older plant, in which primarily auto parts were produced. DGB's success led Barnhouse to allow the company to go public in order to capitalize on a rapidly expanding market. The capital thus generated was put to use in a new shop devoted solely to the production of machine tools.

The business suffered during the depression years, but managed to survive. During World War II the company did very well. After the war, however, the firm's growth became sporadic. Attempts to diversify into a greater variety of industrial products were not uniformly successful. By the late 1950s, DGB was making profits but not at a high rate.

In 1958, D. G. Barnhouse III took over from his father as President and Chief Executive Officer. Under the new leadership, the company's strategy shifted to place greater emphasis on research and development, as well as diversification and expansion into new markets. The company grew rapidly throughout the 1960s and early 1970s as a combined result of the new leadership and the growth conditions in the international economy during that period. The employees at the Grandville plant gained respectable wage and benefit increases annually, and the company itself was able to sustain a reasonable profit margin.

By the mid-1970s a new plant was opened in nearby Newton, Indiana, a relatively rural area that offered low-cost labor. This plant finished and assembled several types of low-cost machine tools. It employed 90 women and 60 men; the employees, who were not unionized, fell into five job classifications from production and assembly workers to a single general mechanic for the maintenance crew. (Blue-collar employment in the Grandville plant numbered 500 at the time.)

By the early 1990s, it became time again to consider a new strategic direction for DGB. Under current consideration was the possibility of investing in new automated manufacturing equipment, which would allow for a total work force reduction in the Grandville plant of about 10 percent. Alternately, the new equipment could be installed in the Newton plant, while the older Grandville plant could slowly be phased out. This option would entail moving some of the existing Grandville plant equipment to Newton and increasing the number of employees at the newer plant.

Labor Relations at D. G. Barnhouse Co., Inc.   The Barnhouse family had always played an active role in directing the company's labor relations. The

good
L.R.

company carefully protected senior employees against shifting economic conditions. During the depression, several skilled employees were given jobs sweeping the floors of the Grandville plant in order to avoid layoffs. The firm's employees were granted life insurance pensions and hospitalization insurance long before these became standard benefits even in unionized companies. It was partly as a result of these long-standing policies that the Steelworkers, the Machinists, and the Auto Workers had been unable to unionize DGB's employees throughout the 1930s.

After World War II the company used overtime work and subcontracting to keep the number of employees low and steady. Then, in the early 1960s, as business picked up for the company, workers were put on a seven-day work schedule, and morale was severely strained. As a result, the employees of DGB decided to form a union of their own, with substantial encouragement from several first-line supervisors, and with the help of a local of the United Metal Products Workers of America (UMP). The company was certain that this effort at unionization simply reflected the work of a handful of "radicals," and was therefore taken completely by surprise when the National Labor Relations Board representation election resulted in a substantial majority in favor of unionization.

Even before the union had been voted in, DGB had generally paid wages more or less equal to those paid in competing unionized plants in the area. It had regularly participated in industry-wide wage surveys in order to keep appraised of the going rates. But, at the same time, DGB had always been reluctant to grant long-term or automatic cost-of-living increases, or to appear to be following the bargaining pattern set in any particular industry. This aversion to automatic wage/benefit increases and to following pattern bargains was reflected in the contracts negotiated with the union until the early 1980s. But in 1982 DGB for the first time, and quite reluctantly, negotiated a cost-of-living clause in its contract with the UMP.

With respect to fringe benefits, DGB has always been relatively liberal. The life insurance plan provides at least two years' pay, as well as double indemnity, with the company paying half of the premium. DGB also pays for half of its employees' Blue Cross Blue Shield insurance. The company's policy has always been to pay regular employees half-pay during periods of sick leave.

The company's pension plan currently provides retiring employees with 2 percent of average earnings based on the last five years of service for each year of service up to 30 years. The company contributes half the cost of the pension. The combined weekly employee contribution for pension and insurance (life and health) is $50.00.

The 1991 Contract

The 1991 contract was difficult to negotiate, since the union was quite unhappy about lagging wages and benefits and because the company was facing very difficult market conditions. The union was unable to gain anything approaching workers' demands. By a 400 to 80 vote (with 20 members not voting), the membership rejected a contract with the following general features:

1. An hourly pay raise of 12 cents to unskilled and 18 cents to skilled workers.

2. A modest cost-of-living (COLA) clause.

3. An agreement to study ways of upgrading the pension plan.

4. An agreement to consider modifications in work rules and job and pay classifications.

After another unsuccessful week of negotiations, the workers began a strike. But three days later, all of the skilled workers and some of the unskilled employees went back to work voluntarily, and DGB was operating at close to full capacity again. Finally, a one-year agreement was signed on December 31, 1990.

The Aftermath   After the strike, all of the employees at DGB were very discontented. Old divisions between skill groups flared up. Unskilled workers were angry with both the company and their union. All the workers began to feel it was time for some sort of change.

Two months after the abortive strike, a young drill press operator named Bill White challenged and narrowly defeated the incumbent local union president, on the basis of a campaign emphasizing the need for more worker input into plant operations and control over technology and investment. The younger workers were in general pleased with White's approach, but the older employees (with less fear of losing their jobs) were not so sanguine, particularly since White seemed to be uninterested in pension plan improvements.

All the workers shared a certain nervousness about their jobs, however, due to increasing publicity about automation in machine tool plants, and about sluggish demand for machine tools themselves. DGB had done nothing to allay the employees' fears of replacement by robots, or about layoffs.

The Community   Grandville, Illinois, has about 160,000 inhabitants. The nearest large city is Detroit. The working population numbers about 70,000 of which fully 10 percent are unemployed. The unemployment rate is significantly higher for minorities and women. Some of the unemployed population secure a nominal income from the sale of small farm produce.

Aside from the Grandville plant of DGB, there are nine organized firms in the city. Their products, unions and employee statistics are shown below:

Company	Principal Products	Union	No. of Employees
1	Hoists	United Steel Workers	315
2	Pumps	Machinists (IAM)	712
3	Controls	Machinists (IAM)	342
4	Electronics	IUE	2,498
5	Truck bodies	Allied Industrial Workers	2,902
6	Metal parts	UAW	1,240
7	Structural steel	Iron Workers	1,198
8	Bakery	Bakery Workers	202
9	Trucking	Teamsters	79

Building construction employees are also extensively organized in Grandville. No other company is organized by the UMP. The largest of a number of unorganized plants manufactures office equipment and employs about 1,000 people. This group of workers has been subject to three unsuccessful organization drives over the last decade.

The Upcoming Negotiations

Employee recommendations as to the substance of the union's position in the upcoming negotiations were being considered by the UMP local leadership. The union had already notified DGB that it wished to renegotiate the contract and that a list of proposals would be sent to the company when the negotiations were to begin. Donald Grayson Barnhouse III responded that the company's counterproposals would be sent to the union as soon as he had received their negotiating demands.

> It is the responsibility of the union and management bargaining teams to formulate their bargaining strategies, to put priorities or weights on various items, to develop specific changes in contract language to implement various proposals, to decide what compromises to make, and to decide what will constitute an acceptable agreement.

COLLECTIVE BARGAINING AGREEMENT

Parties to the Agreement

This Agreement, made and entered into this 31st day of December 1990, is made by and between D. G. Barnhouse Co., Incorporated, of Illinois, hereinafter called the "Company," and Local 245 International Union, United Metal Products, Machinery and Related Equipment Workers of America, hereinafter called the "Union."

ARTICLE I

Intent and Purpose

Section 1—The parties hereto intend and propose herein to set forth and comply with an agreement concerning pay rates, work hours, and employment conditions, and to set procedures for the prompt and equitable adjustment of alleged grievances.

Section 2—The Company shall in no way discriminate against any employee on the grounds of membership in or affiliation with the Union.

ARTICLE II

Recognition

Section 1—The Company recognizes the Union as the sole and exclusive bargaining agent representing the employees in the Grandville, Illinois, plant of the

Company for the purpose of collective bargaining with respect to rates of pay, wages, hours of work, and other conditions of employment.

Section 2—The term "Employees" for the purpose of this Agreement shall mean all of the employees of the Company except office employees, foremen, watchmen and guards, timekeepers, and supervisors who have and exercise the authority to recommend the hiring, promoting, discharge, disciplining of employees, or otherwise effecting changes in the status of employees.

ARTICLE III

Strikes and Lockouts

Section 1—The Company agrees there shall be no lockout of its employees and the Union agrees that neither it nor any of its members shall cause, permit, or take part in any strike during the term of this Agreement.

[handwritten: no lockout / no strike clause / implies arbitration]

ARTICLE IV

Hours of Work

Section 1—The normal work hours for all employees shall be eight (8) per day and forty (40) per week and, for production employees, shall be limited to the period of Monday to Friday (both days included).

Section 2—Hours worked in addition to the normal work hours shall be according to the following schedule: forty (40) to forty-five (45) shall be limited to five (5) days; over forty-five (45) to fifty-five (55) hours shall be limited to five and one-half (5 1/2) days; over fifty-five (55) to sixty (60) hours shall be limited to six (6) days. All other work schedules shall be mutually approved by the Company and the Union.

Section 3—All time worked by an employee in excess of eight (8) hours in any one day and forty hours (40) hours in any one week and all time worked on Saturday shall be paid for at the time and one-half rate; provided, however, employees shall not receive time and one-half for Saturday as such if they were absent during the week except for one of the following reasons: sickness, accident or death in the family, jury duty or subpoena to court. In cases when employees were absent due to one of the above reasons, they shall turn in a slip stating the reason for that absence, not later than Saturday of the week in which they were absent. All time worked on Sunday shall be paid for at the double time rate.

[handwritten: overtime]

Section 4—The company will attempt to distribute overtime as equitably as possible among affected employees; and shall allow union officials to verify same.

Section 5—The Company shall allow Union Bargaining Committee members first priority for working the first shift; and when feasible employees with the greatest seniority within their job classifications shall be granted second priority to work the first shift, and those next in seniority, the second shift. Further, once an employee exercises seniority rights to obtain a transfer from one shift to another, he/she shall not return to the original shift until a period of six (6) months after the transfer shall have elapsed.

[handwritten: seniority]

Section 6—All employees shall be granted two (2) fifteen- (15-) minute rest periods, at a time to be mutually agreed upon by the Company and the Union, and

[handwritten: breaks]

with pay at their hourly base rate. Smoking, other than during rest periods, is prohibited, and then only in the designated places.

Section 7—Employees shall not be absent from work without permission, except for good and sufficient reason, and must, except in an emergency, get word to the Company no later than three (3) hours after the scheduled starting time, when s/he cannot work.

Section 8—Penalty for violation of Section 7 of this Article will be:

absenthsm

1st Offense—Caution by foreman and a written report to Union and Personnel Department

2d Offense—One day suspension without pay

3d Offense—Two days suspension without pay

4th Offense—Cause for dismissal

ARTICLE V

Wages

Section 1—The rates for all employees shall be in accordance with the "Rate Classification of Jobs," which shall be appended hereto as Exhibit 1 and made a part of this Agreement.

Section 2—All employees shall receive a cost-of-living adjustment in pay, as of the first of January 1992, of one (1) cent per hour for each 0.3-point rise in the U.S. Bureau of Labor Statistics All-Cities Consumer Price Index for the period covering January 1991 through December 1991. However, if the Consumer Price Index declines to levels below those of January 1991, there shall be no pay reduction.

Section 3—Newly hired employees with less than thirty (30) days of employment to their credit shall be considered probationary employees: provided, however, the Company may request an extension of the probationary period not to exceed thirty (30) days for employees whose qualifications or capabilities are in doubt. Any employee remaining in the service of the Company beyond his/her probationary period shall automatically receive an increase of five (5) cents per hour and continuing every fourth (4th) week thereafter, until the minimum of his/her classification is reached.

Section 4—Any employee who is placed in his/her regular occupation after a layoff or transfer for reasons beyond his/her control shall be paid the wage rate applicable at the time of the layoff or transfer, plus or minus any general wage increases or decreases effective during that period.

Section 5—Except for the above provisions, no employee's wage rate shall be changed except by mutual agreement between the Company and the Union.

ARTICLE VI

Seniority, Layoffs, and Rehiring

Section 1—The Company shall notify the Union at such time as any newly hired employees who have completed their probationary period will have worked for thirty (30) days.

Seniority →

*layoff /
callbacks*

Section 2—An employee's seniority rights shall be measured on a plantwide and departmental basis, starting from the first day or hour worked. If, however, an employee is hired after having quit voluntarily or after having been duly discharged, that employee's seniority will be measured as of the time of rehiring.

With respect to the scheduled hours of work per week, the Company shall conform with the following provisions:

(*a*)   The hours of work shall be reduced to forty (40) hours a week before any such employees are laid off.

(*b*)   The schedule of hours per week may be increased from between forty (40) to forty-five (45) inclusive without any employee being called back.

(*c*)   The schedule of hours per week may be increased to over forty-five (45) for a maximum period of four (4) weeks, after which time enough employees who have been laid off will be recalled in order to revert to a maximum forty-five (45) hour work week.

Section 3—In the event of a layoff, employees with the least plantwide seniority will be laid off first, and employees with the most seniority will be retained, subject to their ability to perform the available work without being trained.

Section 4—In the event that workers shall be recalled after having been laid off, the last to have been laid off shall be the first to be recalled, as per the conditions noted in Section 2 of this Article, above. Any laid off employees shall accrue seniority, to be credited after his/her return to work, for a grace period of up to three (3) months. However, no employee shall surpass any other employee in seniority solely as a result of the provisions of Section 2 of this Article, above. An employee shall be considered to have quit voluntarily if he/she does not return to work within five (5) days of receiving notification of recall by registered letter to his/her last known address by the Company.

Section 5—On any layoff or return to work the Company shall notify the Union and the employee affected not less than two (2) working days before such layoff or return to work is effected. Any grievances involving such layoff or return to work shall be submitted to the Company no later than five (5) working days after the Company has given due notice of the fact.

Section 6—The Company shall post an updated seniority list on all bulletin boards at the workplace, shall furnish the Union with such lists, and shall consider such lists to be a matter of mutual approval with the Union. Such lists will include the names, hiring dates, and seniority positions, on a plantwide departmental basis, of all employees.

Section 7—In case of layoff, the president of the Union shall have seniority over all other employees during his/her term of office, regardless of length of service with the company.

ARTICLE VII

Discharge

Section 1—If the Company discharges an employee, such action will be taken for good and sufficient reason, and shall be taken after notifying the Union Bargaining

Committee of the action and reasons therefore. If investigation of such an action leads the Union to conclude that the employee affected was discharged unfairly, that employee shall have the right to lodge a grievance against the Company in accordance with the grievance procedure established in Article XII of this document.

ARTICLE VIII

New Jobs, Transfers, Promotion, and Merit Rating

Section 1—The Company shall notify the Union president when any vacancy or a new job of any occupation occurs which is under the jurisdiction of the Union, and which results in the need for additional help in the department affected. Such notification shall include a statement of the required job qualifications, of the approximate wage rate, and of any other pertinent information. Upon receipt of such notification, the Union will post the job opening on the designated bulletin board(s), after which time interested applicants shall submit written bids to the Company's Personnel Office. Any such jobs shall be awarded on the basis of seniority when the qualifications of applicants are approximately equal.

Job Openings w/in Co.

Section 2—All employees accepting promotion or transfer shall be granted a reasonable period of time for training, during which time they shall receive no less pay than the minimum established in Exhibit 1. Any higher rate of pay shall be determined on the basis of experience, application and general qualifications for the job in question, at the time of the employee's reclassification.

Section 3—With the exception of trainees, each employee on rate ranges shall be considered for merit a raise six (6) months after employment in his/her classification, and at six (6) month intervals thereafter until he/she reaches the maximum rate in the classification. Trainees shall receive merit consideration six (6) months after completion of the ninety (90) day training period. Foremen shall submit written reports of all employees' progress to the Personnel Department at six (6) month intervals, with copies of such reports being furnished at the time of their receipt to the president of the Union.

ARTICLE IX

Military Service

Section 1—When an employee with seniority is called or volunteers for service in any of the armed forces of the United States, he shall, upon termination of such service, be restored to his former position, or to a position of similar status and pay; provided, however, that he has received honorable discharge, is physically and mentally competent, notifies the Company of his intention to return to work at least ninety (90) days prior to his discharge, and reports for work not more than ninety (90) days after release from service; and provided further, that the Company's circumstances have not been changed so as to make it impossible or unreasonable to do so.

Section 2—Any employee who is rehired in accordance with the provisions of this Article shall advance in seniority in the same manner as though he had remained in the Company's service.

ARTICLE X

Vacations

Section 1—All employees shall receive a vacation with pay in accordance with the following schedule:

(a)　All employees with between six (6) months and one (1) year service at the start of the vacation period shall receive a one (1) week vacation with forty (40) hours straight time pay, provided they have worked at least 125 hours in each month following the month in which they were employed. The latter provision with respect to the number of hours worked per month may be modified upon mutual agreement between the Union Bargaining Committee and the Company.

(b)　Vacation for all other employees shall be computed from the following table:
　　All employees will receive vacation according to the following criteria, in which the time of service is to be measured at the start of the vacation period. More than one (1) but less than ten (10) years of service—two (2) weeks vacation with eighty (80) hours straight time pay; more than ten (10) but less than twenty (20) years' service—three (3) weeks vacation with one hundred twenty (120) hours straight time pay; more than twenty (20) years' service—four (4) weeks vacation with one-hundred sixty (160) hours straight time pay.

Section 2—Employees voluntarily terminating their service to the Company shall receive vacation pay earned during the previous year at the time of separation. Vacation pay earned the current year shall be paid not later than March of the following year.

Section 3—The vacation period shall be the first two (2) weeks in August, at which time the plant shall shut down; provided, however, that when August 1 occurs later in the week than Wednesday, the vacation period shall start the following Monday.

Section 4—Upon request, any employee with ten (10) to twenty (20) years of service shall be granted a fourth week of unpaid vacation. Employees with twenty (20) or more years of service shall be granted a fifth week of unpaid vacation. For these additional weeks, eligible employees will have the right to select their vacation dates on the basis of seniority provided it does not interfere with the operation of the business.

Section 5—Employees are not permitted to postpone their vacations from one year to another or to omit vacations and draw pay allowance in lieu thereof.

ARTICLE XI

Holidays

Section 1—The following days shall be considered work holidays:

New Year's Day

Memorial Day

The Fourth of July

[handwritten note in left margin: plant shut-down for vacation pd.]

Labor Day

Thanksgiving Day

Christmas Eve ½ day

Christmas Day

The Union shall be able to determine one further floating work holiday per year.

Section 2—When employees perform no work on a holiday, as defined in Section 1, above, they shall receive eight (8) hours pay at their base rate for each such holiday, unless such a holiday occurs on a day not regularly scheduled for work, and unless an employee has not completed his/her probationary period with the Company as of the date of such a holiday.

(*a*)   Employees shall receive pay for each holiday not worked, as outlined above, if they worked the scheduled work days immediately before and immediately after the holiday. If the schedule of work hours exceeds fifty (50) hours per week at the time of a holiday, an employee shall receive holiday pay in accordance with the above provisions if he/she has worked at least 80 percent of the scheduled hours on the scheduled work days immediately preceding and immediately following the holiday. An employee is also qualified for holiday pay if his/her failure to work on the days immediately preceding and following the holiday is caused by any of the following:

(1)   The employee is excused from working because he/she is ill;

(2)   The employee is injured in the plant;

(3)   The employee suffers a death in his/her family;

(4)   The employee must serve on a jury or attend court pursuant to subpoena;

(5)   The employee becomes a parent.

(*b*)   Any employee required to work on a holiday shall be paid at his/her straight time hourly rate for all hours actually worked plus straight time at his/her hourly rate for eight (8) hours.

ARTICLE XII

Grievance Procedure

In the event any employee feels that he/she has a just complaint or grievance with respect to any employer-employee matter, an earnest effort shall be made by the parties thereto to settle such differences at the earliest time and in the following manner:

(*a*)   Between the aggrieved employee and his or her foreman or between the Department Steward and the foreman.

(*b*)   If no satisfactory agreement is reached, the matter in dispute shall be referred in writing to the president of the Union, and the Bargaining Committee shall then bring the matter to the attention of the duly designated representative of the Company.

(*c*) If no satisfactory agreement is reached by the Union and the Company representatives, the matter in dispute may be referred by either party to the American Arbitration Association for final and binding arbitration by an arbitrator to be designated by the Association. The proceedings shall be conducted in accordance with the rules of the Association.

ARTICLE XIII

Insurance and Pensions

The Company will continue in effect the existing insurance covering death and accidental death or dismemberment of full-time regular employees and hospitalization and surgical care of regular full-time employees, except as the terms and conditions of such insurance may be altered by the carrier.

The Company will also continue in effect the existing Pension Plan. (See Exhibit 3.)

ARTICLE XIV

Union Business

Section 1—Any employee who is a member of the Union and who may be called upon to transact Union business, shall, upon application to the proper representatives of the Company and the Union, be allowed to leave work for sufficient time to transact such business or to attend such meetings as may be necessary.

Section 2—Any member of the Union who may be elected or appointed to any office in the Union that requires a leave of absence shall, at the expiration of such term of office, be reinstated to his/her former or equivalent position, including all rights previously held, provided that the Company's circumstances had not changed so as to make it impossible or unreasonable to do so.

Section 3—The Union shall be allowed to collect dues, sign membership application cards, ballot for Union officers and distribute the regular monthly Union publications after working hours on Company property.

Section 4—The Company shall install and maintain bulletin boards for the Union in places mutually agreed upon by both parties. No material shall be posted thereon except that pertaining to the activities and business of the Union.

ARTICLE XV

Duration of Agreement

This Agreement shall be effective January 1, 1991. It shall remain in full force and effect from January 1, 1991 to and including December 31, 1991, and thereafter it shall be automatically renewed from time to time for further periods of one (1) year unless either party at least sixty (60) days prior to December 31, 1991, or any subsequent expiration date, serves on the other party written notice of its desire to amend or terminate the Agreement.

If the notice given is one expressing an election to terminate, then the Agreement shall expire upon such ensuing expiration date. If the notice given is one expressing a desire to amend the Agreement, the party serving such notice to amend shall, within thirty (30) days from the date of such notice to amend is served, transmit to the other party in writing the amendments proposed for negotiation and mutual agreement. If the party upon whom such notice to amend is served desires to amend the Agreement, it shall be no later than ten (10) days after receipt of such notice to amend serve written notice to that effect on the other party; and within thirty (30) days from the date its notice is served shall transmit to the other party in writing the amendments it proposes for negotiation and mutual agreement.

Negotiations between the parties on the amendments so proposed shall begin as soon as possible after the above mentioned notices have been given, but pending consummation of an Agreement on the proposed amendments, the terms and conditions of the old Agreement shall continue in effect.

IN WITNESS WHEREOF, we hereunto set our hands at Fort Jefferson, Indiana, on this 31st day of December 1991.

(Signed)

Company: _____

D. G. Barnhouse Co., Incorporated
D. G. Barnhouse III, President

Union: _____

U.M.P. LOCAL 245
William White, President
James LaPierre, Secretary

BACKGROUND DATA

Exhibit 1

Rate Classification of Jobs

Labor Grade	Job Title	Rate Range (per hour)*
1	Tool and Die Maker	$12.20–$14.48
2	Machinist All Around Mechanical Inspector Plant Electrician Plant Mechanic	$11.97–$13.84
3	Machine Specialist Gauge Inspector	$11.59–$13.53
4	Tool Grinder	$11.52–$13.45
5	Electrician	$11.22–$13.29
6	Carpenter	$10.71–$13.23

Exhibit 1   *(continued)*

Rate Classification of Jobs

Labor Grade	Job Title	Rate Range (per hour)*
7	All Around Instrument Assembler	$10.71–$13.23
8	Mechanical Inspector	$10.71–$13.23
	All Around Mechanical Assembler	$10.71–$13.23
9		$10.63–$12.99
	Turret Lathe Operator	
	Engine Lathe Operator	
	Handscrew Machine Operator	
	Milling Machine Operator	
10	Drill Press Operator	$10.56–$12.72
	Final Assembler	
11	Set-up	$ 9.45–$12.21
	Welder (Tool Room)	
	Grinder Operator	
12	Production Tester	$ 9.45–$12.21
	Receiving Inspector	
13	Instrument Assembler	$ 9.38–$11.96
14	Production Inspector	$ 9.29–$11.89
	Shear Operator	
15	Resolver Assembler	$ 9.29–$11.89
16	Punch Press Operator	$ 9.29–$11.89
	Outside Truck Driver	
17	Expeditor, Machine Shop	$ 9.16–$11.73
	Shipper and Receiver	
	Painter	
	Storekeeper	
	Expeditor, Assembly	
18	Fireman	$ 9.06–$11.66
	Expeditor, Tooling	
	Subassembler	
19	Oiler	$ 9.01–$11.52
	Bonding and Spraying	
	Tool Keeper	
20	Power Trucker	$ 8.91–$11.36
	Timekeeper	
	Bonding	
	Store Clerk	
21	Groundskeeper	$ 8.71–$10.98
	Basic Assembler	
	Routine Assembler	
22	Sweeper	$ 8.34–$10.71
	Assembler	

*A newly hired employee may be paid a rate no more than 23 cents below the minimum of the classification for which he or she was hired and shall be increased to the minimum in accordance with Article V, Section 2.

Exhibit 2

Distribution Table

Job Grade	Number of Current Employees
1	5
2	10
3	11
4	17
5	22
6	26
7	30
8	34
9	36
10	36
11	39
12	38
13	35
14	32
15	32
16	29
17	26
18	14
19	10
20	6
21	7
22	5
Total	500

Exhibit 3

Illinois First Life Insurance Co., Life Insurance and Retirement Benefit Agreement Summary

The employees covered under this agreement include all full-time employees of the Company; new employees become eligible after the probationary period of employment, or immediately if they are over 55 years old. At the option of the Company, employees can remain insured after layoff or become reinsured upon rehiring but with no credit given for the period during which they were not insured.

LIFE INSURANCE

In case of the death of an employee, except by suicide or while serving in the Armed Forces, the beneficiary will receive a death benefit of double the annual salary of the employee, i.e., 2,080 times the employee's last base hourly wage rate. Upon proof that death occurred as a result of accidental injury on the job, this benefit will be doubled. The employee can change his/her beneficiary by notifying the Company in writing. If he/she dies with no beneficiary on record, the benefit will be paid to his/her estate. The beneficiary may elect to be paid the benefit in equal installments of an amount determined by the insurer and based on the age of the beneficiary.

If an employee terminates his/her employment with the Company, he/she may automatically purchase from the insurer insurance providing coverage up to the level of that in force at the time of such termination at the insurer's individual premium rates.

PENSIONS

Upon retirement at age 65 or later eligible employees with at least 10 years of service with the Company will receive pension benefits monthly for life of 2 percent of the average monthly base wage during the 60 months prior to retirement, multiplied by the number of years of service (up to 30), and reduced by 20 percent of the amount the employee would normally receive under the Social Security Act.

Employees with more than 10 years of service who terminate employment with the Company before retirement will receive pensions as per the above, calculated on the basis of the 60-month period prior to termination.

PREMIUMS

The total weekly premium will be paid within 7 days of the end of each calendar week of coverage. Interest will start to accrue on unpaid premiums of the 8th day after the end of the calendar week of coverage. After 26 weeks of failure to pay premiums the agreements will be terminated as outlined below.

If the Company pays less than the full premium per employee, it must collect the balance from the employees and pay the full premium to the insurer. Employees working full time will pay no more than 50 percent of the premium. Employees on layoff or Company-approved leaves of absence can pay up to 100 percent of the premium. All employees within each of these categories will pay the same percentage of the premium.

Employees who have contributed as above and who terminate employment with the Company can receive a refund for their payments with 6 percent annually compounded interest, after which point they lose all rights of future retirement benefits.

FUNDING

The insurer will apply the premiums received to the purchase of term life insurance and permanent annuity coverage sufficient to provide the stipulated benefits for service credited to covered employees before or after the date of the agreement, as appropriate.

ADMINISTRATION

The Company will be responsible for maintaining records for each covered employee, showing the following data on the employee: name and current address; date of birth; name and address of beneficiary; current base hourly rate; number of years and months of credited service both before the date of the agreement and after the date of the agreement; wages received during the preceding sixty (60) month period; and amount and date of each employee contribution to pension coverage premiums.

These records will be available to the Insurer for inspection or audit at any reasonable time.

Upon notification from the Company of the death of a covered employee, the Insured will be responsible for making payment of the death benefit to the beneficiary.

The Insurer will be responsible for regular payment of retirement benefits to retiring employees upon Company notification of retirement by a covered employee or upon notification by a terminated employee with vested retirement benefits. The Insurer will not be responsible for payment of that portion of a benefit which results from the employee's service to the Company prior to the date of the agreement and/or for which the Company has not paid sufficient premiums.

Upon notification from the Company within seven (7) days of the termination of a covered employee, the Insurer will be responsible for notifying the employee of his options, if applicable, to receive refund of pension benefit premiums, if any, with interest, or, if eligible, to vest his or her rights to future retirement benefits under the plan, and to convert to a regular individual life insurance policy available from the Insurer.

Within thirty (30) days of the end of each calendar year or other Company-designated fiscal period, the Insurer will provide the Company with the following information: premiums paid by the Company and by employees during the year for current coverage; premiums paid during the year for coverage prior to the agreement date; contingent liability for unpaid premiums for prior coverage; interest paid on late premiums for current coverage and premiums for prior coverage; interest on premiums for prior coverage which has accrued and has not been paid; and other appropriate information.

APPLICABLE LAW

The terms of this plan are governed by the laws of the State of Illinois.

The Company is responsible for securing approval for the agreement from the Internal Revenue Service.

TERMINATION

The plan may be terminated by either party on any anniversary date, provided that at least sixty (60) days written notice has been given and received. The agreement will terminate automatically if at any time there are fewer than one hundred (100) covered employees.

Upon termination of the agreement, all covered employees will be given the options normally provided, as if they had terminated employment with the Company.

The Insurer will not be released by termination of this agreement from the responsibilities (1) to continue paying retirement benefits to those who have already retired and (2) to initiate retirement benefits to those employees with a vested right to retirement benefits at the date of such termination.

For the Insurer: For the Company:

/s/ James Gordon   /s/ D. G. Barnhouse III
CEO   President
Illinois Cooperative Life   **D. G. Barnhouse Co., Inc.**
   Insurance Co.

December 31, 1990

ILLINOIS COOPERATIVE LIFE INSURANCE COMPANY, D. G. BARNHOUSE CO., INC. PENSION PLAN COMPUTATION OF RETIREMENT BENEFIT FOR 1980 RETIREMENT

Name of employee _____ (sample) _____

Date of hire ___5/1/59___ Date of Retirement ___1/16/80___

Months employed __252__ Less uncredited months __36__ Credit Service __216__

WAGE HISTORY

Year	Gross Pay	FICA Pay	Year	Gross Pay	FICA Pay	60-Month Base Pay
1959	4560	4560	1970	6270	6270	
1960	4530	4530	1971	7110	7110	
1961	4640	4640	1972	7810	7810	
1962	5140	4800	1973	8510	8300	
1963	5200	4800	1974	9105	8900	
1964	5510	4800	1975	9834	9400	8900
1965	5720	4800	1976	10719	10300	10000
1966	5940	4940	1977	12636	12400	11800
1967	6020	6020	1978	14040	13600	13400
1968	6410	6410	1979	15600	15000	14800
1969	6490	6490				

COMPUTATION OF PRIMARY SOCIAL SECURITY BENEFIT

17 years of highest credited FICA earnings ____1963–1979____

Earnings in that period ____$137,350____

Average monthly earnings ____$673____

Primary monthly benefit amount ____$343.60____

COMPUTATION OF BASIC MONTHLY RETIREMENT BENEFIT

Base pay during final 60-month period ____$58,900____

Average monthly earnings ____$981.00____

Service factor ____18____ years of Service × 2% = ____36%____

Average monthly earnings × service factor = basic monthly benefit ____$353.16____

Exhibit 4

Exercise Background Statistics

Table 1

Consumer Price Index (All-Cities Index, 1967= 100)	
January 1981	260.5
January 1982	282.5
January 1983	293.5
January 1984	305.2
January 1985	316.1
January 1986	328.4
January 1987	333.1
January 1988	346.7
January 1989	362.7
January 1990	381.5

Source: Actual data, U.S. Department of Labor, Bureau of Labor Statistics, various years.

Table 2   **D. G. Barnhouse Co., Inc.**
Statement of Financial Position

	Last Year	Two Years Ago
Current Assets		
Cash	$ 1,160,206	$ 1,102,813
Accounts receivable (net)	3,027,476	3,895,825
Inventory	12,040,281	11,707,781
Other	144,506	104,497
Total current assets	$16,372,469	$16,810,916
Fixed Assets		
Investments (at cost)	$ 114,092	$ 114,092
Plant, property, and equipment	22,021,031	21,010,980
Less: Accumulated depreciation	11,976,945	11,784,645
Plant, property, and equipment (net)	10,044,086	9,226,335
Total fixed assets	$10,158,178	$ 9,340,427
Other Assets		
Intangible assets (net)	$ 156,448	$ 164,654
Deferred charges	281,198	307,184
Total other assets	$ 473,646	$ 471,838
Total Assets	$26,968,293	$26,623,181
Liabilities and Equities		
Current Liabilities	$ 1,293,630	915,195
Accounts payable	2,212,900	3,162,500
Notes payable *Debt*	382,689	501,993
Accrued expenses	57,859	501,237
Accrued taxes payable	744,172	727,480
Total current liabilities	$ 4,691,250	$ 5,808,405
(Net working capital)	$11,681,219	$11,002,511
Total Liabilities	$ 4,691,250	$ 5,808,405
Shareholder Equity		
Common stock (par value $1.00, 5,800,000 shares authorized and issued)	$ 6,670,000	$ 6,670,000
Less: Treasure stock (200,000 shares)	230,000	230,000
Common stock outstanding (5,600,000 shares)	$ 6,440,000	$ 6,440,000
Retaining earnings	$15,837,043	$14,374,776
Total shareholder equity (per common share)	$22,277,043	$20,814,776
Total Liabilities and Equities	$26,968,293	$26,623,181

Table 3

D. G. Barnhouse Co., Inc.
Statement of Income and Retained Earnings

	Last Year	Two Years Ago
Income Statement		
Net sales	$30,579,826	$31,025,621
Cost of goods sold	22,023,587	21,292,887
Gross profit on sales	8,556,239	9,732,734
Selling and administrative expense	4,754,001	6,080,616
Net operating profit	$ 3,802,238	$ 3,652,118
Other income and expense		
Income	10,977	61,280
Expense	134,240	175,285
Net other expense	$ 123,263	$ 114,005
Net income before taxes	3,678,975	3,538,113
Income tax expense	1,765,908	1,698,294
Net income (per common share)	$ 1,913,067	$ 1,839,819
Retained Earnings Statement		
Retained earnings, beginning of year	$14,374,776	$12,985,757
Net income for the period	1,913,067	1,839,819
Less: Dividends paid	450,800	450,800
Retained earnings, end of year	$15,837,043	$14,374,776

Table 4

D. G. Barnhouse Co., Inc.
Statement of Sources and Uses of Funds
(Last Year)

Sources of Funds

Net earnings for the period	$1,913,067
Depreciation	192,300
Decrease in intangible assets and deferred charges	34,192
Total	$2,139,559

Uses of Funds

Increase in working capital	$ 678,708
Property, plant, equipment additions	1,010,051
Cash dividends paid	450,800
Total	$2,139,559

Analysis of Increase in Working Capital

Increase (decrease) in current assets

Cash	$ 57,393
Accounts receivable	(868,349)
Inventory	332,500
Other current assets	40,009
	$ 438,447

Decrease (Increase) in current liabilities

Accounts payable	$ (378,435)
Notes payable	949,600
Accrued expenses	119,304
Accrued taxes payable	443,378
Other current liabilities	(16,692)
	$1,117,155
Net Increase in Working Capital	$ 678,708

Table 5
D. G. Barnhouse Co., Inc.
Quarterly Sales and Earnings per Share Record
(Sales in $ Million; Earnings and Dividends in $)

Quarter	Last Year	2 Years Ago	3 Years Ago	4 Years Ago	5 Years Ago	6 Years Ago
First	$8.51	$8.55	$6.95	$5.67	$5.12	$5.07
Second	7.82	8.38	6.20	5.78	4.07	5.59
Third	7.52	7.49	6.34	5.53	5.39	5.50
Fourth	6.73	6.60	5.69	5.37	5.29	5.03
Earnings/share	$0.33	$0.32	$0.30	$0.32	$0.04	$0.20
Dividends/share	$0.09	$0.09	$0.09	$0.09	$0.09	$0.09

Table 6

**D. G. Barnhouse Co., Inc.
Employee Age Groups**

Age	Number of Current Employees
Under 30	164
30–39	112
40–49	90
50–59	73
Over 60	61
Total	500

Seniority

Table 7

**D. G. Barnhouse Co., Inc.
Seniority List**

Term of Service	Number of Current Employees
0–2 years	71
3–9 years	160
10–14 years	49
15–20 years	122
Over 20 years	98
Total	500

Seniority

Appendix B

Public Sector Mock Bargaining Exercise

The following materials provide the basic data for a mock exercise in the public sector. The exercise involves negotiations between Queen City and a police association representing police officers employed by the city, the Queen City Police Association. (Both the city and union names, as well as the material and data, are fictitious.)

The students should divide into union and management teams. Three students per team are preferred. The roles on the union bargaining committee include the union president and chief negotiator, the union attorney, and the union secretary-treasurer. The roles on the management bargaining team include the director of labor relations and chief negotiator, an assistant city attorney, and a deputy police commissioner. More union and management roles may be added if desired.

The task confronting the negotiators is to bargain a new contract covering the police officers. A copy of the current police contract and other pertinent data are provided at the end of the case. The material below presents background material to the police negotiations.

BARGAINING BETWEEN QUEEN CITY, NEW YORK, AND THE QUEEN CITY POLICE ASSOCIATION (IND.)

Background

Queen City is an aging central city of about 350,000 (1991 estimate) located in upstate New York, and is the center of a standard metropolitan statistical area (SMSA) of more than one million people. The city's job base is in heavy manufacturing, but the area has become steadily less attractive to employers because of obsolete plants and equipment, high taxes, high labor costs, and the like. As a result, many of them have moved away, taking thousands of jobs with them. This job decline is reflected in the SMSA's high unemployment rate (9.0 percent in 1991). The hardest-hit part of the area has been Queen City itself.

Note: Peter Feuille developed this exercise and we are grateful for his permission to use it. An earlier version of the exercise appears in David Lewin, Peter Feuille, Thomas A. Kochan, and John T. Delaney, *Public Sector Labor Relations: Analysis and Readings,* 3d ed. (Lexington, MA: Lexington Books, 1987): 597-617.

The city has been losing population for years (in 1950 it had 560,000 residents), and it is no secret that most of the city's emigrants are middle-class white people, fleeing what they perceive as unsafe streets, poor schools, and high taxes. Over the past two decades there has been an influx of black people and Puerto Ricans, to the point where African Americans currently make up about 25 percent of the city's population and Hispanics about 10 percent. Many members of these two groups are indigent; consequently, welfare costs have increased significantly over the past several years. One result of these population changes is a depletion of the city's tax rolls. In short, Queen City is a classic example of the stagnation and subsequent decline of central cities in the northeastern United States.

The city government is organized on a strong-mayor basis (that is, the mayor has appointive, budgetary, and veto powers over the city council), with the city council consisting of 15 seats elected on a ward basis. The mayor and the council members serve four-year terms, with half of the council up for election every two years. The elections are partisan, and the city is solidly Democratic (the mayor and 13 of the 15 council incumbents are Democrats). The mayor is not only the dominant elected official but also the local strongman in the Democratic party—the closest thing Queen City has to a political boss. As a result, the council tends to pass what the mayor wants and to reject what he doesn't want. The annual budget approval process provides the best example of the mayor's hegemony.

City finances strongly reflect the city's weak economic situation. The 1991 city budget totals $350 million (the city school district has its own budget, and the school district has been similarly hit by stagnating revenues and increasing costs), and the city expects that its 1992 budget will require even more money. The current budget includes about $175 million in county- and state-collected revenues of various kinds and about $80 million in federal revenue, so the city has become the fiscal handmaiden of higher level governments. With stagnating local revenues and increasing costs (the city's population decline has not been matched by a similar decline in the demand for city services, especially police and fire services), each year is a struggle to break even.

Next year promises to be tough because of the state's own financial problems and proclaimed inability to increase the amount of aid to local governments. City officials are constantly trying to persuade Queen County to assume various city functions (and, of course, their associated costs); but, given that county government is largely Republican, the usual response is negative. The city has reached the constitutional ceiling on its property tax (taxes equal to 2 percent of the full value of city property), which means that in coming years only minimal additional revenues can be derived from this source. Because of very strong voter resistance to higher taxes (New York citizens on a per capita basis pay among the highest state and local taxes in the nation), city officials are reluctant to increase property taxes and do not dare institute a city sales or income tax (the latter two taxes would need enabling legislation from Albany). For 1992 the city's best estimate is that it will have 2 percent more money to spend on services and functions that it now provides. Labor costs account for about 70 percent of the city budget.

The city government employs about 5,300 people (down from 6,500 in 1970), most of whom are in one of five bargaining units. The independent Queen City Police Association represents the patrol officers and communications operators in the police department; the International Association of Fire Fighters, AFL-CIO, represents the uniformed, nonsupervisory employees in the fire department; the American Federation of State, County, and Municipal Employees, AFL-CIO, represents most of the city's blue-collar employees (the majority of whom are in the public works and parks departments); the independent Queen City Civil Service Association represents most of the city's white-collar employees (who are scattered across virtually all city departments); and the Queen City Building and Construction Trades Council, AFL-CIO, represents the various craft classifications (electrician, carpenter, plumber, and so on).

The city has a reputation as a union town because of the high incidence of unionization in the private sector. Although this union influence contributed to the early and solid organization of the city's employees, and although some private sector union officials plan important roles in local politics, it is not entirely clear how this union context has directly benefitted city employees. Except for special cases, the city has not done any general hiring in the past several years, and municipal employee ranks have been thinned by attrition. City officials contemplate actual layoffs, but in recent years layoffs have not been necessary.

The city's director of labor relations (DLR) heads the city's Office of Labor Relations and is responsible for the negotiation and administration of contracts with all the city unions. He is appointed by and serves at the pleasure of the mayor, and he currently enjoys the mayor's complete confidence. He receives policy (that is, maximum dollar limit) guidance from the mayor and has been able to convince the mayor and the council to shut off union end runs on matters within the scope of bargaining. The DLR also maintains good relations with city department heads and works closely with them on contract language questions so that city labor contracts will not unduly limit managerial prerogatives. The city's collective bargaining takes place under the aegis of New York's Taylor Law (except as expressly modified for the purposes of this case) and the state Public Employment Relations Board's (PERB) decisions regarding the interpretation of the Taylor Law.

The Queen City Police Department is one of the most important of the city's departments. The police budget for 1991 totals about $57 million, of which almost 90 percent goes for labor costs (including fringes, which average about 50 percent of salaries). The average 1991 salary (excluding fringes) in the entire department is about $29,000, and the department consists of about 1,050 sworn officers and about 125 civilian employees, with the civilians employed in a wide variety of jobs (clerical, custodial, mechanical, administrative, communications, and so forth). The police bargaining unit consists of 800 patrol officers (including detectives) and 40 communications officers (CO's). The CO's are civilians, but they wear uniforms and some of them eventually become patrol officers.

The department is directed by the police commissioner, who is appointed by and serves at the pleasure of the mayor. The department is divided into 10 police precincts, each with its own stationhouse. Patrol officers assigned to regular patrol duty work out of the various station houses. Most patrol officers and CO's work rotating shifts, which rotate every three months. The police department has the usual big city problems of poverty, police-minority group friction, and increasing violence (much of which is associated with drug trade).

A recent incident stirred much controversy and antagonism between the police force (who are mostly white males) and community groups representing the black community. A white patrol officer shot a 15-year-old black youth after stopping the youth for questioning. The officer claimed the youth had reached into his pocket as if to go for a gun. Community groups saw this as another in a long series of police actions in which excessive force was used against the black community. These groups demanded the creation of a public review board to investigate this and other police actions. After an investigation directed by the police chief, the police officer in question was exonerated and the mayor pledged to study the possibility of a public review board.

The police union consists of two occupational groups, the patrol officers and the CO's. The patrol officers naturally look down on the CO's because of the latter's civilian status—they have no arrest powers and carry no weapons. The CO's are in the unit, however, because there is some measurable "community of interest" across the two groups and because the union leadership wants the CO's there in case of a strike so that the police communications processes will be disrupted and there will be fewer personnel available for management to use during the stoppage.

The union's membership (which includes 98 percent of the eligibles) is divided along the usual lines: age and seniority (the older officers are interested in pensions; the younger ones are interested in wages and, more recently, job security), duties (the street patrol officers, or the "combatants," sneer at the desk jockeys, or "noncombatants," in headquarters), and so on. There is—for a police union—the usual rank-and-file militance to get "more" and get it yesterday.

The parties negotiated 5 percent pay increases each year in the current two-year contract covering 1990 and 1991. Because these pay raises lagged behind increases in some other New York cities, the union and its members are looking for a nice catch-up increase. In addition, the younger and shorter service officers, concerned over possible layoffs, are looking for job security protection in this year's contract as well as the usual bundle of cash and other benefits.

Currently there is police and fire pay parity—not contractually, but as a result of a long-standing political custom. As a result, pay increases negotiated by one public safety group are given to the other group. In some years the police settle first, and in other years the fire fighters are the pacesetters. Neither group has settled yet for 1992, and each group is keeping a sharp eye on the other.

The city also is engaged in negotiations with all the other unions representing municipal employees. Each of these unions is jockeying for position while keeping an eye on what is going on with the other groups.

Union Demands

After careful evaluation of membership desires, the police union leadership has formulated the following package of contract demands to be submitted to management. They are listed in no particular order of importance, though the weights bargainers may choose to attach to them should reflect the facts of the case. To facilitate cost calculations, background information is provided for some of these demands. The union wants:

1. In light of police salaries elsewhere and increases in inflation, a 12 percent pay increase at all steps for patrol officers and communications operators.

2. The city to pay the entire cost of the family Blue Cross-Blue Shield-major medical coverage. The city already pays the employees' premium and most of the family premium. The current employee-only premium is $1,200 per year; the current family premium is $2,400 per year ($1,200 additional). Blue Cross benefits are the same across all city groups. Premiums have increased about 5 percent annually during the past three years. About 80 percent of the members have family coverage, and about 20 percent have single coverage. The health insurance plan covers all city employees.

3. The mayor and the police chief to go on record opposed to any sort of public review board of police actions. If such a board were to be created, the police want to be guaranteed that they and their representatives will be provided equal participation in any such board.

4. An increase in life insurance coverage from $25,000 to $40,000, and the city to continue to pay the full premium. Premiums currently are $80 per year per employee; the premium for $40,000 coverage would be $120 per year per employee. Police and fire fighters receive the same life insurance benefits, but other city employees receive from $5,000 to $10,000 less coverage, depending on the unit.

5. A dental insurance plan covering each employee and his or her family. Premiums are $125 per year for single coverage and $300 per year ($175 additional) for family coverage. No other city group has dental insurance.

6. A 10 percent shift premium for all hours worked between the hours of 6 P.M. and 6 A.M. No other city group receives such a premium. Approximately 50 percent of all police hours are worked between 6 P.M. and 6 A.M.

7. An increase in annual longevity pay for patrol officers as follows: from the present $300 to $600 after 10 years' service and $900 after 15 years' service; from the present $600 to $1,200 after 20 years' service and $1,500 after 25 years' service. For CO's, increases will be from $150 to $300 after 10 years' service, to $450 after 15 years' service, to $600 after 20 years' service, and to $750 after 25 years' service. Fire fighters receive the same longevity pay as police; other city employees receive lesser amounts depending on the unit.

8. An increase in sick leave accrual to 18 days per year of service (or one and one-half days per month), including the first year, with the maximum accrual increased to 300 days. Whenever an employee is terminated for any reason, the employee shall receive a cash payment equal to the value of all accrued sick leave.

9. An increase in the uniform allowance to $450 for patrol officers and $225 for CO's.

10. Four more paid holidays (Martin Luther King's birthday, Washington's birthday, Lincoln's birthday, and the day after Thanksgiving). Other city employees receive the same number of holidays the police currently receive. All officers are given one day's pay for each holiday. Officers who work on a holiday receive the one day's holiday pay just mentioned plus time-and-one-half for working on that day.

11. An increase in vacation time to three weeks after five years, four weeks after 10 years, five weeks after 15 years, and six weeks after 20 years. At present all city employees, including police, receive the same amount of vacation.

12. An increase in the standby pay rate as follows: 60 percent of the employee's straight time hourly pay rate for the first eight hours; $35 for each 12-hour period (or fraction) thereafter. In an average week approximately 15 officers will be required to stand by for one shift (eight hours) each.

13. A new Section 2.3 to be added to Article II that will establish an agency shop. About 98 percent of the unit already belong to the union, but union leaders

believe that everyone should help pay for the costs of collective bargaining services.

14. Section 5.6 (Civil Service) to be deleted and replaced by a new section: "Just Cause. No disciplinary action shall be taken against any member of the bargaining unit except for just cause." In 1991 seven major disciplinary cases were processed and discipline was levied by the police commissioner according to departmental and civil service regulations. Two of these cases involved discharges (for on-the-job misconduct), and both cases have been appealed to court (with the association's assistance).

15. A no-layoff clause.

16. A requirement that seniority be the determining factor in layoffs, work assignments, transfers, vacation selection, and holiday scheduling. As a result of long-standing custom, seniority is currently used on a de facto basis for vacation selection and holiday scheduling, but this is not a contractual requirement. As in any large city police department, there is the usual griping that many personnel decisions are made according to favoritism and political criteria. Also as usual, there is little hard evidence to support these complaints.

17. A one-year contract expiring on December 31, 1992.

> These union demands are not listed in any particular order of importance beyond the facts presented in the case. It is the responsibility of the union bargaining team to gather supporting evidence, to put priorities or weights on various items, to develop specific contract language to implement various proposals, to develop justifications for its demands, to decide what compromises to make, and to decide what will constitute a minimum acceptable agreement.

Employer Demands

In collective bargaining the employer typically spends much time responding to union demands. However, as a result of problems that have arisen during the life of the existing contract and because of the city's fiscal constraints, the city has formulated the following demands. The city wants:

1. In light of the city's finances and the modest rate of inflation, no increase in pay during 1992, a 2 percent salary increase on January 1, 1993, and another 2 percent on January 1, 1994; and no increase in any fringe benefit at any time. Considering how fringe benefit increases spread to other city bargaining units, the city is especially eager to avoid benefit increases.

2. A reduction in the off-duty court appearance pay minimum guarantee to one hour. About 100 officers per week make off-duty court appearances, and the city estimates that about 50 percent of them complete their appearances in less than three hours.

3. Sick leave accrual to remain the same; however, there shall be no payment to terminated or retired officers.

4. The definition of a grievance to be changed so that everything beyond the comma in Section 5.1 is deleted. During 1991, about 300 step 1 grievances were filed, and five of these went all the way to arbitration. The association won three cases (overtime pay, court appearance pay, and standby pay), and the city won two (sick leave pay at termination, association representation at a step 1 grievance meeting). All five of the arbitration cases involved contractual interpretation disputes, but about one-quarter of the step 1 grievances did not. The city does not want to process city or department rules complaints through the grievance procedure, and it notes that these matters can be processed through the existing civil service appeals procedure.

5. Deletion of the phrase "or at least reasonably close to these time limits" in the second sentence of Section 5.4.

6. Insertion of the following sentence into Article VI so that the second sentence in that article reads: "The Association agrees that if any such activity occurs, the Association and its officers and agents shall work as speedily and diligently as possible for the complete cessation of any such activity." There have been no strikes in the department's history, but at contract negotiation time there are periodic rumblings from some officers about "showing the city we mean business."

7. The elimination of communications operators from the bargaining unit so that the unit will be limited to police patrol officers.

8. A three-year contract expiring on December 31, 1994.

These employer demands are not presented in any particular order of importance. It is the responsibility of the management bargaining team to gather supporting evidence, to put priorities or weights on various items, to develop specific contract language to implement various proposals, to develop justifications for its proposals, to respond to union demands, to decide what compromises to make, and to decide what will constitute an acceptable agreement.

Impasse Resolution

If no agreement is reached by the end of the time set aside for direct negotiations, there are a variety of methods for resolving the impasse: mediation, fact-finding, some form of arbitration, or strike. In light of the increasing use of compulsory arbitration to resolve police and fire fighter bargaining impasses, it would be useful and instructive to have any impasse in this case be resolved by the following arbitration procedures. If two or more negotiations arenas exist, it may be particularly instructive to use two or three of the following methods in order to see what impact the different procedures have on the bargaining process.

Final-Offer Arbitration with Package Selection

If the two sides do not reach full and complete agreement by the end of the time set aside for negotiations, then all unresolved items shall be submitted directly to final-offer arbitration. Specifically, at the next class session, each party shall submit to the arbitrator (the instructor or instructor's designee) and to the other party a written list of all unresolved items and its final offer on each of those items. Each party shall concurrently submit a list of all items, if any, that have been agreed on in direct negotiations. The arbitration hearing shall commence promptly at the beginning of the class period and shall be heard by the single arbitrator with full powers to issue a binding decision.

Each side shall have 20 minutes to present its case and an additional five minutes for rebuttal, and each side shall be responsible for developing and presenting justifications for its final offer. The arbitrator's decision shall be final and binding upon the parties. The decision, together with accompanying explanation, shall be delivered orally to the parties before the end of the class period.

The arbitrator shall be limited in his or her decision to choosing the most reasonable final offer. The arbitrator shall not compromise or alter *in any way* the final offer s/he selects. The arbitrator shall make her/his selection decision on an entire package basis (that is, s/he shall *not* make separate selection decisions on each issue), and her/his selection, together with any previously agreed-on items, shall constitute the new collective bargaining agreement between the parties. In making her/his determination of the most reasonable offer, the arbitrator shall be guided by the arbitration criteria listed at the end of this section.

Nothing in the foregoing shall preclude the parties from requesting a recess during the arbitration hearing in order to resume direct negotiations, nor shall it preclude the arbitrator from recessing the hearing and ordering the parties to resume direct negotiations if the arbitrator believes that such resumption of negotiations may be helpful in resolving the impasse. Similarly, nothing in the foregoing shall limit the arbitrator from rendering any mediation assistance to the parties if the arbitrator believes such assistance will be helpful in resolving the impasse. (Time constraints, however, will limit the amount of additional negotiation or mediation activities during the arbitration session.)

Final-Offer Arbitration with Issue-by-Issue Selection

Everything is the same as stated in the preceding section, with the important exception that the arbitrator will make a separate "most reasonable" selection decision on each issue in dispute.

Conventional Arbitration

In reaching a decision, the arbitrator shall take into consideration the following:

1. Comparisons of the wages, hours, and conditions of employment of the employees involved in the arbitration proceeding with the wages, hours, and conditions of employment of other employees performing similar services or requiring similar skills under similar working conditions in public employment in comparable communities.

2. The interests and welfare of the public and the financial ability of the public employer to pay.

3. The average consumer prices for goods and services in the area, commonly known as the cost of living.

4. The overall compensation currently received by the employees, including direct wages, vacations and other excused time, insurance and pensions, medical and hospitalization benefits, the continuity and stability of employment, and all other benefits received.

5. Changes in any of the foregoing circumstances during the preceding negotiations or during the arbitration proceedings.

6. Such other factors, not confined to the foregoing, that are normally or traditionally taken into consideration in the determination of wages, hours, and conditions of employment through collective bargaining, fact-finding, or arbitration in public employment.

Post-Exercise Analysis

The instructor and the students will find it profitable to spend all or most of a class period analyzing the negotiation and impasse resolution experiences of the various bargaining teams (whether or not they go to arbitration). The students probably will have numerous questions about various facts of the negotiation and impasse processes, and the instructor should have a variety of constructively critical comments to make about how the students tried to obtain a favorable contract.

BACKGROUND DATA

Tables 1 through 4 provide background information for this exercise.

Table 1

Queen City Budget, 1991

Revenues	
Local	
Property taxes	$ 79,025,000
Licenses and permits	2,705,000
Parking meters	2,400,000
Fines and forfeitures	3,550,000
Interest	1,300,000
Other local	5,480,000
County and state distributions	
Sales taxes	70,600,000
Gasoline taxes	4,700,000
State aid	100,115,000
Federal revenues	
Shared revenue	17,900,000
Housing and community development	50,880,000
Other federal	12,045,000
Total Revenues	$350,700,000
Appropriations	
Police department	$57,150,000
Fire department	41,610,000
Public works and sanitation department	60,750,000
Parks and recreation department	11,675,000
Finance and accounting department	5,005,000
City auditor	1,480,000
Total departments	$177,670,000

Table 1
(continued)

Queen City Budget, 1991

Appropriations

City's share of special districts	
School	$8,680,000
Sewers	15,865,000
Public health	6,175,000
Public housing	80,500,000
General administration	61,090,000
Reserve	720,000
Total Appropriations	$350,700,000

Table 2
New York Comparability Information for Patrol Officers, 1991*

City (population)	Maximum Salary	Longevity Pay		Health Insurance (percentage paid by employer)		Dental Insurance (percentage paid by employer)	
		Maximum Amount	No. Years to Maximum	Employee	Family	Employee	Family
Rockville (250,000)	$28,300	$1,000	25	100%	100%	100%	50%
Swinton (180,000)	27,500	800	20	100	90	100	0
York (200,000)	27,400	1,200	30	100	100	75	0
Albert (110,000)	26,700	750	25	100	95	Not Provided	
Queen View (50,000)	26,000	600	20	100	80	Not Provided	
Queen Woods (60,000)	27,400	600	20	100	90	Not Provided	
Queen Falls (85,000)	27,000	900	25	100	100	100	0

	Annual Clothing Allowance	Term Life Insurance Coverage	Sick Leave		Night Shift Premium	No. of Paid Holidays
			No. Days per Year	No. Days Maximum Accrual		
Rockville	$400	$30,000	12	180	None	12
Swinton	325	20,000	12	150	25c/hr.	11
York	350	25,000	12	120	35%	12
Albert	400	20,000	15	200	None	11
Queen View	300	15,000	10	125	None	11
Queen Woods	325	20,000	12	140	None	10
Queen Falls	350	20,000	12	160	None	10

*Over the years the City and the Association have relied heavily on these New York cities for comparison purposes. Queen View, Queen Woods, and Queen Falls are suburbs of Queen City; the other cities are located in upstate New York. None of these cities have negotiated or arbitrated their 1992 contracts. From time to time, the City and the Association also look at similar size cities in other states.

Table 3

Queen City Police Salary History

Year	Step D Patrol Officer	Step D Communication Operator
1981	$18,000*	$13,800*
1982	18,900*	14,700*
1983	20,100*	15,800*
1984	20,900*	16,500*
1985	21,600	17,000
1986	22,300	17,600
1987	23,000	18,200
1988	23,750	18,800
1989	24,600	19,450
1990	25,800	19,750
1991	27,100	21,250

*Salaries were set by an arbitrator; salaries in other years were determined in collective bargaining. The city and the association negotiated a two-year contract for 1990–1991; the arbitrator issued a two-year award in 1981–1982; all other contracts and awards were for one year each.

Table 4

Police Bargaining Unit Seniority Distribution

Years of Service*	No. of Employees
26 or more	90
20–25	160
15–19	230
10–14	225
5–9	100
4	12
3	10
2	8
1	5
Probationary	0

*Within each years-of-service category, employees are distributed on a linear basis.

AGREEMENT BETWEEN QUEEN CITY, NEW YORK, AND QUEEN CITY
POLICE ASSOCIATION

January 1, 1990, through December 31, 1991

Parties to the Agreement

This Agreement is entered into by and between Queen City, New York (here-inafter called the "City"), and the Queen City Police Association (hereinafter called the "Association").

ARTICLE I

Recognition and Representation

The City recognizes the Association as the sole and exclusive bargaining agent with respect to wages, hours, and other conditions of employment for employees classified as Police Patrol Officer and Communications Operator.

ARTICLE II

Check-off

Section 2.1—Check-off Association Dues   Upon receipt of a signed authorization from an employee in the form set forth by the City, the City agrees for the dura-tion of this Agreement to deduct from such employee's pay uniform monthly Association dues. The Association will notify the City in writing of the amount of the uniform dues to be deducted. Deductions shall be made on the second City payday of each month and shall be remitted, together with an itemized statement, to the Treasurer of the Association by the 15th day of the month following the month in which the deduction is made.

Section 2.2—Indemnification   The Association shall indemnify the City and hold it harmless against any and all claims, demands, suits, or other forms of liability that may arise out of, or by reason of, any action taken by the City for the pur-pose of complying with the provisions of this Article.

ARTICLE III

No Discrimination

Section 3.1—General   Neither the City nor the Association shall discriminate against any employees because of race, creed, color, national origin, sex, or Association activity.

Section 3.2—Job Transfer   The City will not use job transfer as a form of disci-plinary action. Violations of this section will be subject to the grievance proce-dure.

ARTICLE IV

Management Rights

The City shall retain the sole right and authority to operate and direct the affairs of the City and the Police Department in all its various aspects, including, but not limited to, all rights and authority exercised by the City prior to the execution of this Agreement. Among the rights retained is the City's right to determine its mission and set standards of service offered to the public; to direct the working forces; to plan, direct, control and determine the operations or services to be conducted in or at the Police Department or by employees of the City; to assign or transfer employees; to hire, promote, demote, suspend, discipline, or discharge for cause, or relieve employees due to lack of work or for other legitimate reasons; to make and enforce reasonable rules and regulations; to change methods, equipment, or facilities; provided, however, that the exercise of any of the above rights shall not conflict with any of the provisions of this Agreement.

ARTICLE V

Grievance Procedures

Section 5.1—Definition of Grievance   A grievance is a difference of opinion between an employee or the Association and the City with respect to the meaning or application of the express terms of this Agreement, or with respect to inequitable application of the Personnel Rules of the City or with respect to inequitable application of the Rules of the Police Department.

Section 5.2—Association Representation   The Association shall appoint an Employee Committee of not more than three members to attend grievance meetings scheduled pursuant to Steps 3 and 4. The Association may appoint three Stewards, one from each shift (who may be the same persons selected for the Employee Committee), to participate in the grievance procedure to the extent set forth in Step 1 and Step 2 of the grievance procedure. The Association shall notify the Director of Labor Relations in writing of the names of employees serving on the Employee Committee and as Stewards. One representative of the Executive Board of the Association and/or the Association's legal counsel shall have the right to participate in Steps 3, 4, and 5 of the grievance procedure.

Section 5.3—Grievance Procedure   Recognizing that grievances should be raised and settled promptly, a grievance must be raised within seven (7) calendar days of the occurrence of the event giving rise to the grievance. A grievance shall be processed as follows:

> *Step 1—Verbal to Immediate Supervisor:* By discussion between the employee, accompanied by the Steward, if the employee so desires, and the employee's immediate supervisor. The immediate supervisor shall answer verbally within seven (7) calendar days of this discussion.

> *Step 2—Appeal to Captain:* If the grievance is not settled in Step 1, the Association may, within seven (7) calendar days following receipt of the immediate supervisor's answer, file a written grievance signed by the employee and her/his Steward on a form provided by the City setting forth the nature of the grievance and the contract provision(s) involved. The Captain shall give a written answer in seven (7) calendar days after receipt of the written grievance.

> *Step 3—Appeal to the Police Commissioner:* If the grievance is not settled in Step 2 and the Association decides to appeal, the Association shall, within

seven (7) calendar days from receipt of the Step 2 answer, appeal in writing to the Police Commissioner. The Employer Committee and the Commissioner will discuss the grievance at a mutually agreeable time. If no agreement is reached in such discussion, the Commissioner will give an answer in writing within seven (7) days of the discussion. The City may join the Step 3 and Step 4 meetings if it so desires, by having in attendance both the Commissioner and the Director of Labor Relations or the Director's designee.

Step 4—Appeal to Director of Labor Relations: If the grievance is not settled in Step 3 and the Association decides to appeal, the Association shall, within seven (7) calendar days after receipt of the Step 3 answer, file a written appeal to the Director of Labor Relations. A meeting between the Director, or his/her designee, and the Employee Committee will be held at a mutually agreeable time. If no settlement is reached at such meeting, the Director, or the designee, shall give an answer in writing within ten (10) calendar days of the meeting.

Step 5—Arbitration: If the grievance is not settled in accordance with the foregoing procedure, the Association may refer the grievance to arbitration by giving written notice to the director of Labor Relations within twenty-one (21) calendar days after receipt of the City's answer in Step 4. The parties shall attempt to agree upon an arbitrator promptly. In the event the parties are unable to agree upon an arbitrator, they shall jointly request the Federal Mediation and Conciliation Service to submit a panel of five arbitrators. The Association shall strike one name and the City shall strike one name; then the Association shall strike another name, and the City shall strike another name, and the person whose name remains shall be the arbitrator; provided that either party, before striking any names, shall have the right to reject one panel of arbitrators. The arbitrator shall be notified of the selection by a joint letter from the City and the Association requesting that he/she set a time and a place for hearing, subject to the availability of the City and Association representative. The arbitrator shall have no right to amend, modify, nullify, ignore, add to, or subtract from the provisions of this Agreement. The arbitrator shall consider and decide only the specific issue submitted, whose decision shall be based solely upon his/her interpretation of the meaning or application of the terms of this Agreement to the facts of the grievance presented. The decision of the arbitrator shall be final and binding. The costs of the arbitration, including the fee and expenses of the arbitrator, shall be divided equally between the City and the Association.

Section 5.4—Time Limits   No grievance shall be entertained or processed unless it is filed within the time limits set forth in Section 5.3. If a grievance is not appealed within the time limits for appeal set forth above, or at least reasonably close to the time limits, it shall be deemed settled on the basis of the last answer of the City, provided that the parties may agree to extend any time limits. If the City fails to provide an answer within the time limits so provided, the Association may immediately appeal to the next Step.

 Section 5.5—Investigation and Discussion   All grievance discussions and investigations shall take place in a manner that does not interfere with City operations.

Section 5.6—Civil Service   It is understood that matters subject to Civil Service, such as promotion, discharge, and disciplinary suspension of seven days or more, are not subject to this grievance procedure. However, in the event a permanent employee is discharged or suspended for seven days or more, the Association may request a meeting to discuss said discharge or suspension prior to institution of a Civil Service appeal. Upon receipt of such request, the City will meet promptly at Step 3 or Step 4 for this purpose.

ARTICLE VI

No Strikes–No Lockouts

The Association, its officers and agents, and the employees covered by this Agreement agree not to instigate, promote, sponsor, engage in, or condone any strike, slowdown, concerted stoppage of work, or any other intentional interruption of operations. Any or all employees who violate any of the provisions of this Article may be discharged or otherwise disciplined by the City. The city will not lock out any employees during the term of this Agreement as a result of a labor dispute with the Association.

ARTICLE VII

Wages and Benefits

Section 7.1—Salary Schedules   The salary schedule and longevity pay effective from January 1, 1990, through December 31, 1990, and from January 1, 1991, through December 31, 1991, is attached hereto as Exhibit 1.

Section 7.2—Fringe Benefits   The fringe benefits in effect during the term of this Agreement shall be as follows:

(*a*)   Holidays shall be as follows:

New Year's Day	Veteran's Day
Good Friday	Thanksgiving
Memorial Day	Christmas Eve
Fourth of July	Christmas
Labor Day	New Year's Eve

(*b*)   Vacation shall be accrued at the following rates:

Recruitment through sixth year	2 weeks
Seventh through fourteenth year	3 weeks
Fifteenth and later years	4 weeks

(*c*)   Uniform allowance: The City shall provide annual uniform allowances as follows:

Patrol Officers	$350
Communications Operators	$175

In the administration of the foregoing uniform allowance, the City will not set any dollar limit on any authorized item.

(*d*)   Group Insurance.   The City's term life insurance program ($25,000 coverage per employee) shall be continued in effect for the term of this Agreement, and the City's 100 percent contribution shall continue. The City's Blue Cross/Blue Shield-major medical program (single and family coverage) shall be continued in effect for the term of this agreement. For the term of this Agreement, the city shall pay the entire cost of "employee only" Blue Cross/Blue Shield or major medical coverage. As of January 1, 1989, the employee's monthly contribution for "family" Blue Cross/Blue Shield or major medical coverage shall be $8.00.

(*e*)   Retiree Blue Cross/Blue Shield or Major Medical Coverage.   An employee who retires on or after January 1, 1989, and is eligible for an immediate pension under the New York Police pension fund, may elect "employee only" or "family" coverage under the City's Blue Cross/Blue Shield or major medical program by paying the entire group premium cost, which may increase from time to time, by means of deduction from the pensioner's pension check.

(*f*)   Sick Leave.   The City's sick leave plan shall be continued in effect for the term of this Agreement (accrual of six days for the first full year of employment and 12 days for subsequent full years of employment), with the maximum accrual increased to 150 days. Whenever an employee with ten years or more of service is terminated for any reason, the employee shall receive one of the following, whichever is greater: (1) payment of all sick days accrued in excess of 50 days (to a maximum of 25 days pay), or (2) the current four-week special retirement allowance for employees who retire with eligibility for current pension benefits.

Section 7.3—Overtime Pay for Emergency Duty   A Patrol Officer shall receive time and one-half his regular straight-time hourly rate when ordered to report for overtime emergency duty or when ordered to remain on the job for overtime emergency duty. A Patrol Officer will not receive overtime pay for any work during his regular working hours.

Section 7.4—Off-Duty Court Appearance Pay   A Patrol Officer shall receive time and one-half his/her regular straight-time hourly rate for required court appearances during his off-duty hours. Patrol Officers shall be guaranteed three hours at the time and one-half rate for each separate off-duty court appearance or actual time spent, whichever is greater.

Section 7.5.—Emergency Standby Pay   Whenever the City places an employee on emergency standby, the employee shall receive standby pay as follows: (1) for the first four hours, 30 percent of the employee's straight-time hourly rate, and (2) for each 12-hour period thereafter, or fraction thereof, $15.00.

ARTICLE VIII

Termination and Legality Clauses

Section 8.1—Savings   If any provision of this Agreement is subsequently declared by legislative or judicial authority to be unlawful, unenforceable, or not in accordance with applicable statutes or ordinances, all other provisions of this Agreement shall remain in full force and effect for the duration of this Agreement.

Section 8.2—Entire Agreement This Agreement constitutes the entire agreement between the parties and concludes collective bargaining on any subject, whether included in this Agreement or not, for the term of this Agreement.

Section 8.3—Term This Agreement shall become effective January 1, 1990, and shall terminate at 11:59 P.M. on December 31, 1991. Not earlier than July 1, 1991, and not later than August 1, 1991, either the City or the Association may give written notice to the other party by registered or certified mail of its desire to negotiate modifications to this Agreement, said modifications to be effective January 1, 1992.

Queen City   Queen City Police Association

Exhibit 1

Annual Salary Schedule and Longevity Pay, Queen City, New York

Table 1

Salary Schedule
(Annual salaries)

Step	Patrol Officers	Communications Operators
Effective January 1, 1990, through December 31, 1990		
A (Probationary)	$22,000	$16,700
B	22,250	17,200
C	23,500	18,450
D	25,800	19,750
Effective January 1, 1991, through December 31, 1991		
A (Probationary)	$22,200	$16,900
B	23,650	18,400
C	25,000	19,700
D	27,100	21,250

Note: On the annual anniversary date of his or her employment, each employee shall advance one step until Step D is reached.

After completing the specified years of service, each eligible employee shall receive an annual longevity stipend, as follows:

Table 2

Longevity Pay
Effective January 1, 1990, through December 31, 1991

	Patrol Officer	Communications Operators
After 10 years	$300	$150
After 20 years	600	300

Appendix C

Grievance Arbitration Exercises

CASE 1

```
In the Matter of Arbitration between
International Brotherhood
of Electrical Workers, AFL—CIO, Local 400,
                    —and—
ABC Wire Making Company
```

The Issue

At the outset of the hearing the parties stipulated the issue to be as follows:

> Was the company's decision to hire Mitchell Carey as a primary operator of the dual-head extruder in violation of Article 10, Section 1(d) of the collective bargaining agreement? If so, what shall be the remedy?

The Facts

On September 26, 1990, the company posted job openings for three shifts for the position of Grade 3 Dual-Head Extruder/Primary Operator. Two employees bid for and were placed in these positions. The company then sought applicants from outside the company for the third position and hired Mr. Mitchell Carey. On October 28, the day after Mr. Carey began work, the union filed a grievance claiming the company violated Article 10, Section 1(d) of the collective bargaining agreement by not offering the job to Mr. Michael Seiss, the most senior maintenance mechanic who was on layoff status at that time.

Article 10.1(d) reads as follows:

> If the job is not filled by (a), (b), or (c) above, the Company may select from the callback list the employee who, in their opinion, is the best qualified for that job; and if, in their opinion, no one is qualified, the Company may hire a new employee.

The union agrees that the company properly followed the procedures called for in paragraphs (a), (b), and (c) of Section 1 of Article 10. Therefore, the dispute focuses on the company's application of paragraph (d).

The Union's Arguments

Michael Seiss testified that he has worked for the company as a maintenance mechanic for eight years. As part of this job he has had responsibility for maintaining, repairing, setting up, and installing machinery in the plant. He also testified that he has done this work on machine #802—the dual-head extruder. While Mr. Seiss testified that he has not set up or run this particular machine by himself, he said that he has set the dies and heat temperature controls and has observed the extruder in operation. It is his belief that he could run this machine. Mr. Seiss also indicated that he was on layoff from September 1990 to February 1991 and would have taken the dual-head extruder operator job if it had been offered to him.

The union argues that maintenance mechanics are qualified to do the job in question and that the company should call back any employee who is qualified for this job before hiring from the outside. Therefore, the union requests that Mr. Seiss be made whole for lost wages and benefits from October 27, 1990, to the time of his recall in February 1991.

The Company's Argument

The company argues that the job of extruder operator requires a more complex level of skill and expertise than do other machine operator jobs in the plant. A letter of agreement on skill progression rates contained in the collective bargaining agreement is cited as evidence for the high level of skill required. That letter provides for a pay rate increase of 15 cents per hour for each year of experience in this job title.

The company's central argument is that Article 10, Section 1(d) indicates that the company may, but is not required to, recall an employee from the callback list after it has complied with the procedures outlined in paragraphs (a), (b), and (c). It stresses that the word "may" in paragraph (d) should be taken for its plain meaning, particularly since it contrasts with the words "shall" in paragraphs (a) and (b) and "will" in paragraph (c). Thus, the company argues that it had the discretion to decide whether any current employees were qualified to perform the job of extruder operator.

The company further argues that it did not act in an unreasonable or arbitrary fashion in deciding that Mr. Seiss's experience as a maintenance mechanic did not qualify him to operate the dual-head extruder. As noted in the letter of agreement cited above, the dual-head extruder job is critical to the plant's operations and, in the company's opinion, requires a higher level of skill and expertise than the other machine jobs in the plant. Mr. John Reilly, Director of Human Resources, testified that he and the company's personnel manager reviewed the employees on layoff status and concluded that, in their opinion, none was qualified for this position or could do the job without extensive training. The company also notes that Mr. Seiss had never run nor been trained on this machine. The company rejects the view that he was qualified to operate this machine because he had worked on it in his capacity as a maintenance mechanic. The company further notes that Article 9, Section 2 of the collective bargaining agreement states: "to be qualified, an employee must be able to perform the job without assistance. . . ."

Questions for Discussion

1. What is the company's contractual responsibility in this case?

2. Who has the burden of proof of the current employee's (Mr. Seiss's) ability or inability to perform the vacant job?

3. Assume you are the arbitrator. What would you decide?

4. Assume you were brought in as a human resource consultant to the company and the union following this case. What changes in practices would you recommend to avoid disputes like this in the future?

CASE 2

In the Matter of Arbitration between
American Federation of Teachers Union, Local 3000,
                              —and—
Homer City School System

The Issue

The parties stipulated the issue in this case as follows:

> Did the school administration have just cause to reprimand teacher Joseph O'Connell? If not, what shall be the remedy?

The Facts

Mr. O'Connell is a white, male gym teacher at Homer City High School. Before classes started on the morning of February 7, 1990, he was assigned to supervise one end of the third-floor corridor until homeroom period began. While performing his duties, Mr. O'Connell noticed a seventh-grade African-American male student in the hall near his locker. Mr. O'Connell instructed the student to go to his homeroom; however, the student said he had permission from his homeroom teacher to go to his locker and walked away. Several minutes later Mr. O'Connell again saw the student in the hall and again instructed him to go to his homeroom, but the student did not do so. A third time Mr. O'Connell instructed the student to return to his homeroom, but the student ran down an adjacent stairway instead.

Mr. O'Connell then encountered the student in the corridor near the stairwell. A verbal confrontation occurred and, Mr. O'Connell testified, the student pushed Mr. O'Connell and shouted obscenities at him. Mr. O'Connell then told the student to go to the office with him. As they approached the top of a set of stairs, the student swung his arm around as if to hit Mr. O'Connell, whereupon Mr. O'Connell grabbed the student from behind and lifted him off the ground to restrain him.

Mr. Steven Smith, another teacher whose duty post was at the other end of the hall, testified that he ran to the scene in response to the noise he heard. Mr. Smith asked Mr. O'Connell to release the student and told the student to go to the office with him. The student did so. The student was subsequently suspended for his actions.

There were no witnesses to the interaction between Mr. O'Connell and the student before Mr. Smith's arrival.

Mr. Michael Rogers, the principal of Homer City High School, testified that he was not at the school on the day of the incident. When he returned to school he reviewed the reports of the incident prepared by his staff and by Mr. Smith and Mr. O'Connell. He also received a letter from the student's mother that was critical of Mr. O'Connell's behavior and demanded that appropriate disciplinary action be taken against him. She also requested a meeting with Mr. Rogers and said she would bring along a prominent local attorney who was formerly associated with the U.S. Office of Civil Rights. This meeting was held on February 10, 1990. Mr. Rogers also met with Mr. O'Connell to discuss the incident.

On March 7th Mr. Rogers wrote a letter to Mr. O'Connell stating, in part:

> I originally accepted your description of the incident. Nevertheless, I am concerned about the use of unnecessary force on your part in handling the situation. My review of all of the statements submitted leads me to conclude that you did indeed use excessive force in dealing with [the student]. You state that [he] threatened you physically and that you felt it necessary to restrain him by clamping him in a bear hug and physically carrying him to the office. I find that your decision to use physical force to restrain [the student] was an unnecessary and inappropriate overreaction.
>
> Since we have spoken on previous occasions about your handling of incidents involving minority students, I have decided to forward my summary of this matter to the Deputy Superintendent/Operations for review and possible further disciplinary action.
>
> A copy of this memorandum has been placed in your personnel folder.

A hearing to review this matter was subsequently conducted by Mr. Richard Hortoy, assistant superintendent of the school system, at which the student, his mother, his attorney, Mr. O'Connell, and appropriate school and union representatives were present. Thereafter Mr. Hortoy and the other school representatives are called the "school administration."

After the hearing, in a letter to Mr. O'Connell, Mr. Hortoy reported the following decision:

> Based on the testimony presented at the hearing, the School administration determined that you did overreact by using unnecessary physical force in a situation that should have been addressed via appropriate school channels. . . . Please be advised that this letter is a written reprimand of poor judgment in handling a difficult situation. The use of excessive physical force in a similar type of situation will result in further disciplinary action, suspension, or dismissal. This letter will be placed in your personnel file.

Mr. O'Connell subsequently filed a grievance claiming that both the Rogers and the Hortoy letters constituted discipline without just cause as required in Article VI, Section B of the collective bargaining agreement. That clause states:

> Any discipline in relation to collective bargaining unit members shall be for just cause.

The Union's Argument

The union begins its argument by noting that there were no direct witnesses to most of the incident. Only the teacher and the student involved were present.

The school principal testified that he had expressed his concern to Mr. O'Connell about Mr. O'Connell's excessive use of force in similar incidents with minority students. However, on this point the union argues that the administration failed to abide by its written rules governing the conduct of disciplinary hearings and issuance of discipline by failing to follow the progressive discipline procedures outlined in the school superintendent's personnel policies. No record of these conversations was ever made or placed in Mr. O'Connell's personnel file.

The School Administration's Argument

The school administration argues that the Management Rights clause of the collective bargaining agreement gives it the right to set and apply disciplinary rules and policies. An arbitrator should only set aside the administration's judgment in disciplinary cases involving the use of physical force if it can be shown that the administration acted in bad faith or in an arbitrary, discriminatory, or capricious manner. Since the administration acted in this case after a careful review of the facts and the conduct of a hearing, its judgment that Mr. O'Connell did use excessive force should stand.

The school administration also argues that while it does have a policy of progressive discipline, it may impose a more severe penalty and skip the oral warning for a first offense when the incident in question is serious in nature. Use of physical force against a student fits this description.

The administration further argues that the sheer differences in physical size and strength between the teacher and the student indicate that the teacher was in no physical danger and therefore his use of a bear hug to restrain the student was a clear overreaction.

Finally, the administration argues that Mr. O'Connell had available and was aware of other, more appropriate alternatives for dealing with the student's actions. He could have asked for Mr. Smith or some other teacher to assist him after the verbal threats were made by the student. Or, Mr. O'Connell could have referred the issue to Ms. Wickett, the assistant principal in charge at the time of the incident.

Questions for Discussion

1. Who has the burden of proof in this case?

2. What relevance, if any, would you give to the fact that the teacher was a large, muscular, white gym teacher and the student was a seventh-grade African-American?

3. What relevance, if any, would you give to the school administration's claim that this teacher had similar cases of excessive force with minority students in the past that had not resulted in disciplinary action?

4. If you were the arbitrator, what would you decide in this case? If you decide Mr. O'Connell was unjustly disciplined, what remedy would you require? If you decide that the school administration acted properly in its discipline of Mr. O'Connell, what, if any, advice would you give to the student's parent?

5. If you were the principal in this school, what would you do to avoid a repetition of this type of case in the future between students and faculty?

CASE 3

In the Matter of Arbitration between
Minnesota Mining & Manufacturing Co. (3M)
                    —and—
Oil, Chemical & Atomic Workers
International Union, Local 6–75

The Issue

The parties stipulated the issue in this case as follows:

> Has the company violated the collective bargaining agreement by following a practice of not using bargaining unit employees to repair personal computers?

The Facts

This grievance was brought by the Oil, Chemical & Atomic Workers International Union, Local 6-75 on behalf of the grievant, Terry Begley, and members of the bargaining unit. The grievant is a systems control technician employed by the Minnesota Mining & Manufacturing Co. (3M), and the union is his sole representative.

The union and the company are parties to a collective bargaining agreement. Article 2.01 in the agreement recognizes the union as the exclusive bargaining agent for all hourly paid employees designated in the bargaining unit. The unit includes all production and maintenance employees, including service control technicians. Furthermore, Article 8.17(c) provides that "Supervisory and other salaried employees will not perform the work of hourly production employees except in cases of emergency." The union argues that the company has violated the contract by giving to salaried employees bargaining unit work that should have been performed by service control technicians.

Two years ago the company purchased 4,000 desktop personal computers. Salaried repair technicians, who are not members of the bargaining unit, were given the responsibility for repairing those personal computers. The company claims that this assignment is a logical extension of its longstanding practice of having salaried repair technicians repair all of the company's office equipment.

The union disagrees and notes that systems control technicians, who are members of the bargaining unit, have historically repaired and maintained equipment associated with the operation, maintenance, and process control of the manufacturing processes. Because this has included working regularly with computers, the introduction of personal computers simply expanded the work that should have been made available to members of the bargaining unit. Furthermore, the union argues that denying service control technicians this work threatens their job security, for as computerization becomes more prevalent, bargaining unit members will be denied the opportunity to keep pace with changing technology. Therefore, the union submits that the company should be directed to assign the work of repairing and maintaining personal computers and ancillary equipment to the systems control technicians.

The Union's Argument

The evidence that members of the bargaining unit are qualified to perform the work in question is compelling. The union presented evidence that service control technicians have extensive training, both to obtain their positions and under a continuing on-the-job training program. Part of that continued training includes work with computers.

Personal computers are electronic devices that serve a purpose similar to the equipment for which service control technicians have always been responsible. Furthermore, bargaining unit members are qualified to service personal computers.

The union rejects the company's argument that the contested work is not bargaining unit work because it involves office rather than production equipment. The evidence shows that bargaining unit members already work extensively in offices, where they perform a variety of tasks in nonproduction areas. For example, service control technicians are responsible for lighting, for the entire heating and cooling system, and for the physical furniture.

The company claims that bargaining unit members cannot work on personal computers because they might gain access to confidential information. Service control technicians, however, are already entering the premises for other reasons; there is no reason to suspect their work with personal computers.

Finally, the union submits that service control technicians must be given the opportunity to grow with their craft. Assigning the repair and maintenance of personal computers and ancillary equipment to service control technicians would be a logical extension of work that they are presently performing and for which they are well qualified. Denying them that right threatens to render them obsolete in the future operations of 3M.

The Company's Argument

The company submits that by this grievance the union seeks to gain for bargaining unit members work that is not rightfully theirs. First, the company argues that the contract does not prohibit the assignment of this work to non-bargaining unit members; rather, it expressly provides this right to the company in Article 4, the Management Rights clause. Thus, the contract clearly supports management's actions in this case.

Second, the company submits that the contested work is properly assigned to non-bargaining unit, salaried employees. The company has never asked or directed office equipment repair workers to perform bargaining unit work, and service control technicians have never been responsible for repairing desktop personal computers. The salaried persons who presently perform this work are highly skilled in a number of areas for which bargaining unit members are limited by experience and training. They are cross trained with respect to both types of equipment and product lines. Service control technicians are not expected to have that expertise. Furthermore, the nature of the contested work makes it ill-suited for assignment to bargaining unit members. The union should not be in a position to gain access to information that relates directly to the management of the company.

Finally, the company is puzzled that the union is alarmed at the possibility that technology may someday eliminate the position of service control technician, when it is technology that created that position in the first place. The company notes that no service control technician has been laid off or had hours reduced as the result of the introduction of personal computers at 3M. In fact, the position of service control technician is one of the more secure jobs at the company.

Questions for Discussion

1. If you were the arbitrator, what would you decide in this case?

2. What responsibilities should the company have to provide career opportunities to workers like service control technicians who are the highest paid members of the bargaining unit.

3. If a company offers training and promotional opportunities to jobs outside of the bargaining unit, should workers have the opportunity to carry over their union membership and coverage under collective bargaining? What would our labor law say in this case? What would good human resource management practice suggest?

4. How should a company and a union handle cases like this? Is arbitration the best option? If you were the arbitrator in this case, what alternative ways might you suggest for handling such issues in the future?

CASE 4
PRODUCTIVITY BARGAINING FOR METER READERS:
A MEDIATION/ARBITRATION PROCESS

In 1991 negotiations between Central City Electric Utility Inc. and the Utility Workers Union reached a settlement on a new contract on all items *except* the proposed revision of the work standards that govern meter readers. The parties were attempting to achieve a significant overhaul of work standards that had been in place since 1959. Because of the complexity of the issues involved, the parties agreed to establish a joint study committee to work on this issue for six months following the ratification of the other terms of the agreement.

If the study committee failed to reach an agreement on new, updated standards, the parties agreed to refer the issue to a mediator. If mediation failed to resolve the issue, the issue would be submitted to arbitration. Both parties wanted to reach an acceptable solution on their own or, if necessary, with the help of a mediator and avoid arbitration. Arbitration was viewed by both sides as undesirable since the issues were extremely complicated. The parties estimated it might take up to 20 days of hearings to "educate" the arbitrator sufficiently to receive an informed decision.

Despite good faith efforts on everyone's part, the joint study committee failed to make any significant progress. Therefore, a mediator was brought in with the understanding that the mediator would arbitrate the dispute if necessary.

Background

The current Meter Route Evaluation Program was developed by a management consulting firm in the mid-1950s and agreed to by the parties in negotiations in 1959. This program continued in existence to the present and consists of the following key features:

> Each meter route is composed of a measured eight-hour work day made up of six and one-half hours of field time and one and one-half hours of paperwork and processing time. Meter readers report for work in the morning and turn in the *prior* day's readings at that time. They then proceed into the field and are free to go home without reporting back to the company office whenever they finish their allotted number of meters.

Travel time and other adjustments for walking time are built into the schedule. Although the meter routes were originally established to require an average of 6.5 hours to complete, a number of improvements in technology and worker-initiated "shortcuts" have reduced the actual time required by most meter readers. Recent data collected by the company suggest that, on average, readers are finishing their routes in 4.5 hours.

Over the 30-plus years the existing system was in place, a number of changes were introduced in the technology and process of meter reading. The most important of these, the use of electronic meter-reading devices called "itrons," was first introduced in 1985 and had spread across the system by 1991. Itrons allow many of the reader's tabulations and reporting tasks that had been done manually to now be done electronically. The itron is also fitted with a clock that provides management with significant additional information and allows for close monitoring of the reader's work practices and workday. Data are collected, for example, on such things as reader identity, car mileage, number of meters assigned, number read, number skipped (for example, because nobody is home), number not read, time the itron is energized, time of first and last read, and time between reads. In addition, the reader can enter valuable discrepancy data or any other notes on observations made during the time in the field that might be helpful to improving or changing routes or other operating procedures.

These data are used for a variety of management and control systems and are fed into a computer program that is used for setting and modifying routes to equalize workloads within the allotted field time.

A bargaining unit member is responsible for setting and adjusting the routes under the direction of a nonbargaining unit manager. Both the manager and the union member who sets the routes sit on their respective bargaining teams for the contract negotiations and therefore both serve as "expert resources" and are available for consultation in joint and/or separate sessions. Since they work closely together, these two individuals, as with most members of the union and management bargaining teams, appear to have good working relationships.

Future Technological Changes   While the itron represents the current stage of technology, new electronic devices are being developed that can be mounted on poles or in some cases on the meters themselves that would eliminate the need for meter readers altogether. Depending on the rate of capital investment by the company, these new devices could cover a majority of the meter readers' current work in 10 years. No significant introduction of this future wave of technology is likely to occur, however, for at least three to five years.

Pressures for Upgrading the Work Standards   Management is pressing hard to update the existing work standards for the following reasons:

1. Itron-generated reports disclose that the actual work time required by the readers to complete their routes has declined to an average of 4.5 hours.

2. The company realizes that it could significantly reduce its read-bill cycle (time between when a meter is read, a bill is sent to the customer, and a payment is received) if the meter readings were returned at the end of the workday rather than the following morning.

3. A 20-company comparison of comparable utilities showed that Central City had:
   a. The *highest* meter-reading expense per customer
   b. The smallest number of meters per route
   c. Average wage rates that were 25.8 percent above the mean for the 20 companies.

   Given that the existing work standards and work rules were designed for an older technology and now produce the highest costs and lowest productivity in a group of 20 comparable firms, it was clear to all parties that some productivity improvements needed to be introduced into the system. The question, however, was what changes?

Management's Proposals

The company proposed the following changes:

1. Each worker would report twice a day—once in the morning and once at the end of his/her route when the itron would be returned to begin immediate processing and billing.

2. It was estimated that it should now take workers one-half hour less each day to complete existing routes due to the greater efficiency of the itron.

3. In light of the 30 minutes saved by the itron, the number of meters to be read per person per day would be increased from the current level of 240 to 300. Management's specific proposal when the study committee broke off deliberations was for a 25 percent increase in productivity, but management also indicated this number was not a firm demand and could be reduced if the overall settlement promised continuous future productivity increases rather than only a one-time improvement.

The Union's Position

The union did not offer a concrete alternative proposal but put a general offer of a 4 percent increase in the number of meters to be read by each worker on the table during the joint study process. The union leaders realized that further compromise from this number would be needed to get a settlement. But the union members were adamantly opposed to management's demand that they report back to the company office at the end of the day with their itron since that would eliminate their "incentive"—that is, the ability to go home as soon as they finished their last read. They understood management's desire for getting the billing out sooner but wondered if there wasn't some other way to accomplish this while preserving their freedom to go home when finished. Moreover, they suspected that management's real motive was to get them back to the office to "hassle" them if they got done "too early." Union negotiators also expressed a concern that this "speed-up" proposed by management was just the first in what would prove to be a continuous speed-up in work standards with no benefit to the workers.

Mediation

When he was selected, the mediator phoned the chief spokesmen for the union and the company bargaining teams to get some background information. Both the union and company negotiators indicated a strong hope that a mediated settlement could be achieved, thereby avoiding a costly, lengthy, and possibly unworkable arbitration award.

The mediator was warned by management that its team was under intense pressure to achieve significant productivity improvements from and greater accountability of the meter readers. Top management was frustrated by the comparative cost and productivity numbers presented above. Management was determined to get the data in at the end of the day to reduce its billing cycle and wanted the workers to report back to the office as a further check on the actual times required to complete different routes.

Although the union recognized the validity of management's case for improvements, there were serious internal differences among young and old union members. Furthermore, a change in union leadership was about to occur as the current president took over his new office as president of the state AFL-CIO. Another member of the bargaining team was to take office as union president. This new president was obviously not interested in accepting an unpopular new agreement as his first act in office!

After listening to a briefing by the union and management negotiating teams, the mediator offered the following preliminary comments:

1. It seems both sides have perverse incentives here. Workers are being asked to accept higher workloads now with no apparent monetary rewards. Moreover, under the current system there are no further incentives for workers to identify additional ways to improve productivity and lower costs.

2. Given that workers don't help find ways to improve productivity under the current system, the incentive increases for management to accelerate the timetable for investing in new technology that will eventually eliminate the meter readers' jobs.

3. The parties have no joint process in place for planning for the introduction of the new technology or for the retraining or transfer of current readers to other jobs in the bargaining unit or the company. Yet the parties do share workday schedule data—a union member manages the schedules with a management supervisor.

At a break the mediator described the problem to himself (as mediators are prone to do from time to time) as follows:

> Here I'm faced with a really complex, outdated system that needs fundamental overhaul and parties that face a lot of internal politics. Their working relationship, however, seems quite good. Moreover, we have on the teams the two best technical experts who know how the system works and clearly have more knowledge than I do about what alternatives might work and how different changes will play out in practice. Somehow I've got to tap and use this joint expertise to find a solution.
>
> Furthermore, there must be a way to create an ongoing structure and compensation arrangement that gives both parties an incentive to plan for the future and to produce *continuous* performance improvements rather than just a *one-time* jump from the results of these negotiations. But to do this we must give the meter readers themselves some incentive to participate with management in the benefits of productivity improvement and to overcome their fear of a continuous speed-up ending in the elimination of their jobs!

Questions for Discussion

1. If you were the mediator, how might you go about helping the parties find a solution? For example, would you spend most of your time working with the parties in separate sessions by shuttling ideas and proposals back and forth between the labor and management teams? Or would you work jointly with both sides in a common session?

2. As mediator, how might you draw out the expertise of the union and management technical experts who work with the key data as part of their jobs? Would a subcommittee be advisable? What guidelines should the subcommittee work under?

3. If mediation failed and you were the arbitrator, what would you decide? How would you increase the chances that your decision was workable and equitable?

Glossary

Ability to pay. Management's financial ability to meet union demands, which is determined by company earnings and assets.

Absolute union wage effect. A measure of how much union workers earn above what those workers would earn if there were no unions.

Accountability. Programs in the public schools that assess how well teachers are meeting school and student goals.

Accretion clause. A clause in a labor contract providing that any new plant not previously represented by a union will be automatically added to the bargaining unit.

Affirmative action. Programs aimed at alleviating past discrimination by giving discriminated workers preference over others in the hiring or promotion process.

AFL-CIO. A federation of national labor unions formed through the merger of the American Federation of Labor and the Congress of Industrial Organizations in 1955, with the goal of promoting the political objectives of the labor movement and assisting the member unions in their collective bargaining activities.

AFL-CIO Committee on the Evolution of Work. A committee created by the AFL-CIO in 1984 to meet, study, and debate alternative union organizing, bargaining, and political strategies. The committee has focused on how changes in the nature of work and demographic composition of the work force create the need for new union strategies.

AFL-CIO Organizing Institute. An institute created by the AFL-CIO in 1989 to engage in the recruitment and training of new organizers; it also provides affiliated unions with strategic planning and analysis concerning organizing campaigns.

Agency shop. A contract clause providing that members of the bargaining unit must pay dues to the union covering the cost of union representation (but individuals do not necessarily have to become members of the union).

American Arbitration Association (AAA). A private nonprofit organization that facilitates the arbitration process by maintaining lists of arbitrators and making available facilities for arbitration hearings.

American Federation of Labor (AFL). A federation of national labor unions founded by Samuel Gompers in 1886 with the goal of organizing craft workers into exclusive unions to achieve improved wages and working conditions and to protect the status of the trade through collective bargaining.

Annual improvement factor. Annual wage increases in auto and other multiyear labor contracts usually equal to 3 percent per year in addition to cost-of-living increases.

Antitrust legislation. Legislation against trusts and monopoly applied to unions in the early part of the twentieth century.

Apprenticeship program. A formal system of training and certification to obtain skilled workers.

Arbitration. A procedure used to settle impasses in which a third party (the arbitrator) makes a binding decision.

Arbitration hearing. A stage of the arbitration procedure when both parties present their positions and evidence to support their cases, usually initiated with opening statements by the union and management representatives.

Arbitrator's decision. The ruling of an arbitrator given either orally or in written form. If written, the decision typically includes a summary of the issues, facts, and claims made by the parties and the arbitrator's resolution of the grievance.

Attitudinal structuring. The degree of trust that exists in a relationship between management and labor.

Authorization cards. Cards signed by unorganized employees declaring their interest in unionization. Before the NLRB can schedule an election, a minimum of 30 percent of the election unit must sign authorization cards.

Bargaining in good faith. A characteristic of collective bargaining that is required of labor and management by the National Labor Relations Act. This has been interpreted to occur when the employer and the representative of the employees meet at reasonable times and exhibit both give and take.

Bargaining outcomes. The results of the negotiations process (the rights and obligations of management and labor) codified in the collective bargaining agreement.

Bargaining power. The ability of either party (management or labor) to achieve its goals. This is heavily influenced by strike leverage and the elasticity of demand for labor.

Bargaining power model of strikes. A model that views strikes as a product of the militance of the union and work force. During periods when the union's bargaining power is weak, the union is less likely to resort to a strike.

Bargaining structure. The scope of employees and employers covered or affected by the terms of a collective bargaining agreement, both formal and informal, centralized or decentralized.

Bargaining unit. The workers or jobs formally covered by a collective bargaining agreement.

Behavioral strike model. A model that views strikes as determined by the extent to which workers are integrated into society.

Board of directors. The top governing board of a company.

Boulwarism. A hard-line management strategy for regaining the initiative in bargaining used by General Electric in the 1950s. Under this strategy management polled workers to determine their interests, and then made one final offer in negotiations that reflected the financial condition of the firm and the results of the workers surveys.

Broad bargaining unit. A bargaining unit that includes a number of skill types of employees. The broadest unit is an industrial unit including all the unionized employees in a plant (skilled and unskilled).

Bureaucratic pattern. A nonunion industrial relations pattern characterized by highly formalized procedures, detailed job classifications, and job evaluation schemes.

Business agent. An individual who operates as the chief administrative officer of a local union by directing the local contract negotiations and handling grievances.

Business cycle. Fluctuations in national output and unemployment. The U.S. economy historically has experienced sizeable, although usually short, business cycles.

Business strategies. High-level management decisions that involve matters such as investments, the sourcing of supplies, and production strategies.

Business unionism. The philosophy of the AFL and the dominant philosophy of U.S. trade unions in which business unions focus on practical objectives, such as improvements in wages and employment conditions, and eschew concern for broad political change.

Captive audience speech. A speech during a management-led meeting on company time and on company facilities during a representation election campaign used to dissuade employees from voting for the union.

Cell manufacturing. A production technique where teams of employees direct the operation of a group of machines.

Centralized bargaining structure. Bargaining that covers all the plants of a company and, in the extreme case, all the companies in an industry with the same collective bargaining agreement.

Chilling effect. A result that occurs when labor and management avoid making compromises they might otherwise be willing to make because they believe the fact finder or arbitrator will split the difference between their final positions.

Civil Rights Act. Federal legislation passed in 1965 that requires equal pay for equal work and disallowing discrimination based on race, sex, color, or creed.

Clayton Act. Federal legislation passed in 1914, which declares that human labor is not an article of commerce.

Clinical approach. An approach to arbitration taken by arbitrators or the courts. Emphasizes the mediation of disputes, informality of procedure, and arbitrator discretion in helping the parties develop a working relationship.

Closed shop. A contractual clause providing that individuals must be a member of the union in order to be eligible for hire into the bargaining unit.

Coalition bargaining. Bargaining that occurs when the unions that represent different groups of employees in a company coordinate their bargaining against that company.

Codetermination. Employee representation on boards of directors and in works councils. This system is mandated by federal law in Germany.

Collective bargaining. A mechanism for organized groups of workers and their employers to resolve conflicting interests and to pursue agreement over common interests.

Collective bargaining agreement. The results of labor-management negotiations codified in written form.

Committee on Political Education (COPE). A committee in the AFL-CIO concerned with educating union members on political issues and lobbying for union-supported legislative and political programs.

Common law. Court decisions that stand until they are overturned by a higher court or altered by legislation.

Commonwealth v. Hunt Case. A landmark case of 1842 that broke the courts from the criminal conspiracy doctrine by ruling that unions had a right to exist but that prohibited them from using coercive pressures to achieve their goals.

Competitive menaces. A term coined by John Commons to refer to the pressures employees faced from market expansion and industrialization. Commons argued that workers formed unions to counteract the effects of competitive menaces such as child, prison, or immigrant labor.

Compulsory arbitration. A dispute resolution procedure in which both parties are required to adhere to the settlement imposed by an arbitrator if they are unable to reach a negotiated settlement on their own.

Concessionary bargaining. The negotiation of pay freezes, pay cuts, rollbacks, or work rule changes that occurred frequently in the 1980s.

Conflict. A situation that arises from a difference in economic interests between workers and employers.

Conflict pattern. An unstable industrial relations union pattern under which labor and management are engaged in a struggle over basic rights.

Congress of Industrial Organizations (CIO). A federation of national labor unions formed in 1938 with the goal of promoting industrial unionism.

Construction Industry Stabilization Committee. A tripartite group that reviewed wage increases and used its authority to reject increases it found were out of line in an attempt to control wage inflation in the construction industry in the 1970s.

Consultation. Informal meetings between labor and management to settle disputes.

Contract administration. The day-to-day implementation and application of the labor contract. The processing of grievances is a central activity here.

Contract ratification. A vote by union members to reject or approve the settlement of a negotiated contract.

Contract zone. The potential contract settlements created by the overlap between what management and labor are willing to accept during negotiations.

Conventional arbitration. A dispute resolution procedure in which the arbitrator is free to fashion any award he or she deems appropriate.

Cordwainers' case. A landmark case of 1806 in which the court ruled that efforts by unions or other combinations of workers to raise wages were illegal and that unions were "criminal conspiracies."

Corporate campaigns. An aggressive tactic by unions designed to increase the probability of organizing new workers by bringing public, financial, and political pressures on management.

Corrective discipline. Penalties that increase incrementally in severity to give employees the opportunity to reform their behavior; usually a part of progressive discipline.

Cost-of-living adjustment (COLA). Increases in worker earnings based on increases in inflation.

Craft unions. Unions organized on the basis of skill or trade.

Criminal conspiracy doctrine. An early view adopted by the courts that labor unions per se were illegal.

Cross-sectional. Data from different individuals or firms (or other observations) at a given point in time.

Cyclical factors. Union growth factors influenced by the state of the economy.

Danbury Hatters case. A landmark antitrust case of 1908 in which the U.S. Supreme Court ruled that unions were covered under the Sherman Antitrust Act.

Davis-Bacon procedures. Procedures that pay workers on government funded projects wages equal to those prevailing in union contracts in the area.

Decentralized bargaining structure. Bargaining that involves either a single or few plants in a firm.

Decertification election. A vote by employees in a bargaining unit to determine whether they desire to maintain their existing union representation.

Deindustrialization. The loss of manufacturing jobs and the industrial base of the U.S. economy.

Demand for labor. The degree to which the quantity of labor employed by a firm or industry changes as the price of labor changes.

Democratization. The spread of political democracy in countries that were previously governed by totalitarianism or dictatorship.

Demographic context. The factors in the environment that influence collective bargaining, such as the racial and sexual composition and educational attainment of the work force.

Dependency ratio. The number of people not in the labor force compared to the number in the labor force.

Dependent variable. The outcome caused (explained) by various independent variables.

Deregulation. The elimination of federal laws that stipulate how firms in an industry should price their services and that restrict the entry of firms into an industry.

Deskilling. The lowering of the skills required in jobs.

Discipline. The punishment given an employee for not abiding by an organization's rules.

Dispute resolution. The process by which labor and management settle their differences (i.e., arbitration, fact-finding, or mediation).

Distribution of income. The extent to which income is distributed evenly in a country.

Distributive bargaining. A win-lose bargaining process in which one side's gains are the other side's losses: also termed zero-sum gain bargaining.

Double-breasting. The existence of separate union and nonunion divisions within a single firm.

Drive system. A workplace in which the supervisor exercises much control over the work force, deciding matters such as discipline, hiring, firing, and pay setting.

Dual image of trade unions. Simultaneous skepticism of the political activities of trade unions and support for the social benefits of collective bargaining activities by U.S. workers.

Due process. Procedures that give employees the opportunity to redress managerial policies with which they disagree.

Duty of fair representation. The responsibility of unions to represent all members of the bargaining unit fairly and impartially.

Economic context. The economic factors of the environment that influence the bargaining process and bargaining outcomes such as the unemployment rate, the growth in the economy, and the rate of inflation.

Elasticity of demand. The degree to which the demand for a good or input changes when its price changes.

Election unit. The group of employees the National Labor Relations

Board determines is eligible to vote in a union representation election.

Employee. The individuals (blue- and white-collar) who work for a firm or organization.

Employee ownership. A form of worker ownership in which employees of a firm also own a sizeable share of the firm.

Employee Retirement Income Security Act (ERISA). Federal legislation passed in 1974 that specifies minimum standards for pensions concerning matters such as funding, vesting, and the disclosure of information.

Employee stock ownership plan (ESOP). A form of worker ownership in which workers, encouraged by favorable federal tax laws, buy company stock.

Employer. The firm or organization that makes decisions about employment practices and the production of goods and services.

Employer election neutrality. A situation in which the employer neither supports nor opposes the union's efforts to organize a plant or company.

Employer federation. A group of employers who join together to pursue their mutual interests. These federations typically provide member firms with advice and engage in political lobbying.

Employment at will. A doctrine stipulating that employers are free to discharge employees without liability and due process, provided that the termination does not violate a statutory or constitutional provisions.

Employment stabilization. Management's use of extensive measures such as transfers, overtime cutbacks, and reductions in subcontracting to avoid layoffs during business downturns.

Enterprise union. A union whose membership includes both the blue- and white-collar workers from only one company. Most Japanese unions are structured in this fashion.

Equal employment opportunity. Programs aimed at providing equal wages for equal work and hiring and promotion decisions that are made without concern for an individual's race, sex, creed, or religion.

European Economic Community (EEC). An organization of 12 European nations that regulates trade and political relations among them.

European integration. The process of accomplishing the EEC's goal of eliminating explicit trade restrictions and standardizing government regulations over labor, product, and tax matters by December 31, 1992.

Exclusive jurisdiction. The right for only one union to represent a designated group of workers.

Executive Order 10988. An order issued by President John F. Kennedy in 1962 that extended collective bargaining rights to federal government employees.

Expedited arbitration. A type of grievance arbitration procedure in which the parties agree to speed the resolution of disputes by bypassing some of the steps in the normal grievance procedure and adhering to tight time limits.

Experimental Negotiations Agreement (ENA). A voluntary interest arbitration plan negotiated in 1972 as part of the Basic Steel Agreement. Under the ENA the parties gave up their rights to strike and lock out during contract negotiations.

External environment. The key dimensions (economic, law and public policy, demography, social attitudes, and technology) that set the context for collective bargaining and strongly influence the bargaining process and bargaining outcomes.

Facilitator. An individual who seeks to create compromises in disputes between quarreling parties.

Fact-finding. The process through which a neutral party analyzes and then conveys the facts of a labor-management dispute. Used frequently in the public sector, but rarely employed in the private sector.

Federal Mediation and Conciliation Service (FMCS). A federal agency that provides mediation services.

Final-offer arbitration. A form of binding interest arbitration in which the arbitrator must select as the settlement the final offer of either the union or management.

Fiscal policy. The tax and expenditure decisions of the federal government that affect the national output of goods and services.

Formal bargaining structure. The bargaining unit (employees and employers) that is bound by the terms of a collective bargaining agreement.

Fractional bargaining. The extension of bargaining down to the work group and shop floor level, where supervisors and workers often negotiate unwritten agreements or ignore certain provisions of the contract.

Free collective bargaining. The negotiation and enforcement of labor agreements by the parties directly affected by those agreements with minimal government intervention.

Fringe benefit. Compensation that supplements wages, such as a pension or health insurance.

Functional level. The middle tier of industrial relations activity that in-

volves the negotiation and administration of a collective bargaining agreement.

Gain sharing. A contingent compensation system that distributes earnings to employees as a function of output or profits.

Government. Local, state, and federal agencies that carry out legislative and executive duties.

Grievance. A complaint by an employee (or union) that management is inaccurately or unfairly implementing the labor contract.

Grievance administration. The processing and resolution of grievances by labor and management.

Grievance arbitration. The final step in most grievance procedures in which a neutral third party is selected to resolve the dispute.

Grievance mediation. A type of mediation in which a third party is selected to function as both mediator and arbitrator with the goal of mediating settlements to grievances, thereby reducing the frequency of arbitrations.

Harmonization. The process of bringing greater standardization in the regulations, laws, and practices of the member nations of the EEC.

Haymarket affair. An outburst of violence that occurred in Chicago in 1886 after a lockout of workers at the McCormick Harvester Works plant.

Hicks model of strikes. A model developed by John R. Hicks which argues that strikes occur as a result of miscalculations by labor and/or management.

High-tech paradox. The surprising finding that plants with the highest technology are not the most productive; generally these plants fail to effectively integrate new technologies and manufacturing practices with innovative industrial relations practices.

Home-based work. The performance of employment tasks at home.

Homestead strike. A strike in 1892 involving the Carnegie Steel Company and the Amalgamated Association of Iron, Steel, and Tin Workers that turned violent when striking workers tried to prevent replacement workers from entering the facility and fought with private security guards.

Hot cargo clause. A clause requiring that unionized employees in a firm not engaged directly in a labor dispute not handle goods from a company that is engaged directly in a strike.

Human relations movement. A school of thought in the 1920s and 1930s that maintained that worker satisfaction would result in higher productivity and stressed the social significance of work and work groups.

Human resource management pattern. A nonunion industrial relations pattern that includes policies such as employment stabilization, team forms of work organization, skill-based pay, and elaborate communication and complaint procedures.

Illegal subjects of bargaining. Topics that may not be lawfully included in contractual negotiations, such as a racially discriminating clause, as stipulated by the NLRA.

Impasse. The point in negotiations where no compromise appears achievable and a strike or lockout is imminent.

Impasse resolution. Efforts including arbitration, fact-finding, and mediation that are used to resolve a dispute between labor and management.

Implied obligations doctrine. The view that while management may have a property right to allocate the resources needed for the proper functioning of the organization, workers should have due process rights. This argument has been used by critics of employment at will.

Income security. Programs that provide income support to laid-off workers provided through a collective bargaining agreement.

Incomes policies. Direct efforts by the government to limit wage increases that have been adopted in some countries during periods of inflation.

Indentured servants. An employment arrangement that prevailed in the colonial period in the United States under which passage to the colonies was gained by individuals in exchange for their services for a specified number of years.

Independent variable. The manipulated or control variables that explain why a particular outcome occurred (i.e., the variables that cause an outcome).

Industrial relations. A broad interdisciplinary field of study that encompasses all aspects of the employment relationship.

Industrial unions. Unions that represent workers across a number of different skill levels.

Industrial Workers of the World (IWW). A union active in the early twentieth century that supported direct action to improve working conditions and the creation of an independent political party to work for the overthrow of capitalism and the establishment of a cooperative commonwealth.

Industrialization. The process of technological change and industrial development that brought forth economic expansion and modernization.

Inelastic. A lack of responsiveness in demand (or supply) to price.

Informal bargaining structure. The employees or employers who, even though they are not a direct party, are affected by the results of a collective bargaining agreement.

Institutional economists. Individuals who reject the view that labor can be viewed and analyzed as a commodity. These economists study the role that history, politics, and conflict play in the determination of employment conditions.

Integrative bargaining. A win-win bargaining process in which solutions to problems provide gains to both labor and management.

Interest arbitration. The binding determination of a collective bargaining agreement by a third party called into play after labor and management have reached impasse, rarely used in the private sector but used extensively in the public sector.

International trade secretariat. An autonomous agency that provides information to member unions and coordinates union activities across national borders.

Intraindustry pattern bargaining. The informal spillover of contract terms across firms in an industry.

Intraorganizational bargaining. The presence of differing interests within the union and/or management.

Jawboning. The attempt by government officials to convince labor and/or management to voluntarily settle on low contract terms so as to assist efforts to lower inflation.

Job classification. A description of the skills needed for and responsibili-

ties of a particular job as formally stated in a contract or personnel manual.

Job control unionism. Unionism characterized by detailed and complex contracts that outline workers' rights and job obligations.

Job definition. The breadth and responsibilities of a job.

Job security. A clause in collective bargaining agreements that provides employment or income protection to workers affected by layoffs or plant closings.

Joint steering committee. An employer-employee committee with the goal of coordinating participation, work restructuring, and collective bargaining activities.

Jones and Laughlin case. A landmark Supreme Court case of 1937 that established the constitutionality of the National Labor Relations Act.

Judicial approach. A formal and legalistic style of arbitration which has the arbitrator act like a judge and not like a mediator.

Judicial deference to arbitration. The view established in the Steelworkers' trilogy cases that the courts would only review arbitrable disputes in exceptional circumstances.

Just cause. The issue of whether management had legitimate reasons to take actions, especially whether management acted appropriately and fairly in disciplining an employee.

Just-in-time inventory system. A system in which the firm maintains few inventories on hand and relies on suppliers for frequent deliveries. One of the central features of Japanese production systems.

Knights of Labor. One of the most important early national labor movements in the United States. It organized workers on a city-by-city basis across crafts in the period 1860 to 1890 under the philosophy that all workers had common interests regardless of skill or occupation.

Labor. A term used to refer to employees and the unions that represent them.

Labor law reform. Legislation introduced into congress to impose harsher penalties on firms that violate labor laws and in other ways limit managerial efforts to defeat union-organizing campaigns.

Labor-management committee. A group of workers (and possibly union representatives) who meet with management in an effort to resolve problems and improve organizational performance outside of formal collective bargaining.

Labor-management cooperation. Efforts by labor and management to jointly solve problems (i.e., pursue integrative bargaining). Often involves work restructuring and participation processes.

Labor-management dialogue. An effort to open communication channels between management and labor to solve mutual problems.

Labor-Management Relations Act (*see* **Taft-Hartley Act**).

Labor-Management Reporting and Disclosure Act (Landrum-Griffin Act). Amendments to the National Labor Relations Act, passed in 1959, that established reporting and disclosure requirements for union finances, specified the rights of individual union members, and imposed a duty on union leaders to represent their members' interests in a fair manner.

Labor relations staff. The management personnel with responsibility for handling union-organizing attempts, negotiations, contract administration, and litigation with regard to union activity.

Laboratory conditions. The notion that workers should be free to judge whether they want union representation in an environment free of coercion and misinformation.

Laundry list (of issues). A long list of proposals and inflated demands used by labor at the start of negotiations.

Lead teacher program. A program that uses experienced committed senior school teachers as mentors and role models for younger teachers.

Lifetime employment. The practice common to Japanese firms of employing employees from the time they finish school until they reach retirement age.

Lloyd-Follette Act. Federal legislation passed in 1912 that provided postal employees with the right to organize.

Local labor market. The employment opportunities within a specific geographic area.

Local union. A branch of a national union often confined to a specific plant or geographic area.

Lockout. The initiative an employer takes to close operations (and lay off employees) after an impasse is reached in contract negotiations.

Locus of power. The amount of power workers and the union exert in society. Labor's power in national political affairs is a major component.

Longitudinal data. Historical data that track individuals or some other observations over time.

Management. A term used to refer to the individuals responsible for promoting the goals of employers and their organizations. Encompasses owners and shareholders of an organization, top executives, line managers, and industrial relations and human resource staff professionals.

Management by stress. The argument that Japanese management techniques pressure workers to work exceedingly fast and under the strain of continuous peer and managerial oversight.

Management rights. Contractual language or understandings that give management the right to take certain actions unfettered by contractual restrictions.

Mandatory subjects of bargaining. Topics required in contractual negotiations, such as wages and other conditions of employment, as stipulated by the NLRA.

Marshall's Conditions. Four factors that influence the elasticity of labor demand: the degree to which labor can be replaced by technology; the demand elasticity of the final product; the elasticity of supply of nonlabor factors of production; and the share of labor costs in total costs.

Means-end doctrine. The decision of the courts in *Commonwealth v. Hunt* to assess whether unions had abused their power or violated the constitutional rights of workers or employers through their actions rather than to conclude that unions per se were illegal.

Mediation. A voluntary form of intervention in labor-management disputes whose objective is to help the parties reach a settlement. Mediators only make suggestions as their advice is not binding.

Mediation-arbitration. An impasse resolution procedure in which a third party first tries to mediate a settlement and then acts as the arbitrator if mediation fails.

Microelectronic technology. Technology that uses computers or microprocessors in its circuits or components.

Miscalculation. Labor contract negotiations in which either labor or management is excessively optimistic regarding what will settle or result from a strike.

Molly Maguires. A militant society of Irish mine workers formed to aid striking miners' resistance to wage cuts.

Monetary policy. The amount of money in circulation and the interest rate; used by the federal government to influence economic growth. Monetary policy is set by the Federal Treasury Department and the Federal Reserve Bank.

Multilateral bargaining. Collective bargaining in which there are many individuals who have some managerial responsibility and input into management's decisions. This form of bargaining is common in the public sector.

Multinational firm. A firm or organization that engages in economic activity in more than one country.

Multinational unionism. Union jurisdiction or coordination that spans national boundaries.

Multiple interests. An industrial relations perspective that recognizes the diversity of goals and conflicts across the parties involved in the employment relationship.

Narrow bargaining unit. A bargaining unit that includes employees of only one occupational or skill type, such as a union that only represents police.

National Academy of Arbitrators (NAA). A professional society of experienced arbitrators.

National emergency dispute. A strike or lockout that emerges from a negotiation impasse in a major industry and which causes major disruptions to the national economy. The NLRA outlines special procedures to be followed to resolve such disputes.

National Industrial Recovery Act (NIRA). Federal legislation passed in 1933 that included language giving employees the right to organize into unions.

National Labor Relations Act (NLRA). Federal legislation passed in 1935 that became the basic law governing private sector collective bargaining and unions in the United States. The purpose of the act is to promote the orderly and peaceful recognition of unions and the use of collective bargaining as a means for establishing the terms and conditions of employment.

National Labor Relations Board (NLRB). Five members appointed by the President and confirmed by the Senate who oversee representation and election questions, and investigate unfair labor practice charges and issue complaints over such charges.

National Mediation Board. A board authorized by a 1934 amendment to the Railway Labor Act to conduct representation elections and to mediate disputes that arise during negotiations covered by the act.

National Trade Union. An effort in the 1830s to bring separate unions together into one organization to promote the interests of all workers.

National union. The national level of a union; the most powerful union body in the U.S. labor movement.

Negotiations process. The efforts by labor and management to resolve conflicts, typically involving tactics, strategies, and counterstrategies, until they reach a collective bargaining agreement.

New Deal. A series of governmental programs designed by President Franklin D. Roosevelt during the great depression to bolster citizens' purchasing power and to assist workers with economic hardships.

New Deal industrial relations system. Industrial relations activities characterized by managerial initiative and prerogatives at the strategic level, a central role for the grievance procedure at the middle level, and job control at the workplace level.

New industrial relations system. An industrial relations system that features employee participation in strategic and workplace decisions, flexibility in the organization of work, and extensive informal communication between labor and management.

Normative argument. An argument based on ethics or morals.

Norris-Laguardia Act. Federal legislation passed in 1932 that outlawed yellow-dog contracts and endorsed workers' rights to form unions.

Occupational Safety and Health Act. Federal legislation passed in 1970 that required employer compliance with safety and health standards. Administration of the act is in the hands of the U.S. Department of Labor.

Ombudsman. An individual selected (typically by management) to mediate workplace complaints or conflicts as an alternative to the traditional grievance procedure.

Open shop movement. A movement that sought to discourage unionization through company-controlled unions and the expansion of pensions, welfare, and profit-sharing programs.

Organizational change. Efforts to reshape relationships between workers and managers through trust building or changes in work assignments.

Organizers. Individuals who rally employee support in favor of union representation during an election campaign.

Participatory pattern. A union pattern of industrial relations characterized by contingent compensation systems, team forms of work organization, employment security programs, and direct participation by workers and unions in strategic and workplace decision making.

Part-time. Working less than a 40-hour week.

Past practice. Customary policies or methods. Arbitrators often give much weight to past practice in deciding grievances.

Paternalistic pattern. A nonunion industrial relations pattern in which personnel policies are informally administered with substantial managerial discretion.

Pattern bargaining. The imitation of collective bargaining settlements by parties not directly involved in the initial negotiations.

Performance appraisal. An evaluation of the productivity and the contribution of an employee through formal evaluative techniques.

Permissible subjects of bargaining. Contractual issues the parties may discuss but which are not mandatory subjects, as stipulated by the NLRA.

Prehearing briefs. Statements presented to the arbitrator before an arbitration hearing in which the parties present their views of the issues, express their positions, and describe the evidence that supports their position.

Primary union effects. The extent to which a union is able to raise worker compensation through contract negotiations.

Private sector. Firms that are privately owned and employment opportunities within those firms (i.e., not in the public sector).

Product market. The firms that compete against one another in the sale or production of a good.

Production standard. Rules for or expectations about the pace of work, such as the speed of an assembly line.

Productivity. The ability to create goods and services; formally measured as a ratio of output to inputs.

Productivity bargaining. Bargaining concerned with improving output and performance through the removal of inefficient practices. Often involves a one-time buyout of outmoded practices to facilitate the efficient operation of new technology.

Professional employee. An employee engaged in work that consistently involves the exercise of discretion and judgment.

Profit sharing. Compensation awarded employees based on the profits of the firm (a form of contingent compensation).

Progressive discipline. Penalties that increase in a stepwise fashion after repeated offenses by an employee, such as the issuance of an oral warning, suspension, and then discharge.

Public sector. Organizations and jobs that are part of the government (i.e., not in the private sector).

Pullman strike. A strike by the American Labor Union led by Eugene Debs in the early 1890s against wage cuts. Federal troops were sent to enforce a court injunction against the striking workers on the grounds that they were impeding the delivery of mail and interstate commerce.

Quality circle (QC). A group of workers and their supervisors who meet with the purpose of solving production problems.

Quality of working life program (QWL). Activities oriented toward improving organizational performance and the working life of employees. QWL activities can include small work group meetings, labor-management committees, study teams, and the discussion of business plans.

Railway Labor Act. The first federal law (passed in 1926) to endorse the process of collective bargaining in the private sector. The act provides railway employees with the rights to organize and to bargain collectively and was amended to include airline employees.

Rank-and-file members. The membership of a union.

Red circle wage rates. Wage rates that cannot be downgraded in the aftermath of technological change or other organizational restructuring.

Relative union wage effect. A comparison of the earnings of union and nonunion workers given the presence of the union. Nonunion earnings are measured without considering what they would be if there were no unions.

Representation election. A vote by employees in an election unit to determine whether a union is desired.

Residual rights doctrine. The view that unions should not have a right to infringe on the ability of management to act on the owners' behalf, except in the case of an issue over which management has agreed to share its authority by way of specific contract language.

Right-to-work laws. Laws that make it illegal to require employees to join unions as a condition of employment (i.e., a union shop is not allowed). The Taft-Hartley Act allows states to pass such a law.

School-based management. Reforms in the public schools that give teachers broader responsibilities. In some of the reforms parents and other community groups are drawn into decision processes.

Scientific management. A school of thought developed by Frederick Taylor in the early part of the twentieth century that blends economic incentives and industrial engineering methods. Scientific management advocates argued that appropriate task designs and wage systems could eliminate the sources of conflict between workers and employers.

Scope of bargaining. The breadth of issues discussed in labor negotiations.

Secondary boycott. An effort by a union to exert bargaining leverage on a firm by convincing customers to boycott stores that sell the firm's products or employees in other firms not to handle the products of the original firm.

Secondary union effects. The extent to which a firm alters work rules and other practices to counteract the measures the firm took in response to the higher wages negotiated by the union. For example, firms often alter employment practices by increasing the pace of work.

Seniority-based pay. A pay system in which wages increase with employee tenure, used widely in Japan.

Seniority rights. The use of an employee's length of service to allocate benefits or job opportunities.

Service sector. Jobs that produce some sort of service rather than a tangible good. Service workers include retail clerks, social workers, teachers, and the like.

Sherman Antitrust Act. Federal legislation passed in 1890 that originally was intended to limit the power of business trusts, but which was applied to unions in the early part of the twentieth century.

Shock effect. Improvements in the performance of the enterprise spurred by management's efforts to pay for the gains won by a union.

Shop steward. An employee who serves as the union representative who provides union services at the shop floor level when a grievance or other dispute arises.

Sit-down strike. Where the workers occupy the factory and refuse to leave the premises in an effort to pressure management. Used in the mid-1930s but later ruled illegal.

Skill (knowledge)-based pay. A wage system that provides greater pay (often in step increases) as a worker becomes competent in more skills and jobs.

Social Charter. A declaration of principles concerning worker rights issued by the EEC. The charter favors giving workers the rights to form unions and to collectively bargain.

Social context. Social factors such as public attitudes toward and the public's image of unions that are a part of the environment influencing the bargaining process.

Social dimension. The regulations, directives, and laws that govern employment and industrial relations policies in the EEC.

Social technical approach. The use of technology to decentralize decision making in organizations and to upgrade worker skills by broadening job tasks.

Solidarity. A Polish labor union led by Lech Walesa. The initial goals of Solidarity, in 1980, were to improve the wages and employment conditions of shipyard workers. Solidarity eventually became a broad social movement and Walesa was elected president of Poland.

Southern strategy. The construction of auto plants in the south by General Motors in the 1970s and the initial operation of these plants on a nonunion basis.

Spring wage offensive. The annual setting of wages in a handful of key firms in the spring in Japan. These settlements set a wage pattern that is followed by many enterprise unions.

Steelworkers' trilogy. A series of Supreme Court decisions (the first appeared in 1960) that elevated the status and role of grievance arbitration. The decisions limited court review of arbitration.

Stipulation. A joint presentation by labor and management made before an arbitration hearing that outlines the areas of agreement and makes it easier for the arbitration hearing to focus on the evidence and the dispute.

Strategic involvement. Participation by workers and/or a union in high-level business decisions such as product planning, sourcing, investment, and other broad issues.

Strategic level. The top tier of industrial relations activity that involves both managerial and union strategies and structures. At this level are shaped the goals that exert long-run influences on collective bargaining.

Strike authorization. A vote by union members expressing their support for a strike.

Strike deadline. The date at which a collective bargaining contract expires and a strike can start if a settlement is not reached.

Strike leverage. The degree to which labor or management is willing and able to sustain a strike.

Structural factors. Historical, political, and social factors that influence union growth.

Subprocesses of bargaining. The various aspects involved in the negotiation of any collective bargaining agreement. The subprocesses include distributive bargaining, integrative bargaining, intraorganizational bargaining, and attitudinal structuring.

Substantive regulation. Direct government regulation of employment conditions, such as a minimum wage law.

Supervisor. An employee who has authority, in the interest of the employer, to hire, transfer, suspend, layoff, recall, promote, discharge, assign, reward, or discipline other employees if such authority is not merely routine or clerical in nature, but requires the use of independent judgment.

Supervisory board. A committee of individuals who control managerial performance and appoint top managers in German firms.

Supplementary unemployment benefit (SUB). Income protection negotiated by some unions to provide benefits during temporary layoffs that supplement unemployment insurance. In some industries, such as the auto industry, SUB benefits (in combination with unemployment insurance) can provide 95 percent of the take-home pay for up to three years.

Supply effect. The lowering of the wages of nonunion workers because of employment reductions in the union sector (and subsequent labor market crowding in the nonunion sector) caused by union-negotiated wage increases.

Surface bargaining. Bargaining opposite a representative who lacks the authority necessary to make commitments that will stick within the organization. Also known as shadow boxing.

Taft-Hartley Act (Labor Management Relations Act). Amendments to the National Labor Relations Act, passed in 1947, that were designed to strengthen management's power by eliminating unions' rights to conduct secondary boycotts and outlining unfair labor practices by unions and rules governing a union's obligation to bargain in good faith.

Taylor Law. Legislation that regulates public sector bargaining in New York State. Deters strikes through a penalty whereby a striking public employee is penalized one day's pay for each strike day in addition to the day's pay the employee loses while striking.

Team form of work organization. A system in which workers are organized into work groups and perform a broader than normal set of tasks. In some teams workers perform material handling, inspection and repair duties, and budget and planning tasks.

Technological context. Technological factors in the environment that influence the bargaining process and bargaining outcomes. Important factors include the extent of new technology and the degree to which technology either leads to labor displacement or requires high-versus low-skilled employees.

Texas and New Orleans Railroad Company v. Brotherhood of Railway and Steamship Clerks Case. A landmark U.S. Supreme Court case of 1930 that upheld the constitutionality of the Railway Labor Act. This ruling marked the first time the Court had recognized the authority of the government to protect the rights of workers to organize into unions and to collectively bargain.

Trade deficit. The amount by which a country's imports exceed its exports.

Trading group. The existence of strong connections (often financially based) between Japanese companies.

Transfer rights. Employee prerogatives that influence how or whether they can transfer to other jobs within the plant or organization.

Two-tiered wage agreements. Wage settlements that decrease the pay rates of future hires while they maintain or increase the pay rates of existing employees.

Unemployment benefits. Payments provided to laid-off workers through unemployment insurance systems. Federal legislation guides these systems, but the level and duration of unemployment benefits is regulated and varies by state governments. The unemployment system is funded by employer tax contributions.

Unfair labor practice by employer. An action by an employer that interferes with or coerces employees or unions in their NLRA rights.

Unfair labor practice by union. An action by a union that interferes with or coerces union members or employers NLRA rights.

Union decertification. An election in which unionized workers vote on whether to terminate their union representation.

Union democracy. The extent to which union members influence union decisions and finances in an open and democratic manner.

Union density. The extent of union membership in a particular work force. This is usually measured as the percentage of the relevant work force that belongs to a union or is covered by a union contract.

Union federation. A coalition of unions that usually provides advice and engages in political lobbying but does not become directly involved in collective bargaining.

Union jurisdiction. The workers represented by a union. U.S. unions follow a practice of exclusive jurisdiction.

Union merger. The consolidation of two unions, usually intended to gain efficiencies, to coordinate bargaining, and reduce rivalry.

Union negotiating committee. The union officers, staff, and members who participate in negotiations. This committee usually prepares for negotiations by meeting a number of times before the start of negotiations to formulate the union's list of demands and to form expectations about what the union can win.

Union Privilege Program. A subsidiary of the AFL-CIO that promotes associate unionism and the provision of consumer benefits (such as credit cards) to members.

Union security. A clause in collective bargaining agreements that provides either a union shop or an agency shop.

Union shop. A contractual clause providing that all members of the bargaining unit as a condition of employment must be dues-paying members of the union.

Union suppression. A management strategy to actively resist union organizing through threats or employee intimidation.

U.S. Department of Labor (DOL). A federal agency that serves as advisor to the President on labor issues, conducts research and collects data on labor matters, and oversees the administration of many labor policies.

Utopian movements. An 1800s social movement that favored the creation of communities of workers, citizens, and consumers who would work and advance together in an effort to avoid the dehumanizing effects of the factory system.

Voluntary arbitration. A dispute resolution procedure in which both parties agree voluntarily to submit a dispute to arbitration. The arbitrator's decision may or may not be binding on the parties.

Voluntary recognition. An employer's voluntarily recognizing that a union may provide representation for their employees without the occurrence of a representation election. The employer can do this when presented with authorization cards signed by at least 50 percent of the election unit.

Wage administration. The implementation of wages and wage adjustments on a daily basis.

Wage and price controls. Direct efforts by the government to restrain wage and price increases, for example, through a wage and price freeze. Some governments have turned to these policies during periods of high inflation.

Wage-employment trade-off. The extent to which a wage increase leads to declines in employment. This trade-off is determined by the elasticity of demand for labor.

Wage incentive systems. The payment of wages based in part on piece rates or some other measure of individual worker performance.

Wage objectives. The wages that management or the union desire to achieve through negotiations.

Wage-price guideposts. Advisory or voluntary limits unions and management negotiators are asked to observe in their wage settlements by the federal government.

Wage reopener. A stipulation through which the contract remains in force over several years, but wages are renegotiated at some specified point during the life of the agreement.

War Labor Board. A government board created in both World War I and II with the purpose of reducing impediments to war production created by labor strife. The boards encouraged union recognition and pattern bargaining and strongly discouraged strikes.

Welfare capitalism. Personnel practices such as job ladders, pensions, and various insurance benefits introduced by management with the hope that these would lead employees to shun unionism.

Whipsawing. Union whipsawing occurs when a union negotiates a bargain at one plant or company and then puts pressure on the next plant or company to equal or surpass the contract terms negotiated at the first site. Employer whipsawing occurs when management wins concessions in one plant or company and then tries to use this as a pattern for concessions in other plants or companies by threatening noncompliant unions with plant closings.

Work restructuring. Rearranging the duties and the responsibilities of jobs or workers in an effort to improve organizational performance. The introduction of work teams, reductions in the number of job classifications, and the broadening of worker duties are forms of work restructuring.

Work rules. Language or understandings that guide the way work is done and influence matters such as the pace and difficulty of work or the number and scope of job classifications.

Worker Adjustment and Retraining Notification Act (S2527). Federal legislation passed in 1989 that requires employers to provide advance notice to employees affected by plant closings.

Workingmen's political parties. Parties that attempted to establish political coalitions to advance labor's interests active in the 19th century.

Workplace level. The bottom tier of industrial relations activity that involves conflict resolution, communication, and complaint procedures on a daily basis on the shop floor.

Works council. A committee of employees that is given the right to discuss a variety of personnel matters and other powers through federal legislation in Germany. Works councils are a major feature of the German codetermination system.

Work-sharing. Contractual provisions geared toward preserving jobs by cutting the workweek during output declines rather than by instigating employee layoffs.

Yellow-dog contract. An agreement between employee and employer stating that the employee will neither join nor participate in union activities as a condition of employment. Such contracts were outlawed by the Norris-LaGuardia Act.

Name Index

Subject Index